THE
HANDBOOK
OF
FINANCIAL
ENGINEERING

THE HANDBOOK OF FINANCIAL ENGINEERING

New Financial Product Innovations, Applications, and Analyses

Clifford W. Smith, Jr.
William E. Simon Graduate School of Business Administration
University of Rochester

Charles W. Smithson
Chase Manhattan Bank

HARPER BUSINESS

A Division of Harper & Row, Publishers, New York

Grand Rapids, Philadelphia, St. Louis, San Francisco
London, Singapore, Sydney, Tokyo, Toronto

International Standard Book Number: 0-88730-448-6

Library of Congress Catalog Card Number: 90-33922

Printed in the United States of America

Library of Congress Cataloging-in-Publication Data

The Handbook of financial engineering : new financial product
   innovations, applications, and analyses / editors, Clifford W.
   Smith, Jr. and Charles W. Smithson.
      p. cm.
   Includes bibliographical references.
   ISBN 0-88730-448-6
   1. Corporations—Finance. 2. Forward exchange. 3. Futures.
4. Swaps (Finance) 5. Options (Finance) I. Smith, Clifford W.
II. Smithson, C. W. (Charles W.)
HG4026.H289 1990
658.159 224—dc20   90-33922
                                                                 CIP

90 91 92 93 HC 9 8 7 6 5 4 3 2 1

To our parents

PREFACE

Over the last two decades, the increase in volatility of financial prices has led to heightened interest in financial engineering (a.k.a. hybrid financial securities). We found that more and more of our colleagues — academic and practitioners — were asking us to suggest references. The result was that we compiled a list of articles that we recommended to our colleagues. This book collected that group of readings.

In such a book of readings, we are most indebted to the people who wrote the articles:

Joan Lordi Amble, Financial Accounting Standards Board
Fischer Black, Goldman, Sachs & Co., New York
Phelim P. Boyle, University of Waterloo
Eric Briys, Centre HEC-ISA, Jouy en Josas, France
Halsey G. Bullen, Financial Accounting Standards Board
Andrew H. Chen, Southern Methodist University
Carl R. Chen, University of Dayton
John C. Cox, Massachusetts Institute of Technology
Michel Crouhy, Centre HEC-ISA, Jouy en Josas, France
Marguerite Del Valle, Hopgood, Calimafde, Kalil, Blaustein and Judlowe,
    New York
Frank H. Easterbrook, University of Chicago Law School
Warren Edwardes, Charterhouse Bank Ltd.
John D. Finnerty, McFarland Dewey & Co. and Fordham University
Kenneth R. French, University of Chicago
Mark B. Garman, University of California at Berkeley
Steven C. Hayden, Kidder Peabody and Company
E. Philip Jones, Harvard Business School
James V. Jordan, Virginia Polytechnic and State University
Stephen Judlowe, Hopgood, Calimafde, Kalil, Blaustein and Judlowe,
    New York
John W. Kensinger, University of Texas at Austin
S. W. Kohlhagen, Stamford Capital, Sterling, Grace & Co.
Edmond Levy, Midland Montague

Robert S. Mackay, Virginia Polytechnic and State University
John D. Martin, University of Texas
Scott P. Mason, Harvard Business School
John J. McConnell, Purdue University
Eugene J. Moriarty, Evergreen Financial Management Inc.
Christopher Petruzzi, New York University
J. William Petty, Abilene Christian University
Mark Pitts, Shearson Lehman, New York
John J. Pringle, University of North Carolina
Stephen A. Ross, Yale University
Mark Rubinstein, University of California at Berkeley
Eduardo S. Schwartz, University of California at Los Angeles
Donald J. Smith, Boston University
John E. Stewart, Arthur Anderson & Co, Chicago
Stuart M. Turnbull, University of Toronto and Australian Graduate
    School of Management
Lee Macdonald Wakeman, Continental Bank, Chicago
Larry D. Wall, Federal Reserve Bank of Atlanta
Ropbert E. Whaley, Duke University
D. Sykes Wilford, Chase Investment Bank, London
Robert C. Wilkins, Financial Accounting Standards Board
Bernard J. Winger, University of Dayton
Clifford C. Woods III, Financial Accounting Standards Board

However, we also wish to express our thanks to the journals which originally
published these papers for giving us permission to reproduce the papers:

Bank Structure and Competition (Federal Reserve Bank of Chicago)
Economic Review of the Federal Reserve Bank of Atlanta
Financial Management
Intermarket
Journal of Accountancy
Journal of Applied Corporate Finance (Formerly *Midland Corporate
    Finance Journal*)
Journal of Business
Journal of Finance
Journal of Financial Economics
Journal of Futures Markets
Journal of International Money and Finance
Journal of Portfolio Management

Clifford W. Smith, Jr.
Charles W. Smithson

CONTENTS

PART I

Introduction

1

Financial Engineering: An Overview

Clifford W. Smith, Jr. & Charles W. Smithson

I. Introduction

While Financial Engineering seems to mean different things to different people, we use the term to describe the creation of financial contracts that have nonstandard packages of cash flows. We believe that financial engineering is most productively analyzed as the combination of the basic capital market instruments to obtain "hybrid" instruments. The analogy originated by Smithson [40] and used in **Smith, Smithson, and Wilford** [35]* and **Smith** [39] is that the basic capital instruments can be viewed as a set of financial building blocks.

Figure 1.1 provides the "instruction sheet" for the financial building blocks. One can think of the financial building blocks as coming in three types: credit extension, price fixing, and price insurance.

Credit Extension Building Blocks

The traditional credit extension building blocks are bonds or loans or private placements. As illustrated in Panel A of Figure 1.1, the credit extension building block appears in four basic forms: zero coupon, level coupon, floating rate coupon, and amortizing.

---

*References to articles reprinted in this volume are in boldface type.

FIGURE 1.1 Panel A   *Credit Extension Instruments*

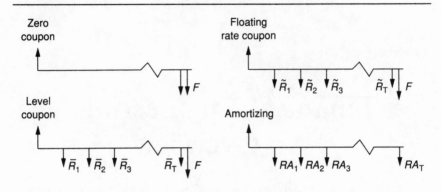

FIGURE 1.1 Panel B   *Forwards, Futures, and Swaps*

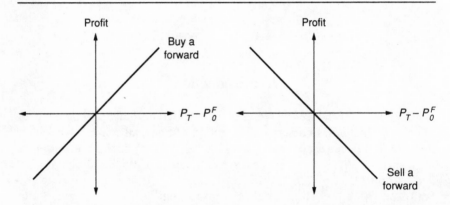

At contract maturity (time = T), the profit to the buyer of a forward contract is equal to the difference between the spot price at T and the exercise price agreed to at contract origination $(P_T - P_0^F)$ times the size of the forward contract. The profit to the seller of the contract is the reverse.

Price Fixing Building Blocks

Forward Contract.   A forward contract obligates its owner to buy a given asset on a specified date at a price (known as the "exercise price") specified at the origination of the contract. If, at maturity, the actual price is higher than the exercise price, the contract owner makes a profit; if the price is lower, he suffers a loss.

FIGURE 1.1 Panel C *Options*

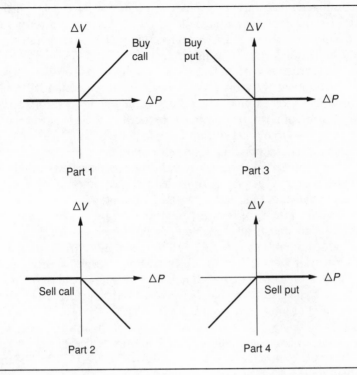

The profit/loss profiles from buying or selling a forward contract are illustrated in Panel B of Figure 1.1. If the price at contract maturity is higher than the exercise price, the owner of the forward contract will gain and the seller of the contract will lose.

Two features of a forward contract should be noted. First, unlike loans or deposits where the credit risk is from the borrower to the lender, the default (credit) risk of a forward contract is two-sided. The contract owner either receives or makes a payment, depending on the price movement of the underlying asset. Thus, both parties must evaluate the default probability if the other party is to make a payment. Second, the value of the forward contract is conveyed only at the contract's maturity; no payment is made either at origination or during the term of the contract.

Futures Contracts.   Although futures contracts on commodities have been traded on organized exchanges in Chicago since 1865, financial futures date from the introduction of foreign currency futures in 1972. The basic form of the futures contract is identical to that of the forward contract: A futures contract obligates its owner to purchase a specified asset at a specified exercise price on the contract maturity date. Thus, the payoff profiles for the forward contract as presented in Panel B of Figure 1.1 also illustrate the payoff to the holder and seller of a futures contract.

Like the forward contract, a futures contract also has two-sided risk. But in contrast to forwards, credit or default risk has been substantially reduced in the futures market through the use of two major devices: First, the performance period of a futures contract is reduced to a single day because the contract is marked to market and cash settled daily. Second, all futures market participants post a bond in the form of margin.[1]

A detailed comparison of forwards and futures is provided by **French** [17] in which he examines the pricing of traded forwards and futures contracts. His evidence indicates that, although there is a potential theoretical difference between the pricing of forward and futures contracts, in practice there appears to be no statistically reliable difference in observed pricing.

Settlement mechanisms specified by the exchanges introduce additional complications for valuing futures contracts. For example, in the case of futures contracts on U.S. Treasury bonds traded on the Chicago Board of Trade, the exchange specifies that delivery will be in the form of any one of a predefined set of long-term government bonds. As **Boyle** [5] indicates, this specification by the exchange provides the seller of the futures contract (the "short") with several potentially valuable options. For example, the short gets to wait until contract maturity to decide which specific bond of the set of eligible bonds is the cheapest to deliver.

Swaps. Because they were publicly introduced only as recently as 1981, swaps are commonly portrayed as one of the latest financing innovations. But, as **Smith, Smithson, and Wakeman** [32, 34] indicate, a swap contract is really nothing more than a series of forward contracts.

As implied by its name, a swap contract obligates two parties to exchange, or "swap," specified cash flows at specified intervals. The most common form is the interest rate swap, in which the cash flows are determined by two different interest rates. Panel A of Figure 1.2 illustrates an interest rate swap from the perspective of a party who is paying a series of cash flows determined by a fixed interest rate ($\bar{R}$) in return for a series of cash flows determined by a floating interest rate ($\tilde{R}$).[2] Panel B of Figure 1.2 illustrates that this swap can be decomposed into a portfolio of forward contracts.

---

1. See Smithson [40].
2. Specifically, the interest rate swap cash flows are determined as follows: The two parties agree to some notional principal, P. (The principal is notional in the sense that it is only used to determine the magnitude of cash flows; it is not paid or received by either party.) At each settlement date, $1, 2, ..., T$ the party illustrated makes a payment $\bar{R} = \bar{r}P$, where $\bar{r}$ is the T-period

FIGURE 1.2 *(a) An Interest Rate Swap; (b) An Interest Rate Swap as a Portfolio of Forward Contracts*

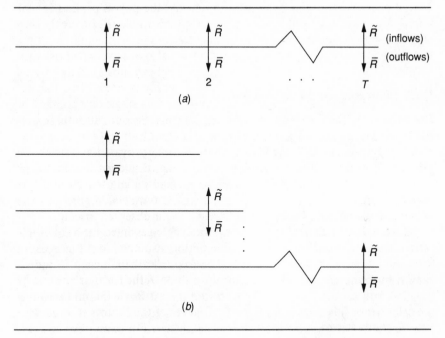

This means that the profit/loss profiles in Panel B of Figure 1.1 also represent the payoffs for a swap contract. Specifically, "long a forward or long a futures" would also illustrate a swap contract in which the party receives cash flows determined by a floating rate (e.g., LIBOR) and makes payments determined by a fixed rate.

Smith, Smithson, and Wakeman [34] argue that the credit risk of swaps is somewhat less than that of a forward contract with the same maturity, but greater than that of a comparable futures contract. The performance period of a forward is equal to its maturity; and because no performance bond is required, a forward contract is a pure credit instrument. Futures both reduce the performance period (to one day) and require a bond, thereby eliminating credit risk. Swap contracts use only one of these mechanisms to reduce credit risk; they reduce the performance period.[3] Thus, given a

---

fixed rate that existed at origination. At each settlement, the party illustrated receives $\tilde{R} = \tilde{r}P$, where $\tilde{r}$ is the floating rate for that period (e.g., at settlement date 2, the interest rate used is the one-period rate in effect at period 1).

3. There are instances in which a bond has been posted in the form of collateral. In this case, the swap becomes more like a futures contract.

swap and an equivalent portfolio of forward contracts, the swap imposes less credit risk on the counterparties to the contract.

Wall and Pringle [43] provide an overview of the demand for and uses of interest rate swaps, as well as a review of the pricing of swap contracts. They also review the evidence on credit risk and the consequent regulation of the market.

Price Insurance Building Blocks

The owner of a forward, futures, or swap contract has an *obligation* to perform. In contrast, an option gives its owner a *right,* not an obligation — the owner of an option has bought some price insurance, rather than fixing the price. The payoff profiles for option positions are displayed in Panel C of Figure 1.1. The payoff profile for an option giving its owner the right to buy an asset — a call option — is provided in Panel C Part 1 of Figure 1.1. The owner of the contract illustrated has the right to purchase the asset at a specified future date at a price agreed upon today. Consequently if at the expiration date P is higher, the value of the option also is higher. But because the option contract owner is not obligated to purchase the asset if P moves against him, the value of the option falls only to zero if P declines.

The payoff profile for the party who sold the call option (also known as the call "writer") is shown in Figure 1.1, Panel C Part 2. Note that, in contrast to the buyer of the option, the seller of the call option does have an *obligation* to perform. A put option gives its owner the right to sell an asset at a specified price. The payoff to the buyer of a put is illustrated in Figure 1.1, Panel C Part 3; the payoff for the seller of the put is shown in Part 4.

While options look very different from forwards (or futures or swaps), it is important to note that combinations of option positions are equivalent to a forward position. Consider a portfolio constructed by buying a call and selling a put with the same exercise price. As Panel A of Figure 1.3 illustrates, the resulting portfolio (long a call, short a put) has a payoff profile equivalent to that of buying a forward contract on the asset. Similarly, Panel B of Figure 1.3 illustrates that a portfolio made up of selling a call and buying a put (short a call, long a put) is equivalent to selling a forward contract. The relationship illustrated in Figure 1.3 is known more formally as put-call parity.

To this point we have considered only the payoffs for the option contracts, sidestepping the thorniest issue — the valuation of option contracts. The breakthrough in option-pricing theory came with Black and Scholes [4]. Black and Scholes employ what might be described as a dynamic "building block" approach to the valuation of options. Look again at the call option illustrated in Panel C Part 1 of Figure 1.1. For increases in the financial price, the payoff profile for the option is that of a forward contract. For decreases

FIGURE 1.3   *Put-Call Parity: (a) Long a Call, Short a Put; (b) Short a Call, Long a Put*

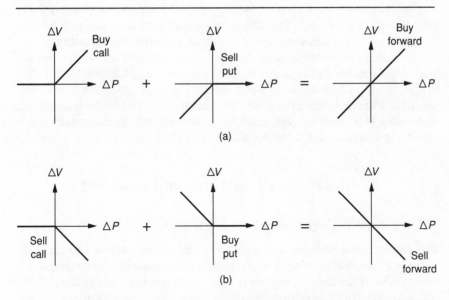

in the price, the value of the option is constant — like that of a "riskless" security such as a Treasury bill.

The Black-Scholes analysis demonstrates that the payoff to a call option could be replicated by a continuously adjusting ("dynamic") portfolio of two securities: (1) forward contracts on the underlying asset and (2) riskless securities. As the financial price rises, the "call option equivalent" portfolio contains an increasing proportion of forward contracts on the asset. Conversely, the replicating portfolio contains a decreasing proportion of the asset as the price of the asset falls. Because this replicating portfolio is effectively a synthetic call option, arbitrage activity should ensure that its value closely approximates the market price of exchange-traded call options. In this sense, the value of a call option — and thus the premium that would be charged its buyer — is determined by the value of its option equivalent portfolio.

The Black-Scholes methodology is described in **Smith** [31]. Smith points out the stringent assumptions used in the Black-Scholes model, a point that is reinforced in **Black** [3].

Subsequent to the publication of the Black-Scholes model, **Cox, Ross, and Rubenstein** [10] provided an analytically simpler method for valuing options. This methodology, referred to as the binominal pricing model, approximates the price distribution of the underlying asset by a series of discrete steps.

Thus, while options do have a payoff profile that differs significantly from that of forward contracts (or futures or swaps), option payoff profiles can be duplicated by a combination of forwards and risk-free securities.

The earliest analyses of options dealt with European-style options on shares. Subsequent research expanded the pricing methodology to consider other options. The manner in which interest rate options are valued is discussed in **Pitts [29]**. The pricing of American options on futures is described in **Whaley [44]**. And the valuation of options on foreign exchanges is described in **Garman and Kohlhagen [18]**.

II. The Rationale for Financial Engineering

Using Financial Engineering for Classic Arbitrage

The conventional wisdom is that financial engineering evolved to take advantage of some kind of arbitrage opportunity. Classic arbitrage refers to a situation in which the firm earns a riskless profit by exploiting pricing differences for the same instrument across markets. However, it is not clear that the activity we have observed in financial engineering has anything to do with classic financial arbitrage. Financial arbitrage should lead to decreasing, not increasing, activity. As the differences are arbitraged, the rate differences would be eliminated and this rationale should disappear. The evidence to date suggests that classic arbitrage opportunities are rare in today's financial markets. Thus, our analysis assumes that financial markets are efficient and focuses on other motives for financial engineering. These general motives for financial engineering are described in **Smith, Smithson, and Wilford [36]**.

Using Financial Engineering to "Arbitrage" Tax and Regulatory Authorities

In contrast to classic arbitrage, tax and regulatory arbitrage is a situation in which the firm can earn a risk-free profit by exploiting opportunities provided by the structure of the tax and regulatory environments.

A firm issuing dollar-denominated, fixed rate bonds in the U.S. capital markets has to comply with the requirements of the U.S. Securities and Exchange Commission. In the less regulated Eurobond market, the costs of issue could be considerably lower — as much as 80 basis points less.[4] However, not all firms have direct access to the Eurobond market. Financial engineering

---

4. Loeys [23].

can provide firms with access and thereby permit more firms to take advantage of this regulatory arbitrage.

Moreover, firms issuing in the U.S. capital markets, as well as the security purchasers, were generally faced with the provisions of the U.S. tax code. The introduction of financial instruments like the swap market permitted some "creative" use of the tax rules. For example, as described in **Smith, Smithson, and Wakeman** [32], a U.S. firm could issue a yen-denominated debt in the Eurobond market, structure the issue so as to receive favorable tax treatment under the Japanese tax code, avoid much of the U.S. securities regulation, and still manage its currency exposure by swapping the transaction back into dollars.

More generally, if a hybrid debt instrument is designed so that it will reduce the volatility of the issuing firm's pre-tax income, the issuing firm can reduce expected taxes. Mayers and Smith [25] and Smith and Stulz [37] demonstrate that point by showing that if the tax function faced by the issuing firm is convex, Jensen's Inequality implies that expected taxes are reduced by reducing the volatility of pre-tax income. And, the more convex the tax schedule, the greater the reduction in expected taxes.

Progressivity causes the tax schedule to be convex; however, the range of progressivity for U.S. corporate income taxes is relatively small. In addition to progressivity, tax preference items—tax loss carryforwards and tax credits, for example—also make the tax schedule convex (see Zimmerman [46]). If the firm's pre-tax income falls below some level, the value of the tax preference items is reduced either by the loss of the tax shield or by postponement of its use. (See DeAngelo and Masulis [12] and Gurel and Pyle [20].)

Using Financial Engineering to Reduce the Expected Costs of Financial Distress

Mayers and Smith [25] and Smith and Stulz [37] argue that reducing the variance of firm value will reduce the probability of the firm encountering financial distress and consequently expected costs of financial distress. Hence, if a hybrid debt instrument is designed so that it will reduce the volatility of the issuing firm's value, the issuing firm can reduce the expected transactions costs of financial distress.

The magnitude of this cost reduction is a positive function of (1) the probability that the firm will encounter financial distress if it does not hedge and (2) the costs the firm faces if it does encounter financial distress.

Using Financial Engineering to Increase the Firm's Debt Capacity

Financial engineering can be used to reduce agency costs and thereby increase the issuing firm's debt capacity. With more debt in the firm's capital structure, the value of shareholders' claims can be reduced if the firm undertakes a positive net present value project, because the gains accrue to the debtholders (see Myers [27]). Mayers and Smith [26] and Bessembinder [2] argue that the underinvestment problem can be controlled by hedging, so firms with more debt in their capital structure would be more likely to hedge.

III. Examples of Financial Engineering

The instruments can be combined with another to give one financial instrument the characteristics of another. Rather than talk about this in the abstract, let's look at some examples of how this has been done in the marketplace.

Combining Forwards with Swaps

Suppose a firm not currently exposed to interest rate movements will, at a known date in the future, be inversely exposed to interest rates: If rates rise, the value of the firm will decrease.[5] To manage this exposure, the firm could use a forward or a futures or a swap, but one commencing at that known date in the future rather than today.

Such a product is the *forward swap* (also referred to as the *delayed start swap*). A forward swap is illustrated in Panel C of Figure 1.4, where one party pays a fixed rate and receives floating *starting in period 5*. This instrument is a forward contract on a swap, but (not surprisingly) it can also be constructed as a package of swaps: As Figure 1.4 illustrates, the forward swap is equivalent to a package of two swaps:

Swap 1   From Period 1 to Period T, the party pays fixed and receives floating.

Swap 2   From Period 1 to Period 4, the party pays floating and receives fixed.

Forwards with Optionlike Characteristics

The addition of optionlike characteristics to forward contracts first appeared in the foreign exchange markets. The evolution of this market is described in **Edwardes and Levy** [14].

Begin with a standard foreign exchange forward contract. Panel A of Figure 1.5 illustrates a forward contract on sterling where the forward sterling exchange rate – the contract rate – is $1.50 per pound sterling. However, the

---

5. For example, the firm may know that in one year it will require funds to be borrowed at a floating rate, thereby giving the firm the inverse exposure to interest rates. Or the firm may be adding a new product line, the demand for which is extremely sensitive to interest rate movements – as rates rise, the demand for the product decreases and cash flows to the firm decrease.

FIGURE 1.4 *Creating a Forward Swap: (a) Pay Fixed, Receive Floating for Periods 1 through T; Plus (b) Pay Floating, Receive Fixed for Periods 1 through 4; Equals (c) A Four-Period Forward Contract on a Pay-Fixed, Receive-Floating Swap*

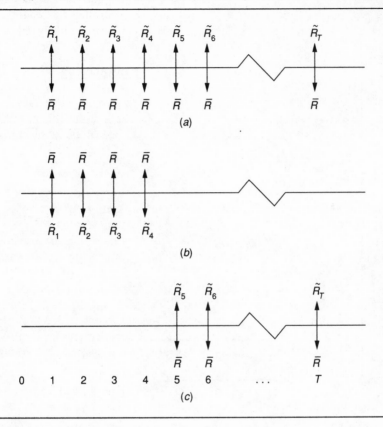

owner of the forward contract might desire a contract that permits him to profit if the price of sterling rises but floors his losses if the price of sterling falls. While such a contract could be obtained using a call option on sterling, the same contract could be obtained by altering the terms of the standard forward contract in two ways:

1. Increase the exercise price of the forward contract from $1.50 to $1.55.

2. Permit the owner of the forward to *break* (i.e., unwind) the agreement at a sterling price of $1.50.

This altered forward contract is referred to as a *break forward contract.*[6]

---

6. According to Srinivasulu (1987), *break forward* is the name given to this construction by Midland Bank. It also goes under other names: Boston Option (Bank of Boston), FOX — Forward with Optional Exit (Hambros Bank), and Cancelable Forward (Goldman Sachs).

FIGURE 1.5 *Optionlike Forwards: (a) A Standard Forward; (b) A Break Forward; (c) A Range Forward*

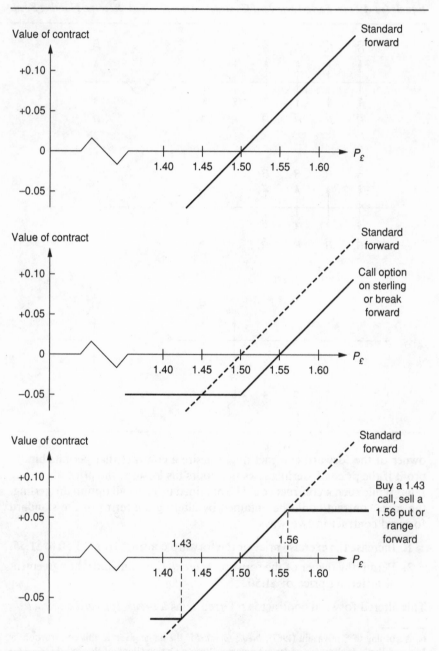

The break forward construction has no explicit option premium, but the premium is still being paid by the owner of the break forward contract in the form of a contract exchange rate above the market. From our discussion of options, we know that a call can be paid for with the proceeds of selling a put. The payoff profile for such a situation is illustrated in Panel C of Figure 1.5 (presuming that the proceeds of a $1.56 put option on sterling would carry the same premium as a $1.43 call option). A payoff profile identical to this option payoff profile could, however, also be generated simply by changing the terms of a standard forward contract to the following:

At maturity, the buyer of the forward contract agrees to purchase sterling at a price of $1.50 per pound sterling.

The buyer of the forward contract has the right to break (unwind) the contract at a price of $1.43 per pound sterling.

The seller of the forward contract has the right to break (unwind) the contract at a price of $1.56 per pound sterling.

Such a forward contract is referred to as a *range forward,*[7] the pricing of which is discussed in **Boyle and Turnbull** [6].

Swaps with Optionlike Characteristics

Given that swaps can be viewed as packages of forward contracts, it should not be surprising that swaps can also be constructed so as to have optionlike characteristics similar to those illustrated for forwards in Panel C of Figure 1.5. Suppose, for example, that a firm with a floating rate liability wanted to limit its outflows should interest rates rise substantially and that it was willing to give up some potential gains should there instead be a dramatic decline in short-term rates. To achieve this end the firm could modify the interest rate swap contract as follows:

As long as the interest rate neither rises by more than 200 basis points nor falls more than 100 basis points, the firm pays a floating rate and receives a fixed rate; but if the interest rate is more than 200 basis points above or 100 basis points below the current rate, the firm receives and pays a fixed rate.

The resulting payoff profile for this flolating *floor-ceiling swap* is illustrated in Panel A of Figure 1.6. Conversely, the interest rate swap contract could have been modified as follows:

---

7. As Srinivasulu (1987) points out, this construction also appears under a number of names: range forward (Salomon Brothers), collar (Midland Montagu), flexible forward (Manufacturers Hanover), cylinder option (Citicorp), option fence (Bank of America), mini-max (Goldman Sachs), and forward band (Chase Manhattan).

FIGURE 1.6   *Payoff Profile for Floor-Ceiling Swaps: (a) Floating Floor-Ceiling Swap; (b) Fixed Floor-Ceiling Swap*

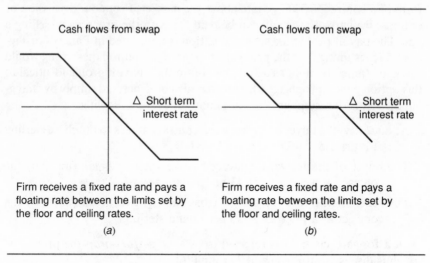

Firm receives a fixed rate and pays a floating rate between the limits set by the floor and ceiling rates.

(a)

Firm receives a fixed rate and pays a floating rate between the limits set by the floor and ceiling rates.

(b)

As long as the interest rate is within 200 basis points of the current rate, the firm neither makes nor receives a payment; but if the interest rate rises or falls by more than 200 basis points, the firm pays a floating rate and receives a fixed rate.

The payoff profile for the resulting fixed floor-ceiling swap is illustrated in Panel B of Figure 1.6.

Redesigned Options

To "redesign" an option, one normally puts two or more options together to change the payoff profile. Examples abound in the world of the option trader. Figure 1.7 illustrates how some of the more colorfully named combinations — *straddles, strangles,* and *butterflys* — are formed.

To see how and why these kinds of creations evolve, consider the hypothetical situation in which a firm desires to hedge an exposure by establishing a floor on losses. The firm could buy an out-of-the-money call option, but to do so a premium must be paid. To eliminate the premium, the out-of-the-money call could be financed by selling an out-of-the-money put — often referred to as a *collar* (or a *zero cost collar*). However, the out-of-the-money call could also be financed by selling a put with precisely the same exercise price (i.e., by selling an in-the-money put). As illustrated in Panel B of Figure 1.8, the proceeds from selling the in-the-money put would exceed the cost of the out-of-the-money call; thus, to finance one out-of-the-money call, one would need sell only a fraction of one in-the-money put. In Panel B, we

FIGURE 1.7 *Option Strategies: (a) The Straddle; (b) The Strangle; (c) The Butterfly*

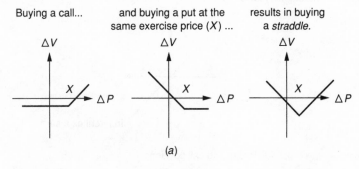

Buying a call...   and buying a put at the same exercise price (*X*) ...   results in buying a *straddle*.

(a)

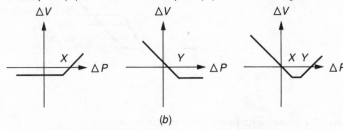

Buying a call at one exercise price (*X*) ...   and buying a put at the lower exercise price (*Y*) ...   results in buying a *strangle*.

(b)

Buying a call at one exercise price (*X*) ...   and buying a put at a higher exercise price (*Y*) ...

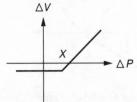
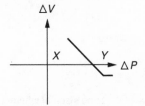

then selling a call and a put at an exercise price in between (*Z*) ...   results in buying a *butterfly*.

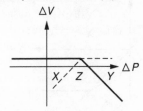
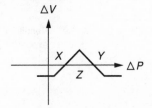

(c)

FIGURE 1.8 *Creating a "Participation"*

Panel A: Inherent risk profile.

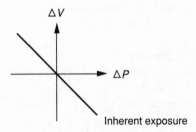

Panel B: Payoff profiles for put and call positions.

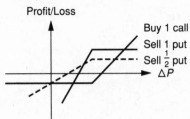

Panel C: Payoff profile for selling $\frac{1}{2}$ put and buying one call.

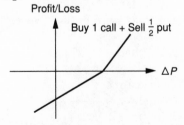

Panel D: Comparison of inherent risk (Panel A) with resulting exposure from purchase of participation (Panel C).

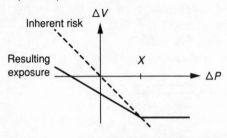

have presumed that the put value is twice the call value, so to finance one call you need sell only $\frac{1}{2}$ put, the payoff profile for which is also illustrated in Panel B. Panel C simply combines the payoff profiles for selling $\frac{1}{2}$ put and buying one call with an exercise price of X. Finally, Panel D of Figure 1.8 combines the option combination in Panel C with the inherent risk profile in Panel A.

Note what happened in the preceding. The firm obtained the floor it wanted, but without any up-front premium; the floor is paid for not with a fixed premium, but with a share of the firm's gains above the floor. The provider of the floor is paid with a share of potential gains, hence the name of this option combination—a *participation*.

This construction has been most widely used in the foreign exchange market, where they are referred to as *participating forwards*. A discussion of this and other optionlike combinations in the currency markets is provided in **Briys and Crouhy** [7].

Options on Other Financial Instruments

In addition to options on shares and options on physical commodities, *options on futures contracts* made their appearance in 1982.[8] Given the relations between futures and forwards and futures and swaps, one might expect that the introduction of options on forwards and options on swaps would have followed close on the heels of the options on futures. However, options on forwards (in particular, *options on forward rate agreements*) and options on swaps (referred to as *swaptions*) appeared only recently. In early 1989, the market for swaptions was particularly active as bond issuers were using swaptions to sell the interest rate option embedded in the call provision of a bond.

For the options discussed so far, the reference price has been a "spot" price; the value of the option at expiration is determined by the difference between the exercise price and the price prevailing at expiration. Recently, *average price options* have appeared that specify the reference price as the average price; at expiration, the value of the option is determined by the difference between the exercise price and the average of the spot prices that have existed over a specified period.

Even more innovative are the so-called *lookback options,* where the exercise price is not set at contract origination but is set instead at expiration—

---

8. Options on T-bond futures were first traded on the CBOT in October 1982, followed by options on Eurodollar futures on the CME in March 1985. Options on currency futures were first traded on the CME in January 1984. Options on commodity futures appeared with options on copper futures on the COMEX in April 1985 and with options on crude oil futures on the NYME in November 1986.

at the most favorable price that occurred during the life of the option. For instance, the owner of a lookback call option is able to buy an asset at expiration for the lowest price that occurred during the lifetime of the option. Such an option can be viewed as the combination of an at-the-money option and a second option that permits the exercise price to be changed with favorable movements in the underlying price.

More complicated analytically is the valuation of an option on an option — a *compound option*.[9] These analytical difficulties notwithstanding, some options on options have begun to be traded. The compound options first appeared with *options on foreign exchange options*. These options are particularly valuable to firms bidding on contracts denominated in foreign currencies. If the firm won the bid an option would be desired, but if the firm lost the bid the option would not be needed; hence, what the bidding firm wanted was an option on the option. However, today the more active market for compound options is for options on interest rate options (caps). Referred to in the trade as *captions,* these compound options are becoming more widely quoted and used.

Hybrid Securities

It's hard to go for a day in the financial markets without hearing of at least one hybrid product. Perhaps the most complete taxonomy of the hybrids issued as of the end of the 1980s is found in **Finnerty** [16].

Notwithstanding the number of products, our position is that there is little new under the sun. The hybrid products generally involve nothing more than putting the building blocks together in a different fashion. For example, combining a conventional fixed rate loan with an interest rate swap results in a *reverse floating rate loan*. As illustrated in Figure 1.9, the net coupon payments on this hybrid are equal to twice the fixed rate minus the floating rate times the principal,

$$\text{Net Coupon} = 2\bar{R} - \tilde{R} = (2\bar{r} - \tilde{r})P$$

so, if the floating rate rises, the net coupon payment falls. These reverse floating rate notes — also called *bull floating rate notes* — are discussed in detail in **Smith** [38].

Hybrids can be created using preferred stock instead of corporate debt as the underlying corporate liability. For example, preferred stock plus an interest rate swap produces an adjustable rate preferred issue, an instrument analyzed in **Winger, Chen, Martin, Petty, and Hayden** [45].

---

9. For a discussion of the compound option problem, see Geske [19] and Cox and Rubenstein [11, pp. 412–415].

FIGURE 1.9 *Using a Swap to Create a Reverse Floating-Rate Loan*

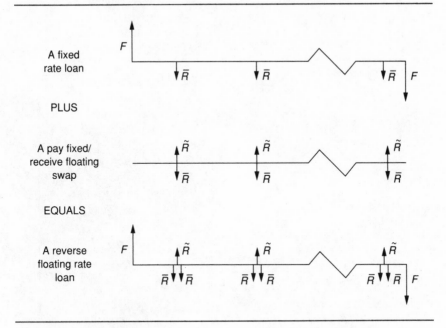

A hybrid security made up of a standard credit extension instrument and a forward contract is a *dual currency bond*. The top of Figure 1.10 illustrates a dual currency bond in which the coupons are paid in dollars, but the principal is paid in yen. The remainder of Figure 1.10 illustrates that this bond is made up of a standard, level coupon dollar bond and a dollar/yen forward contract.

Hybrids also combine interest rate options with credit extension instruments. The most common example is a *callable bond:* The investor's position is equivalent to long a standard bond and short a put option on interest rates. If rates fall, the issuer can call the bonds and issue new bonds at a lower rate. There also exist *extendible notes* wherein the investor's position is equivalent to long a standard bond and short a call option on interest rates. Since the issuer can extend the maturity of the note at some prespecified interest rate, the issuer has a call option on interest rates; that is, if rates rise above the specified rate, the issuer benefits from the extendibility.

While callables and extendibles both contain options purchased by the issuers, *putable notes* contain a call option on interest rates purchased by the investor. If rates rise, the bondholder can put the notes back to the issuer and invest in notes paying a higher interest rate. Moreover, these putable

FIGURE 1.10   *A Dual Currency Bond*

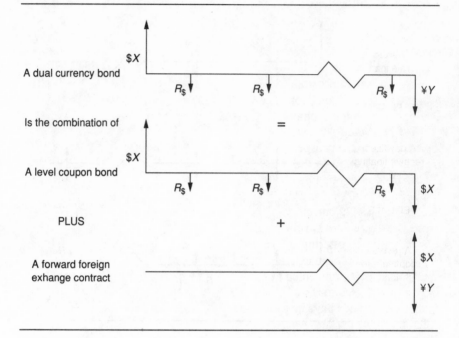

notes can also provide the bondholder with an option on the creditworthiness of the issuer. If the issuer's creditworthiness declines, the bondholder can redeem the bonds at a specified price.[10]

Since putable notes exist, there can also exist *putable stock*. **Chen and Kensinger** [9] analyze a standard putable stock arrangement in which the investors buy units composed of a share of common stock and a right provided by the issuing corporation that entitles the unitholder to claim more stock if market price drops below a stated level prior to a prespecified date.

Perhaps the most common hybrid security is the combination of a debt instrument with an option on the firm's equity. As described in **Jones and Mason** [21], the construction of these hybrids follows our building block theme. The simplest of the equity-linked hybrids is a *bond with attached warrant* — the combination of a level coupon bond and an option on shares

---

10. This idea of providing the bondholder with an option on the creditworthiness of the issuer was used by Manufacturers Hanover in February 1988 when it issued *floating rate, rating sensitive notes*. With these notes, the spread over LIBOR automatically changed if the issuer's credit rating changed. Note that in contrast to the putable notes that combine an interest rate option and an option on the creditworthiness of the issuer, these floating rate, rating sensitive notes contain only options on Manufacturers Hanover's creditworthiness.

of the issuing firm. **Finnerty** [15] contrasts the incentives to issue a bond with a warrant with the incentives to issue a *convertible bond*.

Merrill Lynch combined several options in their *LYONs* (Liquid Yield Option Notes). As described in **McConnell and Schwartz** [24], the LYON is a putable, callable, convertible, zero coupon bond.

By the end of the 1980s, hybrids were being issued that extended the process. Along one dimension, there was an expansion of the kinds of warrants available. In addition to options on shares, options appeared that are exercisable into foreign exchange and gold.

By 1986, Standard Oil was providing oil options with its *Oil Indexed Notes*. As described in the prospectus, at maturity the holder of the 1990 note would receive (in addition to the principal) "the excess...of the Crude Oil Price ...over \$25 multiplied by 170 barrels of Light Sweet Crude Oil...." Hence, at issue the 1990 note was the combination of a standard note and a four-year option on 170 barrels of crude oil. The pricing of this hybrid is also discussed in **Boyle and Turnbull** [6].

In addition to offering options on assets other than shares, the building block process has been extended along another dimension by modifying the timing of the options embedded in the bond. A traditional bond with attached warrant contains only one option exercisable at one point in time. More recent bonds have involved packages of options that are exercisable at different points in time. An example of this type of hybrid is Magma Copper Company's *Copper Interest-Indexed Senior Subordinated Notes,* issued in November 1988. This 10-year issue pays a quarterly interest payment determined by the prevailing price of copper:

Average Copper Price	Indexed Interest Rate
\$2.00 or above	21%
1.80	20%
⋮	⋮
0.90	13%
0.80 or below	12%

Hence, at each coupon date the holder of the debenture has an option position on copper price. That is, this 10-year debenture has embedded in it 40 option positions on the price of copper — one with maturity 3 months, one with maturity 6 months, and so forth each quarter until the final option position with maturity 10 years.

IV. The Stumbling Blocks

In their review of survey results, Rawls and Smithson [30] note that users and potential users consistently report two principal stumbling blocks: (1) the perception that financial engineering is "too complex" and (2) constraints imposed by accounting, taxes, and regulations. With respect to the first stumbling block, we believe that Smithson's building block analogy goes a long way toward demystifying financial engineering; it's hard to think about connecting building blocks as complex. A substantial amount of research has been directed toward the second stumbling block.

Accounting

Uncertainty continues to exist about the correct accounting treatment for the new financial products—particularly for hybrid securities. Consequently, the accounting treatment for these products is receiving a great deal of attention. For example, the November 1989 issue of *Journal of Accountancy* focused on accounting for the risk management products.

Stewart [42] points out that if traditional accounting methods are used for the risk management instruments, fluctuations in accounting statement income will increase, implying to the analyst that the use of the instruments caused the firm to be more risky, when in fact the opposite is true. To develop appropriate accounting methods for instruments used to hedge the firm's exposures, the Financial Accounting Standards Board (FASB) faces two major problems: (1) There is a total absence of accounting guidance for many of the risk management instruments, including interest rate forwards, interest rate swaps, and almost all types of options. (2) The current standards are inconsistent.

Given the building blocks approach we favor, it is rewarding to hear **Bullen, Wilkins, and Woods** [8] reporting that, in developing new accounting standards, the FASB has also adopted a building block approach, attempting to break down complex financial instruments to determine their economic substance and thereby eliminate the inconsistent accounting standards. However, the FASB has not yet sufficiently narrowed down the number of building blocks. Currently, the FASB considers six basic blocks—unconditional receivable (payable), conditional receivable (payable), forward contract, option, guarantee or other conditional exchange, and equity. This taxonomy involves some double counting: A conditional receivable (payable) is an option, as are guarantees[11] and equity.[12] We continue to assert that there are only three basic building blocks. Using the language of the FASB, we can express these three as

1. An unconditional receivable (payable) that can be in the form of a bond or a loan or a deposit.

---

11. A guarantee can be viewed as an option on creditworthiness, as with the option attached to debt instruments by Manufacturers Hanover and Enron in their *rating sensitive notes*.
12. The description of equity as a call option on the value of the firm's assets first appeared in Black and Scholes [4].

2. A forward contract that can be expanded into a futures contract or a swap contract.

3. A conditional receivable (payable) is an option that encompasses guarantees and equity.

Bullen, Wilkins, and Woods also note that a substantial body of authoritative accounting literature may be affected by the development of appropriate accounting methods for the financial instruments. Their list includes Accounting Principles Board Opinion 21, as well as FASB Statements no. 12, 15, 52, 65, 76, 77, 80, and 91.

In July 1989, FASB issued for comment a revised draft dealing with the disclosures firms will be required to make regarding their use of the financial instruments. As described in **Amble** [1], these disclosure requirements — which deal with the extent, nature, and terms of financial instruments used, as well as the amount of credit risk accepted by the firm — are to be effective for calendar year 1989 reporting.

Taxes

Smithson [41] notes that uncertainty also exists about the tax status of some of the financially engineered securities. For example, early in session, the 101st Congress focused attention on the current tax rules that permit a firm to take a deduction today for interest payments deferred into the future, with the House voting to eliminate deductibility entirely (treating the bonds as equity) and the Senate voting to defer the deductibility.[13] By the end of the session, "Congress's attention [on junk bonds and LBO debt] had waned,"[14] but the issue of interest deductibility is one that will continue to receive attention.

Regulation

There are important regulatory issues currently being resolved that will have an important impact on the structure of these markets. One issue is the capital requirements imposed on financial institutions that make markets in the financial instruments. **Smith, Smithson, and Wakeman** [33] indicate that the proposals to date appear to reflect an overestimation of the credit risk of swaps. The capital requirement thus represents a tax on the affected financial institutions and could affect the pricing and organization of the market.

---

13. Kevin G. Salwin, "Two Legislative Proposals Would Raise Cost of Leveraged Buy-Outs Up to 10%," *Wall Street Journal,* October 19, 1989.
14. David E. Rosenbaum, "Legislation on Buyouts Is Unlikely," *The New York Times,* November 6, 1989.

A second issue has to do with regulatory policy affecting the rate of financial innovation. Because of the language of the Commodity Exchange Act, the Commodity Futures Trading Commission (CFTC) — with the Securities and Exchange Commission (SEC) and the federal and state banking regulators — has played a central role in the regulation of financial engineering. In July 1989, the CFTC issued a release giving financial institutions more latitude in the development of commodity-linked transactions and hybrid securities. **Jordan, Mackay, and Moriarty** [22] provide insights into the release and its implications.

Also concerned with the rate of innovation, **Petruzzi, Del Valle, and Judiowe** [28] review the use of copyrights and patents by firms engaged in innovative financial engineering. They indicate that the legal system has begun to apply copyright and patent provisions more broadly. This copyright and patent protection raises the costs of entry to potential competitors, thereby increasing innovative activity, since it allows the innovating institution to capture greater returns from its innovative activity.

Easterbrook [13] analyzes entry restrictions in the futures markets. He argues that, while the possibility of manipulation exists, effective manipulation is very difficult because of competition from the cash markets. Indeed, he argues that the losses from manipulation are strictly less than the gains from trading, so entry restrictions are never correct public policy.

V. The Future for Financial Engineering

In an open memo, Columbia Savings & Loan, Fidelity Investments, Investors Diversified Services, Prudential Insurance, Reliance Insurance, and other large institutional investors[15] expressed their concern about

1. Relative size of the firm's debt as a percent of its net assets.

2. The ability of the issuer to increase the relative size of the debt by making payments to shareholders.

3. Potential changes in creditworthiness of the firm; that is, via changes in control.

4. Maintenance of the firm's net asset value.

This memo points to increased covenant protection as the solution to this problem. Although covenant protection is important, covenants cannot do it all.

Instead, the evidence points toward financially engineered bonds designed to deal explicitly with the problems of the corporate debt market. It seems that two types of these new structures are appearing.

---

15. Memo of April 14, 1989. The firms named were members of the steering committee.

One type is a bond that tries to align the interests of the shareholders and bondholders. Such a bond is the LYON we looked at earlier. The LYON satisfies the issuers' demands by being a subordinated, zero coupon bond. Since the LYON is convertible, the interests of the bondholder are better aligned with those of the shareholder; since the LYON is putable, it addresses investors' concerns about potential changes in creditworthiness of the firm — changes in control of the firm.[16]

The other type is a bond that attempts to reduce directly the default risk. Such a bond is the Magma "Copper Interest Indexed Senior Subordinated Notes" we looked at earlier. If copper prices are low (and the probability of Magma being in financial distress is consequently higher), the coupon payment will be low — so the structure of the bond itself lowers the probability of default. To the extent that issuers want to lever up the firm, financial engineering will be even more widely used.

---

16. The trade press looks at "change of control" puts (a.k.a. "poison puts") as a takeover defense when in fact they are "golden parachutes" for the bondholders. These puts provide the bondholder with insurance against wealth transfers via restructuring.

References

1. Joan Lordi Amble, "The FASB's New ED on Disclosure," *Journal of Accountancy* vol. 168 (no. 5, November 1989), pp. 63–70. **Reprinted in this volume.**
2. H. Bessembinder, "Risk Hedging and Firm Value: Contracting, Investment Incentive, and Capital Structure Effects." Working Paper, University of Rochester, 1987.
3. Fischer Black, "The Holes in Black-Scholes," *Journal of Applied Corporate Finance* vol. 1 (no. 4, 1988), pp. 67–73. **Reprinted in this volume.**
4. Fischer Black and Myron Scholes, "The Pricing of Options and Corporate Liabilities," *Journal of Political Economy* vol. 81 (no. 3, 1973), pp. 637–659.
5. Phelim P. Boyle, "The Quality Option and Timing Option in Futures Contracts," *Journal of Finance* vol. 44 (no. 1, 1989), pp. 101–113. **Reprinted in this volume.**
6. Phelim P. Boyle and Stuart M. Turnbull, "Pricing and Hedging Capped Options," *Journal of Futures Markets* vol. 9 (no. 1, 1989), pp. 41–54. **Reprinted in this volume.**
7. Eric Briys and Michel Crouhy, "Creating and Pricing Hybrid Foreign Currency Options," *Financial Management* vol. 17 (no. 4, 1988), pp. 59–65. **Reprinted in this volume.**
8. Halsey G. Bullen, Robert C. Wilkins, and Clifford C. Woods III, "The Fundamental Financial Instrument Approach," *Journal of Accountancy* vol. 168 (no. 5, November 1989), pp. 71–78. **Reprinted in this volume.**
9. Andrew H. Chen and John W. Kensinger, "Puttable Stock: A New Innovation in Equity Financing," *Financial Management* vol. 17 (no. 1, 1988), pp. 27–37. **Reprinted in this volume.**
10. John C. Cox, Stephen A. Ross, and Mark Rubenstein, "Option Pricing: A Simplified Approach," *Journal of Financial Economics* vol. 7 (no. 3, 1979), pp. 229–263.

28 Introduction

11. John C. Cox and Mark Rubenstein, *Options Markets* (Englewood Cliffs, New Jersey: Prentice-Hall, 1985).
12. Harry DeAngelo and Ronald W. Masulis, "Optimal Capital Structure Under Corporate and Personal Taxation," *Journal of Financial Economics* vol. 8 (1980), pp. 3-29.
13. Frank H. Easterbrook, "Monopoly Manipulation and the Regulation of Futures Markets," *Journal of Business* vol. 59 (no. 2, 1986), pp. 103-127. **Reprinted in this volume.**
14. Warren Edwardes and Edmond Levy, "Break Forwards: A Synthetic Option Hedging Instrument," *Midland Corporate Finance Journal* vol. 5 (no. 2, 1987), pp. 59-67. **Reprinted in this volume.**
15. John D. Finnerty, "The Case for Issuing Synthetic Convertible Bonds," *Midland Corporate Finance Journal* vol. 4 (no. 3, 1986), pp. 73-82. **Reprinted in this volume.**
16. John D. Finnerty, "Financial Engineering in Corporate Finance: An Overview," *Financial Management* vol. 17 (no. 4, 1988), pp. 14-33. **Reprinted in this volume.**
17. Kenneth R. French, "A Comparison of Forward and Futures Prices," *Journal of Financial Economics* vol. 12 (no. 3, 1983), pp. 311-342. **Reprinted in this volume.**
18. Mark B. Garman and S. W. Kohlhagen, "Foreign Currency Option Values," *Journal of International Money and Finance* vol. 2 (1983), pp. 231-237. **Reprinted in this volume.**
19. Robert Geske, "The Valuation of Compound Options," *Journal of Financial Economics* vol. 7 (1979), pp. 63-81.
20. Eitan Gurel and David Pyle, "Bank Income Taxes and Interest Rate Risk Management: A Note," *Journal of Finance* vol. 39 (September 1984), pp. 1199-1206.
21. E. Phillip Jones and Scott P. Mason, "Equity Linked Debt," *Midland Corporate Finance Journal* vol. 3 (no. 4, 1986), p. 46-58. **Reprinted in this volume.**
22. James V. Jordan, Robert S. Mackay, and Eugene J. Moriarty, "Hybrid Debt Instruments: Regulation and Economics," *Journal of Applied Corporate Finance* (forthcoming). **Reprinted with additions in this volume.**
23. Jan Loeys, "Interest Rate Swaps: A New Took for Managing Risk," *Business Review,* Federal Reserve Bank of Philadelphia (May/June 1985), pp. 17-25.
24. John J. McConnell and Eduardo S. Schwartz, "LYON Taming," *Journal of Finance* vol. 41 (no. 3, 1986), pp. 561-577. **Reprinted in this volume.**
25. David Mayers and Clifford W. Smith, Jr., "On the Corporate Demand for Insurance," *Journal of Business* vol. 55 (April 1982), pp. 281-296.
26. David Mayers and Clifford W. Smith, Jr., "Corporate Insurance and the Underinvestment Problem," *Journal of Risk and Insurance* vol. 54 (1987), pp. 45-54.
27. S. C. Myers, "The Determinants of Corporate Borrowing," *Journal of Financial Economics* vol. 5 (November 1977), pp. 147-175.
28. Christopher Petruzzi, Marguerite Del Valle, and Stephen Judiowe, "Patent and Copyright Protection for Innovations in Finance," *Financial Management* vol. 17 (no. 4, 1988), pp. 66-71. **Reprinted in this volume.**
29. Mark Pitts, "The Pricing of Options on Debt Securities," *Journal of Portfolio Management* vol. 9 (1985), pp. 41-50. **Reprinted in this volume.**
30. S. Waite Rawls, III, and Charles W. Smithson, "Strategic Risk Management," *Journal of Applied Corporate Finance* vol. 2 (no. 4, Winter 1990), pp. 6-18.
31. Clifford W. Smith, Jr., "Option Pricing: A Review," *Journal of Financial Economics* vol. 3 (1976), pp. 3-52. **Reprinted in this volume.**

32. Clifford W. Smith, Jr., Charles W. Smithson, and Lee Macdonald Wakeman, "The Evolving Market for Swaps," *Midland Corporate Finance Journal* vol. 3 (no. 4, 1986), pp. 20–32. **Reprinted in this volume.**
33. Clifford W. Smith, Jr., Charles W. Smithson, and Lee Macdonald Wakeman, "Credit Risk and the Scope of Regulation of Swaps," *Bank Structure and Competition* (1987), pp. 166–185. **Reprinted in this volume.**
34. Clifford W. Smith, Jr., Charles W. Smithson, and Lee Macdonald Wakeman, "The Market for Interest Rate Swaps," *Financial Management* vol. 17 (no. 4, 1988), pp. 34–44. **Reprinted in this volume.**
35. Clifford W. Smith, Jr., Charles W. Smithson, and D. Sykes Wilford, "Managing Financial Risk," *Journal of Applied Corporate Finance* vol. 1 (no. 4, 1989a), pp. 27–48. **Reprinted in this volume.**
36. Clifford W. Smith, Jr., Charles W. Smithson, and D. Sykes Wilford, "Financial Engineering: Why Hedge?" *Intermarket* vol. 6 (no. 7, 1989b), pp. 12–16. **Reprinted in this volume.**
37. Clifford W. Smith, Jr., and R. M. Stulz. "The Determinants of Firms' Hedging Policies," *Journal of Financial and Quantitative Analysis* vol. 20 (December 1985), pp. 391–405.
38. Donald J. Smith, "The Pricing of Bull and Bear Floating Rate Notes: An Application of Financial Engineering," *Financial Management* vol. 17 (no. 4, 1988), pp. 72–81. **Reprinted in this volume.**
39. Donald J. Smith, "The Arithmetic of Financial Engineering," *Journal of Applied Corporate Finance* vol. 1 (no. 4, 1989), pp. 49–58. **Reprinted in this volume.**
40. Charles W. Smithson, "A LEGO^R Approach to Financial Engineering: An Introduction to Forwards, Futures, Swaps, and Options," *Midland Corporate Finance Journal* vol. 4 (no. 4, 1987), pp. 16–28.
41. Charles W. Smithson, "The Market for High Yield Debt," unpublished manuscript.
42. John E. Stewart, "The Challenge of Hedge Accounting," *Journal of Accountancy* vol. 168 (no. 5, 1989), pp. 71–78. **Reprinted in this volume.**
43. Larry D. Wall and John J. Pringle, "Interest Rate Swaps: A Review," *Economic Review of the Federal Reserve Bank of Atlanta* (1988), pp. 22–40. **Reprinted in this volume.**
44. Robert E. Whaley, "Valuation of American Futures Options: Theory and Empirical Tests," *Journal of Finance* vol. 41 (no. 1, 1986), pp. 127–150. **Reprinted in this volume.**
45. B. J. Winger, C. R. Chen, J. D. Martin, J. W. Petty, and S. C. Hayden, "Adjustable Rate Preferred Stock," *Financial Management* vol. 15 (no. 1, 1986), pp. 48–57. **Reprinted in this volume.**
46. J. L. Zimmerman, "Taxes and Firm Size," *Journal of Accounting and Economics* (1983), pp. 119–149.

PART II

Foundations of
Financial Engineering

2

Managing Financial Risk*

*Clifford W. Smith, Jr., Charles W. Smithson,
& D. Sykes Wilford*

There is no doubt that the financial environment is a lot riskier today than it was in the 1950s and 1960s. With changes in some macroeconomic institutional structures—notably, the breakdown of the Bretton Woods agreement in 1972—have come dramatic increases in the volatility of interest rates, foreign exchange rates, and commodity prices.

Such increased volatility will not come as news to most corporate executives. Since the 1970s, many CEOs and CFOs have watched the profitability of their firms swing widely in response to large movements in exchange rates, interest rates, and commodity prices. What may be news, however, are the techniques and tools now available for measuring and managing such financial risks.

Recognition of the increased volatility of exchange rates, interest rates, and commodity prices should lead managers of the firm to ask three questions:

1. To what extent is my firm exposed to interest rates, foreign exchange rates, or commodity prices?
2. What financial tools are available for managing these exposures?
3. If my firm is significantly exposed, how do I use the financial tools to manage the exposure?

It is with these three questions that the following discussion deals.

*This article is an abbreviated version of Chapters 2, 3, and 19 of *Managing Financial Risk,* (1990) Ballinger *Institutional Investor Series.* This material is used with the permission of the publisher.

Identifying and Measuring Financial Risk

The Risk Profile

U.S. savings and loans (S&Ls) are a widely cited example of firms subject to interest rate risk. Because S&Ls typically fund long-lived assets (e.g., 30-year fixed rate mortgages) with liabilities that reprice frequently (passbook deposits), their value is negatively related to interest rates. When interest rates rise, the value of S&Ls' assets declines significantly, but the value of their liabilities changes little. So, the value of shareholders' equity falls.

The resulting relation between interest rates and the value of S&Ls is portrayed graphically in a *risk profile* in Figure 2.1. The negative slope reflects the inverse relation between the financial price (i.e., interest rates) and the value of the S&L. The precise measure of the exposure is reflected by the slope of the line; and it is a measure of the slope that the techniques described below will provide.

But before considering the size of the exposure, the first question is: How do we go about identifying such exposures? In the case of S&Ls, the exposure to interest rates is apparent from the firm's balance sheet; the mismatch of

FIGURE 2.1   *The Risk Profile for a U.S. S&L*

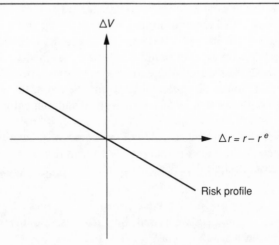

As actual interest rates, r, rise above expected rates, r^e,
$\Delta r > 0$ the value of the S&L's assets declines relative to the
value of its liabilities: so, the value of the firm declines,
$\Delta V < 0$.

maturities between assets and liabilities is obvious. Many companies, however, have economic or "operating" exposures that are not reflected on their balance sheets. Take, for example, the vulnerability of building products firms to increases in interest rates. Increases in interest rates decrease the demand for building products. As sales and thus cash inflows decline—and to the extent that its costs and liabilities are fixed—the value of a building products firm declines.

We can make a similar observation about foreign exchange risk. In some instances, exposures are apparent. For example, a U.S. importer orders product from Germany and is expected to pay in Deutsche Marks (DM) for the products when they are delivered in 90 days. If during those 90 days the price of a DM rises—that is, the value of the dollar declines—the U.S. importer will have to pay more for the product. In this case, an increase in the price of the foreign currency leads to a decrease in the value of the importer.

Since 1972, firms have become adept at dealing with such transaction exposures.[1] However, a firm's exposure to foreign exchange rate risk can be more subtle; even firms that have no foreign receipts or payments may still be exposed to foreign exchange risk. If the dollar is strong, the dollar price of foreign products to U.S. consumers becomes cheaper and foreign firms make inroads into the U.S. market, thereby decreasing net cash flows to the U.S. producers and thus reducing their value. The reverse is true when the value of the dollar falls. Obvious to firms like automakers, this economic or competitive (or "strategic") risk is receiving more attention from the managers of other U.S. firms as well.[2]

Not surprisingly, the same relations appear with respect to commodity price risk. The exposures can be apparent: For example, as the price of oil rises, the costs for an airline rise; so rising oil prices are linked to falling firm values. Or the exposures can be subtle. For example, a primary input in aluminum production is electric energy. Aluminum manufacturers in Iceland use electricity generated by that country's abundant geothermal energy. As the price of oil rises, the costs of competitors rise while the costs of Icelandic producers remain unchanged, thus improving the competitive position and increasing the value of Icelandic firms. It is when oil prices fall and competitors' costs decline that Icelandic producers worry.[3]

---

1. A transaction exposure occurs when the firm has a payment or receipt in a currency other than its home currency. A translation exposure results when the value of foreign assets and liabilities must be converted into home currency values.
2. A case in point is Kodak, which has begun to manage "overall corporate performance in the long run." See Paul Dickens, "Daring to Hedge the Unhedgeable," *Euromoney Corporate Finance,* August 1988.
3. For this useful story about Icelandic aluminum producers, we are indebted to J. Nicholas Robinson of Chase Manhattan Bank.

Financial price risk, then—whether caused by changes in interest rates, foreign exchange, or commodity prices—consists of more subtle economic exposures as well as the obvious balance sheet mismatches and transactional exposures. And the *risk profile* mentioned earlier, in order to provide a useful measure of a firm's overall economic exposure, must reflect the total effect of both kinds of price risk.

The question that naturally arises, then, is: How do you determine the slope of the risk profile? That is, how do you estimate the change in firm value expected to accompany a given change in a financial price ($\Delta V/\Delta P$)?

Quantifying Financial Risk: A Special Case

Financial institutions, particularly banks, were the first to devote significant attention to quantifying financial exposures. Our S&L example is admittedly an extreme case of interest rate exposure, even for a financial institution. Nevertheless, because some mismatch between the maturities of assets and liabilities almost inevitably occurs in the normal course of their business, all financial institutions generally face some degree of interest rate risk. To measure this exposure to interest rates, financial institutions rely on two techniques: *gap* and *duration*.

Gap.   The method most financial corporations use to measure their exposure to interest rate changes is called the "maturity gap" approach.[4] The approach gets its name from a procedure designed to quantify the "gap" between the market values of rate sensitive assets (RSA) and rate sensitive liabilities (RSL); that is, gap = RSA − RSL.[5] The financial institution determines the "gapping period"—the period over which it wants to measure its interest rate sensitivity—say, six months, one year, five years, and so forth. Then, for each of these periods, it measures its gap as defined above. In the context of a gap model, changes in interest rates affect a financial institution's market value by changing the institution's net interest income (NII). Hence, once the gap is known, the impact on the firm of changes in the interest rate can be calculated as follows:

$$\Delta NII = (gap) \times (\Delta r)$$

---

4. For a discussion of the maturity gap model, see Alden L. Toevs, "Measuring and Managing Interest Rate Risk: A Guide to Asset/Liability Models Used in Banks and Thrifts," Morgan Stanley Fixed Income Analytical Research Paper, October 1984. (An earlier version of this paper appeared in *Economic Review,* The Federal Reserve Bank of San Francisco, Spring, 1983).

5. The assets and liabilities that are "rate sensitive" are those that will reprice during the gapping period.

TABLE 2.1 *Calculation of the Value and Duration of the Business Loan*

(1) Time to Receipt (Years)	(2) Cash Flow	(3) Discount Rate	(4) PV	(5) Weight	(6) Weight × Time
0.5	90	7.75%	86.70	0.22	0.11
1.0	90	8.00%	83.33	0.21	0.21
1.5	90	8.25%	79.91	0.20	0.31
2.0	90	8.35%	76.66	0.19	0.38
2.5	90	8.50%	73.40	0.18	0.45
			400.00 Present Value		1.45 Duration

Duration. Some financial institutions use an alternative to the gap approach called "duration analysis" to measure their interest rate exposure.[6] In essence, the duration of a financial instrument provides a measure of when on average the present value of the instrument is received.

For example, let's look at the duration of a business loan with a maturity of 2.5 years and a sinking fund. Because part of the value is received prior to maturity, the duration of the instrument is clearly less than 2.5 years. To find out how much less, we need to ask the question "When on average is the present value received?"

Table 2.1 provides an illustration. Columns 1–4 provide the present value of the bond. To determine *when* on average the present value will be received, we need to calculate the weighted average time of receipt. Column 5 provides the weights. Multiplying these weights (Column 5) by the times the cash flows are received (Column 1) and summing gives the duration of this business loan (1.45 years).

The use of duration effectively converts a security into its zero coupon equivalent. In addition, duration relates changes in interest rates to changes in the value of the security.[7] Specifically, duration permits us to express the percentage change in the value of the security in terms of the percentage

---

6. For a discussion of duration, see George G. Kaufman, "Measuring and Managing Interest Rate Risk: A Primer," *Economic Perspectives,* Federal Reserve Bank of Chicago. See also Stephen Schaefer, "Immunisation and Duration: A Review of the Theory, Performance, and Applications," *Midland Corporate Finance Journal,* Vol. 2 No. 3, Fall 1984.

7. Note the contrast with the gap approach, which relates changes in the interest rate to changes in net interest income.

change in the discount rate $(1+r)$ and the duration of the security, as follows: [8]

$$\frac{\Delta V}{V} = \frac{\Delta(1+r)}{(1+r)} \times D$$

For example, if the duration of a security is 1.45 years, and the discount rate increases by 1% (that is, if $\Delta(1+r)/(1+r) = 0.01$), the market value of the 2.5-year business loan will decrease by 1.45%. The concept of duration, moreover, can be extended to provide a measure of the interest rate exposure of an entire bank or S&L.

Quantifying Financial Price Risk: The General Case

While gap and duration work well for financial institutions, these techniques offer little guidance in evaluating the interest rate sensitivity of a nonfinancial institution, and neither gap nor duration is useful in examining a firm's sensitivity to movements in foreign exchange rates or commodity prices. What is needed is a more general method for quantifying financial price risk—a method that can handle firms other than financial institutions and financial exposures other than interest rates.

To get a measure of the responsiveness of the value of the firm to changes in the financial prices, we must first define a measure of the value of the firm. As with interest rate risk for financial institutions, this value measure could be a "flow" measure (gap analysis uses net interest income) or a "stock" measure (duration uses the market value of the portfolio).

Flow Measures.   Within a specific firm, estimation of the sensitivity of income flows is an analysis that can be performed as part of the planning and budgeting process. The trade press suggests that some firms have begun using simulation models to examine the responsiveness of their pre-tax income to changes in interest rates, exchange rates, and commodity prices. [9] Beginning with base case assumptions about the financial prices, the firm obtains a forecast for revenues, costs, and the resulting pre-tax income. It then considers alternative values for an interest rate or an exchange rate or a commodity price and obtains a new forecast for revenues, costs, and pre-tax income. By observing how the firm's projected sales, costs, and income move in response to changes in these financial prices, management is able to trace out a risk profile similar to that in Figure 2.1.

---

8. The calculations in Table 2.1 are based on the use of MacCauley's duration. If we continue to apply MacCauley's duration (D), this equation is only an approximation. To be exact, modified duration should be used. For a development of this relation, see George G. Kaufman, G. O. Bierwag, and Alden Toevs, eds. *Innovations in Bond Portfolio Management: Duration Analysis and Immunization* (Greenwich, Conn.: JAI Press, 1983).
9. See, for instance, Paul Dickens, cited in Note 2.

In making such an estimation, two inherent problems confront the analyst: (1) This approach requires substantial data and (2) it relies on the ability of the researcher to make explicit, accurate forecasts of sales and costs under alternative scenarios for the financial prices. For both these reasons, such an approach is generally feasible only for analysts within a specific firm.

Stock Measures. Given the data requirements noted above, analysts outside the firm generally rely on market valuations, the most widely used of which is the current market value of the equity. Using a technique much like the one used to estimate a firm's "beta," an outside observer could measure the historical sensitivity of the company's equity value to changes in interest rates, foreign exchange rates, and commodity prices.

For example, suppose we wished to determine the sensitivity of a company's value to the following financial prices:

- the one-year T-bill interest rate;
- the deutsche mark/dollar exchange rate;
- the pound sterling/dollar exchange rate;
- the yen/dollar exchange rate; and
- the price of oil.

We could estimate this relation by performing a simple linear regression as follows:[10]

$$R_t = a + b_1 \left(\frac{\Delta P_{TB}}{P_{TB}} \right)_t + b_2 \left(\frac{\Delta P_{DM}}{P_{DM}} \right)_t + b_3 \left(\frac{\Delta P_{\pounds}}{P_{\pounds}} \right)_t$$
$$+ b_4 \left(\frac{\Delta P_{\yen}}{P_{\yen}} \right)_t + b_5 \left(\frac{\Delta P_{OIL}}{P_{OIL}} \right)_t$$

---

10. In effect, this equation represents a variance decomposition. While it is a multifactor model, it is not related in any important way to the APT approach suggested by Ross and Roll. Instead, it is probably more accurate to view the approach we suggest as an extension of the market model. In its more complete form, as described in Chapter 2 of our book *Managing Financial Risk,* the regression equation would include the rate of return to the market ("beta") as well as the percentage changes in the financial prices, and would thus look as follows:

$$R_t = a + \beta R_{m,t} + b_1 PC(P_{TB}) + b_2 PC(P_{DM}) + b_3 PC(P_{\pounds}) + b_4 PC(P_{\yen}) + b_5 PC(P_{OIL})$$

This more complete model is based on a number of earlier studies: French, Ruback, and Schwert ("Effects of Nominal Contracting on Stock Returns," *Journal of Political Economy* Vol. 91 No. 1, 1983) on the impact of unexpected inflation on share returns, Flannery and James ("The Effect of Interest Rate Changes on Common Stock Returns of Financial Institutions," *Journal of Finance* Vol. 39 No. 4, 1984) and Scott and Peterson ("Interest Rate Risk and Equity Values of Hedged and Unhedged Financial Intermediaries," *Journal of Financing Research* Vol. 9 No. 6, 1986) on the impact of interest rate changes on share prices for financial firms, and Sweeney and Warga ("The Pricing of Interest Rate Risk: Evidence from the Stock Market," *Journal of Finance* Vol. 41 No. 2, 1986) on the impact of interest rate risk on share prices for nonfinancial firms. This model does exhibit the problems of measuring the reaction

TABLE 2.2   *Measurements of Exposures to Interest Rate, Foreign Exchange Rates, and Oil Prices*

Percentage Change In	Chase Manhattan		Caterpillar		Exxon	
	Parameter Estimate	T Value	Parameter Estimate	T Value	Parameter Estimate	T Value
Price of 1-Year T-Bill	2.598[a]	1.56	−3.221[b]	1.76	1.354[c]	1.24
Price of DM	−0.276	0.95	0.344	1.07	−0.066	0.35
Price of Sterling	0.281	1.16	−0.010	0.38	0.237[a]	1.50
Price of Yen	−0.241	0.96	0.045	0.16	−0.278[b]	1.69
Price of WTI Crude	0.065	1.21	−0.045	0.77	0.082[c]	2.33

a. Significant at 90% single tailed.
b. Significant at 90%.
c. Significant at 95%.

where R is the rate of return on the firm's equity; $\Delta P_{TB}/P_{TB}$ is the percentage change in the price of a one-year T-bill; $\Delta P_{DM}/P_{DM}$, $\Delta P_{\pounds}/P_{\pounds}$, and $\Delta P_{Y}/P_{Y}$ are the percentage changes in the dollar prices of the three foreign currencies; and $\Delta P_{OIL}/P_{OIL}$ is the percentage change in the price of crude oil. The estimate of b_1 provides a measure of the sensitivity of the value of the firm to changes in the one-year T-bill rate; b_2, b_3, and b_4 estimate its sensitivity to the exchange rates; and b_5 estimates its sensitivity to the oil price.[11]

To illustrate the kind of results this technique would yield, we present three examples: a bank (Chase Manhattan), an industrial (Caterpillar), and an oil company (Exxon). For the period January 6, 1984, to December 2, 1988, we calculated weekly (Friday close to Friday close) share returns and the corresponding weekly percentage changes in the price of a one-year T-bill rate, the dollar prices of a Deutsche Mark, a Pound Sterling, and a Yen, and the price of West Texas Intermediate crude. Using these data, we estimated our regression equation. The results of these estimations are displayed in Table 2.2.

Given the tendency of banks to accept short-dated deposits to fund longer-dated assets (loans), it is not surprising that our estimates for Chase Manhattan indicate an inverse exposure to interest rates. Although only marginally significant, the positive coefficient indicates that an increase in the one-year

---

of firm value to changes in exchange rates, which are described by Donald Lessard in "Finance and Global Competition: Exploiting Financial Scope and Coping with Volatile Exchange Rates," *Midland Corporate Finance Journal* Fall 1986.

For expositional purposes, we use in this paper the shorter form of the equation. This abbreviated model is acceptable empirically given the small correlations that exist between the percentage changes in the financial prices and the market return.

11. These coefficients actually measure elasticities. Further, had we used the percentage change in the quantity, (1 + one-year T-bill rate), instead of the percentage change in the price of the one-year T-bill, the coefficient b_1 could be interpreted as a "duration" measure.

TABLE 2.3 *Comparison of Five Banks' Sensitivity to One-Year T-Bill Rates*

Bank	Estimated Sensitivity	T-Value
Bank of America	3.2	1.5
Bankers Trust	2.2	1.4
Chase	2.6	1.6
First Chicago	3.0	1.6
Manufacturers Hanover	3.2	1.9

T-bill rate (or a decrease in the price of the T-bill) is expected to lead to a decrease in the bank's value.

Additional information can be obtained by comparing the coefficient estimates among firms in the same industry. For example, we can compare the estimated sensitivity of Chase's value to the one-year T-bill rate to the sensitivities of other banks as shown in Table 2.3.

In contrast to the bank's inverse exposure, Caterpillar appears to have a positive exposure to the one-year T-bill rate. That is, the negative regression coefficient indicates that increases in the one-year T-bill rate (or decreases in the price of the T-bill) lead to increases in the value of the firm.

Even more surprising, given much that has been written about Caterpillar's exposure to foreign currency changes, is the lack of any significant exposure to the yen. This result is more understandable if we break up this five-year span into shorter intervals and look at Caterpillar's sensitivity to the price of the yen on a year-by-year basis. (See Table 2.4.) The data reflect the fact that, as Caterpillar has moved its production facilities, the firm has changed from being positively exposed to the yen (such that an increase in the value of the dollar would harm Caterpillar) to being negatively exposed to the yen (an increase in the value of the dollar now helps Caterpillar).

Unlike the other two firms, the estimate for Exxon's exposure to interest rates is not statistically significant (not, at least, to the one-year T-bill rate). Exxon does exhibit the expected positive exposure to the price of oil. But our estimates also reflect the now common view, reported in the financial

TABLE 2.4 *Caterpillar's Sensitivity to Japanese Yen*

	1984	1985	1986	1987	1988
Parameter estimate for percentage change in price of yen	1.72	0.15	0.33	−1.08	−0.85
T-value	1.59	0.31	0.65	1.08	1.53

TABLE 2.5 *Exxon's Exposure to Price of Oil*

	1984	1985	1986	1987	1988
Parameter estimate for percentage change in price of oil	0.80	0.15	0.09	0.05	−0.01
T-value	3.94	0.85	2.79	0.37	0.17

press and elsewhere, that Exxon's exposure to the price of oil has been declining over time—both in size and consistency as measured by statistical significance. (See Table 2.5.) Given its international production and distribution, as well as its international portfolio of assets, Exxon also exhibits marginally significant exposures to foreign exchange rates. Our estimates suggest Exxon benefits from an increase in the value of the pound but is harmed by an increase in the value of the yen.

Measuring Corporate Exposure: Summing Up

The purpose of this first section, then, has been to outline a statistical technique (similar to that used to calculate a firm's "beta") that can be used to provide management with an estimate of the sensitivity of firm value to changes in a variety of financial variables. Such measures can be further refined by using information from other sources. For example, the same regression technique can be used, only substituting changes in the firm's periodic earnings and cash flows for the changes in stock prices in our model. There are, however, two principal advantages of our procedure over the use of such accounting numbers: (1) Market reactions are likely to capture the entire capitalized value of changes in firm value in response to financial price changes; and (2) regression analysis using stock prices, besides being much faster and cheaper, can be done using publicly available information.

The Tools for Managing Financial Risk:
A Building Block Approach [12]

If it turns out that a firm is subject to significant financial price risk, management may choose to hedge that risk. [13] One way of doing so is by using an

---

12. This section of the article is adapted from Charles W. Smithson, "A LEGO Approach to Financial Engineering: An Introduction to Forwards, Futures, Swaps, and Options," *Midland Corporate Finance Journal* 4, Winter 1987.

13. In this paper we do not address the question of why public corporations hedge. For a discussion of the corporate decision whether or not to hedge financial price exposures, see Alan

on-balance-sheet transaction. For example, a company could manage a foreign exchange exposure resulting from overseas competition by borrowing in the competitor's currency or by moving production abroad. But such on-balance-sheet methods can be costly and, as firms like Caterpillar have discovered, inflexible.[14]

Alternatively, financial risks can be managed with the use of off-balance-sheet instruments. The four fundamental off-balance-sheet instruments are forwards, futures, swaps, and options.

When we first began to attempt to understand these financial instruments, we were confronted by what seemed an insurmountable barrier to entry. The participants in the various markets all seemed to possess a highly specialized expertise that was applicable in only one market to the exclusion of all others (and the associated trade publications served only to tighten the veil of mystery that "experts" have always used to deny entry to novices). Options were discussed as if they were completely unrelated to forwards or futures, which in turn seemed to have nothing to do with the latest innovation, swaps. Adding to the complexities of the individual markets was the welter of jargon that seems to have grown up around each, thus further obscuring any common ground. (Words such as "ticks," "collars," "strike prices," and "straddles" suddenly had acquired a remarkable currency.) In short, we seemed to find ourselves looking up into a Wall Street Tower of Babel, with each group of market specialists speaking its own language.

After observing these instruments over the past several years, we have been struck by how little one has to dig before superficial differences give way to fundamental unity. In marked contrast to the specialized view of most Wall Street practitioners, we take a more "generalist" approach—one that treats forwards, futures, swaps, and options not as four unique instruments and markets, but rather as four interrelated instruments for dealing with a single problem: managing financial risk. In fact, we have come up with a little analogy that captures the spirit of our conclusion: The four basic off-balance-sheet instruments—forwards, futures, swaps, and options—are much like those plastic building blocks children snap together. You can either

---

Shapiro and Sheridan Titman, "An Integrated Approach to Corporate Risk Management," *Midland Corporate Finance Journal* 3, Summer 1985. For other useful theoretical discussions of the corporate hedging decision, see David Mayers and Clifford Smith, "On the Corporate Demand for Insurance," *Journal of Business* 55, April 1982 (a less technical version of which was published as "The Corporate Insurance Decision," *Chase Financial Quarterly* Vol. 1 No. 3, Spring 1982); Rene Stulz, "Optimal Hedging Policies," *Journal of Financial and Quantitative Analysis* 19, June 1984; Clifford Smith and Rene Stulz, "The Determinants of Firms' Hedging Policies," *Journal of Financial and Quantitative Analysis* 20, December 1985.

For some empirical tests of the above theoretical work, see David Mayers and Clifford Smith, "On the Corporate Demand for Insurance: Some Empirical Evidence," working paper, 1988; and Deana Nance, Clifford Smith, and Charles Smithson, "The Determinants of Off-Balance-Sheet Hedging: An Empirical Analysis," working paper 1988.

14. See "Caterpillar's Triple Whammy," *Fortune,* October 27, 1986.

build the instruments from one another, or you can combine the instruments into larger creations that appear (but appearances deceive) altogether "new."

Forward Contracts

Of the four instruments, the forward contract is the oldest and, perhaps for this reason, the most straightforward. A forward contract obligates its owner to buy a specified asset on a specified date at a price (known as the "exercise price") specified at the origination of the contract. If at maturity the actual price is higher than the exercise price, the contract owner makes a profit equal to the difference; if the price is lower, he suffers a loss.

In Figure 2.2, the payoff from buying a forward contract is illustrated with a hypothetical risk profile. If the actual price at contract maturity is higher than the expected price, the inherent risk results in a decline in the value of the firm; but this decline is offset by the profit on the forward contract. Hence, for the risk profile illustrated, the forward contract provides an effective hedge. (If the risk profile were positively instead of negatively sloped, the risk would be managed by selling instead of buying a forward contract.)

Besides its payoff profile, a forward contract has two other features that should be noted. First, the default (or credit) risk of the contract is two-sided. The contract owner either receives or makes a payment, depending on the price movement of the underlying asset. Second, the value of the forward

FIGURE 2.2 *Payoff Profile for Forward Contract*

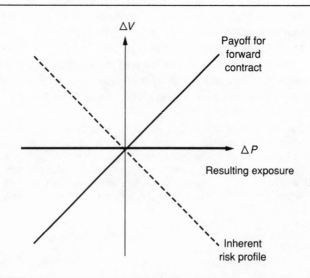

contract is conveyed only at the contract's maturity; no payment is made either at origination or during the term of the contract.

Futures Contracts

The basic form of the futures contract is identical to that of the forward contract; a futures contract also obligates its owner to purchase a specified asset at a specified exercise price on the contract maturity date. Thus, the payoff profile for the purchaser of a forward contract as presented in Figure 2.2 could also serve to illustrate the payoff to the holder of a futures contract.

But, unlike the case of forwards, credit or default risk can be virtually eliminated in a futures market. Futures markets use two devices to manage default risk. First, instead of conveying the value of a contract through a single payment at maturity, any change in the value of a futures contract is conveyed at the end of the day in which it is realized. Look again at Figure 2.2. Suppose that, on the day after origination, the financial price rises and, consequently, the financial instrument has a positive value. In the case of a forward contract, this value change would not be received until contract maturity. With a futures contract, this change in value is received at the end of the day. In the language of the futures markets, the futures contract is "marked to market" and "cash settled" daily.

Because the performance period of a futures contract is reduced by marking to market, the risk of default declines accordingly. Indeed, because the value of the futures contract is paid or received at the end of each day, Fischer Black likened a futures contract to "a series of forward contracts [in which] each day, yesterday's contract is settled and today's contract is written."[15] That is, a futures contract is like a sequence of forwards in which the "forward" contract written on day 0 is settled on day 1 and is replaced, in effect, with a new "forward" contract reflecting the new day 1 expectations. This new contract is then itself settled on day 2 and replaced, and so on until the day the contract ends.

The second feature of futures contracts that reduces default risk is the requirement that all market participants — sellers and buyers alike — post a performance bond called the "margin."[16] If my futures contract increases in value during the trading day, this gain is added to my margin account at the day's end. Conversely, if my contract has lost value, this loss is deducted from my margin account. And, if my margin account balance falls below

---

15. See Fischer Black, "The Pricing to Commodity Contracts," *Journal of Financial Economics* 3, 1976, 167–179.

16. Keep in mind that if you buy a futures contract, you are taking a long position in the underlying asset. Conversely, selling a futures contract is equivalent to taking a short position.

some agreed-upon minimum, I am required to post additional bond; that is, my margin account must be replenished or my position will be closed out.[17] Because the position will be closed before the margin account is depleted, performance risk is eliminated.[18]

Note that the exchange itself has not been proposed as a device to reduce default risk. Daily settlement and the requirement of a bond reduce default risk, but the existence of an exchange (or clearinghouse) merely serves to transform risk. More specifically, the exchange deals with the two-sided risk inherent in forwards and futures by serving as the counterparty to all transactions. If I wish to buy or sell a futures contract, I buy from or sell to the exchange. Hence, I need only evaluate the credit risk of the exchange, not of some specific counterparty.

The primary economic function of the exchange is to reduce the costs of transacting in futures contracts. The anonymous trades made possible by the exchange, together with the homogeneous nature of the futures contracts — standardized assets, exercise dates (four per year), and contract sizes — enable the futures markets to become relatively liquid. However, as was made clear by recent experience on the London Metal Exchange, the existence of the exchange does not in and of itself eliminate the possibility of default.[19]

In sum, a futures contract is much like a portfolio of forward contracts. At the close of business of each day, in effect, the existing forwardlike contract

---

17. When the contract is originated on the U.S. exchanges, an "initial margin" is required. Subsequently, the margin account balance must remain above the "maintenance margin." If the margin account balance falls below the maintenance level, the balance must be restored to the initial level.

18. Note that this discussion has ignored daily limits. If there are daily limits on the movement of futures prices, large changes in expectations about the underlying asset can effectively close the market. (The market opens, immediately moves the limit, and then is effectively closed until the next day.) Hence, there could exist an instance in which the broker desires to close out a customer's position but is not able to immediately because the market is experiencing limit moves. In such a case, the statement that performance risk is "eliminated" is too strong.

19. In November of 1985, the "tin cartel" defaulted on contracts for tin delivery on the London Metal Exchange, thereby making the exchange liable for the loss. A description of this situation is contained in "Tin Crisis in London Roils Metal Exchange," The Wall Street Journal, November 13, 1985.

From the point of view of the market, the exchange does not reduce default risk. The expected default rate is not affected by the existence of the exchange. However, the existence of the exchange can alter the default risk faced by an individual market participant. If I buy a futures contract for a specific individual, the default risk I face is determined by the default rate of that specific counterparty. If I instead buy the same futures contract through an exchange, my default risk depends on the default rate of not just my counterparty, but on the default rate of the entire market. Moreover, to the extent that the exchange is capitalized by equity from its members, the default risk I perceive is further reduced because I have a claim not against some specific counterparty, but rather against the exchange. Therefore, when I trade through the exchange, I am in a sense purchasing an insurance policy from the exchange.

is settled and a new one is written.[20] Combined with the margin requirement, this daily settlement feature allows futures contracts to eliminate the credit risk inherent in forwards.

Swap Contracts[21]

A swap contract is in essence nothing more complicated than a series of forward contracts strung together. As implied by its name, a swap contract obligates two parties to exchange, or "swap," some specified cash flows at specified intervals. The most common form is the interest rate swap, in which the cash flows are determined by two different interest rates.

Panel A of Figure 2.3 illustrates an interest rate swap from the perspective of a party who is receiving a series of cash flows determined by a fixed interest rate ($\bar{R}$) in return for a series of cash flows determined by a floating interest rate ($\tilde{R}$).[22]

Panel B of Figure 2.3 serves to illustrate that this swap contract can be decomposed into a portfolio of forward contracts. At each settlement date, the party to this swap contract has an implicit forward contract on interest rates: the party illustrated is obligated to sell a fixed rate cash flow for an amount specified at the origination of the contract. In this sense, a swap contract is also like a portfolio of forward contracts.

In terms of our earlier discussion, this means that the solid line in Figure 2.2 could also represent the payoff from a swap contract. Specifically, the solid line in Figure 2.3 would be consistent with a swap contract in which the party illustrated receives cash flows determined by one price (say, the U.S. Treasury bond rate) and makes payments determined by another price (say, LIBOR). Thus forwards, futures, and swaps all function in the same way in terms of their ability to manage risk.

---

20. A futures contract is like a portfolio of forward contracts; however, a futures contract and a portfolio of forward contracts become identical only if interest rates are "deterministic" — that is, known with certainty in advance. See Robert A. Jarrow and George S. Oldfield, "Forward Contracts and Futures Contracts," *Journal of Financial Economics* 9, 1981, 373–382; and John A. Cox, Jonathan E. Ingersoll, and Stephen A. Ross, "The Relation between Forward Prices and Futures Prices," *Journal of Financial Economics* 9, 1981, 321–346.
21. This section is based on Clifford W. Smith, Charles W. Smithson, and Lee M. Wakeman, "The Evolving Market for Swaps," *Midland Corporate Finance Journal,* Winter 1986, 20–32.
22. Specifically, the interest rate swap cash flows are determined as follows: The two parties agree to some notional principal, P. (The principal is notional in the sense that it is only used to determine the magnitude of cash flows; it is not paid or received by either party.) At each settlement date, $1, 2, ..., T$, the party illustrated makes a payment $\bar{R} = \bar{r}P$, where $\bar{r}$ is the T-period fixed rate that existed at origination. At each settlement, the party illustrated receives $\tilde{R} = \tilde{r}P$, where $\tilde{r}$ is the floating rate for that period (e.g., at settlement date 2, the interest rate used is the one-period rate in effect at period 1).

FIGURE 2.3   *(a) An Interest Rate Swap; (b) An Interest Rate Swap as a Portfolio of Forward Contracts*

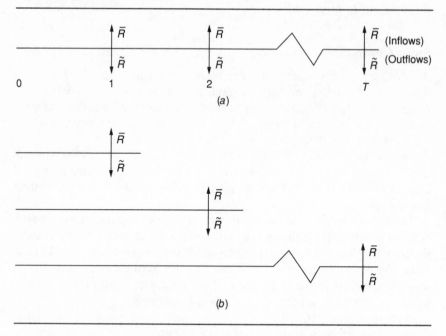

But identical payoff *patterns* notwithstanding, the instruments all differ with respect to default risk. As we saw, the performance period of a forward is equal to its maturity; and because no performance bond is required, a forward contract is a pure credit instrument. Futures both reduce the performance period (to one day) and require a bond, thereby eliminating credit risk. Swap contracts use only one of these mechanisms to reduce credit risk; they reduce the performance period.[23] This point becomes evident in Figure 2.3. Although the maturity of the contract is T periods, the performance period is generally not T periods long but is instead a single period. Thus, given a swap and a forward contract of roughly the same maturity, the swap is likely to impose far less credit risk on the counterparties to the contract than the forward.

At each settlement date throughout a swap contract, the changes in value are transferred between the counterparties. To illustrate this in terms of Figure 2.3, suppose that interest rates rise on the day after origination. The

---

23. There are instances in which a bond has been posted in the form of collateral. As should be evident, in this case the swap becomes very like a futures contract.

value of the swap contract illustrated has risen. This value change will be conveyed to the contract owner not at maturity (as would be the case with a forward contract) nor at the end of that day (as would be the case with a futures contract). Instead, at the first settlement date, part of the value change is conveyed in the form of the "difference check" paid by one party to the other. To repeat, then, the performance period is less than that of a forward, but not as short as that of a futures contract.[24] (Keep in mind that we are comparing instruments with the same maturities.)

Let us reinforce the two major points made thus far. First, a swap contract, like a futures contract, is like a portfolio of forward contracts. Therefore, the payoff profiles for each of these three instruments are identical. Second, the primary difference among forwards, futures, and swaps is the amount of default risk they impose on counterparties to the contract. Forwards and futures represent the extremes, and swaps are the intermediate case.

Option Contracts

As we have seen, the owner of a forward, futures, or swap contract has an *obligation* to perform. In contrast, an option gives its owner a *right,* not an obligation. An option giving its owner the right to buy an asset at a predetermined price—a call option—is provided in Figure 2.4(*a*). The owner of the contract has the right to purchase the asset at a specified future date at a price agreed upon today. Thus, if the price rises, the value of the option also goes up. But because the option contract owner is not obligated to purchase the asset if the price moves against him, the value of the option remains unchanged (at zero) if the price declines.[25]

The payoff profile for the party who sold the call option (also known as the call "writer") is shown in Figure 2.4(*b*). In contrast to the buyer of the option, the seller of the call option has the *obligation* to perform. For example, if the owner of the option elects to exercise his option to buy the asset, the seller of the option is obligated to sell the asset.

Besides the option to buy an asset, there is also the option to sell an asset at a specified price, known as a "put" option. The payoff to the buyer of a put is illustrated in Figure 2.4(*c*), and the payoff to the seller of the put is shown in (*d*).

---

24. Unlike futures, for which all of any change in contract value is paid/received at the daily settlements, swap contracts convey only part of the total value change at the periodic settlements.

25. For continuity, we continue to use the ΔV, ΔP convention in figures. To compare these figures with those found in most texts, treat ΔV as deviations from zero ($\Delta V = V - 0$) and remember that P measures deviations from expected price ($\Delta P = P - P_e$).

FIGURE 2.4   *Payoff Profiles of Puts and Calls: (a) Buy a Call; (b) Sell a Call; (c) Buy a Put; (d) Sell a Put*

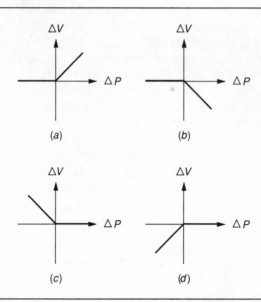

Pricing Options.   Up to this point, we have considered only the payoffs to the option contracts. We have sidestepped the thorniest issue — the valuation of option contracts.

The breakthrough in option-pricing theory came with the work of Fischer Black and Myron Scholes in 1973.[26] Conveniently for our purposes, Black and Scholes took what might be described as a "building block" approach to the valuation of options. Look again at the call option illustrated in Figure 2.4. For increases in the financial price, the payoff profile for the option is that of a forward contract. For decreases in the price, the value of the option is constant — like that of a "riskless" security such as a Treasury bill.

The work of Black and Scholes demonstrated that a call option could be replicated by a continuously adjusting ("dynamic") portfolio of two securities: (1) forward contracts on the underlying asset and (2) riskless securities. As the financial price rises, the "call option equivalent" portfolio contains an increasing proportion of forward contracts on the asset. Conversely, the

---

26. See Fischer Black and Myron Scholes, "The Pricing of Options and Corporate Liabilities," *Journal of Political Economy,* 1973. For a less technical discussion of the model, see "The Black-Scholes Option Pricing Model for Alternative Underlying Instruments," *Financial Analysts Journal,* November-December, 1984, 23–30.

FIGURE 2.5 *"At the Money" vs. "Out of the Money"*

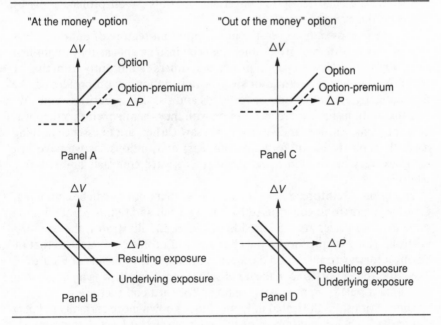

"At the money" option

Panel A

Panel B

"Out of the money" option

Panel C

Panel D

replicating portfolio contains a decreasing proportion of forwards as the price of the asset falls.

Because this replicating portfolio is effectively a synthetic call option, arbitrage activity should ensure that its value closely approximates the market price of exchange-traded call options. In this sense, the value of a call option, and thus the premium that would be charged its buyer, is determined by the value of its option equivalent portfolio.

Panel A of Figure 2.5 illustrates the payoff profile for a call option that includes the premium. This figure (and all of the option figures thus far) illustrates an at-the-money option—that is, an option for which the exercise price is the prevailing expected price. As Panels A and B of Figure 2.5 illustrate, an at-the-money option is paid for by sacrificing a significant amount of the firm's potential gains. However, the price of a call option falls as the exercise price increases relative to the prevailing price of the asset. This means that if an option buyer is willing to accept larger potential losses in return for paying a lower option premium, he would then consider using an out-of-the-money option.

An out-of-the-money call option is illustrated in Panel C of Figure 2.5. As shown in Panel D, the out-of-the-money option provides less downside protection, but the option premium is significantly less. The lesson to be learned here is that the option buyer can alter his payoff profile simply by changing the exercise price.

For our purposes, however, the most important feature of options is that they are not as different from other financial instruments as they might first seem. Options do have a payoff profile that differs significantly from that of forward contracts (or futures or swaps). But, option payoff profiles can be duplicated by a combination of forwards and risk-free securities. Thus, we find that options have more in common with the other instruments than was first apparent. Futures and swaps, as we saw earlier, are in essence nothing more than portfolios of forward contracts; and options, as we have just seen, are very much akin to portfolios of forward contracts and risk-free securities.

This point is reinforced if we consider ways that options can be combined. Consider a portfolio constructed by buying a call and selling a put with the same exercise price. As the left side of Figure 2.6 illustrates, the resulting portfolio (long a call, short a put) has a payoff profile equivalent to that of buying a forward contract on the asset. Similarly, the right side of Figure 2.6 illustrates that a portfolio made up of selling a call and buying a put (short a call, long a put) is equivalent to selling a forward contract.

The relationship illustrated in Figure 2.6 is known more formally as "put-call parity." The special import of this relationship, at least in this context, is the "building block construction" it makes possible: Two options can be "snapped together" to yield the payoff profile for a forward contract, which is identical to the payoff profile for futures and swaps.

At the beginning of this section, then, it seemed that options would be very different from forwards, futures, and swaps—and in some ways they are. But we discovered two building block relations between options and the other three instruments: (1) Options can be replicated by "snapping together" a forward, futures, or swap contract together with a position in risk-free securities; and (2) calls and puts can be combined to become forwards.

The Financial Building Blocks

Forwards, futures, swaps, and options look so different from one another. And if you read the trade publications or talk to the specialists that transact in the four markets, the apparent differences among the instruments are likely to seem even more pronounced.

But it turns out that forwards, futures, swaps, and options are not each unique constructions, but rather more like those plastic building blocks that children combine to make complex structures. To understand the off-balance-sheet instruments, you don't need a lot of market-specific knowledge. All

FIGURE 2.6 *Put-Call Parity: (a) Long a Call, Short a Put Equals Buying a Forward; (b) Short a Call, Long a Put Equals Selling a Forward*

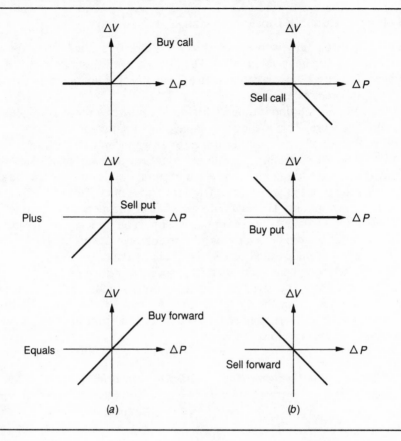

you need to know is how the instruments can be linked to one another. As we have seen, (1) futures can be built by "snapping together" a package of forwards; (2) swaps can also be built by putting together a package of forwards; (3) synthetic options can be constructed by combining a forward with a riskless security; and (4) options can be combined to produce forward contracts — or, conversely, forwards can be pulled apart to replicate a package of options.

Having shown you all the building blocks and how they fit together in simple constructions, we now want to demonstrate how they can be used to create more complicated, customized financial instruments that in turn can be used to manage financial risks.

Assembling the Building Blocks

Using the Building Blocks to Manage an Exposure

Consider a company whose market value is directly related to unexpected changes in some financial price, P. The risk profile of this company is illustrated in Figure 2.7. How could we use the financial building blocks to modify this inherent exposure?

The simplest solution is to use a forward, a futures, or a swap to neutralize this exposure. This is shown in Panel A of Figure 2.8.

But, the use of a forward, a futures, or a swap eliminates possible losses by giving up the possibility of profiting from favorable outcomes. The company might want to minimize the effect of unfavorable outcomes while still allowing the possibility of gaining from favorable ones. This can be accomplished using options. The payoff profile of an at-the-money option (including the premium paid to buy the option) is shown on the left side of Panel B. Snapping this building block onto the inherent exposure profile gives the resuilting exposure illustrated on the right side of Panel B.

A common complaint about options — especially at-the-money options — is that they are "too expensive." To reduce the option premium, you can think about using an out-of-the-money option. As Panel C of Figure 2.8 illustrates, the firm has thereby given up some protection from adverse outcomes in return for paying a lower premium.

FIGURE 2.7 *Risk Profile for Firm with Market Value Related to P*

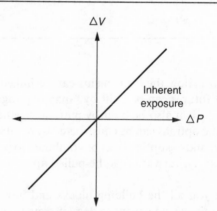

The value of the firm is directly related to financial price P
(i.e., interest rates or foreign exchange rates or commodity
prices). If P rises, the value of the firm rises.

FIGURE 2.8a *Managing an Exposure*

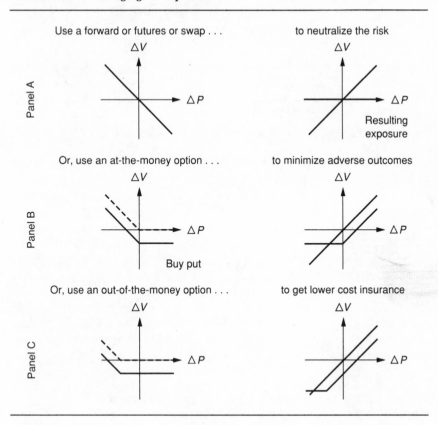

Use a forward or futures or swap . . . to neutralize the risk

Panel A

ΔV / ΔP / Resulting exposure

Or, use an at-the-money option . . . to minimize adverse outcomes

Panel B

ΔV / ΔP / Buy put

Or, use an out-of-the-money option . . . to get lower cost insurance

Panel C

ΔV / ΔP

But, with an out-of-the-money option, some premium expense remains. Panel D illustrates how the out-of-pocket expense can be *eliminated*. The firm can sell a call option with an exercise price chosen so as to generate premium income equal to the premium due on the put option it wishes to purchase. In building block parlance, we snap the "buy-a-put" option onto the inherent risk profile to reduce downside outcomes, and we snap on the "sell-a-call" option to fund this insurance by giving up some of the favorable outcomes.

Panel E reminds us that forwards, futures, and swaps can be used in combination with options. Suppose the treasurer of the company we have been considering comes to you with the following request:

> I think that this financial price, *P*, is going to fall dramatically. And, while I know enough about financial markets to know that *P* could actually rise a little, I am sure it will not rise by much. I want some kind of financial solution that

FIGURE 2.8b *Managing an Exposure*

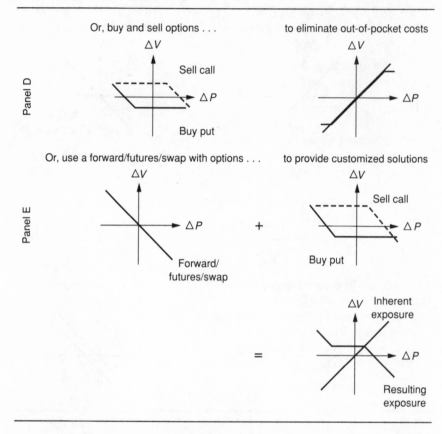

will let me benefit when my predictions come to pass. But I don't want to pay any out-of-pocket premiums. Instead, I want this financial engineering product to pay me a premium.

If you look at the firm's inherent risk profile in Figure 2.7, this seems like a big request. The firm's inherent position is such that it would lose rather than gain from big decreases in P.

The resulting exposure profile shown on the right side of Panel E is the one the firm wants: It benefits from large decreases in P, is protected against small increases in P (though not against large increases) and receives a premium for the instrument.

How was this new profile achieved? As illustrated on the left side of Panel E, we first snapped a forward/futures/swap position onto the original risk profile to neutralize the firm's inherent exposure. We then sold a call option and bought a put option with exercise prices set such that the income from selling the call exceeded the premium required to buy the put.

No high level math was required. Indeed, we did this bit of financial engineering simply by looking through the box of financial building blocks until we found those that snapped together to give us the profile we wanted.

Using the Building Blocks to Redesign Financial Instruments

Now that you understand how forwards, futures, swaps, and options are all fundamentally related, it is a relatively short step to thinking about how the instruments can be combined with each other to give one financial instrument the characteristics of another. Rather than talk about this in the abstract, let's look at some examples of how this has been done in the marketplace.

Combining Forwards with Swaps. Suppose a firm's value is currently unaffected by interest rate movements. But, at a known date in the future, it expects to become exposed to interest rates: If rates rise, the value of the firm will decrease.[27] To manage this exposure, the firm could use a forward, futures, or swap commencing at that future date. Such a product is known as a *forward* or *delayed start* swap. The payoff from a forward swap is illustrated in Panel C of Figure 2.9, where the party illustrated pays a fixed rate and receives floating starting in period 5.

Although this instrument is in effect a forward contract on a swap, it also, not surprisingly, can be constructed as a package of swaps. As Figure 2.9 illustrates, a forward swap is equivalent to a package of two swaps:

Swap 1 — From period 1 to period *T*, the party pays fixed and receives floating.

Swap 2 — From period 1 to period 4, the party pays floating and receives fixed.

Forwards with Optionlike Characteristics. The addition of optionlike characteristics to forward contracts first appeared in the foreign exchange markets. To see how this was done, let's trace the evolution of these contracts.

Begin with a standard forward contract on foreign exchange. Figure 2.10(*a*) illustrates a conventional forward contract on sterling with the forward sterling exchange rate (the "contract rate") set at $1.50 per pound sterling. If, at maturity, the spot price of sterling exceeds $1.50, the owner of this contract makes a profit (equal to the spot rate minus $1.50). Conversely, if at maturity the spot price of sterling is less than $1.50, the owner of this contract

---

27. For example, the firm may know that in one year it will require funds that will be borrowed at a floating rate, thereby giving the firm the inverse exposure to interest rates. Or the firm may be adding a new product line, the demand for which is extremely sensitive to interest rate movements — as rates rise, the demand for the product decreases and cash flows to the firm decrease.

FIGURE 2.9 *Construction of a Forward Swap*

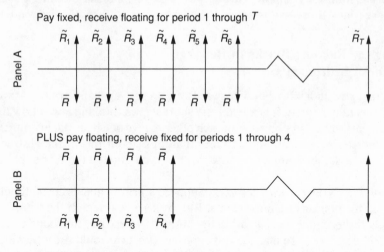

Pay fixed, receive floating for period 1 through T

Panel A

PLUS pay floating, receive fixed for periods 1 through 4

Panel B

EQUALS a four-period forward contract on a pay fixed, receive floating swap

Panel C

suffers a loss. The owner of the forward contract, however, might instead want a contract that allows him to profit if the price of sterling rises, but limits his losses if the price of sterling falls.[28] Such a contract would be a call option on sterling. Illustrated in Figure 2.10(*b*) is a call option on sterling with an exercise price of \$1.50. In this illustration we have assumed an option premium of 5 cents (per pound sterling).

The payoff profile illustrated in Figure 2.10(*b*) could also be achieved by altering the terms of the standard forward contract as follows:

1. Change the contract price so that the exercise price of the forward contract is no longer \$1.50 but is instead \$1.55. The owner of the forward contract agrees to purchase sterling at contract maturity at a price of \$1.55 per unit; and

---

28. This discussion is adapted from Warren Edwardes and Emond Levy, "Break Forwards: A Synthetic Option Hedging Instrument," *Midland Corporate Finance Journal* 5, Summer 1987, 59–67.

FIGURE 2.10 *Forwards with Optionlike Characteristics: (a) Standard Forward; (b) Break Forward; (c) Range Forward*

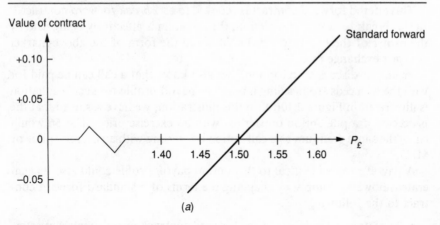

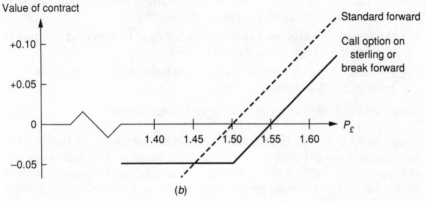

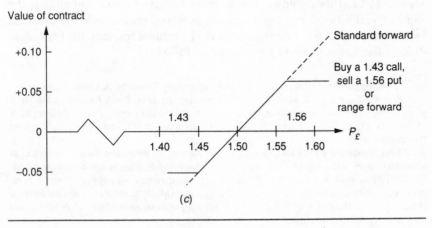

2. Permit the owner of the contract to break (i.e., "unwind") the agreement at a sterling price of $1.50.

This altered forward contract is referred to as a *break forward* contract.[29] In this break forward construction, the premium is effectively being paid by the owner of the break forward contract in the form of the above-market contract exchange rate.

From our discussion of options, we also know that a call can be paid for with the proceeds from selling a put. The payoff profile for such a situation is illustrated in Figure 2.10(c). In this illustration, we have assumed that the proceeds of a put option on sterling with an exercise price of $1.56 would carry the same premium as a call option on sterling with an exercise price of $1.43.[30]

A payoff profile identical to this option payoff profile could also be generated, however, simply by changing the terms of a standard forward contract to the following:

• At maturity, the buyer of the forward contract agrees to purchase sterling at a price of $1.50 per pound sterling;

• the buyer of the forward contract has the right to break the contract at a price of $1.43 per pound sterling; and

• the seller of the forward contract has the right to break the contract at a price of $1.56 per pound sterling.

Such a forward contract is referred to as a *range forward*.[31]

Swaps with Optionlike Characteristics.   Given that swaps can be viewed as packages of forward contracts, it should not be surprising that swaps can also be constructed to have optionlike characteristics like those illustrated for forwards. For example, suppose that a firm with a floating rate liability wanted to limit its outflows should interest rates rise substantially; at the same time, it was willing to give up some potential gains should there instead be a dramatic decline in short-term rates. To achieve this end, the firm could modify the interest rate swap contract as follows:

---

29. According to Sam Srinivasulu in "Second-Generation Forwards: A Comparative Analysis," *Business International Money Report,* September 21, 1987, *break forward* is the name given to this construction by Midland Bank. It goes under other names: Boston Option (Bank of Boston), FOX—Forward with Optional Exit (Hambros Bank), and Cancelable Forward (Goldman Sachs).
30. These numbers are only for purposes of illustration. To determine the exercise prices at which the values of the puts and calls are equal, one would have to use an option-pricing model.
31. As Srinivasulu (cited Note 29) pointed out, this construction also appears under a number of names: range forward (Salomon Brothers), collar (Midland Montagu), flexible forward (Manufacturers Hanover), cylinder option (Citicorp), option fence (Bank of America) and mini-max (Goldman Sachs).

FIGURE 2.11 *Payoff Profile for Floor-Ceiling Swaps*

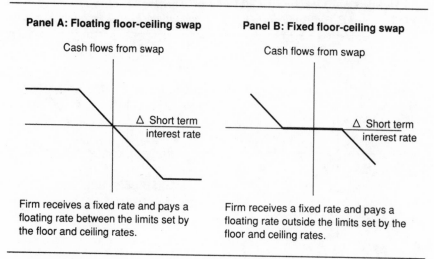

Panel A: Floating floor-ceiling swap

Cash flows from swap

Δ Short term interest rate

Firm receives a fixed rate and pays a floating rate between the limits set by the floor and ceiling rates.

Panel B: Fixed floor-ceiling swap

Cash flows from swap

Δ Short term interest rate

Firm receives a fixed rate and pays a floating rate outside the limits set by the floor and ceiling rates.

> As long as the interest rate neither rises by more than 200 basis points nor falls more than 100 basis points, the firm pays a floating rate and receives a fixed rate. But, if the interest is more than 200 basis points above or 100 basis points below the current rate, the firm receives and pays a fixed rate.

The resulting payoff profile for this floating floor-ceiling swap is illustrated in Panel A of Figure 2.11.

Conversely, the interest rate swap contract could have been modified as follows:

> As long as the interest rate is within 200 basis points of the current rate, the firm neither makes nor receives a payment; but if the interest rate rises or falls by more than 200 basis points, the firm pays a floating rate and receives a fixed rate.

The payoff profile for the resulting fixed floor-ceiling swap is illustrated in Panel B of Figure 2.11.

Redesigned Options. To "redesign" an option, what is normally done is to put two or more options together to change the payoff profile. Examples abound in the world of the option trader. Some of the more colorfully named combinations are *straddles, strangles,* and *butterflies.*[32]

---

32. For a discussion of traditional option strategies like straddles, strangles, and butterflies, see for instance Chapter 7 of Richard M. Bookstaber, *Option Pricing and Strategies in Investing* (Reading, Mass.: Addison-Wesley, 1981).

FIGURE 2.12   *Construction of a Participation: (a) Inherent Exposure of Firm; (b) Finance Out-of-the-Money Call by Selling Fraction ($\frac{1}{2}$) of In-the-Money Put; (c) Combined Payoff Profile for Option Combination (b); (d) Resulting Exposure*

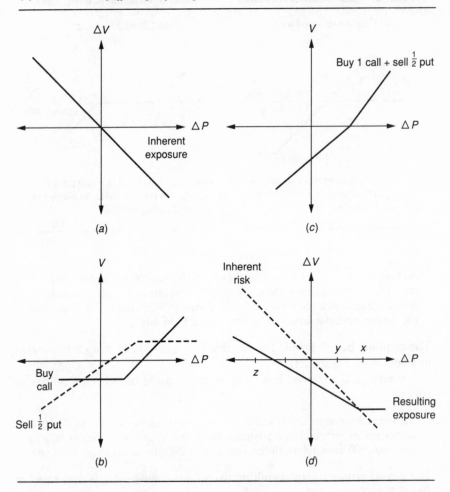

To see how and why these kinds of creations evolve, let's look at a hypothetical situation. Suppose a firm was confronted with the inherent exposure illustrated in Figure 2.12(*a*). Suppose further that the firm wanted to establish a floor on losses caused by changes in a financial price.

As you already know, this could be done by purchasing an out-of-the-money call option on the financial price. As we have seen, a potential problem with this solution is the premium the firm has to pay. Is there a way the premium can be eliminated?

We have already seen that buying an out-of-the-money call can be financed by selling an out-of-the-money put. However, suppose that this out-of-the money call is financed by selling a put with precisely the same exercise price — in which case, the put would be in-the-money. As illustrated in Figure 2.12(*b*), the proceeds from selling the in-the-money put would exceed the cost of the out-of-the-money call. Therefore, to finance one out-of-the-money call, one would need sell only a fraction of one in-the-money put.

In Figure 2.12(*b*), we have assumed that the put value is twice the call value; so, to finance one call, you need sell only $\frac{1}{2}$ put. Figure 2.12(*c*) simply combines the payoff profiles for selling $\frac{1}{2}$ put and buying one call with an exercise price of x. Finally, Figure 2.12(*d*) combines the option combination in (*c*) with the inherent risk profile in (*a*).

Note what has happened. The firm has obtained the floor it wanted, but there is no upfront premium. At the price at which the option is exercised, the value of the firm with the floor is the same as it would have been without the floor. The floor is paid for not with a fixed premium, but with a share of the firm's gains above the floor. If the financial price rises by x, the value of the firm falls to the floor and no premium is paid. If, however, the financial price rises by less, say y, the value of the firm is higher and the firm pays a positive premium for the floor. If the financial price falls, say, by z, the price it pays for the floor rises.

What we have here is a situation where the provider of the floor is paid with a share of potential gains, thereby leading to the name of this option combination — a *participation*. This construction has been most widely used in the foreign exchange market where they are referred to as *participating forwards*.[33]

Options on Other Financial Instruments

Options on futures contracts on bonds have been actively traded on the Chicago Board of Trade since 1982. The valuation of an option on a future is a relatively straightforward extension of the traditional option-pricing models.[34] Despite the close relation between futures and forwards and futures and swaps, the options on forwards (*options on forward rate agreements*) and options on swaps (*swaptions*) are much more recent.

---

33. For more on this construction, see Srinivalsulu cited in Notes 29 and 31.
34. Options on futures were originally discussed by Fischer Black in "The Pricing of Commodity Options," *Journal of Financial Economics* 3, January-March 1976. A concise discussion of the modifications required in the Black-Scholes formula is contained in James F. Meisner and John W. Labuszewski, "Modifying the Black-Scholes Option Pricing Model for Alternative Underlying Instruments," *Financial Analysts Journal,* November/December 1984.

More complicated analytically is the valuation of an option on an option, also known as a *compound option*.[35] Despite their complexity and resistance to valuation formulae, some options on options have begun to be traded. These include options on foreign exchange options and, most notably, options on interest rate options (caps), referred to in the trade as *captions*.

Using the Building Blocks to Design "New" Products

It's rare that a day goes by in the financial markets without hearing of at least one new or hybrid product. But, as you should have come to expect from us by now, our position with respect to "financial engineering" is that there is little new under the sun. The "new" products typically involve nothing more than putting the building blocks together in a new way.

Reverse Floaters.   One example of a hybrid security is provided in Figure 2.13. If we combine the issuance of a conventional fixed rate loan and an interest rate swap where the issuing party pays fixed and receives floating, the

35. For a discussion of the problem of valuing compound options, see John C. Cox and Mark Rubinstein, *Options Markets* (Englewood Cliffs, NJ: Prentice-Hall, 1985), 412–415.

FIGURE 2.13   *Using a Swap to Create a Reverse Floating Rate Loan*

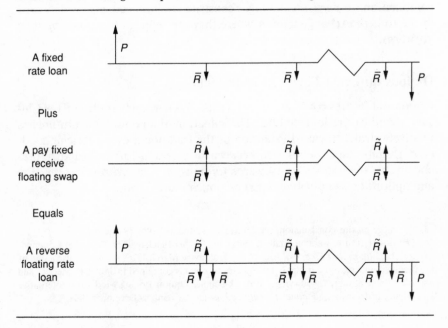

result is a reverse floating rate loan. The net coupon payments on the hybrid loan are equal to twice the fixed rate ($\bar{r}$) minus the floating rate ($\tilde{r}$) times the principal (P), or

$$\text{Net Coupon} = (2\bar{r} - \tilde{r})P = 2\bar{R} - \tilde{R}$$

If the floating rate ($\tilde{r}$) rises, the net coupon payment falls.

Bonds with Embedded Options. Another form of hybrid securities has evolved from bonds with warrants. Bonds with warrants on the issuer's shares have become common. Bond issues have also recently appeared that feature warrants that can be exercised into foreign exchange and gold.

In 1986, Standard Oil issued a bond with an oil warrant. These notes stipulated that the principal payment at maturity would be a function of oil prices at maturity. As specified in the Prospectus, the holders of the 1990 notes will receive, in addition to a guaranteed minimum principal amount, "the excess... of the Crude Oil Price... over $25 multiplied by 170 barrels of Light Sweet Crude Oil." What this means is that the note has an embedded four-year option on 170 barrels of crude oil. If at maturity the value of Light Sweet Oklahoma Crude Oil exceeds $25, the holder of the note will receive (Oil Price − $25) × 170 plus the guaranteed minimum principal amount. If the value of Light Sweet Oklahoma Crude is less than $25 at maturity, the option expires worthless.[36]

The building block process has also been extended to changes in the timing of the options embedded in the bond. For a traditional bond with an attached warrant, there is only one option exercisable at one point in time. More recent bonds have involved packages of options that can be exercised at different points in time.

The first time we saw this extension was in Forest Oil Corporation's proposed *Natural Gas Interest Indexed Debentures.* As set forth in the issue's red herring prospectus of July 1988, Forest Oil proposed to pay a stipulated base rate plus four basis points for each $0.01 by which the average gas spot price exceeds $1.76 per MMBTU (million British Thermal Units). In effect, then, this proposed 12-year hybrid debenture is a package consisting of one standard bond plus 24 options on the price of natural gas with maturities ranging from 6 months to 12 years.[37]

---

36. Note that this issue did have a cap on the crude oil price at $40. Hence, the bondholder actually holds two options positions: long a call option at $25 per barrel and short a call option at $40 per barrel.

37. As reported in *The Wall Street Journal* on September 21, 1988, Forest Oil withdrew its Natural Gas Indexed Bond in favor of a straight issue. However, in November of 1988, Magma Copper did issue senior subordinated notes on which the coupon payments were linked to the price of copper in much the same way as Forest's coupons would have been linked to the price of natural gas.

FIGURE 2.14 *Building Blocks of an Oil-Indexed, Dual Currency Bond*

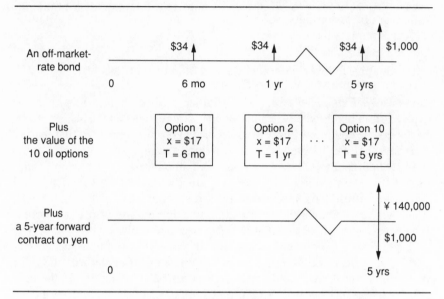

If we want to get a little fancier, we can consider the possibility of an *oil interest-indexed, dual currency bond.*[38] Assume that the maturity of this issue is five years, with the semiannual coupon payments indexed to the price of crude oil and the final principal repayment indexed to the value of yen. More specifically, assume that for each $1000 of principal, the bondholder receives the following: (1) the greater of $34 or the value of two barrels of Sweet Light Crude Oil at each coupon date; and (2) 140,000 yen at maturity.

How would we value such a complicated package? The answer, again, is by breaking it down into the building blocks. As shown in Figure 2.14, this oil-indexed, dual currency bond consists of three basic components: (1) a straight bond paying $34 semiannually; (2) 10 call options on the price of oil with an exercise price of $17 per barrel ($34/2) maturing sequentially every six months over a five-year period; and (3) a five-year forward contract on yen with an exercise price of 140 yen/dollar. As it turns out, then, this complicated-looking bond is nothing more than a combination of a standard bond, a series of options, and a forward contract.

Concluding Remarks

The world is more volatile today than it was two decades ago. Today's corporate risk manager must deal with the potential impact on the firm of sig-

---

38. Unlike the other structures discussed, this one has not yet been issued.

nificant month-to-month (and sometimes day-to-day) changes in exchange rates, interest rates, and commodity prices. Volatility alone could put a well-run firm out of business, so financial price risk deserves careful attention. As this summary has demonstrated, there now exist techniques and tools for accomplishing this task.

This article makes three major points: First, there are simple techniques that allow management (and outsiders as well) to identify and measure a firm's exposures. Besides managing "one-off" exposures (such as interest rate exposures from floating rate borrowings or foreign exchange transaction and translation exposures), many firms are now recognizing their economic exposures. To measure such economic exposures, we have introduced the concept of the *risk profile*. Using this concept, we have proposed simple methods for quantifying the extent of an individual firm's exposures to interest rates, foreign exchange rates, and commodity prices. In the case of a financial firm's exposure to interest rate risk, the techniques of *gap* and *duration* analysis can be applied directly. For the more general case, we demonstrate how simple regression analysis (the same technique used in calculating a firm's "beta") can be used to measure a variety of exposures.

Second, the tools for managing financial risk are simpler than they appear. These financial instruments can be viewed as building blocks. The basic component is a forward contract. Both futures and swaps are like bundles of forward contracts; forwards, in fact, can be combined to yield futures and swaps. The primary differences between these two instruments are the way they deal with default risk and the degree of customization available.

Even options, moreover, can be related to forward contracts. An option on a given asset can be created by combining a position in a forward contract on the same asset with a riskless security; in short, forwards and T-bills can be combined to produce options.[39] Finally, options can be combined to create forward positions; for example, buying a call and shorting a put produces the same position as buying a forward contract.

Third, once you understand the four basic building blocks, it is a straightforward step to designing a customized strategy for managing your firm's exposure. Once the exposure is identified, it can be managed in a number of ways:

- by using one of the financial instruments—for example, by using an interest rate swap to hedge a building products firm's exposure to rising interest rates;

- by using combinations of the financial instruments—for example, buying a call and selling a put to minimize the out-of-pocket cost of the hedge; or

- by combining financial instruments with a debt instrument to create a

---

39. This is most often referred to as a synthetic option or as dynamic option replication.

hybrid security—for example, issuing an oil-indexed bond to hedge a firm's exposure to oil prices.

Our final point in all of this is very simple. Managing financial price risk with "financial engineering" sounds like something you need a degree from Caltech or M.I.T. to do, but designing effective solutions with the financial building blocks is easy.

3

Financial Engineering in Corporate Finance: An Overview

John D. Finnerty *

Financial innovation over the past two decades has rapidly brought about revolutionary changes in financial instruments and processes. Almost daily the financial press carries yet another tombstone advertisement featuring a new security. A variety of factors, among the more important of which are increased interest rate volatility and the frequency of tax and regulatory changes, have stimulated the process of financial innovation. The deregulation of the financial services industry and increased competition within investment banking have undoubtedly placed increased emphasis on the ability to design new products, develop better processes, and implement more effective solutions to increasingly complex financial problems. Financial engineering is the lifeblood of this activity.

Financial engineering involves the design, the development, and the implementation of innovative financial instruments and processes, and the formulation of creative solutions to problems in finance. The term "innovative" is used here to describe a solution that is nontrivial. Innovative financial solutions may involve a new consumer-type financial instrument, such as IRA and Keogh accounts; a new security, such as money market preferred stock; a new process, such as the shelf registration process; or a creative solution

*The author would like to thank James Ang, Laurence Booth, Marek Borun, Dennis Logue, and the anonymous referees for helpful comments on earlier drafts of the paper. Earlier versions of the paper were presented at Florida State University, the University of Tornoto, and the 18th Annual Meeting of the FMA in New Orleans, LA, October 22, 1988.

to a corporate finance problem, such as the design of customized security arrangements for a project financing or a leveraged buyout.

I. Scope of Financial Engineering

The definition of corporate financial engineering distinguishes three types of activities. The first, securities innovation, involves the development of innovative financial instruments, including those developed primarily for consumer applications such as new types of bank accounts, new forms of mutual funds, new types of life insurance products, and new forms of residential mortgages. Innovative financial instruments also include those developed primarily for corporate finance applications, such as new debt instruments; options, futures, and other new risk management vehicles; new types of preferred stock; new forms of convertible securities; and new types of common equity instruments.

The second branch of corporate financial engineering involves the development of innovative financial processes. These new processes reduce the cost of effecting financial transactions and are generally the result of legislative or regulatory changes (for example, the shelf registration process) or of technological developments (electronic security trading).

The third branch involves creative solutions to corporate finance problems. It encompasses innovative cash management strategies, innovative debt management strategies, and customized corporate financing structures such as those involved in various forms of asset-based financing.

II. The Process of Financial Innovation

Miller [38], Silber [46, 47, 48], and Van Horne [53] characterize the process of financial innovation in different terms.[1] Miller finds that regulatory and tax factors have provided the major impetus for financial innovation over the past 20 years. He describes financial innovations as "unforecastable improvements" in the array of available financial products and processes that came into being as a result of unexpected tax or regulatory impulses [38, p. 460]. Zero coupon bonds provide a good example of how a tax impulse led to innovation.

Prior to the passage of the Tax Equity and Fiscal Responsibility Act of 1982 (TEFRA), an issuer of zero coupon bonds could have amortized the

---

1. Other noteworthy contributions to the literature on financial innovations have been made by Atchison, DeMong, and Kling [4]; Black and Scholes [8]; Darrow and Mestres [17]; and Friedman [25].

original issue discount – the difference between the face amount of the bonds and their issue price – on a straight-line basis for tax purposes. Being able to deduct the interest expense faster than the interest implicitly compounded on the bonds produced significant tax benefits, which were greater the higher the bond's offering yield. And the higher the bond's offering yield, the deeper the discount. When interest rates rose sharply in 1981 and 1982, there was a flood of zero coupon bond issues to exploit this tax loophole. (See Fisher, Brick, and Ng [24]; and Yawitz and Maloney [55].) Zero coupon bonds were not a new financial instrument; it took an external shock (rising interest rates that greatly enhanced the potential tax benefits) to spur their use.

Zero coupon bonds also illustrate the interaction between Kane's regulatory dialectic and financial engineering [31, 32, 33]. Kane defines the regulatory dialectic as a cyclical process in which the opposing forces of regulation and regulatee avoidance adapt continually to one another. Finnerty [19] describes how U.S. corporations responded to TEFRA's closing of the domestic tax loophole by issuing zero coupon bonds to Japanese investors in order to exploit a Japanese tax loophole. The Japanese regulatory authorities responded to this activity first by imposing quantitative restrictions on Japanese purchases and then by threatening to close the tax loophole.

Silber [46, 47, 48] views the process of financial innovation differently from Miller. He characterizes innovative financial instruments and processes as attempts by corporations to lessen the financial constraints they face. In his view, firms maximize utility subject to a number of constraints, some of which are imposed by government regulation and the balance of which are imposed either by the marketplace or by the firm itself. Innovative activity responds to economic impulses that increase the cost of adhering to a particular constraint. The increased cost stimulates innovative activity to relax the constraint and thereby reduce the cost of adhering to it. For example, banks are capital-constrained. Considerable effort has gone into designing capital notes, which are debt instruments that qualify as "capital" for bank regulatory purposes. Issuing capital notes enables banks to increase the degree of leverage any particular amount of common equity would otherwise support. As a second example, increasingly volatile interest rates raised the cost of adhering to a policy of investing in fixed-dividend-rate preferred stock, which stimulated the innovative activity that led to the development of various forms of adjustable rate preferred stock.

Both Ben-Horim and Silber [5] and Silber [48] report that Silber's constraint-induced model of innovation explains a large percentage of new commercial bank products introduced during the 1952–1982 period. Nevertheless, Silber's model provides only a partial explanation of the process of financial innovation because it focuses almost exclusively on the securities issuer and leaves investors with an essentially passive role.

Van Horne takes a more critical view of the process of financial innovation than either Miller or Silber. In his 1984 presidential address to the American Finance Association, Van Horne [53] argues that in order for a new financial instrument or process to be truly innovative, it must enable the financial markets to operate more efficiently or make them more complete. If the financial markets were perfect and complete, there would be no opportunities for (nontrivial) financial innovation. Greater efficiency can be achieved by reducing transaction costs, which innovations such as the shelf registration process and electronic funds transfer have accomplished, or by reducing differential taxes and other "deadweight" losses. The financial markets can be made more complete by designing a new security whose contingent after-tax returns cannot be replicated by any combination of existing securities.

Van Horne also notes the excesses that have resulted from the innovative process, citing "innovations" whose only apparent benefit is some sort of desirable accounting treatment (for example, in-substance defeasance) and pointing out the apparently substantial fees that investment bankers and other promoters of financial innovations have reaped.[2] How the innovator shares in the rewards to innovation is an interesting empirical question that deserves careful study. In particular, how do the underwriting spreads on innovative securities vary as additional issuers enter the market? How is the net advantage of financial innovation allocated among the various parties to the transaction, and how does this allocation change as the innovative security becomes seasoned and as imitators enter the market? On this last point, Winger et al. [54] found that, in the case of adjustable rate preferred stock, later issuers achieved more favorable terms than the initial issuers.

The Miller, Silber, and Van Horne papers suggest that the factors responsible for financial innovation can be classified into 11 categories: (1) tax asymmetries that can be exploited to produce tax savings for the issuer, investors, or both and that are not offset by the added tax liabilities of the other; (2) transaction costs; (3) agency costs; (4) opportunities to reduce some form of risk or to reallocate risk from one market participant to another who is either less risk averse or else willing to bear the risk at a lower cost; (5) opportunities to increase an asset's liquidity; (6) regulatory or legislative change; (7) level and volatility of interest rates; (8) level and volatility of prices; (9) academic work that has resulted in advances in financial theories or better understanding of the risk-return characteristics of existing classes of securities;

---

2. Ricks [43] notes that the SEC is concerned that certain innovative financial products have been misrepresented to investors; for example, the index option has been marketed to retail investors as a conservative hedging product. Ricks raises an interesting issue—whether the evolution of financial instruments has outstripped the ability of brokers to understand what they are selling and of brokerage firms to provide adequate supervision.

(10) accounting benefits (which may, and often do, have at best an ephemeral effect on shareholder wealth); and (11) technological advances and other factors. Table 3.1 lists a broad variety of financial innovations and identifies the factors primarily responsible for each.

III. Consumer-Type Financial Instruments

Table 3.1 lists 14 innovative consumer-type financial instruments introduced within the past 20 years. Broker cash management accounts, which permit individuals to earn money market rates of interest on funds not currently invested in securities; money market mutual funds and money market accounts offered by banks, which pay current market interest rates on invested cash balances; NOW accounts, which are interest-bearing checking accounts; and debit cards, which enable bank depositors to shift money between accounts or withdraw cash from accounts at remote teller stations, all owe their existence at least partly to rising interest rates, which increased the opportunity cost of maintaining funds in non-interest-bearing checking or passbook accounts. In particular, money market mutual funds circumvented the outmoded Regulation Q interest rate ceilings. Money market accounts and NOW accounts resulted also from relaxed regulatory restrictions on the types of accounts banks could offer.

Municipal bond funds, IRA/Keogh accounts, and all-saver certificates were initiated by legislation. Municipal bond funds enable smaller individual investors to achieve a degree of portfolio diversification more cheaply than they could on their own. IRA/Keogh accounts conveyed special tax advantages to self-directed retirement accounts. All-saver certificates provided a tax incentive to depositing funds in thrifts, which faced funding problems at least partly brought on by high interest rates.

The equity access account was designed to enable individuals to borrow against the equity built up in their own homes. The Tax Reform Act of 1986 limited full interest deductions to mortgage interest, which stimulated the use of this vehicle. Bull and bear CDs pay a variable interest rate that is tied to changes in the Standard & Poor's 500 Index. They give individuals an indirect way of participating in the market for options on the S&P 500 Index. Tuition futures enable families to prepay the cost of an undergraduate education, which transfers college cost inflation risk to the seller of the tuition futures contract.

The remaining three products are all by-products of the higher level and volatility of interest rates. Universal life insurance and variable life insurance provide a wider choice of investment options than traditional whole life insurance, while retaining the tax deferral of investment earnings that life insurance products provide. Universal life insurance policies build cash

TABLE 3.1 Factors Primarily Responsible for Financial Innovations

Innovation	Factors Primarily Responsible*	Innovation	Factors Primarily Responsible*
Consumer-Type Financial Instruments			
Broker cash management accounts	7	Money market mutual funds	6, 7
Municipal bond funds	2, 4, 6	Money market accounts	6, 7
All-saver certificates	6, 7	NOW accounts	6, 7
Equity access account	1, 6, 8	Bull/Bear CDs	2
Debit card	2, 7, 11	IRA/Keogh accounts	1, 6
Tuition futures	4, 8	Universal or variable life insurance	1, 7, 8
Variable or adjustable rate mortgages	7	Convertible mortgages or reduction option loans	2, 7
Securities			
Deep discount/zero coupon bonds	1, 4, 7	Stripped debt securities	1, 4, 7
Floating rate notes	4, 5, 7	Floating rate, rating-sensitive notes	3, 4, 5, 7
Floating rate tax-exempt notes	4, 5, 7	Auction rate notes/debentures	2, 3, 4, 7
Real yield securities	2, 4, 5, 8	Dollar BILS	4, 7
Puttable-extendible notes	2, 3, 4	Increasing rate notes	3
Interest rate reset notes	3	Annuity notes	11
Extendible notes	2, 4	Variable coupon/rate renewable notes	2, 4, 6
Puttable/adjustable tender bonds	2, 4, 7	Variable duration notes	4, 7
Euronotes/Euro-commercial paper	2, 4	Universal commercial paper	4
Medium term notes	2	Negotiable CDs	2, 5
Mortgage-backed bonds	4	Mortgage pass-throughs	2, 4, 5
Collateralized mortgage obligations	2, 4, 5	Stripped mortgage-backed securities	4
Receivable-backed securities	4, 5	Real estate-backed bonds	4, 5
Letter of credit/surety bond credit support	4, 11	Yield curve/maximum rate notes	4, 6, 7
Interest rate swaps	4, 6, 7	Currency swaps	4, 6
Interest rate caps/floors/collars	4, 7	Remarketed reset notes	2, 3, 4
Foreign-currency-denominated bonds	4, 7	Eurocurrency bonds	7
Dual currency bonds	4, 6	Indexed currency option notes/ principal exchange rate linked securities	4, 6, 7
Commodity-linked bonds	4, 6, 8		

Instrument	Factors	Instrument	Factors
Gold loans	4, 8	High-yield (junk) bonds	2, 5, 7, 9
Exchange-traded options	4, 9	Foreign currency futures	4, 9, 11
Interest rate futures	4, 7, 9	Stock index futures	4, 8, 9
Options on futures contracts	4, 7, 9	Forward rate agreements	4, 7
Warrants to purchase bonds	4, 7	Adjustable rate preferred stock	1, 4, 5, 6, 7
Convertible adjustable preferred stock	1, 4, 5, 7, 11	Auction rate preferred stock	1, 4, 5, 7
Remarketed preferred stock	1, 2, 4, 5, 7	Indexed floating rate preferred stock	1, 4, 5, 7
Single-point adjustable rate stock	1, 2, 3, 4, 5, 7	Stated rate auction preferred stock	1, 3, 4, 5, 7
Variable cumulative preferred stock	1, 10	Convertible exchangeable preferred	1, 2, 10
Adjustable rate convertible debt	3, 4, 7	Zero coupon convertible debt	1, 11
Puttable convertible bonds	1, 10	Mandatory convertible/equity contract notes	1, 6
Synthetic convertible debt	3	Exchangeable auction preferred	1, 2, 4, 5, 7
Convertible reset debentures	1	Participating bonds	3, 4
Master limited partnership	4, 6	Additional class(es) of common stock	11
Americus trust	3, 4, 10	Paired common stock	4
Puttable common stock			

Financial Processes

Process	Factors	Process	Factors
Shelf registration	2, 6, 7	Direct public sale of securities	2, 6
Discount brokerage	2, 6	Automated teller machines	2, 11
Point-of-sale terminals	11	Electronic security trading	2, 11
Electronic funds transfer/automated clearing houses	7, 11	CHIPS (same day settlement)	7, 11
		Cash management/sweep accounts	7, 11

Financial Strategies/Solutions

Strategy	Factors	Strategy	Factors
More efficient bond call strategies	7, 9	Debt-for-debt exchanges	1, 7, 10
Stock-for-debt swaps	1, 7, 10	In-substance defeasance	1, 7, 10
Preferred dividend rolls	1	Hedged dividend capture	1
Leveraged buyout structuring	1, 9, 11	Corporate restructuring	1, 9, 11
Project finance/lease/asset-based financial structuring	4		

*Notation: 1, tax advantages; 2, reduced transaction costs; 3, reduced agency costs; 4, risk reallocation; 5, increased liquidity; 6, regulatory or legislative factors; 7, level and volatility of interest rates; 8, level and volatility of prices; 9, academic work; 10, accounting benefits; and 11, technological developments and other factors.

value at a stated fixed rate, or according to a stated interest rate formula that the insurance company guarantees. Variable life insurance policies are really families of mutual funds wrapped within a life insurance contract. Current yield and redemption value are tied directly to the particular mutual fund around which the policy is wrapped. Variable rate and adjustable rate mortgages allow the mortgage interest rate to adjust over time, which facilitates thrift asset-liability management in a volatile interest rate environment. Convertible mortgages (also referred to as reduction option loans) give borrowers the option to fix the interest rate on a variable rate or adjustable rate mortgage on one or more specified mortgage rate reset dates, provided the "index" rate has fallen more than two percentage points since the mortgage's issue date. To exercise the option, the borrower pays a fee that is typically smaller than the cost of refunding the original mortgage.

IV. Securities Innovation

There has been a more or less steady flow of security innovations in recent years. The investment banks that develop new securities herald each new product's introduction along with its advantages, and the financial press dutifully reports them [18, 37]. However, the process is not without its detractors [45, 53].

In addition to the factors discussed in Section II, a change in the industry environment helps account for the revolution in securities innovation. In recent years, the investment banking business has shifted away from what is known as "relationship banking" and become more competitive and hence more transactional. Developing an innovative security provides an opportunity for the financial engineer to solicit business from companies that have traditionally used other investment bankers. A successful innovator is usually awarded a mandate to sell the new security on a negotiated basis, rather than having to bid for securities "off the shelf" as is the case with conventional debt instruments. Investment banks therefore have a strong financial incentive to engineer innovative securities [26, 34].

A new security is truly "innovative" only if it (1) enables an investor to realize a higher after-tax risk-adjusted rate of return without adversely affecting the issuer's after-tax cost of funds, and/or (2) enables an issuer to realize a lower after-tax cost of funds without adversely affecting investors than had been possible prior to the introduction of the new security. A new security can accomplish this only if it makes the markets more efficient or more complete. It is not enough for a new security just to be different; there must be some real value added to the issuing company's shareholders.

A. Sources of Value Added

The purpose of securities innovation is to develop positive-net-present-value financing mechanisms [44]. Finnerty [22] develops an analytical framework that indicates three principal sources of value added through securities innovation: features that reallocate or reduce risk and in so doing reduce the required offering yield, characteristics that lead to lower issuance expenses during the period the financial obligation is intended to remain outstanding, and features that create a tax arbitrage for the issuer and investors (at the expense of the Internal Revenue Service). The resulting value added will be allocated among the company's shareholders, the purchasers of the innovative security, and the underwriters through the pricing of the innovative security and the setting of underwriting commissions.

If a company can repackage a security's payment stream so that it either involves less risk or reallocates risk from one class of investors to one that is less risk sensitive and thus requires a smaller risk premium, and does so in a manner that investors cannot duplicate as cheaply by utilizing existing securities, then shareholder value will be enhanced. Collateralized mortgage obligations (CMOs) and stripped mortgage-backed securities are examples. If a company can issue a security against a diversified portfolio of assets, it can reduce the investor's risk and hence the required yield. If the issuer can accomplish this more cheaply than the investor can by himself, there is opportunity for gain. Some examples are mortgage pass-through securities and debt backed by a portfolio of automobile receivables. If a company can securitize a loan so that it becomes publicly tradable, the lender's liquidity risk is reduced, resulting in a lower required yield. Negotiable certificates of deposit and nonrecourse notes (i.e., mortgages) secured by commercial real estate are examples. Both can be traded in the public securities markets, unlike conventional certificates of deposit and most commercial mortgages. If a company can design a security that reduces the agency costs that would normally arise in connection with a conventional financing, for example, costs due to informational asymmetries between the issuer and investors, a lower offering yield can result. Floating rate, rating sensitive notes, whose interest rate increases when the issuer's debt rating decreases, are an example.

Second, if a company can structure a securities issue so that underwriting commissions are reduced, shareholder value will be enhanced. Extendible notes are an example. Their maturity can be extended by mutual agreement between the issuer and investors, effectively rolling over the notes without additional underwriting commissions. Third, if a company can structure a new security so as to reduce investor taxes without increasing corporate income taxes, shareholder value will be enhanced as a result of this tax arbitrage.

For example, a company that is not currently a taxpayer can create such an arbitrage by issuing auction rate preferred stock to fully taxable corporate investors in lieu of commercial paper [1, 54]. Fourth, if a company can structure a new security so as to increase the present-value tax shields available to the issuer without increasing the investors' tax liabilities, shareholder value can again be enhanced through tax arbitrage. For example, the selling of zero coupon notes to tax-exempt investors before TEFRA resulted in such an arbitrage because the issuer could deduct the original discount on a straight-line basis. This tax treatment did not adversely affect tax-exempt investors. The balance of this section describes a number of innovative securities listed in Table 3.1 in greater detail.

B. Debt Innovations

Most of the financial innovations in recent years have involved debt securities. Some, such as zero coupon bonds, were issued in large volume for a period of time but have become very rare, either because changes in tax law eliminated their advantages or because more recent innovations superseded them. Other debt innovations such as extendible notes, medium-term notes, and collateralized mortgage obligations have had a more lasting impact. Yet others, such as indexed currency option notes, variable duration notes, certain commodity-linked bonds, and annuity notes, have been introduced and disappeared quickly, in some cases after just a single issue. Table 3.2 lists several of the more significant debt innovations and classifies each innovation's value-enhancing features.

Risk Reallocation / Yield Reduction.   Most of the debt innovations in Table 3.2 involve some form of risk reallocation as compared to conventional debt instruments or some other form of yield reduction mechanism. Involving the reapportioning of interest rate risk, credit risk, or some other form of risk, risk reallocation is beneficial when it transfers risk from those who are less willing to bear it to those who are more willing to bear it, in the sense that they require a smaller yield premium to compensate them for bearing the risk. A yield reduction (or equivalently, an increase in the net proceeds that can be realized from the sale of a given debt service stream) results when repackaging a particular debt service stream and selling the component parts yields greater proceeds than selling the original debt service stream intact.

Serial zero coupon bonds, stripped U.S. Treasury securities, and stripped municipal securities illustrate that the sum of the parts can exceed the whole when a particular debt service stream is subdivided and its constituent parts are sold separately. For example, stripping a bearer U.S. Treasury bond creates a serial zero coupon issue. Each zero coupon bond in the series can be sold to the highest bidder. Because the U.S. Treasury did not issue zero coupon bonds, securities firms created them by stripping bearer Treasury securities and earned an arbitrage profit for their effort. As one would expect, the substantial arbitrage profits earned by the securities firms initially involved in stripping were eliminated over time as competitors entered the market.

Mortgage pass-through certificates and receivable-backed securities can be sold in the marketplace at a lower yield than the assets that back them because they provide investors with a degree of diversification that many (smaller) investors could not achieve as cheaply on their own. In addition, the issuer often retains a subordinated interest in the collateral pool so that much of the apparent yield reduction results from the investors' senior position with respect to mortgage or receivable pool cash flows. Collateralized mortgage obligations (CMOs) and stripped mortgage-backed securities illustrate the benefits that can result from repackaging mortgage payment streams [50]. Most mortgages are prepayable at par at the option of the mortgagor after some brief period. This creates significant prepayment risk for lenders. CMOs package the mortgage payment stream from a portfolio of mortgages into several series of debt instruments—sometimes more than a dozen—which are prioritized in terms of their right to receive principal payments. In the simplest form of CMO, each series must be repaid in full before any principal payments can be made to the holders of the next series in order to reduce prepayment uncertainty. Thus, CMOs may make the capital market more complete by producing specific payoff streams that were previously unavailable. This occurs especially by achieving a specific allocation of prepayment risk across the different tranches. Stripped mortgage-backed securities divide the mortgage payment stream into two separate streams of claims, in the extreme case, one involving interest payments exclusively and the other involving principal repayments exclusively. The introduction of these securities also enhanced market completeness because of their duration and convexity. The apparent failure fully to understand the riskiness of these securities led to a substantial and highly publicized financial loss by a major brokerage house [51].

Adjustable rate notes and floating rate notes expose the issuer to floating interest rate risk but reduce the investor's principal risk. This interest rate risk reallocation can be of mutual benefit to issuers whose assets are interest-rate sensitive, such as banks and credit companies, and certain types of investors. Dollar BILS are a special type of floating rate note, one that has zero duration when duration is measured with respect to the specified index to which the floating rate is tied.

A recently introduced mechanism for transferring interest rate risk goes by two different names because it has two different sponsoring securities firms.

TABLE 3.2 *Selected Debt Innovations*

Security	Distinguishing Characteristics	Risk Reallocation/ Yield Reduction	Enhanced Liquidity
Adjustable Rate Notes and Floating Rate Notes	Coupon rate floats with some index, such as the 91-day Treasury bill rate.	Issuer exposed to floating interest rate risk but initial rate is lower than for fixed-rate issue.	Price remains closer to par than the price of a fixed-rate note of the same maturity.
Auction Rate Notes and Debentures	Interest rate reset by Dutch auction at the end of each interest period.	Coupon based on length of interest period, not on final maturity.	Designed to trade closer to par value than a floating rate note with a fixed interest rate formula.
Bonds Linked to Commodity Price or Index	Interest and/or principal linked to a specified commodity price or index.	Issuer assumes commodity price or index risk in return for lower (minimum) coupon. Can serve as a hedge if the issuer produces the particular commodity.	
Collateralized Mortgage Obligations (CMOs) and Real Estate Mortgage Investment Conduits (REMICs)	Mortgage payment stream is divided into several classes which are prioritized in terms of their right to receive principal payments.	Reduction in prepayment risk to classes with prepayment priority. Designed to appeal to different classes of investors; sum of the parts can exceed the whole.	More liquid than individual mortgages.
Commercial Real Estate–Backed Bonds	Nonrecourse bonds serviced and backed by a specified piece (or portfolio) of real estate.	Reduced yield due to greater liquidity.	More liquid than individual mortgages.
Credit-Enhanced Debt Securities	Issuer's obligation to pay is backed by an irrevocable letter of credit or a surety bond.	Stronger credit rating of the letter of credit or surety bond issuer leads to lower yield, which can more than offset letter of credit/surety bond fees.	
Dollar BILS	Floating rate zero coupon note the effective interest rate on which is determined retrospectively based on the change in the value of a specified index that measures the total return on long-term, high-grade corporate bonds.	Issuer assumes reinvestment risk.	
Dual Currency Bonds	Interest payable in US dollars but principal payable in a currency other than US dollars.	Issuer has foreign currency risk with respect to principal repayment obligation. Currency swap can hedge this risk and lead, in some cases, to yield reduction.	

Reduction in Agency Costs	Reduction in Transaction Costs	Tax Arbitrage	Other Benefits
Interest rate each period is determined in the marketplace, rather than by the issuer or the issuer's investment banker.	Intended to have lower transaction costs than repeatedly rolling over shorter maturity securities.		
			Attractive to investors who would like to speculate in commodity options but cannot, for regulatory or other reasons, purchase commodity options directly.
	Most investors could not achieve the same degree of prepayment risk reduction as cheaply on their own		
			Appeals to investors who like to lend against real estate properties.
			Enables a privately held company to borrow publicly while preserving confidentiality of financial information.
			Useful for hedging and immunization purposes because Dollar BILS have a zero duration when duration is measured with respect to the specified index.
			Euroyen-dollar dual currency bonds popular with Japanese investors who are subject to regulatory restrictions and desire income in dollars without principal risk.

TABLE 3.2 *Continued*

Security	Distinguishing Characteristics	Risk Reallocation/ Yield Reduction	Enhanced Liquidity
Euronotes and Euro-commercial Paper	Euro-commercial paper is similar to US commercial paper.	Elimination of intermediary brings savings that lender and borrower can share.	
Extendible Notes	Interest rate adjusts every 2–3 years to a new interest rate the issuer establishes, at which time note holder has the option to put the notes back to the issuer if the new rate is unacceptable.	Coupon based on 2–3 year put date, not on final maturity.	
Floating Rate, Rating Sensitive Notes	Coupon rate resets quarterly based on a spread over LIBOR. Spread increases if the issuer's debt rating declines.	Issuer exposed to floating interest rate risk but initial rate is lower than for fixed-rate issue.	Price remains closer to par than the price of a fixed-rate note of the same maturity.
Floating Rate Tax-Exempt Revenue Bonds	Coupon rate floats with some index, such as the 60-day high-grade commercial paper rate.	Issuer exposed to floating interest rate risk but initial rate is lower than for fixed-rate issue. Effectively, tax-exempt commercial paper.	
Increasing Rate Notes	Coupon rate increases by specified amounts at specified intervals.	Defers portion of interest expense to later years, which increases duration.	
Indexed Currency Option Notes/Principal Exchange Rate Linked Securities	Issuer pays reduced principal at maturity if specified foreign currency appreciates sufficiently relative to the US dollar.	Investor assumes foreign currency risk by effectively selling the issuer a call option denominated in the foreign currency.	
Interest Rate Caps, Floors, and Collars	Investor who writes an interest rate cap (floor/collar) contract agrees to make payments to the contract purchaser when a specified interest rate exceeds the specified cap (falls below the floor/falls outside the collar range).	Seller assumes the risk that interest rates may rise above the cap (fall below the floor/fall outside the collar range).	

Reduction in Agency Costs	Reduction in Transaction Costs	Tax Arbitrage	Other Benefits
	Corporations invest in each other's paper directly rather than through an intermediary.		
Investor has a put option, which provides protection against deterioration in credit quality or below-market coupon rate.	Lower transaction costs than issuing 2- or 3-year notes and rolling them over.		
Investor protected against deterioration in the issuer's credit quality because of increase in coupon rate when rating declines.			
		Investor does not have to pay income tax on the interest payments but issuer gets to deduct them.	
When such notes are issued in connection with a bridge financing, the step-up in coupon rate compensates investors for the issuer's failure to redeem the notes on schedule.			
			Attractive to investors who would like to speculate in foreign currencies but cannot, for regulatory or other reasons, purchase or sell currency options directly.

\

TABLE 3.2   *Continued*

Security	Distinguishing Characteristics	Risk Reallocation/ Yield Reduction	Enhanced Liquidity
Interest Rate Reset Notes	Interest rate is reset 3 years after issuance to the greater of *(i)* the initial rate and *(ii)* a rate sufficient to give the notes a market value equal to 101% of their face amount.	Reduced (initial) yield due to the reduction in agency costs.	
Interest Rate Swaps	Two entities agree to swap interest rate payment obligations, typically fixed rate for floating rate.	Effective vehicle for transferring interest rate risk from one party to another. Also, parties to a swap can realize a net benefit if they enjoy comparative advantages in different international credit markets.	
Medium-Term Notes	Notes are sold in varying amounts and in varying maturities on an agency basis.	Issuer bears market price risk during the marketing process.	
Mortgage Pass-Through Certificates	Investor buys an undivided interest in a pool of mortages.	Reduced yield due to the benefit to the investor of diversification and greater liquidity.	More liquid than individual mortgages.
Negotiable Certificates of Deposit	Certificates of deposit are registered and sold to the public on an agency basis.	Issuer bears market price risk during the marketing process.	More liquid than non-negotiable CDs.
Puttable Bonds and Adjustable Tender Securities	Issuer can periodically reset the terms, in effect rolling over debt without having to redeem it until the final maturity.	Coupon based on whether fixed or floating rate and on the length of the interest rate period selected, not on final maturity.	
Puttable-Extendible Notes	At the end of each interest period, the issuer may elect to redeem the notes at par or to extend the maturity on terms the issuer proposes, at which time the note holder can put the notes back to the issuer if the new terms are unacceptable. Investors also have series of put options during initial interest period.	Coupon based on length of interest interval, not on final maturity.	

Reduction in Agency Costs	Reduction in Transaction Costs	Tax Arbitrage	Other Benefits
Investor is compensated for a deterioration in the issuer's credit standing within 3 years of issuance.			
			Interest rate swaps are often designed to take advantage of special opportunities in particular markets outside the issuer's traditional market or to circumvent regulatory restrictions.
	Agents' commissions are lower than underwriting spreads.		
	Most investors could not achieve the same degree of diversification as cheaply on their own.		
	Agents' commissions are lower than underwriting spreads.		
Investor has a put option, which provides protection against deterioration in credit quality or below-market coupon rate.	Lower transaction costs than having to perform a series of refundings.		
Put options protect against deterioration in issuer's credit standing and also against issuer setting below-market coupon rate or other terms that might work to investor's disadvantage.			

TABLE 3.2 *Continued*

Security	Distinguishing Characteristics	Risk Reallocation/ Yield Reduction	Enhanced Liquidity
Real Yield Securities	Coupon rate resets quarterly to the greater of *(i)* change in consumer price index plus the "Real Yield Spread" (3.0% in the first such issue) and *(ii)* the Real Yield Spread, in each case on a semi-annual-equivalent basis.	Issuer exposed to inflation risk, which may be hedged in the CPI futures market.	Real yield securities could become more liquid than CPI futures, which tend to trade in significant volume only around the monthly CPI announcement date.
Receivable Pay-Through Securities	Investor buys an undivided interest in a pool of receivables.	Reduced yield due to the benefit to the investor of diversification and greater liquidity. Significantly cheaper for issuer than pledging receivables to a bank.	More liquid than individual receivables.
Remarketed Reset Notes	Interest rate reset at the end of each interest period to a rate the remarketing agent determines will make the notes worth par. If issuer and remarketing agent can not agree on rate, then the coupon rate is determined by formula which dictates a higher rate the lower the issuer's credit standing.	Coupon based on length of interest period, not on final maturity.	Designed to trade closer to par value than a floating-rate note with a fixed interest rate formula.
Stripped Mortgage-Backed Securities	Mortgage payment stream subdivided into two classes, *(i)* one with below-market coupon and the other with above-market coupon or *(ii)* one receiving interest only and the other receiving principal only from mortgage pools.	Securities have unique option characteristics that make them useful for hedging purposes. Designed to appeal to different classes of investors; sum of the parts can exceed the whole.	
Stripped Treasury or Municipal Securities	Coupons separated from corpus to create a series of zero coupon bonds that can be sold separately.	Yield curve arbitrage; sum of the parts can exceed the whole.	
Variable Coupon Renewable Notes	Coupon rate varies weekly and equals a fixed spread over the 91-day T-bill rate. Each 91 days the maturity extends another 91 days. If put option exercised, spread is reduced.	Coupon based on 1-year termination date, not on final maturity.	

Reduction in Agency Costs	Reduction in Transaction Costs	Tax Arbitrage	Other Benefits
	Investors obtain a long-dated inflation hedging instrument that they could not create as cheaply on their own.		Real yield securities have a longer duration than alternative inflation hedging instruments.
	Security purchasers could not achieve the same degree of diversification as cheaply on their own.		
Investors have a put option, which protects against the issuer and remarketing agent agreeing to set a below-market coupon rate, and the flexible interest rate formula protects investors against deterioration in the issuer's credit standing.	Intended to have lower transaction costs than auction rate notes and debentures, which require periodic Dutch auctions.		
	Lower transaction costs than issuing 1-year note and rolling it over.		Designed to appeal to money market mutual funds, which face tight investment restrictions, and to discourage put to isuer.

TABLE 3.2   *Continued*

Security	Distinguishing Characteristics	Risk Reallocation/ Yield Reduction	Enhanced Liquidity
Variable Rate Renewable Notes	Coupon rate varies monthly and equals a fixed spread over the 1-month commercial paper rate. Each quarter the maturity automatically extends an additional quarter unless the investor elects to terminate the extension.	Coupon based on 1-year termination date, not on final maturity.	
Warrants to Purchase Debt Securities	Warrant with 1–5 years to expiration to buy intermediate-term or long-term bonds.	Issuer is effectively selling a covered call option, which can afford investors opportunities not available in the traditional options markets.	
Yield Curve Notes and Maximum Rate Notes	Interest rate equals a specified rate minus LIBOR.	Might reduce yield relative to conventional debt when coupled with an interest rate swap against LIBOR.	
Zero Coupon Bonds (sometimes issued in series)	Non-interest-bearing. Payment in one lump sum at maturity.	Issuer assumes reinvestment risk. Issues sold in Japan carried below-taxable-market yields reflecting their tax advantage over conventional debt issues.	

Yield curve notes and maximum rate notes, collectively "inverse floaters," carry an interest rate that increases (decreases) as interest rates fall (rise) [28, 39, 49]. Typically, the incentive in issuing an inverse floater is to fix the coupon by entering into an interest rate swap agreement. The two transactions together benefit the issuer when they result in a lower cost of funds than a conventional fixed-rate issue. Investors find inverse floaters useful for immunization purposes because of their very long duration, which may exceed the maturity of the security [28, 39, 49].

Three other classes of debt innovations in Table 3.2 also involve some form of risk reallocation. Credit-enhanced debt securities involve credit risk reallocation through bank letters of credit or insurance company surety bonds. When the letter of credit or surety bond fee is less than the resulting reduction in the yield required to sell the securities, the credit risk reallocation is beneficial to the issuer. Dual currency bonds, indexed currency option notes, and principal-exchange-rate-linked securities illustrate two forms of currency

Reduction in Agency Costs	Reduction in Transaction Costs	Tax Arbitrage	Other Benefits
	Lower transaction costs than issuing 1-year note and rolling it over.		Designed to appeal to money market mutual funds, which face tight investment restrictions.
			Useful for hedging and immunization purposes because of very long duration.
		Straight-line amortization of original issue discount pre-TEFRA. Japanese investors realize significant tax savings.	

risk reallocation. Bonds that make interest and/or principal payments that are linked to a specified index or commodity, such as the price of oil or the price of silver, are attractive to institutions that are not permitted to invest directly in commodity options and can serve as a hedge for an issuer who is a producer of the commodity.

Reduced Agency Costs. Five of the debt innovations in Table 3.2 are designed at least partly to reduce agency costs. Increasing rate notes, when used in connection with a bridge financing, provide an incentive for the issuer to redeem the notes (out of the proceeds of a permanent financing) on schedule. Interest rate reset notes protect against deterioration in the issuer's credit standing prior to the reset date. Puttable-extendible notes provide a series of put options that protect against deterioration in the issuer's credit standing. The protection that such an option affords investors is not readily available in the options markets because a well-organized market for long-term corporate bond options does not currently exist. Remarketed reset notes include a put option, which protects against the issuer and remarketing agent conspiring to set a below-market coupon rate, and a flexible interest rate formula (in the event the issuer and the remarketing agent cannot agree on a rate), which provides for a higher interest rate the lower the issuer's credit standing. Similarly, floating rate, rating-sensitive notes bear a coupon rate that varies inversely with the issuer's credit standing.

Reduced Issuance Expenses.   Extendible notes, variable coupon renewable notes, puttable bonds, adjustable tender securities, remarketed reset notes, and euronotes and euro-commercial paper are all designed to reduce issuance expenses and other forms of transaction costs. Extendible notes typically provide for an interest rate adjustment every two or three years, although other adjustment intervals are possible, and thus represent an alternative to rolling over two- or three-year note issues without incurring additional issuance expenses.

Variable coupon renewable notes represent a refinement of the extendible note concept. The maturity of the notes automatically extends 91 days at the end of each quarter — unless the holder elects to terminate the automatic extension, in which case the interest rate spread decreases. A holder wishing to terminate the investment would avoid the reduction in spread by selling the notes in the marketplace. Goodman and Yawitz [28] explain how these features were designed to meet regulatory investment restrictions that money market mutual funds face.[3] In another refinement of the extendible note concept, puttable bonds, adjustable tender securities, and remarketed reset notes give the issuer the flexibility to reset the terms of the security periodically. These securities offer the issuer greater flexibility than extendible notes in the choice of terms on which to extend the maturity of the debt issue.

Euronotes and euro-commercial paper represent the extension of commercial paper to the Euromarket [42]. Transaction cost savings result because corporations invest directly in one another's securities rather than through banks and other intermediaries, as was formerly the case.

Tax Arbitrage.   Zero coupon bonds, as previously noted, provided a form of tax arbitrage prior to the passage of TEFRA. In addition, the investor bears no reinvestment risk, because interest is compounded over the life of the debt issue at the yield at which the investor purchased the bond.

---

3. Variable coupon renewable notes have a nominal maturity of one year, which is the maximum maturity permitted money market mutual fund investments. Also, because of the weekly rate reset, variable coupon renewable notes count as 7-day assets in meeting the 120-day upper limit on a money market mutual fund's dollar-weighted average portfolio maturity.

C. Options, Futures, and Other Interest Rate Risk Management Vehicles

Options, futures, and other interest rate risk management vehicles enable market participants who are averse to certain risks (such as foreign currency risk, interest rate risk, or stock market risk) to transfer that risk to others who are less risk averse, on certain specified terms in exchange for a fee. Miller [38] cites financial futures as the most significant financial innovation of the past 20 years. Block and Gallagher [9] and Booth, Smith, and Stolz [10] catalog the many uses to which interest rate futures may be put for risk management purposes.

Warrants to purchase debt securities, an innovative form of debt option, have been more popular in the Euromarket than in the domestic market. They typically take the form of an option to buy an intermediate-term or long-term bond, and generally have a term of expiration between one and five years. The warrant issuer is effectively writing a covered call option on the issuer's own debt. Issuing the warrant represents a form of hedging by the debt issuer, and it affords investors opportunities not available in the traditional options markets.

Interest rate risk management vehicles include interest rate futures, options on interest rate futures, forward rate agreements, interest rate swaps, interest rate caps, interest rate floors, and interest rate collars [3, 6, 13]. The interest rate swap market has exploded within the past five years, and swap activity currently exceeds $400 billion per year. Bicksler and Chen [6] describe the market imperfections that can create comparative advantages among different borrowers in the fixed rate debt and floating rate debt markets and across national boundaries, and thereby provide economic incentives to engage in interest rate swaps. Arak et al. [3] provide an alternative rationale for swaps. They state that swaps enable borrowers to fix the risk-free rate so that borrowers who believe their credit standing is about to improve have an incentive to borrow short-term funds and swap into fixed payments. Brown and Smith [13] describe the innovative nature of interest rate caps, floors, and collars, all of which impose limits on an entity's exposure to floating-interest-rate risk.

Miller [38] questions whether diminishing returns to financial innovation have already set in. Much of the innovative activity in recent years has involved the development of new futures products. Reports in the financial press have stated that 80% to 90% of new futures products fail and argued that the financial futures industry has already developed perhaps as much as 90% of the potentially useful futures products [41]. Miller notes that the Chicago Board of Trade and the Chicago Mercantile Exchange spent a combined total of $5 to $6 million developing two distinct futures contracts for over-the-counter stocks, both of which failed in the marketplace. The economics of futures innovation is one area of investigation that might yield at least a partial answer to Miller's question.

D. Preferred Stock Innovations

Preferred stock offers a tax advantage over debt to corporate investors, who are permitted to deduct from their taxable income 70% of the dividends they receive from unaffiliated corporations. Corporate money managers have a tax incentive to purchase preferred stock rather than commercial paper or other short-term debt instruments, the interest on which is fully taxable. However, the purchasing of long-term fixed-dividend-rate preferred stock exposes the purchaser to the risk that rising interest rates could lead to a fall in the price of the preferred stock that would more than offset the tax saving. Table 3.3 lists a variety of new securities designed to deal with this problem.

Adjustable rate preferred stock was designed to lessen the investor's principal risk by having the dividend rate adjust as interest rates change. The dividend rate adjusts based on a formula. At times the spread investors have required to value the securities at par has differed significantly from the fixed spread specified in the formula, causing the value of the security to deviate significantly from its face amount. Winger et al. [54] document the high volatility of adjustable rate preferred stock holding-period returns relative to those of alternative money market investments.

Convertible adjustable preferred stock (CAPS) was designed to eliminate this deficiency. CAPS have traded closer to their respective face amounts than adjustable rate preferred stocks. However, there have been only a few CAPS issues, probably because prospective issuers have objected to the possibility of having to issue common stock or raise a large amount of cash on short notice.

Auction rate preferred stock carried the evolutionary process a step further. The dividend rate is reset by Dutch auction every 49 days, which represents just enough weeks to meet the 46-day holding period required to qualify for the 70% dividends-received deduction. (One variation of this security, stated rate auction preferred stock, fixes the dividend rate for several years before the regular Dutch auctions commence.) Alderson, Brown, and Lummer [1] document the tax arbitrage that auction rate preferred stock affords under current tax law. Various versions of auction rate preferred stock are sold under different acronyms (MMP, Money Market Preferred; AMPS, Auction Market Preferred Stock; DARTS, Dutch Auction Rate Transferable Securities; STAR, Short-Term Auction Rate; etc.) coined by the different securities firms that offer the product. The names may differ, but the securities are the same.

In an effort to refine the adjustable rate preferred stock concept further, there have been at least two attempts to design a superior security, but only one was successful. Single-point adjustable rate stock (SPARS) has a dividend rate that adjusts automatically every 49 days to a specified percentage of the 60-day high-grade commercial paper rate. The security is designed to afford the same degree of liquidity as auction rate preferred stock, but with lower transaction costs since no auction need be held. However, the fixed-dividend-rate formula involves a potential agency cost that auction rate preferred stock does not. Investors will suffer a loss if the issuer's managers take actions that cause the issuer's credit standing to deteriorate, because the dividend formula is fixed. Primarily for this reason there have been at most only a few SPARS issues.

Remarketed preferred stock has a dividend rate that is reset at the end of each period to a dividend rate that a specified remarketing agent determines will make the preferred stock worth par. Such issues permit the issuer considerable flexibility in selecting the length of the dividend period, which may be of any length, even one day. Remarketed preferred also offers greater flexibility in selecting the other terms of the issue; in fact, each share of an issue could have different maturity, dividend rate, or other terms, provided the issuer and holders so agree. Remarketed preferred has not proven as popular with issuers as auction rate preferred stock, but that could change due to the greater flexibility remarketed preferred affords.

As a result of the controversy over whether auction rate preferred stock or remarketed preferred stock results in more equitable pricing, variable cumulative preferred stock was invented in order to let the issuer decide at the end of each dividend period which of the two reset methods will determine the dividend rate for the following dividend period.

E. Convertible Debt/Preferred Stock Innovations

Convertible debt innovations share a dominant theme: the creation of additional tax deductions (while preserving the amelioration of moral hazard, which conventional convertible bonds achieve). The creation of additional tax deductions involves a form of tax arbitrage because 80–90% of convertible bond investors are tax-exempt [21]. Table 3.4 describes seven recent innovations involving convertible securities.

Convertible exchangeable preferred stock consists of convertible perpetual preferred stock that the issuer is permitted to exchange for an issue of convertible subordinated debt, having the same conversion terms and an interest rate that equals the dividend rate on the convertible preferred. The exchange feature enables the issuer to reissue the convertible preferred as convertible debt should it become taxable in the future, but without having to pay additional underwriting commissions. A large volume of such securities

TABLE 3.3   *Selected Preferred Stock Innovations*

Security	Distinguishing Characteristics	Risk Reallocation/ Yield Reduction	Enhanced Liquidity
Adjustable Rate Preferred Stock	Quarterly dividend rate reset each quarter based on maximum of 3-month T-bill, 10-year Treasury, and 20-year Treasury rates plus or minus a specified spread.	Issuer bears more interest rate risk than a fixed-rate preferred would involve. Lower yield than commercial paper.	Security is designed to trade near its par value.
Auction Rate Preferred Stock (MMP/DARTS/ AMPS/STAR)	Dividend rate reset by Dutch auction every 49 days (subject to a maximum rate of 110%, or under certain circumstances 125%, of the 60-day "AA" Composite Commercial Paper Rate). Dividend is paid at the end of each dividend period.	Issuer bears more interest rate risk than a fixed-rate preferred would involve. Lower yield than commercial paper.	Security is designed to provide greater liquidity than convertible adjustable preferred stock.
Convertible Adjustable Preferred Stock	Issue convertible on dividend payment dates into variable number of the issuer's common shares, subject to a cap, equal in market value to the par value of the preferred.	Issuer bears more interest rate risk than a fixed-rate preferred would involve. Lower yield than commercial paper.	Security is designed to provide greater liquidity than adjustable rate preferred stock (due to the conversion feature).
Remarketed Preferred Stock (SABRES)	Perpetual preferred stock with a dividend rate that resets at the end of each dividend period to a rate the remarketing agent determines will make the preferred stock worth par (subject to a maximum rate of 110%, or under certain circumstances 125%, of the 60-day "AA" Composite Commercial Paper Rate). Dividend periods may be of any length, even 1 day. Different shares of a single issue may have different periods and different dividend rates.	Issuer bears more interest rate risk than a fixed-rate preferred would involve. Lower yield than commercial paper.	Security is designed to trade near its par value.
Single-Point Adjustable Rate Stock	Dividend rate reset every 49 days as a specified percentage of the high-grade commercial paper rate.	Issuer bears more interest rate risk than a fixed-rate preferred would involve. Lower yield than commercial paper.	Security is designed to trade near its par value.

Reduction in Agency Costs	Reduction in Transaction Costs	Tax Arbitrage	Other Benefits
		Designed to enable short-term corporate investors to take advantage of 70% dividends received deduction.	
Dividend rate each period is determined in the marketplace, which provides protection against deterioration in issuer's credit standing (protection is limited by the dividend rate cap).		Designed to enable short-term corporate investors to take advantage of 70% dividends received deduction.	
		Designed to enable short-term corporate investors to take advantage of 70% dividends received deduction.	
		Designed to enable short-term corporate investors to take advantage of 70% dividends received deduction.	Remarketed preferred stock offers greater flexibility in setting the terms of the issue than auction rate preferred stock, which requires a Dutch auction for potentially the entire issue once every 49 days.
	Security is designed to save on recurring transaction costs associated with auction rate preferred stock.	Designed to enable short-term corporate investors to take advantage of 70% dividends received deduction.	

TABLE 3.3 *Continued*

Security	Distinguishing Characteristics	Risk Reallocation/ Yield Reduction	Enhanced Liquidity
Stated Rate Auction Preferred Stock	Initial dividend period of several years during which the dividend rate is fixed. Thereafter the issuer can elect to have the dividend rate reset every 49 days by Dutch auction.	Issuer bears more interest rate risk than a fixed-rate preferred would involve.	Security is designed to trade near its par value after the initial dividend period has elapsed and the Dutch auctions determine the dividend rate.
Variable Cumulative Preferred Stock	At the end of any dividend period the issuer can select between the auction method and the remarketing method to have the dividend rate reset.	Issuer bears more interest rate risk than a fixed-rate preferred would involve. Lower yield than commercial paper.	Security is designed to trade near its par value.

have been issued by companies that were not currently taxpayers for federal income tax purposes. Similarly, exchangeable auction preferred stock permits the issuer to exchange auction rate notes for auction rate preferred stock on any dividend payment date.

Adjustable rate convertible debt is a security with a purported tax advantage. The security represented an attempt to package equity as debt. The Internal Revenue Service has ruled that the security is equity for tax purposes, thereby denying the interest deductions and rendering the security unattractive. Zero coupon convertible debt reflects a similar theme [36]. If the issue is converted, both interest and principal are converted to common equity, in which case the issuer will have effectively sold common equity with a tax deductibility feature.

Debt with mandatory common stock purchase contracts represents debt that qualifies as primary capital for bank regulatory purposes because conversion is mandatory. In the meantime, the issuer gets a stream of interest tax deductions that simply selling common stock would not afford. Finnerty [21] and Jones and Mason [30] describe how to package a unit consisting of debt and warrants into synthetic convertible debt, the features of which mirror the features of conventional convertible debt. Synthetic convertible bonds enjoy a tax advantage relative to a comparable convertible debt issue because, in effect, the warrant proceeds are deductible for tax purposes over

Reduction in Agency Costs	Reduction in Transaction Costs	Tax Arbitrage	Other Benefits
The maximum permitted dividend rate, expressed as a percentage of the 60-day "AA" Composite Commercial Paper Rate, increases according to a specified schedule if the preferred stock's credit rating falls.		Designed so as eventually to enable short-term corporate investors to take advantage of 70% dividends received deduction.	
The maximum permitted dividend rate, expressed as a percentage of the 60-day "AA" Composite Commercial Paper Rate, increases according to a specified schedule if the preferred stock's credit rating falls.	Security is designed to save on transaction costs the issuer would otherwise incur if it wanted to change from auction reset to remarketing reset or vice versa.	Designed to enable short-term corporate investors to take advantage of 70% dividends received deduction.	Security is designed to enable the issuer to select at the end of each dividend period the method of rate reset it prefers.

the life of the debt issue. Lastly, convertible reset debentures protect holders against deterioration in the issuer's financial prospects within two years of issuance through an interest rate reset mechanism.

F. Common Equity Innovations

There are four principal common equity innovations: additional class(es) of common stock whose dividends are tied to the earnings of a specified subsidiary of the issuer, the Americus Trust, the master limited partnership, and puttable common stock. Table 3.5 indicates the principal benefits resulting from these innovations.

The creation of a new class of common stock that reflects the financial condition and operating peformance of a subsidiary is best illustrated by the General Motors Corporation Class E Common Stock. Class E Stock holders are entitled to only one-half a vote per share, and their dividends are dependent on the paid-in surplus attributable to that particular class of stock and to the separate net income of General Motors' Electronic Data Systems Corporation subsidiary. Such a class of stock enables the marketplace to establish a separate market value for the subsidiary while ensuring that the parent company retains 100% voting control and thus the right to consolidate the subsidiary for federal income tax purposes. It can also prove useful for an

TABLE 3.4 *Selected Convertible Debt/Preferred Stock Innovations*

Security	Distinguishing Characteristics	Risk Reallocation/ Yield Reduction	Enhanced Liquidity
Adjustable Rate Convertible Debt	Debt the interest rate on which varies directly with the dividend rate on the underlying common stock. No conversion premium.		
Convertible Exchangeable Preferred Stock	Convertible preferred stock that is exchangeable, at the issuer's option, for convertible debt with identical rate and identical conversion terms.		
Convertible Reset Debentures	Convertible bond the interest rate on which must be adjusted upward, if necessary, by an amount sufficient to give the debentures a market value equal to their face amount 2 years after issuance.		
Debt with Mandatory Common Stock Purchase Contracts	Notes with contracts that obligate note purchasers to buy sufficient common stock from the issuer to retire the issue in full by its scheduled maturity date.		
Exchangeable Auction Preferred Stock	Auction rate preferred stock that is exchangeable on any dividend payment date, at the option of the issuer, for auction rate notes, the interest rate on which is reset by Dutch auction every 35 days.	Issuer bears more interest rate risk than a fixed-rate instrument would involve.	Security is designed to trade near its par value.
Synthetic Convertible Debt	Debt and warrants package structured in such a way as to mirror a traditional convertible debt issue.		
Zero Coupon Convertible Debt	Non-interest-bearing convertible debt issue.		

Reduction in Agency Costs	Reduction in Transaction Costs	Tax Arbitrage	Other Benefits
		Effectively, tax deductible common equity. Security has since been ruled equity by the IRS.	Portion of the issue carried as equity on the issuer's balance sheet.
	No need to reissue convertible security as debt —just exchange it— when the issuer becomes a taxpayer.	Issuer can exchange debt for the preferred when it becomes taxable with interest rate the same as the dividend rate and without any change in conversion features.	Appears as equity on the issuer's balance sheet until it is exchanged for convertible debt.
Investor is protected against a deterioration in the issuer's financial prospects within 2 years of issuance.			
		Notes provide a stream of interest tax shields, which (true) equity does not.	Commercial bank holding companies have issued it because it counted as "primary capital" for regulatory purposes.
	Issuance of auction rate notes involves no underwriting commissions.	Issuer can exchange notes for the preferred when it becomes taxable.	Appears as equity on the issuer's balance sheet until it is exchanged for auction rate notes.
		In effect, warrant proceeds are tax deductible.	Warrants go on the balance sheet as equity.
		If issue converts, the issuer will have sold, in effect, tax deductible equity.	If holders convert, entire debt service stream is converted to common equity.

TABLE 3.5   *Selected Common Equity Innovations*

Security	Distinguishing Characteristics	Risk Reallocation/ Yield Reduction	Enhanced Liquidity
Additional Class(es) of Common Stock	A company issues a second class of common stock the dividends on which are tied to the earnings of a specified subsidiary.		
Americus Trust	Outstanding shares of a particular company's common stock are contributed to a five-year unit investment trust. Units may be separated into a PRIME component, which embodies full dividend and voting rights in the underlying share and permits limited capital appreciation, and a SCORE component, which provides full capital appreciation above a stated price.	Stream of annual total returns on a share of stock is separated into *(i)* a dividend stream (with limited capital appreciation potential) and *(ii)* a (residual) capital appreciation stream.	
Master Limited Partnership	A business is given the legal form of a partnership but is otherwise structured, and is traded publicly, like a corporation.		
Puttable Common Stock	Issuer sells a new issue of common stock along with rights to put the stock back to the issuer on a specified date at a specified price.	Issuer sells investors a put option, which investors will exercise if the company's share price decreases.	

employee stock option plan or other incentive compensation schemes for employees of the subsidiary.

The first Americus Trust was offered to owners of American Telephone & Telegraph Company common stock on October 25, 1983 [2]. Since then,

Reduction in Agency Costs	Reduction in Transaction Costs	Tax Arbitrage	Other Benefits
			Establishes separate market value for the subsidiary while assuring the parent 100% voting control. Useful for employee compensation programs for subsidiary.
	PRIME component would appeal to corporate investors who can take advantage of the 70% dividends received deduction. SCORE component would appeal to capital-gain-oriented individual investors.		PRIME component resembles participating preferred stock if the issuer's common stock dividend rate is stable. SCORE component is a longer-dated call option than the ones customarily traded in the options market.
		Eliminates a layer of taxation because partnerships are not taxable entities.	
The put option reduces agency costs associated with a new share issue that are brought on by informational asymmetries.			Equivalent under certain conditions to convertible bonds but can be recorded as equity on the balance sheet so long as the company's payment obligation under the put option can be settled in common stock.

more than two dozen other Americus Trusts have been formed. An Americus Trust offers the common stockholders of a company the opportunity to strip each of their common shares into a PRIME Component, which carries full dividend and voting rights and limits capital appreciation rights, and a

SCORE Component, which carries full capital appreciation rights above a threshold price. PRIMEs and SCOREs appear to expand the range of securities available for inclusion in investment portfolios.[4]

Master limited partnerships are publicly traded limited partnerships that operate much like corporations except for their legal status, and many are listed on the New York Stock Exchange. The partnership structure eliminates a layer of taxation. However, if an entity is profitable and needs to retain the bulk of its earnings, the limited partners will owe tax on their respective pro rata shares of the partnership's income. Collins and Bey [16] show that the master limited partnership structure is best suited for companies with high tax rates and low retention rates (i.e., companies in "mature" industries) but is poorly suited for companies in "growth" industries.

Puttable common stock involves the sale of put options along with a new issue of common stock. The package of securities is comparable to a convertible bond [15]. The put option reduces the agency costs associated with a new share issue and could prove useful in reducing or perhaps even eliminating the underpricing of initial public offerings.

V. Innovative Financial Processes

The innovative financial processes listed in Table 3.1 reflect three basic causal factors: (1) efforts aimed at reducing transaction costs, (2) steps taken to reduce idle cash balances in response to higher interest rates, and (3) the availability of relatively inexpensive computer technology to facilitate quicker financial transactions. The shelf registration process, extended to a broad range of corporate issuers by the Securities and Exchange Commission in 1982, has streamlined the process of issuing corporate securities. Kidwell, Marr, and Thompson [34] document the reduction in flotation costs that has resulted from this innovative offering process. Similarly, the direct sale of securities to the public, as evidenced by Green Mountain Power Company's sale of debt securities to its ratepayers beginning in 1970 and Virginia Electric and Power Company's sale of common stock to its ratepayers beginning some ten years later, also reduce transaction costs because the securities are not sold through securities firms. Such offering methods have the potential for reducing a company's cost of capital by appealing to a natural clientele for the company's securities.

---

4. The AT&T Americus Trust was formed prior to the breakup of AT&T. The trust therefore provided an opportunity for investors to acquire units representing shares in pre-reorganization AT&T (i.e., proportionate interests in post-reorganization AT&T and in the seven regional holding companies AT&T spun off) perhaps more cheaply than they could by accumulating the shares of the different entities on their own.

Discount brokerage, which resulted from the elimination of fixed commission rates by the Securities and Exchange Commission on May 1, 1975, has substantially reduced brokerage commission charges below the commission rates the "full-service" brokerage houses charge. Essentially, brokerage services have become unbundled. As a result of discount brokerage, individuals can pay separately for transaction execution. Electronic security trading and automated teller machines were also intended to reduce transaction costs.

Electronic security trading, automated teller machines, point-of-sale terminals, electronic funds transfer, CHIPS (Clearinghouse Interbank Payment System), and cash management/sweep accounts have all been made possible by the availability of inexpensive computer technology. The last three were also motivated by a desire to speed cash collection, to speed check processing, and to ensure the investment of excess cash balances, respectively, all in order to reduce idle cash balances, whose opportunity cost increases with rising interest rates. Gentry [27] provides a comprehensive review of recent developments in corporate cash management. It seems likely that further technological advances will lead to more efficient systems for effecting financial transactions and for managing cash balances.

VI. Creative Solutions to Corporate Finance Problems

Although it does not seem reflected in the relatively small number of items listed in that category in Table 3.1, finding creative solutions to corporate finance problems is an important undertaking. For example, considerable practitioner and academic effort has been expended trying to develop the most efficient strategy for calling high-coupon debt when interest rates decline [11]. Volatile interest rates have also created opportunities for companies to extinguish debt at a discount from its face amount, which produces accounting benefits. Developing techniques for accomplishing this tax-free illustrates the interaction between financial engineering and Kane's regulatory dialectic. The Bankruptcy Tax Act of 1980 eliminated several widely used strategies for obtaining the gain tax-free. Such a gain is the difference between the face amount of the debt and the repurchase price. Investment bankers first developed debt-for-lower-coupon-debt exchanges, and later developed stock-for-debt swaps, in order to achieve tax-free treatment. But the Tax Reform Act of 1984 made the gain realized in such transactions taxable and thereby virtually eliminated all remaining possibilities for refunding discounted debt profitably [20]. Nevertheless, investment bankers came up with in-substance defeasance as a means for extinguishing discounted debt in a tax-free manner. However, Peterson, Peterson, and Ang [40] correctly point out that such transactions are unlikely to enhance shareholder wealth.

Bankers and corporate treasurers have also expended considerable effort to come up with more tax-effective cash management strategies, including preferred dividend rolls (see Joehnk, Bowlin, and Petty [29]) and hedged dividend capture (see Brown and Lummer [12] and Zivney and Alderson [56] and references therein) in addition to the new forms of floating-rate preferred stock discussed earlier.

The third major area of activity encompasses leveraged buyout structuring, corporate restructuring, and project finance/lease/asset-based financial structurings. All involve, among other things, the crafting of contractual and other security arrangements that allocate financial risks and rewards among shareholders and one or more classes of creditors. For example, a leveraged buyout typically involves multiple layers of equity and multiple layers of debt, each with its own particular security arrangements. The capital structure must be engineered to suit the risk-return characteristics of the portfolio of operating assets, to satisfy the risk-return preferences of the various classes of investors, and to minimize potential agency costs.

Recent research has documented the substantial increases in shareholder wealth — on the order of 30% — accompanying the announcements of leveraged buyouts and leveraged recapitalizations [7, 35, 52]. Financial engineering in such cases involves estimating the cash flow stream available to service debt and preferred stock, determining the most appropriate capital structure (including the examining of the advantages of using employee stock ownership plans or other specialized forms of financing to effect the transaction [14]), designing the terms of each issue of securities so as to allocate risks and returns appropriately and minimize potential agency costs, and crafting incentive compensation arrangements for managers to ensure shareholder-wealth-maximizing behavior. Most attention in the financial press has been focused on the restructuring of financially healthy companies, but the same issues arise, and are potentially more challenging, when a troubled company is involved (as for example in the reorganization of First City Bancorporation of Texas into a recapitalized bank holding company and a collecting bank, the latter being given $1.79 billion of nonperforming, past due, and other lesser quality assets that were removed from First City Bancorporation's books [23]).

VII. Conclusion

One of the more important questions raised by Miller [38] is whether the process of financial innovation has reached the point of diminishing returns. If the tax regime remains static, if interest rates stabilize, if the regulatory landscape solidifies, and so on, diminishing returns to financial innovation are bound to set in eventually. But to the extent that financial innovation occurs in response to unexpected economic, tax, and regulatory shocks, such shocks can keep the process of financial innovation going indefinitely without diminishing returns necessarily setting in. Financial innovations symbolize the profit-driven response to the changes in the economic, tax, and regulatory environments. As this environment changes, and as consolidation within the financial services industry intensifies competition, market participants will seek out new ways to conduct financial transactions more efficiently. The rapid pace of financial innovation therefore seems likely to continue.

While much has been written about the process of financial innovation, there has been little empirical analysis of the process. Future research might fruitfully pursue either of two basic lines of inquiry: possible further financial innovations and the economics of financial innovation. With regard to the first line of inquiry, one area that seems particularly fruitful for further investigation is that of mortgage-related securities — specifically, developing the means for further reducing the investor's prepayment risk and perhaps eventually combining a portfolio of mortgages with options and/or futures and/or interest rate swaps so as to eliminate prepayment risk entirely. Other areas include the securitization of additional classes of assets and further applications of futures and options to customize securities issues to suit issuer and investor preferences better.

With regard to the economics of financial innovation, the principal issues concern the profitability of securities innovation and how the process of financial innovation operates. In particular, how are the rewards to securities innovation allocated among the financial institution that develops the innovative security, the issuer, and investors? Are the innovator's profits excessive, as Van Horne seems to suggest that they might have been in some cases, or are they commensurate with the costs and risks of the process that Miller and others have noted? How are the rewards to the innovator affected as competitors introduce similar products or refinements? Who are the principal innovators: securities firms, banks, securities issuers, the academic community, or others? The answers to these and related questions will promote our understanding of financial engineering, an activity that plays a crucial role in promoting market efficiency.

References

1. M. J. Alderson, K. C. Brown, and S. L. Lummer, "Dutch Auction Rate Preferred Stock," *Financial Management* (Summer 1987), pp. 68–73.
2. Americus Trust for AT&T Common Shares, Series A, Prospectus, October 25, 1983.

3. M. Arak, A. Estrella, L. Goodman, and A. Silver, "Interest Rate Swaps: An Alternative Explanation," *Financial Management* (Summer 1988), pp. 12–18.
4. M. D. Atchison, R. F. DeMong, and J. L. Kling, *New Financial Instruments: A Descriptive Guide,* Charlottesville, VA: Financial Analysts Research Foundation, 1985.
5. M. Ben-Horim and W. Silber, "Financial Innovation: A Linear Programming Approach," *Journal of Banking and Finance* (September 1977), pp. 277–296.
6. J. Bicksler and A. H. Chen, "An Economic Analysis of Interest Rate Swaps," *Journal of Finance* (July 1986), pp. 645–655.
7. B. S. Black and J. A. Grundfest, "Shareholder Gains from Takeovers and Restructurings between 1981 and 1986: $162 Billion is a Lot of Money," *The Continental Bank Journal of Applied Corporate Finance* (Spring 1988), pp. 5–15.
8. F. Black and M. Scholes, "From Theory to a New Financial Product," *Journal of Finance* (May 1974), pp. 399–412.
9. S. B. Block and T. J. Gallagher, "The Use of Interest Rate Futures and Options by Corporate Financial Managers," *Financial Management* (Autumn 1986), pp. 73–78.
10. J. R. Booth, R. L. Smith, and R. W. Stolz, "The Use of Interest Futures by Financial Institutions," *Journal of Bank Research* (Spring 1984), pp. 15–20.
11. W. M. Boyce and A. J. Kalotay, "Optimum Bond Calling and Refunding," *Interfaces* (November 1979), pp. 36–49.
12. K. C. Brown and S. L. Lummer, "A Reexamination of the Covered Call Option Strategy for Corporate Cash Management," *Financial Management* (Summer 1986), pp. 13–17.
13. K. C. Brown and D. J. Smith, "Recent Innovations in Interest Rate Risk Management and the Reintermediation of Commercial Banking," *Financial Management* (Winter 1988).
14. R. F. Bruner, "Leveraged ESOPs and Corporate Restructuring," *The Continental Bank Journal of Applied Corporate Finance* (Spring 1988), pp. 54–66.
15. A. H. Chen and J. W. Kensinger, "Puttable Stock: A New Innovation in Equity Financing," *Financial Management* (Spring 1988), pp. 27–37.
16. J. M. Collins and R. P. Bey, "The Master Limited Partnership: An Alternative to the Corporation," *Financial Management* (Winter 1986), pp. 5–14.
17. P. H. Darrow and R. A. Mestres, Jr., *Creative Financing in the 1980s,* New York: Practising Law Institute, 1983.
18. J. Dutt, "What's Hot, What's Not," *Investment Dealers' Digest* (March 17, 1986), pp. 20–28.
19. J. D. Finnerty, "Zero Coupon Bond Arbitrage: An Illustration of the Regulatory Dialectic at Work," *Financial Management* (Winter 1985), pp. 13–17.
20. ———, "Refunding Discounted Debt: A Clarifying Analysis," *Journal of Financial and Quantitative Analysis* (March 1986), pp. 95–106.
21. ———, "The Case for Issuing Synthetic Convertible Bonds," *Midland Corporate Finance Journal* (Fall 1986), pp. 73–82.
22. ———, "An Analytical Framework for Evaluating Securities Innovations," *Journal of Corporate Finance* (Winter 1987), pp. 3–18.
23. First City Bancorporation of Texas, Inc., Proxy Statement, January 26, 1988.
24. L. Fisher, I. E. Brick, and F. K. W. Ng, "Tax Incentives and Financial Innovation: The Case of Zero-Coupon and Other Deep-Discount Corporate Bonds," *Financial Review* (November 1983), pp. 292–305.

25. B. Friedman, "Postwar Changes in the American Financial Markets," in M. Feldstein (ed.), *The American Economy in Transition,* Chicago: University of Chicago Press, 1980.
26. W. K. H. Fung and A. Rudd, "Pricing New Corporate Bond Issues: An Analysis of Issue Cost and Seasoning Effects," *Journal of Finance* (July 1986), pp. 633–643.
27. J. A. Gentry, "State of the Art of Short-Run Financial Management," *Financial Management* (Summer 1988), pp. 41–57.
28. L. S. Goodman and J. B. Yawitz, "Innovation in the U.S. Bond Market," *Institutional Investor Money Management Forum* (December 1987), pp. 102–104.
29. M. D. Joehnk, O. D. Bowlin, and J. W. Petty, "Preferred Dividend Rolls: A Viable Strategy for Corporate Money Managers?," *Financial Management* (Summer 1980), pp. 78–87.
30. E. P. Jones and S. P. Mason, "Equity-Linked Debt," *Midland Corporate Finance Journal* (Winter 1986), pp. 47–58.
31. E. J. Kane, "Good Intentions and Unintended Evil: The Case Against Selective Credit Allocation," *Journal of Money, Credit and Banking* (February 1977), pp. 55–69.
32. ———, "Accelerating Inflation, Technological Innovation, and the Decreasing Effectiveness of Banking Regulation," *Journal of Finance* (May 1981), pp. 355–367.
33. ———, "Technological and Regulatory Forces in the Developing Fusion of Financial-Services Competition," *Journal of Finance* (July 1984), pp. 759–772.
34. D. S. Kidwell, M. W. Marr, and G. R. Thompson, "SEC Rule 415: The Ultimate Competitive Bid," *Journal of Financial and Quantitative Analysis* (June 1984), pp. 183–195.
35. R. T. Kleiman, "The Shareholder Gains from Leveraged Cash-Outs: Some Preliminary Evidence," *The Continental Bank Journal of Applied Corporate Finance* (Spring 1988), pp. 46–53.
36. J. J. McConnell and E. S. Schwartz, "LYON Taming," *Journal of Finance* (July 1986), pp. 561–576.
37. G. Miller, "The Knockoff Artists," *Institutional Investor* (May 1986), pp. 81ff.
38. M. H. Miller, "Financial Innovation: The Last Twenty Years and the Next," *Journal of Financial and Quantitative Analysis* (December 1986), pp. 459–471.
39. J. P. Ogden, "An Analysis of Yield Curve Notes," *Journal of Finance* (March 1987), pp. 99–110.
40. P. Peterson, D. Peterson, and J. Ang, "The Extinguishment of Debt Through In-Substance Defeasance," *Financial Management* (Spring 1985), pp. 59–67.
41. W. Power, "Many of 1987's New Trading Products Are Failing Despite Spirited Marketing," *Wall Street Journal* (January 4, 1988), p. 26.
42. *Recent Innovations in International Banking,* Bank for International Settlements, April 1986.
43. T. E. Ricks, "SEC Chief Calls Some Financial Products 'Too Dangerous' for Individual Investors," *Wall Street Journal* (January 7, 1988), p. 46.
44. A. C. Shapiro, "Guidelines for Long-Term Corporate Financing Strategy," *Midland Corporate Finance Journal* (Winter 1986), pp. 6–19.
45. D. Shirreff, "Down with Innovation!," *Euromoney* (August 1986), pp. 23ff.
46. W. L. Silber (ed.), *Financial Innovation,* Lexington, MA: Lexington Books, 1975.

47. ——, "Innovation, Competition, and New Contract Design in Futures Markets," *Journal of Futures Markets* (No. 2, 1981), pp. 123-156.
48. ——, "The Process of Financial Innovation," *American Economic Review* (May 1983), pp. 89-95.
49. D. J. Smith, "The Pricing of Bull and Bear Floating Rate Notes: An Application of Financial Engineering," *Financial Management* (Winter 1988), pp. 72-81.
50. J. Spratlin and P. Vianna, *An Investor's Guide to CMOs,* New York: Salomon Brothers Inc, May 1986.
51. J. Sterngold, "Anatomy of a Staggering Loss," *New York Times* (May 11, 1987), pp. D1ff.
52. K. Torabzadeh and W. Bertin, "Leveraged Buyouts and Stockholder Wealth," *Journal of Financial Research* (Winter 1987), pp. 313-321.
53. J. C. Van Horne, "Of Financial Innovations and Excesses," *Journal of Finance* (July 1985), pp. 621-631.
54. B. J. Winger, C. R. Chen, J. D. Martin, J. W. Petty, and S. C. Hayden, "Adjustable Rate Preferred Stock," *Financial Management* (Spring 1986), pp. 48-57.
55. J. B. Yawitz and K. J. Maloney, "Evaluating the Decision to Issue Original Issue Discount Bonds: Term Structure and Tax Effects," *Financial Management* (Winter 1983), pp. 36-46.
56. T. L. Zivney and M. J. Alderson, "Hedged Dividend Capture with Stock Index Options," *Financial Management* (Summer 1986), pp. 5-12.

4

The Arithmetic of
Financial Engineering

Donald J. Smith

Financial engineering is the construction of innovative asset and liability structures. The building blocks of financial engineering include traditional instruments, such as fixed income bonds and floating rate notes, as well as the new "off balance sheet" tools of the 1980s: interest rate swaps, caps, floors, collars, and many others. The role of the engineer is to combine such instruments to provide a risk-return configuration otherwise unavailable. Often the objective is simply to replicate an existing product or strategy at a lower transaction cost or with some gain in hedging efficiency. The ultimate prize is a "pure" (that is, riskless) arbitrage opportunity – the chance to buy and sell simultaneously an equivalent product at different prices. In reasonably efficient markets, however, such opportunities are likely to be scarce. More common is an opportunity for "risk arbitrage" – the chance for investors to earn higher expected rates of return, or for borrowers to reduce their expected cost of funds, while bearing a given level of risk.

The search for an arbitrage opportunity (or, alternatively, for a more efficient hedging vehicle) begins with the identification of a synthetic financial structure that mimics the characteristics of another, usually more obvious, type of asset or liability. The process is not as complex as it might seem. The logic of the combinations of the various securities is based on certain simple rules that can be viewed as the "arithmetic" of financial engineering. This arithmetic, the reader should be assured at the outset, involves only the most basic mathematical properties and operations.

The Arithmetic Rules

The statement that a portfolio of security A and security B is equivalent to security C can be expressed as follows:

$$A + B = C \qquad (4.1)$$

The equals sign here means identical promised coupon and principal cash flows in terms of amount, currency, and timing. The maturity and coupon payment frequency are assumed to be the same on each side of the equation. Otherwise, the structures are not comparable and no meaningful statement can be made about an arbitrage opportunity.

Equation 4.1 refers to future *expected* cash flows. The yield to the investor, or cost of funds to the borrower, of $A + B$ and C will be identical only if the current prices are the same. A yield-to-maturity is calculated as an internal rate of return — that is, the particular interest rate such that the present values of all future cash flows discounted by that rate exactly equal the current price. Prices, and therefore yields, can differ because the future cash flows are only promised; hence the notion of credit, or default, risk. If one stream of promised cash flows is viewed as more uncertain than another, the current price would be lower, and thus the calculated internal rate of return would be higher. The greater the credit risk, the higher the promised yield.

Suppose, then, that the credit risks are the same for $A + B$, the synthetic portfolio, as for C, the straight security. If the current prices differ, borrowers and investors would have clear preferences for one alternative over the other, all other things being equal. Obviously, investors would prefer a lower price and borrowers a higher price for the same promised future cash flows. When a synthetic financial structure obtains a preferential price, the relative gain is typically called "arbitrage."

The "other things being equal" condition is important. Financial structures can differ along dimensions other than promised cash flows and current prices. Special covenants in the documentation, such as provisions for early termination (call or put options) as well as material adverse change, cross-default, and negative pledge clauses, can lead to a preference for one structure over another. We will therefore assume, for now at least, that the documentation and all accounting and taxation aspects on each side of the equation are the same to allow for direct comparison.

Financial engineering often involves taking long and/or short positions in different securities within a synthetic structure. In the arithmetic framework a "+" indicates a long position and a "−" indicates a short position. To "go long" means to buy, hold, or invest in a security. To "go short" means to issue, sell, or write a security. Being long represents a lending posture, being short a borrowing one.

Equation 4.1 can thus be rewritten as follows:

$$+A+B = +C \tag{4.2}$$

That is, a synthetic portfolio consisting of long positions in A and B is equivalent to a long position in C.

Multiplying through the above equation by -1 gives us the following:

$$-A-B = -C \tag{4.3}$$

This means that issuing C directly entails making the same future cash payments as issuing both A and B.

Adding or subtracting from each side of the equation creates other configurations. For example, subtract B from each side of Equation 4.2:

$$+A = +C-B \tag{4.4}$$

Buying security A is identical to a combination of buying C and writing B. An investor searching for arbitrage gains would ascertain if the net purchase price of buying C and issuing B is less than the price of buying A.

As another example, add A to each side of Equation 4.3:

$$-B = -C+A \tag{4.5}$$

Issuing security B is equivalent to a portfolio of a long position in A and a short position in C. A borrower would identify an arbitrage gain if the proceeds from selling B exceeded the net proceeds from issuing C and purchasing A.

Interest Rate Swaps

Interest rate swaps are among the most important financial innovations of the 1980s.[1] In a typical "plain vanilla" rate swap, two counterparties exchange fixed for floating coupon payments based on some notional principal amount. The floating rate on the vast majority of swaps is three- or six-month LIBOR. In practice, settlement is often on a "net" basis: the fixed rate is compared to LIBOR and then only the difference times the notional principal, adjusted for the number of days elapsed, is paid by the owing counterparty at the end of the period.

---

1. For more extensive discussion of interest rate swaps, see Jan Loeys, "Interest Rate Swaps: A New Tool for Managing Risk," *Federal Reserve Bank of Philadelphia Business Review* (May/June 1985); James Bicksler and Andrew Chen, "An Economic Analysis of Interest Rate Swaps," *Journal of Finance* (July 1986); Clifford Smith, Charles Smithson, and Lee Wakeman, "The Evolving Market for Swaps," *Midland Corporate Finance Journal* (Winter 1986); and Steven D. Felgran, "Interest Rate Swaps: Use, Risk, and Prices," *New England Economic Review* (November/December 1987).

For example, consider a $10 million notional principal swap with semi-annual settlements on March 15 and September 15 and having a fixed rate of 9%. Suppose that the six-month LIBOR index is determined to be 7.5% on March 15. Assuming that both rates are quoted on a 360 day basis, the fixed payer on the swaps owes (9% − 7.5%) times (184/360) times $10 million, or $76,666.67, to the counterparty at the end of the period on September 15. Note that there are 184 days between March 15 and September 15. If LIBOR had instead been 10.5%, the fixed payer would receive the same amount.

By market convention, the counterparty that agrees to pay the fixed rate and receive the floating rate is named the "buyer" of the swap. The fixed payer has established a long position in the swap transaction and the fixed receiver a short position. This terminology, however arbitrary, fits nicely into our arithmetic framework. A long position in a par value swap is equivalent to a synthetic portfolio of a long position in a par value unrestricted floating rate note (FRN) and a short position in a par value fixed rate note:

$$
\begin{array}{ccccccc}
& \text{Interest Rate} & & \text{Unrestricted} & & \text{Fixed Rate} & \\
+ & \text{Swap} & = + & \text{FRN} & - & \text{Note} & (4.6) \\
& \textbf{pay fixed,} & & \textbf{LIBOR} & & \textbf{Swap fixed} & \\
& \textbf{rec. LIBOR} & & & & \textbf{rate} &
\end{array}
$$

An unrestricted FRN has no constraint (other than a minimum of zero) on the floating rate. As indicated by Equation 4.6, the fixed payer on the swap is obligated to the same future cash flows as if an unrestricted FRN (at LIBOR flat) had been purchased from, and a fixed rate note (at the swap fixed rate) sold to, the counterparty.

Now multiply both sides of Equation 4.6 by −1.

$$
\begin{array}{ccccccc}
& \text{Interest Rate} & & \text{Unrestricted} & & \text{Fixed Rate} & \\
- & \text{Swap} & = - & \text{FRN} & + & \text{Note} & (4.7) \\
& \textbf{rec. fixed,} & & \textbf{LIBOR} & & \textbf{Swap fixed} & \\
& \textbf{pay LIBOR} & & & & \textbf{rate} &
\end{array}
$$

A short position in a par value swap — that is, receiving the fixed rate and paying floating — is equivalent to issuing an unrestricted FRN and buying a fixed rate note.

The term "par value" swap means that there is no initial cash exchange between the two counterparties. This implies that the hypothetical unrestricted FRN and fixed rate note are both par value securities. Therefore, at the outset of the swap, the present values of the long and short positions are exactly offset and any exchange of principal would be redundant.

Caps, Collars, and Floors

Interest rate swaps belong to a general class of risk management tools known as forward contracts. In fact, a swap can be viewed as a series of interest rate forward transactions – one for each of the settlement dates over the life of the contract. The most important characteristic of a forward contract, for our purposes, is its symmetrical payoff distribution. This means that interest rate changes can lead, in principle, to unlimited gains or losses on the contract. When the swap is used as a hedge, however, these value changes are designed to be offset by opposite changes in the underlying exposure.

The other broad class of risk management tools is option contracts. Options, unlike forwards, have an asymmetrical or "truncated" payoff distribution. For example, a long position in an option has unlimited profit potential but losses are limited to just the purchase price of the option itself. Conversely, the short position, usually called the "writer" of the option, can have unlimited losses but gain only the sale price of the contract.

Interest rate caps, collars, and floors are all over-the-counter interest rate options.[2] A *cap* (or *ceiling*) agreement is analogous to a *put* option on a debt security. For an up-front fee known as the "premium," a buyer of a cap will receive from the cap writer the excess of some reference rate (almost always LIBOR) over the given cap rate (called the "strike rate"). The payment, if any, on each settlement date will be the annual rate difference, adjusted for the fraction of a year elapsed, times the specified notional principal. If LIBOR is less than the cap rate, no payment is made.

An interest rate *floor* agreement is analogous to a *call* option on debt. For an up-front premium, the buyer of the floor will receive from the floor writer the excess of the floor rate over LIBOR. Calculation of the settlement payment is the same as that on a cap. If LIBOR is above the floor rate, no payment is forthcoming.

Caps and floors are akin to interest rate insurance contracts. One can use them to insure against losses from LIBOR rising above or falling below certain levels. A rate *collar* is a combination of a cap and a floor. To buy a collar is to buy a cap and to write a floor. Note that a collar will always cost less than a cap for a given ceiling strike rate because the sale price of the floor serves to offset the purchase price of the cap. A long position in a 5–9% collar can be described in the arithmetic framework as follows:

$$+ \text{ Collar } = + \text{Cap} - \text{Floor} \qquad (4.8)$$
$$\quad\; 5\%\text{–}9\% \qquad\quad 9\% \qquad 5\%$$

As above, the plus signs mean long positions and the minus sign a short position. Multiplying both sides of this equation by −1 describes the short side of a collar:

$$- \text{ Collar } = - \text{Cap} + \text{Floor} \qquad (4.9)$$
$$\quad\; 5\%\text{–}9\% \qquad\quad 9\% \qquad 5\%$$

---

2. See Ian Rowley and Henrik Neuhaus, "How Caps and Floors Can Influence Desired Cash Flows," *Euromoney Corporate Finance* (July 1986); and Donald J. Smith, "Putting the Cap on Options," *Euromoney Corporate Finance* (January 1987) for further discussion of interest rate cap and floor agreements.

To write a collar, therefore, is to write a cap and to buy a floor. The cap and floor strike rates are usually set such that the writer of a collar receives a net premium payment. When the strike rates are structured so that the premiums exactly offset each other, the outcome is a *zero cost collar*.

Premiums on option contracts depend on the particular strike rate, the current and expected future interest rate levels as embodied in the shape of the yield curve, the perceived volatility of future interest rates, and the maturity of the contract. For example, premiums on interest rate caps increase for lower strike rates and a steeper yield curve. Premiums on floors increase for higher strike rates and a flatter yield curve. Higher volatility and a longer maturity raise premiums on both caps and floors.

If the strike rates on the cap and the floor are identical, the resulting collar is equivalent to an interest rate swap. For example, buying a 9% cap on LIBOR and writing a 9% floor is the same as going long on a swap to pay 9% fixed and receive LIBOR.

$$+ \text{Cap} - \text{Floor} = + \text{Interest Rate Swap} \qquad (4.10)$$
$$\quad 9\% \qquad 9\% \qquad\qquad \textbf{pay 9\% fixed,}$$
$$\textbf{rec. LIBOR}$$

Intuitively, as the strike rates on the cap and floor get close, the collar "tightens" and eventually becomes a fixd versus floating rate swap. Notice that if 9% is the fixed rate on a "par value" swap (hence no exchange of principal), the premiums on the cap and floor at a 9% strike rate are equal.

Synthetic Structures Using Typical FRNs

Many innovative structures built by financial engineers in recent years have combined floating rate notes with interest rate swaps, caps, and floors. A typical FRN has its coupon rate reset each period at a reference rate, often LIBOR, plus some fixed margin. This margin reflects the credit quality of the issuer and other characteristics of the security—for instance, maximum or minimum coupon rates and call or put options. The margin would be higher if there is more credit risk, if there is a maximum coupon rate, or if the issuer has a call option on the FRN. The margin would be lower if there is less credit risk, if there is a minimum coupon rate, or if the investor has a put option. Although some unrestricted FRNs have been issued, most have a minimum coupon rate on the order of 5%.

In the context of the arithmetic framework, a typical FRN at LIBOR-plus-25 basis points with a 5% minimum coupon can be broken down into an unrestricted FRN at LIBOR flat plus a .25% annuity plus an interest rate floor agreement. The annuity, which represents the fixed margin on the typical FRN, is a series of level payments (if negative) or receipts (if positive).

$$+ \quad \begin{matrix} \text{Typical} \\ \text{FRN} \\ \textbf{LIBOR} + \textbf{0.25\%,} \\ \textbf{min. 5\%} \end{matrix} \quad = + \begin{matrix} \text{Unrestricted} \\ \text{FRN} \\ \textbf{LIBOR} \end{matrix} \quad - \text{Annuity} + \begin{matrix} \text{Floor} \\ \textbf{4.75\%} \end{matrix} \qquad (4.11)$$

A long position in the typical FRN thus offers the same promised future cash receipts as buying the unrestricted FRN and the annuity (which together provide LIBOR + 0.25%) combined with a floor on LIBOR at a 4.75% strike rate.[3]

Synthetic Fixed Rate Debt

Equation 4.11 above can be rewritten to isolate the unrestricted FRN. Formulated in this way, a long position in the unrestricted FRN is equivalent to a long position in the typical FRN and short positions in the annuity and floor agreement. That portfolio can then be substituted into Equation 4.6 to obtain the following relationship between a typical FRN, a fixed rate note, and an interest rate swap.

$$+ \begin{matrix} \text{Interest} \\ \text{Rate} \\ \text{Swap} \\ \textbf{pay} \\ \textbf{fixed,} \\ \textbf{rec.} \\ \textbf{LIBOR} \end{matrix} = + \begin{matrix} \\ \text{Typical} \\ \text{FRN} \\ \textbf{LIBOR} \\ +\textbf{0.25\%,} \\ \textbf{min. 5\%} \end{matrix} - \begin{matrix} \text{Annuity} \\ \textbf{0.25\%} \end{matrix} - \begin{matrix} \text{Floor} \\ \textbf{4.75\%} \end{matrix} - \begin{matrix} \text{Fixed} \\ \text{Rate} \\ \text{Note} \\ \textbf{Swap} \\ \textbf{fixed} \\ \textbf{rate} \end{matrix} \qquad (4.12)$$

Then, by rearranging the terms and combining the annuity and fixed rate note, the following equivalence relationship is obtained:

$$- \begin{matrix} \text{Fixed} \\ \text{Rate} \\ \text{Note} \\ \textbf{Swap fixed} \\ \textbf{rate} + \textbf{0.25\%} \end{matrix} = - \begin{matrix} \\ \text{Typical} \\ \text{FRN} \\ \textbf{LIBOR} + \textbf{0.25\%,} \\ \textbf{min. 5\%} \end{matrix} + \begin{matrix} \text{Interest} \\ \text{Rate} \\ \text{Swap} \\ \textbf{pay fixed,} \\ \textbf{rec. LIBOR} \end{matrix} + \begin{matrix} \text{Floor} \\ \textbf{4.75\%} \end{matrix} \qquad (4.13)$$

A synthetic fixed rate issue equal to the swap rate plus the margin on the

---

3. The floor agreement corresponds to the minimum coupon on the typical FRN. Suppose that LIBOR is only 4% on a particular reset date. The minimum coupon on the typical FRN is binding at 5%. The unrestricted FRN and the annuity provide only 4.25% combined, but the long position in the in-the-money floor pays the additional 0.75%. In general, the required strike rate on the floor is the minimum coupon on the FRN less the fixed margin over LIBOR in the reset formula.

FRN can be constructed by issuing the typical FRN, buying the interest rate swap, and buying the interest rate floor.[4]

Identifying Arbitrage Gains

Equation 4.13 represents one of the highly touted arbitrage opportunities that are claimed to have motivated the development of the swap market in the early 1980s. Companies having a natural preference for fixed rate funding (for example, public utilities or thrift institutions) issued floating rate debt and then "bought" fixed interest rate swaps, thereby achieving a synthetic, fixed rate debt instrument. The flip side to this arbitrage opportunity can be seen by moving the swap and floor agreements to the other side of the equation. Those companies having a natural preference for variable rate debt (e.g., money center banks) issued fixed rate debt and "swapped into" a synthetic floating rate. When those synthetic rates achieved through swaps are less than the explicit fixed and floating rate alternatives, the firms have been able to "arbitrage" the swap market to lower their respective costs of funds.

The conventional explanation for this opportunity is the existence of differential credit risk premiums—that is, a higher credit premium (over the rate charged to a more creditworthy borrower) in the fixed rate market than in the floating rate market. The evidence supporting such an explanation, however, is largely anecdotal and thus unreliable. It is also suspect because of several problems in measuring arbitrage gains.[5] In measuring such gains, it is essential that a comparison is made between debt structures with the same covenants and provisions.

A common pitfall is to neglect the value of the call option included in most medium- to long-term corporate bonds. A callable bond must offer the investor a higher yield than otherwise comparable noncallable debt. The amount of this call premium depends on the length of the deferment period before the insurer can exercise the option, the specified call price, and the probability of exercise as indicated by the expected level and volatility of future rates.

For example, suppose that a corporate borrower undertakes the structure outlined in Equation 4.13 to obtain a swap-driven fixed-rate cost of funds of, say, 9.75%. If the yardstick fixed rate alternative is, say, 10%, the swap structure appears to deliver a 25 basis point arbitrage gain. But if this yard-

---

4. The yield to maturity will differ from that coupon rate as the net proceeds differ from the par value amount, as in any fixed income bond pricing problem. Also, the notional principal on the swap and floor are assumed to match the face value of the FRN.

5. This discussion is based in part on Donald J. Smith, "Measuring the Gains from 'Arbitraging' the Swap Market," *Financial Executive* (March/April 1988).

stick is the yield on a callable bond and the FRN and swap are noncallable, then the comparison is misleading. In this case, any arbitrage gain from the synthetic fixed rate debt instrument must be measured relative to a noncallable debt issue. As a practical matter, call options on corporate debt are very common while similar exit options on interest rate swaps, caps, and floors are rare.

As another example, suppose that the FRN in Equation 4.13 had a put option attached that granted the right of the holder to sell the FRN back to the issuer at par value. Then, the fixed margin of 0.25% would be lower than for an FRN without such an option. That put option could even be implicit, such as a material adverse change clause whereby the lender can advance the maturity date if the issuer's credit standing deteriorates. (Such clauses are quite common on bank revolving credit agreements.) In this case, the synthetic fixed rate structure would have to be compared to an explicit fixed rate security offering investors the same put option.

If measured against a fixed rate note with no such provision (or, worse yet, against one with a call option), the synthetic structure might only appear to be advantageous. The lower cost of funds could merely represent the fair value of the options contained in the documentation.

In comparing the costs of synthetic with conventional fixed rate debt, one must also recognize the role of the floor agreement in the synthetic structure in offsetting the minimum coupon constraint contained in most FRNs on the market. Suppose that the floor on LIBOR is omitted in a structure such as that presented in Equation 4.13. The all-in synthetic fixed rate cost of funds would be reduced by the amount of the amortized cost of the premium on the floor.

In fact, market rates were quite high in the early 1980s, and a floor on LIBOR at 4.75%, even if available, would have been a very inexpensive, deep out-of-the-money option. Nevertheless, if a "quasi-fixed" cost of funds is favorably compared to a truly fixed rate, one can only conclude that the *expected* cost of funds is lowered by the financial engineering.

Still another requirement for comparing synthetic with conventional debt instruments is to account for the degree of credit risk the issuer accepts by entering into the interest rate swap. If the counterparty to the swap defaults, the firm would have to replace the swap to maintain a synthetic fixed rate. If market rates have risen at the time of the default, the firm would pay a higher fixed rate on the replacement swap, raising its all-in cost of funds.[6]

---

6. In fact, the counterparty would never default if rates have fallen since the swap would have positive economic value. Also, if the floor writer defaults when LIBOR is below 4.75%, the firm's cost of funds would rise. Note that the credit risks on the swap and the floor are somewhat offsetting since it is most unlikely that both counterparties would default in the same interest rate environment.

Therefore, the synthetic fixed rate structure always has an element of credit risk. Any gain in the cost of funds over a straight fixed rate alternative should be measured net of the cost of bearing the estimated default risk.

Asset Swaps

Asset swaps are another synthetic structure that have emerged in the last few years.[7] These can be illustrated by multiplying both sides of Equation 4.13 by -1:

	Fixed Rate		Typical		Interest Rate				
+	Note	= +	FRN	−	Swap	−	Floor	(4.14)
	Swap fixed		**LIBOR + 0.25%,**		**rec. fixed,**		**4.75%**	
	rate + 0.25%		**min. 5%**		**pay LIBOR**			

A synthetic fixed rate asset is constructed by buying the FRN, selling the swap to receive the fixed rate, and writing the floor agreement. Notice that a synthetic floating rate asset is obtained simply by moving the swap and floor agreements to the other side of the equation.

The motivation for asset swaps is to change the cash flow characteristics of the underlying asset — in the case of Equation 4.14, the FRN. Consider an institutional investor that would like to carry a certain issuer's name on its books but does not like the coupon characteristics of the debt that is available on the market. For example, a pension fund might want to invest in fixed income securities and prefer, or be constrained, to hold only high-quality debt of top-tier corporate and sovereign names. An investment banker can package an available FRN with a swap — perhaps even mixing in the floor agreement — and deliver the desired asset to the investor. Even in the event of a default on the swap, the investor retains ownership of the underlying high-quality asset.

One final observation should be made before proceeding to the more exotic structures. The synthetic fixed coupon rates and yields-to-maturity implied by Equations 4.13 and 4.14 will not be equal because of the market maker's bid-ask spreads on the interest rate swap and floor agreements. The market maker will set a lower fixed rate on a swap when it pays fixed than when it receives fixed in order to make a profit and cover its own operational costs. Likewise, a market maker will buy a floor at a lower up-front premium than when it writes the option.

---

7. See Daniel Stillet, "Unravelling the Asset Swap," *Euromoney Corporate Finance* (April 1987) for a description and applications of this innovation.

BOOKSTAR

The Complete Discount Bookstore

◆ An

extraordinary

selection

of over

100,000

books

on sale

every day.

◆

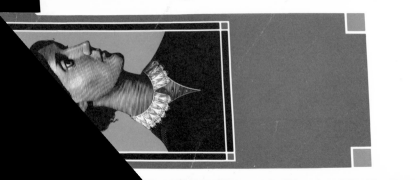

A bookstore

for the

uncommon

reader.

BOOKSTAR
The Complete Discount Bookstore

Therefore, from a firm's perspective, the fixed rate on the swap and the premium on the floor are both higher in Equation 4.13 than in Equation 4.14. As would be expected, the synthetic fixed rate cost of funds for a firm is somewhat higher than the synthetic fixed return on an asset when each is constructed from the same typical FRN.

Synthetic Structures Using Innovative FRNs

Mini-Max Floaters

A security that became popular in 1985 was the "mini-max," or "collared," FRN. This is in essence a typical FRN with the addition of a maximum coupon rate. The investor in a mini-max FRN trades off a ceiling on potential coupon receipts for a higher fixed margin over the variable reference rate. This higher margin can be viewed as the amortized cost of a cap written by the investor and sold back to the issuer.

The structure of a 5-9% mini-max FRN with a coupon reset formula of LIBOR + 0.50% can be broken down using the arithmetic framework as follows:

$$
\begin{array}{llllll}
\text{Mini-Max} & \text{Unrestricted} & & & & \\
+ \quad \text{FRN} = + & \text{FRN} & + \text{Annuity} - & \text{Cap} & + \text{Floor} & (4.15) \\
\quad \textbf{LIBOR} & \textbf{LIBOR} & \textbf{0.50\%} & \textbf{8.50\%} & \textbf{4.50\%} & \\
\quad \textbf{+0.50\%} & & & & & \\
\quad \textbf{min. 5\%,} & & & & & \\
\quad \textbf{max. 9\%} & & & & &
\end{array}
$$

A long position in the mini-max FRN is equivalent in terms of future cash flows to buying a hypothetical unrestricted FRN at LIBOR flat, buying an annuity that pays 0.50%, writing a cap on LIBOR with a strike rate of 8.50%, and buying a floor on LIBOR with a strike rate of 4.50%. The last two transactions are the same as selling a 4.50%–8.50% interest rate collar, similar to Equation 4.9 above. Multiplying through Equation 4.15 by −1 would show that issuing a mini-max FRN is identical to issuing the unrestricted FRN and the annuity, buying the cap, and writing the floor. In sum, the issuer buys an interest rate collar from the investor.

The introduction of FRNs containing an embedded interest rate cap is noteworthy because it led to an arbitrage opportunity in "stripping" the cap and selling it at a profit. To see how this was done, first note that the combination of long positions in the unrestricted FRN, the annuity, and the floor agreement in Equation 4.15 is equivalent to buying a typical FRN with a reset formula of LIBOR + 0.50% and minimum coupon rate of 5% (as in Equation 4.11). Therefore, buying a mini-max FRN is the same as buying a typical FRN with no ceiling and writing an interest rate cap:

$$
\begin{array}{ccccc}
 & \text{Mini-Max} & & \text{Typical} & \\
+ & \text{FRN} & = + & \text{FRN} & - \text{ Cap} \\
 & \text{LIBOR} + 0.50\%, & & \text{LIBOR} + 0.50\%, & 8.50\% \\
 & \text{min. } 5\%, & & \text{min. } 5\% & \\
 & \text{max. } 9\% & & &
\end{array}
\tag{4.16}
$$

Multiplying both sides of Equation 4.16 by -1 and rearranging terms shows that issuing the mini-max FRN and writing the cap agreement is equivalent to issuing a typical FRN.

$$
\begin{array}{ccccc}
 & \text{Mini-Max} & & \text{Typical} & \\
- & \text{FRN} & - \text{ Cap} = - & \text{FRN} & \\
 & \text{LIBOR} + 0.50\%, & 8.50\% & \text{LIBOR} + 0.50\%, & \\
 & \text{min. } 5\%, & & \text{min. } 5\% & \\
 & \text{max. } 9\% & & &
\end{array}
\tag{4.17}
$$

Suppose that the firm could issue a typical FRN directly in the capital market at par value (i.e., a price of 100) assuming that it had a reset formula of LIBOR + 0.50% and a minimum coupon rate of 5%. Also, suppose that the mini-max FRN could be sold only at discount — say, at a price of 98 — to reflect the ceiling rate constraint. Then, if the issuing firm can write a cap agreement and sell it for an up-front premium of more than 200 basis points (times the notional principal equaling the face value of the FRN), a pure arbitrage gain is made. The desired type of variable rate funding is obtained at a lower cost of funds since the net proceeds exceed that of the direct alternative. Moreover, there is no credit risk since the firm is the writer of the option.

This structure was apparently executed a number of times in 1985, initially by Shearson Lehman Brothers and subsequently by other investment and commercial banks.[8] Interest rate cap market makers were willing to buy the "stripped" caps at a price that gave the issuing firms a lower cost of funds because they in turn could sell the caps at a still higher price. Prior to this innovation, the cap market was fairly thin for maturities beyond a few years because hedging exposed positions was difficult due to the absence of exchange-traded futures and options contracts. "Cap stripping" created a supply of options that deepened and extended the maturity range of the market.

Inverse Floaters

An important innovation in the FRN market came in 1986 with the introduction of the inverse floater, also known as a "bull floater" or yield curve note.

---

8. The background to this innovation and strategy is described in David Shirreff, "Caps and Options: The Dangerous New Protection Racket," *Euromoney* (March 1986).

These have a fundamentally different coupon reset formula, one that commonly takes the form of a fixed percentage rate *minus* LIBOR. As LIBOR increases, the coupon payment on an inverse floater decreases. Inverse floaters have been issued by SallieMae, GMAC, and Citicorp, among others. By design, this type of security would be attractive to investors who are bullish on bond prices and expect market rates to fall. The attraction of the inverse floater is that its price increase in percentage terms will be greater than — indeed typically about double — that of a fixed rate note of the same maturity.[9] Also, the initial coupon rate is typically higher than those on traditional FRNs. In this way, inverse FRNs are similar to capped or collared FRNs. There is a pick-up in yield if market rates remain steady or decline but at the risk of larger price declines if rates rise.

One motive for issuers of inverse floaters is to hedge an exposure to floating interest rates. For instance, thrift institutions, which are often exposed to higher deposit rates, could issue inverse floaters to smooth out their cost of funds. The combination of an inverse floater and a traditional floater is in essence a fixed-rate note because the variable reference rate cancels out.

Another motive for issuing inverse floaters is arbitrage gains. Issuers commonly use interest rate swaps and caps to transform the inverse floater to the desired type of fixed rate or traditional floating rate debt. The claim is that such financial engineering lowers the cost of funds.

To see one way in which this innovative structure is put together, first note that issuing an inverse floater with a coupon reset formula of 16% − LIBOR is equivalent to issuing two fixed rate notes at 8%, buying an unrestricted FRN at LIBOR flat, and writing a cap on LIBOR with a strike rate of 16%.

$$
\begin{array}{ccccc}
& & \text{Two} & & \\
\text{Inverse} & & \text{Fixed Rate} & \text{Unrestricted} & \\
-\ \text{Floater} & = - & \text{Notes} & +\quad \text{FRN} & -\ \text{Cap} \qquad (4.18) \\
\mathbf{16\% - LIBOR} & & \mathbf{8\%} & \mathbf{LIBOR} & \mathbf{16\%}
\end{array}
$$

The cap is needed in the structure because the inverse floater would pay a zero coupon rate if LIBOR rises above 16%.

As shown earlier (in Equation 4.6), a long position in an unrestricted FRN can be isolated and set equal to a long position in a fixed rate note at the swap rate and a long position in an interest rate swap. Substituting that relationship into Equation 4.18 gives the following:

---

9. Jess Yawitz, in "Pricing and Duration of Inverse Floating Rate Notes," Goldman Sachs (March 1986), shows that the duration of an inverse floater is typically about double that of a fixed rate note with the same maturity. Twice the duration means twice the price volatility. This result is also obtained by Joseph Ogden, "An Analysis of Yield Curve Notes," *Journal of Finance* (March 1987), by means of a simulation study. See also Donald J. Smith, "The Pricing of Bull and Bear Floating Rate Notes: An Application of Financial Engineering," *Financial Management* (Winter 1988) for further discussion.

	Two	Fixed	Interest		
Inverse	Fixed Rate	Rate	Rate		
− Floater = −	Notes +	Note +	Swap	− Cap	(4.19)
16% −	8%	Swap fixed	pay fixed,	16%	
LIBOR		rate	rec. LIBOR		

Then, after combining the fixed rate notes and rearranging terms, we see how an inverse floater can be converted with a swap into a synthetic fixed rate note.

			Interest		
	Fixed Rate		Inverse	Rate	
−	Note = −	Floater	− Swap	+ Cap	(4.20)
	16% − Swap	16% − LIBOR	rec. fixed,	16%	
	fixed rate		pay LIBOR		

Issuing the inverse floater, receiving the fixed rate on an interest rate swap, and buying a cap on LIBOR with a 16% strike rate creates a synthetic fixed coupon rate of 16% minus the swap rate.

A firm would claim (or its investment banker could claim on its behalf) to have engineered a lower cost of funds if the all-in yield-to-maturity given the net proceeds is less than on a straight fixed rate note issue.[10] However, as with any structure that includes swaps or long positions in options, the inevitable credit risk should be evaluated and subtracted from any claimed arbitrage gain. (And, as emphasized earlier, one cannot directly compare the cost of a noncallable swap-driven structure to the yield on a callable bond.)

Innovations in Interest Rate Risk Management

Besides structuring synthetic funding alternatives and seeking arbitrage opportunities, financial engineers have developed innovative products for managing interest rate risk. The motivation here is typically to provide interest rate protection without major balance sheet restructuring. For instance, suppose that a firm would like to set a ceiling on its floating rate cost of funds but views the up-front premium on an interest rate cap to be prohibitively expensive. One alternative is a collar agreement whereby the firm sells an interest rate floor back to the cap writer, reducing the net premium. In fact,

---

10. For example, Albert Lord, the CFO of SallieMae, in describing their first yield curve note issue which had a reset formula 17.2% minus LIBOR, is quoted in *Euromoney Corporate Finance* (April 1986, page 26) saying, "The formula worked out that the bull floater, or yield curve note, plus the swap resulted in us paying 17.2% and receiving fixed rate funds pegged to Treasuries. . . . The end cost of funds, including the cost of the cap, was very competitive — below the five year Treasury rate."

a floor strike rate can be found for any given cap rate so that the collar has no initial cost.

Another alternative, recently developed by financial engineers, can be generically called a "participation agreement." This is a variation of the zero cost collar described above, but instead of setting the floor strike rate so that the premiums offset, the notional principal of the floor is adjusted. The outcome is that the buyer of a participation agreement has the benefit of a ceiling on LIBOR but makes settlement payments at a constant fraction of the rate differential when LIBOR is below the ceiling.[11]

An example is useful to illustrate this structure. Suppose that in the current interest rate environment a three-year 10% cap on LIBOR costs 150 basis points times the notional principal (NP). For instance, if NP = $10 million, the up-front premium would be $150,000. Also, suppose that a 6.50% floor costs 150 basis points while a 10% floor costs 400 basis points. A firm with $10 million in floating rate debt could get interest rate protection with a 6.50%–10% zero cost collar. Alternatively, it could buy a 10% cap for NP = $10 million and write a 10% floor for NP = $3.75 million. That would represent a zero cost participation agreement because the sale price of the floor also would be $150,000, equalling the cost of the cap. When LIBOR is below the 10% ceiling, the firm, as writer of the floor, would make payments equal to 37.5% of that on a 10% floor if the notional principal had been $10 million. Hence, the firm shares, or "participates" in, 62.5% of the difference between the 10% ceiling rate and LIBOR. The participation rate (PR) is said to be 62.5%.

Using the arithmetic framework, a long position in a 10% ceiling zero cost participation agreement for any given amount of interest rate protection, NP* (e.g., the amount of underlying debt) and a 62.5% PR is equivalent to buying a 10% cap for NP = NP* and writing a 10% floor for NP = $(1 - PR)NP^* = .375NP^*$.

$$
\begin{array}{ccccc}
\text{Participation} & & & & \\
+ \text{ Agreement} & = + & \text{Cap} & - & \text{Floor} \quad (4.21) \\
10\% \text{ ceiling} & & 10\% & & 10\% \\
NP = NP^* & & NP = NP^* & & NP = .375NP^*
\end{array}
$$

In general, the zero cost participation rate will be one minus the ratio of the premiums on the cap and the floor for a given strike rate.

Notice that a cap and a floor at the same strike rate is equivalent to an interest rate swap, as shown earlier (in Equation 4.10).

---

11. See Keith C. Brown and Donald J. Smith, "Recent Innovations in Interest Rate Risk Management and the Reintermediation of Commercial Banking," *Financial Management* (Winter 1988) for an extended analysis of the trade-offs between interest rate collars and participation agreements.

$$
\begin{array}{lll}
& \text{Interest Rate} & \\
+ & \text{Swap} & = +\,\text{Cap} \; - \; \text{Floor} \\
& \textbf{pay 10\% fixed,} & \;\;10\% \quad\;\; 10\% \\
& \textbf{rec. LIBOR} &
\end{array}
\qquad (4.22)
$$

This would be a nonpar value (or "off market") swap if the premiums on the cap and the floor are not equal. For instance, if the fixed rate on a par value swap is only 8.50%, the fixed payer at 10% would require an up-front receipt for the present value of the stream of differences between 10% and 8.5% times the notional principal. The payment would also equal the difference between the premiums on the cap and the floor at a 10% strike rate.

Since a 10% cap on LIBOR for $NP = NP^*$ in Equation 4.21 can be separated into two 10% caps, one at $NP = .375NP^*$ and another at $NP = .625NP^*$, the long position in a zero cost position in a zero cost participation agreement can also be written as follows:

$$
\begin{array}{lllll}
& \text{Participation} & & \text{Interest Rate} & \\
+ & \text{Agreement} & = + \quad \text{Cap} \quad + & \text{Swap} & \\
& \textbf{10\% ceiling} & \qquad\quad \textbf{10\%} & \textbf{pay 10\% fixed,} & \\
& \textbf{NP = NP*} & \textbf{NP = .625NP*} & \textbf{rec. LIBOR} & \\
& \textbf{62.5\% PR} & & \textbf{NP = .375NP*} &
\end{array}
\qquad (4.23)
$$

Therefore, a participation agreement can be viewed as a weighted average of an interest rate cap and an interest rate swap, using the participation rate to determine the respective notional principals. Full 100% participation in rates below the ceiling is a pure cap; zero participation is a pure swap.

Summary and Conclusions

Financial engineering is fundamentally the art and science of designing financial structures that create an otherwise unavailable risk-return tradeoff. Much of this involves combining the new off-balance-sheet products such as interest rate swaps, caps, and floors with traditional on-balance-sheet securities like fixed and floating rate notes. Fortunately, simple arithmetic and the technique of describing long and short positions in a portfolio by pluses and minuses can illustrate the process of creating synthetic securities. Also, although all of the products and structures discussed in this article have been designed for interest rates within a given currency, the same framework can be applied to the foreign exchange market and to currency swaps and options. In fact, many innovations are first seen in the cross-currency Euro-markets and subsequently introduced to the domestic market.

The key to applying the arithmetic approach to financial engineering is to identify structures that provide the same promised future cash flows. Comparisons between synthetic and conventional fixed rate debt, for example, are grossly misleading if the values of the embedded call and put options are not accounted for properly. But, if the cash flows are indeed equivalent, then any difference in the present values of the portfolios represents a genuine arbitrage opportunity. This opportunity ranges from "pure" arbitrage to "risk" arbitrage, depending on the degree of uncertainty about the promised cash receipts. In particular, structures which involve interest rate swaps and long positions in caps and floors always have some degree of credit risk. Given credit enhancements and the quality of the counterparty, these risks might be deemed to be negligible. In that case, financial engineers can confidently claim a higher *expected* return to investors (or lower cost of funds to borrowers). Nevertheless, the outcome should not be mistaken for pure arbitrage that entails no risk.

5

Financial Engineering: Why Hedge?

Clifford W. Smith, Jr., Charles W. Smithson,
& D. Sykes Wilford

The financial environment in which the modern corporation operates has become dramatically more volatile in the last two decades. With this volatility comes greater financial risk. Thus, corporations today are exposed to greater risk in interest rates, currency exchange rates, and commodity prices. Ultimately, this risk can affect the value of a firm itself.

In "Managing Financial Risk" (Chapter 2), we examined several off-balance-sheet instruments that can be used to manage financial price risk. The value of managing financial price risk is illustrated in Figure 5.1. Obviously, volatility—risk to the firm—can be reduced by using these products.

It would seem that every firm exposed to increased risk should hedge. Of course, matters are far more complicated than they first appear. Even with the recent increase in risk, not all firms use risk management products to reduce risk by hedging. We want to focus on the primary question: Why should a company hedge its financial price risk? Or, to rephrase the question, which firms have the best reasons for hedging?

1. The World Has Become a Riskier Place

This is such an obvious answer that it makes the question seem frivolous. Since a great many companies are subject to financial price risk, and since off-balance-sheet instruments are readily available, it would seem to follow that firms with exposures to interest rates, foreign exchange rates, or com-

FIGURE 5.1 *The Effect of Risk Management — Hedging — Is To Reduce the Variance in the Distribution of Firm Value*

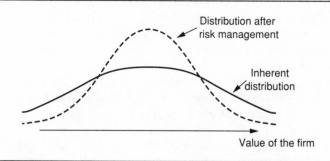

modity prices clearly would want to use forwards, futures, swaps, or options to manage risks.

As straightforward as this logic may appear, the conclusion doesn't follow. What does follow is that firms could reduce their risk by using these instruments, not that they should do so.

To understand why and when a company should manage financial price risk, let's begin by assuming its objective to be the maximization of expected present value. We'll express expected present value (following most corporate finance textbooks) as follows:

$$E(V_j) = \sum_{t=0}^{T} \frac{E(\text{NCF}_{j,t})}{(1+r_j)^t} \tag{5.1}$$

(The discount rate for a firm is the rate at which the firm's present value is derived by discounting the value of future cash flows.)

Given this assumption, a company should manage its financial price risk if that risk management strategy increases expected present value. Let's examine why.

It's natural to think about corporations as if they were individuals. Individuals should want to manage, or reduce, risk because they are risk averse. But companies aren't individuals. They might be described as legal fictions, as creations of individuals who hold claims on them. Since shareholders, the ultimate owners of a corporation, are individuals and since individuals are risk averse, it would seem that shareholders would want management to reduce financial price risk.

But this doesn't necessarily follow. For firms as opposed to individuals, portfolio theory tells us that not managing risk may be the best policy. For individuals, such risks are diversifiable and can be eliminated if the investor holds a well-diversified portolio. Risk aversion per se can be regarded as a rationale for hedging only if the owner of a firm doesn't hold a diversified portfolio. Hence, risk aversion is a compelling reason for hedging only if the firm is a proprietorship or a closely held corporation.

The basic insight inherent in portfolio theory is simple. If assets are combined in a portfolio the riskiness of the resulting portfolio is less than the linear combination of risks for the assets (unless the assets are perfectly and positively correlated).

For the individual investor, managing exposure to financial risks at the level of the firm may not be wise because the individual can more efficiently manage such risks individually by properly diversifying his or her investment portfolio.

Managing financial price risk, if it is to be adopted, must make sense because it adds to a company's value, not because it is inherently wise to reduce risk to the firm (again, unless the firm is held by undiversified owners). But we can draw an even more specific conclusion.

As Equation 5.1 makes clear, if a company's expected present value is to increase, it must be caused either by an increase in expected net cash flows or by a decrease in the discount rate.

Since we're talking about risk, it seems that we might see an effect on value through a decrease in the discount rate. But portfolio theory says that such an effect won't occur. Altering diversifiable risks—and financial price risks are generally diversifiable—can have no effect on a company's discount rate.

Thus, the gains from hedging must show up in expected net cash flows. But how can a financial policy increase the real cash flows of an organization?

We can understand how this can occur by recalling a basic canon of modern finance theory. The relation between a firm's real cash flows and its financial policies has been demonstrated by Franco Modigliani and Merton Miller in what has become known as the M&M proposition. In its original form, this proposition states: If there are no taxes, if there are no transaction costs, and if the investment policy of a firm is fixed, then the financial policies of the firm are irrelevant.

Risk management is one of the firm's financial policies. So one way to understand Modigliani and Miller is that, in a world with no taxes, no transaction costs, and with fixed investment policies, investors can create their own risk management by holding diversified portfolios. This is precisely the conclusion we arrived at earlier.

But we can also stand the M&M proposition on its head: If financial policies—one of which is risk management policy—affect value, they must do so because of their impact on transaction costs, taxes, or investment decisions.

We can use the M&M proposition to determine areas where we expect to see the effect of risk management on net cash flows. It tells us specific reasons why a firm should hedge financial price exposure. It also tells us which firms we can expect to hedge.

2. By Managing Risk a Company Can Reduce Expected Taxes

To see how a risk management strategy can reduce expected taxes, consider a naive example. Say a firm has an equal probability of a pre-tax income of either -400 or $+600$ (see Figure 5.2). This gives it an expected pre-tax income of 100:

$$E(\text{PTI}) = \tfrac{1}{2}(-400) + \tfrac{1}{2}(600) \qquad (5.2)$$

We are concentrating on the tax effect, so we assume there are no transaction costs and that the investment decision is fixed. For simplicity we'll also assume a zero interest rate.

Suppose that the tax rate on pre-tax income is 20% and that the government will refund to the firm 20% of its losses. (In a multiperiod world, this is equivalent to a 100% tax-loss carryforward.) The resulting tax schedule is illustrated in Figure 5.3.

With this tax code, the tax on expected income,

$$T[E(\text{PTI})] = T[100] = 20 \qquad (5.3)$$

is the same as expected tax,

$$E(T) = \tfrac{1}{2}[T(-400)] + \tfrac{1}{2}[T(600)] = \tfrac{1}{2}(-80) + \tfrac{1}{2}(120) = 20 \qquad (5.4)$$

Consequently, there is no benefit to the firm from hedging.

Suppose that the tax rate on pre-tax income remains at 20% but that the government will refund to the firm only 10% of its losses. (In a multiperiod world this is equivalent to a 50% tax-loss carryforward.) As illustrated in Figure 5.4, the tax schedule has a kink at zero; it has become convex.

FIGURE 5.2 *Equal Probability of Pre-Tax Income of -400 or $+600$*

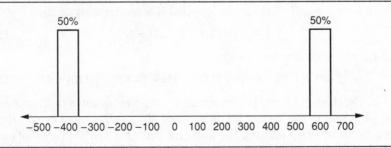

FIGURE 5.3 *Linear Tax Schedule (100% Tax-Loss Carryforward)*

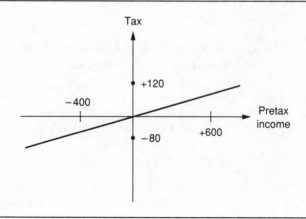

FIGURE 5.4 *Convex Tax Schedule (50% Tax-Loss Carryforward)*

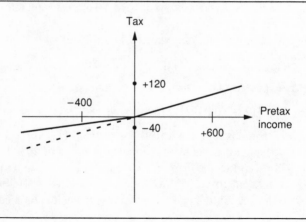

With this convex tax schedule, tax on expected income and expected tax are no longer equal. The tax on expected income remains at 20,

$$T[E(\text{PTI})] = T[100] = 20 \qquad (5.5)$$

But the expected tax rises to 40,

$$E(T) = \tfrac{1}{2}[T(-400)] + \tfrac{1}{2}[T(600)] = \tfrac{1}{2}(-40) + \tfrac{1}{2}(120) = 40 \qquad (5.6)$$

Clearly, the firm would prefer the tax on expected income to the expected tax—it would prefer to pay 20 rather than 40. As illustrated below, this is done by completely hedging the firm. Instead of a 50/50 probability of a

FIGURE 5.5   *Completely Hedged Firm has 100% Probability of Pre-Tax Income of 100*

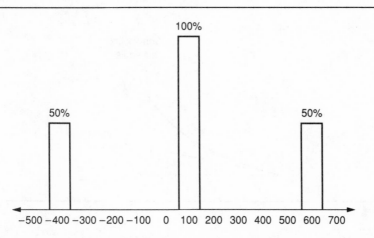

pre-tax profit of 600 or a loss of 400, the firm would have a 100% probability of a pre-tax income of 100 (see Figure 5.5).

With the convex tax schedule, hedging has provided a tax benefit. In the case in point, the benefit is 20.

The tax benefit of hedging is a positive function of the convexity of the tax schedule. Let's make the tax schedule more convex. Suppose that the tax rate on profits is 20% and that none of the losses are refunded. (Again, in the multiperiod world, the tax-loss carryforward drops to 0%.) In this case, the tax benefit rises from 20 to 40.

The tax benefit of hedging is a positive function of the percentage of the distribution of pre-tax income in the convex region of the tax schedule. Let's keep volatility of pre-tax income the same but move the distribution to the right. Instead of −400 to +600, let the distribution be −200 to +800. Now less of the distribution lies around the kink in the tax schedule, and the tax benefit of hedging declines from 20 to 10. Finally, the tax benefit of hedging is a positive function of the volatility of pre-tax income. If we reduce the range of pre-tax income to −200 to +400 (instead of −400 to +600), the tax benefit falls from 20 to 10.

This illustrates that, for a risk management strategy to produce tax benefits, the tax schedule must be convex in the range of the firm's pre-tax income. And the more convex the tax schedule, the greater the tax benefits. As illustrated in Figure 5.6, tax schedule convexity means simply that the marginal tax rate exceeds the average tax rate.

FIGURE 5.6   *Tax Schedule Convexity Means the Marginal Tax Rate Exceeds the Linear Rate*

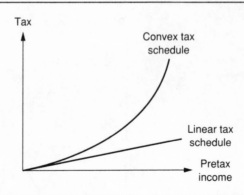

Hence the tax benefit of risk management is improved by increases in the progressivity of the tax code, tax-loss carryforwards, and tax credits. And since the alternate minimum tax makes the individual firm's tax schedule convex, the tax benefit of risk management is also increased by the introduction of an alternate minimum tax.

3. Hedging Can Reduce the Firm's Potential Costs of Financial Distress

As illustrated in Figure 5.7, risk management reduces the probability of a company encountering financial distress by reducing the volatility of its value. Consequently, risk management reduces the costs the firm would face if it met with financial distress. Let's consider the positive benefits of hedging as the reduction in a company's expected costs as a result of financial distress.

The magnitude of the cost reduction depends on two obvious factors: the probability that the firm will encounter financial distress if it doesn't hedge, and the costs it will face if it does run into financial distress. The cost savings — the benefit from risk management — will vary directly with the probability of financial distress if the firm doesn't hedge, and also directly with the cost of financial distress (if encountered).

Two factors determine the probability of default. First, since default results when a firm is unable to pay its fixed claims, the larger the ratio of service on fixed claims to cash inflows, the higher the probability of default. As the coverage of fixed claims declines, the probability of default rises. Second, since default is triggered when income is too low to pay fixed claims,

FIGURE 5.7 *Define V_{FD} as that Value of the Firm below which Financial Distress is Encountered; Risk Management Reduces the Probability of V_{FD} from P_{FD} to P'_{FD}*

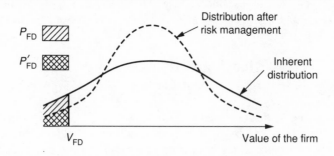

volatility of a firm's income is important. The more volatile the income, the more likely the prospect of default.

The cost of financial distress itself depends on a number of factors. Financial distress can lead to bankruptcy or to reorganization or liquidations. These are obviously situations where a company would face significant direct legal and accounting costs. These attendant costs of bankruptcy tend to have a substantial fixed component — it doesn't take many more accountants or lawyers to reorganize a large firm than it does to reorganize a small one. Hence, the per-dollar costs are higher for small firms than for large ones. So small companies should have greater incentive to hedge.

Even if financial distress didn't lead to bankruptcy, the firm should expect to encounter a number of indirect costs. These result from higher contracting costs with customers, employees, and suppliers. Firms that provide service agreements or warranties have a higher degree of contracting with their customers. These firms would consequently face higher costs if the company had financial problems. The value consumers place on service agreements and warranties depends on the firm's financial viability. If it is less viable, consumers will place less value on service agreements and warranties.

In the same way, contracting costs would be higher for firms that produce credence goods — goods for which quality is important but for which the quality is difficult to judge prior to consumption (e.g., pharmaceuticals or air travel). Consumers of credence goods must use other characteristics to determine product quality. If the firm is in financial trouble, the consumer's concern is that product quality is being reduced.

Contracting costs of the firm with its employees are higher as the firm uses more specialized labor or as it spends more time and money training workers. If the firm is perceived to have financial difficulties, it would experience more turnover in employees, so the cost of financial distress rises.

Contracting costs with suppliers are higher as the firm requires more customization from its suppliers or as the firm has fewer potential suppliers. As it encounters financial distress, it is more likely to receive unfavorable credit terms, delivery schedules, and service. Moreover, its suppliers may be less willing to tailor their production facilities to meet custom requirements.

4. Hedging Can Increase a Firm's Debt Capacity

Modigliani and Miller assumed a world in which a firm's investment policy was fixed. And, if the objective is to maximize shareholder value, the optimal fixed investment policy is simple: Accept all positive net present value projects and reject all negative ones.

But there are cases where a firm will reject a positive net present value project. Consider a firm subject to oil price risk:

Outcome	Probability	Firm Value in Period 1
Price of oil rises	0.5	1000
Price of oil falls	0.5	200

The firm has available a positive net present value project. An outlay of $600 in Period 1 will result in a certain income of $800 in Period 2.

The firm plans to issue bonds with a face value of $500 in Period 1 and pass on the proceeds to the shareholders. For simplicity, assume no transaction costs, no taxes, and risk-free interest rate of zero.

As shown below, if the price of oil falls, this firm will pass up the positive net present value project—that is, if the value of the firm in Period 1 is $200, the shareholders will not undertake the positive net present value investment project.

Period 1		Period 2			
Value of Firm		Value of Firm	Value of Debt	Value of Equity	Project Undertaken?
1000	undertake	1200	500	700	yes
	do not	1000	500	500	
200	undertake	400	500	−100	no
	do not	200	200	0	

As noted, the debt will sell for $350, not $500, the proceeds of which will be distributed to the shareholders. The expected present value of the equity is $350. The total value to the shareholders (including dividends) is $700.

This illustrates a classic conflict between shareholders and bondholders. Financial economists call it the underinvestment problem. If the firm's value is low, the shareholders will opt not to undertake the positive net present value project because the gains accrue to the bondholders. The problem is the amount of debt in the firm's capital structure. As illustrated below, if it reduces its debt/equity ratio, the underinvestment problem disappears. Suppose that a firm had issued debt with a face value of $350 instead of $500:

Period 1		Period 2			
Value of Firm		Value of Firm	Value of Debt	Value of Equity	Project Undertaken?
1000 {	undertake	1200	350	850 }	yes
	do not	1000	350	650	
200 {	undertake	400	350	50 }	yes
	do not	200	200	0	

With less debt in the capital structure the positive net present value project will always be undertaken. The debt sells at its face value of $350, the proceeds of which will go to the shareholders. The expected present value of the equity is $450, so the total value of the shareholders' position is (including dividends) $450 + $350 = $800, rather than the $700 when the face value of the debt was $500. By reducing the face value of the debt, the shareholders have gained $100.

As an alternative to altering the debt/equity ratio, the underinvestment problem can be controlled by using risk management techniques.

Suppose a company could hedge its exposure to oil prices so that regardless of what happens to oil prices, the value of the firm will remain $600. With the firm's value hedged against oil prices, the positive net present value project will always be undertaken.

Period 1		Period 2			
Value of Firm		Value of Firm	Value of Debt	Value of Equity	Project Undertaken?
600 {	undertake	800	500	300 }	yes
	do not	600	500	100	

With the hedge against oil prices, the firm can issue debt with a face value of $500 and still avoid the underinvestment problem. In this case the total value of the shareholders' wealth is $800 — the dividend paid from the proceeds of the debt issue ($500) plus the value of equity ($300).

The more debt a firm has in its capital structure, the greater the benefit from using risk management to control the underinvestment problem. Alternatively, the more risk management a firm does, the more debt it can support.

Portfolio Theory

Portfolio theory is based on a simple statistical relation. The variance of a combination of random variables involves not only the variances of random variables but also the covariance,

$$\text{Var}(A+B) = \text{Var}(A) + \text{Var}(B) + 2\text{Cov}(A, B)$$

Define the risk for security A as the standard deviation of its returns, σ_A. Likewise, define the risk for security B as σ_B. Then, consider a simple portfolio made up of one of security A and one of B. If risk were additive, the variance for this portfolio would be given by

$$(\sigma_A + \sigma_B)^2 = \sigma_A^2 + \sigma_B^2 + 2\sigma_A\sigma_B$$

But, using the variance formula noted above, the variance of the portfolio is given by

$$\sigma_P^2 = \sigma_A^2 + \sigma_B^2 + 2\rho_{AB}\sigma_A\sigma_B$$

where ρ_{AB} is the correlation between the returns of securities A and B and the product $\rho_{AB}\sigma_A\sigma_B$ is $\text{Cov}(A, B)$. Comparing the two equations above, the riskiness of the portfolio is less than the linear combination of the risks for the individual securities,

$$\sigma_P < \sigma_A + \sigma_B$$

unless the two securities are perfectly positively correlated—that is, unless $\rho_{AB} = 1$.

---

5. Managing Risk Can Reduce a Firm's Borrowing Costs

The underinvestment problem is but one difficulty resulting from the conflict between bondholders and shareholders—a conflict that is a special case of what is sometimes called the agency problem. This problem refers to conflicts of interests that occur in virtually all cooperative activities among self-interested individuals. It results from different claims held by bondholders and shareholders. The bondholders hold fixed claims while shareholders hold claims that are like call options on the firm's value.

We have already seen that an increase in debt/equity ratio increases the probability of conflict between shareholders and bondholders—and that it thereby increases the value of a hedging strategy to reduce the cost of this conflict. Another determinant of the conflict (and consequently of the value of a hedging strategy) can be found in the range of investment projects available for a firm. Like any other option, the value of shareholders' equity rises as volatility in the returns of the underlying asset increases. If shareholders could switch from low-variance investment projects to high-variance ones, the shareholders would transfer wealth from the bondholders to themselves. But since bondholders realize that this opportunistic behavior could occur, they protect themselves against the shareholders' temptation to select high-variance projects by lowering the price they are willing to pay for bonds. To get the bondholders to pay more for the bonds, the shareholders must assure them that these wealth transfers won't take place. These assurances can take the form of restrictive covenants or, most importantly for our purposes, hedging.

It then follows that, in addition to the level of debt in the firm's capital structure, the value of the risk management program to a firm depends on the range of available investment projects. The wider the range of investment projects (i.e., the greater the variance in returns for an available project), the greater the potential for conflict between shareholder and bondholder. But it also increases the value of a hedging program that would reduce the conflict.

PART III

The Building Blocks
of Financial Engineering

6

A Comparison of Futures and Forward Prices*

Kenneth R. French

1. Introduction

Futures and forward contracts are very similar; both contracts represent an agreement to trade an asset at a specific time in the future. Because of this similarity, these contracts are often treated as though they are identical. However, futures and forward contracts are not identical; the daily gain or loss from holding a futures contract is transferred between the traders at the end of each day, while the profits or losses from holding a forward contract accumulate until the contract matures. A number of recent papers have examined the theoretical implications of this difference for the relation between futures and forward prices. For example, Margrabe (1976), Cox, Ingersoll,

*This paper is based on my doctoral thesis at the University of Rochester. I am very grateful to my dissertation committee, G. William Schwert (Chairman), Michael Jensen, John Long, and Charles Plosser, for their guidance. I have also received helpful comments from Robert Jarrow, Scott Richard, Richard Roll, Richard Ruback, Dennis Sheehan, René Stulz, Lee Wakeman, Jerold Zimmerman, and the referee, Douglas Breeden. Financial support was generously provided by the Managerial Economics Research Center, Graduate School of Management, University of Rochester; the Center for the Study of Futures Markets, Graduate School of Business, Columbia University; the Foundation for Research in Economics and Education; and the Richard D. Irwin Foundation. I would also like to thank Christopher Snyder of Data Resources, Inc., and Richard Brealey for providing data. This work was completed while I was a postdoctoral fellow at the University of California, Los Angeles.

and Ross (1977), and Jarrow and Oldfield (1981) demonstrate that these prices will not be equal unless interest rates are nonstochastic. Cox, Ingersoll, and Ross (1981), Richard and Sundaresan (1981), and French (1982) build models of futures and forward prices that allow them to make more specific predictions about the relation between these prices. This paper examines the accuracy of many of these predictions for silver and copper contracts.

A forward contract is simply a sales agreement in which delivery and payment are deferred. All of the terms of the sale, such as the asset to be delivered, the time of delivery, and the purchase price (called the forward price), are specified when the contract is written. No payments are made until the contract matures. At that time the seller delivers the asset and the buyer pays the forward price. Since the asset can be purchased just before delivery and re-sold immediately afterward, a forward contract can be viewed as a bet about the maturity price of the commodity. The payoff on this bet is equal to the difference between the forward price and the maturity spot price.

A futures contract can also be viewed as a bet about the maturity price of the asset, but the parties to this bet settle up daily.[1] At the end of each day's trading, the current futures price is compared with the closing price from the previous day. If the futures price has fallen, the investor who is long in the contract (committing himself to purchase the commodity) must pay the short investor the amount of the decrease. If the futures price has risen, the long investor receives the amount of the increase from the short investor. When the contract matures, the long investor purchases the commodity at the previous day's closing, or settlement, price. Since the commodity can be re-sold immediately at the prevailing spot price, the sum of the cash flows between the two futures traders is equal to the difference between the original futures price and the maturity spot price. This is very similar to the cash flow from the forward contract "bet." However, with a forward contract the profits are transferred at maturity, while the profits from a futures contract are transferred at the end of each day.[2]

Despite the differences between these contracts, most commodity traders treat futures contracts as though they are forward contracts. For example, by implicitly modeling futures contracts as forward contracts, futures traders have developed several "arbitrage" conditions relating futures prices, spot prices, and storage costs. Many economists seem to agree that the daily settling up has a negligible effect on futures prices. In developing their models of futures prices, Dusak (1973), Grauer (1977), and Grauer and Litzenberger (1979) abstract from the settling-up provisions of these contracts entirely. Other authors, such as Black (1976), explicitly recognize the daily settling up, but they still conclude that futures and forward prices will be the same.

---

1. This settling up is often called "marking-to-market."
2. Strictly speaking, each futures contract is a bet about the next day's futures price.

In light of this consensus about the similarity between futures and forward prices, the empirical evidence in this paper may be surprising. There are significant differences between these prices for both copper and silver contracts. For example, during the 1974–1980 sample period, the average futures–forward price differences are about 0.1%, 0.4%, and 0.8% for 3-, 6-, and 12-month silver contracts, respectively.

The next section of this paper outlines the pricing models of Cox, Ingersoll, and Ross (1981), Richard and Sundaresan (1981), and French (1982). These models imply that futures and forward prices will differ in predictable ways. For example, the models predict that the price for a forward contract is related to the interest rate on a long-term bond that matures at the same time as the contract, while the futures price is related to the return from rolling over one-day bonds until the contract matures. These prices will be identically equal only if interest rates are nonstochastic.

Section 3 compares futures and forward prices for copper and silver and tests many of the predictions of the pricing models outlined in Section 2. In general, the average price differences are consistent with the predictions. However, the models are not helpful in describing intrasample variations in the futures–forward price differences. This failure is apparently caused by measurement errors in both the price differences and in the explanatory variables.

Section 4 contains a brief summary and some conclusions.

2. Models of Futures and Forward Prices

This section uses models developed by Cox, Ingersoll, and Ross (1981), Richard and Sundaresan (1981), and French (1982) to examine the theoretical differences between futures and forward prices. All of these models assume that there are no taxes or transaction costs and that individuals can borrow and lend at the same nominal interest rate.[3]

2.1. Arbitrage Models

Futures and forward contracts provide a wide variety of intertemporal exchange opportunities. For example, by initiating a long forward contract and purchasing risk free bonds, an individual can buy an asset today that will be delivered in the future. To see the mechanics of this transaction, define $f(t, T)$ as the forward price on day t for a contract that matures on day T and define $R(t, T)$ as the yield to maturity on a riskless discount bond that pays one dollar on day T. The current price of this bond is

---

3. The models also assume that investors will not default on any contract. This implies that there is a finite upper bound on the daily price changes and on the daily interest rates.

$$B(t, T) \equiv \exp[-(T-t)R(t, T)] \tag{6.1}$$

A trader can make a delayed purchase by initiating one forward contract and investing $f(t, T)B(t, T)$ dollars in riskless bonds. When the contract matures, he receives $f(t, T)$ dollars from the bonds and exchanges this for one unit of the commodity. In effect, an investment of $f(t, T)B(t, T)$ today yields one unit of the commodity on day T. Alternatively, the trader could reverse the strategy and obtain $f(t, T)B(t, T)$ dollars today in exchange for the asset at time T.

Because this intertemporal exchange is available, investors must be marginally indifferent between $f(t, T)B(t, T)$ dollars today and one unit of the commodity on day T. By defining $\tilde{P}(T)$ as the (unknown) price of the commodity at time T, this indifference can be expressed in purely dollar terms; $f(t, T)B(t, T)$ must be the value on day t of $\tilde{P}(T)$ dollars on day T. Equivalently, the forward price must equal the present value of the maturity spot price times the gross return from a long-term bond,

$$f(t, T) = \exp[(T-t)R(t, T)]PV_{t, T}[\tilde{P}(T)] \tag{6.2}$$

In Equation 6.2, $PV_{t, T}(\cdot)$ denotes the present value at time t of a payment received at time T.

For example, consider a forward contract on a stock that pays no dividends. Since the current stock price must be the present value of the future stock price, the forward price is equal to

$$f(t, T) = \exp[(T-t)R(t, T)]P(t) \tag{6.3}$$

This result is intuitively appealing. Using a forward contract to purchase the stock on day T is equivalent to purchasing the stock today, except the forward contract allows the payment to be deferred. Therefore, the forward price is equal to the deferred value of the current stock price.

The present value of the maturity spot price is not observable for most commodities; a more complete model must be introduced to evaluate the payment in Equation 6.2 and to determine the forward price. However, Equation 6.2 is useful for highlighting the differences between futures and forward prices.

Cox, Ingersoll, and Ross (1981) and French (1982) develop a similar expression for futures prices. They demonstrate that the futures price must equal the present value of the product of the maturity spot price and the gross return from rolling over one-day bonds,

$$F(t, T) = PV_{t, T}\left\{\exp\left[\sum_{\tau=t}^{T-1} \tilde{R}(\tau, \tau+1)\right]\tilde{P}(T)\right\} \tag{6.4}$$

In this equation, $F(t, T)$ is the futures price on day t for a contract that matures on day T and $R(\tau, \tau+1)$ is the continuously compounded interest rate on a one-day bond from day τ to day $\tau+1$.

Equations 6.2 and 6.4 indicate that the difference between forward and futures prices is related to the difference between holding a long-term bond and rolling over a series of one-day bonds. The only cash flow that is relevant to the forward trader is agreed on today and paid on the maturity date. Therefore, the relevant interest rate in determining the forward price is the known yield on a multiperiod bond. On the other hand, while the futures trader knows the total payments he will have to make, the timing of these cash flows is only determined as the contract matures. Because of this uncertainty, the futures price is a function of the unknown one-day interest rates that are expected to arise over the life of the contract. In general, the futures price will not equal the forward price unless these interest rates are nonstochastic.

Cox, Ingersoll, and Ross use the arbitrage models in Equations 6.2 and 6.4 to develop several propositions about the relation between forward and futures prices. In a continuous-time, constinuous-state economy, they find that the difference between these prices is equal to

$$F(t,T) - f(t,T) = -PV_{t,T}\left\{\left\{\int_t^T \tilde{F}(w,T)\,\text{cov}[\tilde{F}(w,T), \tilde{B}(w,T)]\,dw\right\}\middle/ B(t,T)\right.$$
(6.5)

In this equation, $\text{cov}[\tilde{F}(w,T), \tilde{B}(w,T)]$ is defined as the local covariance at time w between the percentage change in the futures price and the percentage change in the bond price. This result has several implications. For example, the local covariance between the futures and bond prices is almost certainly positive for financial assets, such as treasury bills. Therefore, the forward price should be above the futures price for these assets. On the other hand, one would expect the futures price to be above the forward price for most real commodities. Unexpected inflation and changes in expected inflation probably play a major role in determining the covariance between bond prices and commodity prices. Since unexpected inflation moves bond prices and commodity prices in opposite directions, the covariance should be negative and the futures–forward price difference should be positive.[4]

Equation 6.5 also implies that the difference between the futures and forward prices will be related to the variance of both the futures prices and the bond prices. Specifically, if the correlation between the futures and bond prices is constant, the absolute value of the price difference will be an increasing function of the market's expectation of both the futures and bond price variances.

---

4. The local covariance between the futures price and the bond price may be positive for some commodities. For example, if a commodity is used in the production of a durable good, an increase in the expected real interest rate will reduce the demand for the commodity. Therefore, changes in the expected real interest rate will tend to make the commodity and bond prices move together. However, since the inflation rate is much more volatile than the expected real interest rate, the covariance is still expected to be negative for most commodities.

Cox, Ingersoll, and Ross also use the arbitrage models to show that the difference between the futures and forward prices can be expressed as

$$F(t,T) - f(t,T) = PV_{t,T}\left\{ \exp\left[\int_t^T \tilde{r}(w)\,dw\right]\int_t^T [\tilde{P}(w)/\tilde{B}(w,T)]\right.$$
$$\left. \times \{\text{var}[\tilde{B}(w,T)] - \text{cov}[\tilde{P}(w), \tilde{B}(w,T)]\}\,dw \right\} \quad (6.6)$$

if the commodity is stored costlessly over the contract period. In this equation, $\tilde{r}(w)$ is the instantaneous interest rate at time w, $\text{var}[\tilde{B}(w,T)]$ is the local variance of the percentage change in the bond price, and $\text{cov}[\tilde{P}(w), \tilde{B}(w,T)]$ is the local covariance between the percentage change in the spot price and the percentage change in the bond price. This result implies that the futures–forward price difference will be a decreasing function of the market's expectation of the spot price variance if the price difference is negative and if the local correlation between the spot and bond prices is constant.

2.2. Utility Based Models

The relation between futures and forward prices can be explored further by assuming that markets are complete and that there is some rational individual who acts to maximize a time-additive expected utility function of the form

$$J = E_t\left\{ \sum_{\tau=t}^{\infty} \exp[-\rho(\tau - t)]U[\tilde{C}(\tau)]\right\} \quad (6.7)$$

In Equation 6.7, $\tilde{C}(\tau)$ is a vector indicating the (nonnegative) quantity of each good consumed on day τ, and ρ is a utility discount factor. Further, $U(\cdot)$ is a single period, von Neumann–Morgenstern utility function that is increasing, strictly quasi-concave, and differentiable. Finally, define $\tilde{\lambda}(\tau)$ as the marginal value of a dollar that is received at time τ. For notational convenience, this marginal value is discounted back to day t. In other words, $\tilde{\lambda}(\tau)$ is the discounted marginal utility of money on day τ,

$$\tilde{\lambda}(\tau) = \exp[-\rho(\tau - t)]\tilde{u}(i,\tau)/\tilde{P}(i,\tau) \quad (6.8)$$

In this expression, $\tilde{P}(i,\tau)$ is the price of any commodity that is consumed on day τ and $\tilde{u}(i,\tau)$ is the marginal utility of this commodity on day τ. Notice that, unlike $\tilde{\lambda}(\tau)$, $\tilde{u}(i,\tau)$ is not discounted back to day t.

The discussion in the previous section shows that investors must be marginally indifferent between $f(t,T)$ dollars today and $\exp[(T-t)R(t,T)]\tilde{P}(T)$ dollars on day T. For an individual with the time-additive utility function in Equation 6.7, this indifference can be expressed as

$$f(t,T)\lambda(t) = \exp[(T-t)R(t,T)]E_t[\tilde{P}(T)\tilde{\lambda}(T)] \quad (6.9)$$

the marginal utility of $f(t,T)$ dollars today must equal the expected marginal utility of $\exp[(T-t)R(t,T)]\tilde{P}(T)$ dollars at time T. Equivalently, the forward price must equal

$$f(t, T) = \exp[(T-t)R(t, T)]E_t[\tilde{P}(T)\tilde{\lambda}(T)/\lambda(t)] \qquad (6.10)$$

If this condition were not satisfied, the individual could increase his lifetime expected utility by using a portfolio of forward contracts and bonds to transfer money between day t and day T.[5]

The time-additive utility function can also be used to characterize futures prices. Equation 6.4 implies that, in equilibrium,[6] investors are indifferent between $F(t, T)$ dollars today and $\exp[\sum_{\tau=t}^{T-1} \tilde{R}(\tau, \tau+1)]\tilde{P}(T)$ dollars at time T. This indifference can be expressed as

$$F(t, T)\lambda(t) = E_t\left\{\exp\left[\sum_{\tau=t}^{T-1} \tilde{R}(\tau, \tau+1)\right]\tilde{P}(T)\tilde{\lambda}(T)\right\} \qquad (6.11)$$

or

$$F(t, T) = E_t\left\{\exp\left[\sum_{\tau=t}^{T-1} \tilde{R}(\tau, \tau+1)\right]\tilde{P}(T)\tilde{\lambda}(T)/\lambda(t)\right\} \qquad (6.12)$$

Equations 6.10 and 6.12 reemphasize that the forward price is a function of the gross return from holding a long-term bond while the futures price is a function of the gross return from rolling over one-day bonds.[7]

3. A Comparison of Futures and Forward Prices

As the discussion in Section 1 indicates, the similarity between futures and forward prices often leads people to view them as identical contracts. The models of futures and forward prices described in the previous section highlight the theoretical differences between these contracts. This section examines the empirical effects of these differences and tests several predictions of the models.

3.1. Matching Futures and Forward Prices

The tests in this section compare futures and forward prices for silver and copper from 1968 through 1980. Most of the organized forward activity during this period occurred on the London Metal Exchange (LME).[8] Members of this exchange trade spot and forward contracts on silver, copper, and

---

5. Equation 6.10 and Equation 6.12 below actually follow directly from Equations 6.2 and 6.4 using the relation $PV_{t, T}(\tilde{Y}) = E_t[\tilde{Y}\tilde{\lambda}(T)/\lambda(t)]$.
6. In equilibrium, no investor wants to make additional trades at the existing prices.
7. The models in Equations 6.10 and 6.12 are developed by Richard and Sundaresan (1981) and French (1982). In addition, the forward price model in Equation 6.10 is similar to the futures price models in Grauer (1977) and Grauer and Litzenberger (1979).
8. Silver contracts began trading on the LME in February 1968. The London Bullion Market prices for silver spot and forward contracts are used before 1973.

several other metals. Although other contracts are available, the standard silver contracts have maturities of 3, 6, and 12 months and the standard copper contract has a 3-month maturity. A new set of contracts is written each day. For example, the 3-month silver contract initiated on February 10, 1977, matured on May 10, while the contract written on February 11 matured on May 11.

The futures prices reflect trading on two exchanges in the United States — the Commodity Exchange (Comex) in New York and the Chicago Board of Trade (CBT).[9] The contract maturities used in these markets follow a different convention than that used in forward markets. While forward traders write contracts with a specific time until maturity, such as three months, futures contracts are traded continually for up to two years. For example, an investor could initiate a December 1978 silver contract any time from January 1977 until it matured two years later.

In comparing futures and forward prices, one would like to simultaneously observe futures and forward contracts for the same commodity and the same maturity. The different maturity structures used in the futures and forward markets make this difficult. The discussion in the first two sections assumes that futures and foward contracts have precise maturity dates. While this is true for forward contracts, it is not true for most futures contracts, including those examined here. Instead, a short futures trader may choose to make delivery any time during the maturity month. The exchange's clearinghouse then assigns the shipment to the long trader with the "oldest" contract. The tests reported in this section assume that futures contracts mature in the first week of the delivery month.[10]

The futures and forward prices have several other characteristics that make comparisons between them difficult. For example, both Comex and the CBT impose limits on the daily price movement of any futures contract that is not in its delivery month. These limits constrain the futures price to lie within a range determined by the previous day's settlement price. If a limit is reached, the day's trading is effectively stopped unless the equilibrium price moves back within the limits. In other words, when a limit move occurs, the reported price may be significantly different from the unobserved market-clearing price. To reduce the effect of this measurement error, any futures price that reflects a limit move is not included in the tests.

---

9. The commodity price data are obtained from several sources: the Commodity Services, Inc., data bank, provided by the Center for the Study of Futures Markets at Columbia University; the Data Resources, Inc., commodities data bank; the *Wall Street Journal;* and the *Journal of Commerce.*

10. Specifically, the tests use prices observed on Fridays. The relevant Friday for each futures contract is chosen so that the matching forward contract matures during the first week of the futures delivery month. All of the tests have been replicated using four other maturity periods: the second, third, and fourth week of the maturity month and the first business day of that month. The results are not substantially different for the different maturity assumptions.

Perhaps the biggest problems encountered in trying to match futures and forward prices arise because the forward contracts are traded in Great Britain while the futures contracts are traded in the United States.[11] Ideally, the futures and forward prices should be observed simultaneously. In fact, prices from the London exchanges are recorded several hours before the American prices are observed. This difference introduces measurement error between the futures and forward prices.

Two other complications are potentially more serious. First, American futures prices are denominated in dollars while London forward contracts are denominated in pounds sterling. Before these prices can be compared, they must be converted into the same currency. Second, silver or copper in London is not exactly the same commodity as it is in New York or Chicago because of transportation costs and international trade restrictions.

One way to deal with these problems is to assume that the expected difference between the exchange-adjusted spot prices is a constant fraction of the expected spot prices,

$$E_t[\tilde{P}(T, \$)] = (1+b)E_t[\tilde{P}(T, £)\tilde{X}(T, T)] \qquad (6.13)$$

In this expression, $\tilde{P}(T, \$)$ is the spot price at time T denominated in dollars, $\tilde{P}(T, £)$ is the spot price in pounds, and $\tilde{X}(T, T)$ is the spot exchange rate between dollars and pounds at time T. Although the expected basis differential, b, is assumed to be constant through time, it may vary across commodities. For example, since the cost of transporting silver between London and the United States is small relative to the value of the commodity, one expects that the absolute value of the basis differential for silver is small. On the other hand, the basis differential for copper may be higher because the relative transportation costs are higher.

Under this constant-expected-basis-differential model, the American forward price can be estimated by the product of the London forward price, the forward exchange rate, and the basis adjustment,[12]

---

11. The price controls imposed in the United States from August 15, 1971, through April 30, 1974, could cause more problems. Both the spot prices and the futures prices for copper and silver were subject to these controls. For example, during the first 90 days of the control period none of the futures contracts was allowed to trade above its May 25, 1970, price or the average of the prices for the 30 days preceding August 15, 1971, whichever was higher. Because of the potential distortions caused by the price controls, all of the tests have been duplicated using three separate subperiods: a pre-control period, from January 1, 1968, through August 14, 1971; a price control period from August 15, 1971, through April 30, 1974; and a post-control period from May 1, 1974, through December 31, 1980. Surprisingly, the price controls do not affect the results of these tests. For a more complete description of the price controls imposed on the copper and silver markets and some tests of the effect of these controls, see Levich and White (1981).

12. This conversion also assumes that, conditional on the information available at time t, the covariance of the marginal utility of a dollar with the difference between the basis-adjusted

$$f(t, T, \$) = (1 + b)f(t, T, \pounds)X(t, T) \tag{6.14}$$

Table 6.1 presents estimates of the basis differential for silver and copper as a percentage of the spot price.[13] The British spot prices used in these estimates are measured by prices from the London Metal Exchange. Explicit spot prices for copper and silver are not available from the American futures exchanges. Instead, the price for the deliverable futures contract — called the cash price — is used. For example, the December silver futures price is used to estimate the American spot price during December.

The estimates of the basis differential for silver in Table 6.1 are very small. For example, the average differential over the full 1968–1980 sample period is less than 0.1%, with a t-statistic of 0.53.[14] This is consistent with the relatively small transportation costs for silver. The estimates for copper are much larger; the average basis differential for the full sample period is −0.34% and the average for the first subperiod, from 1968 through 1973, is −1.87%.

The forward prices that are converted from pounds to dollars in the tests below all have maturities of three months or more. Therefore, it is only necessary to assume that the expected basis differential is constant for forecast horizons of at least three months. This is weaker than assuming that the basis differential always equals b,

$$P(t, \$) = (1 + b)P(t, \pounds)X(t, t) \tag{6.15}$$

The expectational model does not rule out differences between the basis-adjusted spot prices. However, since the conditional expected value of these differences is zero, differences that are at least three months apart must be independent. The autocorrelations reported in Table 6.1 provide a test of this implication.

The estimates for silver support the constant-expected-basis-differential model. Since these estimates use monthly observations, the autocorrelations

---

maturity spot prices is zero; $\text{cov}_t[\bar{\lambda}(T, \$), (1 + b)\tilde{P}(T, \pounds)\tilde{X}(T, T) - \tilde{P}(T, \$)] = 0$.

French (1982) demonstrates that Equation 6.14 holds under the assumption that this covariance is zero and that the expected basis differential, b, is zero. Extending this result to the general case of any constant expected basis differential is straightforward.

13. Although the model in Equation 6.13 is specified in terms of the levels of the spot prices, these estimates and all of the tests below use the logarithms of the prices. This eliminates some heteroskedasticity.

The exchange rates used in Table 6.1 and in the tests below are obtained from the *Bank of England Quarterly Bulletin,* the Federal Reserve Bank of New York, and Data Resources, Inc. Although daily data are available during most of the period, only the exchange rates for Friday are available from 1968 through 1970. This does not cause problems for most of the tests because they only use futures and forward prices that are observed on Friday. However, for tests involving daily data, the Friday exchange rate is used for the next four days during this period.

14. The t-statistics in Table 6.1 are adjusted for autocorrelation at lags one and two since these are allowed under the constant-expected-basis-differential model.

TABLE 6.1 *Estimates of the Basis Differentials and Tests of the Constant-Expected-Basis-Differential Model*[a]

	Number	Mean	Std. dev.	t-stat.	$S(r_3)$	r_1	r_2	r_3	r_4	r_5	r_6
					Silver						
1/68–12/80	146	0.080	1.863	0.526	0.086	0.025	−0.044	−0.011	0.249	0.053	0.018
1/68–12/73	66	−0.015	1.533	0.056	0.160	0.446	0.179	−0.002	0.182	0.269	0.259
1/74–12/80	80	0.158	2.104	1.000	0.120	−0.149	−0.143	−0.019	0.283	0.011	−0.065
					Copper						
1/68–12/80	112	−0.349	3.558	0.605	0.178	0.795	0.520	0.576	0.428	0.376	0.400
1/68–12/73	37	−1.868	3.955	2.236	0.395	0.897	0.146	0.682	0.409	0.366	0.716
1/74–12/80	75	0.400	3.107	0.578	0.218	0.839	0.665	0.580	0.411	0.288	0.219

a. The percentage basis differential is estimated by $\log[P(t, \$)/P(t, £)X(t, t)] * 100$. Under the constant-expected-basis-differential model, the auto-correlations after lag 2 should not be significantly different from zero. The autocorrelation at lag i is denoted by r_i and $S(r_3)$ is the standard error for the autocorrelation at lag 3, estimated using Bartlett's (1946) approximation. Copper has fewer observations than silver during the first sample period because fewer copper contracts were traded during this period.

should be approximately zero after the second lag. In fact, almost all of the autocorrelations for the silver price differences are close to zero. For example, only the autocorrelation at lag 4 is significant during the 1968–1980 period.[15] The results for copper are less consistent with the model. For example, all of the estimates for the 1968–1980 sample period are significantly positive. Because of these large autocorrelations, the futures and forward price comparisons involving converted copper prices should be interpreted cautiously.[16]

3.2. A Preliminary Look at the Data

Before comparing individual futures and forward prices, it is helpful to examine the general properties of the cash, spot, futures, and forward prices that are used in the tests below. Tables 6.2 and 6.3 summarize the daily percentage changes in the prices for silver and copper contracts. These changes are equal to the daily logarithmic price relatives. For example, the daily percentage change in the spot price for London silver is equal to $\log[P(t, £)/P(t-1, £)] * 100$.

Most of the tests in this paper use copper and silver prices from 1968 through 1980. However, metal prices were unusually volatile during the last two years of this sample period. For example, the cash price for silver rose from $5.98 per ounce on January 2, 1979, to $52.25 on January 21, 1980. By the end of 1980, the cash price had fallen back down to $16.58. Because of this unusual behavior during 1979 and 1980, Tables 6.2 and 6.3 summarize the daily price changes when these two years are included in the sample and when they are not.

Comparisons of the behavior of futures and forward prices are complicated by the price limits in the futures markets. Although limit moves are not included in the futures price series (nor in any of the tests below), the price limits reduce the apparent volatility of the futures prices because they make it impossible to observe large price changes. Because of this problem, Tables 6.2 and 6.3 report estimates for two different sets of converted forward prices. The first set includes all of the forward prices that are available during the sample period. The second set is more restrictive; it only includes a forward price if a matching futures price is also available. In other words,

---

15. The standard errors for the autocorrelations beyond the second lag are estimated using Bartlett's (1946) approximation. Under the hypothesis that the differences are uncorrelated after lag 2, these standard errors are equal to $S(r_3) = \{N^{-1}[1+2r_1^2+2r_2^2]\}^{1/2}$.

16. All of the tests below were also performed using a second conversion technique. This technique assumes that the market uses the current basis differential as its forecast of the future differential, so the American forward price is estimated as $f(t, T, \$) = f(t, T, £)X(t, T) \times \{P(t, \$)/P(t, £)X(t, t)\}$. The results using this conversion technique are very similar to the results reported below.

a forward price is not included if the matching futures contract was not traded or if its price reflects a limit move.

The standard deviations for silver in Table 6.2 indicate that the price limits do have a noticeable effect. For example, the estimated standard deviation for the daily change in the three-month futures prices over the full 1968–1980 sample period is 1.5%, while the London forward prices and the first set of converted forward prices have standard deviations of approximately 2.7%. If the converted forward price series is restricted to days when non-limit futures prices are available, the estimate falls to 1.6%. However, the evidence still suggests that unconstrained American prices would be less volatile than the London or converted prices. First, the standard deviations for the restricted forward prices remain higher than the standard deviations for the futures prices. While this difference may still be caused by the price limits,[17] the second piece of evidence is not affected by this bias. Since silver (and copper) futures prices are not constrained by price limits during a contract's delivery month, the standard deviations for the cash prices are not artificially reduced. Therefore, direct comparisons between the cash and spot prices are appropriate. These comparisons indicate that the standard deviations for the American cash prices are consistently lower than the standard deviations for the London or converted spot prices.

Because of the price limits, the standard deviations for the futures prices are fairly constant through time. However, the estimates for the cash, spot, and forward prices indicate that the silver price volatility increased dramatically over the sample period. For example, even if the very turbulent 1979–1980 period is excluded, the standard deviations for the spot and forward prices increased by more than 50% from the first to the second subperiod. It is also interesting that the estimated standard deviations for the forward prices do not appear to be related to the maturity of the contracts.

The summary statistics for the daily changes in the copper prices are presented in Table 6.3. These results are slightly different from the results in Table 6.2. For example, the standard deviations for the futures prices are approximately equal to the standard deviations for both the restricted and the unrestricted forward price series during both the 1968–1973 subperiod and the 1974–1978 subperiod. The effect of the future price limits is only

---

17. Selection bias can still occur because the futures and forward prices are not perfectly correlated. A large change in the forward price can be included in the sample if it is associated with a smaller change in the futures price. However, large changes in the futures price are never included.

It may appear that the difference between the closing times of the London and American markets can also contribute to the selection bias problem. For example, if a limit move is caused by information that arrives after the London market closes on day t, this information will lead to a large change in the forward price on day $t+1$. However, a limit move on day t eliminates the price changes for both day t and day $t+1$.

TABLE 6.2   Means, Standard Deviations, and t-Statistics of the Daily Percentage Changes in the Futures and Forward Prices for Silver[a]

		American prices	London prices	Converted prices	Restricted converted prices	American prices	London prices	Converted prices	Restricted converted prices
		1/68–12/80				*1/68–12/78*			
Cash or spot contracts	Mean	0.085	0.060	0.054	0.034	0.059	0.047	0.037	0.034
	Std. dev.	2.372	2.849	2.880	2.923	1.831	2.223	2.223	2.332
	t-stat.	1.805	1.190	1.046	0.574	1.502	1.092	0.855	0.657
	Number	2,563	3,145	3,145	2,441	2,166	2,662	2,662	2,064
3-month contracts	Mean	0.060	0.059	0.058	0.017	0.053	0.047	0.044	0.017
	Std. dev.	1.479	2.719	2.772	1.623	1.451	2.019	2.047	1.518
	t-stat.	1.941	1.225	1.164	0.480	1.662	1.199	1.101	0.491
	Number	2,266	3,143	3,070	2,167	2,044	2,662	2,599	1,955
		1/68–12/73							
Cash or spot contracts	Mean	0.022	0.045	0.042	0.025				
	Std. dev.	1.549	1.586	1.610	1.645				
	t-stat.	0.488	1.092	0.983	0.510				
	Number	1,166	1,456	1,456	1,124				
3-month contracts	Mean	0.040	0.046	0.041	0.036				
	Std. dev.	1.431	1.586	1.630	1.466				
	t-stat.	0.909	1.119	0.934	0.795				
	Number		1,456	1,405	1,026				

		1/74–12/80				1/74–12/78		
Cash or spot contracts	Mean	0.137	0.074	0.064	0.042	0.102	0.050	0.032	0.044
	Std. dev.	2.883	3.599	3.635	3.679	2.113	2.180	2.809	2.952
	t-stat.	1.771	0.839	0.726	0.410	1.530	0.614	0.391	0.459
	Number	1,397	1,689	1,689	1,317	1,000	1,206	1,206	940
3-month contracts	Mean	0.079	0.017	0.073	−0.001	0.069	0.047	0.048	−0.005
	Std. dev.	1.522	3.406	3.454	1.753	1.472	2.442	2.449	1.573
	t-stat.	1.792	0.851	0.864	0.018	1.449	0.674	0.683	0.091
	Number	1,187	1,687	1,665	1,141	965	1,206	1,194	929
6-month contracts	Mean	0.020	0.086	0.089	−0.003	0.014	0.052	0.056	−0.021
	Std. dev.	1.470	3.852	3.887	2.150	1.463	3.189	3.183	2.154
	t-stat.	0.460	0.876	0.899	0.037	0.288	0.567	0.608	0.288
	Number	1,159	1,551	1,525	1,024	951	1,191	1,175	886
12-month contracts	Mean	0.076	0.074	0.074	0.007	0.081	0.049	0.049	0.083
	Std. dev.	1.623	3.487	3.538	2.219	1.635	2.653	2.672	2.274
	t-stat.	1.590	0.839	0.817	0.104	1.531	0.635	0.623	0.109
	Number	1,167	1,545	1,515	1,021	957	1,191	1,171	881

a. The percentage price change is defined as $\log(P_t/P_{t-1})*100$. The American prices are cash and futures prices. The London prices are spot and futures prices. The converted prices are London spot and forward prices converted to dollars. The estimates for the forward prices denominated in pounds sterling. The converted prices are London spot and forward prices converted to dollars. The estimates for the unrestricted series use all of the available converted prices, while the restricted estimates use prices only if the matching American prices are also available.

TABLE 6.3 *Means, Standard Deviations, and t-Statistics of the Daily Percentage Changes in the Futures and Forward Prices for Copper*[a]

		American prices	London prices	Converted prices	Restricted converted prices	American prices	London prices	Converted prices	Restricted converted prices
		1/68–12/80				*1/68–12/78*			
Cash or spot contracts	Mean	-0.011	0.010	0.006	-0.021	-0.023	0.012	0.004	-0.037
	Std. dev.	1.793	1.904	1.926	1.895	1.553	1.717	1.726	1.466
	t-stat.	-0.272	0.303	0.164	0.473	-0.574	0.372	0.112	0.939
	Number	1,793	3,216	3,216	1,751	1,440	2,728	2,728	1,413
3-month contracts	Mean	-0.013	0.009	0.005	-0.419	-0.018	0.011	0.003	-0.042
	Std. dev.	1.540	1.879	1.924	1.371	1.445	1.343	1.373	1.267
	t-stat.	-0.322	0.273	0.138	1.176	-0.457	0.427	0.117	1.187
	Number	1,542	3,215	3,136	1,483	1,333	2,727	2,660	1,283
		1/68–12/73							
Cash or spot contracts	Mean	0.032	0.038	0.036	-0.038				
	Std. dev.	1.500	1.863	1.869	1.594				
	t-stat.	0.484	0.781	0.733	0.542				
	Number	519	1,481	1,481	512				
3-month contracts	Mean	-0.013	0.035	0.029	-0.022				
	Std. dev.	1.298	1.271	1.312	1.180				
	t-stat.	0.266	1.051	0.823	0.501				
	Number	745	1,482	1,427	713				

		1/74–12/80				1/74–12/78			
Cash or spot contracts	Mean	−0.029	−0.013	−0.020	−0.014	−0.055	−0.018	−0.034	−0.036
	Std. dev.	1.899	1.939	1.974	2.006	1.582	1.525	1.539	1.389
	t-stat.	0.548	0.288	0.423	0.254	1.049	0.419	0.748	0.773
	Number	1,274	1,735	1,735	1,239	921	1,247	1,247	901
3-month contracts	Mean	−0.013	−0.013	−0.015	−0.060	−0.025	−0.017	−0.026	−0.067
	Std. dev.	1.736	2.274	2.314	1.527	1.634	1.424	1.441	1.369
	t-stat.	0.205	0.236	0.271	1.093	0.375	0.428	0.643	1.165
	Number	797	1,733	1,709	770	588	1,245	1,233	570

a. The percentage price change is defined as $\log(P_t/P_{t-1})*100$. The American prices are cash and futures prices. The London prices are spot and forward prices denominated in pounds sterling. The converted prices are London spot and forward prices converted to dollars. The estimates for the unrestricted series use all of the available converted prices, while the restricted estimates use prices only if the matching American prices are also available.

noticeable when the more volatile 1979 and 1980 prices are included in the sample.[18]

The behavior of the copper price variances through time is also slightly different from the behavior for silver. The standard deviations for the copper and silver price changes are all about 1.5% during the first subperiod. However, the estimates for copper are much lower than the estimates for silver from 1974 through 1980; while silver's variance increases from the first to the second subperiod, copper's variance remains fairly constant. In fact, the standard deviations for copper do not increase unless 1979 and 1980 are added to the sample period.

Autocorrelations for the daily copper and silver price changes are presented in Table 6.4. The autocorrelations for the spot, cash, and 3-month price series are estimated using data from 1968 through 1980, while the autocorrelations for the 6- and 12-month series are estimated from 1974 through 1980. The most striking result in Table 6.4 is that almost all of the first-order autocorrelations are negative and relatively large. Only five of these autocorrelations are within four standard errors of zero. This serial correlation would seem to suggest a profitable trading opportunity; buy on the day after a price drop and sell after a rise. However, it is more likely that the correlation is caused by measurement error than by market inefficiency. For example, suppose the measurement error in today's reported spot price for silver is positive. This introduces a positive bias in today's price change and a negative bias in tomorrow's price change. This pattern would cause a negative first-order autocorrelation in the observed price changes. If the measurement error is negative, the pattern is reversed but the final result is the same. In view of this measurement error hypothesis, it is interesting to note that four of the five smallest first-order autocorrelations are for cash and futures prices.

To summarize the results from Tables 6.2 through 6.4, there are some noticeable differences between the behavior of the futures prices and the behavior of the forward prices. For example, the evidence in Tables 6.2 and 6.3 indicates that, because of the futures price limits, the variance of the observed futures prices is generally lower than the variance of the forward prices. In addition, the first-order autocorrelations in Table 6.4 suggest that the London spot and forward prices contain more measurement error than the American cash and futures prices. The data also indicate that the variability of the daily price changes increases from 1968 to 1980. The silver price volatility appears to grow over the whole sample period. Although the variance of the copper prices is fairly constant from 1968 through 1978, the variances for both commodities increase significantly during the 1979–1980 period.

---

18. In fact, only 3% of the three-month copper futures prices observed from 1968 though 1978 reflect limit moves, while 9% of the prices for 1979 and 1980 are limit moves.

TABLE 6.4   Autocorrelations of the Daily Percent Changes in the Cash, Spot, Futures and Forward Prices for Copper and Silver[a]

	Number	$S(r_1)$	r_1	r_2	r_3	r_4	r_5	r_6
			Silver					
Cash prices	2,364	0.021	0.050	0.008	−0.026	0.018	−0.057	0.036
London spot prices	3,054	0.018	−0.172	−0.025	0.052	0.020	−0.054	−0.035
Converted spot prices	3,054	0.018	−0.170	−0.029	0.048	0.016	−0.052	−0.034
Restricted spot prices	2,213	0.021	−0.216	0.006	0.025	0.037	−0.015	0.013
3-month contracts								
Futures prices	2,081	0.022	−0.111	0.010	−0.044	0.081	−0.083	0.034
London forward prices	3,051	0.018	−0.131	−0.023	0.045	0.026	−0.051	−0.045
Converted forward prices	2,947	0.018	−0.133	−0.028	0.041	0.022	−0.048	−0.037
Restricted forward prices	1,954	0.023	−0.203	−0.021	0.012	0.020	−0.012	0.036
6-month contracts								
Futures prices	1,037	0.031	−0.148	0.020	−0.015	0.028	−0.062	0.005
London forward prices	1,505	0.026	−0.195	−0.045	0.038	0.018	−0.054	−0.043
Converted forward prices	1,467	0.026	−0.195	−0.042	0.026	0.026	−0.059	−0.045
Restricted forward prices	905	0.033	−0.244	0.007	−0.038	0.078	−0.028	−0.019
12-month contracts								
Futures prices	1,057	0.031	−0.018	0.038	−0.015	0.017	−0.043	0.019
London forward prices	1,496	0.026	−0.150	−0.028	0.038	0.034	−0.075	−0.064
Converted forward prices	1,452	0.026	−0.150	−0.028	0.022	0.039	−0.079	−0.058
Restricted forward prices	906	0.033	−0.141	−0.035	0.038	0.035	−0.017	−0.018

160   The Building Blocks of Financial Engineering

TABLE 6.4 *Continued*

	Number	$S(r_1)$	r_1	r_2	r_3	r_4	r_5	r_6
			Copper					
Cash prices	1,636	0.025	-0.023	-0.039	0.042	0.027	0.069	-0.060
London spot prices	3,160	0.018	-0.106	-0.050	0.058	0.015	0.015	0.003
Converted spot prices	3,160	0.018	-0.093	-0.048	0.052	0.015	0.016	0.008
Restricted spot prices	1,585	0.025	-0.137	-0.062	0.054	0.036	0.056	-0.003
3-month contracts								
Futures prices	1,407	0.027	-0.064	-0.039	0.007	0.001	0.081	-0.058
London forward prices	3,158	0.018	-0.192	-0.020	-0.013	0.064	0.005	0.018
Converted forward prices	3,043	0.018	-0.188	-0.024	-0.020	0.056	0.009	0.019
Restricted forward prices	1,329	0.027	-0.053	-0.057	0.048	0.064	0.061	-0.056

a. r_τ is the autocorrelation at lag τ; $S(r_1)$ is the standard error of the first-order correlation. The cash, spot, and 3-month autocorrelations are estimated from 1/68 to 12/80. The 6- and 12-month autocorrelations are estimated from 1/74 to 12/80. The converted prices are London spot and forward prices converted to dollars. The estimates for the unrestricted series use all of the available converted prices, while the restricted estimates use the converted prices only if the matching American prices are also available.

3.3. The Differences between Futures and Forward Prices and Tests of the Cox–Ingersoll–Ross Propositions

The simplest way to examine whether there is an empirically relevant difference between futures and forward prices is to compare them individually. Table 6.5 summarizes the percentage differences between matching futures and forward prices, defined as $\log[F(t, T)/f(t, T)] * 100$, for both copper and silver. These differences are measured at 3 months to maturity for the copper contracts and at 3, 6, and 12 months to maturity for the silver contracts. Since the futures contracts mature at monthly intervals, this process generates monthly observations.[19] For example, the January price difference for the 3-month silver series reflects futures and forward contracts that mature in April, while the February difference involves contracts that mature in May. The forward prices in Table 6.5 (and in the tests below) are converted from pounds sterling to dollars using three different estimates of the basis differential for each commodity. The forward prices in the 1968–1980 comparisons are converted using the full-period estimates of the basis differential. The conversions for the subperiod tests use the basis differential estimated over the matching subperiod.

The futures–forward price differences for silver in Table 6.5 indicate that, on average, the futures prices are larger than the forward prices. Four of the five estimates are significantly positive at the 5% level. Moreover, the difference between the futures and forward prices increases with the maturity of the contract; the average differences from 1974 through 1980 are about 0.1%, 0.4%, and 0.8% for the 3-, 6-, and 12-month contracts, respectively.

The relation between the futures and forward prices for copper is less clear-cut. It appears that the futures prices are lower than the forward prices during the first subperiod and higher than the forward prices during the second subperiod; the average price differences are −0.9% and 0.1%, respectively. However, the t-statistics for these estimates are only 1.55 and 0.21.[20]

Table 6.5 also contains some evidence about two of the propositions developed by Cox, Ingersoll, and Ross (1981). They hypothesize that the futures–forward price difference is equal to

$$F(t, T) - f(t, T) = -PV_{t, T} \left\{ \int_t^T \tilde{F}(w, T) \, \text{cov}[\tilde{F}(w, T), \tilde{B}(w, T)] \, dw \right\} \bigg/ B(t, T) \tag{6.16}$$

---

19. Futures contracts do not mature every month, so some months will not be represented in these series.

20. It is interesting that, although the average price difference for the second subperiod is positive, the t-statistic for the average difference of the full period, −1.68, is more negative than the t-statistic for the first subperiod, −1.55. This happens because different estimates of the basis differential are used for the full sample period and for each subperiod.

TABLE 6.5 *Futures-Forward Price Differences and Tests of the Cox-Ingersoll-Ross Propositions* [a]

		log(fut/for)*100	cov(F, B)	var(B) − cov(P, B)
		1968–1980		
3-month	Mean	0.297	0.231	0.803
silver	Std. dev.	1.325	1.917	4.203
	t-stat.	2.372	0.889	1.319
	Number	112	140	154
3-month	Mean	−0.701	0.371	0.158
copper	Std. dev.	3.744	1.442	0.843
	t-stat.	1.685	2.556	1.506
	Number	81	127	154
		1968–1973		
3-month	Mean	0.485	0.139	0.110
silver	Std. dev.	1.332	0.530	0.795
	t-stat.	2.651	1.193	0.653
	Number	53	68	70
3-month	Mean	−0.861	0.189	0.008
copper	Std. dev.	3.464	0.734	0.310
	t-stat.	1.552	1.195	0.150
	Number	39	56	70
		1974–1980		
3-month	Mean	0.136	0.318	1.380
silver	Std. dev.	1.325	2.630	5.595
	t-stat.	0.788	0.648	1.267
	Number	59	72	84
6-month	Mean	0.444	0.019	1.543
silver	Std. dev.	1.489	2.338	4.985
	t-stat.	2.251	0.041	1.369
	Number	57	63	84
12-month	Mean	0.846	−1.945	2.187
silver	Std. dev.	1.678	5.240	4.038
	t-stat.	3.670	1.533	2.294
	Number	53	72	79
3-month	Mean	0.109	0.515	0.283
copper	Std. dev.	3.325	1.808	1.094
	t-stat.	0.212	2.347	1.556
	Number	42	71	84

a. Under the first CIR proposition, if the covariance between the daily percentage change in the futures price and the daily percentage change in the bond price is positive, the futures-forward price difference should be negative. If the covariance is negative, the price difference should be positive. Under the second CIR proposition, if the bond price variance is larger than its covariance with the spot price, the futures-forward price difference should be positive. If the variance-covariance difference is negative, the price difference should also be negative. The t-statistics for the covariances and the variance-covariance differences are adjusted for serial correlation.

where $\text{cov}[\tilde{F}(w, T), \tilde{B}(w, T)]$ is the local covariance at time w between the percentage change in the futures price and the percentage change in the bond price. This instantaneous covariance may be changing stochastically as the futures contract and the bond contract move toward maturity at time T. However, if the covariance is always positive during the contract period, the integral in Equation 6.16 will be positive and the forward price should be higher than the futures price. On the other hand, if the local covariance is always negative, the futures price should be above the forward price.

Cox, Ingersoll, and Ross (CIR) also show that the futures–forward price difference can be expressed as

$$F(t, T) - f(t, T) = PV_{t, T} \left\{ \exp\left[\int_t^T \tilde{r}(w)\, dw \right] \int_t^T [\tilde{P}(w)/\tilde{B}(w, T)] \right.$$
$$\left. \times \{\text{var}[\tilde{B}(w, T)] - \text{cov}[\tilde{P}(w), \tilde{B}(w, T)]\}\, dw \right\} \quad (6.17)$$

if the commodity is stored costlessly over the contract period. This leads to the prediction that, if the local variance of the bond price is always larger than the local covariance between the spot price and the bond price, the futures price will be above the forward price. If the variance is smaller than the covariance, the futures price should be below the forward price.

The simplest way to test these hypotheses is to assume that the local variances and covariances are constant and the same for all contracts.[21] Under this assumption the local covariance in Equation 6.16 is measured in two steps. First, the covariance between the daily percentage change in the futures price and the daily percentage change in the bond price is estimated for each pair of futures and forward contracts. These covariances are then averaged across contracts. The local variances and covariances in Equation 6.17 are estimated in the same way. The results of this process are reported in the second and third columns of Table 6.5.[22]

---

21. This assumption cannot be strictly true since the local variances and covariances must converge to zero as the contracts approach maturity and the bond prices converge to one. However, estimates of the variances and covariances measured over the full contract period can be used to predict whether the relevant integrals are positive or negative. For example if the futures price is roughly constant, the average covariance between the futures price and the bond price is approximately proportional to the integral in Equation 6.16.

22. All of the variances and covariances in Table 6.5 have been multiplied by 10^6. The bond prices used to estimate these variables are measured by the 3-, 6-, and 12-month Treasury bill prices provided by the Federal Reserve Bank of New York and Data Resources, Inc. For example, when a futures contract has 12, 11, or 10 months to maturity, its daily price changes are compared with the price changes for Treasury bills that will mature in approximately 12 months. When the futures contract has between 9 and 5 months to maturity, the 6-month Treasury bill series is used. The 3-month bills are used during the last four months of the contract period. A 1-month Treasury bill series is also available, but its bid/ask spread is very large. For example, the average daily spread from 1973 through 1980 is 0.32%. The average daily bid/ask spread for the 3-month series over this period is 0.025%.

Under the first CIR proposition, if the covariance between the bond prices and the futures prices is positive the futures–forward price difference should be negative. The results in Table 6.5 provide some support for this hypothesis. For example, the average covariance for copper from 1968 through 1980 is 0.37, with a t-statistic of 2.56.[23] Using the CIR model, this implies that the futures prices will be below the forward prices. The average price difference of -0.7% is consistent with this prediction. The results for 12-month silver contracts also support the CIR hypothesis; the average covariance from 1974 through 1980 is -1.9, and, as the model predicts, the average futures–forward price difference is significantly positive. Unfortunately, the other comparisons do not provide much evidence. All but one of the other average covariances are approximately zero. The estimated covariance for 3-month copper contracts from 1974 through 1980 is significantly positive. However, since the t-statistic for the average futures–forward price difference for these contracts is only 0.21, one cannot reject the hypothesis that the true difference is negative, as the model predicts.

The results in Table 6.5 provide more support for the second CIR proposition. Under this hypothesis, a positive difference between the variance of the bond prices and the covariance of the bond and spot prices should be associated with a positive difference between the futures and forward prices. The estimates for silver are all consistent with this model. For example, the average variance–covariance difference for 12-month silver contracts is 2.2, with a t-statistic of 2.29, and, as the model predicts, the price difference is significantly positive. Only the negative price differences for copper do not support the model.

The evidence in Table 6.5 indicates that the average differences between the observed futures and forward prices are consistent with the CIR propositions. These propositions may also help to explain variations among the futures–forward price differences. For example, if the covariance between futures prices and bond prices in Equation 6.16 is not constant across contracts, changes in this covariance should be related to changes in the price differences. To examine this hypothesis, the covariance is estimated over each 3-, 6-, and 12-month contract period. Then the futures contracts (and the matching forward contracts) are divided into two groups. Contracts with negative estimated covariances are assigned to one group, while those with positive estimates are assigned to the other. Under the null hypothesis, the futures prices for the first group should be larger than the matching forward prices. In the second group, the futures prices should be below the forward prices.

---

23. The t-statistics for the covariances and the variance–covariance differences are adjusted to reflect the serial correlation caused by the overlapping estimation periods.

The first half of Table 6.6 describes the results of this segmentation. The 3-month contracts in this table are compared over the full 1968–1980 sample period, while the 6- and 12-month contracts are compared from 1974 through 1980.[24] In general, the covariances are not useful in discriminating among the price differences. The comparisons between the two groups are randomly distributed about zero. For example, three of the four *t*-statistics comparing the two groups are between −0.3 and 0.3 and none is larger than 1.2.[25]

The second CIR proposition can be tested in the same way. First, the variance of the percentage change in the bond price and the covariance between the percentage change in the bond price and the percentage change in the spot price are estimated over the life of each pair of futures and forward contracts. Then the contracts are sorted into two groups. If the bond price variance is larger than the covariance between the bond and spot prices, the futures and forward contracts are assigned to the first group. If this difference is negative, the contracts are assigned to the second group. Using the CIR model, the futures–forward price differences should be positive in the first group and negative in the second.

The results of this stratification process are summarized in the second half of Table 6.6. Again, the 3-month contracts are compared over the full 1968–1980 sample period, while the 6- and 12-month contracts are compared from 1974 through 1980. The results in Table 6.6 do not provide any support for the second CIR hypothesis. For example, although the model predicts that the price difference should be negative when the variance is smaller than the covariance, three of the four differences for the second group are positive. Moreover, although the average difference for the first group should be larger than the average for the second group, the comparisons between the groups are distributed randomly about zero.[26]

Although the results in Table 6.6 do not support the CIR propositions, they are not as inconsistent with the models as they seem. First, the tests

---

24. To be included in the sample, each pair of contracts must have a futures price and a converted forward price available on the contracting date described in Footnote 10. In addition, there must be at least 10 days of futures and bond price data available during each month of the contracts' life.

25. Two other methods for stratifying the sample were also tried. One approach assigns contracts to the two groups only if the correlation between the bond and futures prices is significantly different from zero. The second method only assigns those contracts whose monthly covariances are either all positive or all negative. The results using these stratification techniques are similar to those reported.

26. A second stratification technique was also tried. If the difference between the variance and the covariance is positive in each month during the estimation period, the contract pair is assigned to the first group. If this difference is negative during each month, the contracts are assigned to the second group. All other futures–forward pairs are dropped from the sample. There is no discernible difference between the futures–forward prices differences for these two groups.

TABLE 6.6 Futures–Forward Price Differences Sorted by Covariances and Variance–Covariance Differences[a]

		cov(F,B)<0	cov(F,B)>0	Difference	var(B)>cov(P,B)	var(B)<cov(P,B)	Difference
3-month silver	Mean	0.328	0.270	0.058	0.363	0.236	0.127
	Std. dev.	1.097	1.522	0.260	1.119	1.499	0.251
	t-stat.	2.071	1.374	0.225	2.384	1.199	0.508
	Number	48	60	108	54	58	112
6-month silver	Mean	0.380	0.496	-0.116	0.459	0.434	0.025
	Std. dev.	1.114	2.041	0.430	1.348	1.589	0.405
	t-stat.	1.930	1.114	-0.270	1.597	1.616	0.062
	Number	32	21	53	22	35	57
12-month silver	Mean	0.662	1.255	-0.594	0.605	0.925	-0.319
	Std. dev.	1.226	2.405	0.508	1.579	1.721	0.536
	t-stat.	3.149	2.152	-1.169	1.381	3.399	-0.596
	Number	34	17	51	13	40	53
3-month copper	Mean	-0.591	-0.775	0.185	-0.661	-0.729	0.068
	Std. dev.	4.358	3.364	0.863	3.881	3.688	0.847
	t-stat.	-0.779	-1.563	0.214	-0.978	-1.369	0.080
	Number	33	46	79	33	48	81

a. Under the first CIR proposition, the futures–forward price difference should be positive if the covariance between the bond prices and the futures prices is negative, and it should be negative if the covariance is positive. The difference between the two groups should be positive. Under the second CIR proposition, if the variance of the bond price changes is larger than the covariance between the bond price changes and the spot price changes, the futures–forward price differences should be positive. If the variance is less than the covariance, the price difference should be negative. The difference between the two groups should be positive.

involving the 3-, 6-, and 12-month silver contracts are not independent. For example, the variance–covariance difference for the 6-month contract that matures in June is estimated with bond and spot prices from January through June, while the estimate of the difference for the 3-month June contracts uses the same data during April, May, and June. A more important problem arises because the models imply that the futures–forward price differences are related to the market's expectations of the relevant variances and covariances; these expectations are unobservable. The tests in Table 6.6 use estimates of the realized variances and covariances as proxies for the market's expectations. Since these proxies contain measurement error, many of the price pairs may be assigned to the wrong group in Table 6.6. This could mask the true relation between the price differences and the expected variances and covariances.

The Cox, Ingersoll, and Ross models make several other predictions that may be less sensitive to these measurement error problems. For example, if the local correlation between futures price changes and bond price changes is constant, the first CIR proposition implies that the absolute value of the futures–forward price difference is an increasing function of the market's expectation of both the futures price variance and the bond price variance. Analogously, the second proposition implies that the price difference is a decreasing function of the spot price variance if the price difference is negative and if the local correlation between the spot and bond prices is constant.

As Cox, Ingersoll, and Ross demonstrate, their second proposition can be re-expressed as

$$F(t, T) - f(t, T) = -PV_t \left\{ \exp\left[\int_t^T \tilde{r}(w)\, dw\right] \int_t^T \tilde{f}(w, T) \right.$$
$$\left. \times \text{cov}[\tilde{f}(w, T), \tilde{B}(w, T)]\, dw \right\} \qquad (6.18)$$

This leads to one more prediction; if the local correlation between the forward price and the bond price is constant, the absolute value of the futures–forward price difference is an increasing function of the market's expectation of the forward price variance.

To test these predictions, the variances of the relevant variables are regressed against the futures–forward price differences. These variances are estimated over the life of the matching contracts.[27] For example, each futures price variance is computed using the daily price changes for an individual futures contract as it approaches maturity. The bond price variances are measured in two different ways. Under the first approach, which is also used for the forward prices, the variances for the 3-, 6-, and 12-month regressions

---

27. These tests have been replicated using variances estimated over the period immediately before the contract date. The results from the two sets of variances are very similar.

are estimated using the matching 3-, 6-, and 12-month price series. Under the second approach, the bond price variances are estimated by the variance of the percentage changes in the daily federal funds return during each contract period.[28]

Table 6.7 presents regressions of these variances against the futures–forward price differences.[29] The 3-month regressions in this table are estimated over the full 1968–1980 sample period. The 6- and 12-month regressions are estimated from 1974 through 1980.

The results in Table 6.7 are similar to the results in Table 6.6; although they are consistent with the CIR propositions, they do not provide much support for these propositions. For example, the models imply that the absolute value of the price differences will increase with the variance of the futures, forward, and bond prices. Since the futures price is generally above the forward price for silver, this means that the slope coefficient in the silver regressions involving these variances should be positive. On the other hand, the price differences for copper are usually negative. Therefore, the slope coefficients for all of the copper regressions – including the spot price regression – should be negative. In fact, the estimates appear to be randomly distributed about zero.[30] These results are particularly ambiguous because only two of the twenty estimates are significantly different from zero. The results in Table 6.7 neither support nor refute the CIR propositions.[31]

It appears that the Cox, Ingersoll, and Ross propositions are useful in describing the average differences between futures and forward prices. However, without better estimates of the market's expectations of the relevant variances and covariances, neither hypothesis is able to discriminate among the individual differences.

---

28. The federal funds returns are provided by the Federal Reserve Bank of New York.

29. The regressions in Table 6.7 suffer from at least two econometric problems. First, the error terms are serially correlated and, second, each futures–forward price difference may be correlated with the previous error terms. Generalized least squares (GLS) is usually used to solve the first problem. However, as Hansen and Hodrick (1980) demonstrate, GLS would lead to inconsistent estimates in this case. Fortunately, the ordinary least squares estimators (OLS) in Table 6.7 are consistent and asymptotically normal [see Hansen (1980)]. The usual estimated covariance matrix for the OLS coefficients, appropriately modified to reflect the serial correlation in the error terms, provides a consistent estimate of the covariance matrix of the asymptotic distribution; writing the regressions in Table 6.7 in matrix notation, $Y = X\gamma + e$, the estimated covariance matrix for the OLS coefficients is $\hat{\Sigma} = (X'X)^{-1}X'\hat{\Omega}X(X'X)^{-1}$, where $\hat{\Omega}$ is the estimated covariance matrix for the error terms. The standard errors in Table 6.7 are based on this estimated covariance matrix.

30. These regressions have also been estimated using the absolute value of the futures–forward price differences. The coefficients in these regressions are very similar to the estimates reported in Table 6.7.

31. Part of this ambiguity may be caused by measurement errors in the observed futures–forward price differences. The effect of these measurement errors is discussed in the next section.

TABLE 6.7 Regressions of Variances against Futures–Forward Price Differences[a]

	Number	Intercept	Slope	R^2	Number	Intercept	Slope	R^2
	Treasury Bill Prices				*Federal Funds Returns*			
3-month silver	112	0.007 (3.893)	0.018 (0.176)	0.00	112	0.744 (5.440)	−17.733 (2.535)	0.07
6-month silver	57	0.026 (2.544)	0.139 (0.459)	0.00	57	0.339 (2.312)	2.587 (0.746)	0.01
12-month silver	51	0.102 (1.923)	−0.150 (0.087)	0.00	51	0.250 (1.961)	5.517 (1.430)	0.04
3-month copper	81	0.011 (3.598)	0.051 (0.653)	0.01	81	0.621 (4.712)	−11.520 (3.522)	0.21
	Futures Prices				*Converted Forward Prices*			
3-month silver	86	0.036 (5.348)	0.335 (0.814)	0.01	90	0.270 (1.325)	−0.712 (0.062)	0.00
6-month silver	55	0.037 (2.990)	0.361 (1.006)	0.01	56	0.132 (2.527)	−0.373 (0.269)	0.00
12-month silver	54	0.042 (1.996)	0.826 (0.981)	0.10	51	0.118 (2.407)	−1.943 (1.187)	0.02
3-month copper	73	0.031 (6.953)	−0.110 (0.977)	0.02	63	0.618 (1.043)	11.655 (0.731)	0.01

TABLE 6.7 *Continued*

	Number	Intercept	Slope	R^2
		Converted Spot Prices		
3-month silver	111	0.266 (1.604)	0.368 (0.040)	0.00
6-month silver	57	0.440 (1.298)	0.800 (0.084)	0.00
12-month silver	51	0.445 (1.440)	−6.554 (0.663)	0.01
3-month copper	80	0.031 (3.840)	−0.275 (1.424)	0.04

a. The dependent variable in these regressions is the variance of the indicated variable, estimated over the contract period. The independent variable is the percentage difference between the futures price and the converted forward price. The *t*-statistics, adjusted for the serial correlation caused by the overlapping estimation periods, are in parentheses.

3.4. Futures–Forward Price Differences and Interest Rate Differences

The models in Section 2 imply that the difference between futures and forward prices should be related to the difference between short- and long-term interest rates. In fact, if the marginal utility of the commodity, $\tilde{P}(T)\tilde{\lambda}(T)$, is assumed to be independent of the nominal interest rate,[32] Equations 6.8 and 6.10 can be used to write the ratio of the futures and forward prices as

$$F(t, T)/f(t, T) = E_t\left\{\exp\left[\sum_{\tau=t}^{T-1} \tilde{R}(\tau, \tau+1)\right]\right\} \Big/ \exp[(T-t)R(t, T)] \qquad (6.19)$$

The ratio of the futures price and the forward price should equal the ratio of the expected gross return from rolling over one-day bonds and the gross return from investing in a $(T-t)$ day bond.

Since the expected return from rolling over one-day bonds is unobservable, the prediction in Equation 6.19 cannot be tested directly. One alternative is to use the actual return, which is observed at time T,

$$\frac{F(t, T)}{f(t, T)} = \exp\left[\sum_{\tau=t}^{T-1} R(\tau, \tau+1) - \epsilon(t, T)\right] \Big/ \exp[(T-t)R(t, T)] \qquad (6.20)$$

In this expression, $\epsilon(t, T)$ is equal to the market's error in forecasting the cumulated one-day returns. Equation 6.20 can be tested by estimating the regression

$$\sum_{\tau=t}^{T-1} R(\tau, \tau+1) - (T-t)R(t, T) = \alpha + \beta \log[F(t, T)/f(t, T)] + \epsilon(t, T) \qquad (6.21)$$

Table 6.8 presents ordinary least squares (OLS) estimates of this regression for copper and silver.[33] Under the null hypothesis, the intercept should equal zero and the slope should equal one. This hypothesis can be rejected for all of the regressions summarized in Table 6.8. Although most of the estimates of α are not significantly different from zero, all of the estimates of β are quite significantly different from one. For example, the largest slope coefficient is estimated for the 3-month silver price regression from 1974

---

32. The following set of conditions is sufficient for this assumption to hold:
    1. The price of some commodity (commodity N) is independent of the marginal utility of all commodities.
    2. The expected value of the continuously compounded real rate of return on nominal bonds is constant. This real rate is defined in terms of commodity N.
33. The regressions in Table 6.8 suffer from the same econometric problems as the regressions in Table 6.7. These problems are discussed in Footnote 29.

The one-day bond returns used to estimate the regressions in Table 6.8 are measured by the overnight federal funds rate. The long-term interest rates — with maturities of 3, 6, and 12 months — are measured by the return on U.S. Treasury bills.

TABLE 6.8 *Regressions of Interest Rate Differences on Futures–Forward Price Differences* [a]

	Number	Intercept	Slope	R^2
		3-Month Silver		
1/68–12/80	110	0.031	0.035	0.03
		(0.045)	(0.022)	
1/68–12/73	53	0.109	0.002	0.00
		(0.063)	(0.029)	
1/74–12/80	57	−0.033	0.058	0.09
		(0.057)	(0.029)	
		6-Month Silver		
1/74–12/80	57	−0.128	0.006	0.00
		(0.133)	(0.048)	
		12-Month Silver		
1/74–12/80	53	−0.034	0.001	0.00
		(0.167)	(0.055)	
		3-Month Copper		
1/68–12/80	79	0.050	−0.028	0.12
		(0.047)	(0.011)	
1/68–12/73	39	−0.019	−0.043	0.27
		(0.067)	(0.015)	
1/74–12/80	40	0.077	−0.022	0.05
		(0.073)	(0.019)	

a. The dependent variable in this regression is the cumulated one-day federal funds interest rate minus the Treasury bill interest rate over the contract period. The independent variable is the percentage difference between the futures price and the converted forward price. Under the null hypothesis, the intercept should be zero and the slope coefficient should be one. The asymptotic standard errors are in parentheses.

through 1980. The value of this coefficient is 0.058 and it has a standard error of 0.029. In other words, the largest estimate of β is more than 30 standard errors below one. The values of F-statistics testing the joint hypothesis that α equals zero and β equals one are over 50 for all of the regressions.

The evidence in Table 6.8 indicates that the observed differences between the short- and long-term interest rates are not useful in explaining the observed differences between the futures and forward prices. However, these results do not necessarily imply that the underlying model is wrong. Instead, they may be caused by measurement errors in the observed price differences. For example, each day's forward prices are recorded in London about five hours before the futures prices are recorded in America. Many of the largest positive and negative price differences are probably caused by information that arrives after the London market closes but before the American markets do. These measurement errors in the price differences bias the slope coefficients in Table 6.8 toward zero. This problem is particularly troublesome because, under the null hypothesis, the variation in the true, unobserved price differences is probably small relative to the variance of the measurement errors.[34]

4. Summary and Conclusions

This paper uses the pricing models of Cox, Ingersoll, and Ross (1981), Richard and Sundaresan (1981), and French (1982) to examine the relation between futures and forward prices for copper and silver. There are significant differences between these prices. The average differences are generally consistent with the predictions of both arbitrage and utility-based models. However, these models are not helpful in explaining intrasample variations in the futures–forward price differences.

There are several possible reasons why the futures and forward price models do not help in discriminating among the price differences. The most obvious explanation is that the models are incomplete. For example, the models abstract from market imperfections such as taxes and transactions costs. If these factors play an important role in determining the futures and forward prices, one may observe differences in these prices that are unrelated to the factors examined here.

An alternative interpretation of the evidence in this paper says that the theoretical models do describe the underlying price differences, but, because of measurement errors, the models are not useful in discriminating among the observed differences. Under this hypothesis, the models fail to capture movements in the observed price differences because measurement errors mask the variations in the true price differences. However, the models correctly predict the average observed price differences because aggregating across contracts reduces the effect of measurement errors.

These measurement errors take two forms. First, the futures–forward price differences are measured with error. For example, the individual prices are only recorded in discrete steps, such as eighths of a dollar or tenths of a pound. Also, the prices in each pair are not matched precisely. This problem is especially acute because the forward prices are observed in London and the futures prices are observed approximately five hours later in New York

---

34. Ignoring the econometric problems discussed in Footnote 29, the probability limit of the estimated slope coefficient is equal to plim $\hat{\beta} = \beta / [1 + \sigma_u^2 / \sigma_x^2]$, where σ_u^2 is the variance of the measurement errors and σ_x^2 is the variance of the true price differences. Therefore, the bias in the slope coefficient increases as the relative variance of the measurement errors increases.

and Chicago. These errors in measuring the futures–forward price differences can have a particularly large effect if the variation in the true price differences is small.

A second type of measurement error arises because all of the predictions involve variables that must be estimated. The tests involving the Cox, Ingersoll, and Ross predictions provide good examples of this problem. The CIR propositions indicate that the futures–forward price differences should be related to the market's expectations of local variances and covariances. However, neither these expectations nor the realized values of the variables are observable. Although several approaches are used to estimate the variances and covariances, none of them is powerful enough to discriminate among the various price differences.

Earlier studies of the empirical relation between futures and forward prices do not provide much help in determining if the results reported here are caused by problems with the theoretical models or by problems with the data. Several papers have been written comparing the prices for Treasury bill futures contracts with the forward prices implied by the interest rates on Treasury bills traded in the spot market.[35] The evidence in these papers indicates that, on average, the futures prices for contracts with approximately four or more months to maturity are significantly lower than the matching forward prices. As the contracts approach maturity, this relation is reversed; the implied forward prices tend to be lower than the matching futures prices. Cornell and Reinganum (1981) compare futures and forward prices for foreign exchange contracts. Although they observe differences between individual prices, they find that the average difference is not significantly different from zero. Unfortunately, none of these papers examines the relation between the observed price differences and the theoretical models studied here. More tests are needed to support or reject these models.

The results in this paper have important implications for other research. Most commodity exchanges in the United States trade futures contracts. However, since forward contracts are easier to analyze, many economists treat the observed prices as though they were forward prices. This simplification can be misleading. The studies comparing the futures prices and implied forward prices for Treasury bills provide a good example of the problems this may cause. The authors of many of these studies claim that the futures prices should equal the forward prices implied in the spot market. When they observe differences between these prices, they interpret this as evidence of market inefficiency. The results in this paper suggest that these price differences may actually be caused by differences between futures and forward contracts.

---

35. See, for example, Puglisi (1978), Capozza and Cornell (1979), Rendleman and Carabini (1979), and Vignola and Dale (1980).

References

Bartlett, M. S. 1946. On the theoretical specification of sampling properties of auto-correlated time series. *Journal of the Royal Statistical Society (Suppl.)* 8, 27–41.

Black, F. 1976. The pricing of commodity contracts. *Journal of Financial Economics* 3, Jan./March, 167–179.

Capozza, D., and B. Cornell. 1979. Treasury bill pricing in the spot and futures markets. *Review of Economics and Statistics* 61, Nov., 513–520.

Cornell, B., and M. Reinganum. 1981. Forward and futures prices: Evidence from the foreign exchange markets. *Journal of Finance* 36, Dec., 1035–1045.

Cox, J., J. Ingersoll, and S. Ross. 1977. A theory of the term structure of interest rates and the valuation of interest-dependent claims. Working paper (Graduate School of Business, Stanford University, Stanford, CA).

Cox, J., J. Ingersoll, and S. Ross. 1981. The relation between forward prices and futures prices. *Journal of Financial Economics* 9, Dec., 321–346.

Dusak, K. 1973. Futures trading and investor returns: An investigation of commodity market risk premiums. *Journal of Political Economy* 81, Nov./Dec., 1387–1406.

French, K. R. 1982. The pricing of futures and forward contracts. Ph.D. dissertation (University of Rochester, Rochester, NY).

Grauer, F. 1977. Equilibrium in commodity futures markets: Theory and tests. Ph.D. dissertation (Stanford University, Stanford, CA).

Grauer, F., and R. Litzenberger. 1979. The pricing of commodity futures contracts, nominal bonds and other risky assets under commodity price uncertainty. *Journal of Finance* 34, March, 69–83.

Hansen, L., 1980. Large sample properties of generalized method of moments estimators. Working paper (Graduate School of Industrial Administration, Carnegie-Mellon University, Pittsburgh, PA).

Hansen, L., and R. Hodrick. 1980. Forward exchange rates as optimal predictors of future spot rates: An econometric analysis. *Journal of Political Economy* 88, Oct., 829–853.

Jarrow, R., and G. Oldfield. 1981. Forward contracts and futures contracts. *Journal of Financial Economics* 9, Dec., 373–382.

Levich, R., and L. White. 1981. Price controls and futures contracts: An examination of the markets for copper and silver during 1971–1974. Working paper (Center for the Study of Futures Markets, Columbia Business School, New York, NY).

Margrabe, W. 1976. A theory of forward and futures prices. Working paper (The Wharton School, University of Pennsylvania, Philadelphia, PA).

Puglisi, D. 1978. Is the futures market for treasury bills efficient? *Journal of Portfolio Management* 4, Winter, 64–67.

Rendleman, R., and C. Carabini. 1979. The efficiency of the treasury bill futures market. *Journal of Finance* 39, Sept., 895–914.

Richard, S. F., and M. Sundaresan. 1981. A continuous time equilibrium model of forward prices and futures prices in a multigood economy. *Journal of Financial Economics* 9, 347–372.

Vignola, A., and C. Dale. 1980. The efficiency of the treasury bill futures market: An analysis of alternative specifications. *Journal of Financial Research* 3, Fall, 169–188.

7

The Quality Option and Timing Option in Futures Contracts

*Phelim P. Boyle**

Often in futures contracts, the short position has some flexibility with regard to when, where, how much, and what will be delivered. These flexibilities have been described as the timing option, the location option, the quantity option, and the quality option. There are many examples of such delivery options in traded futures contracts. For example, the Treasury Bond Futures Contract traded on the Chicago Board of Trade permits the short to deliver any one of a predefined set of long-term government bonds. The wheat futures contract on the same exchange permits the short position to deliver any one of eleven different types of wheat at either Chicago or Toledo at any time during the delivery month. These delivery options have attracted considerable research interest[1] in the last few years. The basic intuition is that

*The author thanks Gord Willmot for very helpful suggestions. He is also grateful to Eric Kirzner, George Blazenko, Len Eckel, Tony Atkinson, Bill Scott, Duane Kennedy, and Keith Sharp for useful comments. He is grateful to Mark Rubinstein for helpful suggestions and acknowledges the useful comments of an anonymous referee and the editor of this Journal. An earlier version of this paper was presented at the Research Seminar of the Canadian International Futures Conference in Toronto. Research support from the Canadian Securities Institute, the Centre for Accounting Research and Education at the University of Waterloo, and the Natural Sciences and Engineering Research Council of Canada is gratefully acknowledged.
1. Contributions to this literature include Arak and Goodman [2], Benninga and Smirlock [3], Cheng [5, 6], Garbade and Silber [9], Gay and Manaster [10, 11], Hegde [12, 13], Hemler [14], Kamara and Siegel [17], Kane and Marcus [18, 19], Kilcollin [20], Livingston [21], and Margrabe [23].

these options, which are available to the seller, are reflected in a somewhat lower futures price.

The aim of the present paper is to develop a procedure for computing the impact of the quality option when there are several deliverable assets. In addition, we analyze the timing option and explore its interaction with the quality option. This interaction between these two types of options may be of interest. We show that if there is only one deliverable asset, then the short position should optimally deliver this asset at the first available opportunity. When there is more than one deliverable asset, delivery at the first permitted opportunity need no longer be optimal.

Section I describes the approach used to value the quality option when there are several deliverable assets. We show how known results concerning order statistics of the multivariate normal can be used to obtain accurate numerical estimates of the value of the quality option. Some specimen numerical results are given to illustrate how the number of deliverable assets affects the futures price of the contract. We also illustrate the sensitivity of the value of the quality option to the correlation among the prices of the deliverable assets.

Section II of the paper uses arbitrage arguments to analyze the timing option when there is just one deliverable asset. In this case, the optimal strategy for the short is to deliver at the first permitted opportunity. The interaction between the timing option and the quality option is probed. We assume that the short position can select any time within a given period to deliver either of two deliverable assets. Arbitrage arguments are used to develop inequalities that illustrate the interaction. In addition, numerical estimates are derived that suggest that the value of the timing option is quite small for plausible parameter values.

I. Quality Option with n Deliverable Assets

We first describe our basic notation and assumptions. In the one asset case, it is well known that a long forward contract is equivalent to a long call and a short put. The generalization of this result to the n asset case plays an important role in the development of our method for the valuation of a futures contract when the short position has a quality option.

Assumptions.   We assume perfect frictionless markets. We assume a known constant interest rate of R percent per annum so that futures prices are equal to the corresponding forward prices.[2]

---

2. This assumption is often made in discussions of the quality option. Hence, we will use the terms forward price and futures price interchangeably in the sequel. For a discussion of the

It is assumed that there are n deliverable assets, the prices of which follow a multivariate lognormal distribution. When the futures contract matures, we assume that the short will deliver the cheapest of the n assets at that time.

Notation.   We use the following notation:

- t: current time.
- $t+T$: delivery date under futures (forward) contract.
- $A_i(t)$: current price of asset, i, $1 \le i \le n$.
- $[\sigma_{ij}T]$: variance-covariance matrix of asset returns over any time interval, T. The variables

$$\log_c \left[\frac{A_i(t+T)}{A_i(t)} \right]$$

  have a multivariate normal distribution with variance covariance matrix $[\sigma_{ij}T]$. Instead of σ_{ij}, we sometimes use $\sigma_i \sigma_j \rho_{ij}$.

- K: strike price of European options (both call and put).
- $F(t, [A_1, ..., A_n], (t+T))$: forward (futures) price at time t of contract where short can deliver any one of assets $1, ..., n$.
- $EC[t, [A_1, ..., A_n], K, (t+T)]$: price of a European call option at time t on the minimum of the n assets, with a strike price of K and an expiration date of $(t+T)$. At maturity, the value of this call is

$$\max[[\min(A_1, A_2, ..., A_n) - K], 0]$$

- $EP[t, [A_1, A_2, ..., A_n], K, (t+T)]$: current price at time t of a European put option on the minimum of the n assets, with strike price K and expiration date $(t+T)$. The value of this option at expiration is

$$\max[[K - \min(A_1, A_2, ..., A_n)], 0]$$

To motivate the n-dimensional case, it may be helpful to start with the one- and two-dimensional cases. Note that when there is just one deliverable asset (with delivery date $(t+T)$), we can replicate a long forward contract to purchase one unit of the underlying asset with a portfolio consisting of a long European call option and a short European put option on one unit of the same underlying asset. In this case, both option contracts expire at $(t+T)$, and the exercise price of each option is equal to the equilibrium forward price. This can be written as

$$VF(t, [A_1], F, (t+T)) = EC[t, [A_1], F, (t+T)]$$
$$-EP[t, [A_1], F, (t+T)] \qquad (7.1)$$

---

relationship between forward and futures prices, see Cox, Ingersoll, and Ross [7], Jarrow and Oldfield [15], and Richard and Sundaresan [25].

where $VF(t, [A_1], F, (t+T))$ is the current value of the forward contract at time t and $F = F(t, [A_1], (t+T))$ is the forward price.

At inception, the value of the forward contract is zero, and so in this case the call option value is equal to the value of the put option. In fact, one method of deriving the forward price in this case would be to find the exercise price that made the two options have the same value.[3] We recall from the put-call parity theorem that the option portfolio on the right-hand side of Equation 7.1 is equal in value to

$$A_1(t) - F \exp(-RT)$$

Since this is zero for the equilibrium forward price, we have

$$F(t, [A_1], (t+T)) = A_1(t) \exp(RT) \tag{7.2}$$

Equation 7.2 depicts the well-known cost of carry relationship when there is just one deliverable asset and no frictions.

In the case of two deliverable assets, the value of the forward contract is equal to a long call on the minimum of the two assets plus a short put position on the minimum of the two assets. Thus, the value of the forward contract in this case is equal to

$$EC[t, [A_1, A_2], K, (t+T)] - EP[t, [A_1, A_2], K, (t+T)] \tag{7.3}$$

At inception, the value of the forward contract is zero, and so the value of the option combination is also zero where the strike price K of the options is equal to the forward price

$$F(t, [A_1, A_2], (t+T))$$

Stultz [27] developed an extension of the put-call parity theorem for option combinations such as Expression 7.3. He noted that Expression 7.3 could also be expressed as[4]

$$EC[t, [A_1, A_2], 0, (t+T)] - Ke^{-RT} \tag{7.4}$$

where the European call option in Expression 7.4 has a zero exercise price and entitles its owner to the minimum of asset one and asset two at time $(t+T)$. We note that, in general, the current value of this option is less than the minimum of $A_1(t)$ and $A_2(t)$ and that it corresponds to the "correct" spot price to use when there are two deliverable assets. Margrabe [22] noted that options of this nature on the minimum of two assets with a zero strike price could be further simplified.

---

3. It turns out that, while this appears a little awkward in the one-asset case, it is a useful approach when there are two (or more) underlying assets, and it is also helpful in the analysis of the timing option.

4. To obtain the equilibrium forward price in the two-asset case, we can find the value of K which makes Expression 7.4 zero. This value of K represents the required forward price.

The generalization of Stulz's and Margrabe's results to the n-dimensional case has been discovered by several authors. In the case of a forward contract where the short can deliver any one of n assets, the value of the forward contract can be expressed as a long call plus a short put:

$$EC[t, [A_1, A_2, ..., A_n], K, (t+T)]$$
$$-EP[t, [A_1, A_2, ..., A_n], K, (t+T)] \quad (7.5)$$

At inception, the value of the forward contract is zero, and, in this case, the strike price, K, is equal to the forward price,

$$F(t, [A_1, A_2, ..., A_n], (t+T))$$

In analogy with the two-dimensional case, Expression 7.5 may be written as

$$EC[t, [A_1, A_2, ..., A_n], 0, (t+T)] - Ke^{-RT} \quad (7.6)$$

Since the value of the forward contract, at inception, is zero, this implies that

$$F(t, [A_1, A_2, ..., A_n], (t+T))$$
$$= e^{RT} EC[t, [A_1, A_2, ..., A_n], 0, (t+T)] \quad (7.7)$$

Hence, the forward price can be obtained if we can value the call option on the minimum of the n assets, with strike price zero and expiration date $(t+T)$.

For small numbers of deliverable assets, $n = 2$ or 3, it is fairly straightforward to evaluate the option on the right-hand side of Equation 7.7. However, for larger numbers of assets, the computations involve integrations over $(n-1)$-dimensional[5] multivariate normal integrals. By making some simplifying assumptions, we can develop a procedure for evaluating the option on the minimum of the n assets. This enables us to obtain the forward price of a contract where the short can deliver any one of n assets.

To explore the behavior of the quality option as the number of assets gets large, it is convenient to assume that all the assets have the same current price and the same standard deviation and are equicorrelated. This symmetry makes the analysis simpler.[6]

To compute the value of the quality option, we use known results for the multivariate normal distribution. The option on the minimum of the n assets can be analyzed in terms of order statistics. Apart from a discount factor, the option (with zero strike price) on the minimum of the n assets is equal

---

5. The n-dimensional integral in this case can be converted into an $(n-1)$-dimensional integral using the technique suggested by Margrabe [22].
6. We suspect that this symmetry should simplify the integrals developed by Johnson [16], but we do not pursue this point here.

to the expected value of the lowest extreme order statistic. In the case of the standardized multivariate normal distribution, the moments of the order statistics when the variables are independent have been published by Ruben [26] and Teichroew [28]. Owen and Steck [24] developed simple expressions for the moments of the order statistics in the case of an equicorrelated multivariate normal distribution in terms of the moments of the order statistics of the uncorrelated multivariate normal distribution.[7] Owen and Steck [24] give the numerical values of the first four moments of the extreme (highest) order statistic from the multivariate normal distribution with zero correlation for values of n ranging from 2 to 50. The moments of the lowest order statistic are obtained by changing the sign of the odd order moments in their Table I.

Let $X^{(i)}$ denote the ith order statistic from the multivariate normal distribution in the uncorrelated case where

$$X^{(1)} \geq X^{(2)} \geq \cdots \geq X^{(n)}$$

Let $Z^{(i)}$ be the corresponding order statistics in the case of the equicorrelated multivariate normal distribution with common correlation coefficient, ρ. Then Owen and Steck show that the moments of the $X^{(i)}$ and the $Z^{(i)}$ are related as follows:

$$E(Z^{(i)}) = \sqrt{(1-\rho)}\, E(X^{(i)}) \tag{7.8a}$$

$$E[Z^{(i)} - E(Z^{(i)})]^2 = \rho + (1-\rho)[E(X^{(i)} - E(X^{(i)}))^2] \tag{7.8b}$$

$$E[Z^{(i)} - E(Z^{(i)})]^3 = (1-\rho)^{3/2}[E(X^{(i)} - E(X^{(i)}))^3] \tag{7.8c}$$

$$E[Z^{(i)} - E(Z^{(i)})]^4 = 3\rho^2 + 6\rho(1-\rho)E[X^{(i)} - E(X^{(i)}))^2]$$
$$+ (1-\rho)^2 E[(X^{(i)} - E(X^{(i)}))^4] \tag{7.8d}$$

From these relations, we can find the moments in the equicorrelated case.

In the case of the quality option with n deliverable assets, we are seeking the expected value of the lowest order statistic in the case of an equicorrelated multivariate normal distribution. We can use the moments of the equicorrelated multivariate lognormal case to obtain a series expansion for this expectation. The essential idea is that if we know the central moments of a random variable X, then the expected value of a function g of X can be obtained as follows:[8]

---

7. Afonja [1] provides expressions for the moments of the order statistics in the general case of a multivariate normal distribution with unequal means, variances, and correlations. However, his expressions involve multiple integrals, and it would probably be as simple in the general case to evaluate the options directly using Johnson's [16] results.

8. This expression can be obtained from a Taylor series expansion. The symbols $\mu_3(x)$ and $\mu_4(x)$ denote the third and fourth central moments of X.

$$E\{g(X)\} = g\{E(X)\} + \frac{g^{ii}}{2}\{E(X)\}\,\mathrm{var}\,X + \frac{g^{iii}}{6}\{E(X)\}\mu_3(X)$$
$$+ \frac{g^{iv}}{24}\{E(X)\}\mu_4(X) + \cdots \tag{7.9}$$

Numerical Examples. The standard assumptions used for our numerical examples are

$$T = 0.75 \text{ years}$$
$$R = 10\% \text{ per annum}$$
$$\sigma_i = 25\% \text{ per annum}, \quad 1 \le i \le n$$
$$\rho_{ij} = 0.95, \quad 1 \le i \le j \le n$$
$$A_i(t) = 40, \quad 1 \le i \le n$$

With just one deliverable asset, the futures price under the above assumptions is 43.1154. This futures price is used as a benchmark against which to measure the impact of the quality option. When there are just two deliverable assets, the futures price given by Equation 7.4[9] is 41.9380, so that the ratio relative to the one asset benchmark futures price is 97.27 percent. We use this ratio as the metric to illustrate the significance of the quality option.

In order to compute the impact of the quality option when there are several deliverable assets, we used the isomorphism between the lowest order statistic and the call option on the minimum of the n assets with zero strike price. Equation 7.9 is used to obtain the order statistics of the multivariate normal distribution in terms of the known order statistics of the multivariate lognormal distribution. The results are given in Table 7.1. As a check on our procedure, the computed results for $n = 2$ and $n = 3$ agreed to three decimal places with the exact results obtained by independent methods. For $n = 4$, we used Monte Carlo simulations to confirm the accuracy of the approximation.

Note from Table 7.1 that the impact of the quality option increases as the number of deliverable assets increases. Thus, for five deliverable assets, the impact is twice as large as if there were just two assets. As the correlation coefficient increases, the impact of the quality option is reduced. However, note that even when the correlation coefficient is as high as 0.995, the impact of the quality option is nontrivial, especially if there is a large set of deliverable assets.

II. The Timing Option

In several types of futures contracts, the short position has some flexibility regarding the timing of the actual delivery. For example, delivery may take

9. We use the formulas given by Stulz [27] to evaluate the European call option in Equation 7.4.

TABLE 7.1 *Relationship of Quality Option to the Number of Deliverable Assets*[a]

Number of Deliverable Assets (n)	Correlation Coefficient = 0.95		Correlation Coefficient = 0.995	
	Value ($) of Option on the Minimum of the n Assets Strike Price = 0	Ratio of Futures Price to Reference Futures Price	Value ($) of Option on the Minimum of the n Assets Strike Price = 0	Ratio of Futures Price to Reference Futures Price
2	38.908	97.27	39.654	99.14
3	38.374	95.94	39.483	98.71
4	38.033	95.08	39.372	98.43
5	37.786	94.46	39.292	98.23
10	37.100	92.75	39.066	97.66
20	36.511	91.28	38.869	97.17
30	36.201	90.50	38.765	96.91
40	35.994	89.99	38.695	96.74
50	35.840	89.60	38.643	96.61

a. Assets are assumed to have an equicorrelated multivariate lognormal distribution. All assets are assumed to have same current price (= $40) and same standard deviation (= 25% per annum). Two basic situations are considered: first, the correlation coefficient = 0.95; second, the correlation coefficient = 0.995.

place on any business day within the delivery month. In this section, we examine how the timing option affects the futures price and we analyze the interaction between the timing option and the quality option. We again assume a frictionless market and that the underlying assets pay no dividends and have no associated service flow. Initially, we analyze the timing option when there is only one deliverable asset and obtain a simple expression for the futures price in this case. When there is more than one deliverable asset, there is an interaction between the timing option and the quality option. We discuss this relationship and develop a numerical procedure to evaluate the timing option in this case. Some numerical examples are presented to illustrate the size of the timing option and to indicate the circumstances where it is likely to have the greatest value.

A. Timing Option with One Deliverable Asset

To discuss this case, it is convenient to introduce some additional notation. We assume that the futures contract expires at time $(t + T_3)$. The short position can deliver the underlying asset at any time during the interval $[t+T_1, t+T_3]$. Let us denote the time that delivery occurs by $[t+T_2]$. We have

$$T_1 \le T_2 \le T_3$$

The current price of the deliverable asset is $A_1(t)$, and the riskless interest rate is R percent per annum (continuously compounded). We assume that the choice of the delivery time is made by the short position in such a way as to maximize his or her benefits under the contract. We also assume that forward prices and futures prices are equal as before. Let $F(t, [A_1], (t+T_1)) = F_1$ denote the futures price, at time t, of a futures contract where delivery takes place at time $(t+T_1)$. Thus there is no timing option in this case. Let $F(t, [A_1], (t+T_2)) = F_2$ denote the futures price, at time t, of a futures contract where delivery can occur at time $(t+T_2)$; $T_1 \le T_2 \le T_3$. Thus, F_2 corresponds to the case where there is a timing option.

We can show that to prevent arbitrage, F_2 must equal F_1. First, suppose that $F_2 > F_1$. Consider the following investment strategy at time t. Take a long position in the contract with no timing option and a short position in the contract with the timing option. Note that the short position decides when the asset is to be delivered under the contract with the timing option. At time $(t+T_1)$, the long position is worth

$$A_1(t+T_1) - F_1$$

The short position can be liquidated at time $(t+T_1)$, at which time it is worth

$$-(A_1(t+T_1) - F_2)$$

The net profit on the strategy is

$$F_2 - F_1$$

which by assumption is strictly positive. This strategy yields a strictly positive payoff with zero initial investment and is accordingly in conflict with the no-arbitrage principle. Hence, our assumption that $F_2 > F_1$ is untenable, and so

$$F_2 \le F_1 \qquad (7.10)$$

To prove[10] the converse, assume that $F_1 > F_2$. Consider the following strategy. At current time t an investor goes long one futures contract with the timing option and simultaneously goes short a futures contract that has no timing option and calls for delivery at time $(t+T_1)$. At the same time, the investor purchases one unit of the underlying asset (planning to sell it at time $(t+T_1)$). He or she also goes short one unit of the asset (planning to liquidate the position at time $(t+T_2)$) when delivery occurs under the futures contract with the timing option.

---

10. The author thanks Mark Rubinstein for suggestions that improved an earlier proof of this result.

TABLE 7.2   *Portfolio Strategy to Illustrate That F_2 Must Be Greater Than or Equal to F_1, Where F_2 Is Futures Price with Timing Option and F_1 Is Futures Price without Timing Option* [a]

		Cash Flow to Investor	
Action	Time t	$t + T_1$	$t + T_2$
Long Futures (with Timing Option), Delivery at $(t + T_2)$	0	–	$A_1(t + T_2) - F_2$
Short Futures (without Timing Option), Delivery at $(t + T_1)$	0	$F_1 - A_1(t + T_1)$	
Buy Asset (Sell at $t + T_1$)	$-A_1(t)$	$A_1(t + T_1)$	$F_1 e^{R(T_2 - T_1)}$
Short Asset (Liquidate at $t + T_2$)	$+A_1(t)$	–	$-A_1(t + T_2)$
Total	0	0	$F_1 e^{R(T_2 - T_1)} - F_2$

a. $A_i(t + T_i)$ is the price of the deliverable asset 1 at time $(t + T_i)$, where $i = 1, 2$.

The time pattern of cash flows under this portfolio strategy is illustrated in Table 7.2. The table illustrates the cash flows to the investor under the assumed strategy. At time $(t + T_1)$, the investor takes delivery of the asset under the futures contract without the timing option and simultaneously sells the asset. The proceeds from this are $(F_1 - A_1(t + T_1))$ and $A_1(t + T_1)$, that is, F_1. Assume that the investor places this amount in a risk free account until time $(t + T_2)$. At time $(t + T_2)$, it will have accumulated to

$$F_1 \exp(R[T_2 - T_1])$$

At time $(t + T_2)$, the short position in the futures contract with the timing option delivers the asset. Simultaneously, the investor liquidates the short asset position. The net value of these two transactions to the investor is

$$[A_1(t + T_2) - F_2)] - A_1(t + T_2) = -F_2$$

Hence, the total value of the investor's portfolio at time $(t + T_2)$ is

$$F_1 e^{R(T_2 - T_1)} - F_2$$

By our initial assumption, this is strictly positive (since R is assumed positive). However, this result violates the no-arbitrage principle, so our initial assumption is untenable.

Hence,

$$F_1 \leq F_2 \tag{7.11}$$

Combining Expressions 7.10 and 7.11, it must be that $F_1 = F_2$. Thus, when there is just one deliverable asset, the timing option has no value [11] and the

---

11. It has no value when the comparison is made with the contract that calls for delivery at time

short position should optimally deliver the asset at the first permitted opportunity.

Recall that F_1 can be obtained from the cost of carry model so that

$$F_1 = A_1(t) \exp[RT_1] \tag{7.12}$$

When there is just one deliverable asset, this is also equal to F_2. The intuition is that the seller is committed to deliver the asset during the delivery window and that there are no gains to waiting since the asset pays no dividend.

B. Timing Option with Two Deliverable Assets

When the terms of the futures contract permit more than one deliverable asset, there is an interaction between the timing option and the quality option. In this case, it is no longer true that the futures price when there is a timing option is equal to the futures price assuming earliest delivery. It is instructive to see where the arbitrage arguments used for one deliverable asset fail. The first stage of the argument leading to Equation 7.10 still goes through. To see where the argument leading to Inequality 7.11 breaks down, assume that there are two deliverable assets denoted by i and j. Assume that

$$F_1(t, [A_i, A_j], (t + T_1)) = F_1$$

denotes the current futures price of a contract which involves the delivery of the asset with the lowest price at time $(t + T_1)$. Let

$$F(t, [A_i, A_j], (t + T_2)) = F_2$$

denote the futures price of the contract where delivery of the either asset i or asset j can take place at any time during the interval $[t + T_1, t + T_3]$ at the option of the short position.

When there is uncertainty as to which asset will be delivered, then the argument leading to Equation 7.11 no longer goes through. It could happen that the first asset is the cheapest to deliver under the futures contract without the timing option, whereas the second asset is the cheaper at time $(t + T_2)$. Under these circumstances it is not possible to guarantee a riskless profit to the previous strategy. Hence, when there is a timing option and more than one deliverable asset, there is an interaction between the timing option and the quality option.

To explore the magnitude and significance of the timing option when there are two underlying deliverable assets, we have developed a numerical algorithm. This involves an extension of the Cox, Ross, and Rubinstein [8] approach to option pricing developed recently by Boyle [4]. A binomial lattice

---

$(t + T_1)$. Of course, the forward price for the contract with the timing option, F_2, will generally be less than F_3 when there is just one asset.

framework is constructed to value contingent claims, the payoffs of which are a function of two state variables. In our case, the state variables are the prices of the two deliverable assets. The method proceeds by obtaining the value of the contingent claim on the boundary and working recursively backwards through the lattice to arrive at its current value. The method lends itself to the incorporation of any type of early exercise policy. In the case of a futures contract with a timing option, we assume that the asset is delivered when it is to the advantage of the short position to do so.

Suppose that F_2 is the current futures price of the contract with a timing option when either asset i or asset j can be delivered by the short position. The value of a long position in this contract at time $(t + T_2)$ is

$$\min[[A_i(t + T_2), A_j(t + T_2)] - F_2]$$

Note that this value can be either positive or negative. The early exercise strategy conducted by the short position is designed to minimize the value of the contract held by the long position. Thus, at each node of the lattice, delivery is assumed to occur if it minimizes the contract value. The equilibrium futures price F_2 is obtained by recognizing that the initial contract value is zero. The solution design recognizes that the short position will deliver the minimum of the two assets at the time during the permitted interval when it is in its best interest to do so.

Table 7.3 provides values of futures prices when there are two deliverable assets and a timing option. It is assumed that delivery can take place during the last three weeks of the life of the contract. We have computed futures prices for different contract maturities and different assumptions as to the correlation between the two assets. The main conclusion from Table 7.3 is that the impact of the timing option on the equilibrium futures price is small. As the correlation between the two assets increases, the futures price of the contract with the timing option F_2 moves closer to the futures price for the single asset case F_1. The impact of the timing option is small—smaller than the impact of the quality option. Note that when the correlation between the assets is less than one, the futures price for the contract with the timing option F_2 is less than the futures price assuming delivery at the first permitted date F_1. Note that F_2 is also less than the futures price assuming delivery at the last permitted date F_3.

It is important to emphasize that the model developed here does not apply directly to the Treasury bond futures contracts. In the case of the Treasury bond futures contract, the underlying assets make coupon payments. In addition, stochastic interest rates drive a wedge between futures prices and forward prices, and it is slightly inconsistent to maintain that they are equal in this situation. Empirical results (Hemler [14]) indicate that participants in the Chicago T-Bond futures contract tend to postpone delivery toward the end of the delivery month.

TABLE 7.3   *Futures Prices with and without Timing Option When There Are Two Deliverable Assets*[a]

	$T_3 = 6$ weeks $T_1 = 3$ weeks	$T_3 = 13$ weeks $T_1 = 10$ weeks	$T_3 = 39$ weeks $T_1 = 36$ weeks
Futures Price	\$	\$	\$
	Correlation Coefficient = 1.00		
F_1	40.23	40.78	42.87
F_2	40.23	40.78	42.87
F_3	40.46	41.01	43.12
	Correlation Coefficient = 0.90		
F_1	39.80	39.98	41.28
F_2	39.74	39.94	41.27
F_3	39.85	40.10	41.45
	Correlation Coefficient = 0.50		
F_1	39.27	38.99	39.32
F_2	39.01	38.84	39.23
F_3	39.09	38.97	39.40

a. Both assets are currently worth \$40 and have the same standard deviation, 25% per annum. The timing option is available during the last three weeks of each contract. The futures prices are as follows:
F_1: futures price when delivery occurs at $t + T_1$.
F_2: futures price when delivery occurs during $[t + T_1, t + T_3]$ at the option of the short; i.e., there is a timing option.
F_3: futures price when delivery occurs at $t + T_3$.

III. Conclusion

In this paper we have explored the price implications of some of the delivery options that are often found in futures contracts. In the case of the quality option, a method was developed for analyzing the significance of this option when there are several deliverable assets. Numerical simulations were carried out to illustrate the significance of the quality option when there are several deliverable assets. Even when the underlying assets have highly correlated returns, this option continues to have nontrivial value. The timing option was also analyzed and found to be much less important. Some aspects of the interaction between the timing option and the quality option were analyzed.

The present analysis applies to the situation where the underlying deliverable assets follow a joint lognormal distribution. Hence, it is more applicable to commodity futures than to interest rate futures. An important area of further research would be the analysis of Treasury bond futures contracts. Recently Kane and Marcus [19] used a simulation approach to analyze delivery options in this case and concluded that the delivery option had a significant impact on futures prices. For the parameter values used, they concluded that the delivery option resulted in a 2 to 6% reduction in the futures price.[12]

Clearly, these delivery options are of economic significance in many types of futures contracts. The quality option has an impact on the futures price, and thus it will also affect hedging strategies. Further extensions of this work could tackle some of these issues. It would also be interesting to provide an empirical examination of the results developed in the present paper. These extensions are left for future research.

---

12. Hemler [14] produces somewhat lower values for the quality option in the case of Treasury bond futures contracts.

References

1. B. Afonja. "The Moments of the Maximum of Correlated Normal and *t*-Variates," *Journal of the Royal Statistical Society (Series B)* 34 (1972), 251–62.
2. M. Arak and L. Goodman. "Treasury Bond Futures: Valuing the Delivery Options," *Journal of Futures Markets* 7 (June 1987), 269–86.
3. S. Benninga and M. Smirlock. "An Empirical Analysis of the Delivery Option, Marking to Market, and the Pricing of Treasury Bond Futures," *Journal of Futures Markets* 5 (Fall 1985), 361–74.
4. Phelim P. Boyle. "A Lattice Framework for Option Pricing with Two State Variables," *Journal of Financial and Quantitative Analysis* 23 (March 1988), 1–12.
5. S. Cheng. "Pricing Models for Multiple-Currency Option Bonds," Working paper, Graduate School of Business, Columbia University, NY, 1985.
6. ———. "Multi-Asset Contingent Claims in a Stochastic Interest Rate Environment," Working paper, Graduate School of Business, Columbia University, NY, 1985.
7. J. Cox, J. Ingersoll, and S. Ross. "The Relation between Forward Prices and Futures Prices," *Journal of Financial Economics* 9 (December 1981), 321–46.
8. J. Cox, S. Ross, and M. Rubinstein. "Option Pricing: A Simplified Approach," Journal of Financial Economics 7 (September 1979), 229–63.
9. K. Garbade and W. Silber, "Futures Contracts on Commodities with Multiple Varieties: An Analysis of Premiums and Discounts," *Journal of Business* 56 (July 1980), 249–72.
10. G. Gay and S. Manaster. "The Quality Option Implicit in Futures Contracts," *Journal of Financial Economics* 13 (September 1984), 353–70.

11. ———. "Implicit Delivery Options and Optimal Delivery Strategies for Financial Futures Contracts," *Journal of Financial Economics* 16 (May 1986), 41–72.
12. S. Hegde. "An Empirical Analysis of Implicit Delivery Options in the Treasury Bond Futures Market," Unpublished manuscript, College of Business Administration, University of Notre Dame, IN, 1986.
13. ———. "The Value of the Implicit Quality Option in the Treasury Bond Futures Contract: An Empirical Evaluation," Unpublished manuscript, College of Business Administration, University of Notre Dame, IN, 1986.
14. Michael J. Hemler. "The Quality Delivery Option in Treasury Bond Futures Contracts," Unpublished Ph.D. dissertation, Graduate School of Business, University of Chicago, IL, March 1988.
15. R. A. Jarrow and G. S. Oldfield. "Forward Contracts and Futures Contracts," *Journal of Financial Economics* 9 (December 1981), 373–82.
16. H. Johnson. "Options on the Maximum or the Minimum of Several Assets," *Journal of Financial and Quantitative Analysis* 22 (September 1987), 277–83.
17. A. Kamara and A. F. Siegel. "Optimal Hedging in Futures Markets with Multiple Delivery Specifications," *Journal of Finance* 42 (September 1987), 1007–21.
18. A. Kane and A. Marcus. "Valuation and Optimal Exercise of the Wild Card Option in the Treasury Bond Futures Market," *Journal of Finance* 41 (March 1986), 195–207.
19. ———. "The Quality Option in the Treasury Bond Futures Market: An Empirical Assessment," *Journal of Futures Markets* 6 (Summer 1986), 231–48.
20. T. Kilcollin. "Difference Systems in Financial Futures Markets," *Journal of Finance* 37 (December 1982), 1183–98.
21. M. Livingston. "The Delivery Option on Forward Contracts," *Journal of Financial and Quantitative Analysis* 22 (March 1987), 79–87.
22. W. Margrabe. "The Value of an Option to Exchange One Asset for Another," *Journal of Finance* 33 (March 1978), 177–86.
23. ———. "A Theory of the Price of a Claim Contingent on n Asset Prices," Working Paper 82-01, George Washington University, Washington, D.C., September 1982.
24. D. B. Owen and G. P. Steck. "Moments of Order Statistics from the Equi-Correlated Multivariate Normal Distribution," *Annals of Mathematical Statistics* 33 (December 1962), 1286–91.
25. S. F. Richard and M. Sundaresan. "A Continuous Time Model of Forward Prices and Futures Prices in a Multigood Economy," *Journal of Financial Economics* 9 (December 1981), 347–71.
26. H. Ruben. "On the Moments of Order Statistics in Samples from Normal Populations," *Biometrika* 41 (June 1954), 200–27.
27. R. M. Stulz. "Options on the Minimum or the Maximum of Two Risky Assets: Analysis and Applications," *Journal of Financial Economics* 10 (July 1982), 161–85.
28. D. Teichroew. "Tables of Expected Values of Order Statistics and Products of Order Statistics for Samples of Size Twenty or Less from the Normal Distribution," *Annals of Mathematical Statistics* 27 (June 1956), 410–26.

8

The Evolving Market for Swaps

Clifford W. Smith, Jr., Charles W. Smithson, & Lee Macdonald Wakeman

A recent advertisement extols swaps as "a tool no financial manager can ignore."[1] While this statement has the hyperbolic ring of Madison Avenue prose, it is nevertheless quite clear that the swaps market — a relatively new and rapidly developing market — has become increasingly important. As with other evolving markets in the past, there exists confusion about certain economic implications of this market, especially among some corporate treasurers to whom these instruments are being marketed. Questions that deserve consideration include: (1) How does the swaps market relate to other financial markets? (2) How (and why) did the swaps market evolve? (3) What goes into the pricing of a swap, particularly the evaluation of credit risk? (4) What direction might the swaps market be expected to take in the future? Our paper focuses on these questions, and in so doing it proposes a general analytical framework that should prove helpful in evaluating both the broad variety of swaps now available and those that are yet to be devised.

Analysis of Swap Transactions

As its name implies, a swap is normally defined as an exchange. More specifically, it is an exchange of cash flows over time between two parties (generally

---

1. Bankers Trust Company, "The International Swap Market," Advertising Supplement to *Euromoney Corporate Finance,* September 1985.

FIGURE 8.1   *Cash Flows in a Parallel Loan Agreement*

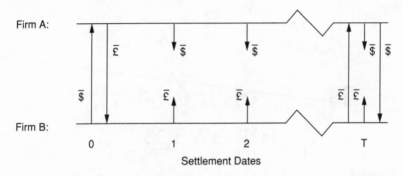

The British firm A simultaneously borrows dollars from American firm B and loans an equivalent amount denominated in pounds to firm B at time 0. During the term of the loan, firm A makes interest payments in dollars to firm B, while firm B makes interest payments in pounds to firm A. At maturity (timeT) the two firms make their final interest payments and return the principals. Firm A returns dollars and firm B returns pounds.

referred to as the "counterparties"). The first swaps developed from parallel loans arranged between two companies in different countries, a form popular in the 1970s. To illustrate a parallel loan, suppose a British company makes a loan denominated in pounds to a U.S. company, which in turn makes a loan of equal value denominated in dollars to the British company. As illustrated in Figure 8.1, these loans have parallel interest and principal repayment schedules. By entering into this parallel loan agreement, the British company is able to transform a debt incurred in pounds into a fully hedged U.S. dollar liability. There are, however, two potentially important problems with parallel loans: (1) Default by one party does not release the other from making its contractually obligated payments; (2) although the loans effectively cancel one another, they remain on-balance-sheet items for accounting and regulatory purposes. Early in the 1980s a new transaction known as a "currency swap" was devised to overcome these problems; and because of its success, it effectively displaced the use of parallel loans.

The Currency Swap

A currency swap involves the same pattern of cash flows as a parallel loan. Indeed, without any modification, Figure 8.1 could be used to illustrate the cash flows for a fixed currency swap where firm A pays a fixed interest rate in dollars and receives a fixed rate in pounds, while the counterparty, firm B, pays fixed rate pounds and receives fixed rate dollars. (In this context, the

FIGURE 8.2   *Cash Flows from a Fixed Currency Swap*

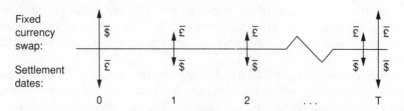

The British firm A pays interest at a fixed dollar rate ($\bar{\$}$) and receives interest at a fixed pound rate ($\bar{£}$). The long arrows denote the initial exchange of principal and the reexchange at maturity; the short arrows denote the cash flows exchanged over the course of the agreement.*

short arrows in Figure 8.1 denote the cashflows exchanged during the term of the agreement, while the long arrows denote the initial exchange of principals at time 0 and the reexchange at maturity, time T.) Alternatively, a swap transaction could be illustrated by looking at the cash flows paid and received over time by one of the counterparties. Figure 8.2 illustrates the position of the British firm A in this fixed currency swap.*

Although a swap is defined as an "exchange" of cash flows, there need not be an actual exchange of payments. Instead, at specified intervals, only the net cash flows could be exchanged, and the party that would have received the lower of the cash flows could simply pay the other the difference in the two cash flows. In the case of currency swaps, the counterparties do exchange interest payments; however, the exchange is conditional in the sense that if one party defaults, the other is released from its obligation. In currency swaps, moreover, the counterparties generally exchange the principals at an agreed-upon rate of exchange and then reexchange at the end of the agreement; but this exchange also need not occur. The principal could instead be "notional," as is generally the case in interest rate swaps (which we take up later).

By thus converting the older parallel loan transaction into a conditional exchange of the cash flows, the currency swap reduces the probability and magnitude of default. Furthermore, as implied above, current regulatory and accounting practice treats swap contracts as off-balance-sheet items. Thus, as stated earlier, the currency swap accomplishes the goals of its predecessor, the parallel loan agreement, while eliminating the major remaining problems with that transaction.

---

*In this figure and in similar figures to follow, we adopt the convention of showing inflows above the line and outflows below the line.

Swaps as Packages of Forward Contracts

One of the major themes of this paper, to which we shall return throughout, is the fundamental similarity between swaps and forward contracts. In fact, it is our contention that any swap can be decomposed into a series of forward contracts.

Again consider Figure 8.2, which illustrates the cash flows in a fixed currency swap — one in which the firm pays fixed rate interest in one currency and receives fixed rate interest in another. The cash flows for the counterparty receiving pounds and paying dollars at settlement date 1 are equivalent to those from holding a long position in pounds in a pound-dollar forward contract. This also applies to each settlement date between 2 and T; hence this currency swap for firm A is equivalent to a package of T long forward contracts in pounds. The positions are reversed for the counterparty.

We believe this decomposition of swaps into forward contracts is the most productive way of evaluating swaps, particularly the pricing of swaps. Simple swaps have been standardized and are now quoted virtually as commodities, and for such swaps this method of analysis will seem roundabout. But, as we will demonstrate, for more complicated swaps, where the timing of cash flow exchanges differ or where the principal changes, decomposition of cash flows into forward contracts is the simplest, most effective analytical approach.

Currency Coupon Swaps

In a currency swap, as we have seen, the counterparties agree on the timing of the exchanges, the principal amounts of the currencies that will be exchanged, the interest rates (which reflect credit market forward prices) that will determine the future cash flows, and the exchange rates used to calculate the net cash flows. The earliest currency swaps were fixed currency swaps, which specified fixed interest rates in both currencies. Soon after came a variant of the fixed currency swap called the currency coupon swap. In such an arrangement, the interest rate in one currency is fixed and the other is floating.

Interest Rate Swaps

The interest rate swap, which was introduced shortly after currency swaps, is a special case of the currency coupon swap — one in which all the cash flows are denominated in a single currency. Figure 8.3 illustrates a simple interest rate swap. The primary difference between Figures 8.2 and 8.3 is that the exchanges of principal flows at time 0 and T net to zero because they are of the same amount and denominated in the same currency.

FIGURE 8.3 *Cash Flows in an Interest Rate Swap*

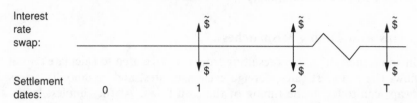

The firm illustrated pays a fixed dollar interest rate ($\bar{\$}$) and receives interest computed on a floating dollar rate ($\tilde{\$}$). The counterparty pays floating and receives fixed.

Basis Rate Swaps

To this point, we have described swaps in which both interest rates are fixed (fixed currency swaps) and swaps in which one interest rate is fixed and one is floating (simple interest rate swaps and currency coupon swaps). In a basis rate swap, both interest rates are floating. The primary effect of such swaps is to allow floating rate cash flows calculated on one basis to be exchanged for floating rate cash flows calculated on another. For example, it permits firms to make conversions from one-month LIBOR to six-month LIBOR, or from LIBOR to U.S. commercial paper rates. A basis rate swap is equivalent to pairing two simple interest rate swaps such that the flows are converted from floating to fixed, and then converted from fixed to floating (but on a different basis).

Commodity Swaps

A swap is in effect an exchange of net cash flows calculated to reflect changes in designated prices. So far, we have considered only two prices, interest rates and exchange rates. However, swaps defined in prices other than interest rates and foreign exchange rates are also possible. Once a principal amount is determined and that principal contractually converted to a flow, any set of forward prices can be used to calculate the cash flows (and thus the difference checks).

Consider, for example, the possibility of swaps denoted in commodities such as oil and wheat. The counterparties could agree to some notional principal and to the conversion of this principal to flows using a fixed dollar interest rate and the U.S. price of wheat. Such a swap is analytically no different from a currency swap where forward prices of wheat replace the forward currency prices. In addition, neither firm need be in the wheat business; the difference checks are paid in dollars, not wheat. Moreover, in a swap in which the firm elects to pay with wheat, it can receive either fixed or floating rates in any currency or commodity.

Swaps with Timing Mismatches

In addition to differences resulting from the price used to calculate the cash flows (i.e., interest rates, foreign exchange rates, and commodity prices), swaps can differ in the timing of the cash flows. At the simplest level, it could be that one party is paying on a monthly basis while the other is on a quarterly schedule. More significant differences in the timing of the cash flows include so-called "zero" swaps — swaps in which one party makes no payment until maturity — and customized swaps in which the payments from one party vary, either in terms of timing or amount.

Swaps with Optionlike Payoffs

We have stressed the similarity of swaps to forward contracts. Indeed, the payoff profile for a simple swap contract is identical to that of a forward contract. Figure 8.4 presents a simple case in which the firm pays a floating interest rate and receives a fixed rate. This firm has positive net cash flows when the short-term interest rate is below that existing at the contract origination date.

Swaps can also be constructed so as to have optionlike provisions that limit the range of outcomes. For example, suppose that a firm with a floating rate liability wanted to limit its outflows should interest rates rise substantially and was willing to give up some potential gains should there instead be a dramatic decline in short-term rates. To achieve this end the firm could modify a simple interest rate swap contract to read as follows: As long

FIGURE 8.4 *Payoff Profile of an Interest Rate Swap for Firm Paying Floating Rate and Receiving Fixed Rate*

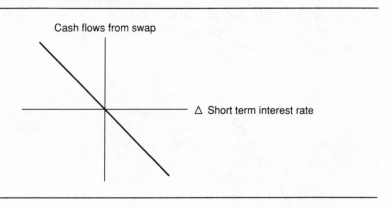

FIGURE 8.5   *Payoff Profile for Floor-Ceiling Swaps*

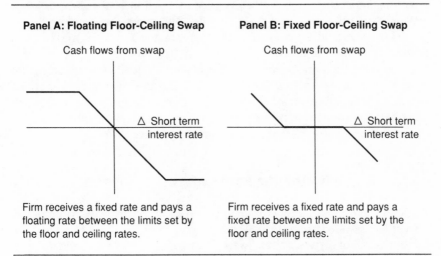

Panel A: Floating Floor-Ceiling Swap

Cash flows from swap

Δ Short term interest rate

Firm receives a fixed rate and pays a floating rate between the limits set by the floor and ceiling rates.

Panel B: Fixed Floor-Ceiling Swap

Cash flows from swap

Δ Short term interest rate

Firm receives a fixed rate and pays a fixed rate between the limits set by the floor and ceiling rates.

as the interest rate neither rises by 200 basis points nor falls more than 100 basis points, the firm pays a floating rate and receives a fixed rate; but, if the interest is more than 200 basis points above or 100 basis points below the current rate, the firm receives and pays a fixed rate. The resulting payoff profile for this floating floor-ceiling swap is illustrated in Panel A of Figure 8.5. (It is also the payoff profile for a "spread.")[2]

Conversely, the contract could have been modified as follows: As long as the interest rate is within 200 basis points of the current rate, the firm receives and pays a fixed rate; but if the interest rate rises or falls by more than 200 basis points, the firm pays a floating rate and receives a fixed rate. The payoff profile for the resulting fixed floor-ceiling swap is illustrated in panel B of Figure 8.5.

Given the range of swaps described above, we agree with the market participant who noted that "the future potential structures...are limited only by the imagination and ingenuity of those participating in the market."[3]

Development of the Swaps Market

The swaps market is still relatively new. As we noted, its origins can be traced to the parallel loan products of the 1970s. However, a market for swaps did

---

2. Note also that if the floor and ceiling rates are equal, this side of the contract is equivalent to a fixed rate obligation since a long call plus a short put with the same terms equals a long forward contract.
3. Bankers Trust Company, "The International Swap Market," cited earlier.

not exist in any meaningful sense until the 1980s. Currency swaps are slightly older than interest rate swaps; their public introduction was the World Bank–IBM transaction in August 1981. U.S. dollar-denominated interest rate swaps started in 1982. While not as old as the currency swaps market, the U.S. interest rate swaps market is now the largest of the swaps markets.

Given the growth in swaps that has occurred, there are two questions we want to consider in this section: (1) Since swaps are so similar to forward contracts, *why* did this market evolve? (2) In order to provide a framework for looking at the future of this market, what path has the evolution of this market followed so far—*how* did this market evolve?

Why Did the Swaps Market Evolve?

Trade journals and market participants agree that the growth of the swaps market has resulted from the ability to receive "significant cost savings" by combining a bond issue with a swap.[4] Using swaps, the firm ends up with lower borrowing costs than it could have obtained with a single transaction. For example, with the use of swaps, companies have obtained funding at LIBOR minus 75–100 basis points. Obviously, a satisfying explanation of why the swaps market evolved must identify the source of this cost saving.

Financial Arbitrage

The popular argument seems to be that the cost savings is based on some kind of financial arbitrage across different capital markets. That is, prices in various world capital markets are not mutually consistent; and firms can lower their borrowing costs by going to foreign capital markets with lower rates, borrowing there, and then swapping their exposure back into their domestic currency, thereby ending with cheaper funding than that obtainable from simply borrowing at home.

The problem with this argument, however, is that the very process of exploiting this kind of opportunity should soon eliminate it. The opening and expansion of a swap market effectively increases the demand for loans in low-rate markets and reduces the demand in higher-rate markets, thereby eliminating the supposed rate differences. Moreover, if this were the only economic basis for swaps, the benefits to one party would come at the expense of the other. Thus, in reasonably efficient and integrated world capital markets, it seems difficult to attribute the continuing growth of the swaps market simply to interest rate differences, and thus financial arbitrage, among world capital markets.

---

4. As as example of the popular literature on swaps, see Tanya S. Arnold, "How to Do Interest Rate Swaps," *Harvard Business Review,* September-October 1984, pp. 96–101.

Tax and Regulatory Arbitrage

Swaps allow companies to engage in what might be termed tax and regulatory arbitrage. Prior to the existence of a well-functioning swap market, a firm issuing dollar-denominated, fixed rate bonds generally did so in U.S. capital markets and thus had to comply with U.S. securities regulation. Moreover, the issuing firm, as well as the security purchasers, were generally faced with the provisions of the U.S. tax code. The introduction of the swap market allows an "unbundling," in effect, of currency and interest rate exposure from the regulation and tax rules in some very creative ways. For example, with the introduction of swaps, a U.S. firm could issue a yen-denominated issue in the Eurobond market, structure the issue so as to receive favorable tax treatment under the Japanese tax code, avoid much of the U.S. securities regulation, and yet still manage its currency exposure by swapping the transaction back into dollars. Unlike the classic financial arbitrage described above, there is no reason for opportunities for tax or regulatory arbitrage to disappear (barring changes, of course, in the various tax and regulatory codes).

To illustrate the manner in which tax and regulatory arbitrage induces swaps, consider the way one U.S. firm used swaps to take advantage of special tax and regulatory conditions in Japan:

1. Until recently, zero coupon bonds received extremely favorable treatment under the Japanese tax code: Taxes were not due until maturity, and at maturity the difference between the purchase price and the face value of the bond was taxed at the capital gains rate.

2. The Ministry of Finance limited the amount a pension fund could invest in non-yen-denominated bonds issued by foreign corporations to at most 10% of their portfolio.

In response to these conditions, a U.S. firm issued a zero coupon yen bond plus a dual currency bond with interest payments in yen and principal repayment in dollars. The zero coupon yen bond permitted the firm to take advantage of the tax treatment of yen zeros. The Ministry of Finance ruled that the dual currency bonds qualified as a yen issue for purposes of the 10% rule, even though the dual currency bond has embedded within it a dollar-denominated zero. Hence, by issuing the dual currency bond, the U.S. firm was able to capitalize on the desire of Japanese pension funds to diversify their portfolios internationally, while at the same time adhering to the regulation imposed by the Ministry of Finance.

The same U.S. firm, however, also wanted to transform its resulting yen exposure to a U.S. dollar exposure. To transform the bond issues, the firm used a currency swap together with a spot $/¥ transaction. (There is less liquidity in nonstandard annuity-type swaps. By combining the principal repayment of the yen zero with the coupon payments of the dual currency

FIGURE 8.6   *Cash Flows in a Dual Currency Bond Issue Plus a Zero Coupon Yen Issue Combined with a Fixed Currency Swap and Spot Currency Transaction*

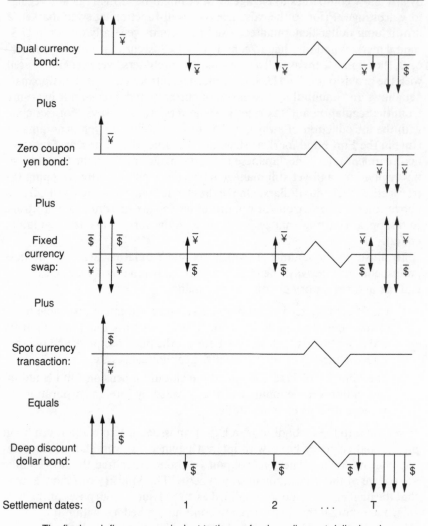

Dual currency bond:

Plus

Zero coupon yen bond:

Plus

Fixed currency swap:

Plus

Spot currency transaction:

Equals

Deep discount dollar bond:

Settlement dates: 0   1   2   . . .   T

The final cash flows are equivalent to those of a deep discount dollar bond.

bond, a standard bond-type swap could be used to hedge.) The resulting cash flows are solely in dollars (see Figure 8.6). Indeed, the swap transaction has created a synthetic deep discount dollar bond, and the rates were such that the firm lowered its total borrowing costs. By using the swap transaction, the firm capitalized on both the favorable regulatory ruling concerning dual currency bonds and the favorable tax treatment of zero coupon bonds, while retaining a fixed dollar interest rate exposure.

Exposure Management

Swaps also allow firms to lower the transactions costs of managing their exposure to interest rates, currency prices, or commodity prices. As we noted, a fixed currency swap can be used by a firm to transform a debt incurred in pounds into a dollar liability. This transformation is illustrated in Figure 8.7. The payoff profile for a loan incurred in pounds relative to changes in the £/$ exchange rate is shown as the dashed line. The payoff profile for the swap is shown as the solid line. Viewed in this context, the swap contract behaves like a conventional long-dated foreign exchange forward contract; losses on the dollar-based loan resulting from exchange rate changes will be offset by gains on the swap contract.

FIGURE 8.7 *Payoff Profile of a Currency Swap Used to Hedge the Financial Risk Exposure from its Underlying Business*

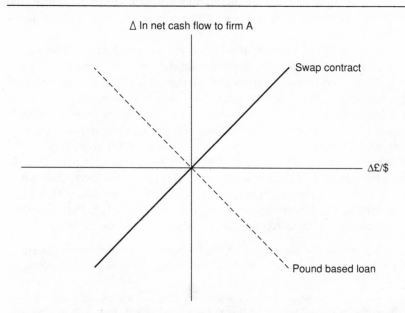

The dashed line represents the exposure of the firm's net cash flow to changes in the £/$ exchange rate without hedging. The payoff profile for the swap is the solid line. Thus, after the swap, the firm is completely hedged against changes in this exchange rate.

For example, consider the case of a firm just entering a foreign market. Although well-known at home, the company might have difficulty placing debt in the foreign credit market where access to information about the firm is more expensive. In this case, it might be less expensive to issue debt in domestic capital markets and swap into the foreign currency exposure.

Conversely, suppose a firm's cash flow exposure in Deutschemarks declines, reducing the amount of DM-denominated debt desired in the firm's balance sheet. Without swaps, the firm would have to call outstanding DM bonds to manage its exposure, an expensive alternative if German interest rates have risen. With access to a liquid swap market, the firm may have a lower-cost means of reducing its DM-denominated liabilities.[5]

Completing Markets

Finally, the swaps market contributes to the integration of financial markets by allowing market participants to fill gaps left by missing markets. An obvious gap filled by the swaps market is the forward market in interest rates. Until recently, there were no forward interest rate contracts available. But, because an interest rate swap behaves like a series of forward contracts, a swap could be used in place of the missing forward contract. Hence, the swap market can be used as a way of synthetically "completing" the financial markets.

Less obvious is the manner in which currency and interest rates swaps have been used to fill gaps in the international financial markets. For example, there is no Swiss Treasury Bill market. Currency and interest rate swaps, however, can be used to create this market synthetically.

In sum, there are four primary reasons *why* the swaps market evolved: (1) classic financial arbitrage opportunities; (2) profit opportunities from regulatory and tax arbitrage; (3) lower transaction costs for some types of financial risk exposure management; and (4) financial market integration. It appears that the first of these is significantly less important today than when swaps markets first opened. Spreads that were initially available have been substantially reduced by the very process of financial arbitrage that produced the original cost savings. As one market observer has commented,

... at the outset of the market, a 'AAA' issuer could reasonably expect to achieve 75–100 basis points below LIBOR on a bond/swap; under current conditions,

---

5. For discussions of corporate motives for hedging, see David Mayers and Clifford Smith, "The Corporate Insurance Decision," *Chase Financial Quarterly* (Spring 1982), and "Corporate Insurance and the Underinvestment Problem," Working Paper, The University of Rochester Managerial Economics Research Center, 1985. See also Clifford Smith and Rene Stulz, "The Determinants of Firms' Hedging Policies," *Journal of Financial and Qualitative Analysis,* December 1985; and Alan Shapiro and Sheridan Titman, "An Integrated Approach to Corporate Risk Management," *Midland Corporate Finance Journal* (Summer 1985).

this same issuer might expect only 25–30 basis points below.... Many issuers now find it more cost-effective to approach the floating rate note market than the bond/swap market.[6]

But if the opportunities for classic financial arbitrage have been eroded by competition, the other three factors remain important and can be expected to stimulate further activity in swaps.

How Did the Swaps Market Evolve?

A picture of the historical development of the swaps market can be obtained by looking either at the evolution of the products or at changes in the market's participants. Both tell the same story. We first look at the products.

As we noted, currency swaps were the first to appear. The earliest swaps were done on a one-off basis, which involved a search for matching counterparties — matching not only in the currencies, but also in the principal amounts desired. These early swaps were custom-tailored products. Because the deals were all one-off, they involved a great deal of work by the financial institution arranging the swap; but — and this is a crucial point — they involved no direct exposure for the intermediary. In the language of the market participants, the early swaps required "creative problem solving" rather than capital commitment from the intermediary.

As interest rate swaps began to appear, the movement toward a more standardized product began. With the U.S. dollar interest rate swaps, there were fewer areas in which counterparties might not match than had been the case for currency swaps. The product had become more homogeneous, and because the product had become more homogeneous, there was less demand for one-off deals. Instead of requiring an exactly matching counterparty, the intermediary could bundle counterparties.

With the move toward homogeneity and the reduced reliance on an identifiable counterparty, markets for swaps — in particular, interest rate swaps — began to look more and more like markets for commodities. Increased competition forced down the spreads. And, with the increased competition, an extensive search for a counterparty or group of counterparties was unprofitable for the intermediary. Instead, the intermediaries began to accept swap contracts without a counterparty, taking the risk into their own books and either matching it internally with an offsetting position or hedging it with government securities or instruments in the financial futures market.

Hence, the evolution of the products offered in the swaps market paralleled that of most markets; swaps evolved from a customized, client-specific product to a standardized product. With the customized product, the role of the

---

6. Bankers Trust Company, "The International Swap Market," cited earlier.

intermediary had been one of problem solving. As the product became more standardized, the role of the intermediary changed considerably, with less emphasis on arranging the deal and more on transactional efficiency and capital commitment.

Looking at the participants in the swaps market, the dominant intermediaries in the early stage of development were investment banks. As the market evolved, the entrants into this market were more highly capitalized firms, in particular commercial banks. This evolution fits precisely with that of the products. In the early stages the emphasis was on the intermediary arranging the transaction rather than accepting risk from the transaction; thus investment banks were the natural intermediaries. But, as the swaps became more standardized, it became essential for the intermediary to be willing and able to accept part or all of a potential transaction into its books. Hence commercial banks, with their greater capitalization, became a more significant factor.

As we noted, the path the swaps market followed in its evolution is similar to that other markets have taken—most notably, the development of the options market. Prior to 1973, the market for put and call options in the United States was an over-the-counter market. Members of the Put and Call Dealer's Association would write options, but only on a one-off basis. Each option was virtually unique because (1) the maturity date was set 181 days from the date the contract was written and (2) the exercise price was set as a function of the prevailing stock price (usually at the stock price). The result was that, for options, there was little volume, little liquidity, and virtually no secondary market. The growth of the options market occurred after the Chicago Board Options Exchange standardized the contracts (maturity dates and exercise prices) and developed an active secondary market. Dealing with a homogeneous product rather than individual customized deals, market makers were able to manage their risks by managing bid-ask spreads to maintain a neutral exposure rather than hedging each transaction on a one-off basis. While over-the-counter options are still offered, the real liquidity in the options market is in exchange-listed options. The options market evolved by moving from an individualized, custom-made product to one resembling a commodity.

While swaps have not evolved to the point of becoming exchange-traded instruments (a point to which we will return in our final section), the paths of evolution—particularly the major factors—have been similar. As was the case with options, contract standardization has played a major role. One market observer put it well by noting that "swaps have become a high volume, lower margin business, rather than the personalized, corporate financial deal of the past."[7] As we have pointed out, the standardization has been more

---

7. K. Henderson Schuyler, "The Constraints on Trading Swaps," *Euromoney,* May 1985, pp. 63–64.

pronounced for interest rate swaps, which may go a long way in explaining why this market has grown more rapidly than that for currency swaps.

Also paralleling the development of options markets, the growth of the swap market corresponded to the liquidity available through the secondary market. While positions can be traded, the secondary market in swaps normally involves the reversing (unwinding) of a position. The simplest method to unwind a swap would involve a cancellation of the agreement, with a final difference check determined on the basis of the remaining value of the contract. However, since this simple "unwind" could result in taxable income, the more common method of unwinding a swap is by writing a "mirror" swap to cancel out the original. Most market observers indicate that this market is sufficiently deep to decrease risks in the primary market, particularly for short-term swaps. Indeed, a 24-hour market now exists for dollar interest rate swaps of up to 12-year maturities and amounts to $500 million.

Pricing Swaps

The pricing of a swap transaction is the aspect of the swap market that has received the most attention, especially that part of pricing that concerns credit risk. The pricing of a swap involves more, however, than just that single dimension. In fact, swap pricing can be viewed as having three major components: forward prices, transaction costs, and the credit risk inherent in the transaction.

Forward Prices

Central to any swap agreement is the forward price—whether it be the forward interest rate, the forward exchange rate, or the forward price of a commodity—embodied in the exchange. Earlier we demonstrated that a swap contract is fundamentally a series of forward contracts.[8] In this view, the forward rate embodied in a swap contract must be the same as the forward rates employed in other corresponding financial contracts such as bonds and futures. And the empirical evidence bears this out: The difference between the two-year swap rate and the forward rate implied by Eurodollar futures declined from over 50 basis points in 1982 and 1983 to less than 20 basis points in 1984; the remaining 20 basis points essentially reflect the difference in transaction costs and credit risk. This development also confirms our expectation that once the initial financial arbitrage opportunities discussed earlier are exhausted, the forward rates for swaps must conform to the market's view of the future as reflected in the prevailing term structure.

---

8. Floor-ceiling swaps also involve options.

The forward rate component of the pricing of a swap, then, is determined neither by the intermediary nor by the swap market. It is determined by competition from other credit market instruments. Because a swap is a package of forward contracts, the forward rates reflected in the swap must conform to the market's view of the forward rate, or financial arbitrage will be profitable.

Transaction Costs

This component would be reflected in the bid-ask spread for a risk free transaction plus any origination fees that are charged.[9] The primary determinant of the bid-ask spread is the demand for liquidity. Put another way, the bid-ask spread is determined not by the market maker but, like the forward rate component, by competition in the market. The bid-ask spread, in short, is a market-determined price that reflects the costs of market-making activities.[10]

Credit Risk

In contrast to the preceding components, both of which are independent of the counterparties, the credit risk premium is determined by the specific credit risk of the intermediary and/or the counterparties. The premium added to the bid-ask spread to reflect nonperformance risk depends on characteristics of the counterparty and of the intermediary arranging the swap; it must therefore reflect an appropriate compensation for the probability of default.

It has been argued by some observers that credit risk in a swap contract is priced "too low" relative to the pricing of credit risk in the loan market. To attempt to evaluate such a statement, we examine the determinants of the credit risk premium.

In a loan, the lender has at risk not only the obligated interest payments, but also the loan principal. In a swap the intermediary has at risk only the net cash flow difference at each settlement date. The difference in exposure implies that for equal levels of nonperformance risk, the credit risk premium associated with a swap would be far smaller than for a loan of comparable size.

As with a loan, the exposure of the intermediary issuing the swap contract to this firm — or, more precisely, its portfolio exposure to similar firms — is

---

9. In this paper, we do not differentiate betwee⁻ transaction costs reflected in the bid-ask spread and those reflected in upfront origination fees. In essence, we assume that the firm is indifferent about the manner in which it receives its fee for transaction costs.

10. See Harold Demsetz, "The Cost of Transacting," *Quarterly Journal of Economics,* 1968, pp. 33–53; and Jack Treynor, "The Only Game In Town," *Financial Analysts Journal,* March-April 1971, pp. 12–22.

a determinant of the credit risk premium. However, one element is significantly more important in the case of a swap contract. If the counterparty is arranging the swap as a hedge and if the counterparty has outstanding lines of credit with the intermediary, the swap decreases expected nonperformance losses of the loan. A counterparty that uses a swap to hedge its financial exposure is reducing its overall probability of financial distress.[11] The probability of default for a swap, and therefore the risk premium, depend critically on whether the swap has been arranged as a hedge.

Consider the situation in which the swap is a hedge. During periods when the firm would be in financial distress, the swap contract would be in the firm's favor; the firm would be receiving difference checks. For example, consider a firm that experiences some financial difficulty if short-term interest rates rise. Suppose that this firm has entered into an interest rate swap to hedge its interest rate exposure. When short-term interest rates rise, the firm does indeed experience a decline in operating cash flow from its core business, but at the same time the firm is receiving inflows from the swap contract. In such a situation, even a firm in financial distress would have no incentive to default on the swap contract.

Therefore, if the swap is a hedge, the probability of default on the swap contract, as well as the probability of default on other liabilities such as loan contracts, are reduced by this active financial risk exposure management, and the credit risk premiums attached to swap contracts should reflect this difference.

By contrast, if the swap had been used *not* to create a hedge, but rather to speculate on movements in financial markets, the probability of default on the swap is higher and the risk premium should be correspondingly greater. In the same way, if the swap is acting as a reverse hedge, the swap would increase the intermediary's exposure.

The above argument suggests that the credit risk assigned to a swap contract should not be based solely on a credit review of the counterparty. The credit risk associated with a swap contract depends on the exposure of the intermediary to firms similar to the one seeking a swap contract and on whether the swap acts as a hedge.

We have purposely not dealt with more technical aspects of credit risk, such as the degree to which risks change if a swap is unwound, the credit risk implications of trading swap positions, and the legal standing of swap contracts in a bankruptcy. (Some of these will be considered in the next section.) Instead, our objective has been to point out what we think are the special features in evaluating the credit risk of a swap: (1) There is no principal at

---

11. Another way of looking at this is that a hedge can make the cost of credit endogenous. It may be advantageous to negotiate swaps and lines of credit simultaneously, since a swap used as a hedge could reduce the cost of the credit line.

risk so we have "settlement risk" rather than "credit risk" per se, and (2) whether the swap is used as a hedge is an important factor. On the basis of what we have seen, we tend to be more optimistic than many observers about the probability of defaults. One piece of evidence consistent with our view is the fact that in June of 1985, Citicorp determined that it had been overcautious and thus reduced its assessment of credit risk, in its pricing of swaps.

Pricing Restrictions from Arbitrage

Our major emphasis has been on viewing swaps as packages of forward contracts. We believe that the approach of pricing swaps by breaking them down into a set of fundamental cash flows is by far the most general, and thus the least restrictive, framework for evaluating new products; it is also likely to be the most flexible in solving pricing problems for very tailored swaps. At the same time, however, we have suggested that complicated swaps can also be decomposed into more simple swaps. For example, as Figure 8.8 demonstrates, a currency coupon swap is equivalent to a fixed currency swap plus

FIGURE 8.8 *A Currency Coupon Swap from Fixed-Rate Pounds to Floating-Rate Dollars Viewed as a Combination of a Fixed Currency Swap from Pounds to Dollars Plus an Interest Rate Swap from Fixed-Rate Dollars to Floating-Rate Dollars*

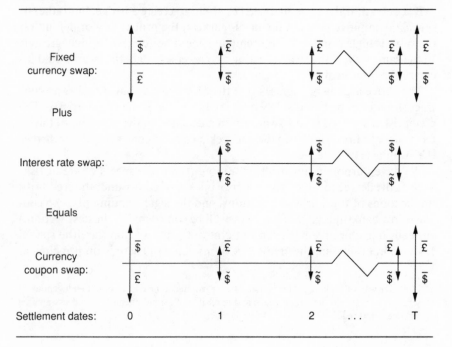

a simple interest rate swap. The idea of unbundling swaps into other swaps can be important in identifying arbitrage opportunities within the market. For example, the cost of a currency coupon swap should be compared to the cost of a simple interest rate swap plus a fixed currency swap. Because they are equivalent transactions, the sum of the prices of the least costly alternative for each component is the best guide to pricing the complex swap.

Moreover, from the perspective of the intermediary, swap decomposition is important for exposure management by the intermediary. Again considering a currency swap, it may be easier to find counterparties for a currency coupon swap by looking for separate counterparties for the interest rate and the currency swap components.

The Future of the Swap Market

We do not purport to be able to predict the future for this market. Indeed, we subscribe to the adage that "he who lives by the crystal ball ends up eating ground glass." Certain factors, however, are likely to have the largest impact on the future evolution of this market. In this section, we will point out those factors we think are more important and suggest possible outcomes.

Liability of the Intermediary

Much of what we have read in the trade journals and heard from the market participants involves conjecture about the swap market "after the first major default." This reflects uncertainty about the legal standing of swap contracts and, more significantly, a good deal of controversy over the liability borne by the intermediary (both the current level and the appropriate level).

At one extreme, there are those who argue that the intermediary should assume no liability. Proponents of this view recommend making swaps more like exchange-traded instruments. Suggestions include marking swaps to market with callable margins (or with variable fees) and collateralization (with or without a clearinghouse).

At the other extreme are those who argue that the intermediary should always retain part of the risk. Arguing against the move toward exchange trading, proponents of this position note that, because swaps are like bundles of forward contracts, credit risk of the counterparties is an important element and the intermediary (who has a comparative advantage in assessing the credit risk) is effectively a counterparty to each side of the contract.

Secondary Market

As we noted, the growth of the secondary market has made possible much of the growth of the swaps market, and future growth depends on the existence of an active secondary market. Whether a still broader secondary market should be encouraged inevitably throws us back on the earlier question of the liability of the intermediary. Proponents of making swaps exchange-traded instruments point out that marking to market or collateralizing allow contract standardization as well as providing effective guarantees against contractual default. Furthermore, if contracts are effectively bonded, as would be the case with marking to market or collateralizing, the secondary markets can be more anonymous.

Opponents of the move toward exchange trading for swaps point out that secondary markets can be active even if the assets are not homogeneous. For example, there exists an active secondary market for mortgage-backed securities. In this market, performance is guaranteed by mortgage insurance and the reputation of the originating institution. And it is argued that similar mechanisms are also possible in the swaps market.

Regulation

As might be expected, the divisions evident in the preceding issues are also evident when it comes to questions concerning appropriate regulation of the market. One group argues that additional contractual guarantees are necessary if abuses in this market are to be avoided. Hence, in this view, regulation should take the form of codifying the contractual guarantees — for example, requiring that the contracts be marked to market or collateralized. Those taking the opposite position argue that this market is simply an extension of credit markets and that imposing liability on the financial intermediary is the best way to limit potential abuses.

Besides this controversy over how to regulate, there is also the issue of who should regulate swaps. There are differences in regulatory bodies across countries, and also multiple regulatory bodies within the same country, that need to be considered. (For example, in the United States, the interested regulatory authorities include the Federal Reserve, the SEC, and the Financial Accounting Standards Board.) Under such circumstances, effective regulation will be difficult if not impossible because it requires coordination both within and among countries. If the United States, for example, decided to place burdensome regulations on swaps, the principal effect on swap activity would be to change the location of swap transactions. Even if a group of the major countries acted in concert, the economic incentives for swaps discussed earlier suggest that there would be strong motive for some country to supply a favorable legal environment.

The future of the swaps market, then, appears to turn on whether that market moves further in the direction of becoming a widely traded exchange. While we are not comfortable in predicting the direction the market will actually take, we are confident that the future composition of this market, both the users and the intermediaries, will depend strongly on the resolution of this uncertainty. If swaps move further toward exchange trading, investment banks will be the major beneficiary. Removing the liability for the intermediary by marking to market or collateralizing would diminish the emphasis on capital commitment; if so, investment banks might well regain the dominance they enjoyed in the earliest stages of the evolution of this market. On the other hand, if the intermediary continues to bear risk (or if the liability for the intermediary is increased), commercial banks will be the beneficiary.

The degree to which the swap market moves toward exchange trading will also determine the users of this market. With credit risk borne by the intermediaries, entry to the swaps market may well be denied to lesser credits. Hence, the predominant users of swaps will be the best credit risks. If the swaps market moves toward exchange trading, however, this composition will change. Lesser credit risks will be able to enter the swap market. Furthermore, to the extent that collateralization or some other form of bonding raises the cost of a swap transaction, the best credits will be expected to exit the market, refusing to pay the implicit insurance premium.

Because of the considerable dispute about the appropriateness of moving further toward exchange trading, there is no consensus about the future form of the swaps market. But there are issues where a consensus is possible. Most observers agree, for example, that while the market will continue to develop a more homogeneous set of products with greater liquidity, there will continue to exist a subset of swaps which are custom tailored. The commercial banks should dominate in the homogeneous swaps market, which will be characterized by high volume, low spreads, and a significant capital commitment. Investment banks should continue to have a comparative advantage in the customized end of the market.

9

The Market for
Interest Rate Swaps*

*Clifford W. Smith, Jr., Charles W. Smithson,
& Lee Macdonald Wakeman*

A swap involves an exchange of cash flows between the parties to the contract; in an interest rate swap, one party periodically pays a cash flow determined by a fixed interest rate and receives a cash flow determined by a floating interest rate. Although the instrument only first appeared in 1982,[1] U.S. dollar interest rate swaps have grown into a market with 1987 volume estimated at $542 billion.[2] With such growth has come concern about the risks in this market. Indeed, in their capital adequacy proposal, the Federal Reserve and the Bank of England suggest, "The credit risks inherent in such contracts now constitute a significant element of the risk profiles of some banking organizations, notably the large multinational banking organizations

*This research was partially supported by the John M. Olin Foundation and the Managerial Economics Research Center, William E. Simon Graduate School of Business Administration, University of Rochester. We thank George Benston, Wayne Marr, David Mayers, René Stulz, our colleagues at the Simon School, and the two referees of *Financial Management* for their comments.
1. The first swap contract to appear was the currency swap, publicly introduced via the transaction between IBM and the World Bank in 1981 (although several private currency swaps had been arranged earlier). The currency coupon swap extended the fixed-fixed nature of a currency swap to the exchange of a cash flow based on a fixed interest rate in one currency for one based on a floating interest rate in another. The interest rate swap evolved as a special case of a currency coupon swap in which all payments are made in a single currency. For more on these and other swap contracts see Smith, Smithson, and Wakeman [23].
2. The notional principal of outstanding U.S. dollar interest rate swaps as reported in the International Swap Dealers Association, Survey of Members, July 1988.

that act as intermediaries between end-users of these contracts."[3] The Bank for International Settlements asserts that the credit risk of swaps is underpriced, "gross income from the transaction is insufficient, on average, to compensate fully for their inherent risks."[4] These statements reflect a misconception about default risks inherent in interest rate swaps as well as about the motivation for the growth of the market — misconceptions that have their root in misunderstandings of the instrument.

I. Analysis of an Interest Rate Swap

A simple interest rate swap contract is illustrated in Panel A of Figure 9.1. The cash flows are based on a "notional" principle P that is used to calculate the cash flows but is not normally exchanged. At stipulated settlement dates (typically every six months) the firm in Figure 9.1 pays a "coupon" determined by the fixed interest rate prevailing at contract origination $(\bar{R}_t)$. In return, the firm receives a "coupon" based on the relevant floating interest rate, $\tilde{R}_t$ (the six-month rate in effect at $t-1$).[5] Hence, throughout the swap the cash flow at the next settlement is nonstochastic. Operationally, gross cash flows are not exchanged; only the net is paid as a difference check from the party that would have received the smaller payment. Thus, the firm illustrated in Figure 9.1 receives a difference check, $D_t = \tilde{R}_t - \bar{R}_t$, at time t.[6]

A. An Interest Rate Swap as a Portfolio of Loans

As illustrated in Figure 9.1, the swap cash flows in Panel A are equivalent to the pair of loan contracts in Panel B — borrowing at a fixed rate and simultaneously lending at a floating rate. To prevent arbitrage, the value at origination of the T-period swap, $S(O,T)$, must equal the difference between the values of a T-period floating rate note, $\tilde{L}(O,T)$, and a T-period fixed rate note, $\bar{L}(O,T)$,[7]

$$S(O,T) = \tilde{L}(O,T) - \bar{L}(O,T) \qquad (9.1)$$

---

3. See the Federal Reserve Bank and Bank of England ([7], p. 3). Also see, E. N. Berg, "Fed Urges Swap Plan for Banks," *New York Times,* (March 3, 1987).

4. See the Bank for International Settlements ([1], p. 3).

5. Swaps generally specify that the rate for the next period is set using the appropriate floating interest rate two days prior to the current period's settlement date.

6. An expected coupon payment for the floating rate loan is $\tilde{R}_t = \tilde{r}(t-1,t)P$, where $\tilde{r}(t-1,t)$ is the forward rate. The coupon payments for the fixed rate loan are $\bar{R}_t = r(O,T)P$, where $r(O,T)$ is the par rate — i.e., the rate for T-period bond that pays a level coupon and sells at par at origination. Therefore, the difference checks for the swap in Figure 9.1 are $D_t = [\tilde{r}(t-1,t) - r(O,T)]P$.

7. Note that this arbitrage result does not depend on the assumption that the contracts are default risk free. With default risk, as long as the borrowing is collateralized with the lending agreement, the cash flows in Panels A and B are always equivalent.

FIGURE 9.1   Decomposition of a Simple Interest Rate Swap

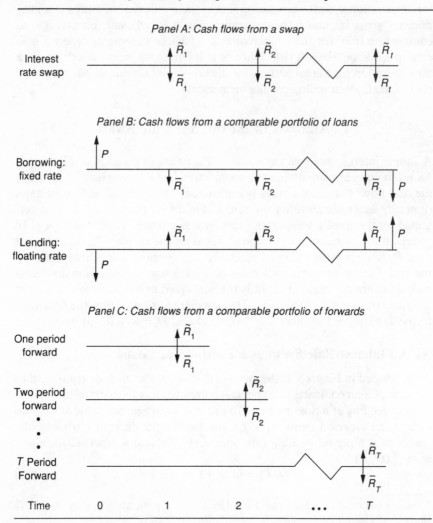

In Panel A the party receives cash flows $(\tilde{R}_t)$ determined by the relevant floating interest rate and pays cash flows $(\bar{R}_t)$ determined by the fixed interest rate at origination. Note that inflows are denoted by up arrows and outflows by down arrows; the magnitude of the cash flow is indicated by the length of the arrow. In Panel B the swap is decomposed into a portfolio of two loan contracts: borrowing at a fixed-rate and lending at a floating-rate, where $\bar{R}_t$ are the fixed coupon payments, $\tilde{R}_t$ are the floating coupon payments, and P is the principal. In Panel C, the swap is decomposed into a portfolio of T forward contracts in which the party illustrated has agreed at origination to pay at period t in the future a known amount $(\bar{R}_t)$ to receive an amount determined by the prevailing single-period interest rate $(\tilde{R}_t)$.

Employing market rates, the value of each loan is zero at origination; hence, the value of the swap contract must also be zero at origination, $S(O, T) = 0$. After origination the swap value is determined by realized rates.

The value of the fixed rate loan, $\bar{L}(O, T)$, can be decomposed into the net present value of a fixed rate annuity with a vector of payments $\bar{R}_T$ and a T-period zero coupon bond with face value P_T,

$$\bar{L}(O, T) = NPV[\bar{R}_T] + NPV[P_T] \tag{9.2}$$

The value of the floating rate loan, $\tilde{L}(O, T)$, can be decomposed into the values of a vector of floating rate annuity payments $\tilde{R}_T$ and the same T-period zero,

$$\tilde{L}(O, T) = NPV[\tilde{R}_T] + NPV[P_T] \tag{9.3}$$

Thus, the value of the swap in Figure 9.1 also is the difference between the values of floating and fixed-rate annuities,

$$S(O, T) = NPV[\tilde{R}_T] - NPV[\bar{R}_T] \tag{9.4}$$

The Impact of Interest Rate Changes on Swap Value. Increases in market rates reduce the value of the fixed rate loan by reducing the value of both the fixed rate annuity and the embedded zero coupon bond,

$$\frac{\partial \bar{L}(O, T)}{\partial \bar{r}(t, t+1)} = \frac{\partial NPV[\bar{R}_T]}{\partial \bar{r}(t, t+1)} + \frac{\partial NPV[P_T]}{\partial \bar{r}(t, t+1)} < 0 \tag{9.5}$$

However, on interest rate reset dates, rate increases leave the value of a default-free floating rate note unaffected. That is, at a settlement date,

$$\frac{\partial \tilde{L}(O, T)}{\partial \bar{r}(t, t+1)} = \frac{\partial NPV[\tilde{R}_T]}{\partial \bar{r}(t, t+1)} - \frac{\partial NPV[P_T]}{\partial \bar{r}(t, t+1)} = 0 \tag{9.6}$$

Since increases in rates unambiguously reduce the value of the embedded zero, they must increase the value of the floating rate annuity by an equal amount. Thus, higher rates increase the swap value,

$$\frac{\partial S(O, T)}{\partial \bar{r}(t, t+1)} = \frac{\partial NPV[\tilde{R}_T]}{\partial \bar{r}(t, t+1)} - \frac{\partial NPV[\bar{R}_T]}{\partial \bar{r}(t, t+1)} > 0 \tag{9.7}$$

As Equation 9.7 indicates, the derivative of the swap value with respect to rate changes is greater than that of either the fixed or floating rate annuity. The relative contribution of the fixed and floating rate terms to interest rate responsiveness depends on the maturity of the swap. For shorter-term swaps, the change in the value of the floating rate annuity dominates, but for longer-term swaps, the change in the fixed rate annuity dominates.

Equation 9.7 demonstrates that on reset dates the value of the Figure 9.1 swap is inversely related to the value of a comparable maturity fixed rate bond. This is obvious from using Equation 9.5 to combine Equations 9.6 and 9.7 to obtain,

$$\frac{\partial S(O,T)}{\partial \tilde{r}(t,t+1)} = -\frac{\partial \tilde{L}(O,T)}{\partial \tilde{r}(t,t+1)} \tag{9.8}$$

This restatement of the relation explains why, at rate reset dates, the interest rate sensitivity of a swap is equal in magnitude to the interest rate sensitivity of a fixed rate bond of the same maturity and coupon, even though the swap principal is only notional.

Thus far we have focused on rate-induced changes in the value of the swap at a settlement date. Between settlement dates, the amount of the next floating rate payment is known. Therefore, Equation 9.6 does not hold for all $r(t,t+1)$ and the responsiveness of the swap value to interest rate changes is reduced, since the derivative of the floating rate loan value with respect to the spot rate is negative. Thus, the sign of the Equation 9.7 derivative can be reversed. For example, in period T if the party in Figure 9.1 is to receive the final difference check, subsequent increases in interest rates lower the remaining swap value.

B. An Interest Rate Swap as a Portfolio of Forward Contracts

Panel C of Figure 9.1 illustrates that a default-free interest rate swap can also be decomposed into a portfolio of forwards, one maturing at each settlement date. Figure 9.2 illustrates the payoff profile for one settlement date. If rates rise, the firm receives an inflow; if rates fall, the firm makes an outflow. Hence, a swap is like a portfolio of forward contracts, with maturities corresponding to the settlement dates specified in the swap. At each settlement the losses or gains in the currently maturing forward are realized. However, since a swap specifies the T-period par rate, $\tilde{r}(O,T)$, in each embedded forward rather than the individual time-zero forward rates, $\tilde{r}(t,t+1)$, the cash flows from a swap and those from a portfolio of forwards will differ unless the term structure is flat.

II. Swaps and Default Risk

The appropriate swap default premium is an issue of major concern to market participants. The chairman of the International Swap Dealers Association (ISDA) effectively summarized the views of many market participants when he asserted: "The credit aspect of swaps is not being adequately remunerated in the market. There's a credit spread of 150 basis points in the loan market but of only 5 to 10 basis points in swaps. The weakest credits are

FIGURE 9.2   *Payoff Profile for a Swap at a Representative Settlement Date*

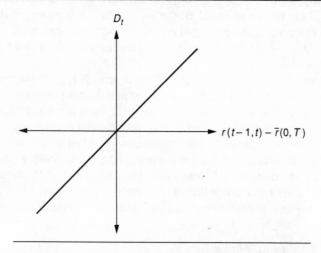

The value of a typical swap difference check, D_t, received by the party paying fixed and receiving floating. The value of the check increases as the realized forward rate, $r(t-1,t)$, is greater than the par rate at origination, $\bar{r}(0, T)$. This figure also can be used to illustrate the relation between swap, forward, and futures contracts. The value to the seller of a forward contract behaves similarly, but the par rate is replaced by the forward rate, $\bar{r}(t-1,t)$. The value of the day t settlement to the seller for a futures contract also behaves similarly, but the rate difference is between the futures rate calculated on day t and that from day $t-1$.

getting a terrific deal."[8] This assertion that the credit/default risk of swaps is mispriced relative to that of loans requires that we examine the differences between default on a loan versus a swap. Yet it is by viewing swaps as a portfolio of forward contracts that we gain the most insights into the default risk of an interest rate swap.

A. Default Risk of Swaps vs. Loans

A crucial difference between default on interest rate swaps and default on loans is that the principal in an interest rate swap is only notional, whereas a

---

8. A quote from Patrick de Saint-Aignan as reported in David Shirreff, "The Fearsome Growth of Swaps," *Euromoney* (October 1985), pp. 247–261.

major component of the expected loss in lending involves principal repayment. Suppose the firm in Figure 9.1 defaults at time t. For default on a fixed rate loan like the one in Panel B, the loss to the counterparty is the sum of the present values of the principal P and the coupon payments $\bar{R}_t, ..., \bar{R}_T$. In contrast, Panel A demonstrates that the counterparty in a swap will suffer no principal loss.

Moreover, in a swap the lost cash flow in periods $t, ..., T$ is reduced from $\bar{R}_t$ to $\bar{R}_t - \tilde{R}_t$ — the difference between fixed and floating rates rather than the level of the rate. If rates have fallen since the contract was originated, the remaining cash flows look like those of an off-market-rate swap. Consider again the swap in Figure 9.1, but suppose the specified fixed rate exceeds the current rate, producing off-market coupons, $\bar{R}_i' > \bar{R}_i$. Defining P' as the value of a bond with coupons of $\bar{R}_i'$ and a principal repayment of P, this off-market swap with a net principal inflow at origination is illustrated in Panel A of Figure 9.3. Panel B decomposes the swap into two loans where the coupon

FIGURE 9.3   *An Off-Market-Rate Swap*

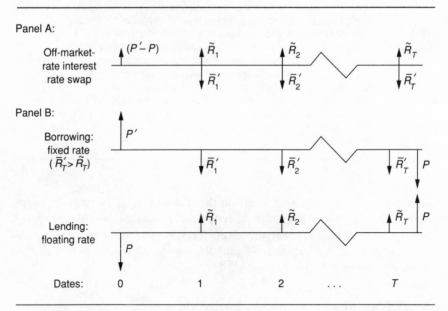

The party pays cash flows $(\bar{R}_t')$ determined by a fixed interest rate above the current market rate and receives cash flows $(\tilde{R}_t)$ determined by the relevant floating interest rate. In Panel A, a principal exchange $(P'-P)$ occurs at origination, with P' equal to the market value of a bond with coupons $\bar{R}_t'$ and a principal repayment of P. In Panel B this swap is decomposed into two loan contracts: borrowing at a fixed rate higher than the prevailing market rate and lending at the market floating rate.

payment $\bar{R}'_i$ is higher than $\bar{R}_i$ and the final principal payment P is less than P'. Hence, in an off-market-rate swap, the party receives a principle inflow at origination and expects to pay difference checks over the term of the swap. Thus the required initial principal exchange, $P' - P$, reflects the current market loss to the floating rate payer were the fixed rate payer to default.

Finally, when comparing swaps and loans, it must be remembered that rational default requires the remaining value of the contract to be negative. For example, if rates have risen since origination, then for the swap in Figure 9.1 the remaining net present value of the contract is positive. Therefore, default by the fixed rate payer would be irrational since it would result in the cancellation of a profitable contract.[9] Consequently, the pricing implications of default are significantly smaller for a swap than for a loan.

B. Default Risk in Forwards, Futures, and Swaps

In many ways, the probability of default on a swap is more like the default problem in forward and futures contracts than loans. As with forwards and futures, swap default risk is two-sided. However, loans, annuities, deposits, and nonassessable insurance policies are structured so that, after origination, payments go in only one direction — one of the parties to the contract bears all the default risk. Consequently, insights into swap default risk can be gained by comparing default control mechanisms for swaps with those of forwards and futures.[10] We examine three of these mechanisms: the way contract value is distributed, the way the contract is traded, and performance bonds.

Distributing Contract Value. The way value changes are distributed to the contracting parties differs across forward, futures, and swap contracts. At one extreme is the futures contract, where the total change in the value of the contract is distributed daily. At the other extreme is the forward contract, where value is distributed to the owners only at contract maturity. Swaps fall between these extremes; difference checks distribute value changes periodically over the contract life, not just at maturity. However, since the difference check in an interest rate swap reflects only the maturing embedded forward contract, a difference check generally does not distribute the entire value change.

---

9. In the special case where the term structure is flat and interest rates have remained unchanged since origination of the swap, $\bar{R}_t - \tilde{R}_t = O$ for all $t = 1, ..., t$; so, the remaining value of the swap is the same as the value at origination $[S(t, T) = S(O, T) = O]$. Hence in this special case, default costs are limited to the transaction costs of locating a replacement counterparty.

10. There exists a wealth of literature on the valuation of default-free forward and futures contracts. See Black [3], Oldfield and Messina [17], Kane [11], Jarrow and Oldfield [9], Cox, Ingersoll, and Ross [6], and Richard Sundaresan [19]. French [8] provides empirical tests of the relation between forward prices and futures prices.

These differences in the distribution of contract value have implications for the probability of default. Since a futures contract is cash-settled daily, losses from default are limited to a one-day value change. Conversely, since a forward contract requires no settlement prior to maturity, the value change can be significantly larger. Hence, potential default risk is greater for forward contracts than futures contracts, all else being equal. Swaps are again an intermediate case; difference checks provide a periodic partial settlement. Moreover, default on any of the required difference-check payments accelerates the remaining payments. With default, the swap reverts from a portfolio of forward contracts to a single, currently due contract.

Trading the Contracts.   Forward, futures, and swap contracts differ with respect to the manner in which they are traded. Futures contracts are always exchange traded. While the exchange itself takes no positions, it guarantees the performance of all participants through its clearinghouse. Hence, the problem of two-sided default risk is addressed by the exchange interposing itself between parties in each transaction. Most forward contracts (for example, on foreign exchange and interest rates) are marketed by financial institutions. Since a bank is one of the counterparties to every transaction, economies of scale in credit evaluation can be achieved, but default risk is still counterparty specific. Some forward contracts are exchange traded, notably forward contracts on tin and several other metals on the London Metal Exchange. That exchange's recent experience demonstrates that the existence of an exchange does not eliminate default risk (the "tin cartel" defaulted on contracts for tin delivery, making the exchange liable for the loss[11]). With an exchange, the cost of default is spread over all the traded contracts rather than imposed on a specific counterparty (as with most forward contracts).

Early in their evolution, swaps were negotiated on an individual basis (particularly currency swaps). A financial intermediary would arrange a swap between two parties known to each other. Development of a secondary market allowing firms to trade swaps was necessarily limited. With matched counterparties, there was an understandable reluctance to permit transferring swap contracts, since such transference would rationally induce the uninvolved party to expend resources to evaluate the prospective new counterparty's default risk.

As the interest rate swap market has evolved, banks have taken more of the intermediary role. Today, the majority of interest rate swaps involve a bank as a counterparty, thereby achieving significant economies in credit evaluation. Furthermore, problems related to the transferring of swaps have been reduced, since the firm can cancel an interest rate swap contract with a

---

11. See "Tin Crisis in London Roils Metal Exchange" in *The Wall Street Journal* of November 13, 1985.

bank via a cash settlement or by "unwinding" the contract (entering into another swap with provisions the reverse of the first).

Performance Bonds. The exchange-traded futures contracts require an explicit performance bond to be posted. This bond, the initial margin, typically is equal to the maximum daily fluctuation permitted in the value of the contract. Each day, the contract is settled by drawing down or adding to the margin account. The futures contract also requires that the margin account balance exceed a specified minimum (the maintenance margin). If as the result of daily settlements the account balance falls below that minimum, the contract owner is required to bring the margin account back to the initial level or the contract is closed out. These mechanisms, in place and functioning, substantially reduce the treat of default for futures contracts.

Exchanges also impose other rules to reduce default risk. Some markets allow collateralization as a substitute for posting margin, thereby lowering the cost of market participation to hedgers. Futures exchanges impose limits on daily price moves, a practice that Brennan [4] argues is a partial substitute for posting margin (but one that is less effective in financial markets where alternative sources of information about equilibrium prices are available). Finally, exchange transactions must be executed through a member firm that endorses the transaction—and thus effectively imposes a potential liability on itself should its customer fail to perform. Hence, this broker endorsement increases the broker's incentive to monitor its customers' margin accounts (Sharpe [21], p. 528).

In the swap market, margin or other forms of explicit performance bonds are not required for good credits, but they are employed for poor credits. The most frequently employed performance bond is to require a poor credit to post collateral in the form of a portfolio of financial securities.

In addition, performance bonding through insurance has also been employed. The World Bank established a swap insurance program that divides the cash flows from the swap between the Word Bank and the Aetna Casualty and Surety Company—the World Bank retains the interest rate risk and Aetna assumes the default risk. This swap insurance program acts like private mortgage insurance; the insurer (here Aetna) bonds the counterparty against default.

C. Other Determinants of Default Risk for Interest Rate Swaps

The Use of the Swap. As suggested above, default requires that both the contract value be negative and the contract owner be in bankruptcy. An interest rate swap could be used either to speculate on or hedge against changes in interest rates. Clearly, the risk of default on the contract is influenced by the use to which the instrument is put. If a firm's cash flows are sensitive to interest rate changes and if it enters into a swap contract as a hedge, the probability of financial distress and bankruptcy is reduced — and outflow is required only when the hedging firm's other net cash flows are expected to be higher. In contrast, if a swap contract is used to speculate, an outflow may well be required when the firm is in financial distress. Thus, with a swap contract, default risk is endogenous, so the default risk and therefore the appropriate risk premium is partially determined by the use to which the instrument is put.

Term Structure.   Given that the credit risk assessment process is in place, default implies a deterioration in the firm's financial position since contract origination. Hence, the probability of default is a positive function of the time since contract initiation. As we note above, a fixed rate payer like the one illustrated in Figure 9.1 will make payments determined by the par rate at origination and will receive payments determined by future floating rates. If the term structure is upward sloping, as in Figure 9.4, the fixed-rate payer

FIGURE 9.4   *The Impact of a Rising Structure of Interest Rates on Swap Payments and Default*

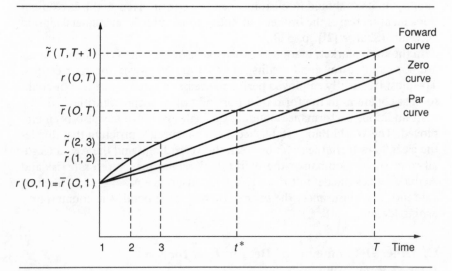

The zero curve displays the yields to maturity of zero coupon bonds. The forward curve displays the implied one-period forward interest rates. The par curve displays the per period rate for a bond that pays a level coupon and sells at par for different maturities. At time t^*, the implied forward rate, $\tilde{r}(t^*-1, t)$, equals the T-period par rate.

expects to pay difference checks for periods 1, 2, ..., t^* and receive difference checks thereafter. Hence, if the term structure is upward sloping, the expectation is that the party paying fixed and receiving floating (the party in Figure 9.1) will pay difference checks early in the term of the swap and receive net payments in the later periods. In terms of Figure 9.4, this means that $\tilde{r}(t-1, t) - r(O, T)$ is expected to be negative in the early periods and positive in the later periods. Thus, the probability that the fixed rate payer will default is less than would be the case if the term structure were flat or had a negative slope.

III. The Rationale for Interest-Rate Swaps

So far we have seen that interest rate swaps fit on a continuum between forward and futures contracts. But this relation between swaps, forwards, and futures raises another question: Since forwards and futures are substitutes for swaps, what explains the dramatic growth of the interest rate swap market?

A. Financial Arbitrage

The argument most frequently advanced to explain the growth of the swap market is that swaps exploit market inefficiencies. For example, Mr. Robin Leigh-Pemberton, governor of the Bank of England, argued that swaps enable borrowers to "arbitrage" the credit markets, allowing ". . . a good credit rating in one part of the currency/maturity matrix to be translated into relatively cheap borrowing in another."[12] Bicksler and Chen [2] reiterated this position by asserting that pricing is inconsistent across financial markets and that the "difference in the quality spreads presents a market arbitrage opportunity" that can be exploited via a swap. An illustration of borrowers taking advantage of the differential quality spreads to which Bicksler and Chen alluded is provided in Table 9.1.[13] In this table, the quality spread in the fixed rate market is 1.2%, but only 0.5% in the floating rate market. The assertion is that this quality-spread differential can be "arbitraged"—the AAA borrows fixed, the BBB borrows floating, and via a swap each ends up with lower borrowing costs.[14]

---

12. A quote in "The Risk Game: A Survey of International Banking," by Merril Stevenson in *The Economist*, March 21, 1987.
13. This illustration was taken from "The International Swap Market," an advertising supplement by Bankers Trust Company to *Euromoney Corporate Finance*, September 1985.
14. The implicit assertion that the quality differential can be used to the benefit of all parties — the two borrowers and the financial intermediary — was examined by Turnbull [27]. He shows that with perfect makets, swaps must be a zero sum game.

TABLE 9.1   *Illustration of the Purported Gains from Credit Risk Arbitrage via an Interest Rate Swap*

Credit Rating of Firm	AAA	BBB
Cost of Directly Borrowing Fixed	10.8%	12.0%
Cost of Directly Borrowing Floating	LIBOR + 0.25%	LIBOR + 0.75%
	Fund	
AAA Borrows Fixed	10.8%	
BBB Borrows Floating		LIBOR + 0.75%
	Swap	
AAA Receives Fixed	10.9%	
AAA Pays Floating	LIBOR	
BBB Receives Floating		LIBOR
BBB Pays Fixed		10.9%
All-in cost of funding	LIBOR − 0.1%	11.65%
Savings	0.35%	0.35%

The illustration in Table 9.1 is consistent with both available data on quality differentials and the observation that fixed rate payers are predominantly the less creditworthy counterparty. However, it is less clear that this behavior is consistent with classic financial arbitrage. First, arbitrage should lead to decreasing, not increasing, swap volume; as the quality spread is arbitraged, the rate differences would be eliminated and this rationale for interest rate swaps should disappear. Second, the underlying reason for the quality differentials is ignored.

Comparative Advantage.   The trade press explains quality differentials by asserting that firms have a "comparative advantage" in one of the credit markets. The AAA has a comparative advantage in the fixed rate market, and the BBB in the floating rate market. The interest rate swap permits them to exploit their comparative advantages and produce interest rate savings. However, the comparative advantage argument does neglect arbitrage. With no barriers to capital flows, this argument from elementary trade theory cannot hold. Arbitrage eliminates any comparative advantage.

Underpriced Credit Risk.   It has been suggested that fixed rate and that floating rate lenders assess risk differently. For example, Ramaswamy and Sundaresan [18] find that default premiums for floating rate loans are lower than predicted. While underpriced credit risk for floating rate loans would explain the growth of interest rate swaps, swaps effectively increase the demand for floating rate debt by lower-rated companies and the demand for fixed rate debt by higher-rated companies. This should eliminate the supposed differential pricing.

Differential Prepayment Options. The apparent savings from obtaining funding via a swap can be explained by considering options available to the borrower. Most fixed rate loans also include a prepayment option.[15] In contrast, interest rate swaps normally contain no such prepayment option. Early termination of a swap agreement requires that the remaining contract be marked to market and paid in full.[16]

Hence, the positions of the firm that has borrowed fixed directly and the one that has borrowed floating and swapped to fixed are quite different. The former owns a put option on interest rates; the latter does not. And, in this context, the transaction between the AAA firm and the BBB firm looks less like financial arbitrage and more like an option transaction. The BBB firm can borrow at a fixed rate more cheaply by swapping from floating because the borrowing-floating/swap-to-fixed alternative does not include the interest rate option contained in the borrow-fixed alternative. The BBB firm has in effect sold an interest rate option. The funding cost "savings" obtained by the BBB firm (and the AAA firm) come from the premium on this option.[17]

B. Liquidity

An important factor in the growth in this market is the substantial reduction in bid-ask spreads. In 1982, spreads exceeded 200 basis points; now they are frequently less than ten. Thus, the dramatic increase in volume has been accompanied by an equally dramatic increase in the liquidity of the market.

C. Exposure Management

Since swaps can be used to manage a corporation's exposure to interest rate risk, part of the growth in interest rate swaps simply reflects the general increase in corporate hedging activities. In addition to risk aversion of the owner of a closely held firm, Smith and Stulz [24] demonstrate that value-

---

15. This is the call provision in standard corporate bonds. See Smith and Warner [25].
16. See Article 12 of the International Swap Dealers Association's *Code of Standard Wording, Assumptions and Provisions for Swaps,* 1986 edition.
17. It is important to ensure that the quoted rates in Table 9.1 are complete and consistent. In addition to differential prepayment options, differential fees, commissions, or expenses can eliminate the apparent advantage. It is also important to ensure that the rates are quoted employing the same compounding and days-of-the-year conventions. See Smith [26].

maximizing firms can have incentives to hedge because: (1) convexities in the corporate tax schedule makes the expected after-tax value of the firm a decreasing function of the volatility of taxable income; (2) expected costs of financial distress are increasing in the volatility of firm value; and (3) managerial risk aversion reduces the value of ill-diversified fixed compensation claims. Mayers and Smith [15] show that hedging can control an aspect of Myers' [16] underinvestment problem, thus reducing expected costs of financial distress. And Shapiro and Titman [20] point out that firms with product warranties, service networks, and the like, have greater incentives to hedge. To this list we offer two additions. First, given current and anticipated future asset structure, corporations have incentives to carefully structure the liability side of their balance sheet to control potential incentive problems.[18] Consider then the firm's long-term debt. When realizations deviate from forecasts, recapitalization of the firm is sometimes beneficial, but most long-term bond contracts include penalties for prepaying or calling the bonds. Interest rate swaps allow the financial manager additional flexibility to restructure the firm's long-term fixed rate obligations while avoiding the costs of calling the bonds. Second, thrifts have a comparative advantage in attracting short-term deposits, but in placing long-term mortgage loans. However, a policy of simply exploiting this institutional advantage exposes them to significant interest rate risk (Smith [22]). As an alternative to offering adjustable rate mortgages or selling mortgages and reinvesting the proceeds in short-term assets, this risk can be managed by using interest rate swaps to manage the gap between asset and liability maturities.[19]

D. Synthetic Instruments

A final reason for the growth of the swap market is their usefulness in the creation of new financial instruments. For example, the market for long-dated interest rate forward contracts was historically very illiquid. But since interest rate swaps can be viewed as portfolios of forward interest rate contracts, long-term swaps have been stripped to increase liquidity in the market for long-dated forward rate agreements. Conversely, interest rate swaps have been combined with other instruments to create new products. For example, the combination of a fixed rate loan and an interest rate swap where the party pays fixed produces a "reverse floating rate loan"; if interest rates rise, then the coupon payments on the loan fall.

---

18. See Myers [16], and Jensen and Smith [10].
19. We believe that these exposure management arguments help explain the active participation of thrift institutions and insurance companies in the interest rate swap market. And Edward Kane reminded us that, in addition to those thrifts wanting to hedge their exposures, there are hundreds of "zombie" thrifts whose managers want to make endgame plays. See Kane [13].

IV. Conclusions

One must be struck by the growth of the U.S. dollar interest rate swap market—from zero in 1981 to an outstanding volume of $542 billion at the end of 1987. The argument that arbitrage of quality spreads is the reason for this growth is unsatisfying. Since swap cash flows are equivalent to those from portfolios of existing financial products, arbitrage among inconsistently priced instruments is feasible. But successful arbitrage should eliminate pricing inconsistencies and should therefore lead to decreasing volume rather than the observed increase. Moreover, we see no convincing evidence that swaps are mispriced—that the quality spread for swaps is lower than for loans is not sufficient to imply mispriced credit risk. Indeed, credit spreads should be lower for swaps than for loans because (1) the principal in a swap is only notional; (2) the difference check is a function of the difference rather than the level of rates; and (3) rational default requires that both the firm be in bankruptcy and the remaining swap value be negative. Indeed, the apparent funding cost savings may well reflect differential prepayment options rather than arbitrage profit. Instead, we propose that the growth of this market has been the result of reductions in the bid-ask spread, a general increase in the corporate demand for risk management instruments (including swaps), and the ability to use swaps to create synthetic financial instruments.

With the dramatic growth in volume has come concern about the credit risk of swaps, including proposals from the Fed and the Bank of England for the imposition of capital adequacy requirements on banks that intermediate swaps. Intermediation in the swap market imposes claims on a firm's capital, so additional capital would perform a potentially valuable bonding function. However, since banks can fully capture the benefits of an increase in demand for their market-making services from better bonding, there will exist a market-determined optimal capital reserve. Therefore, the rationale for the proposed requirements must be based on the nonactuarial pricing of FDIC insurance (see Busser, Chen, and Kane [5]) or on the subsidization of risk-taking behavior that results when government regulators are reluctant to liquidate large financial institutions (see Kane [12, 14]).

While our analysis is not sufficient to permit the quantification of the optimal capital requirement, two general conclusions seem warranted. First, the appropriate capital requirement should be related to the default characteristics of those swaps that the bank intermediates. Our analysis indicates that the default risk of an individual swap is dramatically less than that of a comparable loan, and is more closely related to the default risk of forward and futures contracts. By contrasting the swap with forward and futures contracts, it becomes clear that the default risk for an interest rate swap is determined by the credit rating of the contracting firm, the correlation between the contracting firm's value and interest rates, the volatility of interest rates, the slope of the term structure, the maturity of the swap, the frequency of the difference checks, and whether some form of performance bond is posted.

Second, the cash flow implications of default for a portfolio of swaps are significantly different than those of a single contract. If a bank maintains a relatively balanced portfolio of swaps, it will generally receive payments from half its book and make payments to the other half. Thus, at any time only half its outstanding swaps would be candidates for default. Moreover, since default on the swap requires both that the firm be in financial distress and that the remaining value of the contract be negative, default on swaps by hedgers should be more idiosyncratic than default on loans. Therefore, default risk faced by a bank in the interest rate swap market seems especially well-suited to be managed through diversification by holding a portfolio of swaps.

References

1. Bank for International Settlements, *Recent Innovations in International Banking,* Basle: Author, 1986.
2. J. Bicksler and A. H. Chen, "An Economic Analysis of Interest Rate Swaps," *The Journal of Finance* (July 1986), pp. 645–655.
3. F. Black, "The Pricing of Commodity Contracts," *Journal of Financial Economics* (January 1976), pp. 167–179.
4. M. J. Brennen, "A Theory of Price Limits in Futures Markets," *Journal of Financial Economics* (June 1986), pp. 213–233.
5. S. A. Busser, A. H. Chen, and E. J. Kane, "Federal Deposit Insurance, Regulatory Policy, and Optimal Bank Capital," *Journal of Finance* (March 1981), pp. 51–60.
6. J. C. Cox, J. E. Ingersoll, Jr., and S. A. Ross, "The Relation Between Forward Prices and Futures Prices," *Journal of Financial Economics* (December 1981), pp. 321–346.
7. Federal Reserve Board and Bank of England, "Agreed Proposal of the United States Federal Banking Supervisory Authorities and the Bank of England on Primary Capital and Capital Adequacy Assessment," and Staff Memo: "Treatment of Interest Rate and Exchange Rate Contracts in the Risk Asset Ratio," March 3, 1987.
8. K. R. French, "A Comparison of Futures and Forward Prices," *Journal of Financial Economics* (November 1983), pp. 311–342.
9. R. A. Jarrow and G. S. Oldfield, "Forward Contracts and Futures Contracts," *Journal of Financial Economics* (December 1981), pp. 373–382.
10. M. C. Jensen and C. W. Smith, Jr., "Stockholder, Manager, and Creditor Interests: Applications of Agency Theory," *Recent Advances in Corporate Finance,* E. Altman and M. Subrahmanyam (eds.), Homewood, IL: Irwin, 1987, pp. 93–131.
11. E. J. Kane, "Market Incompleteness and Divergences Between Forward and Futures Interest Rates," *Journal of Finance* (May 1980), pp. 221–234.

12. ———, "Appearance and Reality in Deposit Insurance: The Case for Reform," *Journal of Banking and Finance* (June 1986), pp. 175–188.
13. ———, "Dangers of Capital Forbearance: The Case of the FSLIC and 'Zombie' S&Ls," *Contemporary Policy Issues* (January 1987), pp. 77–83.
14. ———, "How Incentive-Incompatible Deposit Insurance Funds Fail," working paper, Ohio State University, 1988.
15. D. Mayers and C. W. Smith, Jr., "Corporate Insurance and the Underinvestment Problem," *Journal of Risk and Insurance* (March 1987), pp. 45–54.
16. S. Myers, "Determinants of Corporate Borrowing," *Journal of Financial Economics* (November 1977), pp. 147–175.
17. G. Oldfield and R. Messina, "Forward Exchange Price Determination in Continuous Time," *Journal of Financial and Quantitative Analysis* (September 1977), pp. 473–479.
18. K. Ramaswamy and S. M. Sundaresan, "The Valuation of Floating Rate Instruments: Theory and Evidence," *Journal of Financial Economics* (December 1986), pp. 251–272.
19. S. F. Richard and M. Sundaresan, "A Continuous Time Equilibrium Model of Forward Prices and Futures Prices in a Multigood Economy," *Journal of Financial Economics* (December 1981), pp. 347–371.
20. A. C. Shapiro and S. Titman, "An Integrated Approach to Corporate Risk Management," *Midland Corporate Finance Journal* (Summer 1985), pp. 41–56.
21. W. Sharpe, *Investments,* Englewood Cliffs, NJ: Prentice-Hall, 1985.
22. C. W. Smith, Jr., "Pricing Mortgage Originations," *American Real Estate and Urban Economics Association Journal* (Fall 1982), pp. 313–330.
23. C. W. Smith, Jr., C. W. Smithson, and L. M. Wakeman, "The Evolving Market for Swaps," *Midland Corporate Finance Journal* (Winter 1986), pp. 20–32.
24. C. W. Smith, Jr., and R. Stulz, "The Determinants of Firm's Hedging Policies," *Journal of Financial and Quantitative Analysis* (December 1985), pp. 391–405.
25. C. W. Smith, Jr., and J. Warner, "On Financial Contracting: An Analysis of Bond Covenants," *Journal of Financial Economics* (June 1979), pp. 117–161.
26. D. J. Smith, "Measuring the Gains from 'Arbitraging' the Swap Market," unpublished manuscript, Boston University, 1987.
27. S. M. Turnbull, "Swaps: A Zero Sum Game?" *Financial Management* (Spring 1987), pp. 15–21.

10

Interest Rate Swaps:
A Review of the Issues*

Larry D. Wall & John J. Pringle

In the last two decades a myriad of new instruments and transactions have brought about significant changes in financial markets. Some of these innovations have attracted considerable publicity; stock index futures and options, for example, were an important element in the studies of the October 19, 1987, stock market crash.[1] However, not all of these new developments are well-known to the public. One recent innovation that is quietly transforming credit markets is interest rate swaps—an agreement between two parties to exchange interest payments for a predetermined period of time.

The interest rate swap market begain in 1982. By 1988 the outstanding portfolios of 49 leading swap dealers totaled $889.5 billion in principal, of which $473.6 billion represented new business in 1987.[2] Reflecting their rapid growth, swaps have gained considerable importance in the capital markets. Thomas Jasper, the head of Salomon Brothers' swap department, has estimated that 30 to 40% of all capital market transactions involve an interest rate, foreign-exchange, or some other type of swap.[3]

Their rapid growth is one reason swaps have generated considerable interest among academics, regulators, accountants, and market participants alike. Paramount among the questions surrounding swaps are the reasons for their use and the basis of their pricing. Regulators are also keenly concerned with the risks swaps pose to financial firms, while accountants are debating appropriate reporting. This article reviews the current literature

*The authors wish to thank William Curt Hunter and Peter Abken for their comments.

and presents some new research on interest rate swaps. Among the issues addressed are the workings of interest rate swaps, the reasons that firms use such swaps, the risks associated with interest rate swaps, the price of these swaps, the regulation of participants in the swap market, and the disclosure of swaps on firms' financial statements.

What Is an Interest Rate Swap?

Interest rate swaps serve to transform the effective maturity (or, more accurately, the repricing interval) of two firms' assets or liabilities. This type of swap enables firms to choose from a wider variety of asset and liability markets without having to incur additional interest rate risk, that is, risk that arises because of changes in market interest rates. For instance, a firm that traditionally invests in short-term assets, whose returns naturally fluctuate as the yield on each new issue changes, may instead invest in a long-term, fixed rate instrument and then use an interest rate swap to obtain floating rate receipts. In this situation, one firm agrees to pay a fixed interest rate to another in return for receiving a floating rate.

Interest rate swaps have fixed termination dates and typically provide for semiannual payments. Either interest rate in a swap may be fixed or floating.[4] The amount of interest paid is based on some agreed-upon principal amount, which is called the "notional" principal because it never actually changes hands. Moreover, the two parties do not exchange the full amounts of the interest payments. Rather, at each payment a single amount is transferred to cover the net difference in the promised interest payments.

An example of an interest rate swap is provided in Figure 10.1. Atlanta Hi-Tech agrees to pay Heartland Manufacturing a floating rate of interest equal to the London Interbank Offered Rate (LIBOR), which is commonly used

FIGURE 10.1 *An Interest Rate Swap without a Dealer*

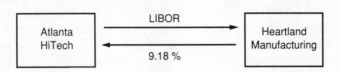

In this example, Atlanta HiTech agrees to pay Heartland Manufacturing a floating rate of interest equal to the London Interbank Offered Rate. In return, Heartland agrees to pay Atlanta HiTech a fixed 9.18% rate of interest. These two companies do not actually exchange the full amounts of the interest payments, but at each payment, a single amount is transferred to cover the net difference in the promised interest payments.

FIGURE 10.2   *An Interest Rate Swap with a Dealer*

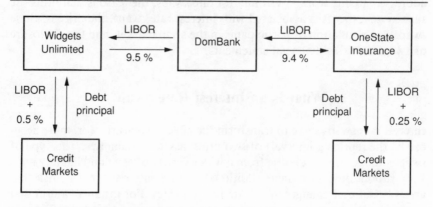

This chart demonstrates three aspects of the swaps market:

(1) Converting floating-rate debt to fixed-rate debt (Widgets Unlimited)
(2) Converting floating-rate assets to fixed-rate assets (OneState Insurance)
(3) Using an intermediary (DomBank) to facilitate the swap

in international loan agreements.[5] In return, Heartland Manufacturing promises to pay Atlanta HiTech a fixed 9.18% rate of interest. The swap transaction is ordinarily arranged at current market rates in order for the net present value of payments to equal zero. That is, the fixed rate on a typical interest rate swap is set so that the market value of the net floating rate payments exactly equals the market value of the net fixed rate payments. If the swap is not arranged as a zero-net-present-value exchange, one party pays to the other an amount equal to the difference in the payments' net present value when the swap is arranged.

Figure 10.2 demonstrates three aspects of the swaps market: converting floating rate debt to fixed rate debt, converting a floating rate asset to a fixed rate asset, and using an intermediary in the swap transaction. In Figure 10.2, Widgets Unlimited can issue short-term debt but is averse to the risk that market interest rates will increase. To avoid this risk, Widgets enters into a swap in which it agrees to pay the counterparty a fixed rate of interest and receive a floating rate. This arrangement resembles long-term, fixed rate debt in that the Widgets' promised payments are independent of market interest rate changes. If market interest rates rise, Widgets will receive payments under the swap that will offset the higher cost of its short-term debt. Should market rates fall, though, under the terms of the swap Widgets will have to pay its counterparty money.

The combination of short-term debt and swaps is not identical to the use of long-term debt. One difference is that Widgets' interest payments are not truly fixed. The company is protected from an increase in market rates but not from changes in its own risk premium. The swap would not compensate Widgets if its own cost of short-term debt increased from LIBOR plus 0.5% to LIBOR plus 0.75%. If the cost of short-term debt to Widgets decreased to LIBOR plus 0.30%, however, the cost of the debt issue would fall by 0.20%. In addition, the counterparty to the combination generally does not provide the corporation with the interest rate option implicit in many bonds issued in the United States whereby they can be called in at a fixed price regardless of current market rates. Call options allow issuers to exploit large changes in market interest rates.[6] In contrast, standard interest rate swap contracts may be unwound or canceled only at prevailing market interest rates.

The other swap user in this example illustrates a swap's potential to convert a floating rate asset to one in which the rate is fixed. OneState Insurance, a small life insurance company, has long-term, fixed-rate obligations but would like to invest part of its portfolio in short-term debt securities. OneState Insurance can invest in short-term securities without incurring interest rate risk by agreeing to a swap in which the insurer pays a floating rate of interest and receives a fixed rate of interest. This combination provides the insurance company with a stream of income that does not fluctuate with changes in short-term market interest rates.

This example also demonstrates the usefulness of an intermediary in a swap. Although Widgets and OneState Insurance could have entered into a swap agreement with each other, in this example (see Figure 10.2), both Widgets Unlimited and OneState Insurance actually have a swap agreement with DomBank. Numerous large commercial and investment banks as well as insurance companies have entered into the swap market as intermediaries. DomBank is compensated in an amount equal to the difference between what is received on one swap and what is paid under the other one. In this example, the fee is equal to 10 basis points.

Using DomBank is advantageous to Widgets and OneState Insurance for two reasons. First, the use of an intermediary reduces search time in establishing a swap agreement. DomBank is willing to enter into a swap at any time, whereas Widgets and OneState Insurance might take several days to discover each other, even with a broker's help. Second, an intermediary can reduce the costs of credit evaluation. Either of the participants in an interest rate swap may become bankrupt and unable to fulfill their side of the contract. Thus, each swap participant should understand the credit quality of the other party. In this example, Widgets and OneState are not familiar with each other, and each would need to undertake costly credit analysis on the other before agreeing to deal directly. However, total credit analysis costs are significantly reduced since both parties know the quality of DomBank and DomBank knows their respective credit standings.

Reasons for Interest Rate Swaps

Why do two firms agree to swap interest payments? They could either acquire assets or issue liabilities with their desired repricing interval (or maturity) and eliminate the need to undertake a swap. An early explanation for swaps was that they reduce corporations' funding costs by allowing firms to exploit market inefficiencies.[7] Although this explanation remains popular with some market participants, academic analysis has questioned the ability of market inefficiencies to explain the existence and growth of the swap market. Several other explanations for the swap market's popularity that do not rely on market inefficiency have also been provided. The next section of this article presents both original research and a review of recent literature to determine alternative reasons for the surge in use of interest rate swaps.

Quality Spread Differential

The cost savings explanation of swaps claims that swaps allow corporations to arbitrage quality spread differentials. A *quality spread* is the difference between the interest rate paid for funds of a given maturity by a high-quality firm — that is, one with low credit risk — and that required of a lower-quality firm. The quality spread *differential* is the difference in quality spreads at two different maturities. Table 10.1 provides the calculation of the quality spread differential based on the example provided in Figure 10.1. Atlanta Hi-Tech, which as a AAA rating, can obtain short-term financing at six-month LIBOR plus 0.20% or fixed rate financing at 9.00%. Heartland Manufacturing can obtain floating rate funding at six-month LIBOR plus 0.70% or fixed rate funds at 10.20%. For floating rate funding, the quality spread, or difference in rates, between the two firms is 50 basis points, but it widens to

TABLE 10.1 *Numerical Example of a Quality Spread Differential*

	Atlanta HiTech	Heartland Manufacturing	Quality Spread
Credit Rating	AAA	BBB	
Cost of Raising Fixed-Rate Funding	9.00%	10.20%	1.20%
Cost of Raising Floating-Rate Funding	6-month LIBOR plus 0.20%	6-month LIBOR plus 0.70%	0.50%
Quality Spread Differential			0.70%

TABLE 10.2 *Numerical Example of a Swap's Ability to Reduce a Firm's Cost of Funding*

	Atlanta HiTech	Heartland Manufacturing
Direct Funding Cost		
Fixed-rate funds raised directly by Atlanta HiTech	(9.00%)	
Floating-rate funds raised directly by Heartland		(6-month LIBOR + 0.70%)
Swap Payments		
Atlanta HiTech pays Heartland floating rate	(LIBOR)	LIBOR
Heartland pays Atlanta HiTech fixed rate	9.18%	(9.18%)
All-in cost of funding	LIBOR − 0.18%	9.88%
Comparable cost of equivalent direct funding	LIBOR + 0.20%	10.20%
Savings	38 basis points	32 basis points

120 basis points for fixed rate funding. The difference in quality spread, or the quality spread differential, in this example is 70 basis points.

The quality spread differential may be exploitable if Atlanta HiTech desires floating rate funds and Heartland Manufacturing seeks a fixed rate. Table 10.2 shows how the quality spread differential is exploited through an interest rate swap. Atlanta HiTech issues fixed rate debt, and Heartland issues floating rate debt. Then the two firms enter into an interest rate swap. The net result is that Atlanta HiTech obtains funds at LIBOR minus 18 basis points and Heartland obtains fixed rate funds at 9.88%. Compared with their cost of funds had they not used the interet rate swap strategy, this result represents a 38-basis-point savings for Atlanta HiTech and a 32-basis-point savings for Heartland. Note that the division of the gain in this example is arbitrary and that the two parties could split the gains differently. However, the total gains to the swapping parties will always equal the quality spread differential − 70 basis points in this example.

Table 10.2 clearly demonstrates the ability of swaps to help exploit apparent arbitrage opportunities. However, some observers question whether arbitrage opportunities actually exist. Stuart Turnbull (1987) argues that swaps are zero-sum games in the absence of market imperfections and swap externalities. He also suggests that quality spread differentials may arise for reasons that are not subject to arbitrage. Clifford W. Smith, Charles W. Smithson, and Lee Macdonald Wakeman (1986) note that even if quality spread differential arbitrage were possible, such activity by itself would not explain swap market growth. In fact, the annual volume of new swaps should be declining as arbitrage becomes more effective.

If the quality spread differential is not entirely the result of market inefficiencies, why does it exist? In a 1987 research paper, the authors of this article point out that quality spread differentials could arise for a number of reasons, including differences in expected bankruptcy costs. Because the expected discounted value of bankruptcy-related losses increases at a faster pace for lower-rated corporations than for higher-rated ones, quality spreads increase with maturity. In this case, the lower initial cost of swap financing is offset by higher costs later.

Alternatively, Jan G. Loeys (1985) suggests that quality spread differentials could arise as risk is shifted from creditors to shareholders. Creditors have the option of refusing to roll over their debt if the firm appears to be riskier than when the debt was incurred, and short-term creditors have more opportunities to exercise this option. Thus, the creditors of a firm that issues short-term debt bear less risk than the creditors of a firm that issues long-term debt. If the creditors of firms that issue short-term debt bear less risk, the equity holders and long-term creditors necessarily bear more risk.

A third possible explanation for the quality spread differential involves differences in short- and long-term contracts. Long-term contracts frequently include a variety of restrictive covenants and may incorporate a call option that is typically not present in short-term debt contracts. The differences in these contract provisions may be reflected in the interest rates charged on various debt contracts. For example, Smith, Smithson, and Wakeman (1988) point out that the long-term corporate debt contracts issued by U.S. firms in domestic markets typically have a call provision that is not adjusted for changes in market interest rates. However, long-term debt contracts issued in the Eurobond markets frequently have call provisions that adjust call prices for market rate changes. Thus, quality spread differentials will reflect differences in contract terms if they are calculated using domestic U.S. market rates for lower-quality firms and Eurobond rates for higher-quality firms.

In a forthcoming paper, one of the authors of this article suggests that the quality spread differential may reflect differences in the agency costs associated with short- and long-term debt. Agency costs arise because managers, owners, and creditors have different interests, and managers or owners may take actions that benefit themselves at the expense of the other parties and at the expense of total firm value. In particular, Larry D. Wall notes that the owners of firms that issue long-term, noncallable debt create an incentive to underinvest and to shift investments from low-risk to high-risk projects.[8] A firm may underinvest in new projects because most of the benefit of some projects is received by creditors in the form of a reduced probability that the firm will default. Owners will prefer a high-risk project to a low-risk project because they receive the gains on successful high-risk projects while creditors suffer most of the losses if the projects fail. Creditors recognize the incentives created by long-term debt and demand a higher risk premium in compensation. The problems created by long-term debt may be reduced or eliminated by short-term debt, that is, debt that matures shortly after the investment decision.[9] An interest rate swap allows lower-quality firms to issue short-term debt while avoiding exposure to changes in market interest rates. Thus, the combination of short-term debt and swaps may be less costly than long-term debt.

In their 1987 paper, the authors also point to another agency cost—that of liquidating insolvent firms—that may be reduced by using short-term debt. Insolvent firms have an incentive to underinvest because, according to David Mayers and Clifford W. Smith (1987), creditors receive almost all of the benefit. Creditors of these firms can reduce the costs associated with underinvestment by taking control of the firm as soon as possible after the firm becomes insolvent. However, creditors may not gain control of a firm until it fails to make a promised debt payment. Short-term debt may hasten creditors' gaining control when a firm has adequate funds to pay interest but lacks the resources to pay interest on its debt and repay the principal.

According to Wall and John J. Pringle, the quality spread differential is not exploitable to the extent that it arises from differences in the expected costs of bankruptcy, shifts in risk from creditors to equityholders, or actual differences in contract terms. However, the quality spread differential can be exploited to the extent that it arises from agency costs. Moreover, arbitrage may eliminate differentials that arise from market inefficiencies, whereas one firm's swap does not reduce the potential agency cost savings to another firm. Thus, agency cost explanations could provide at least a partial explanation for the continuing growth of the swap market.

An important question facing explanations based on the quality spread differential is the extent to which the differential reflects exploitable factors. The authors note that the various explanations of the quality spread differential are not mutually exclusive. For example, if the differential is 70 basis points, then perhaps only 30 basis points may be exploitable.

One empirical study that has some bearing on the quality spread differential is by Robert E. Chatfield and R. Charles Moyer (1986). This study examines the risk premium on 90 long-term putable bonds issued between July 24, 1974, and August 2, 1984, and a control sample of 174 nonputable bonds. The put option on long-term, floating rate debt gives creditors the option to force the firm to repay its debt if the firm becomes riskier.[10] The study finds that the put feature reduces the rate that the market requires on long-term debt by 89 basis points for the bonds in the sample. Chatfield and Moyer provide strong evidence that at least part of the quality spread differential does not arise due to inefficiencies in the markets for short- and long-term debt. However, the observed savings arising from the put feature may be attributable to some of the factors discussed earlier, including bankruptcy costs, risk shifting from creditors to equityholders, and agency costs. Thus, the Chatfield and Moyer results cannot be used to determine the magnitude of agency cost savings available through interest rate swaps.

Other Explanations

Several explanations for the increased use of the interest rate swap market that do not depend on exploiting the quality spread differential are available. One is that swaps may be used to adjust the repricing interval (or maturity) of a firm's assets or liabilities in order to reduce interest rate risk. For example, a firm may start a period with an acceptable degree of exposure to changes in market interest rates. Subsequently, though, it desires a change in its exposure because of shifts in its product environment or in the volatility of interest rates. Swaps provide a low-cost method of making immediate changes in exposure to market interest rates. For example, suppose that a firm is initially fully hedged with respect to interest rate changes but that a subsequent change in its product markets increases its revenues' sensitivity to interest rates. This company may be able to offset the increased sensitivity by entering into a swap whereby it agrees to pay a floating rate of interest, which better matches revenues, and receives a fixed rate of interest to cover payments on its outstanding debt.[11]

Smith, Smithson, and Wakeman (1988) suggest that swaps may allow firms greater flexibility in choosing the amount of their outstanding debt obligations. In particular, reducing debt levels may be a problem if swaps are not used. To reduce its outstanding long-term debt, a firm may need to pay a premium (that is, the call price may exceed the current market value of the debt). On the other hand, if it issues short-term debt without a swap, it may be exposed to adverse changes in market interest rates. However, by issuing a combination of short-term debt and swaps, the firm avoids the need to pay a premium to retire debt and simultaneously eliminates its exposure to changes in market interest rates.

Marcelle Arak and others (1988) present a general model in which firms will choose the combination of short-term debt and interest rate swaps over short-term debt; long-term, fixed rate debt; and long-term, variable rate debt. The model suggests that the combination will be preferred if the firm expects higher risk-free interest rates than does the market, the firm is more risk averse than the market with respect to changes in risk-free rates, the firm expects its own credit spread to be lower than that expected by the market, and the borrower is less risk averse to changes in its credit spread than is the market. The researchers also note that not all four conditions need to be met at the same time.

Arak and her colleagues' model is very broad and could include the agency cost models as subsets. An additional implication of their model is that firms may use swaps to exploit information asymmetries. Suppose that a company desires fixed rate financing to fund a project. It could issue long-term debt, but if management thought that the company would soon receive a better credit rating, issuing long-term debt would force the firm to pay an excessive risk premium. By issuing short-term debt, the firm could obtain a lower cost of long-term funds in the future when its credit rating improved. However, this strategy would expose the firm to interest rate risk. By instead issuing a combination of short-term debt and interest rate swaps the firm's managers can exploit their information about the true credit risk of the firm without exposing the organization to changes in market interest rates.[12] When the good news comes, the firm's floating rate payments to outside creditors falls while its payments under the swap remain the same, thus reducing the firm's total financing costs. One important limitation of this explanation is that it applies only to firms that expect improved credit ratings in the near future.

In yet another alternative to the quality spread differential explanation, Loeys points out that swaps may allow firms to exploit differences in regulation. He notes that Securities and Exchange Commission (SEC) registration requirements raise the cost of issuing bonds in the United States by approximately 80 basis points above the cost of issuing bonds in the Eurobond markets. However, not all firms have access to the Eurobond market. Thus, the costs of obtaining fixed rate funding may be reduced by having companies with access to the Eurobond market issue long-term debt and then enter into a swap with firms that lack access to but prefer fixed rate funding. Smith, Smithson, and Wakeman (1986), observing that a variety of regulations differ across countries in ways that can be exploited, refer to this explanation as tax and regulatory arbitrage.

A Review of the Explanations

The various explanations of interest rate swaps discussed above are not mutually exclusive, since different firms may use swaps for different reasons. One of the most popular explanations of interest rate swaps — that they allow arbitrage of the quality spread differential — is also the explanation with the weakest theoretical support. The other explanations are all theoretically plausible. Unfortunately, published empirical evidence on the reasons for using swaps is almost nonexistent. Linda T. Rudnick (1987) provides anecdotal evidence that reductions in financing costs are one of the primary reasons that firms enter into interest rate swaps. In research currently in progress, the authors of this article are examining the financial characteristics of firms that reported the use of swaps in the notes to their 1986 financial statements.

One limitation of the nonarbitrage explanations of swaps is that they provide only one reason for floating rate payers to enter into swaps, namely, the ability to change the maturity structure of the firm's assets and liabilities.

Moreover, this single explanation fails to provide a sound reason for a firm to issue long-term, fixed rate debt and then enter into a swap agreement. If a company does issue long-term debt and then enters into a swap agreement as a floating rate payer, either fixed rate payers are sharing part of their gains with the floating rate payer or floating rate payers obtain some as yet undiscovered benefit from swaps.

Risks Associated with Swaps

Interest rate swap contracts are subject to several types of risk. Among the more important are interest rate, or position, risk and credit risk. Interest rate risk arises because changes in market interest rates cause a change in a swap's value. Credit risk occurs because either party may default on a swap contract. Both participants in a swap are subject to each type of risk.

Interest Rate Risk

As market interest rates change, interest rate swaps generate gains or losses that are equal to the change in the replacement cost of the swap. These gains and losses allow swaps to serve as a hedge that a company can use to reduce its risk or to serve as a speculative tool that increases the firm's total risk. A swap represents a hedge if gains or losses generated by the swap offset changes in the market values of a company's assets, liabilities, and off-balance-sheet activities such as interest rate futures and options. However, a swap is speculative to the extent that the firm deliberately increases its risk position to profit from predicted changes in interest rates.

The determination of whether and how to use a swap is straightforward for a firm that is a user, one that enters into a swap agreement solely to adjust its own financial position.[13] First, the company evaluates its own exposure to future changes in interest rates, including any planned investments and new financings. Then, its views on the future levels and volatility of interest rates are ascertained. Firms wishing greater exposure to market rate changes enter into swaps as speculators. Alternatively, if less exposure is desired, the company enters into a swap as a hedge.

The problem facing a dealer — a firm that enters into a swap to earn fee income — is more complicated. A dealer may enter into a swap to hedge changes in market rates or to speculate in a manner similar to users. However, a dealer may also enter a swap to satisfy a customer's request even when the dealer wants no change in its interest rate exposure.[14] In this case, the dealer must find some way of hedging the swap transaction.

The simplest hedge for one swap transaction by a dealer is another swap transaction whose terms mirror the first swap. An example of this arrangement is given in Figure 10.2, in which the dealer's promised floating rate payments of LIBOR to Widgets Unlimited is exactly offset by OneState's promise to pay LIBOR. Similarly, the fixed payments to OneState Insurance are covered by Widgets' promised fixed payments, and DomBank is left with a small spread. This combination of swaps is referred to as a *matched pair*. One problem with relying on matched pairs to eliminate interest rate risk is that the dealer is exposed to interest rate changes during the time needed to find another party interested in a matching swap. Another problem is that the dealer may be relatively better at arranging swaps with fixed rate payers and, thus, have problems finding floating rate payers to execute the matching swap (or vice versa).

An alternative to hedging one swap with another swap is to rely on debt securities, or on futures or options on debt securities, to provide a hedge. Steven T. Felgran (1987) gives an example whereby a dealer agrees to pay a fixed rate and receive a floating rate from a customer. The dealer uses the floating rate receipts to support a bank loan, which is then used to purchase a Treasury security of the same maturity and value as the swap. Any gains or losses on the swap are subsequently offset by losses or gains on the Treasury security. Felgran does note one problem with using Treasury securities to hedge a swap: The spread between them and interest rate swaps may vary over time.[15] According to Felgran, dealers are unable to hedge floating rate payments perfectly. Sources of risk include differences in payment dates and floating-rate reset days, disparities in maturity and principal, and "basis risk," that is, the risk associated with hedging floating payments based on one index with floating payments from another index.

Using the futures market to hedge swaps also entails certain drawbacks. Wakeman (1986) points to the "additional risk created by the cash/futures basis volatility." He also notes that matching the fixed rate payments from a swap with the Treasury security of the closest maturity may not be optimal when the Treasury security is thinly traded. As an alternative he suggests that "on-the-run" (highly liquid) Treasury issues be used for hedging. The investment amount and type of issues to be used may be determined applying a duration matching strategy. Still, this approach is unlikely to eliminate interest rate risk for the swap dealer since duration matching provides a perfect hedge only under very restrictive assumptions.

Credit Risk

Aside from interest rate and basis risk, both interest rate swap participants are subject to the risk that the other party will default, causing credit losses. The maximum amount of the loss associated with this credit risk is measured by the swap's replacement cost, which is essentially the cost of entering a new swap under current market conditions with rates equal to those on the swap being replaced.

A simple example can demonstrate the credit risk of swaps. Suppose that Widgets Unlimited agrees to pay a fixed rate of 9.5% to DomBank, and in return Widgets will receive LIBOR on a semiannual basis through January 1994. If the market rate on new swaps maturing in January 1994 falls to 8%, the swap has positive value to DomBank—that is, DomBank would have to pay an upfront fee to entice a third party to enter into a swap whereby Dom-Bank receives a fixed rate of 9.5%. DomBank will suffer a credit loss if Widgets becomes bankrupt while the rate is 8% and pays only a fraction of its obligations to creditors. On the other hand, if the rate on swaps maturing in January 1994 rises to 10.5% and DomBank defaults, Widgets may suffer a credit loss.

This example demonstrates that both of the parties to an interest rate swap may be subject to credit risk at some time during the life of a swap contract. However, only one party at a time may be subject to credit risk. If rates in the above example fall to 8%, DomBank can suffer credit losses, but Widgets is not exposed to credit risk. That is, the swap has negative value to Widgets when the market rate is 8%; Widgets would be happy to drop the swap agreement if DomBank were to go bankrupt. In practice, though, Widgets is unlikely to receive a windfall from DomBank's failure. The swap contracts may provide for Widgets to continue making payments to DomBank or, if the contract is canceled, provide for Widgets to pay DomBank the replacement cost of the swap.[16]

One way of reducing the credit risk associated with swaps is for the party to whom the swap has negative value to post collateral equal to the swap's replacement cost. Some swaps provide for collateral but most do not. According to Felgran, swap collateralization is of uncertain value because such documentation has yet to be adequately tested in court. Moreover, some parties that would be happy to receive collateral are themselves reluctant to post it when swap rates move against them. Certain commercial banks in particular have a strong incentive to avoid collateralization. Such institutions take credit risks in the ordinary course of business and are comfortable with assuming credit risk on interest rate swaps. Investment bankers, on the other hand, are typically at risk for only short periods of time with their nonswap transactions and are not as experienced in evaluating credit risk. Thus, the continued presence of credit risk in the swap market strengthens the relative competitive position of commercial banks.

Several simulation studies have explored the magnitude of the credit risk associated with individual swaps or matched pairs of swaps. Arak, Laurie S. Goodman, and Arthur Rones (1986) examine the credit exposure—or maximum credit loss—of a single interest rate swap to determine the amount of a firm's credit line that is used by a swap.[17] They assume that short-term rates follow a random walk with no drift; in other words, the change in short-term rates does not depend on the current level of, or on past changes in, short-term rates. After the swap begins, the floating rate component of the swap is assumed to move one standard deviation each year in the direction of maximum credit exposure. The standard deviation of interest rates is calculated using 1985 data on Treasury issues. Their results suggest that until the swap matures, maximum annual credit loss on swaps is likely to be between 1 and 2% of notional principal.

J. Gregg Whittaker (1987b) investigates the credit exposure of interest rate swaps in order to develop a formula for swap pricing. Using an options pricing formula to value swaps and assuming that interest rates follow a lognormal distribution and volatility amounts to one standard deviation, Whittaker finds that the maximum exposure for a 10-year matched pair of swaps does not exceed 8% of the notional principal.

The Federal Reserve Board and the Bank of England studied the potential increase in credit exposure of a matched pair of swaps.[18] The study's purpose is to develop a measure of the credit exposure associated with a matched pair of swaps that is comparable to the credit exposure of on-balance-sheet loans. The results are used to determine regulatory capital requirements for interest rate swaps. The joint central bank research assumes that for regulatory purposes the swaps' credit exposure should be equal to its current exposure, that is, the replacement cost plus some surcharge to capture potential increases in credit exposure. The investigation uses a Monte Carlo simulation technique to evaluate the probabilities associated with different potential increases in credit exposure.[19] Interest rates are assumed to follow a lognormal, random walk distribution with the volatility measure equal to the 90th percentile value of changes in interest rates over six-month intervals from 1981 to mid-1986. The credit exposure of each matched pair is calculated every six months and the resulting exposures are averaged over the life of the swap. The study concludes with 70% confidence that the average potential increase in credit exposure will be no greater than 0.5% of the notional principal of the swap per complete year; at the 95% confidence level it finds the average credit risk exposure to be no greater than 1% of the notional principal.

Terrence M. Belton (1987) follows this line of research in analyzing the potential increase in swap credit exposure, but he uses a different method of simulating interest rates. Belton estimates a vector autoregressive model over the period from January 1970 to November 1986 to estimate seven different Treasury rates. (Vector autoregressive models estimate current values of some dependent variables, in this case interest rates at various maturities, as a function of current and past values of selected variables. Belton uses current and past interest rates as explanatory variables.) Changes in the term structure are then simulated by drawing a set of random errors from the joint distribution of rates and solving for future values at each maturity. In effect, Belton's procedure allows the historical shape in the yield curve and historical changes in its level and shape to determine the value of various interest rates in his simulations. Belton's analysis differs from prior studies in that he uses stochastic, or random, default rates rather than focusing exclusively on maximum credit exposure. His results imply that the potential increase in credit exposure of swaps caused by rate changes can be covered by adding a surcharge of 1% to 5% of the notional principal to the current exposure for swaps with a maturity of 2 to 12 years.

While the foregoing analyses suggest several ways of estimating the increased credit exposure associated with matched pairs of swaps, these approaches might not be applicable to swap portfolios. Starting with the assumption that dealers use matched pairs of swaps and that the swaps are entered into at market interest rates, Wall and Kwun-Wing C. Fung (1987) note that the fixed rate on the matched pairs will change over time as interest rates move up and down. Wall and Fung point out that if rates have fluctuated over a certain range, a bank may have credit exposure on some swaps in which it pays a fixed rate and on others in which it pays a floating rate. In this case, an increase in rates generates an increase in the credit exposure of swaps in which the dealer pays a fixed rate but also causes a decrease in the exposure of swaps in which the dealer pays a floating rate. Similarly, a decrease in rates will increase the exposure on the swaps in which the dealer pays a floating rate and decrease exposure on those in which the dealer pays a fixed rate.[20]

In a more empirical vein, Kathleen Neal and Katerina Simons (1988) simulate the total credit exposure of a portfolio of 20 matched pairs of interest rate swaps. The initial portfolio is generated by originating one pair of five-year swaps per quarter from the fourth quarter of 1981 through the fourth quarter of 1986 at the prevailing interest rate. For the period 1987 through 1991, the interest rates are generated randomly based on the volatility observed in historical rates.[21] The maturing matched pair is dropped each quarter from the sample and a new five-year swap is added to the portfolio at the simulated interest rates. After running "several thousand" simulations and assuming a portfolio of interest rate swaps with a notional principal of $10 million, Neal and Simons find the average maximum credit loss to be $185,000 and the 90th percentile exposure, $289,000.

No single correct approach is available to determine the expected credit exposure on an interest rate swap. The results may be influenced by the assumptions that are made about the distribution of future interest rates. However, several studies using different methodologies have reached the conclusion that the maximum exposure on a matched pair of swaps is unlikely to exceed a small fraction of the swap's notional principal. Moreover, the analysis of a single matched pair may overstate the expected exposure of a swap portfolio. Therefore, additional simulations of portfolio analysis risk may be appropriate to determine the risk exposure of swap dealers. Dominique Jackson (1988) reports that a survey of 71 dealers showed that 11 firms had experienced losses with "total write-offs accounting for $33 million on port-folios which totaled a notional (principal) of $283 billion."

How Should Swaps Be Priced?

In addition to considering the reasons for engaging in swaps and the at-tendant risks, the literature on interest rate swaps addresses two important pricing qustions: (1) How should the overall value of a swap be established, and (2) what spread between higher-rated and lower-rated firms is appropri-ate to cover swap credit risk? James Bicksler and Andrew H. Chen (1986) provide an analysis of a swap's overall value. They suggest that an interest rate swap be treated as an exchange of a fixed rate bond for a floating rate bond. According to this approach, the fixed rate payer has in effect sold a fixed rate bond and purchased a floating rate bond. Bicksler and Chen sug-gest that pricing an interest rate swap is essentially the same as pricing a floating rate bond.

Insight into the appropriate spreads between high- and lower-rated firms can be obtained by comparing the quality spreads on bonds versus those on swaps. Patrick de Saint-Aignan, the chairman of the International Swap Dealers Association and a managing director at Morgan Stanley, remarks that, "There's a credit spread of 150 basis points in the loan market but of only 5 to 10 basis points in swaps."[22] However, Smith, Smithson, and Wake-man (1988) note that the risk exposure as a proportion of notional principal for swaps is far less than the exposure on loans. Lenders have credit expo-sure for all principal and interest payments promised on the loan, whereas a swap participant's credit exposure is limited to the difference between two interest rates. Thus, the credit risk borne by swap dealers is a far smaller proportion of the (notional) principal than that assumed by lenders.

Belton also addresses the question of appropriate spreads to compensate for swaps' credit risk by considering the default premium required to com-pensate one party for the expected value of the default losses from the other. For low-risk firms — companies with 0.5% probability of default in one year and zero payment on default — the required premium is 0.70 basis points for a two-year swap and 3.02 basis points for a ten-year swap. For firms below investment grade — firms with a 2% probability of default per year and zero payment on default — the required premium ranges from 2.83 basis points for a two-year swap to 14.24 basis points for a ten-year swap. The differ-ences in default premium of 2 to 14 basis points found by Belton for swaps is approximately in the 5 to 10 basis point range of the credit spread charged in swaps markets.

Whittaker (1987b) applies his options pricing method for calculating swaps' credit risk to the issue of swap pricing. He views a swap as a set of options to buy and sell a fixed rate bond and a floating rate bond. In his model default by the fixed rate payer is analogous to a decision to exercise jointly a call option to purchase the fixed rate bond and a put option to sell a floating rate security. From this perspective, the decision to exercise one option is not independent of the decision to exercise another. Thus, one option may be exercised even though it is unprofitable to do so, provided that it is sufficiently profitable to exercise the other option. He then estimates the value of these options and suggests that "the market does not adequately take account of the exposure and pricing differentials across varying maturities." However, Whittaker claims that his results may not necessarily imply that the market is on average underpricing swap credit risk.

One limitation of the above studies is that they fail to combine into an integrated framework the distribution of interest rates and the credit risk associated with swaps. A conceptually superior approach to interest rate swap valuation begins by separating the payments. The result looks like a series of forward contracts in which the floating rate payer agrees to buy a zero coupon Treasury security from the fixed rate payer. This forward contract may then be decomposed into two options, one in which the floating rate payer buys a call from the fixed rate payer on the zero coupon Treasury security and one in which the floating rate payer sells a put on the security to the fixed rate payer.

Unfortunately, the options derived from this analysis cannot be valued using standard options pricing formulas because both options are subject to credit risk. Herb Johnson and René Stulz (1987) analyze the problem of pricing a single option subject to default risk. However, swaps are a series of linked options whose payments in one period are contingent on the terms of the swap contract being fulfilled in prior periods. Thus, as Smith, Smithson, and Wakeman (1987) suggest, to derive an optimal default strategy for swaps requires analysis of compound option issues similar to those discussed by Robert Geske (1977) for corporate coupon bonds.

The theoretical and pedagogical advantages of splitting a swap into a series of default-risky options are that the decomposition clearly illustrates the primary determinants of swap value: the distribution of the price of default-risk-free bonds (interest rates), the possibility of default by either participant, and the linked nature of the options though time. The practical problem with the decomposition is that developing a pricing formula is not straightforward.

Requirements Imposed on Swaps

Regulation

In contrast to most other financial markets in the United States, the interest rate swap market is subject to remarkably little regulation and does not have a central exchange or even a central clearing mechanism. The terms of a swap agreement are determined by the parties to the contract and need not be disclosed. Nor does the existence of a swap need to be disclosed at the time the agreement is executed. (The financial statements' disclosure requirements for individual firms are discussed later in this article.) While certain regulators have a general responsibility for the financial soundness of some participants in the swap market, no public or private organization has overall responsibility for its regulation.

In general, this lack of regulation has not resulted in any major problems. Legislatures could make one potentially valuable contribution, though, by providing specific statutory language on the treatment of swap contracts when one party defaults. Market participants are currently waiting for the courts to determine if default procedures will follow the language of the swap contract or if the courts will impose some other settlement procedure. For example, many swaps are arranged under a master contract between two parties that provides for the netting of payments across swaps. This clause is desirable because it reduces the credit risk borne by both parties. However, the risk exists that a bankruptcy court will ignore this clause and treat each swap separately.

Even though the swap market is not subject to regulation, individual participants are. In particular, federal banking regulators in the United States are including interest rate swaps in the recently adopted risk-based capital standards. These standards are designed to preserve and enhance the safety and soundness of commercial banks by requiring them to maintain capital commensurate with the levels of credit risk they incur.[23]

Banks' capital standards first translate credit exposure on swaps into an amount comparable to on-balance-sheet loans. The loan equivalent amount for swaps is equal to the replacement cost of the swap plus 0.5% of the notional principal. This loan equivalent amount is then multiplied by 50% to determine a risk-adjusted asset equivalent. Banks are required to maintain tier-one (or core) capital equal to 4% of risk-adjusted assets and total capital equal to 8% by 1992.[24]

The central banks of 12 major industrial powers have agreed to apply similar risk-based capital requirements to their countries' financial firms.[25] However, these standards do not apply to U.S. investment banks or insurance companies. Thus, capital requirements are not being applied to all swap dealers. Some market participants are concerned that the standards will place dealers that are subject to capital regulation at a competitive disadvantage.[26]

Accounting

Like regulatory requirements, accounting standards for swaps are minimal at best, owing largely to their rapid development. Existing accounting standards provide a general requirement that a firm disclose all material matters but do not require a company to disclose its participation in the interest rate swap market. Different firms appear to be following many of the same rules in accounting for the gains and losses under swap contracts, but some important discrepancies exist in practice.

Keith Wishon and Lorin S. Chevalier (1985) note that swap market participants generally do not recognize the existence of swaps on their balance sheets, a practice that is consistent with the treatment of futures agreements. However, they aver that the notes to the firm's financial statements should disclose the existence of material swap agreements and discuss the swap's impact on the repricing interval of the firm's debt obligations. Harold Bierman, Jr. (1987) recommends that firms also disclose the transaction's effects on their risk position.

Another issue at the inception of some swap contracts is accounting for upfront payments. Wishon and Chevalier believe that any upfront payments that reflect yield adjustments should be deferred and amortized over the life of the swap. While acknowledging that payers appear to be following this policy, the researchers note that some recipients have taken the position that all upfront fees are arrangement fees and may be immediately recognized in income. Bierman argues that yield-adjusting fees cannot be distinguished from others. Thus, all fees should be treated in the same manner. He further maintains that the most appropriate treatment is to defer recognition and amortize the payments over the life of the contract.

According to Wishon and Chevalier, regular payments and receipts under a swap agreement are frequently recorded as an adjustment to interest income when the swap is related to a particular debt issue. Though the receipts and payments are technically not interest, this approach is informative, especially if footnote disclosure is adequate. They report, nonetheless, that changes in the market value of the swap are generally not recognized in the income statement if gains and losses are not recognized on the security hedged by the swap. This treatment parallels that of futures, which meets the hedge criteria in the Financial Accounting Standards Board's Statement Number 80, "Accounting for Futures Contracts."

Another issue arising during the life of an interest rate swap is the presentation of the credit risk. For a nondealer, credit risk may not be material and, therefore, need not be reported. However, Wishon and Chevalier argue that the credit risk taken by a dealer is likely to be material and should be disclosed.

Some firms may enter into swaps as a speculative investment. Wishon and Chevalier contend that speculative swaps should be accounted for in the same manner as other speculative investments. Among the alternatives they discuss are using either the lower of cost or market method of valuation, with writedowns only for losses that are not "temporary," and the lower of cost or market in all cases. Both approaches are flawed. The treatment of some swap losses as "temporary" is inappropriate because objective and verifiable predictions of changes in interest rates are impossible.[27] Yet using the lower-of-cost-or-market method of valuation in all cases will always result in a swap's being valued at its historical low, an excessively conservative position. Probably the best approach is to report the swap's replacement cost and to recognize any gains or losses in the current period.

Bierman suggests that, when a speculative swap is terminated prior to maturity, the gain or loss should be recognized immediately. However, no consensus exists on the treatment if the swap is a hedge. Wishon and Chevalier report widespread disagreement on the appropriate treatment of a swap's termination. One common approach would defer and amortize any gains or losses on the swap over the life of the underlying financial instrument. The other calls for immediate recognition of any gains or losses. The treatment of gains or losses on futures hedges suggests that the deferral and amortization of early swaps termination is appropriate.

Eugene E. Comiskey, Charles W. Mulford, and Deborah H. Turner (1987–88), surveying the financial statements of the 100 largest domestic banks in 1986, discovered that some banks are deferring gains or losses in accordance with hedge accounting treatment even though hedge accounting would not be permitted in similar circumstances for futures.[28] They also found that five banks disclosed their maximum potential credit loss in the extremely unlikely event that every counterparty defaulted on all swaps that were favorable to the bank.

The Financial Accounting Standards Board issued an Exposure Draft of a proposed Statement of Financial Accounting Standards titled "Disclosures about Financial Instruments." The statement proposes disclosing a variety of new information about financial instruments, including the maximum credit risk; the reasonably possible credit loss; probable credit loss; the amount subject to repricing within one year, one to five years, and over five years; and the market value of each class of financial instrument. This statement specifically includes interest rate swaps in its definition of financial instruments. If, when, and in what form this proposal will be adopted is unclear.

Commercial banks in the United States are currently required to disclose the notional principal on their outstanding interest rate swap portfolio to the federal bank regulators.[29] It would seem that regulators should also consider requiring disclosure of the replacement cost of outstanding swaps given that replacement cost is an element of the risk-based capital standards.

Conclusion

This article surveys the literature and some research in progress on interest rate swaps. The extremely rapid growth of the market has left academics trying to explain the existence of the market and the pricing of these instruments, regulators attempting to determine what risks these instruments pose to financial firms, and accountants endeavoring to determine how institutions should report their use of swaps. Evidence is beginning to accumulate to dispel some of the early misconceptions about this market, but far more analysis remains before interest rate swaps can be fully understood.

Notes

1. See Abken (1988) for a review of the studies of the stock market crash.
2. The size of the interest rate swap market is typically stated in terms of the notional principal of the outstanding swaps. See the explanation of interest rate swap transactions for a discussion of the role of the notional principal. Refer to Jackson (1988) for a discussion of the size of the interest rate and currency swap markets.
3. See Celarier (1987): 17. This estimating appears to encompass the effect of both interest rate swaps and a related instrument called a currency swap. A *currency swap* is an arrangement between two organizations to exchange principal and interest payments in two different currencies at prearranged exchange rates. For example, one corporation agrees to pay a fixed amount of dollars in return for receiving a fixed number of Japanese yen from another corporation. This article focuses on interest rate swaps, and hereafter the term *swaps* will be used as a synonym for interest rate swaps. Beckstrom (1986) offers a discussion of different types of swaps.
4. Both fixed rate interest payment to floating rate payment swaps and floating rate to floating rate swaps whereby, for example, one party pays the London Interbank Offered Rate (LIBOR) while the other party pays the commercial paper rate, are observed in the market.
5. LIBOR is the most common floating rate in interest rate swap agreements, according to Hammond (1987).
6. However, the call option is not a free gift provided by the bond market to corporations. Corporations pay for this call option by paying a higher rate of interest on their bonds.
7. See Bicksler and Chen (1986) as well as Whittaker (1987a) and Hammond (1987) for further discussion.
8. See Myers (1977); Bodie and Taggart (1978); and Barnea, Haugen, and Senbet (1980).
9. Long-term, callable debt may also reduce the agency problems of underinvestment and risk shifting problems. However, Barnea, Haugen, and Senbet (1980) point out that callable debt does not eliminate the underinvestment problem. Wall (forthcoming) suggests that callable bonds may not solve the risk shifting problem in all cases and also notes that short-term debt will solve both problems if it matures shortly after the firm makes its investment decision.
10. Investors may also have an incentive to exercise the put option on fixed rate bonds when interest rates increase. An easy way to control for this feature is to focus exclusively on floating rate bonds. However, Chatfield and Moyers' study (1986) contained fixed rate, putable bonds. Their research controlled for the interest rate feature of the put option on these bonds by including a variable for

the number of times per year the coupon rate on a bond adjusts and a measure of interest rate uncertainty.

11. Bennett, Cohen, and McNulty (1984) discuss the use of swaps for controlling interest rate exposure by savings institutions.

12. Robbins and Schatzberg (1986) suggest that callable bonds are superior to short-term debt in that they permit firms to signal their lower risk and to reduce the risk borne by equityholders. However, their results depend on a specific example. Wall (1988) demonstrates that the callable bonds may fail to provide a separating equilibrium if seemingly small changes are made to their example.

13. This analysis does not consider the use of the futures, forward, and options markets. See Smithson (1987) for a discussion of the various financial instruments that may be used to control interest rate risk.

14. The dealer may enter into a swap for a customer even though the dealer desires a change in exposure in a direction opposite to the swap.

15. Indeed, some variation in the spread should be expected since the Treasury yield curve incorporates coupon interest payments and principal repayments at the maturity of the swap, whereas the swap contract provides only for periodic interest payments.

16. Widgets would probably prefer to cancel the contract and enter into a new swap contract with a different party. Otherwise, market rates could increase above 9.5% and then DomBank might be unable to make the promised payments. See Henderson and Cates (1986) for a discussion of terminating a swap under the insolvency laws of the United States and the United Kingdom.

17. One way that banks typically limit their risk to individual borrowers is to establish a maximum amount that the organization is willing to lend to the borrower, called the borrower's credit line. The amount of a credit line used by a loan is the principal of the loan; however, the amount of the line used by a swap is less clear since a swap's maximum credit loss is a function of market interest rates.

18. See also Muffet (1987).

19. The Monte Carlo technique involves repeated simulations wherein a key value, in this case an interest rate, is drawn from a random sample.

20. Consider two matched pairs of swaps. For the first matched pair the bank agrees to two swaps: (1) The bank pays a fixed rate of 11% and receives LIBOR on the first swap, and (2) the bank pays LIBOR and receives 11%. For the second matched pair the bank pays and receives a 9% fixed rate for LIBOR. Assume that the notional principal, maturity, and repricing interval of all swaps are equal. If the current market rate for swaps of the same maturity is 10%, the bank has credit exposure on the 9% fixed rate swap in which it pays a fixed rate of interest and has credit exposure on the 11% fixed rate swap in which it pays a floating rate of interest. If the market rate on comparable swaps increases to 10.5%, credit exposure increases on the 9% swap in which the dealer pays a fixed rate and decreases on the 11% swap in which the dealer pays a floating rate. Given the assumptions of this example, the change in exposure is almost zero when the market rate moves from 10 to 10.5%.

21. The paper does not explain how swap replacement values and interest rate volatility were calculated.

22. David Shirreff (1985): 253.

23. The standards do not include any framework for evaluating the overall interest rate risk being taken by banking organizations.
24. The standards effective in 1992 define core (tier-one) capital as common stockholders equity, minority interest in the common stockholders' equity accounts of consolidated subsidiaries, and perpetual, noncumulative preferred stock. (The Federal Reserve will also allow bank holding companies to count perpetual, cumulative preferred stock.) Total capital consists of core capital plus supplementary (tier-two) capital. Supplementary capital includes the allowance for loan and lease losses; perpetual, cumulative preferred stock; long-term preferred stock, hybrid capital instruments including perpetual debt, and mandatory convertible securities; and subordinated debt and intermediate-term preferred stock.
25. The framework for risk-based capital standards has been approved by the Group of Ten countries (Belgium, Canada, France, the Federal Republic of Germany, Italy, Japan, the Netherlands, Sweden, the United Kingdom, and the United States) together with Switzerland and Luxembourg.
26. Pitman (1988) discusses the capital standards' implications for various swap market participants.
27. If the predicted changes in interest rates were subject to objective verification, that would suggest that arbitrage opportunities exist. That is, investors may be able to earn a profit with no net investment (financing the purchase of one debt security with the sale of another) and without assuming any risk (since objective verification proved that interest rates will move in the predicted direction). However, efficient markets theory implies that the market will immediately compete away any arbitrage opportunities.
28. Deferral of gains or losses on futures is permitted only if the future is designated as a hedge for an "existing asset, liability, firm commitment or anticipated transactions," according to Comiskey, Mulford, and Turner (1987–88): 4, 9.
29. See Felgran (1987) for a listing of the top 25 U.S. banks by notional principal of swaps outstanding.

References

Abken, Peter A. 1988. Stock market activity in October 1987: The Brady, CFTC, and SEC reports. Federal Reserve Bank of Atlanta *Economic Review* 73, 36–43.

Arak, Marcelle, Arturo Estrella, Laurie Goodman, and Andrew Silver. 1988. Interest rate swaps: An alternative explanation. *Financial Management* 17, 12–18.

Arak, Marcelle, Laurie S. Goodman, and Arthur Rones. 1986. Credit lines for new instruments: Swaps, over-the-counter options, forwards and floor-ceiling agreements. Federal Reserve Bank of Chicago, *Conference on Bank Structure and Competition*, 437–56.

Barnea, Amir, Robert A. Haugen, and Lemma W. Senbet. 1980. A rationale for debt maturity structure and call provisions in the agency theoretic framework. *Journal of Finance* 35, 1223–34.

Beckstrom, Rod. 1986. The development of the swap market. In Boris Antl (ed.), *Swap Finance, vol. I*. London: Euromoney Publications Limited, pp. 31–51.

Belton, Terrence M. 1987. *Credit-risk in interest rate swaps.* Board of Governors of the Federal Reserve System unpublished working paper, April.

Bennett, Dennis E., Deborah L. Cohen, and James E. McNulty. 1984. *Interest rate swaps and the management of interest rate risk.* Paper presented at the Financial Management Association meetings, Toronto, October.

Bicksler, James, and Andrew H. Chen. 1986. An economic analysis of interest rate swaps. *Journal of Finance* 41, 645-55.

Bierman, Harold, Jr. 1987. Accounting for interest rate swaps. *Journal of Accounting, Auditing, and Finance* 2, 396-408.

Black, Fischer, and Myron Scholes. 1973. The pricing of options and corporate liabilities. *Journal of Political Economy* 81, 637-59.

Bodie Zvi, and Robert A. Taggart. 1978. Future investment opportunities and the value of the call provision on a bond. *Journal of Finance* 33, 1187-1200.

Celarier, Michelle. 1987. Swaps' judgement day. *United States Banker* July, 16-20.

Chatfield, Robert E., and R. Charles Moyer. 1986. "Putting" away bond risk: An empirical examination of the value of the put option on bonds. *Financial Management* 15, 26-33.

Comiskey, Eugene E., Charles W. Mulford, and Deborah H. Turner. 1987-88. Bank accounting and reporting practices for interest rate swaps. *Bank Accounting and Finance* 1, 3-14.

Federal Reserve Board and Bank of England. 1987. Potential exposure on interest rate and exchange rate related instruments. Unpublished staff paper.

Felgran, Steven D. 1987. Interest rate swaps: Use, risk and prices. *New England Economic Review* November/December, 22-32.

Geske, Robert. 1977. The valuation of corporate liabilities as compound options. *Journal of Financial and Quantitative Analysis* 12, 541-52.

Hammond, G. M. S. 1987. Recent developments in the swap market. *Bank of England Quarterly Review* 27, 66-79.

Henderson, Schuyler K., and Armel C. Cates. 1986. Termination provisions of swap agreements under U.S. and English insolvency laws. In Boris Antl (ed.), *Swap Finance, vol. 2.* London: Euromoney Publications Limited, pp. 91-102.

Jackson, Dominique. 1988. Swaps keep in step with the regulators. *Financial Times* August 10, 22.

Johnson, Herb, and René Stulz. 1987. The pricing of options with default risk. *Journal of Finance* 42, 267-80.

Loeys, Jan G. 1985. Interest rate swaps: A new tool for managing risk. Federal Reserve Bank of Philadelphia *Business Review* May/June, 17-25.

Mayers, David, and Clifford W. Smith. 1987. Corporate insurance and the underinvestment problem. *Journal of Risk and Insurance* 54, 45-54.

Muffet, Mark. 1987. Modeling credit exposure on swaps. Federal Reserve Bank of Chicago, *Conference on Bank Structure and Competition,* 473-96.

Myers, Stewart C. 1977. Determinants of corporate borrowing. *Journal of Financial Economics* 5, 147-76.

Neal, Kathleen, and Katerina Simons. 1988. Interest rate swaps, currency swaps, and credit risk. *Issues in Bank Regulation* Spring, 26-29.

Pitman, Joanna. 1988. Swooping on swaps. *Euromoney* January, 68-80.

Robbins, Edward Henry, and John D. Schatzberg. 1986. Callable bonds: A risk reducing, signalling mechanism. *Journal of Finance* 41, 935-49.

Rudnick, Linda T. 1987. Discussion of practical aspects of interest rate swaps. Federal Reserve Bank of Chicago, *Conference on Bank Structure and Competition,* 206-13.

Shirreff, David. 1985. The fearsome growth of swaps. *Euromoney* October, 247-61.

Smith, Clifford W., Charles W. Smithson, and Lee Macdonald Wakeman. 1986. The evolving market for swaps. *Midland Corporate Finance Journal* 3, 20–32.

———. 1987. Credit risk and the scope of regulation of swaps. Federal Reserve Bank of Chicago, *Conference on Bank Structure and Competition,* 166–85.

———. 1988. The market for interest rate swaps. *Financial Management* 17, 34–44.

Smithson, Charles W. 1987. A LEGO® approach to financial engineering: An introduction to forwards, futures, swaps, and options. *Midland Corporate Finance Review* 4, 16–28.

Stulz, René M., and Herb Johnson. 1985. An analysis of secured debt. *Journal of Financial Economics* 14, 501–21.

Turnbull, Stuart M. 1987. Swaps: A zero sum game? *Financial Management* 16, 15–21.

Wakeman, Lee Macdonald. 1986. *The portfolio approach to swaps management.* Chemical Bank Capital Markets Group unpublished working paper, May.

Wall, Larry D. 1986. Alternative financing strategies: Notes versus callable bonds. *Journal of Finance* 43, 1057–65.

———. Forthcoming. Interest rate swaps in an agency theoretic model with uncertain interest rates. *Journal of Banking and Finance.*

Wall, Larry D., and Kwun-Wing C. Fung. 1987. *Evaluating the credit exposure of interest rate swap portfolios.* Federal Reserve Bank of Atlanta Working Paper 87-8, December.

Wall, Larry D., and John J. Pringle. 1987. Alternative explanations of interest rate swaps. Federal Reserve Bank of Chicago, *Conference on Bank Structure and Competition,* 186–205.

Weiner, Lisabeth. 1988. Dollar dominates swaps, survey shows: Deals in U.S. currency outstrip yen, deutsche mark by far. *American Banker* February 26, 2.

Whittaker, J. Gregg. 1987a. Interest rate swaps: Risk and regulation. Federal Reserve Bank of Kansas City *Economic Review* March, 3–13.

———. 1987b. *Pricing interest rate swaps in an options pricing framework.* Federal Reserve Bank of Kansas City unpublished working paper RWP 87-02. Presented at the Financial Management Association meetings, Las Vegas, October.

Wishon, Keith, and Lorin S. Chevalier. 1985. Interest rate swaps—your rate or mine? *Journal of Accountancy* September, 63–84.

11

Option Pricing: A Review*

Clifford W. Smith, Jr.

1. Introduction

Although much interest in option pricing has been generated from the development of new options markets such as the Chicago Board Options Exchange, the recent rapid development of theory and the application of that theory can be traced to the path-breaking paper by Fischer Black and Myron Scholes (1973). In that paper, they provide the first explicit general equilibrium solution to the option-pricing problem for simple puts and calls.[1] They then suggest that this analysis could provide a basis for the general analysis of contingent claim assets, assets whose value is a nonproportional function of the value of another asset. Because puts and calls are perhaps the simplest

*The rate of development of the body of literature on option pricing has been extremely rapid in recent times. These rapid advances make the task of a survey such as this not only somewhat more difficult, but also probably more valuable. I would like to thank those authors who have kindly agreed to allow me to reference their results, which in some cases are as yet unpublished, and I apologize in advance to those authors whose work is not referenced. This paper cannot be an exhaustive survey but is meant only to convey the major thrust of the work on option pricing. An extensive list of references to books and articles on options and option pricing has been included to aid the interested reader. The author would like to thank W. A. Avera, F. Black, H. A. Latané, P. Lloyd-Davies, R. C. Merton, M. Scholes, J. L. Zimmerman, and especially M. C. Jensen and J. B. Long for comments and suggestions.
1. A call is an option to buy a share of stock at the maturity date of the contract for a fixed amount, the exercise price. A put is an option to sell.

form of a contingent claim asset, the study of these simple instruments provides keys to unlock difficult questions of other more complex contingent claims pricing situations.

In deriving their model, Black and Scholes employ the following assumptions:

1. There are no penalties for short sales.
2. Transactions costs and taxes are zero.
3. The market operates continuously.
4. The risk-free interest rate is constant.
5. The stock price is continuous.[2]
6. The stock pays no dividends.
7. The option can only be exercised at the terminal date of the contract.

They derive the solution to the option pricing problem as a function of only five variables:

1. the stock price,
2. the variance on the stock price,
3. the exercise price of the option,
4. the time to maturity of the option,
5. the risk-free interest rate.

Two points should be noted about this list of arguments. First, variables such as the expected rate of return to the stock, or parameters denoting investor attitudes toward risk do not appear as arguments in the general equilibrium option-pricing solution. Second, the only argument of the solution that is not directly observable, the variance rate, can be approximated using the sequence of past prices.

Subsequent modification of the basic Black-Scholes model by Merton (1973b, 1974, 1976) and others shows that the analysis is quite robust with respect to relaxation of the basic assumptions under which the model is derived. No single assumption seems crucial to the analysis. Thorpe (1973) examines the effects of restrictions against the use of the proceeds of short sales. Ingersoll (1976) explicitly considers the effect of differential taxes on capital gains and ordinary income. Merton (1976) argues that the continuous trading solution approximates the asymptotic limit of the discrete trading solution when the stock price movement is continuous. Merton (1973b) also generalizes the model to the case of a stochastic interest rate. Thus, it appears that the relaxation of the first four assumptions involving the specification

---

2. Continuous here means "no jumps." Roughly speaking, in a graph of stock price against time, the stock price can be drawn without lifting the pen.

of the behavior of the capital market environment modifies the analysis in no significant way. In addition, the analytical technique developed by Black and Scholes remains valid even if the last three assumptions dealing with the specification of the stock and option are relaxed. Merton (1976) and Cox and Ross (1976) successfully employ a Black-Scholes type analysis to examine a case in which stock price movements are discontinuous. Merton (1973b) and Thorpe (1973) modify the model to account for dividend payments on the underlying stock. Finally, Merton (1973b) shows that the Black-Scholes solution for an option that can be exercised only at maturity can be appropriate to value a call option that may be exercised prior to the maturity date.

After deriving the general equilibrium option-pricing equation, Black and Scholes make what may be one of the most important observations in the field of finance in the past ten years. They suggest that the equilibrium solution to the option-pricing problem can be utilized to value other complex contingent claim assets, specifically the equity of a levered firm. They argue that the position of the stockholders is equivalent to that of the purchaser of a call; and the position of the bondholders, to that of the writer of a call; that is, the stockholders have the right to buy the firm back from the bondholders by paying the face value of the bonds to the bondholders. The model is also applied by Merton (1974) to analyze the effects of risk on the value of corporate debt; by Galai and Masulis (1976) to examine the effect of mergers, acquisitions, scale expansions, and spin-offs on the relative values of the debt and equity claims of the firm; by Ingersoll (1976) to value the shares of dual-purpose funds; and by Black (1976) to value commodity options, forward contracts, and future contracts. This paper provides a summary of (1) the models of simple option pricing, (2) the empirical verification of these models, and (3) the applications of option-pricing models to value other assets.

Section 2 introduces the terminology employed in the trading of options and develops basic relationships between the values of options and the underlying assets, based only on the assumption that investors prefer more to less. The arguments in this section follow Merton (1973b) and offer insight into the relationships that must hold between asset values for markets to be in equilibrium. The generality of the arguments in this section prohibits a specific solution to the option-pricing problem, but does define limits between which any acceptable general equilibrium solution must fall.

Sections 3 and 4 review the development of explicit solutions to the call option-pricing problem.[3] To derive an explicit solution, each of the works

---

3. Option pricing models seem to fall into two categories: (1) Ad hoc models, and (2) equilibrium models. The ad hoc models generally appear in the nonacademic literature and are the result of casual empiricism or curve-fitting exercises—not of maximizing behavior on the part of the market participants. Examples include Hallingby (1947), Morrison (1957), Giguere (1958), Pease (1963), Kassouf (1962, 1968a, 1969), Thorpe and Kassouf (1967), Shelton (1967b) and Turov (1973). For a summary of many of these models, see Shelton (1967a). These models will not be reviewed in this paper.

reviewed in this section chooses a specific description of the statistical process, which describes the movement of the stock price through time. Then, given that statistical hypothesis, the equilibrium relationship between the call price, the stock price, and other variables of the economy is explored. The statistical assumptions employed are Arithmetic Brownian Motion (leading to a normally distributed stock price), Geometric Brownian Motion (leading to a log-normally distributed stock price), and the Poisson Process (or Jump Process). Section 3 reviews selected papers written prior to the Black-Scholes paper. These papers provide an indication of the development of the thought at this early stage, but more importantly, they offer useful insight into the Black-Scholes general equilibrium call-pricing solution. The Black-Scholes model and its subsequent modifications by Merton and others are discussed in Section 4.

Section 5 provides an analysis of the put-option-pricing model. Useful relationships are defined by use of dominance arguments, including the equilibrium relationship between the price of a put option, which can only be exercised at maturity, and the value of a portfolio consisting of a call, the stock, and riskless bonds. Using this relationship, the Black-Scholes put-option-pricing model is derived.

Section 6 reviews empirical tests of the option-pricing model and evidence on the efficiency of the option market.

Section 7 examines the application of the option-pricing model to value other contingent claim assets. These applications include pricing the equity and debt of the firm, analyzing the risk structure of interest rates, and valuing the shares of a dual-purpose fund.

2. Definition of Terminology and Some Fundamental Constraints on Option Prices

2.1. Terminology

An option is defined as a right to buy or sell designated securities or commodities at a specified price during the period of the contract. The specified price is referred to as the exercise price, striking price, or contract price. The terminal date of the contract is called the expiration date or maturity date. Options to purchase securities that are written by individuals are termed calls; options to sell, puts.[4] If the option may be exercised before the expiration date, then it is referred to as an American option; if only on the expiration

---

4. The above terminology is employed to describe simple options. However, elements of option pricing can arise in other contexts as well. First, convertible preferred stocks and convertible bonds are essentially call options in concert with another basic security. Second, option contracts may be combined to form strips, straddles or spreads. See Kruizenga (1964a).

date, a European option. Options granted by corporations are termed warrants or rights. Rights are usually exercisable for very short periods of time; warrants, generally for longer time periods. Contracts to purchase commodities rather than financial instruments are called commodity options.

Notation. In the option literature, no set of notation is regarded as standard. To facilitate comparisons between different models, one set of notation will be employed. (This will be extended to quotations.) The symbols to be used are:

t current date,

t^* expiration date of the option,

T time to expiration (t^*-t),

B price of a default-free pure discount bond with a face value of one dollar,

C price of an American call option at t,

c price of a European call option at t,

κ expected average rate of growth in the call price [$e^{\kappa T}=E(C^*/C)$],

P price of an American put option at t,

p price of a European put option at t,

r risk-free interest rate,

S stock price at t,

ρ expected average rate of growth in the stock price [$e^{\rho T}=E(S^*/S)$],

X exercise price of the option,

V_a value of portfolio A at t.

Starred variables such as C^*, c^*, S^*, etc., refer to prices at t^*, the expiration date of the option.

2.2. Stochastic Dominance and Some Fundamental Restrictions on Call Option Prices

Merton (1973b) sets forth the most exhaustive set of equilibrium restrictions on call option pricing which is free of distributional assumptions. Merton makes no assumptions about the process generating the stock price over time; the restrictions he derives depend only on dominance arguments. Portfolio A is dominant over portfolio B if over some given time interval the return to A is not less than the return to B for all states of the world, and the return to A is strictly greater than the return to B for at least one state of the world. In equilibrium no dominant or dominated security can exist. If a dominant security existed, everyone would prefer to hold that security. The price would be bid up until the dominance disappeared and vice versa. The results derived through the use of dominance arguments are completely general. If the implications of a specific model based on a specific distributional description of the stock price movement violate these restrictions, then that model must be deficient in some way. The results of these dominance arguments will be used as general consistency criteria against which subsequent models may be conveniently measured.

Call prices are nonnegative. From the definition of a call option, exercise is voluntary. Since exercise will be undertaken only when in the best interests of the option holders,

$$
\begin{aligned}
C(S, T; X) &\geq 0 \quad \text{[American call]} \\
c(S, T; X) &\geq 0 \quad \text{[European call]}
\end{aligned}
\tag{11.1}
$$

At the expiration date, t^*, the call will be priced at the maximum of either the difference between the stock price and the exercise price, $S^* - X$, or zero. When the time to expiration, T, of a call option is zero, then arbitrage is possible since the option can be converted into the common for the option plus the exercise price,

$$
\begin{aligned}
C(S^*, 0; X) &= \text{Max}(0, S^* - X) \\
c(S^*, 0; X) &= \text{Max}(0, S^* - X)
\end{aligned}
\tag{11.2}
$$

At any date before the maturity date an American call option must sell for at least the difference between the stock price and the exercise price. An American call can be exercised at any time before the expiration date, therefore,

$$
C(S, T; X) \geq \text{Max}(0, S - X)
\tag{11.3}
$$

Note that this condition cannot be deduced for a European call, since arbitrage is not possible until $T = 0$.

If two American calls differ only as to expiration date, then the one with the longer term to maturity, T_1, must sell for no less than that of the shorter term to maturity, T_2. At the expiration date of the shorter option, its price will be equal to the maximum of zero and the difference between the stock price and the exercise price by (11.2). This then is the minimum price of the longer option by (11.3). Therefore, to prevent dominance,

$$
C(S, T_1; X) \geq C(S, T_2; X)
\tag{11.4}
$$

Since no correspondence to (11.3) exists for European calls, (11.4) cannot be deduced in that case by this argument.

An American call must be priced no lower than an identical European call. Since the American call confers all the rights of the European call plus the privilege of premature exercise, then, to avoid dominance,

$$
C(S, T; X) \geq c(S, T; X)
\tag{11.5}
$$

If two options differ only in exercise price, then the option with the lower exercise price must sell for a price which is no less than the option with the

Option Pricing: A Review 261

TABLE 11.1 *Terminal Values of Portfolios A and B for Different Relationships Between Stock Price and Exercise Price at the Expiration Date* $(T = 0)$ *of the Call*

Portfolio	Current Value	Stock Price at $T = 0$		
		$S^* \leq X_2$	$X_2 < S^* < X_1$	$X_1 \leq S^*$
A	$C(S, T; X_2)$	0	$S^* - X_2$	$S^* - X_2$
B	$C(S, T; X_1)$	0	0	$S^* - X_1$
Relationship between terminal values of portfolios A and B		$V_a^* = V_b^*$	$V_a^* > V_b^*$	$V_a^* > V_b^*$

higher exercise price to avoid dominance. This may be demonstrated by constructing two portfolios, A and B, where portfolio A contains one call with exercise price X_2, $C(S, T; X_2)$, and portfolio B contains one call with exercise price X_1, $C(S, T; X_1)$ with $X_1 > X_2$.

Since for all possible terminal stock prices above the lower exercise price X_2, the terminal value of portfolio A, V_a^*, exceeds that of portfolio B, V_b^*, then the current price of A must be greater than or equal to the current price of B. If the current price of B were greater than that of A, the return to portfolio A would be greater than the return to B for all states of the world and B would be a dominated portfolio. Therefore,

$$C(S, T; X_1) \leq C(S, T; X_2)$$
$$c(S, T; X_1) \leq c(S, T; X_2)$$
$$(11.6)$$

where $X_1 > X_2$.

Table 11.1 demonstrates that a call with a lower exercise price, X_2, will have dollar payoffs greater than or equal to a call with a higher exercise price, X_1.

The common stock is at least equivalent to a perpetual call (*i.e.,* $T = \infty$) *with a zero exercise price.* Then from (11.4) and (11.6) it follows that

$$S \geq C(S, \infty; 0) \geq C(S, T; X) \tag{11.7}$$

[S may exceed $C(S, \infty; 0)$ because of dividends, voting rights, etc.][5] From (11.7) if a stock is worthless (i.e., $S = 0$), the option must be also:

$$C(0, T; X) = c(0, T; X) = 0 \tag{11.8}$$

---

5. Bachelier's (1900) model violates this restriction. In his model, the stock does not possess the property of limited liability, i.e., that the maximum loss that can be sustained by an asset holder is limited to the size of his investment.

TABLE 11.2 *Terminal Values of Portfolios A and B for Different Relationships Between Stock Price and Exercise Price at the Expiration Date ($T=0$) of the Call*

		Stock Price at $T=0$	
Portfolio	Current Value	$S^* < X$	$X \leq S^*$
A	$c(S,T;X) + XB(T)$	$0 + X$	$(S^* - X) + X$
B	S	S^*	S^*
Relationship between terminal values of portfolios A and B		$V_a^* > V_b^*$	$V_a^* = V_b^*$

An American call on a non–dividend-paying stock will not be exercised before the expiration date. To demonstrate this, first let $B(\tau)$ be the price of a risk-free, pure discount bond, which pays one dollar τ years from now. Then, assuming interest rates are positive, at a given point in time bonds with a longer time to maturity will be priced less than bonds with a shorter time to maturity; that is,

$$0 = B(\infty) < B(\tau_1) < B(\tau_2) < B(\tau_3) < B(0) = 1 \qquad (11.9)$$

where $\infty > \tau_1 > \tau_2 > \tau_3 > 0$.
Now consider two portfolios A and B:

A Purchase one European call for $c(S,T;X)$
      Purchase X bonds for $XB(T)$
B Purchase stock for S

Table 11.2 demonstrates that a call plus discount bonds with a face value of X yield a terminal value greater than or equal to that of the respective stock if the stock pays no dividends.

Since V_a^*, the terminal value of portfolio A, is not less than the V_b^*, the current value of A must be greater than or equal to that of B to avoid dominance. Therefore, for a security paying no dividends, this restriction may be rearranged to yield

$$c(S,T;X) \geq \text{Max}[0, S - XB(T)] \qquad (11.10)$$

Note that if dividends are paid over the life of the option, the return to portfolio B is no longer $(S^* - S)/S$. The proviso of no dividend payments can be dropped if adequate dividend protection exists for the option.[6]

---

6. See Merton (1973b) for a discussion of appropriate protection for options from dividend payments.

From (11.5) and (11.10) it follows that (assuming no dividends and in the absence of transaction costs) the price of an American call is no less than the difference between the stock price and the present value of the exercise price,

$$C(S, T; X) \geq c(S, T; X) \geq \text{Max}[0, S - XB(T)] \qquad (11.11)$$

If exercised, the value of an American option is $\text{Max}[0, S - X]$, which is less than $\text{Max}[0, S - XB(T)]$, since $B(T)$ is less than 1 if T is greater than zero. Therefore, prior to expiration, the holder of an American call will always choose to sell rather than exercise the option. This implies that if there are no dividends paid over the life of the option (or changes in exercise price) an American call will never be exercised before its expiration date and will therefore have the same value as a European option. This is an important result because European calls are simpler instruments than the more familiar American calls. Further, differences between American and European calls (implying some positive probability of premature exercise) must arise from changes in exercise price or dividends rather than from assumptions about distributions of returns or shapes of investors' utility functions.[7]

It has been generally suggested that the minimum justifiable price or the "intrinsic value" of a call is $\text{Max}[0, S - X]$ from (11.3), but Equation 11.11 implies that the "intrinsic value" of an option on a non-dividend-paying stock should be $\text{Max}[0, S - XB(T)]$, which is greater than $\text{Max}(0, S - X)$ prior to the expiration date. Equation 11.11 is a stronger condition than (11.3). That (11.3) obtains can be ensured directly with arbitrage by placing simultaneous orders. Arbitrage in the usual sense does not guarantee (11.11) will hold; but if the condition is violated, the common stock will be a dominated security, and in equilibrium, no dominated security will exist.

A perpetual option on a non-dividend-paying stock must sell for the same price as the stock. Equation 11.11 reflects the fact that the exercise price need not be paid until the option is exercised at the expiration date. Therefore, $XB(T)$ represents the present value of that payment. This adjustment becomes significant as T gets large. For a perpetual option (i.e., $T = \infty$) then from (11.11),

$$C(S, \infty; X) \geq \text{Max}[0, S - XB(\infty)] \qquad (11.12)$$

But the present value of one dollar paid an infinite time in the future is zero, therefore $B(\infty) = 0$, and

$$C(S, \infty; X) \geq S \qquad (11.13)$$

From (11.7), the call price is not greater than the stock price,

$$S \geq C(S, \infty; X)$$

---

7. Samuelson's (1965) model implies that as long as the option is more risky than the stock, there exists some positive probability of premature exercise. This implication is obviously at variance with the above result. See Section 3 for an analysis of Samuelson's model.

TABLE 11.3 *Terminal Values of Portfolios A and B for Different Relationships Between Stock Price and Exercise Price at the Expiration Date ($T = 0$) of the Call*

| Port- | | Stock Price at $T = 0$ | | | |
folio	Current Value	$S^* \leq X_3$	$X_3 < S^* < X_2$	$X_2 < S^* < X_1$	$X_1 \leq S^*$
A	$\lambda C(S, T; X_1) +$	$0+$	$0+$	$0+$	$\lambda(S^* - X_1) +$
	$(1-\lambda)C(S, T; X_3)$	0	$(1-\lambda)(S^* - X_3)$	$(1-\lambda)(S^* - X_3)$	$(1-\lambda)(S^* - X_3)$
B	$C(S, T; X_2)$	0	0	$S^* - X_2$	$S^* - X_2$
Relationship between terminal values of portfolios A and B		$V_a^* = V_b^*$	$V_a^* > V_b^*$	$V_a^* > V_b^*$	$V_a^* = V_b^*$

Therefore, (11.7) and (11.13) imply that a perpetual option on a non–dividend-paying stock must sell for the same price as the security itself,[8]

$$C(S, \infty; X) = S \qquad (11.14)$$

The call price is a convex function of the exercise price. Convexity implies that if $X_2 = \lambda X_1 + (1 - \lambda)X_3$, then

$$C(S, T; X_2) \leq \lambda C(S, T; X_1) + (1 - \lambda)C(S, T; X_3) \qquad (11.15)$$

where $X_1 \geq X_2 \geq X_3$ and $0 \leq \lambda \leq 1$.

To demonstrate this restriction, form two portfolios, A and B, where portfolio A contains λ calls with exercise price X_1 and $(1 - \lambda)$ calls with exercise price X_3, and portfolio B contains one call with exercise price X_2. Table 11.3 demonstrates that a convex combination of calls with different exercise prices yields a terminal value greater than or equal to that of a call with an exercise price which is the convex combination of the other two exercise prices. Table 11.3 shows that V_a^* is greater than or equal to V_b^*; therefore, to avoid dominance the current value of B must be less than or equal to that of A. This is (11.15).

If the call price can be expressed as a differentiable function of the exercise price, the derivative must be negative and be no larger in absolute value than the price of a pure discount bond of the same maturity. To demonstrate this, consider two portfolios A and B;

---

8. It may seem that a stock that will never pay dividends would sell for a zero price and therefore Equation 11.14 would hold with $S = C = 0$. However, this is not the case. Consider two firms, identical in every respect except one has a policy of paying dividends at stated dates while at those dates the second firm takes the same number of dollars, enters the market and purchases as many shares of the firm's stock as possible at the current market price, and retires the shares. Given a world with efficient markets and no taxes, these two firms would have the same market value.

TABLE 11.4 *Terminal Values of Portfolios A and B for Different Relationships Between Stock Price and Exercise Price at the Expiration Date* $(T = 0)$ *of the Call*

		Stock Price at $T = 0$		
Portfolio	Current Value	$S^* \leq X_2$	$X_2 < S^* < X_1$	$X_1 \leq S^*$
A	$c(S, T; X_2) +$	$0 +$	$0 +$	$(S^* - X_1) +$
	$B(T)(X_1 - X_2)$	$(X_1 - X_2)$	$(X_1 - X_2)$	$(X_1 - X_2)$
B	$c(S, T; X_2)$	0	$(S^* - X_2)$	$(S^* - X_2)$
Relationship between terminal values of portfolios A and B		$V_a^* > V_b^*$	$V_a^* > V_b^*$	$V_a^* = V_b^*$

$A \quad c(S, T; X_1) + B(T)(X_1 - X_2)$

$B \quad c(S, T; X_2)$

Table 11.4 shows that V_a^* is not less than V_b^*; therefore, unless the current price of A is not less than that of B, $c(S, T; X_2)$ will be a dominated security,

$$B(T)(X_2 - X_1) \leq c(S, T; X_1) - c(S, T; X_2) \leq 0 \qquad (11.16)$$

where $X_1 > X_2$.

That this is less than zero follows from (11.6).

If $c(S, T; X)$ is a differentiable function of X, then the partial derivative of the call price with respect to the exercise price will be no more negative than minus a bond price with the same maturity date as the option,

$$-B(T) \leq \partial c(S, T; X)/\partial X \leq 0 \qquad (11.17)$$

This can be seen by dividing both sides of (11.16) by $(X_1 - X_2)$ and taking the limit as X_2 approaches X_1.

With dividend payments on the stock, premature exercise of an American call may occur. To examine the effect of dividend payments, consider a security that goes ex-dividend and pays a certain payment (D) on the expiration date of an option. Consider two portfolios A and B:

$A \quad$ Buy one European call and $X + D$ bonds

$B \quad$ Buy one share of stock

See Table 11.5. Since the terminal value of A is not less than that of B, to prevent dominance the current price of A must not be less than B. Then,

$$c(S, T; X) \geq \text{Max}[0, S - (X + D)B(T)] \qquad (11.18)$$

TABLE 11.5   Terminal Values of Portfolios A and B for Different Relationships Between Stock Price and Exercise Price at the Expiration Date ($T = 0$) of the Call

Portfolio	Current Value	Stock Price at $T = 0$	
		$S^* < X$	$X \leq S^*$
A	$c(S, T; X) +$ $(X + D)B(T)$	$0 +$ $X + D$	$S^* - X +$ $X + D$
B	S	$S^* + D$	$S^* + D$
Relationship between terminal values of portfolios A and B		$V_a^* > V_b^*$	$V_a^* = V_b^*$

Note that the value of a pure discount bond with a face value equal to the sum of the exercise price plus the dividend may be greater or less than the exercise price, therefore $\text{Max}[0, S - (X + D)B(T)] \lesssim \text{Max}[0, S - X]$. Then, with dividend payments, it may be advantageous to exercise an American option before expiration.

The above dominance arguments define limits between which the equilibrium call price must fall.[9] Because of the generality of dominance arguments, no specific functional relationship can be defined between the call option price and variables such as the stock price, exercise price, time to maturity, and the like. Most previous efforts to define the equilibrium option price have taken another approach to the problem. A specific description of the statistical process that describes the movement of the stock price through time is assumed. Then, given that statistical assumption, the equilibrium relationship between the call price, the stock price, and other parameters of the economy is explored. Several different hypotheses have been offered to describe the movement of the stock price.

The next two sections trace the development of the general equilibrium specification of the option-pricing model. Section 3 reviews the models developed prior to the Black-Scholes model. This section not only traces the development of thought in this area, but provides useful insight into the Black-Scholes Option Pricing Model. The reader who is not primarily interested in these aspects may wish to skip to Section 4, below, which discusses the first general equilibrium model by Black and Scholes and the subsequent modifications by Merton and others.

---

9. See Merton (1973b) for additional restrictions requiring additional assumptions. Further restrictions are not crucial to address the major issues of this paper but the interested reader is encouraged to refer to Merton's paper for this is a useful and intuitive approach.

3. Incomplete Equilibrium Models of Call Option Pricing

Prior to the Black-Scholes option pricing model, only two assumptions about the statistical process generating the stock price had been offered. Bachelier (1900) suggests an Arithmetic Brownian Motion process. This assumption leads to unacceptable general equilibrium implications.[10] The major objections to Bachelier's model may be summarized as: (1) The assumption of Arithmetic Brownian Motion in the description of expected price movements implies both a positive probability of negative prices for the security and option prices greater than their respective security prices for large T. (2) The assumption that the mean expected price change is zero suggests both zero interest rates and risk neutrality. (3) The implicit assumption that the variance is finite a priori rules out members of the stable-Paretian family other than the normal.

Geometric Brownian Motion. Since the assumption of normality seems to lead to unacceptable implications, most models have used an alternate hypothesis—that the log of the stock price follows a Wiener process (or the stock price follows Geometric Brownian Motion).[11] This hypothesis involves four assumptions:

1. The distribution of price ratios is independent of the price level,

$$\text{Prob}\{\tilde{S}^* \le S^* \,|\, \tilde{S} = S\} = F(S^*/S; T) \tag{11.19}$$

where F is the cumulative distribution function of the stock price relatives.

2. Price ratios are independent. Since $(S^*/S) = (S^*/S')(S'/S)$,

$$F(S^*/S; T) = \int_0^\infty F(S^*/S'; T - T')F'(S'/S; T')\, dS' \tag{11.20}$$

where F' is the density function for F, S' is the stock price T' from now, and $T > T' > 0$.

3. There is a zero probability that the stock price will become zero; therefore logarithms may be employed.

4. The variance of the price relatives is finite—thereby ruling out other members of stable-Paretian distribution of logs.

---

10. Bachelier's (1900) model is explicitly discussed in Appendix 11.A below.
11. Arithmetic Brownian Motion without drift implies that the probabilities of the stock price either rising or falling by one dollar are equal, independent of the level of the stock price. Geometric Brownian Motion without drift implies that the probabilities of the stock price either rising or fall by 1% are equal, independent of the stock price.

Given these four assumptions, the only solution to (11.20) is the log-normal distribution,

$$F(S^*/S; T) = L(S^*; S, \rho T, \sigma\sqrt{T})$$
$$= N\left(\frac{\ln(S^*/S) - (\rho - \sigma^2/2)T}{\sigma\sqrt{T}}\right) \tag{11.21}$$

where L is the cumulative log-normal distribution function for S^*.

A useful theorem in solving integrals involving the log-normal distribution follows.

Theorem 11.1.[12] *If $L'(S^*)$ is a log-normal density function with*

$$Q = \begin{cases} \lambda S^* - \gamma X & \text{if } S^* - \psi X \geq 0 \\ 0 & \text{if } S^* - \psi X < 0 \end{cases}$$

then

$$E(Q) \equiv \int_{\psi X}^{\infty} (\lambda S^* - \gamma X) L'(S^*)\, dS^*$$
$$= e^{\rho T} \lambda S \cdot N\left\{\frac{\ln(S/X) - \ln\psi + [\rho + (\sigma^2/2)]T}{\sigma\sqrt{T}}\right\}$$
$$- \gamma X \cdot N\left\{\frac{\ln(S/X) - \ln\psi + [\rho - (\sigma^2/2)]T}{\sigma\sqrt{T}}\right\} \tag{11.22}$$

where λ, γ, and ψ are arbitrary parameters, ρ is the expected average rate of growth in the stock price $[e^{\rho T} \equiv E(S^*/S)]$, and N is the cumulative standard normal distribution function,

$$N\{q\} = \int_{-\infty}^{q} \frac{1}{\sqrt{2\pi}} e^{-z^2/2}\, dz$$

The Sprenkle Model. Sprenkle (1964) partially removes the first two objections to Bachelier's formulation. Sprenkle assumes that stock prices are log-normally distributed, thus explicitly ruling out the possibility of nonpositive prices for securities and removing the associated infinite prices for options. Further, he allows for drift in the random walk, thus allowing for positive interest rates and risk aversion.

The expected value of the option at the expiration date is

$$E(C^*) = \int_X^{\infty} (S^* - X) L'(S^*)\, dS^* \tag{11.23}$$

and by the above theorem (Equation 11.22) with $\lambda = \gamma = \psi = 1$,

---

12. The proof of this theorem follows the proof of a less general result in the appendix of Sprenkle (1964).

$$E(C^*) = e^{\rho T} S \cdot N \left\{ \frac{\ln(S/X) + [\rho + (\sigma^2/2)]T}{\sigma\sqrt{T}} \right\}$$

$$-X \cdot N \left\{ \frac{\ln(S/X) + [\rho - (\sigma^2/2)]T}{\sigma\sqrt{T}} \right\} \tag{11.24}$$

Sprenkle also assumes that "it is in general not true that the investor would be willing to pay a price for the warrant exactly equal to the expected value of it to him. In fact, he would be willing to pay exactly this price only if he were neutral to risk." Von Neumann–Morgenstern utility functions do not imply that risk-neutral individuals would be indifferent between the choice of C dollars today and a gamble with expected value $E(C^*)$ dollars at the expiration of the option. It must be assumed further that interest rates are zero. Additionally, it is self-contradictory to assume that the random walk of stock prices has a positive bias, while assuming that investors pay the expected value for options.

The final form of Sprenkle's model containing a modification for risk is

$$C = e^{\rho T} S \cdot N \left\{ \frac{\ln(S/X) + [\rho + (\sigma^2/2)]T}{\sigma\sqrt{T}} \right\}$$

$$-(1-k)X \cdot N \left\{ \frac{\ln(S/X) + [\rho - (\sigma^2/2)]T}{\sigma\sqrt{T}} \right\} \tag{11.25}$$

where k is an adjustment for the degree of market risk aversion.

Since the time value of money is ignored, this model is flawed.

The Boness Model. Boness (1964a) allows for the time value of money and thus avoids Sprenkle's error. However, his assumptions are such that different levels of risk for the stock and the options are ignored. Boness assumes that:

(1) The market is competitive in the sense that the equilibrium price of all stocks of the same risk class imply the same expected yield on investment. *For convenience and in default of better information, all stocks on which options are traded are defined to be of the same risk class.*

(2) The probability distribution of expected percentage changes in the price of any stock is log-normal.

(3) Variance of returns is directly proportional to time, $\sigma^2 = \sigma^2 T$.

(4) Investors are indifferent to risk.[13]

Boness expresses the expected terminal value of the option in terms of conditional expected values as

---

13. Boness (1964a, p. 167), emphasis in original.

$$E(C^*) = [E(S^*|S^*>X) - E(X|S^*>X)]\,\text{Prob}(S^*>X) \qquad (11.26)$$

From the definition of conditional expected values, the conditional expected value of S^* given that $S^*>X$ is

$$E(S^*|S^*>X) = \int_X^\infty S^*L'(S^*)\,dS^*/\int_X^\infty L'(S^*)\,dS^* \qquad (11.27)$$

Since the exercise price is nonstochastic,

$$E(X|S^*>X) = X \qquad (11.28)$$

and the probability that S^* will be greater than the exercise price is

$$\text{Prob}(S^*>X) = \int_X^\infty L'(S^*)\,dS^* \qquad (11.29)$$

Substituting these definitions into (11.26), Boness derives the expected terminal price of the option,

$$E(C^*) = \int_X^\infty (S^*-X)L'(S^*)\,dS^* \qquad (11.30)$$

To allow for the time value of money, he then discounts the expected terminal call price back to the present using the expected rate of return to the stock, ρ,

$$C = e^{-\rho T}\int_X^\infty (S^*-X)L'(S^*)\,dS^* \qquad (11.31)$$

To solve (11.31), use the above theorem with $\lambda = \gamma = e^{-\rho T}$ and $\psi = 1$. Then,

$$C = S\cdot N\left\{\frac{\ln(S/X)+[\rho+(\sigma^2/2)]T}{\sigma\sqrt{T}}\right\}$$

$$-e^{-\rho T}X\cdot N\left\{\frac{\ln(S/X)+[\rho-(\sigma^2/2)]T}{\sigma\sqrt{T}}\right\} \qquad (11.32)$$

Boness' fourth assumption would suggest that he uses ρ as a proxy for the expected rate of return on the option, $\kappa\ [e^{\kappa T} \equiv E(C^*/C)]$. However, a different use of this assumption could make his task easier. If Boness notes that Assumption 4 also implies that in equilibrium the returns to all assets would be equal, $\rho \overset{e}{=} \kappa \overset{e}{=} r$, then he could use the appropriate risk-free rate and thus avoid the estimation of the expected average rate of growth in the stock price, ρ.

The Samuelson Model.   Samuelson (1965) assumes stock prices follow Geometric Brownian Motion with positive drift ρ, thus allowing for positive interest rates and risk premiums,

$$E(S^*/S) = e^{\rho T}$$

If the option price also grows at the rate κ,

$$E(C^*/C) = e^{\kappa T}$$

With the addition of the assumptions that the terminal stock price distribution is log-normal, the value of the option is

$$C = e^{-\kappa T} E(C^*)$$
$$= e^{-\kappa T} \int_X^\infty (S^* - X) L'(S^*)\, dS^* \tag{11.33}$$

To solve, let $\lambda = \gamma = e^{-\kappa T}$, $\psi = 1$ and apply the theorem stated in (11.22); then,

$$C = e^{(\rho - \kappa)T} S \cdot N\left\{ \frac{\ln(S/X) + [\rho + (\sigma^2/2)]T}{\sigma\sqrt{T}} \right\}$$

$$- e^{-\kappa T} X \cdot N\left\{ \frac{\ln(S/X) + [\rho - (\sigma^2/2)]T}{\sigma\sqrt{T}} \right\} \tag{11.34}$$

With the additional assumption that $\rho = \kappa$, then $e^{(\rho - \kappa)T} = 1$.

Samuelson examines the more difficult question — the value of an option if the return on the option is greater than the return on the stock, $\kappa > \rho$. Samuelson suggests two situations in which $\rho < \kappa$: (1) If the stock pays a dividend at the rate δ, it would be expected that at least $\rho + \delta = \kappa$, and (2) if the market perceives the option to be more risky than the security, then investors require that $\kappa > \rho$. In the appendix to the Samuelson paper, McKean (1965) solves this problem for a perpetual option and log-normally distributed security prices. His solution is[14]

$$\frac{C}{X} = \frac{(\xi - 1)^{\xi - 1}}{\xi^\xi} \left(\frac{S}{X} \right)^\xi \tag{11.35}$$

where $\xi \equiv (\frac{1}{2} - \rho/\sigma^2) + [(\frac{1}{2} + \rho/\sigma^2)^2 + 2(\kappa/\sigma^2 - \rho/\sigma^2)]^{1/2}$.

Samuelson posits a biased random walk following a Geometric Brownian Motion. Further, he does not rule out the fat-tailed, infinite variance distributions. He does say: (1) that they are mathematically intractable, and (2) that he is "inclined to believe in Merton's conjecture that a strict Levy-Pareto distribution on $\log(S^*/S)$ would lead, with $1 < \alpha < 2$, to a 5-minute warrant or call being worth 100% of the common."[15]

---

14. Note that if $\xi = 2$, $C/X = \frac{1}{4}(S/X)^2$, $C = (S^2/4X)$, which is the ad hoc formula Giguere (1958) assumes to define the relationship between the call and stock prices.

15. The basis for this assertion can be demonstrated as follows: If $\ln(S^*/S)$ is distributed according to a nonnormal stable-Paretian distribution, then to find the expected value of S^*/S note that $\exp[\ln(S^*/S)] = S^*/S$. Let $\alpha \equiv \ln(S^*/S)$. Then the expected value of $\ln(S^*/S)$, ρT, can be expressed as

$$\rho T = \int_0^T e^\alpha f(\alpha)\, d\alpha$$

where $f(\alpha)$ is the nonnormal stable-Paretian density function. This can be written as

$$\rho T = \int_0^\alpha e^\alpha f(\alpha)\, d\alpha + \int_\alpha^\infty e^\alpha f(\alpha)\, d\alpha$$

Choose a so that e^a is greater than a^2. Then the second integral is larger than the same integral with e^α replaced by α^2,

The motivation Samuelson offers for his model is admittedly incomplete. He allows that "a deeper theory would deduce the value of ρ [and presumably also of κ] for each category of stocks." More pointed is the criticism by Black and Scholes (1973) that "there seems to be no model for the pricing of securities under conditions of capital market equilibrium that would make this an appropriate procedure for determining the value of a warrant." Without further qualification, Samuelson's procedure of assuming κ is a constant is inappropriate as a base for a theory of option pricing under capital market equilibrium.

Samuelson's arguments as to why ρ and κ might be expected to differ are general-equilibrium in origin, but the implications of this analysis are at variance with the more general restrictions of Merton. Samuelson finds with $\kappa > \rho$ that there is a positive probability of premature exercise for the option. Merton (1973b) shows that, for a simple option on a stock that pays no dividends, it will never be advantageous to exercise before maturity [see (11.11)].

4. General Equilibrium Call-Option-Pricing Models

4.1. The Black-Scholes Call-Pricing Model

Black and Scholes demonstrate that it is possible to create a riskless hedge by forming a portfolio containing stock and European call options. The sources of change in the value of the portfolio must be the prices, since at a point in time the quantities of the assets are fixed. If the call price is a function of the stock price and the time to maturity, then changes in the call price can be expressed as a function of the changes in the stock price and changes in the time to maturity of the option. Black and Scholes then observe that at any point in time the portfolio can be made into a riskless hedge by choosing an appropriate mixture of stock and calls. For example, if the hedge portfolio is established with a long position in the stock and a short position in the European call and if the stock price rises, then the increase in the value of the portfolio from the profit on the long position in the stock is offset by the decrease in the value of the portfolio from the loss that the increase in the stock price generates through the short position on the option, and vice versa. If quantities of the stock and option in the hedge portfolio are continuously adjusted in the appropriate manner as the asset prices change

---

$$\int_\alpha^\infty \alpha^2 f(\alpha)\, d\alpha < \int_\alpha^\infty e^\alpha f(\alpha)\, d\alpha$$

Since the stable-Paretian is not squared summable, this new integral is infinite. Therefore, ρT is infinite. If ρT is infinite, then in equilibrium it is conjectured rT would have to be infinite also. Then (11.11) would imply $C = S$. I would like to thank R. C. Merton for this explanation and J. C. Cox for the demonstration that ρT is infinite.

over time, then the return to the hedge portfolio becomes riskless. Therefore, the portfolio must earn the riskless rate.

The value of the hedge portfolio, V_H, can be expressed as the stock price times the number of shares of stock plus the call price times the number of calls in the hedge,

$$V_H \equiv SQ_s + cQ_c \tag{11.36}$$

where V_H is the value of the hedge portfolio, Q_s the quantity of stock and Q_c the quantity of calls (for one share each).

The change in the value of the hedge, dV_H, is the total derivative of (11.36),

$$dV_H = Q_s \, dS + Q_c \, dc \tag{11.37}$$

Black and Scholes use stochastic calculus to express dc, the change in the call price. Itô's lemma provides a technique by which certain functions of Wiener processes may be differentiated. If it is assumed that the stock price S follows Geometric Brownian Motion,[16] then Itô's lemma can be employed to express dc as

$$dc = \frac{\partial c}{\partial S} \, dS + \frac{\partial c}{\partial t} \, dt + \frac{1}{2} \frac{\partial^2 c}{\partial S^2} \sigma^2 S^2 \, dt \tag{11.38}$$

Note that the only stochastic term in the expression for dc is dS. The rest are deterministic. Substituting (11.38) for dc in (11.37) yields

$$dV_H = Q_s \, dS + Q_c \left[\frac{\partial c}{\partial S} \, dS + \frac{\partial c}{\partial t} \, dt + \frac{1}{2} \frac{\partial^2 c}{\partial S^2} \sigma^2 S^2 \, dt \right] \tag{11.39}$$

For arbitrary quantities of stock and options, the change in the value of the hedge, dV_H, is stochastic, but if the quantities of each asset are chosen so that $Q_s \, dS + Q_c(\partial c/\partial S) \, dS$ equals zero (i.e., so that the ratio of stock to calls, Q_s/Q_c is equal to $-\partial c/\partial S$),[17] then the return to the hedge becomes riskless. Setting $Q_s = 1$ and $Q_c = -1/(\partial c/\partial S)$ in (11.39) yields

$$dV_H = -\left(\frac{1}{\partial c/\partial S} \right) \left[\frac{\partial c}{\partial t} + \frac{1}{2} \frac{\partial^2 c}{\partial S^2} \sigma^2 S^2 \right] dt \tag{11.40}$$

In equilibrium, two perfect substitutes must earn the same return; therefore, since the hedge is riskless, its return must equal the risk-free rate,[18]

---

16. It is assumed that the motion of the stock price can be described as $dS/S = \mu dt + \sigma dz$, where μ is the instantaneous expected return on S, σ^2 the instantaneous variance of return and dz is a Wiener process. For an exposition of Itô processes and Itô's lemma see Merton (1971) or McKean (1969).

17. Note that this restriction is placed on the ratio Q_s/Q_c. It makes no difference which asset is short. If the stock were sold short instead of the call, the number of shares sold short per call should be $-\partial c/\partial S$.

18. The equality sign $\overset{e}{=}$ should be read "equal in equilibrium." This notation is used to highlight economic interpretation of this equation, which is very different from that of functional relations ($=$) or definitions ($\equiv$).

$$dV_H/V_H \overset{e}{=} r\,dt \tag{11.41}$$

Substituting (11.36) and (11.40) into (11.41) defines a differential equation for the value of the option,

$$\frac{\partial c}{\partial t} = rc - rS\frac{\partial c}{\partial S} - \frac{1}{2}\frac{\partial^2 c}{\partial S^2}\sigma^2 S^2 \tag{11.42}$$

subject to the boundary condition that at the terminal date, the option price must be equal to the maximum of either the difference between the stock price and the exercise price or zero (Equation 11.2),

$$c^* = \text{Max}[0, S^* - X]$$

The differential equation (11.42) can be solved for the equilibrium call price. Black and Scholes transform the equation into the heat exchange equation from physics to find the solution.

A more intuitive solution technique is suggested in a paper by Cox and Ross (1975). To solve the equation, note two observations: First, whatever the solution to the differential equation, it is a function only of the variables in (11.42) and (11.2), that is, r, S, T, σ^2, X. Second, in generating the hedge, the sole assumption involving the preferences of the individuals in the market is that two assets that are perfect substitutes must earn the same equilibrium rate of return; no assumptions involving risk are employed. This suggests that if a solution to the problem can be found that assumes one particular preference structure, it must be the solution to the differential equation for any preference structure that permits equilibrium; therefore, choose the structure that proves most tractable mathematically.

To apply this solution technique,[19] assume the market is composed only of risk-neutral investors. In that case, the equilibrium rate of return to all assets is equal, $r \overset{e}{=} \rho \overset{e}{=} \kappa$; then the option must be priced so that the current call price is the discounted expected terminal price,

$$c = e^{-rT}E(c^*) = e^{-rT}\int_X^\infty (S^* - X)L'(S^*)\,dS^* \tag{11.43}$$

Equation 11.43 may be solved by applying Theorem 11.1 (Equation 11.22) with $\lambda = \gamma = e^{-rT}$ and $\psi = 1$. Substituting r for ρ yields the general equilibrium solution to the call pricing problem,

$$c = S \cdot N\left\{\frac{\ln(S/X) + [r + (\sigma^2/2)]T}{\sigma\sqrt{T}}\right\}$$

$$- e^{-rT}X \cdot N\left\{\frac{\ln(S/X) + [r - (\sigma^2/2)]T}{\sigma\sqrt{T}}\right\} \tag{11.44}$$

---

19. This solution technique, independently derived by Cox and Ross, is similar to a technique employed in an early unpublished version of the Black-Scholes paper. It also corresponds to a technique Merton has employed in lectures but not in print.

Equation 11.44 is the Black-Scholes pricing equation;[20] that it satisfies the differential equation in (11.42) may be established by substitution.[21]

Note that the assumptions used in this derivation are essentially those employed by Boness in deriving (11.32) However, Boness fails to demonstrate that a riskless hedge can be created, a hedge that does not depend on the preference structure of the market—he does not justify his procedure in a general equilibrium framework.[22]

The Black-Scholes model is a function of only five variables: the stock price, the exercise price, the time to maturity of the option, the risk-free interest rate, and the instantaneous variance rate on the stock price. The first four of these variables are directly observable; only the variance rate must be estimated. Further, other unobservable variables that have appeared in earlier models do not appear as arguments in this general equilibrium solution,

---

20. To derive a more intuitive understanding of this equation, consider the equilibrium call price in a world of perfect certainty. Given certainty, the terminal call price would be a positive number (or no one would have ever purchased a call) equal to the terminal stock price minus the exercise price: $C^* = S^* - X$. In equilibrium in a world of certainty, the return to all assets must be equal in equilibrium, therefore: $r \triangleq \rho \triangleq \kappa$. Then, since $S^* = Se^{\rho T}$, the current call price can be expressed as $C = e^{-\kappa T}(e^{\rho T}S - X)$. Substituting r for ρ and κ yields $C = S - e^{-rT}X$. This expression differs from (11.44) only in the multiplication by the cumulative standard normal terms. These terms can be viewed as probabilities reflecting the uncertainty about the terminal stock price. See Footnote 22.

21. An interesting caveat has been pointed out by John Long. In the analysis leading to the differential equation, the option pricing formula has been assumed to be twice differentiable everywhere. The economics of the option pricing problem would suggest that the solution be continuous, but there is no obvious argument that it be differentiable everywhere. If it were postulated that the solution be continuous and satisfy the differential equation only where it is differentiable, then any convex combination of the Black-Scholes equation and $\text{Max}[0, S - XB(T)]$ would satisfy these conditions. An infinite number of solutions can be generated by this process, of which the Black-Scholes solution is the only smooth solution. This point may lead to a closer analysis of the economic implications of smoothness.

22. A comparison of Boness' model can yield a better intuitive understanding of the terms in (11.44). Boness shows that in a world of risk neutrality the equilibrium call price can be expressed in terms of conditional expected values as $C = e^{-\kappa T}E(S^* | S^* > X) \text{Prob}(S^* > X) - e^{-\kappa T}X \text{Prob}(S^* > X)$. In a risk-neutral world the equilibrium-expected rates of return on all assets would be equal, therefore $r \triangleq \rho \triangleq \kappa$. Substituting r for ρ and κ in (11.32) yields (11.44), the Black-Scholes solution. Hence, in a risk-neutral economy, the two terms in (11.44) have natural interpretations: the first term is the discounted expected value of the terminal stock price, given the terminal stock price exceeds the exercise price, times the probability the terminal stock price is greater than the exercise price. The second term is the discounted exercise price times the probability the terminal stock price exceeds the exercise price. *Warning:* This analogy is only suggestive, as this interpretation is predicated on a world of risk neutrality. An uncritical reading of the solution technique above might suggest that this interpretation is valid for all worlds. This is not the case. The solution technique above is *only* a procedure to derive a solution to a differential equation. It suggests that where a risk-free hedge can be established, the solution is independent of the degree of risk aversion in the economy, and therefore the mathematical solutions will be identical in any economy with any degree of risk aversion that permits a solution.

arguments such as the expected rate of return on the stock, the expected rate of return on the option, or a measure of market risk aversion.

The responses of the model to changes in the value of its arguments conforms to the restrictions placed on the option price by the dominance arguments of Merton:[23]

1. As the stock price rises, so does the call price,

$$\frac{\partial c}{\partial S} = N\left\{\frac{\ln(S/X) + [r + (\sigma^2/2)]T}{\sigma\sqrt{T}}\right\} > 0 \qquad (11.45)$$

With a log-normal distribution of stock prices, the expected terminal price is a positive function of the current price; therefore an increase in the stock price increases the expected payoff to the option.

2. As the exercise price rises, the call price falls,

$$\frac{\partial c}{\partial X} = -e^{-rT}N\left\{\frac{\ln(S/X) + [r - (\sigma^2/2)]T}{\sigma\sqrt{T}}\right\} < 0 \qquad (11.46)$$

This conforms to the restriction derived in (11.18) that implies $\partial c/\partial X$ should be between zero and the negative of the bond price, $-e^{-rT}$.

3. As the time to expiration increases, the price of the call rises,

$$\frac{\partial c}{\partial T} = Xe^{-rT}\left[\frac{\sigma}{2\sqrt{T}}N\left\{\frac{\ln(S/X) + [r - (\sigma^2/2)]T}{\sigma\sqrt{T}}\right\} \right.$$
$$\left. + rN\left\{\frac{\ln(S/X) + [r - (\sigma^2/2)]T}{\sigma\sqrt{T}}\right\}\right] > 0 \qquad (11.47)$$

This reflects the fact that the present value of the exercise payment is lower if the time to expiration is greater.

4. As the riskless rate of interest rises, the call price rises,

$$\frac{\partial c}{\partial r} = T \cdot Xe^{-rT}N\left\{\frac{\ln(S/X) + [r - (\sigma^2/2)]T}{\sigma\sqrt{T}}\right\} > 0 \qquad (11.48)$$

When the riskless rate rises the present value of the exercise price falls.

5. As the variance rate rises, so does the call price,

$$\frac{\partial c}{\partial \sigma^2} = Xe^{-rT}N'\left\{\frac{\ln(S/X) + [r - (\sigma^2/2)]T}{\sigma\sqrt{T}}\right\}\frac{\sqrt{T}}{2\sigma} > 0 \qquad (11.49)$$

When the variance rate on the underlying stock price is higher, then the probability of a large positive price change is greater. Of course, the probability of large negative changes is also greater, but the terminal option price cannot be below zero.

---

23. See Merton (1973b) and Section 2.2 above.

FIGURE 11.1 *Diagram of Black-Scholes Call Option Price for Different Stock Prices, with a Given Interest Rate, Variance Rate, and Time to Maturity*

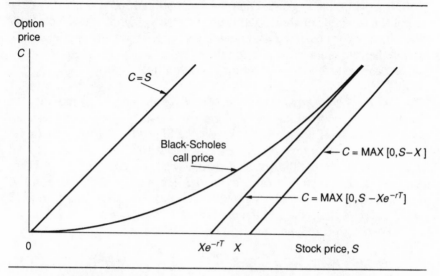

Notes: The Black-Scholes call option price lies below the maximum possible value, $C = S$ (except where $S = 0$), and above the minimum value, $C = \text{Max}[0, S - Xe^{-rT}]$. Note that the curve relating the Black-Scholes call price with the stock price asymptotically approaches $C = \text{Max}[0, S - Xe^{-rT}]$ line.

Although the solution technique employed here assumes a general equilibrium configuration of prices, the specification of the equilibrium call price does not require the current stock price to be a general equilibrium price. A riskless hedge can be formed so long as the stock price follows an Itô process; therefore, (11.44) describes the equilibrium call price given the stock price.

Black and Scholes suggest that discounting the expected value of the distribution of possible values of the call when it is exercised is not an appropriate procedure. But the solution technique employed here does precisely that and yields the same equation that Black and Scholes derived. There is nothing inappropriate in this approach itself, only in the prior implementation of that approach.

4.2. Extensions of the Black-Scholes Model

In developing the basic Black-Scholes model, several assumptions were made. Many of these assumptions have been relaxed in the subsequent work by Merton and others. First, Merton (1973b) has shown that if a stock pays no dividends, then it will not be exercised prematurely and thus will command the same price as a European call [see (11.11) above]. Therefore, the Black-

Scholes option pricing model may be applied to value American options on non–dividend-paying stocks.

Thorpe (1973) has suggested that the assumption of no restrictions on the use of the proceeds of short sales is not necessary. If individuals hold well-diversified portfolios of securities, adding a hedge consisting of a long position in the call and a short position in the stock can be achieved by buying the call and reducing an existing long position in the stock.

The Merton Proportional Dividend Model.　Merton (1973b) modifies the Black-Scholes model along several dimensions. The original model assumes no dividend payments on the stock over the life of the option. Merton relaxes this assumption for a rather special dividend policy—dividends are paid continuously such that the dividend yield, $\delta \equiv D/S$, is constant. For a European call, a hedge can be created as in (11.36). Now, however, the return to the stock consists of price changes plus dividend payments. Equation 11.38 again describes the change in the call price. Substituting into (11.37) to obtain an expression for the change in the value of the hedge,

$$dV_H = Q_s(dS + \delta S\, dt) + Q_c\left(\frac{\partial c}{\partial s}\, dS + \frac{\partial c}{\partial t}\, dt + \frac{1}{2}\frac{\partial^2 c}{\partial s^2}\sigma^2 S^2\, dt\right) \tag{11.50}$$

Again, by forming the hedge so that the ratio of the number of shares of the stock to the number of calls is equal to $-\partial c/\partial S$ the hedge becomes riskless. Setting $Q_s = \partial c/\partial S$ and $Q_c = -1$ yields

$$dV_H = \frac{\partial c}{\partial S}\delta S\, dt - \left(\frac{\partial c}{\partial t} + \frac{1}{2}\frac{\partial^2 c}{\partial s^2}S^2\right) dt \tag{11.51}$$

Again, since the hedge generates a certain return, in equilibrium it must earn the risk-free rate. Therefore, (11.41) again holds. Equation 11.2 is still the boundary condition for the implicit differential equation defined by (11.41) and (11.51). If the above solution procedure is reapplied with $r \stackrel{\underline{c}}{=} \rho + \delta \stackrel{\underline{c}}{=} \kappa$, then the solution becomes

$$c = e^{-\kappa T}\int_X^{\infty}(S^* - X)L'(S^*)\, dS^* \tag{11.52}$$

This can be solved by applying the above theorem, Equation 11.22, with $\lambda = \gamma = e^{-\kappa T}$ and $\psi = 1$ and substituting r for $\rho + \delta$ and κ,[24]

$$c = e^{-\delta T}S \cdot N\left\{\frac{\ln(S/X) + [r - \delta + (\sigma^2/2)]T}{\sigma\sqrt{T}}\right\}$$

$$-e^{-rT}X \cdot N\left\{\frac{\ln(S/X) + [r - \delta - (\sigma^2/2)]T}{\sigma\sqrt{T}}\right\} \tag{11.53}$$

---

24. This equation differs slightly from that reported in Merton (1973b, p. 171), but agrees with the solution, referenced by Merton, of Samuelson (1965).

This is the solution to the European call-option-pricing problem when the underlying stock pays dividends continuously at the rate δ. Note that since dividends are paid, this equation may not be applied to value American call options; Merton (1973b) has shown that there is always some probability of premature exercise of such options.

Ingersoll Differential Tax Model. Ingersoll (1975) modifies the option pricing model to account for the effect of differential tax rates on capital gains versus ordinary income. To take the simplest case, assume that dividends are paid continuously at the rate $\delta = D/S$, that dividends and interest income are taxed at the rate τ, and that capital gains taxes are zero. A risk-free hedge can again be created as in (11.36), with the quantity of stock, Q_s, times the stock price, plus the quantity of calls, Q_c, times the call price,

$$V_H \equiv Q_s S + Q_c c \tag{11.36}$$

But now, returns must be adjusted for the existence of taxes. The change in the stock price is composed of nontaxable capital gains and dividends taxable at the rate τ. The change in the value of the call is still described by

$$dc = \frac{\partial c}{\partial S} dS + \frac{\partial c}{\partial t} dt + \frac{1}{2} \frac{\partial^2 c}{\partial S^2} \sigma^2 S^2 dt \tag{11.38}$$

Therefore, the after-tax change in the value of the hedge can be expressed as

$$dV_H = Q_s (dS + (1 - \tau)\delta S \, dt)$$
$$+ Q_c \left(\frac{\partial c}{\partial S} dS + \frac{\partial c}{\partial t} dt + \frac{1}{2} \frac{\partial^2 c}{\partial S^2} \sigma^2 S^2 dt \right) \tag{11.54}$$

If the ratio of the number of shares of stock to the number of calls is again set equal to $-\partial c/\partial S$, the hedge becomes nonstochastic. Then setting $Q_c = \partial c/\partial S$ and $Q_c = -1$ yields

$$dV_H = \frac{\partial c}{\partial S} \delta (1 - \tau) S \, dt - \left(\frac{\partial c}{\partial t} + \frac{1}{2} \frac{\partial^2 c}{\partial S^2} \sigma^2 S^2 \right) dt \tag{11.55}$$

Since this hedge yields a certain return, it must yield the after-tax, risk-free return in equilibrium. Therefore the equilibrium condition for a world with taxes is that

$$dV_H / V_H \stackrel{e}{=} (1 - \tau) r \, dt \tag{11.56}$$

The boundary condition remains unchanged from (11.42) (Equation 11.2),

$$c^* = \text{Max}[0, S^* - X]$$

To apply the above solution technique to solve the implicit differential equation defined by (11.55) and (11.56), note that equilibrium in a risk-neutral economy would imply that the after-tax expected yield on all assets would be equal; that is, $\rho + (1 - \tau)\delta \stackrel{e}{=} \kappa \stackrel{e}{=} (1 - \tau)r$. The problem then becomes

$$c = e^{-\kappa T} \int_X^\infty (S^* - X) L'(S^*) \, dS^* \qquad (11.57)$$

To solve, apply the above theorem, Equation 11.22, with $\lambda = \gamma = e^{-\kappa T}$, $\psi = 1$, and substitute $r(1 - \tau)$ for $\rho + (1 + \tau)\delta$ and κ,

$$c = e^{-\delta(1-\tau)T} S \cdot N \left\{ \frac{\ln(S/X) + [(r-\delta)(1-\tau) + (\sigma^2/2)]T}{\sigma\sqrt{T}} \right\}$$

$$- e^{r(1-\tau)T} X \cdot N \left\{ \frac{\ln(S/X) + [(r-\delta)(1-\tau) - (\sigma^2/2)]T}{\sigma\sqrt{T}} \right\} \qquad (11.58)$$

This is the solution to the option pricing problem for a world in which the stock pays dividends continuously at the rate δ, dividend and interest income are taxed at the rate τ while capital gains are not taxed.

The Merton Variable Interest Rate Model.   The next model to be considered is Merton's model in which he relaxes the assumption of a constant interest rate. He assumes that the interest rate can vary over the life of the option in such a way that the return to a discount bond can be expressed as an Itô process.[25]

A hedge can again be established. Let the hedge consist of three assets — the call, the stock, and the bond,

$$V_H \equiv Q_c c + Q_s S + Q_B B \qquad (11.59)$$

Then the change in the value of the hedge comes from three sources — the stock price, the bond price, and the call price,

$$dV_H = Q_c \, dc + Q_s \, dS + Q_B \, dB \qquad (11.60)$$

If it is assumed that the call price can be expressed as a function of the bond price as well as the stock price and time to maturity, then applying Itô's lemma yields

$$dc = \frac{\partial c}{\partial S} \, dS + \frac{\partial c}{\partial B} \, dB + \frac{\partial c}{\partial t} \, dt$$

$$+ \frac{1}{2} \left[\frac{\partial^2 c}{\partial S^2} \sigma_s^2 S^2 + 2 \frac{\partial^2 c}{\partial S \partial B} \rho_{sB} \sigma_s \sigma_B SB + \frac{\partial^2 c}{\partial B^2} \sigma_B^2 B^2 \right] dt \qquad (11.61)$$

Substituting into (11.59) yields

$$dV_H = Q_c \left[\frac{\partial c}{\partial S} \, dS + \frac{\partial c}{\partial B} \, dB + \Psi \, dt \right] + Q_s \, dS + Q_B \, dB \qquad (11.62)$$

---

25. Specifically, the change in the bond price is described by $dB/B(T) = \bar{r} \, dt + \sigma_B(T) \, dz(t, T)$, where $\bar{r}$ is the instantaneous expected return to the bond and $\sigma_B^2(T)$ is the instantaneous variance of return to the bond. Since $B(T)$ is a default risk-free bond, $B(0) = 1$. σ_B will be a function of T with $\sigma_B(0) = 0$. In the special case of a constant interest rate, $\bar{r} = r$, $\sigma_B = 0$, $B(T) = e^{-rT}$.

where

$$\Psi \equiv \left[\frac{\partial c}{\partial t} + \frac{1}{2} \left(\frac{\partial^2 c}{\partial S^2} \sigma_s^2 S^2 + 2 \frac{\partial^2 c}{\partial S \partial B} \rho_{sB} \sigma_s \sigma_B SB + \frac{\partial^2 c}{\partial B^2} \sigma_B^2 B^2 \right) \right]$$

and ρ_{sB} is the instantaneous correlation coefficient between the return to the stock and bond.

If a hedge is formed in such a way that the sum of the weights is zero, then the equilibrium return to the hedge must be zero; if there were non-zero returns, then perfectly certain returns could be generated requiring no capital — a situation obviously inconsistent with general equilibrium. But in this case it cannot be guaranteed that it will be possible to define simultaneously a riskless hedge *and* ensure that the weights sum to zero. The problem has three unknowns but has four restrictions: (1) that, by construction, the value of the hedge is zero; (2) that the hedge is nonstochastic and therefore insulated from changes in the stock price; (3) that the hedge is nonstochastic and therefore insulated from unanticipated changes in the bond price; and (4) that a nonstochastic hedge employing no capital in equilibrium must generate a zero return. These restrictions can be stated as

$$V_H \equiv Q_c c + Q_s S + Q_B B = 0$$

$$Q_c \frac{\partial c}{\partial S} dS + Q_s \, dS = 0$$

$$Q_c \frac{\partial c}{\partial B} dB + Q_B \, dB = 0 \tag{11.63}$$

$$Q_c \, dc + Q_s \, dS + Q_B \, dB \overset{\epsilon}{=} 0$$

Merton assumes that these equations are mutually consistent with a nontrivial solution and derives the implications of equilibrium.[26] These equations implicitly define two differential equations that have been assumed to hold simultaneously for the same values of Q_c, Q_s, and Q_B. Two boundary conditions are (1) that at maturity the call will sell for the maximum of either zero or the difference between the stock price and the exercise price, and (2) that a stock with a price of zero will have a zero call price,

$$C(S^*, 0, 1; X) = \text{Max}[0, S^* - X]$$

$$C(0, T, B; X) = 0 \tag{11.64}$$

---

26. The first three restrictions can be combined to yield $c - (\partial c/\partial S)S - (\partial c/\partial B)B = 0$. A sufficient condition for this equation to have a nontrivial solution is homogeneity of c in S and B. A dominance argument as in Merton (1973b) can be used to establish that if returns are independent of the level of the stock price (as in the log-normal) then the call price will be homogeneous in the stock and bond prices.

To solve this set of equations the above solution technique will again be used with two changes applied. First, since the riskless hedge now involves purchasing default-free bonds, the appropriate expression for the risk-free rate is $-\ln B(T)/T$.[27] Therefore, equilibrium in a risk-neutral economy implies that $-\ln B(T)/T \overset{e}{=} \rho \overset{e}{=} \kappa$. Second, variance arises from two sources — the stock and the bond. Therefore, the instantaneous variance is $\hat{\sigma}^2(t) = \sigma_S^2 + \sigma_B^2(t) - 2\rho_{SB}\sigma_S\sigma_B(t)$. It follows that the variance over the life of the option will be the integral of the instantaneous variance,

$$\hat{\sigma}^2 T \equiv \int_0^T \hat{\sigma}^2(t)\,dt \equiv \int_0^T [\sigma_S^2 + \sigma_B^2(t) - 2\rho_{SB}\sigma_S\sigma_B(t)]\,dt \qquad (11.65)$$

Then the solution to this model becomes

$$c = B(T)\int_X^\infty (S^* - X)L'(S^*)\,dS^* \qquad (11.66)$$

To derive the general equilibrium solution to the European call-pricing problem when the interest rate is stochastic, apply Theorem 11.1 (Equation 11.22) with $\lambda = \gamma = B(T)$ and $\psi = 1$,

$$c = S \cdot N\left\{\frac{\ln(S/X) - \ln B(T) + (\hat{\sigma}^2/2)T}{\hat{\sigma}\sqrt{T}}\right\}$$

$$- B(T)X \cdot N\left\{\frac{\ln(S/X) - \ln B(T) - (\hat{\sigma}^2/2)T}{\hat{\sigma}\sqrt{T}}\right\} \qquad (11.67)$$

Equation 11.67 is the Merton (1973b, p. 167) solution.[28] Note that since there are no dividends, then by (11.11) this solution also applies to American calls.

Call Pricing with Poisson Processes.   Thus far, two assumptions about stock price movements have been reviewed in this paper: the Arithmetic Brownian Motion of Bachelier, and the Geometric Brownian Motion of Sprenkle et al. One additional hypothesis is being examined, that of Poisson processes. A Poisson process or jump process offers a statistical description of the movement in the stock price, which allows discontinuous changes. This process provides that, with a low probability, the stock price will jump to a new level.[29] Since a corollary to Itô's lemma can be used to differentiate functions of Poisson processes, the technique employed by Black and Scholes to derive the option price may be used in this context as well.

---

27. In the case of a constant interest rate the bond price would be $B(T) = e^{-rt}$. Then $r = -(1/T)\ln B(T)$.

28. Merton states his solution in terms of the error complement function (erfc). The relationship $\tfrac{1}{2}\mathrm{erfc}(-Q/\sqrt{2}) = N\{Q\}$ has been substituted.

29. A simple Poisson or jump process can be described as $dS/S = \mu dt + (\gamma - 1)$ with probability λdt, and $dS/S = \mu dt + 0$ with probability $(1 - \lambda)dt$. Therefore, with probability λdt the stock price will jump to γS. The parameter λ is the intensity of the process, and $(\gamma - 1)$ is the amplitude of the jump.

Merton (1976) examines the most general specification of the stock price movement where both the Geometric Brownian Motion and the Poisson process are present. He demonstrates that hedging both against the continuous changes and the discrete changes is not possible, and thus the risk-free hedge cannot be created. However, if the jumps are uncorrelated across securities, then the risk associated with the jump is unsystematic risk, and therefore the risk associated with the jump is a diversifiable risk that can be minimized by holding a portfolio of hedges. If the equilibrium return to a security is determined by its nondiversifiable risk (risk that cannot be removed by simply holding additional assets), then the continuous part of the stock price movement can be hedged using Black-Scholes techniques. Since by assumption the risk associated with the jump is nonsystematic, the Capital Asset Pricing Model suggests that the equilibrium rate of return on such an asset must be equal to that of the risk-free asset. Then, if the magnitude of the jump is distributed log-normally, Merton derives an expression for the option price that is a weighted average of the Black-Scholes solution conditional on the number of jumps.

Cox and Ross (1975) demonstrate that if the stochastic part of the stock price movement is defined only as a simple Poisson process, that is, that the jump is in only one direction and of a given amplitude, then a risk-free hedge, like the Black-Scholes hedge, can be created. Although this jump process is very simple, by careful specification of the parameters of the process, the movement of the stock price can be made to approximate that of Geometric Brownian Motion.

These two models suggest that the assumption of a continuous sample path for the stock price, that is, that the stock price can only move "locally," is not crucial to the analysis. In certain cases, the basic Black-Scholes technique can be applied to processes that allow discontinuous sample paths, that is, jumps in the stock price. However, the solution to the option-pricing problem when the stock price movement is discontinuous involves the unobservable expected return on the stock.

This section has reviewed the major models developed on call option pricing. The next section will briefly cover the much smaller body of work on put option pricing.

5. General Equilibrium Put-Option-Pricing Models

5.1. Restrictions from Stochastic Dominance

Merton (1973b) develops general equilibrium restrictions on put prices using dominance arguments. *A put at expiration will be worth either the difference between the exercise price and the stock price or zero, whichever is greater,*

TABLE 11.6   *Terminal Values of Portfolios A and B for Different Relationships Between Stock Price and Exercise Price at the Expiration Date ($T = 0$) of the Call*

Portfolio	Current Value	Stock Price at $T = 0$	
		$S^* \leq X$	$X < S^*$
A	$S + p(S, T; X)$	$S^* + X - S^*$	$S^* + 0$
	$- XB'(T)$	$- X$	$- X$
B	$c(S, T; X)$	0	$S^* - X$
Relationship between terminal values of portfolios A and B		$V_a^* = V_b^*$	$V_a^* = V_b^*$

$$P(S^*, 0; X) = p(s^*, 0; X) = \text{Max}[0, X - S^*] \qquad (11.68)$$

This follows from the definition of a put, since the put will be exercised only if it is advantageous to do so, and from the ability to engage in arbitrage at the expiration date of the put.

When borrowing and lending rates are equal, then the price of a European put is equal to the value of a portfolio of a European call with the same terms as the put, riskless bonds with a face value of X, and a short position in the stock. To demonstrate this relationship, let $B'(T)$ be the current value of one dollar payable T years from now at the borrowing rate. Now consider two portfolios A and B where A contains one share of stock, one European put, and X dollars borrowed for T time periods; and B contains one European call with the same exercise price and maturity date as the put. Table 11.6 demonstrates that a portfolio containing one share of stock, one European put, and X dollars borrowed for T periods yields a terminal value equal to that of a European call with the same exercise price and time to maturity.

Since $V_a^* = V_b^*$, to avoid domination the call must be priced so that

$$c(S, T; X) \leq S + p(S, T; X) - XB'(T) \qquad (11.69)$$

Again, consider two portfolios where A contains one European call, one share of stock sold short, and X bonds; B contains one European put with the same terms as the call. Table 11.7 demonstrates that a portfolio containing a European call, one share of stock sold short, and discount bonds with a face value of X will yield the same terminal value as a European put.

Since $V_a^* = V_b^*$, to avoid domination the put must be priced so that

$$p(S, T; X) \leq c(S, T; X) - S + XB(T) \qquad (11.70)$$

Therefore, if the borrowing and lending rates are equal, a European put must be priced so that

TABLE 11.7 *Terminal Values of Portfolios A and B for Different Relationships Between Stock Price and Exercise Price at the Expiration Date* $(T = 0)$ *of the Call*

Portfolio	Current Value	Stock Price at $T = 0$	
		$S^* \leq X$	$X < S^*$
A	$c(S, T; X) - S$	$0 - S^*$	$S^* - X - S^*$
	$+ XB(T)$	$+ X$	$+ X$
B	$p(S, T; X)$	$X - S^*$	0
Relationship between terminal values of portfolios A and B		$V_a^* = V_b^*$	$V_a^* = V_b^*$

$$p(S, T; X) = c(S, T; X) - S + XB(T) \tag{11.71}$$

This is an extremely useful relationship, for Equation 11.71 can be employed with the restrictions established on call prices in the previous section to establish a number of restrictions on the price of the put. *The price of a European put must not be greater than that of a pure discount bond with a face value of X.* Since the call price is not greater than the stock price from (11.7),

$$p(S, T; X) \leq XB(T) \tag{11.72}$$

A perpetual European put on a stock that pays no dividends must have a price of zero, since a perpetual European call would sell for the stock price S by (11.14),

$$p(S, \infty; X) = c(S, \infty; X) - S + XB(\infty) = S - S + 0 = 0 \tag{11.73}$$

The value of a European put on a stock that has a price of zero is the discounted exercise price. Since from (11.8), $c(0, T; X) = 0$, substituting into (11.71) yields

$$p(0, T; X) = 0 - 0 + XB(T) \tag{11.74}$$

Finally, *an American put must be priced no lower than a similar European put,* $P(S, T; X) \geq p(S, T; X)$, since an American put contains all the features of a European put plus the right to early exercise. Merton argues that an American put will virtually always have a positive probability of premature exercise and will therefore command a greater price than its European counterpart. For example, suppose the stock price falls far below the exercise price, the maximum price that the put can attain is X (the exercise price) and that price will be attained only if the stock price is zero. If the put can be exercised, then discount bonds can be purchased with the proceeds that earn the riskless rate. For stock prices far below the exercise price, since the maximum put price is bounded from above, the return to holding the put may be less than the return to exercising the put and purchasing bonds. Therefore, the put may be more valuable if exercised.

5.2. Put Pricing with Geometric Brownian Motion

Use of (11.71) leads Black and Scholes (1973) to a direct application of their call-pricing equation to derive a solution to the European put-pricing problem. Substituting (11.44) into (11.71),

$$
\begin{aligned}
p = S \cdot N & \left\{ \frac{\ln(S/X) + [r + (\sigma^2/2)]T}{\sigma\sqrt{T}} \right\} \\
& - Xe^{-rT} \cdot N \left\{ \frac{\ln(S/X) + [r - (\sigma^2/2)]T}{\sigma\sqrt{T}} \right\} - S + Xe^{-rT} \\
= -S \cdot N & \left\{ \frac{-\ln(S/X) + [r + (\sigma^2/2)]T}{\sigma\sqrt{T}} \right\} \\
& + Xe^{-rT} \cdot N \left\{ \frac{-\ln(S/X) + [r - (\sigma^2/2)]T}{\sigma\sqrt{T}} \right\}
\end{aligned}
\tag{11.74}
$$

This is the solution to the European put-pricing problem given the Black-Scholes assumptions. To modify the model to account for dividends and the like, substitute the appropriate solution from Section 4.2 into (11.71) and solve.

In Sections 2 through 5 the major thrust of the models of option pricing has been reviewed. There has been some testing of these equilibrium statements. Section 6 reviews these empirical tests.

6. Empirical Tests of Option Pricing

6.1. Tests of the Level of Option Prices

Little empirical testing of the general equilibrium restrictions on option pricing has appeared in print. Black and Scholes (1972) test several implications of their model. They create a hedge with zero market value involving the option, the stock, and risk-free bonds, by employing the Black-Scholes Option-Pricing Model to establish the quantities of the respective assets that minimize risk of the hedge,

$$
V_H = Q_c c + Q_s S + Q_B B = 0
\tag{11.75}
$$

with

$$
Q_s / Q_c = -\partial c / \partial S
$$

and

$$
[Q_c c + Q_s S]/B = Q_B
$$

As an approximation to continuous rebalancing, they rebalance the hedge daily. Since the proportions are not adjusted continuously, the hedge generates an uncertain return. However, Black and Scholes argue that this return will be uncorrelated with the market; this uncertainty is therefore diversifiable risk that can be minimized by holding a portfolio of hedges. If the market prices assets such that an investor is only compensated for accepting nondiversifiable risk, then the expected change in the value of the hedge over the single-day holding periods is zero; that is,

$$\Delta V_H \equiv \Delta c - \frac{\partial c}{\partial S} \Delta S - \left[c - \frac{\partial c}{\partial S} S \right] r \Delta T \overset{e}{=} 0 \qquad (11.76)$$

Black and Scholes obtained the diaries of an option broker from 1966 to 1969 and recorded the six-month calls and straddles written on New York Stock Exchange securities. Their sample consists of 2,039 calls and 3,052 straddles. After estimating the instantaneous variance from the historical series of daily stock prices, they compute the theoretical option price using the Black-Scholes pricing equation (11.44). If the market price is greater than the model price, they refer to the option as "overvalued," and conversely.

Four portfolios are created using four different strategies:

1. Buy all calls at model prices.

2. Buy all calls at market prices.

3. Buy undervalued calls and sell overvalued calls at model prices.

4. Buy undervalued calls and sell overvalued calls at market prices.

The first two strategies test if the market or model prices are on average too high or too low. If abnormal positive returns are generated by either strategy, then the price used by that strategy (model or market) would be on average too low, and conversely. The third and fourth strategies expand the information set to include knowledge of the relationship between the market and model prices. These strategies test if the respective prices efficiently incorporate this additional information. The third strategy is another, more powerful, test of whether the model can be used to price options. If the hedge is formed by purchasing options when they are undervalued and selling options short when they are overvalued, and if this strategy generates abnormal negative returns, then the model price is too high for undervalued options and too low for overvalued options. This would suggest that the market contains information not fully reflected in the model prices. The fourth strategy tests for profit opportunities over the sample period. If this strategy generates abnormal positive returns, then the market price is too low for undervalued options and too high for overvalued options. This would suggest that the Black-Scholes option pricing model contains information that is not being efficiently incorporated into the market price.

TABLE 11.8 *Measures of the Average Return to Portfolios in Dollars per Contract per Day Adjusted for Systematic Risk, and Measures of Significance for Four Portfolio Strategies Constructed Using Estimates of the Variance Derived from the Sequence of Past Stock Prices* [a]

Portfolio Employing Strategy Number	α [b]	$t - \alpha$	α_τ [c]	$t - \alpha_\tau$
1	−0.10	−2.02	−0.12	−0.68
2	−0.06	−1.18	−0.08	−0.47
3	−0.56	−11.60	−0.56	−5.45
4	+0.56	11.73	+0.56	6.64

a. Adapted from Black and Scholes (1972).
b. α = regression intercept (in dollars per contract per day).
c. α_τ = average intercept for the 10 subperiods.

To test if the risk of the hedge is actually uncorrelated with the market, Black and Scholes regress the daily returns from the portfolios against the excess returns of the market. The slope of the regression, β, measures the systematic risk of the hedge, and the intercept, α, measures the average return to the hedge adjusted for systematic risk. Black and Scholes find no significant slope coefficients either over the entire period or for ten subperiods of approximately 75 days each. Since β is uniformly insignificant, only the intercept α is reported. The results of the regressions testing the above four strategies appear in Table 11.8.

Whether bought at market or model prices, the returns to either of the first two strategies over the entire period are not significant; therefore, neither model nor market prices appear to be consistently above or below the correct level. But both the portfolios constructed by buying undervalued and selling overvalued options yield returns significantly different from zero. The third strategy generates significantly negative returns, while the fourth strategy yields significant positive returns. This result could occur in several different ways, but one hypothesis that explains the observed results is that the estimate of the variance actually employed by the market is too narrow, and the historical estimates of the variance include an attenuation bias; that is, the spread of estimates is greater than the spread of the true variance. This would imply that for securities with a relatively high variance, the market would underestimate the variance, while using the historical price series would overestimate the variance; and conversely for relatively low variance securities. To test this possible hypothesis, Black and Scholes group the options into four categories based only on the estimate of the variance derived from past prices.

TABLE 11.9 *Measures of the Average Return to Portfolios in Dollars per Contract per Day Adjusted for Systematic Risk, and Measures of Significance for Four Portfolios Formed by Ranking Securities Using Estimates of the Variance Derived from the Sequence of Past Stock Prices* [a]

Portfolio (low to high variance)	Buy at Model Prices		Buy at Market Prices	
	$\alpha(\$)$	$t - \alpha$	$\alpha(\$)$	$t - \alpha$
1	0.15	2.57	−0.43	−7.47
2	0.06	0.87	−0.04	−0.56
3	−0.35	−4.39	−0.10	−1.76
4	−0.36	−5.57	0.17	2.60

a. Adapted from Black and Scholes (1972).

The results in Table 11.9 indicate that in forming portfolios of hedges using model prices, significant positive returns are generated using low-variance securities. This indicates that the model price is too low and, therefore, the estimate of the variance is too low. The use of high-variance securities generates significant negative returns, indicating that those prices and variance estimates are too high. The results employing the market prices are just the reverse. The results in Table 11.9 are consistent with the hypothesis that the model overprices high-variance securities and the market underprices them. This also suggests market inefficiency in the absence of transactions costs.

To test whether the model values securities correctly when the true variance rate of the stock is known, Black and Scholes estimate the variance rate from the actual price history over the life of the options. Since future information is required, this strategy cannot be implemented in practice but will indicate the efficacy of the approach. The previous test suggests that there may be error in the estimate of the variance. If this is the case, the analysis above mixes a test of the model with a test of the estimate of the variance. By employing the actual variance that occurs over the life of the option, a test of the model alone is derived, a test independent of errors in the estimate of the variance of the stock returns.

The results in Table 11.10 indicate that if the subsequent variance is known, the Black-Scholes model performs very well.

Black and Scholes then proceed to the question of option market efficiency. Their tests establish that options prices do not appear to conform to a general equilibrium configuration: The results of Table 11.9 indicate that higher returns are available to individuals who establish riskless hedges on high-variance securities over the returns available to riskless hedges involving low-

TABLE 11.10 *Measures of the Average Return to Portfolios in Dollars per Contract per Day Adjusted for Systematic Risk, and Measures of Significance for Four Portfolio Strategies Constructed Using Estimates of the Variance Derived from the Sequence of Stock Prices over the Life of the Option* [a]

Portfolio Employing Strategy Number	α [b]	$t-\alpha$	α_τ [c]	$t-\alpha_\tau$
1	-0.04	-1.04	-0.06	-0.75
2	-0.09	-2.00	-0.11	-0.68
3	-0.06	-1.19	-0.06	-1.03
4	1.11	21.64	1.11	11.05

a. Adapted from Black and Scholes (1972).
b. α = regression intercept (in dollars per contract per day).
c. α_τ = average intercept for the 10 subperiods.

variance securities. Market efficiency is a weaker condition that that of general equilibrium. A market is termed efficient if, after transactions costs, no abnormal returns are available. Black and Scholes estimate the transactions costs incurred by individual traders and conclude that these costs are higher than the abnormal returns Black and Scholes generate, excluding transactions costs. They therefore conclude that this market is efficient. However, market efficiency is usually stated in terms of the lowest-cost trader — usually a member of the exchange. Although individuals do not appear to be able to generate abnormal returns including transactions costs, the Black-Scholes evidence is not sufficient to conclude that exchange members cannot generate abnormal returns after including their lower transactions costs.

Two final points should be noted about the procedures employed by Black and Scholes in dealing with Put and Call Dealers Association options: (1) Market prices are observed only on the first day of the contract, and (2) stock prices used are closing quotes. Since only initial market prices are observed, subsequent days' prices had to be created artificially.[30]

It seems unlikely that this artificial series would correspond to the time path of option prices if a secondary market existed. Furthermore, given that stock price quotes are ending quotes, differences between market and model prices could arise from changes in stock prices between the time the option

---

30. To calculate the "market" price for days after the first, Black and Scholes used the following procedure: (1) At the initial date, compute the Black-Scholes model price from (11.44). (2) Take the difference between the model price and the market price. (3) Amortize that difference over the life of the option. (4) Then for the "market" price on day $t+1$, take the "market" price on day t and add the appropriate amortization factor plus the change in option price implied by the Black-Scholes model (reflecting changes in time to maturity of the option plus changes in stock prices from t to $t+1$).

was written and the close that day. The effects of these points can be minimized by utilizing data from the Chicago Options Board Exchange or the American Options Exchange with their active secondary markets.

Galai (1975) repeats the Black-Scholes tests and extends their analysis along several dimensions using data from the first seven months of trading on the Chicago Options Board Exchange. In replicating the earlier tests and in the extensions of these tests, the implications of the analysis basically support the earlier Black-Scholes results.

Galai constructs tests that would be feasible to implement. A trading rule, considered by Galai, is formulated based on the closing prices for day t, and the transactions take place at the closing prices for day $t+1$. The returns to this strategy are generally positive but usually statistically insignificant. Furthermore, the inclusion of minimal transactions costs (less than one percent) eliminates these abnormal positive returns.

6.2. Tests of Relative Option Prices

While Black and Scholes (1972) and Galai (1975) test the absolute level of the observed call prices, Stoll (1969) and Gould and Galai (1974) test the relative spreads between put and call prices. For European options with the exercise price equal to the current stock price, (11.71) can be rewritten as

$$p(S, T; S) + S - c(S, T; S) = SB(T) \qquad (11.77)$$

The left-hand side of (11.77) generates a certain, terminal payoff of S; therefore, over the life of the options, the return to the left-hand side must equal the T-period risk-free rate (R),

$$\frac{S}{p(S, T; S) + S - c(S, T; S)} - 1 = R \qquad (11.78)$$

Stoll (1969) tested (11.78) using data on American options. Again, this restriction does not hold for American options because there is a positive probability of premature exercise for an American put option. For American options, a weaker condition can be established. Since the value of an American put is no less than that of a European put, the American counterpart of (11.77) can be expressed as

$$C(S, T; S) - P(S, T; S) - S(1 - B(T)) \leq 0 \qquad (11.79)$$

Gould and Galai (1974) test (11.79) using both Black and Scholes' and Stoll's data. To examine market efficiency, Gould and Galai demonstrate that the existence of taxes cannot change the direction of the inequality in (11.79). Next, they take an indirect approach to account for transaction costs. If transaction costs are incurred in trading, market efficiency implies that

$$C(S, T; S) - P(S, T; S) - S(1 - B(T)) \leq TC \qquad (11.80)$$

where TC represents the transaction costs incurred by the lowest-cost trader.

TABLE 11.11   *Cases of Potential Market Inefficiency in Relative Put and Call Pricing for 190-Day Options Using Data from 1969* [a]

Stock Price	Lowest Observation	Lowest Quartile	Median	Upper Quartile	Highest Observation	Number of Observations	
< $20	*	$7.02	$25.51	$39.05	$64.04	131	(L)
	*	2.03	14.95	30.72	51.90	89	(H)
$20–$40	*	*	8.10	20.41	100.15	234	(L)
	*	*	3.94	15.52	87.85	240	(H)
$40–$70	*	*	*	*	66.27	73	(L)
	*	*	*	*	56.58	140	(H)
> $70	*	*	*	*	388.82	29	(L)
	*	*	*	*	3329.86	34	(H)

a. The quantity $[C(S, T; S) - P(S, T; S) - S(1 - B(T))]$ is calculated for every pair of puts and calls. Negative magnitudes are consistent with market efficiency and are therefore not reported, while positive magnitudes are consistent with efficiency only if they are less than transactions costs. Asterisk indicates "less than zero." Adapted from Gould and Galai (1974, Table 4, p. 116). The available data does not specify the stock price when the options were written. Gould and Galai compute the figures in Table 11.11 using both the low (L) and high (H) stock price for the week in which the options were written.

Gould and Galai are unable to measure accurately the actual magnitude of exchange members' transaction costs, therefore they compute the left-hand side of (11.80) to see how large the transaction costs would have to be to imply market efficiency. Their results are summarized in Table 11.11.

Gould and Galai estimate individual trader's transactions costs to be generally greater than the magnitudes in Table 11.11. However, some of the figures are above reasonable estimates of the transaction costs incurred by exchange members. Since the magnitudes that appear in Table 11.11 are observable ex ante, only those hedges that have total payoffs in excess of total costs need be created. Since abnormal positive returns can be generated by employing a strategy that only requires knowledge of current prices, what Roberts (1967) has termed the weak form of the efficiency markets hypothesis seems to have been violated in trading in the Put and Call Dealers Association options market.

7. Other Applications of the Option-Pricing Model

7.1. The Equity of a Levered Firm

Black and Scholes (1973) suggest that the Option-Pricing Model can be used to price other contingent claim assets. They suggest viewing the equity of a levered firm as an option purchased from the bondholders. Assume a firm issues pure discount bonds that prohibit any dividend payments until after the bonds are paid off. If the bonds mature at the end of T periods at which time the firm is liquidated, if the bondholders are paid (if possible), and if the residual is paid to the stockholders, then the Black-Scholes Option-Pricing Model can be applied to value the equity and debt of the firm. In essence, this situation can be thought of as one in which the stockholders sell the firm to the bondholders for the proceeds of the bond issue, and the stockholders have the option to buy back the firm from the bondholders at the maturity date of the bonds for an amount equal to the face value of the bonds. Applying the Black-Scholes solution, the value of the equity of the firm is

$$\hat{S} = V \cdot N\left\{\frac{\ln(V/\hat{B}^*) + [r + (\sigma_v^2/2)]T}{\sigma_v\sqrt{T}}\right\}$$

$$- e^{-rT}\hat{B}^* \cdot N\left\{\frac{\ln(V/\hat{B}^*) + [r - (\sigma_v^2/2)]T}{\sigma_v\sqrt{T}}\right\} \tag{11.81}$$

and the value of the debt is

$$\hat{B} = V - \hat{S} \tag{11.82}$$

where $\hat{S}$ is the total value of the stock (equity), V is the total value of the firm, $\hat{B}^*$ is the total face value of the bonds, $\hat{B}$ is the total current value of the bonds, σ_v^2 is the variance rate on the total value of the firm V.

Black and Scholes then briefly sketch the applicability of this analysis for important issues in corporate finance and managerial economics. They suggest that: (1) The discount due to default risk in corporate bonds may be measured by subtracting the value of the bonds given by their formula from the value of risk-free bonds of the same maturity and face value. (2) Changes in capital structure such as issuing bonds and using the proceeds to retire common stock will affect the distribution of the value of the firm between the stockholders and bondholders. (3) Dividend payments are capable of affecting the division of the total value of the firm between the stock and the bonds. (4) It is conjectured that these possibilities for effecting a change in the value of the claims represented by the stock and bonds frequently make it optimal to include restrictions in bond indentures prohibiting these activities. (5) Coupon bonds are like compound options. By paying the last coupon, the stockholders buy the option to purchase the firm by paying the bondholders the face value of a debt. At the time of the next-to-last payment, the stockholders have an option on an option on an option. (6) Callable bonds add another option to the analysis. With a call provision, the firm can either make the coupon payment or retire the bonds. Many applications of the option-pricing model examine and expand the analysis in this list of suggested uses.

7.2. The Risk Structure of Interest Rates

Merton (1974) examines the risk structure of interest rates on corporate debt. He assumes the total value of the firm is unaffected by capital structure. Long (1974) emphasizes the point that to apply stochastic calculus it must be assumed that the process describing the total value of the firm can be fully specified without reference to the value of the firm's bonds or stock, or equivalently, that the total value of the firm is independent of its capital structure. Therefore, this analysis applies to a Miller-Modigliani (1958) world with no taxes or transactions costs of bankruptcy. Jensen and Meckling (1975) suggest that the existence of any agency cost [31] would cause the total value of the firm to be a function of the debt/equity ratio and would therefore invalidate the specific conclusions of this analysis.

Merton substitutes (11.81) into (11.82) to derive

$$\hat{B} = V \cdot N \left\{ \frac{-\ln(V/\hat{B}^*) - [r + (\sigma_v^2/2)]T}{\sigma_v \sqrt{T}} \right\}$$

$$+ \hat{B}^* e^{-rT} \cdot N \left\{ \frac{\ln(V/\hat{B}^*) + [r - (\sigma_v^2/2)]T}{\sigma_v \sqrt{T}} \right\} \tag{11.83}$$

The results of the examination of the partial effects on European calls can be used in this context to find the functional relationship between the value of the firm's debt and the value of the firm, the face value of the bonds, the time to maturity of the bonds, the variance rate on the value of the firm, and the risk-free rate.[32] Therefore this technique allows valuation of the equity and debt, given the total value of the firm.

Merton then suggests that since discussions of bond pricing frequently employ yields rather than bond prices, it is convenient to transform (11.83) into an excess return by using the transformation

$$e^{-r_B(T)T} \equiv \hat{B}/\hat{B}^* \tag{11.84}$$

where $r_B(T)$ expresses the yield to maturity of a risky corporate bond with T periods to maturity, provided that it does not default.

Then the risk premium on risky corporate debt can be measured by

$$r_B(T) - r \equiv -\ln(\hat{B}/\hat{B}^*)T - r \tag{11.85}$$

---

31. Agency costs are taken by Jensen and Meckling (1975) to mean any cost borne by one class of owners of the firm that are imposed by managers of the firm or by another class of owners. These costs include costs arising from restrictive covenants within bond contracts, auditing costs, costs of monitoring managers' activities, and the like.

32. From (11.45)–(11.49): $0 < \partial \hat{S}/\partial V < 1$, $\partial \hat{S}/\partial \hat{B}^* < 0$, $\partial \hat{S}/\partial T > 0$, $\partial \hat{S}/\partial \sigma^2 > 0$, $\partial \hat{S}/\partial r > 0$. Since it has been assumed that $\hat{B} = V + \hat{S}$, these relationships can be employed to derive $0 < \partial \hat{B}/\partial V = (1 - \partial \hat{S}/\partial V) < 1$, $\partial \hat{B}/\partial \hat{B}^* = -(\partial \hat{S}/\partial \hat{B}^*) > 0$, $\partial \hat{B}/\partial T = -(\partial \hat{S}/\partial T) < 0$, $\partial \hat{B}/\partial \sigma^2 = -(\partial \hat{S}/\partial \sigma^2) < 0$, $\partial \hat{B}/\partial r = -(\partial \hat{S}/\partial r) < 0$.

This implicitly defines a risk structure of interest rates. Because of the relationship between the bond price and the other variables in the system, $\hat{B} = \hat{B}[V, \hat{B}^*, T, \sigma^2, r]$, the risk structure can also be expressed as a function of these variables.

7.3. The Effects of Corporate Policy

Galai and Masulis (1976) extend the Black-Scholes analysis of the effect on the distribution of ownership between the stockholders and bondholders to include various changes in investment policy of the firm. They assume that both the capital asset pricing model and the option pricing model simultaneously hold. They then explore the implications of this joint hypothesis.

The capital asset pricing model implies that the equilibrium rate of return to an asset at every point in time is

$$\bar{r}_j = r + \beta_j(\bar{r}_m - r) \tag{11.86}$$

where $\bar{r}_j$ is the instantaneous expected return to asset j, $\bar{r}_m$ is the instantaneous expected return to the market, β_j [$\equiv \text{cov}(\bar{r}_j, \bar{r}_m)/\sigma^2(\bar{r}_m)$] measures the systematic, nondiversifiable risk of a security.

Galai and Masulis demonstrate that if the systematic risk of the firm, β_v, is constant over time, the instantaneous risk of the equity, β_s, will not be stable.

By (11.39) the change in the total value of the stock, $\hat{S}$, is given by

$$d\hat{S} = \frac{\partial \hat{S}}{\partial V} dV + \Psi\, dt \tag{11.87}$$

where

$$\Psi = \frac{\partial \hat{S}}{\partial t} + \frac{1}{2} \frac{\partial^2 \hat{S}}{\partial V^2} \sigma_v^2 V^2$$

and the instantaneous return to the stockholders can be expressed as

$$\tilde{r}_s \equiv \frac{d\hat{S}}{\hat{S}} = \frac{\partial \hat{S}}{\partial V} \frac{V}{\hat{S}} \frac{dV}{V} + \frac{\Psi}{\hat{S}} dt \equiv \frac{\partial \hat{S}}{\partial V} \frac{V}{\hat{S}} \tilde{r}_v + \frac{\Psi}{\hat{S}} dt \tag{11.88}$$

Substituting into the definition of the systematic risk of the equity, β_s, yields[33]

$$\beta_s \equiv \frac{\text{cov}(\tilde{r}_s, \tilde{r}_m)}{\sigma^2(\tilde{r}_m)} = \frac{\partial \hat{S}}{\partial V} \frac{V}{\hat{S}} \frac{\text{cov}(\tilde{r}_v, \tilde{r}_m)}{\sigma^2(\tilde{r}_m)} \equiv \frac{\partial \hat{S}}{\partial V} \frac{V}{\hat{S}} \beta_v \tag{11.89}$$

Therefore, the beta of the stock can be expressed as the elasticity of the value of the stock with respect to the value of the firm, $\epsilon(\hat{S}, V)$, times the beta of the firm,

$$\beta_s = \epsilon(\hat{S}, V)\beta_v \tag{11.90}$$

where

---

33. Again, note that Ψ is nonstochastic; see (11.39).

$$\epsilon(\hat{S}, V) \equiv \frac{\partial \hat{S}}{\partial V} \frac{V}{\hat{S}}$$

Since $\epsilon(\hat{S}, V)$ is greater than 1,[34] the systematic risk of the stock is greater than the systematic risk of the total firm.[35] Because $\epsilon(\hat{S}, V)$ is a function of V, $\hat{B}^*$, r, σ_v^2, and T; if β_v is stationary, β_s will be nonstationary.

Galai and Masulis then demonstrate that if the value of the firm is unaffected by the capital structure (i.e., $V = \hat{S} + \hat{B}$), then from (11.81) and (11.83) the value of the equity and debt is a function of (1) the value of the firm, (2) the face value of the debt, (3) the risk-free rate, (4) the time to maturity of the debt, and (5) the variance rate of the value of the firm. Therefore, unanticipated changes in any of these variables can affect the market value of the stockholders' and bondholders' claims. This descriptive power makes the option-pricing model extremely useful in analyzing changes in corporate investment policy. They employ comparative statics analysis to examine the effect of different policies. Given appropriate assumptions, Galai and Masulis show that: (1) Acquisitions that increase the variance rate of the firm will increase the value of the equity and reduce the value of the debt. (2) Conglomerate mergers that reduce σ_v^2 increase the value of the debt and decrease the value of the equity. (3) Only increases in the scale of operations that are financed by proportional increases in debt and equity cause no redistributions of ownership. (4) Spin-offs where assets are distributed only to stockholders reduce the value of the debt.

7.4. Dual-Purpose Funds

Ingersoll (1976) applies the option-pricing model to the analysis of dual-purpose funds. Dual-purpose funds are closed-end funds that issue two classes of shares: income shares that have the rights to all income earned by the fund, subject to a stated minimum cumulative dividend, plus a fixed payment at the maturity of the fund; and capital shares that pay no dividends and are redeemable at net asset value at the maturity date.

---

34. From (11.83), (11.76), and (11.46),

$$\epsilon(\hat{S}, V) = \frac{\partial \hat{S}}{\partial V} \frac{V}{\hat{S}} = N\left\{ \frac{\ln(V/\hat{B}^*) + [r + (\sigma_v^2/2)]T}{\sigma_v \sqrt{T}} \right\} \frac{V}{\hat{S}}$$

$$= \frac{\left(V \cdot N\left\{ \dfrac{\ln(V/\hat{B}^*) + [r + (\sigma_v^2/2)]T}{\sigma_v \sqrt{T}} \right\} \right)}{\left(V \cdot N\left\{ \dfrac{\ln(V/\hat{B}^*) + [r + (\sigma_v^2/2)]T}{\sigma_v \sqrt{T}} \right\} - \hat{B}^* e^{-rT} \cdot N\left\{ \dfrac{\ln(V/\hat{B}^*) + [r - (\sigma_v^2/2)]T}{\sigma_v \sqrt{T}} \right\} \right)} > 1$$

Note that the denominator is equal to the numerator minus a positive magnitude; the elasticity is therefore greater than 1.

35. For $\beta_v > 0$.

The capital shares of a dual-purpose fund are analogous to a European option on a dividend-paying stock, with an exercise price equal to the required payment to the holders of the income shares. Therefore, in the simplest case — where the interest rate is constant over time, dividends and management fees are paid continuously at a fixed fraction of the asset value of the fund, and taxes are zero — (11.53) can be applied to value the capital shares,

$$c = e^{-\delta T} S \cdot N \left\{ \frac{\ln(S/X) + [r - \delta + (\sigma^2/2)]T}{\sigma\sqrt{T}} \right\}$$

$$- e^{-rT} X \cdot N \left\{ \frac{\ln(S/X) + [r - \delta - (\sigma^2/2)]T}{\sigma\sqrt{T}} \right\} \tag{11.91}$$

where c is the value of the capital shares, $\delta \equiv \delta_1 + \delta_2$ (δ_1 being the dividend payment $[D \equiv \delta_1 S]$; and δ_2, the management fee $[M \equiv \delta_2 S]$); S, the net asset value of the fund; X, the payment to the income shareholders; and σ^2, the variance rate on the net asset value.

Ingersoll derives the value of the income shares as[36]

$$I = S \left[e^{-\delta T} \left(1 - \frac{\delta_1}{\delta_1 + \delta_2} \right) + \frac{\delta_1}{\delta_1 + \delta_2} \right] - c \tag{11.92}$$

First, note that the market value of the fund (or any closed-end fund) will typically be less than the net asset value of the fund because of the management fees incurred by the holders of the shares of the closed-end fund. The difference between the net asset value of the fund and the market value of the fund's shares can be expressed as

$$S - (c + I) = S \frac{\delta^2}{\delta} (1 - e^{-\delta T}) \tag{11.93}$$

Second, because there are no provisions for liquidation of the fund prior to the maturity date of the fund, the payments of dividends and management

---

36. To gain a more intuitive understanding of this equation, it can also be derived in case of perfect certainty. In that case, the terminal value of the fund would be $e^{(r-\delta)T}S$, and the capital share would be priced so that

$$C = e^{-rT}(e^{(r-\delta)T}S - X) = e^{-\delta T}S - e^{-rT}X$$

The income share would be priced so that

$$I = \int_0^T e^{-r\tau} \delta e^{(r-\delta)\tau} S \, d\tau + X e^{-rT} = \frac{\delta_1}{\delta_1 + \delta_2} S(1 - e^{-(\delta_1 + \delta_2)T}) + X e^{-rT}$$

This can be rewritten as

$$I = S \left[e^{-(\delta_1 + \delta_2)T} \left(1 - \frac{\delta_1}{\delta_1 + \delta_2} \right) + \frac{\delta_1}{\delta_1 + \delta_2} \right] - c$$

which is identical to (11.92).

fees are capable of making the capital shares sell below the "intrinsic value," the difference between the net asset value of the fund and the fixed payment owed to the holders of the income shares. This is analogous to a European option on a dividend-paying stock selling below the difference between the stock price and exercise price.

Ingersoll tests this model using market data on the seven dual-purpose funds. His tests suggest that the option-pricing model describes fluctuations in the capital shares quite well.

8. Conclusion

The Black-Scholes Option-Pricing Model provides an explicit general equilibrium solution to the problem of valuing simple puts and calls. Further, the model contains testable hypotheses; the variables of the model are either readily observable or are subject to reasonably accurate estimation. However, at this time it would appear that the development of theoretical hypotheses is far ahead of the empirical work in this area. Several modifications of the basic option-pricing model have been suggested, but the importance of these modifications cannot be judged in the absence of empirical work that is yet to be completed.

The development of organized secondary markets for options, such as the Chicago Board Options Exchange; the American Options Exchange; and the Philadelphia, Baltimore, Washington Options Exchange can provide valuable data for testing the implications of these models for option pricing. However, that the Black-Scholes analysis has generated substantial interest seems to derive more from its implications for a general theory of the valuation of contingent claims than for its direct application to value simple puts and calls. Nevertheless, to date, the only example of empirical verification of this analysis that employs data other than that for put and call trading is by Ingersoll (1976). The potential benefits of empirical research in this area appear to be large.

Appendix A

The Bachelier Model

Bachelier (1900) assumes that the stock price is a random variable, that price changes are independent and identically distributed, and that

$$\text{Prob}\{\tilde{S} \le S^* \mid \tilde{S} = S\} = F(S^* - S; T) \qquad (11.\text{A}.1)$$

where F is the cumulative distribution function of the stock price changes.[37]

---

37. Tildes represent random variables. Equation 11.A.1 says that the probability that the stock

This describes a Wiener Process (or Arithmetic Brownian Motion). Bachelier's choice is unfortunate, for as T approaches infinity, the Prob$\{\tilde{S}^* < S^*\}$ approaches $\frac{1}{2}$ for all S^*. Since nothing in the formulation restricts S^* to the positive numbers, there is a positive probability of negative stock prices; a violation of the property of limited liability.

Bachelier incorrectly deduces that (11.A.1) implies that the density function must be that of the normal,

$$F(S^* - S; T) = N\left(\frac{S^* - (S + \mu T)}{\sigma\sqrt{T}}\right) \qquad (11.A.2)$$

where μ is the mean expected price change per time period; σ^2, the variance per time period; N, the cumulative standard normal distribution.

Equation 11.A.1 is insufficient to deduce (11.A.2). Any member of the stable-Paretian family of distribution satisfies (11.A.1). To deduce normality, it must be assumed further that the variance is finite.

Bachelier's next assumption suggests that his specification of the process that generates the stock price is unsuitable as an equilibrium specification. He assumes that the mean expected price change per unit time (μ) equals zero. Bachelier then assumes that the call is also priced to yield a mean expected return of zero. Bachelier views the stock market as a gamble; he feels that competition will reduce the expected return to zero, which seems to deny both positive interest rates and risk aversion.

Bachelier applies the same logic to the pricing of the call option — he feels the call will be priced so that the current call price is the expected terminal call price. From (11.2), the terminal call price is the maximum of either the difference between the terminal stock price and the exercise price or zero, $C^* = \text{Max}[0, S^* - X]$, therefore Bachelier's model suggests that

$$C = E(C^*) \equiv \int_X^\infty (S^* - X)N'(S^*)\, dS^* \qquad (11.A.3)$$

where $N'(S^*)$ is the normal density function for S^*.

Changing variables,

$$C = \int_{X - S/\sigma\sqrt{T}}^\infty (z\sigma\sqrt{T} + S - X)N'(z)\, dz \qquad (11.A.4)$$

where $z \equiv (S^* - S)/\sigma\sqrt{T}$, and

$$C = S \cdot N\left\{\frac{S - X}{\sigma\sqrt{T}}\right\} - X \cdot N\left\{\frac{S - X}{\sigma\sqrt{T}}\right\} + \sigma\sqrt{T} \cdot N'\left\{\frac{X - S}{\sigma\sqrt{T}}\right\} \qquad (11.A.5)$$

where $N\{\cdot\}$ is the cumulative standard normal, and $N'\{\cdot\}$ is the standard normal density function.

---

price T periods from now ($\tilde{S}^*$) is less than or equal to a given number, S^*, given that the current stock price ($\tilde{S}$) has assumed the value S, can be expressed as a function of the distance $(S^* - S)$ and T.

Note that as the time to expiration is increased, the call price increases without bound.[38] This implication seems to violate the restriction, established in Section 2.2, that the maximum value the call price can assume is equal to the stock price. This result arises because, while Merton assumes the stock possesses limited liability, Bachelier implicitly does not.[39]

To summarize, the major objections to Bachelier's model are: (1) the assumption of Arithmetic Brownian Motion in the description of expected price movements, implying both a positive probability of negative prices for the security and option prices greater than their respective security prices for large T; (2) the assumption that the mean expected price change is zero, suggesting both no time preference and risk neutrality; (3) the implicit assumption that the variance is finite, thereby ruling out other members of the stable-Paretian family except the normal.

---

38. The cumulative standard normal expressions in the first two terms of (11.A.5) go to ½ as $T \to \infty$; therefore the first two terms go to $\frac{1}{2}[S-X]$. In the third term, the argument of the standard normal density function goes to zero; therefore that third term goes to $\lim_{t \to \infty} \sigma\sqrt{T}$ (0.3989), which is infinity.

39. Bachelier assumes the mean future price is positive and, because he specifies a process without drift, equal to the current stock price. The process is such that if the total integral from minus to plus infinity as T is increased, the left half goes to minus infinity and the right to plus infinity, in such a way as to keep the mean unchanged at S. This property, that the expected value of 'half' the distribution rises without bound as T is increased coupled with a zero discount rate, yields the anomalous result that the call price increases without bound as T is increased.

References

Ayers, H. F., 1964. Risk aversion in the warrant markets. In P. Cootner (ed.), *The random character of stock market prices*. Cambridge, MA: MIT Press, 1964, pp. 497–505.

Bachelier, L. 1900. Theory of speculation (English translation). In P. Cootner (ed.), *The random character of stock market prices*. Cambridge, MA: MIT Press, 1964, pp. 17–78.

Baumol, W. J., B. G. Malkiel, and R. E. Quandt. 1966. The valuation of convertible securities. *Quarterly Journal of Economics* 80, 48–59.

Bierman, H., Jr. 1967. The valuation of stock options. *Journal of Financial and Quantitative Analysis* 2, 327–334.

Black, F. 1974. *The pricing of complex options and corporate liabilities*. Mimeo. Chicago, IL: University of Chicago.

Black, F. 1975. Fact and fantasy in the use of options. *Financial Analysts Journal* 31, 36–72.

Black, F. 1976. The pricing of commodity contracts. *Journal of Financial Economics* 3, 167–179.

Black, F., and M. Scholes. 1972. The valuation of option contracts and a test of market efficiency. Papers and Proceedings of the Thirtieth Annual Meeting of the American Finance Association, 27–29 Dec. 1971, *Journal of Finance* 27, 399–417.

Black, F., and M. Scholes. 1973. The pricing of options and corporate liabilities. *Journal of Political Economy* 81, 637–659.

Boness, A. J. 1964a. Elements of a theory of stock-option value. *Journal of Political Economy* 72, 163–175.

Boness, A. J. 1964b. Some evidence on the profitability of trading in put and call options. In P. Cootner (ed.), *The random character of stock market prices.* Cambridge, MA: MIT Press, 1964, pp. 475–496.

Campbell, E. D. 1961. Stock options should be valued. *Harvard Business Review,* 52–58.

Chen, A. H. Y. 1970. A model of warrant pricing in a dynamic market. *Journal of Finance* 25, 1041–1060.

Cox, J. C. 1975. *The valuation of financial claims.* Mimeo. Philadelphia, PA: University of Pennsylvania.

Cox, J. C., and S. A. Ross. 1975. *The pricing of options for jump processes.* Rodney L. White Center for Financial Research Working Paper 2-75. Philadelphia, PA: University of Pennsylvania.

Cox, J. C., and S. A. Ross. 1976. The valuation of options for alternative stochastic processes. *Journal of Financial Economics* 3, 145–166.

Fama, E. F. 1970. Efficient capital markets: A review of theory and empirical work. *Journal of Finance* 25, 383–417.

Fried, S. 1971. *Speculating with warrants.* New York: RHM Associates.

Galai, D. 1975. *Pricing of options and the efficiency of the Chicago Board Options Exchange.* Unpublished Ph.D. dissertation. Chicago, IL: University of Chicago.

Galai, D., and R. W. Masulis. 1976. The option pricing model and the risk factor of the stock. *Journal of Financial Economics* 3, 53–81.

Giguere, G. 1958. Warrants, A mathematical method of evaluation. *Analysts Journal* 14, 17–25.

Gould, J. P., and D. Galai. 1974. Transactions costs and the relationship between put and call prices. *Journal of Financial Economics* 1, 105–129.

Hallingby, P., Jr. 1947. Speculative opportunities in stock purchase warrants. *Analysts Journal* 3, 48–49.

Harbaugh, A. W. 1963. *Operations research in the stock market.* El Segundo, CA: Computer Sciences Corp., 1963.

Hausman, W. H., and W. L. White. 1968. Theory of option strategy under risk aversion. *Journal of Financial and Quantitative Analysis* 3, 343–358.

Hettenhouse, G. W., and D. J. Puglisi. 1975. Investor experience with put and call options. *Financial Analysts Journal* 31, 53–58.

Holland, D. M., and W. G. Lewellen. 1962. Probing the record of stock options. *Harvard Business Review,* 132–150.

Ingersoll, J. 1976. A theoretical and empirical investigation of the dual purpose funds: An application of contingent claims analysis. *Journal of Financial Economics* 3.

Jensen, M. C., and W. H. Meckling. 1975. *Theory of the firm: Managerial behavior, agency costs, and capital structure.* Working Paper. Rochester, NY: University of Rochester.

Kassouf, S. T. 1962. *Evaluation of convertible securities.* Maspeth, NY: Analytic Investors.

Kassouf, S. T. 1965. *A theory and an economic model for common stock purchase warrants.* Unpublished Ph.D. thesis. New York, NY: Columbia University.

Kassouf, S. T. 1968a. Stock price random walks: Some supporting evidence. *Review of Economics and Statistics* 50, 275–278.

Kassouf, S. T. 1968b. Warrant pricing behavior–1945 to 1964. *Financial Analysts Journal* 24, 123–126.

Kassouf, S. T. 1969. An econometric model for option price with implications for investors' expectations and audacity. *Econometrica* 37, 685–696.

Kate, R. C. 1963. The profitability of put and call option writing. *Industrial Management Review* 5, 56–69.

Kruizenga, R. J. 1956. *Put and call options: A theoretical and market analysis.* Unpublished Ph.D. thesis. Cambridge, MA: MIT.

Kruizenga, R. J. 1964a. Introduction to the option contract. In P. Cootner (ed.), *The random character of stock market prices.* Cambridge, MA: MIT Press, pp. 277–391.

Kruizenga, R. J. 1964b. Profit returns from purchasing puts and calls. In P. Cootner (ed.), *The random character of stock market prices.* Cambridge, MA: MIT Press, pp. 392–411.

Leonard, R. J. 1971. *An empirical examination of a new general equilibrium model for warrant pricing.* Unpublished MS thesis. Cambridge, MA: MIT.

Lloyd-Davies, P. 1974. *Risk and optimal leverage.* Mimeo. Rochester, NY: University of Rochester.

Malkiel, B. G., and R. E. Quandt. 1969. *Strategies and rational decision in the securities option market.* Cambridge, MA: MIT Press.

McGuigan, J. R. 1971. *Timing strategies in the call option market.* Unpublished Ph.D. dissertation. Pittsburgh, PA: University of Pittsburgh.

McGuigan, J. R., and W. R. King. 1973. Security option strategy under risk aversion: An analysis. *Journal of Financial and Quantitative Analysis* 8, 1–15.

McKean, H. P., Jr. 1965. Appendix: A free boundary problem for the heat exchange equation arising from a problem in mathematical economics. *Industrial Management Review* 6, 32–39.

McKean, H. P., Jr. 1969. *Stochastic integrals.* New York, NY: Academic Press.

Merton, R. C. 1970. *Analytical optimal control theory as applied to stochastic and nonstochastic economics.* Unpublished Ph.D. thesis. Cambridge, MA: MIT.

Merton, R. C. 1971. *Theory of rational option pricing.* Sloan School of Management Working Paper 574-71. Cambridge, MA: MIT.

Merton, R. C. 1973. Appendix: Continuous time speculative processes. *Mathematical topics in economic theory and computation, SIAM Review* 15, 34–38.

Merton, R. C. 1973a. The relationship between put and call option prices: Comment. *Journal of Finance* 28, 183–184.

Merton, R. C. 1973b. Theory of rational option pricing. *Bell Journal of Economics and Management Science* 4, 141–183.

Merton, R. C. 1974. On the pricing of corporate debt: The risk structure of interest rates. *Journal of Finance* 29, 449–470.

Merton, R. C. 1976. Option pricing when underlying stock returns are discontinuous. *Journal of Financial Economics* 3, 125–144.

Modigliani, F., and M. H. Miller. 1958. The cost of capital, corporation finance, and the theory of investment. *American Economic Review* 48, 261–297.

Morrison, R. J. 1957. The warrants or the stock? *Analysts Journal* 13, 52.

Nast, D. A. 1972. *An economic study of warrant prices.* Paper presented at the Applachian Finance Association Meeting.

Pease, F. 1963. The warrant – its powers and its hazards. *Financial Analysts Journal* 19, 28.

Plum, V. L., and T. J. Martin. 1966. The significance of conversion parity in valuing common stock warrants. *The Financial Review* 1, 26.

Poensgen, O. H. 1965. The valuation of convertible bonds. *Industrial Management Review* 7.

Pye, G. 1966. The value of the call option on a bond. *Journal of Political Economy* 74, 200–205.

Rebalk, R. 1975. Risk and return in CBOE and AMEX option trading. *Financial Analysts Journal* 34, 42–52.

Roberts, H. 1967. *Clinical vs. statistical forecasts of security prices.* Unpublished speech at the Seminar on the Analysis of Security Prices. Chicago, IL: University of Chicago.

Ross, S. A. 1976. Options and efficiency. *Quarterly Journal of Economics* 90, 75–89.

Samuelson, P. A. 1965. Rational theory of warrant pricing. *Industrial Management Review* 6, 13–31.

Samuelson, P. A. 1968. Review of beat the market. *Journal of American Statistical Association* 63, 1049–1051.

Samuelson, P. A. 1973. Mathematics of speculative price. *SIAM Review* 15, 1–42.

Samuelson, P. A., and R. C. Merton. 1969. A complete model of warrant pricing that maximizes utility. *Industrial Management Review* 10, 17–46.

Shelton, J. P. 1967a. The relation of the pricing of a warrant to the price of its associated stock, part I. *Financial Analysts Journal* 23, 143–151.

Shelton, J. P. 1967b. The relation of the pricing of a warrant to the price of its associated stock, part II. *Financial Analysts Journal* 23, 84–99.

Snyder, G. 1969. Alternate forms of options. *Financial Analysts Journal* 25, 93–99.

Sprenkle, C. M. 1964. Warrant prices as indicators of expectations and preferences. In P. Cootner (ed.), *The random character of stock market prices.* Cambridge, MA: MIT Press, pp. 412–474.

Stoll, H. R. 1969. The relationship between put and call option prices. *Journal of Finance* 24, 802–824.

Taylor, H. M. 1967. Evaluating a call option and optimal timing strategy in the stock market. *Management Science,* 111–120.

Thorpe, E. O. 1973. Extensions of the Black-Scholes option model. *39th Session of the International Statistical Institute* (Vienna, Austria), pp. 522–529.

Thorpe, E. O., and S. T. Kassouf. 1967. *Beat the market.* New York, NY: Random House.

Turov, D. 1973. New look in calls. *Barron's.*

Van Horne, J. C. 1969. Warrant valuation in relation to volatility and opportunity costs. *Industrial Management Review* 10, 17–32.

Wilburn, D. S. 1970. *A model of the put and call option market.* Unpublished Master's thesis. Cambridge, MA: MIT, Sloan School of Management.

12

How to Use the Holes in Black-Scholes*

Fischer Black

The Black-Scholes formula is still around, even though it depends on at least 10 unrealistic assumptions. Making the assumptions more realistic hasn't produced a formula that works better across a wide range of circumstances.

In special cases, though, we can improve the formula. If you think investors are making an unrealistic assumption like one of those we used in deriving the formula, there is a strategy you may want to follow that focuses on that assumption.

The same unrealistic assumptions that led to the Black-Scholes formula are behind some versions of "portfolio insurance." As people have shifted to more realistic assumptions, they have changed the way they use portfolio insurance. Some people have dropped it entirely or have switched to the opposite strategy.

People using incorrect assumptions about market conditions may even have caused the rise and sudden fall in stocks during 1987. One theory of the crash relies on incorrect beliefs, held before the crash, about the extent to which investors were using portfolio insurance and about how changes in stock prices cause changes in expected returns.

---

*This article is a revised version of an earlier article, "The Holes in Black-Scholes," which appeared in Vol. 1 No. 4 of *Risk* in March of 1988.

The Formula

The Black-Scholes formula looks like this:

$$w(x, t) = xN(d_1) - ce^{-r(t^* - t)}N(d_2)$$

where

$$d_1 = \frac{\ln(x/c) + (r + \frac{1}{2}v^2)(t^* - t)}{v\sqrt{t^* - t}}$$

and

$$d_2 = \frac{\ln(x/c) + (r - \frac{1}{2}v^2)(t^* - t)}{v\sqrt{t^* - t}}$$

In this expression, w is the value of a call option or warrant on the stock, t is today's date, x is the stock price, c is the strike price, r is the interest rate, t^* is the maturity date, v is the standard deviation of the stock's return, and N is something called the "cumulative normal density function." (You can approximate N using a simple algebraic expression.)

The value of the option increases with increases in the stock's price, the interest rate, the time remaining until the option expires, and the stock's volatility. Except for volatility, which can be estimated several ways, we can observe all of the factors the Black-Scholes formula requires for valuing options.

Note that the stock's expected return doesn't appear in the formula. If you are bullish on the stock, you may buy shares or call options, but you won't change your estimate of the option's value. A higher expected return on the stock means a higher expected return on the option, but it doesn't affect the option's value for a given stock price.

This feature of the formula is very general. I don't know of any variation of the formula where the stock's expected return affects the option's value for a given stock price.

How to Improve the Assumptions

In our original derivation of the formula, Myron Scholes and I made the following unrealistic assumptions:

- The stock's volatility is known, and doesn't change over the life of the option.
- The stock price changes smoothly: It never jumps up or down a large amount in a short time.
- The short-term interest rate never changes.

- Anyone can borrow or lend as much as he wants at a single rate.
- An investor who sells the stock or the option short will have the use of all the proceeds of the sale and receive any returns from investing these proceeds.
- There are no trading costs for either the stock or the option.
- An investor's trades do not affect the taxes he pays.
- The stock pays no dividends.
- An investor can exercise the option only at expiration.
- There are no takeovers or other events that can end the option's life early.

Since these assumptions are mostly false, we know the formula must be wrong. But we may not be able to find any other formula that gives better results in a wide range of circumstances. Here we look at each of these 10 assumptions and describe how we might change them to improve the formula. We also look at strategies that make sense if investors continue to make unrealistic assumptions.

Volatility Changes

The volatility of a stock is not constant. Changes in the volatility of a stock may have a major impact on the values of certain options, especially far-out-of-the-money options. For example, if we use a volatility estimate of 0.20 for the annual standard deviation of the stock, and if we take the interest rate to be zero, we get a value of $0.00884 for a six-month call option with a $40 strike price written on a $28 stock. Keeping everything else the same, but doubling the volatility to 0.40, we get a value of $0.465.

For this out-of-the-money option, doubling the volatility estimate multiplies the value by a factor of 53.

Since the volatility can change, we should really include the ways it can change in the formula. The option value will depend on the entire future path that we expect the volatility to take and on the uncertainty about what the volatility will be at each point in the future. One measure of that uncertainty is the "volatility of the volatility."

A formula that takes account of changes in volatility will include both current and expected future levels of volatility. Though the expected return on the stock will not affect option values, expected changes in volatility will affect them. And the volatility of volatility will affect them, too.

Another measure of the uncertainty about the future volatility is the relation between the future stock price and its volatility. A decline in the stock price implies a substantial increase in volatility, while an increase in the stock price implies a substantial decrease in volatility. The effect is so strong that it is even possible that a stock with a price of $20 and a typical daily move of $0.50 will start having a typical daily move of only $0.375 if the stock price doubles to $40.

John Cox and Stephen Ross have come up with two formulas that take account of the relation between the future stock price and its volatility.[1] To see the effects of using one of their formulas on the pattern of option values for at-the-money and out-of-the-money options, let's look at the values using both Black-Scholes and Cox-Ross formulas for a six-month call option on a $40 stock, taking the interest rate as zero and the volatility as 0.20 per year. For three exercise prices, the values are as follows:

Exercise Price	Black-Scholes	Cox-Ross
40.00	2.2600	2.2600
50.00	0.1550	0.0880
57.10	0.0126	0.0020

The Cox-Ross formula implies lower values for out-of-the-money call options than the Black-Scholes formula. But putting in uncertainty about the future volatility will often imply higher values for these same options. We can't tell how the option values will change when we put in both effects.

What should you do if you think a stock's volatility will change in ways that other people do not yet understand? Also, suppose that you feel the market values options correctly in all other respects.

You should "buy volatility" if you think volatility will rise and "sell volatility" if you think it will fall. To buy volatility, buy options; to see volatility, sell options. Instead of buying stock, you can buy calls or buy stock and sell calls. Or you can take the strongest position on volatility by adding a long or short position in straddles to your existing position. To buy pure volatility, buy both puts and calls in a ratio that gives you no added exposure to the stock; to sell pure volatility, sell both puts and calls in the same ratio.

Jumps

In addition to showing changes in volatility in general and changes in volatility related to changes in stock price, a stock may have jumps. A major news development may cause a sudden large change in the stock price, often accompanied by a temporary suspension of trading in the stock.

When the big news is just as likely to be good as bad, a jump will look a lot like a temporary large increase in volatility. When the big news, if it comes, is sure to be good, or is sure to be bad, the resulting jump is not like a change in volatility. Up jumps and down jumps have different effects on

---

1. See John Cox and Stephen Ross, *Journal of Financial Economics* (January/March 1976).

option values than symmetric jumps, where there is an equal chance of an up jump or a down jump.

Robert Merton has a formula that reflects possible symmetric jumps.[2] Compared to the Black-Scholes formula, his formula gives higher values for both in-the-money and out-of-the-money options. The differences are especially large for short-term options.

Short-term options also show strikingly different effects for up jumps and down jumps. An increase in the probability of an up jump will cause out-of-the-money calls to go way up in value relative to out-of-the-money puts. An increase in the probability of a down jump will do the reverse. After the crash, people were afraid of another down jump, and out-of-the-money puts were priced very high relative to their Black-Scholes values, while out-of-the-money calls were priced very low.

More than a year after the crash, this fear continues to affect option values.

What should you do if you think jumps are more likely to occur than the market thinks? If you expect a symmetric jump, buy short-term out-of-the-money options. Instead of stock, you can hold call options or more stock plus put options. Or you can sell at-the-money options. Instead of stock, you can hold more stock and sell call options. For a pure play on symmetric jumps, buy out-of-the-money calls and puts, and sell at-the-money calls and puts.

For up jumps, use similar strategies that involve buying short-term out-of-the-money calls, or selling short-term out-of-the-money puts, or both. For down jumps, do the opposite.

Interest Rate Changes

The Black-Scholes formula assumes a constant interest rate, but the yields on bonds with different maturities tell us that the market expects the rate to change. If future changes in the interest rate are known, we can just replace the short-term rate with the yield on a zero coupon bond that matures when the option expires.

But, of course, future changes in the interest rate are uncertain. When the stock's volatility is known, Robert Merton has shown that the zero-coupon-bond yield will still work, even when both short-term and long-term interest rates are shifting.[3] At a given point in time, we can find the option value by using the zero-coupon-bond yield at that moment for the short-term rate. When both the volatility and the interest rate are shifting, we will need a more complex adjustment.

---

2. See John Cox, Robert Merton, and Stephen Ross, *Journal of Financial Economics* (January/March 1976).

3. Robert Merton, *Bell Journal of Economics and Management Science* (1977).

In general, the effects of interest rate changes on option values do not seem nearly as great as the effects of volatility changes. If you have an opinion on which way interest rates are going, you may be better off with direct positions in fixed income securities rather than in options.

But your opinion may affect your decisions to buy or sell options. Higher interest rates mean higher call values and lower put values. If you think interest rates will rise more than the market thinks, you should be more inclined to buy calls (and more inclined to buy more stocks and sell puts) as a substitute for a straight stock position. If you think interest rates will fall more than the market thinks, these preferences should be reversed.

Borrowing Penalties

The rate at which an individual can borrow, even with securities as collateral, is higher than the rate at which he can lend. Sometimes his borrowing rate is substantially higher than his lending rate. Also, margin requirements or restrictions put on by lenders may limit the amount he can borrow.

High rates and limits on borrowing may cause a general increase in call option values, since calls provide leverage that can substitute for borrowing. The interest rates implied by option values may be higher than lending rates. If this happens and you have borrowing limits but no limits on option investments, you may still want to buy calls. But if you can borrow freely at a rate close to the lending rate, you may want to get leverage by borrowing rather than by buying calls.

When implied interest rates are high, conservative investors might buy puts or sell calls to protect a portfolio instead of selling stock. Fixed income investors might even choose to buy stocks and puts (and sell calls) to create a synthetic fixed income position with a yield higher than market yields.

Short-Selling Penalties

Short-selling penalties are generally even worse than borrowing penalties. On U.S. exchanges, an investor can sell a stock short only on or after an uptick. He must go to the expense of borrowing stock if he wants to sell it short. Part of his expense involves putting up cash collateral with the person who lends the stock; he generally gets no interest, or interest well below market rates, on this collateral. Also, he may have to put up margin with his broker in cash and may not receive interest on cash balances with his broker.

For options, the penalties tend to be much less severe. An investor need not borrow an option to sell it short. There is no uptick rule for options. And an investor loses much less interest income in selling an option short than in selling a stock short.

Penalties on short selling that apply to all investors will affect option values. When even professional investors have trouble selling a stock short, we will want to include an element in the option formula to reflect the strength of these penalties. Sometimes we approximate this by assuming an extra dividend yield on the stock, in an amount up to the cost of maintaining a short position as part of a hedge.

Suppose you want to short a stock but you face penalties if you sell the stock short directly. Perhaps you're not even allowed to short the stock directly. You can short it indirectly by holding put options or by taking a naked short position in call options. (Though most investors who can't short stock directly also can't take naked short positions.)

When you face penalties in selling short, you often face rewards for lending stock to those who want to short it. In this situation, strategies that involve holding the stock and lending it out may dominate other strategies. For example, you might create a position with a limited downside by holding a stock and a put on the stock, and by lending the stock to those who want to short it.

Trading Costs

Trading costs can make it hard for an investor to create an optionlike payoff by trading in the underlying stock. They can also make it hard to create a stocklike payoff by trading in the option. Sometimes they can increase an option's value, and sometimes they can decrease it.

We can't tell how trading costs will affect an option's value, so we can think of them as creating a "band" of possible values. Within this band, it will be impractical for most investors to take advantage of mispricing by selling the option and buying the stock, or by selling the stock and buying the option.

The bigger the stock's trading costs are, the more important it is for you to choose a strategy that creates the payoffs you want with little trading. Trading costs can make options especially useful if you want to shift exposure to the stock after it goes up or down.

If you want to shift your exposure to the market as a whole rather than to a stock, you will find options even more useful. It is often more costly to trade in a basket of stocks than in a single stock. But you can use index options to reduce your trading in the underlying stocks or futures.

Taxes

Some investors pay no taxes; some are taxed as individuals, paying taxes on dividends, interest, and capital gains; and some are taxed as corporations, also paying taxes on dividends, interest, and capital gains, but at different rates.

The very existence of taxes will affect option values. A hedged position that should give the same return as lending may have a tax that differs from the tax on interest. So if all investors faced the same tax rate, we would use a modified interest rate in the option formula.

The fact that investor tax rates differ will affect values too. Without rules to restrict tax arbitrage, investors could use large hedged positions involving options to cut their taxes sharply or to alter them indefinitely. Thus, tax authorities adopt a variety of rules to restrict tax arbitrage. There may be rules to limit interest deductions or capital loss deductions, or rules to tax gains and losses before a position is closed out. For example, most U.S. index option positions are now taxed each year—partly as short-term capital gains and partly as long-term capital gains—whether or not the taxpayer has closed out his positions.

If you can use capital losses to offset gains, you may act roughly the same way whether your tax rate is high or low. If your tax rate stays the same from year to year, you may act about the same whether you are forced to realize gains and losses or are able to choose the year you realize them.

But if you pay taxes on gains and cannot deduct losses, you may want to limit the volatility of your positions and have the freedom to control the timing of gains and losses. This will affect how you use options, and may affect option values as well. I find it hard to predict, though, whether it will increase or decrease option values.

Investors who buy a put option will have a capital gain or loss at the end of the year or when the option expires. Investors who simulate the put option by trading in the underlying stock will sell after a decline and buy after a rise. By choosing which lots of stock to buy and which lots to sell, they will be able to generate a series of realized capital losses and unrealized gains. The tax advantages of this strategy may reduce put values for many taxable investors. By a similar argument, the tax advantages of a simulated call option may reduce call values for most taxable investors.

Dividends and Early Exercise

The original Black-Scholes formula does not take account of dividends. But dividends reduce call option values and increase put option values, at least when there are no offsetting adjustments in the terms of the options. Dividends make early exercise of a call option more likely and early exercise of a put option less likely.

We now have several ways to change the formula to account for dividends. One way assumes that the dividend yield is constant for all possible stock price levels and at all future times. Another assumes that the issuer has money set aside to pay the dollar dividends due before the option expires. Yet another assumes that the dividend depends in a known way on the stock price at each ex-dividend date.

John Cox, Stephen Ross, and Mark Rubinstein have shown how to figure option values using a "tree" of possible future stock prices.[4] The tree gives the same values as the formula when we use the same assumptions. But the tree is more flexible and lets us relax some of the assumptions. For example, we can put on the tree the dividend that the firm will pay for each possible future stock price at each future time. We can also test, at each node of the tree, whether an investor will exercise the option early for that stock price at that time.

Option values reflect the market's belief about the stock's future dividends and the likelihood of early exercise. When you think that dividends will be higher than the market thinks, you will want to buy puts or sell calls, other things equal. When you think that option holders will exercise too early or too late, you will want to sell options to take advantage of the opportunities the holders create.

Takeovers

The original formula assumes that the underlying stock will continue trading for the life of the option. Takeovers can make this assumption false.

If Firm A takes over Firm B through an exchange of stock, options on Firm B's stock will normally become options on Firm A's stock. We will use A's volatility rather than B's in valuing the option.

If Firm A takes over Firm B through a cash tender offer, there are two effects. First, outstanding options on B will expire early. This will tend to reduce values for both puts and calls. Second, B's stock price will rise through the tender offer premium. This will increase call values and decrease put values.

But when the market knows of a possible tender offer from Firm A, B's stock price will be higher than it might otherwise be. It will be between its normal level and its normal level increased by the tender offer. Then if A fails to make an offer, the price will fall or will show a smaller-than-normal rise.

All these factors work together to influence option values. The chance of a takeover will make an option's value sometimes higher and sometimes

---

4. John Cox, Mark Rubinstein, and Stephen Ross, "Option Pricing: A Simplified Approach," *Journal of Financial Economics* 7 (1979), 229–263.

lower. For a short-term out-of-the-money call option, the chance of a takeover will generally increase the option value. For a short-term out-of-the-money put option, the chance of a takeover will generally reduce the option value.

The effects of takeover probability on values can be dramatic for these short-term out-of-the-money options. If you think your opinion of the chance of a takeover is more accurate than the market's, you can express your views clearly with options like these.

The October 19 crash is the opposite of a takeover as far as option values go. Option values then, and since then, have reflected the fear of another crash. Out-of-the-money puts have been selling for high values, and out-of-the-money calls have been selling for low values. If you think another crash is unlikely, you may want to buy out-of-the-money calls or sell out-of-the-money puts, or do both.

Now that we've looked at the 10 assumptions in the Black-Scholes formula, let's see what role, if any, they play in portfolio insurance strategies.

Portfolio Insurance

In the months before the crash, people in the United States and elsewhere became more and more interested in portfolio insurance. As I define it, portfolio insurance is any strategy whereby you reduce your stock positions when prices fall and increase them when prices rise.

Some investors use option formulas to figure how much to increase or reduce their positions as prices change. They trade in stocks or futures or short-term options to create the effect of having a long-term put against stock or a long-term call plus T-bills.

You don't need synthetic options or option formulas for portfolio insurance. You can do the same thing with a variety of systems for changing your positions as prices change. However, the assumptions behind the Black-Scholes formula also affect portfolio insurance strategies that don't use the formula.

The higher your trading costs, the less likely you are to create synthetic options or any other adjustment strategy that involves a lot of trading. On October 19, the costs of trading in futures and stocks became much higher than they had been earlier, partly because the futures were priced against the portfolio insurers. The futures were at a discount when portfolio insurers wanted to sell. This made all portfolio insurance strategies less attractive.

Portfolio insurance using synthetic strategies wins when the market makes big jumps, but without much volatility. It loses when market volatility is high, because an investor will sell after a fall and buy after a rise. He loses money on each cycle.

But the true cost of portfolio insurance, in my view, is a factor that does not even affect option values. It is the mean reversion in the market — the rate at which the expected return on the market falls as the market rises.[5]

Mean reversion is what balances supply and demand for portfolio insurance. High mean reversion will discourage portfolio insurers because it will mean they are selling when expected return is higher and buying when expected return is lower. For the same reason, high mean reversion will attract "value investors" or "tactical asset allocators," who buy after a decline and sell after a rise. Value investors use indicators like price/earnings ratios and dividend yields to decide when to buy and sell. They act as sellers of portfolio insurance.

If mean reversion were zero, I think that more investors would want to buy portfolio insurance than to sell it. People have a natural desire to try to limit their losses. But, on balance, there must be as many sellers as buyers of insurance. What makes this happen is a positive normal level of mean reversion.

The Crash

During 1987, investors shifted toward wanting more portfolio insurance. This increased the market's mean reversion. But mean reversion is hard to see; it takes years to detect a change in it. So investors did not understand that mean reversion was rising. Since rising mean reversion should restrain an increase in portfolio insurance demand, this misunderstanding caused a further increase in demand.

Because of mean reversion, the market rise during 1987 caused a sharper-than-usual fall in expected return. But investors didn't see this at first. They continued to buy, as their portfolio insurance strategies suggested. Eventually, though, they came to understand the effects of portfolio insurance on mean reversion, partly by observing the large orders that price changes brought into the market.

Around October 19, the full truth of what was happening hit investors. They saw that at existing levels of the market, the expected return was much lower than they had assumed. They sold at those levels. The market fell and expected return rose until equilibrium was restored.

---

5. For evidence of mean reversion, see Eugene Fama and Kenneth French, "Permanent and Temporary Components of Stock Prices," *Journal of Political Economy* 96, No. 2 (April 1988), 246–273; and James Poterba and Lawrence Summers, "Mean Reversion in Stock Prices: Evidence and Implications," *Journal of Financial Economics* 22, No. 1 (October 1988), 27–60.

Mean Reversion and Stock Volatility

Now that we've explained mean reversion, how can you use your view of it in your investments?

If you have a good estimate of a stock's volatility, the stock's expected return won't affect option values. Since the expected return won't affect values, neither will mean reversion.

But mean reversion may influence your estimate of the stock's volatility. With mean reversion, day-to-day volatility will be higher than month-to-month volatility, which will be higher than year-to-year volatility. Your volatility estimates for options with several years of life should generally be lower than your volatility estimates for options with several days or several months of life.

If your view of mean reversion is higher than the market's, you can buy short-term options and sell long-term options. If you think mean reversion is lower, you can do the reverse. If you are a buyer of options, you will favor short-term options when you think mean reversion is high, and long-term options when you think it is low. If you are a seller of options, you will favor long-term options when you think mean reversion is high, and short-term options when you think it's low.

These effects will be most striking in stock index options. But they will also show up in individual stock options, through the effects of market moves on individual stocks and through the influence of "trend followers." Trend followers act like portfolio insurers, but they trade individual stocks rather than portfolios. When the stock rises, they buy; and when it falls, they sell. They act as if the past trend in a stock's price is likely to continue.

In individual stocks, as in portfolios, mean reversion should normally make implied volatilities higher for short-term options than for long-term options. (An option's implied volatility is the volatility that makes its Black-Scholes value equal to its price.) If your views differ from the market's, you may have a chance for a profitable trade.

13

Option Pricing: A Simplified Approach*

John C. Cox, Stephen A. Ross, & Mark Rubinstein

1. Introduction

An option is a security that gives its owner the right to trade in a fixed number of shares of a specified common stock at a fixed price at any time on or before a given date. The act of making this transaction is referred to as exercising the option. The fixed price is termed the striking price, and the given date, the expiration date. A call option gives the right to buy the shares; a put option gives the right to sell the shares.

Options have been traded for centuries, but they remained relatively obscure financial instruments until the introduction of a listed options exchange in 1973. Since then, options trading has enjoyed an expansion unprecedented in American securities markets.

Option-pricing theory has a long and illustrious history, but it also underwent a revolutionary change in 1973. At that time, Fischer Black and Myron Scholes presented the first completely satisfactory equilibrium option-pricing model. In the same year, Robert Merton extended their model in several im-

*Our best thanks go to William Sharpe, who first suggested to us the advantages of the discrete-time approach to option pricing developed here. We are also grateful to our students over the past several years. Their favorable reactions to this way of presenting things encouraged us to write this article. We have received support from the National Science Foundation under Grant Nos. SOC-77-18087 and SOC-77-22301.

Option Pricing: A Simplified Approach 317

portant ways. These path-breaking articles have formed the basis for many subsequent academic studies.

As these studies have shown, option-pricing theory is relevant to almost every area of finance. For example, virtually all corporate securities can be interpreted as portfolios of puts and calls on the assets of the firm.[1] Indeed, the theory applies to a very general class of economic problems — the valuation of contracts where the outcome to each party depends on a quantifiable uncertain future event.

Unfortunately, the mathematical tools employed in the Black-Scholes and Merton articles are quite advanced and have tended to obscure the underlying economics. However, thanks to a suggestion by William Sharpe, it is possible to derive the same results using only elementary mathematics.[2]

In this article we will present a simple, discrete-time option-pricing formula. The fundamental economic principles of option valuation by arbitrage methods are particularly clear in this setting. Sections 2 and 3 illustrate and develop this model for a call option on a stock that pays no dividends. Section 4 shows exactly how the model can be used to lock in pure arbitrage profits if the market price of an option differs from the value given by the model. In Section 5, we will show that our approach includes the Black-Scholes model as a special limiting case. By taking the limits in a different way, we will also obtain the Cox-Ross (1975) jump process model as another special case.

Other more general option-pricing models often seem immune to reduction to a simple formula. Instead, numerical procedures must be employed to value these more complex options. Michael Brennan and Eduardo Schwartz (1977) have provided many interesting results along these lines. However, their techniques are rather complicated and are not directly related to the economic structure of the problem. Our formulation, by its very construction, leads to an alternative numerical procedure that is both simpler and, for many purposes, computationally more efficient.

Section 6 introduces these numerical procedures and extends the model to include puts and calls on stocks that pay dividends. Section 7 concludes the paper by showing how the model can be generalized in other imortant ways and discussing its essential role in valuation by arbitrage methods.

---

1. To take an elementary case, consider a firm with a single liability of a homogeneous class of pure discount bonds. The stockholders then have a "call" on the assets of the firm, which they can choose to exercise at the maturity date of the debt by paying its principal to the bondholders. In turn, the bonds can be interpreted as a portfolio containing a default-free loan with the same face value as the bonds and a short position in a put on the assets of the firm.
2. Sharpe (1978) has partially developed this approach to option pricing in his excellent new book, *Investments*. Rendleman and Bartter (1978) have recently independently discovered a similar formulation of the option-pricing problem.

2. The Basic Idea

Suppose the current price of a stock is $S = \$50$, and at the end of a period of time its price must be either $S^* = \$25$ or $S^* = \$100$. A call on the stock is available with a striking price of $K = \$50$, expiring at the end of the period.[3] It is also possible to borrow and lend at a 25% rate of interest. The one piece of information left unfurnished is the current value of the call, C. However, if riskless profitable arbitrage is not possible, we can deduce from the given information *alone* what the value of the call *must* be!

Consider forming the following levered hedge:

1. Write three calls at C each,

2. buy two shares at $50 each, and

3. borrow $40 at 25% to be paid back at the end of the period.

Table 13.1 gives the return from this hedge for each possible level of the stock price at expiration. Regardless of the outcome, the hedge exactly breaks even on the expiration date. Therefore, to prevent profitable riskless arbitrage, its current cost must be zero; that is,

$$3C - 100 + 40 = 0$$

The current value of the call must then be $C = \$20$.

If the call were not priced at $20, a sure profit would be possible. In particular, if $C = \$25$ the above hedge would yield a current cash inflow of $15 and would experience no further gain or loss in the future. On the other hand, if $C = \$15$, then the same thing could be accomplished by buying three calls, selling short two shares, and lending $40.

---

3. To keep matters simple, assume for now that the stock will pay no cash dividends during the life of the call. We also ignore transaction costs, margin requirements, and taxes.

TABLE 13.1   *Arbitrage Table Illustrating the Formation of a Riskless Hedge*

	Present Date	Expiration Date	
		$S^* = \$25$	$S^* = \$100$
Write 3 calls	$3C$	—	-150
Buy 2 shares	-100	50	200
Borrow	40	-50	-50
Total	—	—	—

Table 13.1 can be interpreted as demonstrating that *an opportunity levered position in stock will replicate the future returns of a call.* That is, if we buy shares and borrow against them in the right proportion, we can, in effect, duplicate a pure position in calls. In view of this, it should seem less surprising that all we needed to determine the *exact* value of the call was its *striking price, underlying stock price, range of movement in the underlying stock price, and the rate of interest.* What may seem more incredible is what we do not need to know: Among other things, *we do not need to know the probability that the stock price will rise or fall.* Bulls and bears must agree on the value of the call, relative to its underlying stock price!

This example is very simple, but it shows several essential features of option pricing. And we will soon see that it is not as unrealistic as it seems.

3. The Binomial Option-Pricing Formula

In this section, we will develop the framework illustrated in the example into a complete valuation method. We begin by assuming that the stock price follows a multiplicative binomial process over discrete periods. The rate of return on the stock over each period can have two possible values: $u - 1$ with probability q, or $d - 1$ with probability $1 - q$. Thus, if the current stock price is S, the stock price at the end of the period will be either uS or dS. We can represent this movement with the following diagram:

$$S < \begin{matrix} uS & \text{with probability } q \\ dS & \text{with probability } 1 - q \end{matrix}$$

We also assume that the interest rate is constant. Individuals may borrow or lend as much as they wish at this rate. To focus on the basic issues, we will continue to assume that there are no taxes, transaction costs, or margin requirements. Hence, individuals are allowed to sell short any security and receive full use of the proceeds.[4]

Letting r denote one plus the riskless interest rate over one period, we require $u > r > d$. If these inequalities do not hold, there would be profitable riskless arbitrage opportunities involving only the stock and riskless borrowing and lending.[5]

To see how to value a call on this stock, we start with the simplest situation: The expiration date is just one period away. Let C be the current value of the call, C_u be its value at the end of the period if the stock price goes to uS, and C_d be its value at the end of the period if the stock price goes to dS.

---

4. Of course, restitution is required for payouts made to securities held short.
5. We will ignore the uninteresting special case where q is zero or one and $u = d = r$.

Since there is now only one period remaining in the life of the call, we know that the terms of its contract and a rational exercise policy imply that $C_u = \max[0, uS-K]$ and $C_d = \max[0, dS-K]$. Therefore,

$$C \begin{cases} C_u = \max[0, uS-K] & \text{with probability } q \\ C_d = \max[0, dS-K] & \text{with probability } 1-q \end{cases}$$

Suppose we form a portfolio containing Δ shares of stock and the dollar amount B in riskless bonds.[6] This will cost $\Delta S + B$. At the end of the period, the value of this portfolio will be

$$\Delta S + B \begin{cases} \Delta uS + rB & \text{with probability } q \\ \Delta dS + rB & \text{with probability } 1-q \end{cases}$$

Since we can select Δ and B in any way we wish, suppose we choose them to equate the end-of-period values of the portfolio and the call for each possible outcome. This requires that

$$\Delta uS + rB = C_u$$
$$\Delta dS + rB = C_d$$

Solving these equations, we find

$$\Delta = \frac{C_u - C_d}{(u-d)S} \qquad B = \frac{uC_d - dC_u}{(u-d)r} \qquad (13.1)$$

With Δ and B chosen in this way, we will call this the hedging portfolio.

If there are to be no riskless arbitrage opportunities, the current value of the call, C, cannot be less than the current value of the hedging portfolio, $\Delta S + B$. If it were, we could make a riskless profit with no net investment by buying the call and selling the portfolio. It is tempting to say that it also cannot be worth more, since then we would have a riskless arbitrage opportunity by reversing our procedure and selling the call and buying the portfolio. But this overlooks the fact that the person who bought the call we sold has the right to exercise it immediately.

Suppose that $\Delta S + B < S - K$. If we try to make an arbitrage profit by selling calls for more than $\Delta S + B$, but less than $S - K$, then we will soon find that we are the source of arbitrage profits rather than their recipient. Anyone could make an arbitrage profit by buying our calls and exercising them immediately.

We might hope that we will be spared this embarrassment because everyone will somehow find it advantageous to hold the calls for one more period as an investment rather than take a quick profit by exercising them immediately. But each person will reason in the following way. If I do not exercise

---

6. Buying bonds is the same as lending; selling them is the same as borrowing.

now, I will receive the same payoff as a portfolio with ΔS in stock and B in bonds. If I do exercise now, I can take the proceeds, $S-K$, buy this same portfolio and some extra bonds as well, and have a higher payoff in every possible circumstance. Consequently, no one would be willing to hold the calls for one more period.

Summing up all of this, we conclude that if there are to be no riskless arbitrage opportunities, it must be true that

$$C = \Delta S + B$$

$$= \frac{C_u - C_d}{u - d} + \frac{uC_d - dC_u}{(u-d)r}$$

$$= \left[\left(\frac{r-d}{u-d} \right) C_u + \left(\frac{u-r}{u-d} \right) C_d \right] \Big/ r \qquad (13.2)$$

if this value is greater than $S-K$, and if not, $C = S - K.$[7]

Equation 13.2 can be simplified by defining

$$p \equiv \frac{r-d}{u-d} \quad \text{and} \quad 1-p \equiv \frac{u-r}{u-d}$$

so that we can write

$$C = [pC_u + (1-p)C_d]/r \qquad (13.3)$$

It is easy to see that in the present case, with no dividends, this will always be greater than $S-K$ as long as the interest rate is positive. To avoid spending time on the unimportant situations where the interest rate is less than or equal to zero, we will now assume that r is always greater than one. Hence, (13.3) is the exact formula for the value of a call one period prior to expiration in terms of S, K, u, d, and r.

To confirm this, note that if $uS \le K$, then $S < K$ and $C = 0$, so $C > S - K$. Also if $dS \ge K$, then $C = S - (K/r) > S - K$. The remaining possibility is $uS > K > dS$. In this case, $C = p(uS - K)/r$. This is greater than $S - K$ if $(1-p)dS > (p-r)K$, which is certainly true as long as $r > 1$.

This formula has a number of notable features. First, the probability q does not appear in the formula. This means, surprisingly, that even if different investors have different subjective probabilities about an upward or downward movement in the stock, they could still agree on the relationship of C to S, u, d, and r.

---

7. In some applications of the theory to other areas, it is useful to consider options that can be exercised only on the expiration date. These are usually termed European options. Those that can be exercised at any earlier time as well, such as we have been examining here, are then referred to as American options. Our discussion could easily be modified to include European calls. Since immediate exercise is then precluded, their values would always be given by (13.2), even if this is less than $S - K$.

Second, the value of the call does not depend on investors' attitudes toward risk. In constructing the formula, the only assumption we made about an individual's behavior was that he prefers more wealth to less wealth and therefore has an incentive to take advantage of profitable riskless arbitrage opportunities. We would obtain the same formula whether investors are risk averse or risk preferring.

Third, the only random variable on which the call value depends is the stock price itself. In particular, it does not depend on the random prices of other securities or portfolios, such as the market portfolio containing all securities in the economy. If another pricing formula involving other variables were submitted as giving equilibrium market prices, we could immediately show that it was incorrect by using our formula to make riskless arbitrage profits while trading at those prices.

It is easier to understand these features if it is remembered that the formula is only a relative pricing relationship giving C in terms of S, u, d, and r. Investors' attitudes toward risk and the characteristics of other assets may indeed influence call values indirectly through their effect on these variables, but they will not be separate determinants of call value.

Finally, observe that $p \equiv (r-d)/(u-d)$ is always greater than zero and less than one, so it has the properties of a probability. In fact, p is the value q would have in equilibrium if investors were risk neutral. To see this, note that the expected rate of return on the stock would then be the riskless interest rate, so

$$q(uS) + (1-q)(dS) = rS$$

and

$$q = (r-d)/(u-d) = p$$

Hence, the value of the call can be interpreted as the expectation of its discounted future value in a risk-neutral world. In light of our earlier observations, this is not surprising. Since the formula does not involve q or any measure of attitudes toward risk, then it must be the same for any set of preferences, including risk neutrality.

It is important to note that this does not imply that the equilibrium expected rate of return on the call is the riskless interest rate. Indeed, our argument has shown that, in equilibrium, holding the call over the period is exactly equivalent to holding the hedging portfolio. Consequently, the risk and expected rate of return of the call must be the same as that of the hedging portfolio. It can be shown that $\Delta \geq 0$ and $B \leq 0$, so the hedging portfolio is equivalent to a particular levered long position in the stock. In equilibrium, the same is true for the call. Of course, if the call is currently mispriced, its risk and expected return over the period will differ from that of the hedging portfolio.

Now we can consider the next simplest situation: a call with two periods remaining before its expiration date. In keeping with the binomial process, the stock can take on three possible value after two periods,

$$
S \Bigg\langle \begin{array}{c} uS \Big\langle \begin{array}{c} u^2 S \\ duS \end{array} \\ dS \Big\langle \begin{array}{c} \\ d^2 S \end{array} \end{array}
$$

similarly, for the call,

$$
C \Bigg\langle \begin{array}{c} C_u \Big\langle \begin{array}{l} C_{uu} = \max[0, u^2 S - K] \\ C_{du} = \max[0, duS - K] \end{array} \\ C_d \Big\langle \begin{array}{l} \\ C_{dd} = \max[0, d^2 S - K] \end{array} \end{array}
$$

C_{uu} stands for the value of a call two periods from the current time if the stock price moves upward each period; C_{du} and C_{dd} have analogous definitions.

At the end of the current period there will be one period left in the life of the call and we will be faced with a problem identical to the one we just solved. Thus, from our previous analysis, we know that when there are two periods left,

$$
C_u = [pC_{uu} + (1-p)C_{ud}]/r
$$

and

$$
C_d = [pC_{du} + (1-p)C_{dd}]/r \tag{13.4}
$$

Again we can select a portfolio with ΔS in stock and B in bonds whose end-of-period value will be C_u if the stock price goes to uS, and C_d if the stock price goes to dS. Indeed, the functional form of Δ and B remains unchanged. To get the new values of Δ and B, we simply use Equation 13.1 with the new values of C_u and C_d.

Can we now say, as before, that an opportunity for profitable riskless arbitrage will be available if the current price of the call is not equal to the new value of this portfolio or $S - K$, whichever is greater? Yes, but there is an important difference. With one period to go, we could plan to lock in a riskless profit by selling an overpriced call and using part of the proceeds to buy the hedging portfolio. At the end of the period, we knew that the market price of the call must be equal to the value of the portfolio, so the entire position could be safely liquidated at that point. But this was true only because the end of the period was the expiration date. Now we have no such guarantee. At the end of the current period, when there is still one period left, the market price of the call could still be in disequilibrium and be greater than the value of the hedging portfolio. If we closed out the position then, selling the portfolio and repurchasing the call, we could suffer a loss that would more than offset our original profit. However, we could always avoid this loss by maintaining the portfolio for one more period. The value of the portfolio at the end of the current period will always be exactly sufficient to purchase the portfolio we would want to hold over the last period. In effect, we would have to readjust the proportions in the hedging portfolio, but we would not have to put up any more money.

Consequently, we conclude that even with two periods to go, there is a strategy we could follow that would guarantee riskless profits with no net investment if the current market price of a call differs from the maximum of $\Delta S + B$ and $S - K$. Hence, the larger of these is the current value of the call.

Since Δ and B have the same functional form in each period, the current value of the call in terms of C_u and C_d will again be $C = [pC_u + (1-p)C_d]/r$ if this is greater than $S - K$, and $C = S - K$ otherwise. By substituting from Equation 13.4 into the former expression and noting that $C_{du} = C_{ud}$, we obtain

$$
\begin{aligned}
C &= [p^2 C_{uu} + 2p(1-p)C_{ud} + (1-p)^2 C_{dd}]/r^2 \\
&= [p^2 \max[0, u^2 S - K] + 2p(1-p) \max[0, duS - K] \\
&\quad + (1-p)^2 \max[0, d^2 S - K]]/r^2
\end{aligned}
\tag{13.5}
$$

A little algebra shows that this is always greater than $S - K$ if, as assumed, r is always greater than one, so this expression gives the exact value of the call.[8]

All of the observations made about Equation 13.3 also apply to Equation 13.5, except that the number of periods remaining until expiration, n, now emerges clearly as an additional determinant of the call value. For Equation 13.5, $n = 2$. That is, the full list of variables determining C is S, K, n, u, d, and r.

We now have a recursive procedure for finding the value of a call with any number of periods to go. By starting at the expiration date and working backwards, we can write down the general valuation formula for any n:

---

8. In the current situation, with no dividends, we can show by a simple direct argument that if there are no arbitrage opportunities, then the call value must always be greater than $S - K$ before the expiration date. Suppose that the call is selling for $S - K$. Then there would be an easy arbitrage strategy that would require no initial investment and would always have a positive return. All we would have to do is buy the call, short the stock, and invest K dollars in bonds. See Merton (1973). In the general case, with dividends such an argument is no longer valid, and we must use the procedure of checking every period.

$$C = \left[\sum_{j=0}^{n} \left(\frac{n!}{j!\,(n-j)!} \right) p^j (1-p)^{n-j} \max[0, u^j d^{n-j} S - K] \right] \bigg/ r^n \qquad (13.6)$$

This gives us the complete formula, but with a little additional effort we can express it in a more convenient way.

Let a stand for the minimum number of upward moves that the stock must take over the next n periods for the call to finish in the money. Thus a will be the smallest nonnegative integer such that $u^a d^{n-a} S > K$. By taking the natural logarithm of both sides of this inequality, we could write a as the smallest nonnegative integer greater than $\log(K/Sd^n)/\log(u/d)$.

For all $j < a$,

$$\max[0, u^j d^{n-j} S - K] = 0$$

and for all $j \geq a$,

$$\max[0, u^j d^{n-j} S - K] = u^j d^{n-j} S - K$$

Therefore,

$$C = \left[\sum_{j=a}^{n} \left(\frac{n!}{j!\,(n-j)!} \right) p^j (1-p)^{n-j} [u^j d^{n-j} S - K] \right] \bigg/ r^n$$

Of course, if $a > n$ the call will finish out of the money even if the stock moves upward every period, so its current value must be zero.

By breaking up C into two terms, we can write

$$C = S \left[\sum_{j=a}^{n} \left(\frac{n!}{j!\,(n-j)!} \right) p^j (1-p)^{n-j} \left(\frac{u^j d^{n-j}}{r^n} \right) \right]$$

$$- K r^{-n} \left[\sum_{j=a}^{n} \left(\frac{n!}{j!\,(n-j)!} \right) p^j (1-p)^{n-j} \right]$$

Now, the latter bracketed expression is the complementary binomial distribution function $\Phi[a; n, p]$. The first bracketed expression can also be interpreted as a complementary binomial distribution function $\Phi[a; n, p']$, where

$$p' \equiv (u/r)p \quad \text{and} \quad 1 - p' \equiv (d/r)(1-p)$$

p' is a probability, since $0 < p' < 1$. To see this, note that $p < (r/u)$ and

$$p^j (1-p)^{n-j} \left(\frac{u^j d^{n-j}}{r^n} \right) = \left[\frac{u}{r} p \right]^j \left[\frac{d}{r} (1-p) \right]^{n-j} = p'^j (1-p')^{n-j}$$

In summary, the binomial option-pricing formula is

$$C = S\Phi[a; n, p'] - K r^{-n} \Phi[a; n, p]$$

where

$p \equiv (r-d)/(u-d)$ and $p' \equiv (u/r)p$,

$a \equiv$ the smallest nonnegative integer greater than $\log(K/Sd^n)/\log(u/d)$.

If $a > n$ then $C = 0$.

It is now clear that all of the comments we made about the one-period valuation formula are valid for any number of periods. In particular, the value of a call should be the expectation, in a risk-neutral world, of the discounted value of the payoff it will receive. In fact, that is exactly what Equation 13.6 says. Why then should we waste time with the recursive procedure when we can write down the answer in one direct step? The reason is that while this one-step approach is always technically correct, it is really useful only if we know in advance the circumstances in which a rational individual would prefer to exercise the call before the expiration date. If we do not know this, we have no way to compute the required expectation. In the present example, a call on a stock paying no dividends, it happens that we can determine this information from other sources: The call should never be exercised before its expiration date. As we will see in Section 6, with puts or with calls on stocks that pay dividends we will not be so lucky. Finding the optimal exercise strategy will be an integral part of the valuation problem. The full recursive procedure will then be necessary.

For some readers, an alternative "complete markets" interpretation of our binomial approach may be instructive. Suppose that π_u and π_d represent the state-contingent discount rates to states u and d, respectively. Therefore, π_u would be the current price of one dollar received at the end of the period, if and only if state u occurs. Each security—a riskless bond, the stock, and the option—must all have returns discounted to the present by π_u and π_d if no riskless arbitrage opportunities are available. Therefore,

$$1 = \pi_u r + \pi_d r$$
$$S = \pi_u(uS) + \pi_d(dS)$$
$$C = \pi_u C_u + \pi_d C_d$$

The first two equations, for the bond and the stock, imply

$$\pi_u = \left(\frac{r-d}{u-d}\right)\frac{1}{r} \quad \text{and} \quad \pi_d = \left(\frac{u-r}{u-d}\right)\frac{1}{r}$$

Substituting these equalities for the state-contingent prices in the last equation for the option yields Equation 13.3.

It is important to realize that we are not assuming that the riskless bond and the stock and the option are the only three securities in the economy, or that other securities must follow a binomial process. Rather, however these securities are priced in relation to others in equilibrium, among themselves they must conform to the above relationships.

From either the hedging or complete markets approaches, it should be clear that three-state or trinomial stock price movements will not lead to an option-pricing formula based solely on arbitrage considerations. Suppose, for example, that over each period the stock price could move to uS or dS or remain the same at S. A choice of Δ and B that would equate the returns in two states could not in the third. That is, a riskless arbitrage position could not be taken. Under the complete markets interpretation, with three equations in now three unknown state-contingent prices, we would lack the redundant equation necessary to price one security in terms of the other two.

4. Riskless Trading Strategies

The following numerical example illustrates how we could use the formula if the current *market price M* ever diverged from its *formula value C*. If $M > C$ we would hedge, and if $M < C$, "reverse hedge," to try and lock in a profit. Suppose the values of the underlying variables are

$$S = 80, \quad n = 3, \quad K = 80, \quad u = 1.5, \quad d = 0.5, \quad r = 1.1$$

In this case, $p = (r - d)/(u - d) = 0.6$. The relevant values of the discount factor are

$$r^{-1} = 0.909, \quad r^{-2} = 0.826, \quad r^{-3} = 0.751$$

The paths the stock price may follow and their corresponding probabilities (using probability p) are, when $n = 3$, with $S = 80$,

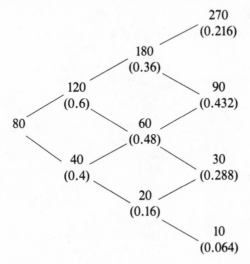

when $n = 2$, if $S = 120$,

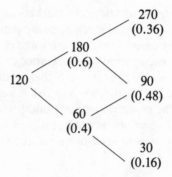

when $n = 2$, if $S = 40$,

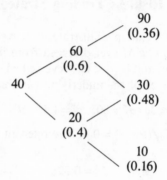

Using the formula, the current value of the call would be

$$C = 0.751[0.064(0) + 0.288(0) + 0.432(90 - 80) + 0.216(270 - 80)]$$
$$= 34.065$$

Recall that to form a riskless hedge, for each call we sell, we buy and subsequently keep adjusted a portfolio with ΔS in stock and B in bonds, where $\Delta = (C_u - C_d)/(u - d)S$. The following tree diagram gives the path the call value may follow and the corresponding values of Δ:

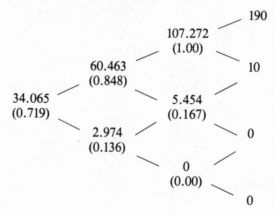

With this preliminary analysis, we are prepared to use the formula to take advantage of mispricing in the market. Suppose that when $n = 3$, the market price of the call is 36. Our formula tells us the call should be worth 34.065. The option is overpriced, so we could plan to sell it and assure ourselves of a profit equal to the mispricing differential. Here are the steps you could take for a typical path the stock might follow.

Step 1 ($n = 3$): Sell the call for 36. Take 34.065 of this and invest it in a portfolio containing $\Delta = 0.719$ shares of stock by borrowing $0.719(80) - 34.065 = 23.455$. Take the remainder, $36 - 34.065 = 1.935$, and put it in the bank.

Step 2 ($n = 2$): Suppose the stock goes to 120 so that the new Δ is 0.848. Buy $0.848 - 0.719 = 0.129$ more shares of stock at 120 per share for a total expenditure of 15.480. Borrow to pay the bill. With an interest rate of 0.1, you already owe $23.455(1.1) = 25.801$. Thus, your total current indebtedness is $25.801 + 15.480 = 41.281$.

Step 3 ($n = 1$): Suppose the stock price now goes to 60. The new Δ is 0.167. Sell $0.848 - 0.167 = 0.681$ shares at 60 per share, taking in $0.681(60) = 40.860$. Use this to pay back part of your borrowing. Since you now owe $41.281(1.1) = 45.409$, the repayment will reduce this to $45.409 - 40.860 = 4.549$.

Step 4d ($n = 0$): Suppose the stock price now goes to 30. The call you sold has expired worthless. You own 0.167 shares of stock selling at 30 per share, for a total value of $0.167(30) = 5$. Sell the stock and repay the $4.549(1.1) = 5$ that you now owe on the borrowing. Go back to the bank and withdraw your original deposit, which has now grown to $1.935(1.1)^3 = 2.575$.

Step 4u ($n = 0$): Suppose, instead, the stock price goes to 90. The call you sold is in the money at the expiration date. Buy back the call, or buy one share of stock and let it be exercised, incurring a loss of $90 - 80 = 10$ either way. Borrow to cover this, bringing your current indebtedness to $5 + 10 = 15$. You own 0.167 shares of stock selling at 90 per share, for a total value of $0.167(90) = 15$. Sell the stock and repay the borrowing. Go back to the bank and withdraw your original deposit, which has now grown to $1.935(1.1)^3 = 2.575$.

In summary, if we were correct in our original analysis about stock price movements (which did not involve the unenviable task of predicting whether the stock price would go up or down) and if we faithfully adjust our portfolio as prescribed by the formula, then we can be assured of walking away in the clear at the expiration date while still keeping the original differential and the interest it has accumulated. It is true that closing out the position before the expiration date, which involves buying back the option at its then current market price, might produce a loss that would more than offset our profit, but this loss could always be avoided by waiting until the expiration date. Moreover, if the market price comes into line with the formula value before the expiration date, we can close out the position then with no loss and be rid of the concern of keeping the portfolio adjusted.

It still might seem that we are depending on rational behavior by the person who bought the call we sold. If instead he behaves foolishly and exercises at the wrong time, could he make things worse for us as well as for himself? Fortunately, the answer is no. Mistakes on his part can only mean greater profits for us. Suppose that he exercises too soon. In that circumstance, the hedging portfolio will always be worth more than $S - K$, so we could close out the position then with an extra profit.

Suppose instead that he fails to exercise when it would be optimal to do so. Again there is no problem. Since exercise is now optimal, our hedging portfolio will be worth $S - K$.[9] If he had exercised, this would be exactly sufficient to meet the obligation and close out the position. Since he did not, the call will be held at least one more period, so we calculate the new values of C_u and C_d and revise our hedging portfolio accordingly. But now the amount required for the portfolio, $\Delta S + B$, is less than the amount we have available, $S - K$. We can withdraw these extra profits now and still maintain the hedging portfolio. The longer the holder of the call goes on making mistakes, the better off we will be.

Consequently, we can be confident that things will eventually work out right no matter what the other party does. The return on our total position, when evaluated at prevailing market prices at intermediate times, may be negative. But over a period ending no later than the expiration date, it will be positive.

In conducting the hedging operation, the essential thing was to maintain the proper proportional relationship: For each call we are short, we hold Δ shares of stock and the dollar amount B in bonds in the hedging portfolio. To emphasize this, we will refer to the number of shares held for each call as the hedge ratio. In our example, we kept the number of calls constant and made adjustments by buying or selling stock and bonds. As a result, our profit was independent of the market price of the call between the time we initiated the hedge and the expiration date. If things got worse before they got better, it did not matter to us.

Instead, we could have made the adjustments by keeping the number of shares of stock constant and buying or selling calls and bonds. However, this could be dangerous. Suppose that after initiating the position, we needed

---

9. If we were reverse hedging by buying an undervalued call and selling the hedging portfolio, then we would ourselves want to exercise at this point. Since we will receive $S - K$ from exercising, this will be exactly enough money to buy back the hedging portfolio.

to increase the hedge ratio to maintain the proper proportions. This can be achieved in two ways:

1. buy more stock, or
2. buy back some of the calls.

If we adjust through the stock, there is no problem. If we insist on adjusting through the calls, not only is the hedge no longer riskless, but it could even end up losing money! This can happen if the call has become even more overpriced. We would then be closing out part of our position in calls at a loss. To remain hedged, the number of calls we would need to buy back depends on their value, not their price. Therefore, since we are uncertain about their price, we then become uncertain about the return from the hedge. Worse yet, if the call price gets high enough, the loss on the closed portion of our position could throw the hedge operation into an overall loss.

To see how this could happen, let us rerun the hedging operation where we adjust the hedge ratio by buying and selling calls.

Step 1 ($n = 3$): Same as before.

Step 2 ($n = 2$): Suppose the stock goes to 120, so that the new $\Delta = 0.848$. The call price has gotten further out of line and is now selling for 75. Since its value is 60.463, it is now overpriced by 14.537. With 0.719 shares, you must buy back $1 - 0.848 = 0.152$ calls to produce a hedge ratio of $0.848 = 0.719/0.848$. This costs $75(0.152) = 11.40$. Borrow to pay the bill. With the interest rate of 0.1, you already owe $23.455(1.1) = 25.801$. Thus, your total current indebtedness is $25.801 + 11.40 = 37.201$.

Step 3 ($n = 1$): Suppose the stock goes to 60 and the call is selling for 5.454. Since the call is now fairly valued, no further excess profits can be made by continuing to hold the position. Therefore, liquidate by selling your 0.719 shares for $0.719(60) = 43.14$ and close out the call position by buying back 0.848 calls for $0.848(5.454) = 4.625$. This nets $43.14 - 4.625 = 38.515$. Use this to pay back part of your borrowing. Since you now owe $37.20(1.1) = 40.921$, after repayment you owe 2.406. Go back to the bank and withdraw your original deposit, which has now grown to $1.935(1.1)^2 = 2.341$. Unfortunately, after using this to repay your remaining borrowing, you still owe 0.065.

Since we adjusted our position at Step 2 by buying overpriced calls, our profit is reduced. Indeed, since the calls were considerably overpriced, we actually lost money despite apparent profitability of the position at Step 1. We can draw the following adjustment rule from our experiment: *To adjust a hedged position, never buy an overpriced option or sell an underpriced option.* As a corollary, whenever we can adjust a hedged position by buying more of an underpriced option or selling more of an overpriced option, our profit will be enhanced if we do so. For example, at Step 3 in the original hedging illustration, had the call still been overpriced, it would have been better to adjust the position by selling more calls rather than selling stock. In summary, by choosing the right side of the position to adjust at intermediate dates, *at a minimum* we can be assured of earning the original differential and its accumulated interest, and we may earn considerably more.

5. Limiting Cases

In reading the previous sections, there is a natural tendency to associate with each period some particular length of calendar time, perhaps a day. With this in mind, you may have had two objections. In the first place, prices a day from now may take on many more than just two possible values. Furthermore, the market is not open for trading only once a day, but, instead, trading takes place almost continuously.

These objections are certainly valid. Fortunately, our option-pricing approach has the flexibility to meet them. Although it might have been natural to think of a period as one day, there was nothing that forced us to do so. We could have taken it to be a much shorter interval — say an hour, or even a minute. By doing so, we have met both objections simultaneously. Trading would take place far more frequently, and the stock price could take on hundreds of values by the end of the day.

However, if we do this, we have to make some other adjustments to keep the probability small that the stock price will change by a large amount over a minute. We do not want to stock to have the same percentage up and down moves for one minute as it did before for one day. But again there is no need for us to have to use the same values. We could, for example, think of the price as making only a very small percentage change over each minute.

To make this more precise, suppose that h represents the elapsed time between successive stock price changes. That is, if t is the fixed length of calendar time to expiration, and n is the number of periods of length h prior to expiration, then

$$h \equiv t/n$$

As trading takes place more and more frequently, h gets closer and closer to zero. We must then adjust the interval-dependent variables r, u, and d in such a way that we obtain empirically realistic results as h becomes smaller, or, equivalently, as $n \to \infty$.

When we were thinking of the periods as having a fixed length, r represented both the interest rate over a fixed length of calendar time and the interest rate over one period. Now we need to make a distinction between these two meanings. We will let r continue to mean one plus the interest rate over a fixed length of calendar time. When we have occasion to refer to one plus the interest rate over a period (trading interval) of length h, we will use the symbol $\hat{r}$.

Clearly, the size of $\hat{r}$ depends on the number of subintervals, n, into which t is divided. Over the n periods until expiration, the total return is $\hat{r}^n$, where $n = t/h$. Now not only do we want $\hat{r}$ to depend on n, but we want it to depend on n in a particular way — so that as n changes the total return $\hat{r}^n$ over the fixed time t remains the same. This is because the interest rate obtainable over some fixed length of calendar time should have nothing to do with how we choose to think of the length of the time interval h.

If r (without the "hat") denotes one plus the rate of interest over a *fixed* unit of calendar time, then over elapsed time t, r^t is the total return.[10] Observe that this measure of total return does not depend on n. As we have argued, we want to choose the dependence of $\hat{r}$ on n, so that

$$\hat{r}^n = r^t$$

for any choice of n. Therefore, $\hat{r} = r^{t/n}$. This last equation shows how $\hat{r}$ must depend on n for the total return over elapsed time t to be independent of n.

We also need to define u and d in terms of n. At this point, there are two significantly different paths we can take. Depending on the definitions we choose, as $n \to \infty$ (or, equivalently, as $h \to 0$), we can have either a continuous or a jump stochastic process. In the first situation, very small random changes in the stock price will be occurring in each very small time interval. The stock price will fluctuate incessantly, but its path can be drawn without lifting pen from paper. In contrast, in the second case, the stock price will usually move in a smooth deterministic way, but will occasionally experience sudden discontinuous changes. Both can be derived from our binomial process simply by choosing how u and d depend on n. We examine in detail only the continuous process that leads to the option-pricing formula originally derived by Fischer Black and Myron Scholes. Subsequently, we indicate how to develop the jump process formula originally derived by John Cox and Stephen Ross.

Recall that we supposed that over each period the stock price would experience a one plus rate of return of u with probability q, and d with probability $1 - q$. It will be easier and clearer to work, instead, with the natural logarithm of the one plus rate of return, $\log u$ or $\log d$. This gives the continuously compounded rate of return on the stock over each period. It is a random variable that in each period will be equal to $\log u$ with probability q, and $\log d$ with probability $1 - q$.

Consider a typical sequence of five moves, say u, d, u, u, d. Then the final stock price will be $S^* = uduudS$; $S^*/S = u^3 d^2$, and $\log(S^*/S) = 3 \log u + 2 \log d$. More generally, over n periods,

---

10. The scale of this unit (perhaps a day, or a year) is unimportant as long as r and t are expressed in the same scale.

$$\log(S^*/S) = j \log u + (n-j) \log d = j \log(u/d) + n \log d$$

where j is the (random) number of upward moves occurring during the n periods to expiration. Therefore, the expected value of $\log(S^*/S)$ is

$$E[\log(S^*/S)] = \log(u/d) \cdot E(j) + n \log d$$

and its variance is

$$\text{var}[\log(S^*/S)] = [\log(u/d)]^2 \cdot \text{var}(j)$$

Each of the n possible upward moves has probability q. Thus, $E(j) = nq$. Also, since the variance each period is $q(1-q)^2 + (1-q)(0-q)^2 = q(1-q)$, then $\text{var}(j) = nq(1-q)$. Combining all of this, we have

$$E[\log(S^*/S)] = [q \log(u/d) + \log d]n \equiv \hat{\mu}n$$

$$\text{var}[\log(S^*/S)] = q(1-q)[\log(u/d)]^2 n \equiv \hat{\sigma}^2 n$$

Let us go back to our discussion. We were considering dividing up our original longer time period (a day) into many shorter periods (a minute or even less). Our procedure calls for, over a fixed length of calendar time t, making n larger and larger. Now if we held everything else constant while we let n become large, we would be faced with the problem we talked about earlier. In fact, we would certainly not reach a reasonable conclusion if either $\hat{\mu}n$ or $\hat{\sigma}^2 n$ went to zero or infinity as n became large. Since t is a fixed length of time, in searching for a realistic result we must make the appropriate adjustments in u, d, and q. In doing that, we would at least want the mean and variance of the continuously compounded rate of return of the assumed stock price movement to coincide with that of the actual stock price as $n \to \infty$. Suppose we label the actual empirical values of $\hat{\mu}n$ and $\hat{\sigma}^2 n$ as μt and $\sigma^2 t$, respectively. Then we would want to choose u, d, and q so that

$$\begin{aligned} [q \log(u/d) + \log d]n &\to \mu \\ q(1-q)[\log(u/d)]^2 n &\to \sigma^2 t \end{aligned} \quad \text{as } n \to \infty$$

A little algebra shows we can accomplish this by letting

$$u = e^{\sigma\sqrt{t/n}} \qquad d = e^{-\sigma\sqrt{t/n}} \qquad q = \tfrac{1}{2} + \tfrac{1}{2}(\mu/\sigma)\sqrt{t/n}$$

In this case, for any n,

$$\hat{\mu}n = \mu t \quad \text{and} \quad \hat{\sigma}^2 n = [\sigma^2 - \mu^2(t/n)]t$$

Clearly, as $n \to \infty$, $\hat{\sigma}^2 n \to \sigma^2 t$, while $\hat{\mu}n = \mu t$ for all values of n.

Alternatively, we could have chosen u, d, and q so that the mean and variance of the future stock price for the discrete binomial process approach the prespecified mean and variance of the actual stock price as $n \to \infty$. However, just as we would expect, the same values will accomplish this as well. Because this would not change our conclusions and it is computationally more convenient to work with the continuously compounded rates of return, we will proceed in that way.

This satisfies our initial requirement that the limiting means and variances coincide, but we still need to verify that we are arriving at a sensible limiting probability distribution of the continuously compounded rate of return. The mean and variance only describe certain aspects of that distribution.

For our model, the random continuously compounded rate of return over a period of length t is the sum of n independent random variables, each of which can take the value log u with probability q, and log d with probability $1 - q$. We wish to know about the distribution of this sum as n becomes large and q, u, and d are chosen in the way described. We need to remember that as we change n, we are not simply adding one more random variable to the previous sum, but instead are changing the probabilities and possible outcomes for every member of the sum. At this point, we can rely on a form of the central limit theorem that when applied to our problem says that, as $n \to \infty$, if

$$\frac{q|\log u - \hat{\mu}|^3 + (1 - q)|\log d - \hat{\mu}|^3}{\hat{\sigma}^3 \sqrt{n}} \to 0$$

then

$$\text{Prob}\left[\left(\frac{\log(S^*/S) - \hat{\mu}n}{\hat{\sigma}\sqrt{n}}\right) \leq z\right] \to N(z)$$

where $N(z)$ is the standard normal distribution function. Putting this into words, as the number of periods into which the fixed length of time to expiration is divided approaches infinity, the probability that the standardized continuously compounded rate of return of the stock through the expiration date is not greater than the number z approaches the probability under a standard normal distribution.

The initial condition says roughly that higher-order properties of the distribution (such as how it is skewed) become less and less important, relative to its standard deviation, as $n \to \infty$. We can verify that the condition is satisfied by making the appropriate substitutions and finding

$$\frac{q|\log u - \hat{\mu}|^3 + (1 - q)|\log d - \hat{\mu}|^3}{\hat{\sigma}^3 \sqrt{n}} = \frac{(1 - q)^2 + q^2}{\sqrt{nq(1 - q)}}$$

which goes to zero as $n \to \infty$ since $q = \frac{1}{2} + \frac{1}{2}(\mu/\sigma)\sqrt{t/n}$. Thus, the multiplicative binomial model for stock prices includes the lognormal distribution as a limiting case.

Black and Scholes began directly with continuous trading and the assumption of a lognormal distribution for stock prices. Their approach relied on some quite advanced mathematics. However, since our approach contains continuous trading and the lognormal distribution as a limiting case, the two resulting formulas should then coincide. We will see shortly that this is indeed true, and we will have the advantage of using a much simpler method. It is important to remember, however, that the economic arguments we used to link the option value and the stock price are exactly the same as those advanced by Black and Scholes (1973) and Merton (1973, 1977).

The formula derived by Black and Scholes, rewritten in terms of our notation as the Black-Scholes option-pricing formula, is

$$C = SN(x) - Kr^{-t}N(x - \sigma\sqrt{t})$$

where

$$x \equiv \frac{\log(S/Kr^{-t})}{\sigma\sqrt{t}} + \frac{1}{2}\sigma\sqrt{t}$$

We now wish to confirm that our binomial formula converges to the Black-Scholes formula when t is divided into more and more subintervals, and $\hat{r}$, u, d, and q are chosen in the way we described—that is, in a way such that the multiplicative binomial probability distribution of stock prices goes to the lognormal distribution.

For easy reference, let us recall our binomial option-pricing formula:

$$C = S\Phi[a; n, p'] - K\hat{r}^{-n}\Phi[a; n, p]$$

The similarities are readily apparent. $\hat{r}^{-n}$ is, of course, always equal to r^{-t}. Therefore, to show the two formulas converge, we need only show that as $n \to \infty$,

$$\Phi[a; n, p'] \to N(x) \quad \text{and} \quad \Phi[a; n, p] \to N(x - \sigma\sqrt{t})$$

We will consider only $\Phi[a; n, p]$, since the argument is exactly the same for $\Phi[a; n, p']$.

The complementary binomial distribution function $\Phi[a; n, p]$ is the probability that the sum of n random variables, each of which can take on the value 1 with probability p and 0 with probability $1 - p$, will be greater than or equal to a. We know that the random value of this sum, j, has mean np and standard deviation $\sqrt{np(1-p)}$. Therefore,

$$1 - \Phi[a; n, p] = \text{Prob}[j \leq a - 1] = \text{Prob}\left[\frac{j - np}{\sqrt{np(1-p)}} \leq \frac{a - 1 - np}{\sqrt{np(1-p)}}\right]$$

Now we can make an analogy with our earlier discussion. If we consider a stock that in each period will move to uS with probability p, and dS with probability $1 - p$, then $\log(S^*/S) = j\log(u/d) + n\log d$. The mean and variance of the continuously compounded rate of return of this stock are

$$\hat{\mu}_p = p\log(u/d) + \log d \quad \text{and} \quad \hat{\sigma}_p^2 = p(1-p)[\log(u/d)]^2$$

Using these equalities, we find that

$$\frac{j - np}{\sqrt{np(1-p)}} = \frac{\log(S^*/S) - \hat{\mu}_p n}{\hat{\sigma}_p\sqrt{n}}$$

Recall from the binomial formula that

$$a-1 = \log(K/Sd^n)/\log(u/d) - \epsilon = [\log(K/S) - n \log d]/\log(u/d) - \epsilon$$

where ϵ is a number between zero and one. Using this and the definitions of $\hat{\mu}_p$ and $\hat{\sigma}_p^2$, with a little algebra, we have

$$\frac{a-1-np}{\sqrt{np(1-p)}} = \frac{\log(K/S) - \hat{\mu}_p n - \epsilon \log(u/d)}{\hat{\sigma}_p \sqrt{n}}$$

Putting these results together,

$$1 - \Phi[a; n, p] = \text{Prob}\left[\frac{\log(S^*/S) - \hat{\mu}_p n}{\hat{\sigma}_p \sqrt{n}} \le \frac{\log(K/S) - \hat{\mu}_p n - \epsilon \log(u/d)}{\hat{\sigma}_p \sqrt{n}}\right]$$

We are now in a position to apply the central limit theorem. First, we must check if the initial condition,

$$\frac{p|\log u - \hat{\mu}_p|^3 + (1-p)|\log d - \hat{\mu}_p|^3}{\hat{\sigma}_p \sqrt{n}} = \frac{(1-p)^2 + p^2}{\sqrt{np(1-p)}} \to 0$$

as $n \to \infty$, is satisfied. By first recalling that $p \equiv (\hat{r} - d)/(u - d)$, and then $\hat{r} = r^{t/n}$, $u = e^{\sigma\sqrt{t/n}}$, and $d = e^{-\sigma\sqrt{t/n}}$, it is possible to show that as $n \to \infty$,

$$p \to \frac{1}{2} + \frac{1}{2}\left(\frac{\log r - \frac{1}{2}\sigma^2}{\sigma}\right)\sqrt{\frac{t}{n}}$$

As a result, the initial condition holds, and we are justified in applying the central limit theorem.

To do so, we need only evaluate $\hat{\mu}_p n$, $\hat{\sigma}_p^2 n$ and $\log(u/d)$ as $n \to \infty$.[11] Examination of our discussion for parameterizing q shows that as $n \to \infty$,

---

11. A surprising feature of this evaluation is that although $p \ne q$ and thus $\hat{\mu}_p \ne \hat{\mu}$, and $\hat{\sigma}_p \ne \hat{\sigma}$, nonetheless $\hat{\sigma}_p \sqrt{n}$ and $\hat{\sigma}\sqrt{n}$ have the same limiting value as $n \to \infty$. By contrast, since $\mu \ne \log r - (\frac{1}{2}\sigma^2)$, $\hat{\mu}_p n$ and $\hat{\mu} n$ do not. This results from the way we needed to specify u and d to obtain convergence to a lognormal distribution. Rewriting this as $\sigma\sqrt{t} = (\log u)\sqrt{n}$, it is clear that the limiting value σ of the standard deviation does not depend on p or q, and hence must be the same for either. However, at any point before the limit, since

$$\hat{\sigma}^2 n = \left(\sigma^2 - \mu^2\frac{t}{n}\right)t \quad \text{and} \quad \hat{\sigma}_p^2 n = \left[\sigma^2 - (\log r - \frac{1}{2}\sigma^2)^2\frac{t}{n}\right]t$$

$\hat{\sigma}$ and $\hat{\sigma}_p$ will generally have different values.

The fact that $\hat{\mu}_p n \to (\log r - \frac{1}{2}\sigma^2)t$ can also be derived from the property of the lognormal distribution that

$$\log E[S^*/S] = \mu_p t + \frac{1}{2}\sigma^2 t$$

where E and μ_p are measured with respect to probability p. Since $p = (\hat{r} - d)/(u - d)$, it follows that $\hat{r} = pu + (1-p)d$. For independently distributed random variables, the expectation of a product equals the product of their expectations. Therefore,

$$E[S^*/S] = [pu + (1-p)d]^n = \hat{r}^n = r^t$$

Substituting r^t for $E[S^*/S]$ in the previous equation, we have

$$\mu_p = \log r - \frac{1}{2}\sigma^2$$

$$\hat{\mu}_p n \rightarrow (\log r - \tfrac{1}{2}\sigma^2)t \quad \text{and} \quad \hat{\sigma}_p\sqrt{n} \rightarrow \sigma\sqrt{t}$$

Furthermore, $\log(u/d) \rightarrow 0$ as $n \rightarrow \infty$.

For this application of the central limit theorem, then, since

$$\frac{\log(K/S) - \hat{\mu}_p n - \epsilon\log(u/d)}{\hat{\sigma}_p\sqrt{n}} \rightarrow z = \frac{\log(K/S) - (\log r - \tfrac{1}{2}\sigma^2)t}{\sigma\sqrt{t}}$$

we have

$$1 - \Phi[a; n, p] \rightarrow N(z) = N\left[\frac{\log(Kr^{-t}/S)}{\sigma\sqrt{t}} + \tfrac{1}{2}\sigma\sqrt{t}\right]$$

The final step in the argument is to use the symmetry property of the standard normal distribution that $1 - N(z) = N(-z)$. Therefore, as $n \rightarrow \infty$,

$$\Phi[a; n, p] \rightarrow N(-z) = N\left[\frac{\log(S/Kr^{-t})}{\sigma\sqrt{t}} - \tfrac{1}{2}\sigma\sqrt{t}\right] = N(x - \sigma\sqrt{t})$$

Since a similar argument holds for $\Phi[a; n, p']$, this completes our demonstration that the binomial option pricing formula contains the Black-Scholes formula as a limiting case.[12, 13]

As we have remarked, the seeds of both the Black-Scholes formula and a continuous-time jump process formula are both contained within the binomial formulation. At which end point we arrive depends on how we take limits. Suppose, in place of our former correspondence for u, d, and q, we instead set

---

12. The only difference is that, as $n \rightarrow \infty$, $p' \rightarrow \tfrac{1}{2} + \tfrac{1}{2}[(\log r + \tfrac{1}{2}\sigma^2)/\sigma]\sqrt{t/n}$.

   Further, it can be shown that as $n \rightarrow \infty$, $\Delta \rightarrow N(x)$. Therefore, for the Black-Scholes model, $\Delta S = SN(x)$ and $B = -Kr^{-t}N(x - \sigma\sqrt{t})$.

13. In our original development, we obtained the following equation (somewhat rewritten) relating the call prices in successive periods:

$$\left(\frac{\hat{r} - d}{u - d}\right)C_u + \left(\frac{u - \hat{r}}{u - d}\right)C_d - \hat{r}C = 0$$

By their more difficult methods, Black and Scholes obtained directly a partial differential equation analogous to our discrete-time difference equation. Their equation is

$$\tfrac{1}{2}\sigma^2 S^2\frac{\partial^2 C}{\partial S^2} + (\log r)S\frac{\partial C}{\partial S} - \frac{\partial C}{\partial t} - (\log r)C = 0$$

The value of the call, C, was then derived by solving this equation subject to the boundary condition $C^* = \max[0, S^* - K]$.

Based on our previous analysis, we would now suspect that, as $n \rightarrow \infty$, our difference equation would approach the Black-Scholes partial differential equation. This can be confirmed by substituting our definitions of $\hat{r}, u, d$ in terms of n in the way described earlier, expanding C_u, C_d in a Taylor series around $(e^{\sigma\sqrt{h}}S, t - h)$ and $(e^{-\sigma\sqrt{h}}S, t - h)$, respectively, and then expanding $e^{\sigma\sqrt{h}}$, $e^{-\sigma\sqrt{h}}$, and r^h in a Taylor series, substituting these in the equation and collecting terms. If we then divide by h and let $h \rightarrow 0$, all terms of higher order than h go to zero. This yields the Black-Scholes equation.

$$u = u \qquad d = e^{\zeta(t/n)} \qquad q = \lambda(t/n)$$

This correspondence captures the essence of a pure jump process in which each successive stock price is almost always close to the previous price ($S \to dS$) but occasionally, with low but continuing probability, significantly different ($S \to uS$). Observe that as $n \to \infty$, the probability of a change by d becomes larger and larger, while the probability of a change by u approaches zero.

With these specifications, the initial condition of the central limit theorem we used is no longer satisfied, and it can be shown the stock price movements converge to a log-Poisson rather than a lognormal distribution as $n \to \infty$. Let us define

$$\Psi[x; y] \equiv \sum_{i=x}^{\infty} \frac{e^{-y} y^i}{i!}$$

as the complementary Poisson distribution function. The limiting option-pricing formula, or jump process option-pricing formula, for the above specifications of u, d, and q is then

$$C = S\Psi[x; y] - Kr^{-t}\Psi[x; y/u],$$

where

$y \equiv (\log r - \zeta)ut/(u-1)$,

$x \equiv$ the smallest nonnegative integer greater than $(\log(K/S) - \zeta t)/\log u$.

A very similar formula holds if we let $u = e^{\zeta(t/n)}$, $d = d$, and $1 - q = \lambda(t/n)$.

6. Dividends and Put Pricing

So far we have been assuming that the stock pays no dividends. It is easy to do away with this restriction. We will illustrate this with a specific dividend policy: The stock maintains a constant yield, δ, on each ex-dividend date. Suppose there is one period remaining before expiration and the current stock price is S. If the end of the period is an ex-dividend date, then an individual who owned the stock during the period will receive at that time a dividend of either δuS or δdS. Hence, the stock price at the end of the period will be either $u(1-\delta)^v S$ or $d(1-\delta)^v S$, where $v = 1$ if the end of the period is an ex-dividend date and $v = 0$ otherwise. Both δ and v are assumed to be known with certainty.

When the call expires, its contract and a rational exercise policy imply that its value must be either

$$C_u = \max[0, u(1-\delta)^v S - K]$$

or

$$C_d = \max[0, d(1-\delta)^v S - K]$$

Therefore,

$$C \begin{cases} C_u = \max[0, u(1-\delta)^v S - K] \\ C_d = \max[0, d(1-\delta)^v S - K] \end{cases}$$

Now we can proceed exactly as before. Again we can select a portfolio of Δ shares of stock and the dollar amount B in bonds which will have the same end-of-period value as the call.[14] By retracing our previous steps, we can show that

$$C = [pC_u + (1-p)C_d]/\hat{r}$$

if this is greater than $S - K$, and $C = S - K$ otherwise. Here, once again, $p = (\hat{r} - d)/(u - d)$ and $\Delta = (C_u - C_d)/(u - d)S$.

Thus far the only change is that $(1 - \delta)^v S$ has replaced S in the values for C_u and C_d. Now we come to the major difference: Early exercise may be optimal. To see this, suppose that $v = 1$ and $d(1 - \delta)S > K$. Since $u > d$, then, also, $u(1 - \delta)S > K$. In this case, $C_u = u(1 - \delta)S - K$ and $C_d = d(1 - \delta)S - K$. Therefore, since $(u/\hat{r})p + (d/\hat{r})(1-p) = 1$,

$$[pC_u + (1-p)C_d]/\hat{r} = (1-\delta)S - (K/\hat{r})$$

For sufficiently high stock prices, this can obviously be less than $S - K$. Hence, there are definitely some circumstances in which no one would be willing to hold the call for one more period.

In fact, there will always be a critical stock price, $\hat{S}$, such that if $S > \hat{S}$, the call should be exercised immediately. $\hat{S}$ will be the stock price at which $[pC_u + (1-p)C_d]/\hat{r} = S - K$.[15] That is, it is the lowest stock price at which the value of the hedging portfolio exactly equals $S - K$. This means $\hat{S}$ will, other things equal, be lower the higher the dividend yield, the lower the interest rate, and the lower the striking price.

We can extend the analysis to an arbitrary number of periods in the same way as before. There is only one additional difference, a minor modification in the hedging operation. Now the funds in the hedging portfolio will be increased by any dividends received, or decreased by the restitution required for dividends paid while the stock is held short.

Although the possibility of optimal exercise before the expiration date causes no conceptual difficulties, it does seem to prohibit a simple closed-form solution for the value of a call with many periods to go. However, our analysis suggests a sequential numerical procedure that will allow us to calculate the continuous-time value to any desired degree of accuracy.

Let C be the current value of a call with n periods remaining. Define

---

14. Remember that if we are long the portfolio we will receive the dividend at the end of the period; if we are short, we will have to make restitution for the dividend.
15. Actually solving for $\hat{S}$ explicitly is straightforward but rather tedious, so we will omit it.

$$\bar{v}(n,i) \equiv \sum_{k=1}^{n-i} v_k$$

so that $\bar{v}(n,i)$ is the number of ex-dividend dates occurring during the next $n-i$ periods. Let $C(n,i,j)$ be the value of the call $n-i$ periods from now, given that the current stock price S has changed to $u^j d^{n-i-j}(1-\delta)^{\bar{v}(n,i)}S$, where $j = 0, 1, 2, ..., n-i$.

With this notation, we are prepared to solve for the current value of the call by working backward in time from the expiration date. At expiration, $i = 0$, so that

$$C(n,0,j) = \max[0, u^j d^{n-j}(1-\delta)^{\bar{v}(n,0)}S - K] \quad \text{for } j = 0, 1, ..., n$$

One period before the expiration date, $i = 1$ so that

$$C(n,1,j) = \max[u^j d^{n-1-j}(1-\delta)^{\bar{v}(n,1)}S - K,$$
$$[pC(n,0,j+1) + (1-p)C(n,0,j)]/\hat{r}]$$
$$\text{for } j = 0, 1, ..., n-1$$

More generally, i periods before expiration

$$C(n,i,j) = \max[u^j d^{n-i-j}(1-\delta)^{\bar{v}(n,i)}S - K,$$
$$[pC(n,i-1,j+1) + (1-p)C(n,i-1,j)]/\hat{r}]$$
$$\text{for } j = 0, 1, ..., n-i$$

Observe that each prior step provides the inputs needed to evaluate the right-hand arguments of each succeeding step. The number of calculations decreases as we move backward in time. Finally, with n periods before expiration, since $i = n$,

$$C = C(n,n,0) = \max[S - K, [pC(n,n-1,1) + (1-p)C(n,n-1,0)]/\hat{r}]$$

and the hedge ratio is

$$\Delta = \frac{C(n,n-1,1) - C(n,n-1,0)}{(u-d)S}$$

We could easily expand the analysis to include dividend policies in which the amount paid on any ex-dividend date depends on the stock price at that time in a more general way.[16] However, this will cause some minor complications. In our present example with a constant dividend yield, the possible stock prices $n-i$ periods from now are completely determined by the total number of upward moves (and ex-dividend dates) occurring during that interval. With other types of dividend policies, the enumeration will be more complicated, since then the terminal stock price will be affected by the timing

---

16. We could also allow the amount to depend on previous stock prices.

of the upward moves as well as their total number. But the basic principle remains the same. We go to the expiration date and calculate the call value for all of the possible prices that the stock could have then. Using this information, we step back one period and calculate the call values for all possible stock prices at that time, and so forth.

We will now illustrate the use of the binomial numerical procedure in approximating continuous-time call values. In order to have an exact continuous-time formula to use for comparison, we will consider the case with no dividends. Suppose that we are given the inputs required for the Black-Scholes option-pricing formula: S, K, t, σ, and r. To convert this information into the inputs d, u, and $\hat{r}$ required for the binomial numerical procedure, we use the relationships:

$$d = 1/u \qquad u = e^{\sigma\sqrt{t/n}} \qquad \hat{r} = r^{t/n}$$

Table 13.2 gives us a feeling for how rapidly option values approximated by the binomial method approach the corresponding limiting Black-Scholes values given by $n = \infty$. At $n = 5$, the values differ by at most \$0.25, and at $n = 20$, they differ by at most \$0.07. Although not shown, at $n = 50$ the greatest difference is less than \$0.03, and at $n = 150$ the values are identical to the penny.

To derive a method for valuing puts, we again use the binomial formulation. Although it has been convenient to express the argument in terms of a particular security, a call, this is not essential in any way. The same basic analysis can be applied to puts.

TABLE 13.2 *Binomial Approximation of Continuous-Time Call Values for (1) January, (2) April, and (3) July Options; $S = 40$ and $r = 1.05$*[a]

		$n = 5$			$n = 20$			$n = \infty$		
σ	K	(1)	(2)	(3)	(1)	(2)	(3)	(1)	(2)	(3)
	35	5.14	5.77	6.45	5.15	5.77	6.39	5.15	5.76	6.40
0.2	40	1.05	2.26	3.12	0.99	2.14	2.97	1.00	2.17	3.00
	45	0.02	0.54	1.15	0.02	0.51	1.11	0.02	0.51	1.10
	35	5.21	6.30	7.15	5.22	6.26	7.19	5.22	6.25	7.17
0.3	40	1.53	3.21	4.36	1.44	3.04	4.14	1.46	3.07	4.19
	45	0.11	1.28	2.12	0.15	1.28	2.23	0.16	1.25	2.24
	35	5.40	6.87	7.92	5.39	6.91	8.05	5.39	6.89	8.09
0.4	40	2.01	4.16	5.61	1.90	3.93	5.31	1.92	3.98	5.37
	45	0.46	1.99	3.30	0.42	2.09	3.42	0.42	2.10	3.43

a. The January options have one month to expiration; the Aprils, four months; and the Julys, seven months; r and σ are expressed in annual terms.

Letting P denote the current price of a put, with one period remaining before expiration we have

$$P \Big\langle \begin{array}{l} P_u = \max[0, K - u(1-\delta)^v S] \\ P_d = \max[0, K - d(1-\delta)^v S] \end{array}$$

Once again, we can choose a portfolio with ΔS in stock and B in bonds that will have the same end-of-period values as the put. By a series of steps that are formally equivalent to the ones we followed in Section 3, we can show that

$$P = [pP_u + (1-p)P_d]/\hat{r}$$

if this is greater than $K - S$, and $P = K - S$ otherwise. As before,

$$p = (\hat{r} - d)/(u - d) \quad \text{and} \quad \Delta = (P_u - P_d)/(u - d)S$$

Note that for puts, since $P_u \leq P_d$, then $\Delta \leq 0$. This means that if we sell an overvalued put, the hedging portfolio that we buy will involve a short position in the stock.

We might hope that with puts we will be spared the complications caused by optimal exercise before the expiration date. Unfortunately, this is not the case. In fact, the situation is even worse in this regard. Now there are always some possible circumstances in which no one would be willing to hold the put for one more period.

To see this, suppose $K > u(1-\delta)^v S$. Since $u > d$, then also $K > d(1-\delta)^v S$. In this case, $P_u = K - u(1-\delta)^v S$ and $P_d = K - d(1-\delta)^v S$. Therefore, since $(u/\hat{r})p + (d/\hat{r})(1-p) = 1$,

$$[pP_u + (1-p)P_d]/\hat{r} = (K/\hat{r}) - (1-\delta)^v S$$

If there are no dividends (that is, $v = 0$), then this is certainly less than $K - S$. Even with $v = 1$, it will be less for a sufficiently low stock price.

Thus, there will now be a critical stock price $\hat{S}$ such that if $S < \hat{S}$, the put should be exercised immediately. By analogy with our discussion for the call, we can see that this is the stock price at which $[pP_u + (1-p)P_d]/\hat{r} = K - S$. Other things being equal, $\hat{S}$ will be higher the lower the dividend yield, the higher the interest rate, and the higher the striking price. Optimal early exercise thus becomes more likely if the put is deep in the money and the interest rate is high. The effect of dividends yet to be paid diminishes the advantages of immediate exercise, since the put buyer will be reluctant to sacrifice the forced declines in the stock price on future ex-dividend dates.

This argument can be extended in the same way as before to value puts with any number of periods to go. However, the chance for optimal exercise before the expiration date once again seems to preclude the possibility of expressing this value in a simple form. But our analysis also indicates that with slight modification, we can value puts with the same numerical techniques

TABLE 13.3 *Stock Prices, Put Values, and Deltas for Riskless Trading Example (see Section 4)*

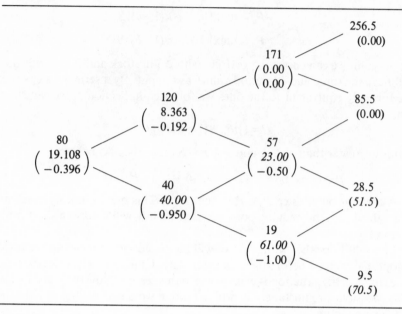

we use for calls. Reversing the difference between the stock price and the striking price at each stage is the only change.[17]

The diagram presented in Table 13.3 shows the stock prices, put values, and values of Δ obtained in this way for the example given in Section 4. The values used here were $S = 80$, $K = 80$, $n = 3$, $u = 1.5$, $d = 0.5$, and $\hat{r} = 1.1$. To include dividends as well, we assume that a cash dividend of 5% ($\delta = 0.05$) will be paid at the end of the last period before the expiration date. Thus, $(1 - \delta)^{v(n, 0)} = 0.95$, $(1 - \delta)^{v(n, 1)} = 0.95$, and $(1 - \delta)^{v(n, 2)} = 1.0$. Put values in italics indicate that immediate exercise is optimal.

---

17. Michael Parkinson (1977) has suggested a similar numerical procedure based on a trinomial process where the stock price can either increase, decrease, or remain unchanged. In fact, given the theoretical basis for the binomial numerical procedure provided, the numerical method can be generalized to permit $k + 1 \le n$ jumps to new stock prices in each period. We can consider exercise only every k periods, using the binomial formula to leap across intermediate periods. In effect this means permitting $k + 1$ possible new stock prices before exercise is again considered. That is, instead of considering exercise n times, we would only consider it about n/k times. For fixed t and k, as $n \to \infty$, option values will approach their continuous-time values.

This alternative procedure is interesting, since it may enhance computer efficiency. At one extreme, for calls on stocks that do not pay dividends, setting $k + 1 = n$ gives the most efficient results. However, when the effect of potential early exercise is important and greater accuracy is required, the most efficient results are achieved by setting $k = 1$, as in our description above.

7. Conclusion

It should now be clear that whenever stock price movements conform to a discrete binomial process or to a limiting form of such a process, options can be priced solely on the basis of arbitrage considerations. Indeed, we could have significantly complicated the simple binomial process while still retaining this property.

The probabilities of an upward or downward move did not enter into the valuation formula. Hence, we would obtain the same result if q depended on the current or past stock prices or on other random variables. In addition, u and d could have been deterministic functions of time. More significantly, the size of the percentage changes in the stock price over each period could have depended on the stock price at the beginning of each period or on previous stock prices.[18] However, if the size of the changes were to depend on any other random variable not itself perfectly correlated with the stock price, then our argument will no longer hold. If any arbitrage result is then still possible, it will require the use of additional assets in the hedging portfolio.

We could also incorporate certain types of imperfections into the binomial option-pricing approach, such as differential borrowing and lending rates and margin requirements. These can be shown to produce upper and lower bounds on option prices, outside of which riskless profitable arbitrage would be possible.

Since all existing preference-free option-pricing results can be derived as limiting forms of a discrete two-state process, we might suspect that two-state stock price movements with the qualifications mentioned above must be in some sense necessary, as well as sufficient, to derive option-pricing formulas based solely on arbitrage considerations. To price an option by arbitrage methods, there must exist a portfolio of other assets that exactly replicates in every state of nature the payoff received by an optimally exercised option. Our basic proposition is the following. Suppose, as we have, that markets are perfect, that changes in the interest rate are never random, and that changes in the stock price are always random. In a discrete-time model, a necessary and sufficient condition for options of all maturities and striking prices to be priced by arbitrage using only the stock and bonds in the portfolio is that in each period,

1. The stock price can change from its beginning-of-period value to only two ex-dividend values at the end of the period, and

---

18. Of course, different option-pricing formulas would result from these more complex stochastic processes. See Cox and Ross (1976) and Geske (1979). Nonetheless, all option-pricing formulas in these papers can be derived as limiting forms of a properly specified discrete two-state process.

2. The dividends and the size of each of the two possible changes are presently known functions depending at most on: (1) current and past stock prices, (2) current and past values of random variables whose changes in each period are perfectly correlated with the change in the stock price, and (3) calendar time.

The sufficiency of the condition can be established by a straightforward application of the methods we have presented. Its necessity is implied by the discussion at the end of Section 3.[19, 20, 21]

This rounds out the principal conclusion of this paper: The simple two-state process is really the essential ingredient of option-pricing by arbitrage methods. This is surprising, perhaps, given the mathematical complexities of some of the current models in this field. But it is reassuring to find such simple economic arguments at the heart of this powerful theory.

---

19. Note that option values need not depend on the present stock price alone. In some cases, formal dependence on the entire series of past values of the stock price and other variables can be summarized in a small number of state variables.

20. In some circumstances, it will be possible to value options by arbitrage when this condition does not hold by using additional assets in the hedging portfolio. The value of the option will then in general depend on the values of these other assets, although in certain cases only parameters describing their movement will be required.

21. Merton's (1976) model, with both continuous and jump components, is a good example of a stock price process for which no exact option-pricing formula is obtainable purely from arbitrage considerations. To obtain an exact formula, it is necessary to impose restrictions on the stochastic movements of other securities, as Merton did, or on investor preferences. For example, Rubinstein (1976) has been able to derive the Black-Scholes option-pricing formula, under circumstances that do not admit arbitrage, by suitably restricting investor preferences. Additional problems arise when interest rates are stochastic, although Merton (1973) has shown that some arbitrage results may still be obtained.

References

Black, F., and M. Scholes. 1973. The pricing of options and corporate liabilities. *Journal of Political Economy* 3, 637–654.

Brennan, M. J., and E. S. Schwartz. 1977. The valuation of American put options. *Journal of Finance* 32, 449–462.

Cox, J. C., and S. A. Ross. 1975. *The pricing of options for jump processes.* Rodney L. White Center Working Paper no. 2-75 (University of Pennsylvania, Philadelphia, PA).

Cox, J. C., and S. A. Ross. 1976. The valuation of options for alternative stochastic processes. *Journal of Financial Economics* 3, 145–166.

Geske, R. 1979. The valuation of compound options. *Journal of Financial Economics* 7, 63–81.

Harrison, J. M., and D. M. Kreps. 1979. Martingales and arbitrage in multiperiod securities markets. *Journal of Economic Theory* 20, 381–408.

Merton, R. C. 1973. The theory of rational option pricing. *Bell Journal of Economics and Management Science* 4, 141–183.

Merton, R. C. 1976. Option pricing when underlying stock returns are discontinuous. *Journal of Financial Economics* 3, 125–144.

Merton, R. C. 1977. On the pricing of contingent claims and the Modigliani-Miller theorem. *Journal of Financial Economics* 5, 241–250.

Parkinson, M. 1977. Option pricing: The American put. *Journal of Business* 50, 21–36.

Rendleman, R. J., and B. J. Bartter. 1978. Two-state option pricing. Unpublished paper (Graduate School of Management, Northwestern University, Evanston, IL).

Rubinstein, M. 1976. The valuation of uncertain income streams and the pricing of options. *Bell Journal of Economics* 7, 407–425.

Sharpe, W. F. 1978. *Investments*. Englewood Cliffs, NJ: Prentice-Hall.

14

The Pricing of Options on Debt Securities

Mark Pitts

While managers of equity portfolios have long been acquainted with traded options, managers of debt portfolios frequently find the emerging markets in debt options difficult to understand. Furthermore, while much of our knowledge of equity options can be transferred directly to the debt option markets, this is not true for one of the most difficult questions that must be addressed, namely, the fair value of an options contract. That question is the subject of this article.

I shall show that equity option models are not directly applicable to debt options but that we can use them in an altered form to value options on some debt securities. We should note at the outset, however, that an equity option model altered to take into account the characteristics of a debt security will not result in all cases in a good model for valuing debt options. These cases are discussed in more detail in the sections that follow.

Options on Actuals and Options on Futures

Traded options on debt securities fall into two large categories: options on actual (or spot) debt securities and options on futures contracts on debt securities.[1] Options on actuals are probably the more familiar, since the equity options market has traditionally been based on actual securities. If a call

---

1. Notes appear at the end of the article.

option on an actual security is exercised, the owner of the option acquires a long position in the actual security; if a put option is exercised, the owner delivers the actual security.

In many ways, options on futures are similar to options on actual securities — although they are not similar to futures contracts. The only significant difference between an option on an actual and an option on a future is that the underlying instrument in the latter case is a futures contract rather than a spot security. Thus, if a call is exercised, the owner of the option acquires a long position in the underlying futures contract and the option writer acquires the offsetting short position in the same futures contract. If a put option on futures is exercised, the owner of the option acquires a short position in the futures contract, and the option writer acquires a long position in the contract. Naturally, any prior positions in the same futures contract held by either party may be totally or partially cancelled out as a result of exercising the option.

For example, suppose that an owner of one put option on December Treasury bonds has previously established a long position in two December T-Bond futures contracts. If he decides to exercise the put, he acquires a short position in December T-Bonds that, when netted against his prior position, leaves him long one December futures contract.

Another difference between options on actuals and options on futures arises from the way in which spot prices and futures prices are quoted. For instance, a quote of 80 on an actual Treasury bond means that one can establish a long position in the actual bond for a price of 80% of par, or $80,000 for a bond with a $100,000 face value. On the other hand, if a futures contract in the same bond is quoted at 80, one can establish a long position in the futures contract essentially for free. The only "cost" in establishing a long position in futures is the initial margin, which is more in the nature of a good-faith deposit than of an actual cost. Therefore, a futures price of 80 does not mean that it costs 80% of the face amount to establish a long position in futures.

This method of quoting futures prices carries over to options on futures. For example, a call option on a futures contract on Treasury bonds struck at 80 does not mean that the owner of the option will pay the seller of the option $80,000 if the option is exercised; it simply means that the owner of the position has the right to establish a long futures position at 80, and the option writer is obligated to take the offsetting short futures position at 80.

Generally, an exchange would effect this transaction by establishing the futures positions at 80 and then immediately marking each position to market. For instance, if futures prices are currently at 85 and a call struck at 80 is exercised, the owner of the option acquires a long futures position at 80 and the writer of the option acquires a short futures position at 80. The exchange then immediately marks each position to market, meaning that the long receives 5 points ($5,000) in cash and the short position pays in 5 points, and the respective futures positions are reestablished at the prevailing futures price of 85.[2]

Finally, an option cannot "outlive" the underlying instrument: The expiration date of an option on a futures contract must be on or before the delivery date of the futures contract. In contrast, the expiration date for an option on an actual security is theoretically unlimited in the case of an equity option, and limited only by the maturity date of the underlying fixed income security in the case of a debt option.

We do have a special case in which a European option on an actual security and a European option on a futures contract on the same security both expire on the futures delivery date. Here, the option on the actual and the option on the futures (with the same strike price) have the same value, even if one option is currently deep in the money and the other is currently deep out of the money. This equality of value occurs because arbitrage will force futures prices and spot prices to converge on delivery date; therefore, the futures and the actual become one and the same instrument at the only point at which the option can be exercised.[3] Hence, there can never be any advantage to owning one option over the other.

Riskless Hedge Valuation

The riskless hedge model is the most widely accepted model for valuing options. Basically, the riskless hedge model involves working backward from the expiration date using a risk-free portfolio to derive the value of the option today. This technique underlies the Black-Scholes [2] model for equity options, the Black [1] model for options on commodity futures, and the binomial option model developed by Cox, Ross, and Rubinstein [5].

To illustrate the technique, we suppose the objective is to value a call option.

The riskless hedge models implicitly assume that the current value of the call option will depend on the current price of the underlying security. This assumption is reasonable since with all other relevant factors held constant, one would expect the value of a call to increase when the price of the underlying security increases, and decrease when the price of the underlying security decreases — but usually not by equal amounts.

The riskless hedge models are based on a portfolio that is long one unit of the underlying security and short just enough calls so that the value of the portfolio will not change for infinitesimally small moves in the price of the underlying security, in effect creating a "riskless hedge." We can think of the resulting portfolio as a risk-free asset that in equilibrium will grow in value at the risk-free rate of return. Using this equilibrium argument and starting at option expiration, when the value of the option is easily derived, we can work *backward* through time to derive the value of the option in the current period, that is, the value of the option "today."

Before explaining how we would apply the riskless hedge technique to options on debt securities, let us use a simple example to illustrate how investors use it to value options on equities. The following one-branch binomial model captures the essence of the riskless hedge model.[4]

Assume for now that the underlying security is a share of stock that pays no dividends until after the option expires. As shown in Figure 14.1, the current stock price is $81, and at option expiration (one month hence) the price will either rise to $83 or fall to $79. We assume that the interest rate is 1% per month. The objective in this example is to find the current value of a European call option with a strike price of $80.

Naturally, it is easy to find the value of the option at expiration if we know what the price of the stock will be at that time – the value of a call is just the price of the stock minus the strike price, or zero, whichever is larger. In this

FIGURE 14.1   *One-Branch Binomial Model for a Riskless Hedge*

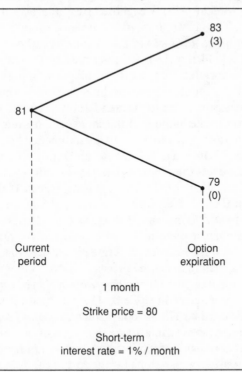

Current
period

Option
expiration

1 month

Strike price = 80

Short-term
interest rate = 1% / month

TABLE 14.1   *Results of Changes in Stock Price*

Stock Price	Value of Stock	Liability of $\frac{4}{3}$ Calls	Portfolio Value
Rises to 83	$83	($4)	$79
Declines to 79	$79	0	$79

example, the value of the option will be $3 if the stock price rises to $83, and $0 if it declines to $79 (at which point the option would expire worthless). These option values appear in parentheses below the expiration prices in Figure 14.1.

The valuation problem is one of finding the current fair value of the option with the stock price currently at $81. The riskless hedge technique enters here. To apply the technique, consider the following risk-free portfolio that can be purchased in the current period:

portfolio = long 1 stock share and short $\frac{4}{3}$ call options

We assume that options contracts are completely divisible so that shorting $\frac{4}{3}$ calls poses no problem. Also, we ignore taxes, transaction costs, and margin requirements. The portfolio is riskless because its value will be the same whether the stock price advances to 83 or declines to 79.

As shown in Table 14.1, if the stock price rises by the end of the period to $83, the liability associated with the short call position is $4 (i.e., $3 \times [\frac{4}{3}]$). On the other hand, if the stock price declines to $79, the options will expire worthless and there will be no associated liability. Adding the value of the long stock position to the liability of the short call position gives the resulting portfolio value of $79 regardless of which direction the stock moves!

This risk-free portfolio is a risk-free asset and must, in equilibrium, return no more than and no less than the risk-free rate of return (i.e., the T-Bill rate or the rate on some other totally risk-free investment). If the portfolio returned more than the risk-free rate, no one would buy T-Bills; they would buy the risk-free portfolio instead. If it returned less than the risk-free rate, arbitrageurs would short the risk-free portfolio (i.e., short the stock and buy $\frac{4}{3}$ calls) and invest the proceeds at a rate higher than their effective "borrowing" cost, thus reaping risk-free profits.

Given that the risk-free portfolio will be worth $79 in one month and given that the portfolio must grow in value by 1% per month (the assumed risk-free rate), its value must be $78.22 today (since $79/1.01 = 78.22$). By the construction of the portfolio we can also see that the cost, or value, of the portfolio is the cost of one share of stock minus the premium received for the $\frac{4}{3}$ calls. Equating these two expressions for the cost of the portfolio, we obtain:

$78.22 = (\text{price of 1 share of stock}) - [(\tfrac{4}{3}) \times (\text{price of 1 call})]$

Since the price of the stock is $81 at the time the portfolio is created this reduces to

$$78.22 = 81 - [(\tfrac{4}{3}) \times (\text{price of 1 call})]$$

Consequently, the current price of a call option must be $2.085. The problem has been solved.

The implications of the riskless hedge models for options on actuals are several.[5] Briefly, holding other factors constant:

1. If the price of the underlying security increases, the value of a call increases, but the value of a put decreases.

2. A higher strike price implies a higher value for the put option but a lower value for the call option.

3. If the rate of interest for borrowing and lending over the life of the option is higher, the value of a call will be higher but the value of a put will be lower.

4. If the volatility of the price of the underlying security is higher, the value of both the put and the call will be higher.

5. A longer time until expiration implies a greater value for both the American call and put options.

6. Finally, the most surprising result: The drift, or trend, in the price of the underlying security has no effect on the value of either put or call options. (This means, for example, that with other factors equal, the value of a call on a stock with a strong upward trend will be the same as the value of a call on a stock with a strong downward trend.)

These results apply to options on actuals and are equally true for options on futures contracts, except that, with other factors held constant, a higher short-term interest rate for borrowing and lending over the life of the option on a futures contract decreases the value of the call as well as the value of the put.

The following sections will show how to generalize the equity option model to deal with options on debt securities. Not surprisingly, it turns out that the foregoing rules are also true for options on debt securities.

Assumptions Underlying the Equity Option Models

We are now in a position to answer one of the most frequently asked questions about debt options; namely, why can't we use equity option models to value options and debt securities?

The answer is straightforward. Like most other mathematical models in finance, the riskless hedge model is based upon many simplifying assumptions. Since the model was originally constructed specifically for equity options, some of the underlying assumptions are unrealistic for options on debt securities. Hence, if equity option models were applied directly to debt securities, the resulting theoretical values would be misleading indicators of true option values.

While there are many variants of the riskless hedge model, the most widely used is the Black-Scholes model for options on (actual) equity securities. To clarify the limitations of the equity option models when applied to options on debt securities, let us examine the assumptions that underlie the Black-Scholes formula:

Assumption 1. Taxes, transaction costs, margin, and other frictions can be ignored.

Assumption 2. When the markets are open, the security underlying the options contract is traded continuously and its price can change very rapidly, but cannot jump. In other words, the price-time relationship is a continuous function. When the markets are closed, the price cannot change; thus, it is assumed that the opening price each day will equal the previous closing price.

Assumption 3. Proportional changes in price are normally distributed.

Assumption 4. The rate of interest for very short-term borrowing and lending over the life of the option is fixed and known.

Assumption 5. The option cannot be exercised prior to expiration.

Assumption 6. The underlying security will not make payouts of any kind during the life of the option.

Assumption 6 can be relaxed using the modification of the Black-Scholes formula proposed by Merton [6] that allows for payouts that are proportional to the price of the underlying security.

Examination of these assumptions will show why it is inappropriate to apply equity option models to debt securities. Perhaps the most inappropriate is Assumption 6, since the underlying securities on all options on actual debt securities that currently trade in any size are coupon bearing. Furthermore, since accrued interest is continuously adding to the (full) price of a bond, accrued interest is essentially a continuous payout to the holder of the debt security. Thus, Assumption 6 will almost always be violated for options on actual debt securities, even if coupons are not paid during the life of the option. Moreover, since coupons are fixed in dollar amount and not proportional to the price of the debt security, Merton's modification of the formula is of little help. In the next section we show how to modify the riskless hedge models to account for coupon flows.

Now let us turn to the assumptins about the price of the underlying security (Assumptions 2 and 3). Since full price (i.e., quoted, or flat, price plus accrued interest) exhibits a saw-toothed pattern through time, it would be unrealistic to think of full price as the variable that exhibits normally distributed price changes (Assumption 3). Furthermore, because full price will immediately plunge to a lower level when coupons are paid, Assumption 2 would necessarily be violated as well. Thus, we should think of the "price" for options on debt securities as the flat price of the underlying security.

Unfortunately, another question arises upon deeper reflection. Is it reasonable to assume that even the flat price fulfills Assumption 3, that is, that proportional changes in the flat price are normally distributed? If proportional price changes are normally distributed, negative prices are precluded, but negative yields may result since no upper bound is placed on prices.

For example, if a 10-year, 8% note sells at any price above 180 (the undiscounted sum of all future cash flows), the associated yield to maturity is negative. This result would be unreasonable since an investment in cash would dominate an investment in the note. As we show in later sections, the riskless hedge model can be modified so that both negative prices and negative yields are prohibited.

Assumption 4 states that the short-term rate of interest for borrowing and lending over the life of the option is constant. Since interest rate changes are the variables that drive price changes on debt securities (or vice versa), it would be ridiculous in some cases to hold the short-term rate of interest constant while the price of the underlying debt security is allowed to vary.

Suppose, for example, that we are considering a 1-year American option on a 1-year debt security. To hold the rate of interest for very short-term borrowing constant over the 1-year period and let the price (or yield) of the 1-year instrument vary would constitute a gross departure not only from reality but also from equilibrium. On the other hand, if the underlying instrument is a long-term bond, Assumption 4, while not totally realistic, is less likely to invalidate the resulting theoretical value. The conclusion of this paper proposes other solution techniques to provide partial solutions to this and other problems that are ignored in the riskless hedge models.

Finally, it is also usually assumed that the option cannot be exercised prior to expiration (Assumption 5). With debt options, as well as equity options, this is usually not the case. Subsequent discussion will indicate how the binomial model can be modified to allow for early exercise.

Thus, Assumptions 3 through 6 are particularly inappropriate for options on debt securities and may produce unrealistic values for those options. In the next section we show how to deal with some of these problems for options on actual debt securities, while in the subsequent section we modify the model for options on futures on debt securities.

Riskless Hedge Valuation of Options on Actual Debt Securities[6]

When a riskless hedge model is used to value options on equities, we assume that proportional changes in price are normally distributed. In the binomial model, for example, this assumption, together with the other inputs to the model, dictates the shape and dispersion of the binomial tree. In practice, the tree has a very large number of branches, with the highest possible price much higher than the current price and the lowest possible price approaching zero. As noted above, this construction will lead to problems if applied to debt securities since negative yields to maturity will result.

We can resolve this problem by an alternative approach, which is probably already more intuitive for those involved in the fixed income markets. Instead of constructing the binomial tree in terms of price, we construct it in terms of yield. The assumption that proportional changes in yield rather than price are normally distributed precludes the possibility of a negative yield, but yields will have no bound on the upside—a realistic touch that fixed income managers will be able to appreciate. As yields rise higher and higher, bond prices fall very low but will never go below zero. If yields fall very low and approach zero, bond prices become very high but never exceed the sum of the undiscounted cash flows.

Now let us return to the one-branch binomial model to show how this approach works for an option on an (actual) 8% 20-year bond currently selling at 81. For simplicity, let us assume that coupons are paid once a month, resulting in a yield to maturity on the bond of approximately 10.236%.

By the end of the month (at which time the option expires), we let the yield to maturity either rise by 25 basis points to 10.486% or fall by 25 basis points to 9.986%. As in our previous example, the strike price is 80 (a yield to maturity of 10.380%); however, we assume coupons are paid just before option expiration, and therefore no interest has accrued if the option is exercised and full price equals flat price. (It is common practice to quote the strike price in terms of a flat price but to require the buyer to pay full price if the option is exercised. Consequently, the actual strike price exhibits a saw-toothed pattern over time.) The very short-term rate of interest for borrowing and lending over the life of the option is 1% per month. Figure 14.2a illustrates these assumptions.

The problem, as before, is to find the fair value of a call option, except that now it is a call on a bond instead of a call on a share of stock. The first step in the process is to convert yields to prices—a simple matter since the yield to maturity uniquely determines the price.

Figure 14.2b shows the tree in (flat) prices that corresponds to the tree in yields. Remember that the bond is aging over time: When we calculate

FIGURE 14.2a   *One-Branch Binomial Tree for Yields (%) of an Option Currently Selling at 81*

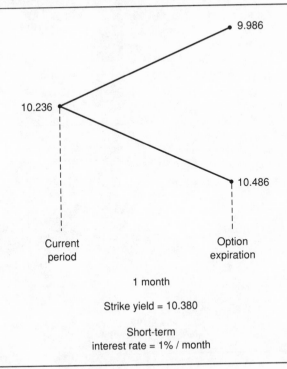

Current period

Option expiration

1 month

Strike yield = 10.380

Short-term interest rate = 1% / month

prices at option expiration, the underlying security is an 8% 19-year-11-month bond.[7]

We are now in a position to proceed in a manner similar to that used in valuing an equity option. As before, we will construct a risk-free portfolio (long the underlying bond and short call options) and impose the equilibrium condition that a risk-free portfolio returns the risk-free rate of return. An important difference in this case will be the coupon received by the holder of the risk-free portfolio. As we have assumed that coupons are paid monthly, this means that the bond pays a coupon of .667 points each month.

Starting at expiration, we can fill in the values of the option for a given price of the underlying bond. If yields fall to 9.986% and prices rise to 82.856, a call struck at 80 is obviously worth 2.856. If yields rise to 10.486% and prices fall to 79.256, the option expires worthless. These values appear in parentheses in Figure 14.2b beneath the bond prices at expiration.

Consider now the following risk-free portfolio:

portfolio = long 1 8% 20-year bond and short 1.2605 call options

FIGURE 14.2b *One-Branch Binomial Tree: Flat Prices*

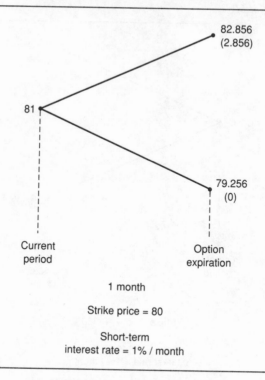

82.856
(2.856)

81

79.256
(0)

Current
period

Option
expiration

1 month

Strike price = 80

Short-term
interest rate = 1% / month

As illustrated in Table 14.2, this portfolio is risk-free because its value at the end of one month is predetermined. If yields rise, the options expire worthless and the value of the portfolio is 79.923 (i.e., 79.256 for the bond and .667 in coupon income). If yields fall, each short call is equivalent to a liability of 2.856 points, or 3.60 points for the short option position as a whole. Combined with the bond and the coupon income, this gives a net value of 79.923.

TABLE 14.2 *Example of Risk-Free Portfolio*

Yields	Value of Bond	Liability of 1.2605 Calls	Coupon Payment	Portfolio Value
Fall to 9.986	82.856	(3.60)	0.667	79.923
Rise to 10.486	79.256	0	0.667	79.923

We can easily calculate the cost of purchasing the risk-free portfolio. It is just the cost of buying the bond in the current period, minus the price received for each call. Letting c denote the price of each call we have

$$\text{cost} = 81 - 1.2605c$$

If the portfolio will be worth 79.923 in one month, and if it must return the risk-free rate of return, then its cost must be the discounted value of 79.923. That is,

$$\text{cost} = 79.923/1.01 = 79.1317$$

Equating these two expressions for the cost and solving for c, we obtain

$$c = 1.4882$$

In other words, the option must be worth 1.4822 percentage points of par.

When we examined the riskless hedge model applied to options on equities, we showed how each relevant factor affected the value of the option. Each factor has the same effect when applied to options on debt securities.

Riskless Hedge Valuation of Options on Futures on Debt Securities[8]

With the foundation laid in the previous section, we can show how to apply the riskless hedge model to options on futures contracts on debt securities. For convenience, we will assume that Figure 14.2a represents the possible quoted *futures* yields, but make no assumption whatsoever about the possible yields for actual debt securities.

Conversion of yields to prices requires a procedure that differs from the procedure used in the last section. For futures on coupon-bearing securities, the established method for linking quoted futures prices to quoted futures yields is to use the price-yield function of a standard nonaging instrument, such as a 20-year, 8% bond.[9] Thus, to derive the appropriate tree of futures prices, we simply find the price of a 20-year, 8% bond that corresponds to each of the yields shown in Figure 14.2a. (For simplicity we retain the assumption of monthly coupon payments.) Since there is no aging, we do not use a 19-year-11-month bond to obtain the prices at option expiration.

Figure 14.3 displays the futures prices. Note that the values of the option at expiration appear in parentheses below the futures prices at expiration.

For call options on futures on debt securities, the risk-free portfolio comprises a long position in futures contracts and a short position in options. Unlike the risk-free portfolio for options on actual debt securities, however, the holder of this risk-free portfolio receives no coupon income. Although the bond that is deliverable in satisfaction of the futures contract may make

FIGURE 14.3   *One-Branch Binomial Tree Showing Futures Prices*

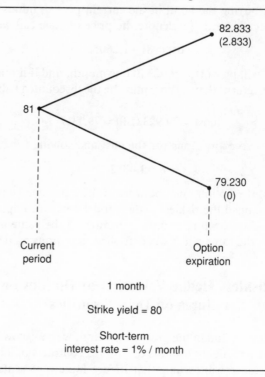

periodic coupon payments and the quoted price may be derived from the price-yield function for a coupon-bearing security, a long position in futures does not entitle the holder to receive coupons.

This is not to say that coupons are completely irrelevant in the context of pricing options on futures. Obviously, coupons are a major factor in the cost-of-carry and have a major impact upon the current futures price; in turn, the current futures price has a predominant impact on the price of the option. On the other hand, since the coupon payment is not received by the holder of the risk-free portfolio, it never enters the calculations. In other words, since the coupon is already incorporated into the prevailing futures price, it need not be explicitly considered in the option valuation procedure.

With this fact in mind, we consider the following risk-free portfolio:

portfolio = long 1 futures contract and short 1.2718 calls

Table 14.3 demonstrates that this portfolio is, indeed, riskless and its value will be *negative* 1.770 whether futures yields rise or fall.

TABLE 14.3 *Riskless Portfolio with Negative Value*

Futures Yields	Margin Flow	Liability of 1.2718 Calls	Portfolio Value
Fall to 9.986	1.833	(3.603)	(1.770)
Rise to 10.486	(1.770)	0	(1.770)

A negative final value for the risk-free portfolio may seem paradoxical, but the paradox is resolved when we calculate the cost of establishing the portfolio. Since futures are "free," there are no economic costs associated with establishing the long futures position. Nevertheless, revenue is raised when the calls are sold. Thus, there is no cost in establishing the risk-free portfolio; in fact, we are paid to establish it. A position in the risk-free portfolio in the earlier cases was like a long position in a risk-free asset (i.e., we were lenders). Now the risk-free position is like a short position in a risk-free asset (i.e., we are borrowers).

Fortunately, the foregoing considerations do not complicate the valuation process. The rate of return on the portfolio must, in equilibrium, equal the risk-free rate. Thus, the present value of the portfolio must be the discounted value of -1.770. The value of the portfolio, however, is also equal to the cost of the calls. Denoting the price of the calls as c, we have

$$1.2718(-c) = -1.770/1.10$$

or equivalently,

$$c = 1.378$$

American Options

The foregoing sections have not dealt with the problem raised by the assumption that the options cannot be exercised prior to expiration (Assumption 5). The right to early exercise can only increase the value of an option: Obviously, it cannot decrease the value of the option since the holder is not obligated to exercise early and can always wait until expiration to exercise, when this is a more favorable alternative.

The practical means by which an option can be Americanized is simple, especially in light of the highly mathematical treatment it receives in the academic press. We proceed to value an American option almost exactly as before: Construct a tree of possible yields, derive the tree of possible prices, and fill in the option values at expiration. We then use the riskless hedge argument to step back through time. The only difference is that the resulting option value each time we move back one step is either the value derived from the riskless hedge procedure or the value of immediate exercise, whichever is greater. This process guarantees that the final value of the option reflects the possibility that the option may be exercised at any point up to and including the expiration date.

To illustrate, consider the example in the last section for options on futures contracts. To show that we might want to exercise early in this example, we will have to use an extremely high interest rate. Suppose, for illustrative purposes, that the interest rate is 50% per month. Then the last equation becomes:

$$1.2718c = 1.770/1.50$$

Solving for c, the value of the call, we find $c = .928$. If the call is exercised immediately, however, it is worth 1 point $(81 - 80)$. Therefore, the derived value of .928 cannot be correct if early exercise is allowed, and we should ignore it. In all subsequent calculations, 1 point should be considered the correct option value for this point in the binomial tree.

Admittedly, an example that depends upon such a high interest rate is unrealistic. There are, however, many realistic examples in which early exercise is optimal. The possibility of early exercise will generally be greatest for in-the-money options and, in the case of call options on actuals, options on securities with high coupon payments. On the other hand, high volatility and a long time to expiration will tend to decrease the chances of immediate exercise by causing the value of the option to exceed its intrinsic value. As the foregoing example shows, the short-term rate of interest for borrowing and lending over the life of the option also plays a role in early exercise. In this particular example, an increase in the short-term rate made early exercise the optimal policy. The issue is not always as clear-cut for options on actual debt securities, but one general rule remains the same: Those factors that make early exercise more advantageous also make the American option more valuable than its European counterpart.

Finally, a model that accounts for the early exercise privilege of American options not only produces a theoretical value for the American option, but also provides the only general method by which we can determine when to exercise the option. The option should be exercised as soon as the value of immediate exercise exceeds the value of the option if immediate exercise were not allowed.

Problems, Complications, and Conclusion

We have made the implicit assumption in each of our examples that the short-term rate of interest for borrowing and lending over the life of the option is constant (Assumption 4). This assumption can be relaxed, but in order to use the riskless hedge, we must assume that the short-term rate is a known function of the rate (or price) of the underlying security. Consequently, more complicated yield curve movements such as parallel shifts or snap-ups and snap-downs can be incorporated into the model.

Since interest rates are the driving variable behind the price of debt securities, we must treat any assumption about the short-term rate of interest with extreme care.

First, any assumption that we make concerning this rate must be consistent with the possible rates for the underlying security. For example, a high short-term rate and an extremely low long-term rate might mean that the long-term debt is a dominated security—clearly, an unrealistic scenario. A second and closely related problem is that the riskless hedge models do not take into consideration the equilibrium structure of the yield curve. There are, however, a number of more complex models that start by modeling the yield curve and derive the value of options on debt securities as a byproduct. (See, for example, Cox, Ingersoll, and Ross [4] and Brennan and Schwartz [3].) While the more complicated models are frequently more theoretically sound, they are almost always more difficult to implement and require many additional assumptions.

In conclusion, the riskless hedge models provide a relatively simple means of valuing options on debt securities. They are not, however, appropriate for all debt options. A 3-month option on a 20-year bond futures contract can be reasonably valued using the riskless hedge, but the model would be totally inappropriate for a 1-year option on a 1-year bond. As is always the case with option models, the most critical step is to decide whether the underlying assumptions are or are not reasonable for the particular option that must be valued.

Notes

1. In this paper we limit the discussion to options that are currently traded in size on an exchange or over the counter. Thus, for example, we do not explicitly consider the call provision attached to most long bonds.
2. One can also think of an option on a futures contract as an option struck at $0 on the *value* of the futures contract (not to be confused with the price of the futures contract). In the foregoing example, the value of the contract at 80 is 5 points when futures prices are at 85.
3. This is somewhat idealized in that it assumes that there is only one security that can be delivered in satisfaction of the futures contract and that there is a single moment at which delivery must be made. However, the established exchanges generally allow the short futures position some choice as to deliverable instrument and time of delivery.
4. See Cox, Ross, and Rubinstein [5] for a rigorous development of the binomial model. The reader who is already familiar with the binomial model and riskless

hedge models for options on equities can proceed to the next section without loss of continuity.

5. Proof of each conjecture appears in Black and Scholes [2].
6. For a more detailed analysis of debt options and the binomial model, see Pitts [7].
7. Note that the tree in Figure 14.2a was constructed for yields on 20-year 8% instruments, not 19-year-11-month 8% instruments and, therefore, the conversion to prices is not as simple as we have indicated. This is probably of little importance in the example at hand; one could think of the yields in Figure 14.2a as yields on "long" instruments trading at a discount. Obviously, this technique becomes highly questionable for options with long lives.
8. For more details on this subject, see Pitts [7].
9. The quoted price determines the daily mark to market. The actual sale price, that is, the amount of money that changes hands at delivery, will depend upon which one of several bonds are delivered. The literature published by the exchanges describes these considerations in detail.

References

1. Fischer Black, "The Pricing of Commodity Contracts," *Journal of Financial Economics* (January/March 1976), pp. 167–179.
2. Fischer Black and Myron Scholes, "The Pricing of Options and Corporate Liabilities," *Journal of Political Economy* (May/June 1973), pp. 637–654.
3. Michael Brennan and Eduardo Schwartz. "Savings Bonds: Theory and Empirical Evidence," monograph 1979-4, Salomon Brothers Center for the Study of Financial Institutions, 1980.
4. John Cox, Jonathan Ingersoll, and Stephen Ross, "A Theory of the Term Structure of Interest Rates," working paper, Stanford University, 1978.
5. John Cox, Stephen Ross, and Mark Rubinstein, "Option Pricing: A Simplified Approach," *Journal of Financial Economics* (September 1979), pp. 229–263.
6. Robert Merton, "Theory of Rational Option Pricing," *Bell Journal of Economics and Management Science* (1973), pp. 141–181.
7. Mark Pitts, "An Introduction to the Pricing of Options on Debt Instruments," Chapter 3 in Frank J. Fabozzi (ed.), *Winning the Interest Game: A Guide to Debt Options,* New York, NY: Probus Publishing Co., 1985.

15

Valuation of American Futures Options: Theory and Empirical Tests

Robert E. Whaley*

Futures option contracts now trade on every major futures exchange and on a wide variety of underlying futures contracts. The Chicago Mercantile Exchange, the Chicago Board of Trade, the New York Futures Exchange, and the Commodity Exchange now collectively have more than 20 options written on futures contracts where the underlying spot commodities are financial assets such as stock portfolios, bonds, notes and Eurodollars, foreign currencies (such as West German marks, Swiss francs, and British pounds), precious metals such as gold and silver, livestock commodities such as cattle and hogs, and agricultural commodities such as corn and soybeans. Moreover, new contract applications are before the Commodity Futures Trading Commission and should be actively trading in the near future.

With the markets for these new contingent claims becoming increasingly active, it is appropriate that the fundamentals of futures option valuation be reviewed and tested. Black [5] provides a framework for the analysis of commodity futures options. Although his work is explicitly directed at pricing European options on forward contracts, it applies to European futures contracts as well if the riskless rate of interest is constant during the futures

*This research was supported by the Finance Research Foundation of Canada. Comments and suggestions by Fred D. Arditti, Warren Bailey, Giovanni Barone-Adesi, Bruce Cooil, Theodore E. Day, Thomas S. Y. Ho, Hans R. Stoll, and a referee and an associate editor of the *Journal of Finance* are gratefully acknowledged.

option life.[1] The options currently trading, however, are American options, and only recently has theoretical work begun to focus on the American futures option-pricing problem.[2]

The purpose of this paper is to review the theory underlying American futures option valuation and to test it on transaction prices from the S&P 500 equity futures option market. In the first section of the paper, the theory of futures option pricing is reviewed. The partial differential equation of Black [5] is presented, and the boundary conditions of the American and European futures option-pricing problems are shown to imply different valuation equations. For the American futures options, efficient analytic approximations of the values of the call and put are presented, and the magnitude of the early exercise premium is simulated.

In the second section of the paper, the American futures option valuation principles are tested on S&P 500 futures option contract data for the period January 28, 1983, through December 30, 1983. Included are an examination of the systematic biases in the mispricing errors of the option-pricing models, a test of the stationarity of the volatility of the futures price change relatives, and a test of the joint hypothesis that the American futures option models are correctly specified and that the S&P market is efficient. The paper concludes with a summary of the major results of the study.

I. Theory of Futures Option Valuation

An option on a futures contract is like an option on a common stock in the sense that it provides its holder with the right to buy or sell the underlying security at the exercise price of the option. Unlike a stock option, however, a cash exchange in the amount of the exercise price does not occur when the futures option is exercised. Upon exercise, a futures option holder merely acquires a long or short futures position with a futures price equal to the exercise price of the option. When the futures contract is marked to market at the close of the day's trading, the option holder is free to withdraw in cash an amount equal to the futures price less the exercise price in the case of a call and the exercise price less the futures price in the case of a put. Thus, exercising a futures option is like receiving in cash the exercisable value of the option.

---

1. Cox, Ingersoll, and Ross [11, p. 324] demonstrate that the price of a futures contract is equal to the price of a forward contract when interest rates are nonstochastic.

2. Following Black's [5] seminal article, Moriarity, Phillips, and Tosini [18], Asay [1], Wolf [24], and others discussed the European futures option-pricing problem. Other than the studies by Whaley [22] and Stoll and Whaley [21], the theoretical work on American futures options is unpublished and includes studies by Ramaswamy and Sundaresan [19] and Brenner, Courtadon, and Subrahmanyam [9].

A. Assumptions and Notation

Black [5] provides the groundwork for futures option valuation. Although his work is directed at pricing a European call option, it is general in the sense that the partial differential equation describing the dynamics of the call option price through time applies to put options as well as call options and to American options as well as European options. The assumptions necessary to develop Black's partial differential equation are as follows:

A1. There are no transaction costs in the option, futures, and bond markets. These include direct costs such as commissions and implicit costs such as the bid-ask spread and penalties on short sales.

A2. Markets are free of costless arbitrage opportunities. If two assets or portfolios of assets have identical terminal values, they have the same price, and/or, if an asset or portfolio of assets has a future value that is certain to be positive, the initial value (cost) of the asset or portfolio is certain to be negative (positive).

A3. The short-term riskless rate of interest is constant through time.

A4. The instantaneous futures price change relative is described by the stochastic differential equation,

$$dF/F = \mu\, dt + \sigma\, dz$$

where μ is the expected instantaneous price change relative of the futures contract, σ is the instantaneous standard deviation, and z is a Wiener process.

Assumptions (A1) and (A2) are fairly innocuous. Transaction costs are trivial for those making the market in the various financial assets, and available empirical evidence suggests investors behave rationally. Assumption (A3) may appear contradictory, since some futures options are written on long-term debt instrument futures contracts[3] where the driving force behind the volatility of the futures price change relatives is interest rate uncertainty. The two interest rates are to some degree separable, however. Assumption (A3) describes the behavior of the short-term interest rate on, say, Treasury bills, while the volatility of T-bond futures prices, for example, is related to the volatility of the long-term U.S. Treasury bond forward rate.[4] Assumption (A4) describes the dynamics of the futures price movements through

---

3. The Chicago Board of Trade, for example, lists options on U.S. T-bond and T-note futures contracts.

4. A priori, the assumption of constant short-term interest rate is untenable for all option-pricing models. A constant short-term rate implies a constant, flat term structure, with interest rate uncertainty having no bearing on the volatility of the underlying asset prices. Such is hardly the case. The validity of such option-pricing models, however, need not be evaluated on the basis of their assumptions and can be judged on the merits of their predictions.

time. It is important to note that no assumption about the relationship between the futures price and the price of the underlying spot commodity has been invoked.[5] The valuation results presented in this section, therefore, apply to any futures option contract, independent of the nature of the underlying spot commodity.

For expositional purposes, the following notation is adopted in this study to describe futures options and their related parameters:

$$F = \text{current futures price}$$

$$F_T = \text{random futures price at expiration}$$

$$C(F, T; X)[c(F, T; X)] = \text{American [European] call option price}$$

$$P(F, T; X)[p(F, T; X)] = \text{American [European] put option price}$$

$$\epsilon_C(F, T; X)[\epsilon_p(F, T; X)] = \text{early exercise premium of American call [put] option}$$

$$r = \text{riskless rate of interest}$$

$$T = \text{time to expiration of futures options}$$

$$X = \text{exercise price of futures options.}$$

---

5. Note that Assumption (A4) defines the dynamics of the futures price movements with no reference to the relationship between the futures price and the price of the underlying spot commodity. Whether such an assumption is more appropriate for the futures price dynamics or the underlying spot commodity dynamics is an open empirical question.

Assumption (A4) is consistent with the assumption that the underlying spot price S follows the stochastic differential equation

$$dS/S = \alpha \, dt + \sigma \, dz$$

where α is the expected relative spot price change, and σ is the instantaneous standard deviation if there is (1) a constant, continuous riskless rate of interest r and (2) a constant, continuous proportional rate of receipt (payment) d for holding the underlying spot commodity. To show this result, apply Ito's lemma to the cost-of-carry relationship, $S_t = F_t e^{-(r-d)(T-t)}$, where F_t is defined in (A4). The expected futures price change relative, μ, is equal to the expected spot price change relative less the difference between the riskless rate of interest and the continuous rate of receipt, $\alpha - (r - d)$, and the standard deviation, σ, is the same for both the underlying spot commodity and futures price changes.

The interpretation of d depends on the nature of the underlying spot commodity. For example, in the foreign currency futures market, d represents the foreign interest rate earned on the investment in the foreign currency. For agricultural commodity futures, d is less than zero and represents the rate of cost for holding the spot commodity (i.e., storage costs, insurance costs, etc.), and for stock index futures, d represents the continuous proportional dividend yield on the underlying stock portfolio.

A continuous proportional dividend yield assumption may not be appropriate for a stock index since dividend payments are discrete and have a tendency to cluster according to the day of the week and the month of the year. With uncertain discrete dividend payments during the future's life, the cost-of-carry relationship between the prices of the stock index and stock index futures is unclear; however, as long as (A4) holds for the futures price dynamics, the option-pricing relationships contained in the paper will hold.

B. Solution to Futures Option-Pricing Problem

Under the assumptions stated above, Black demonstrates that, if a riskless hedge can be formed between the futures option and its underlying futures contract, the partial differential equation governing the movements of the futures option price (V) through time is

$$\tfrac{1}{2}\sigma^2 F^2 V_{FF} - rV + V_t = 0 \tag{15.1}$$

This equation applies to American call $(C=V)$ and put $(P=V)$ options, as well as European call $(c=V)$ and put $(p=V)$ options. What distinguishes the four valuation problems is the set of boundary conditions applied to each problem.

C. European Futures Options

The boundary condition necessary to develop an analytic formula for the European call option is that the terminal call price is equal to the maximum value of 0 or the in-the-money amount of the option, that is, $\max(0, F_T - X)$. Black shows that when this terminal boundary condition is applied to Equation 15.1 where $c = V$, the value of a European call option on a futures contract is

$$C(F, T; X) = e^{-rT}[FN(d_1) - XN(d_2)] \tag{15.2}$$

where $d_1 = [\ln(F/X) + 0.5\sigma^2 T]/\sigma\sqrt{T}$, and $d_2 = d_1 - \sigma\sqrt{T}$, and where $N(\ )$ is the cumulative univariate normal distribution. When the lower boundary condition for the European put, $\max(0, X - F_T)$, is applied to the partial differential Equation 15.1, the analytic solution is

$$p(F, T; X) = e^{-rT}[XN(-d_2) - FN(-d_1)] \tag{15.3}$$

where all notation is as it was defined above.

D. American Futures Options

The European call formula (15.2) provides a convenient way of demonstrating that the American call option may be exercised early. As the futures price becomes extremely large relative to the exercise of the option, the values of $N(d_1)$ and $N(d_2)$ approach one, and the European call value approaches $(F-X)e^{-rT}$. But the American option may be exercised immediately for $F - X$, which is higher than the European option value. Thus, the American call option may be worth more "dead" than "alive"[6] and will command a higher price than the European call option.

---

6. Merton [17] demonstrates that, because the exercisable value of an American call option on a non-dividend-paying stock, $S - X$, is always below the lower price bound of the corresponding

FIGURE 15.1   *European and American Call Option Prics as a Function of the Underlying Futures Contract Price*

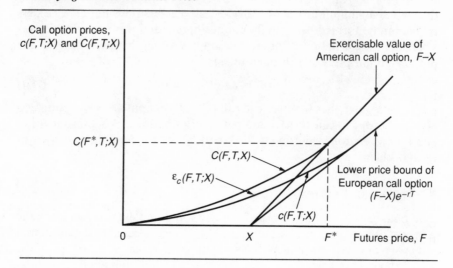

Figure 15.1 illustrates the value of the American call option's early exercise privilege. In the figure, F^* represents the critical current futures price level where the American call option holder is indifferent about exercising his option immediately or continuing to hold it. Below F^*, the value of the early exercise premium $- \epsilon_C(F, T; X) -$ is equal to the difference between the American and European call functions, $C(F, T; X) - c(F, T; X)$. Above F^*, $\epsilon_C(F, T; X)$ is equal to $(F-X) - c(F, T; X)$. Note that as the futures price becomes large relative to the exercise price, the European call option value approaches $(F-X)e^{-rT}$, and the early exercise premium approachs $(F-X)(1 - e^{-rT})$. In other words, the maximum value the early exercise premium may attain is the present value of the interest income that can be earned if the call option is exercised immediately.

Unlike the European option case, there are no known analytic solutions to the partial differential Equation 15.1, subject to the American call option on a futures contract boundary condition, $C(F, t; X) \geq \max(0, F_t - X)$ for all $0 \leq t \leq T$, and, subject to the American put option on a futures contract boundary condition, $P(F, t; X) \geq \max(0, X - F_t)$ for all $0 \leq t \leq T$. Usually, the valuation of American futures options has resorted to finite difference approximation methods.[7] Ramaswamy and Sundaresan [19] and Brenner,

---

European option, $S - Xe^{-rT}$, the American call option is always worth more alive than dead, and will therefore not be exercised early.

7. The first applications of finite difference methods to option-pricing problems were by Schwartz [20], who valued warrants written on dividend-paying stocks, and by Brennan and

Courtadon, and Subrahmanyam [9], for example, use such techniques. Unfortunately, finite difference methods are computationally expensive because they involve enumerating every possible path the futures option price could travel during its remaining time to expiration.

Whaley [23] adapts the Geske-Johnson [13] compound option analytic approximation method to price American futures options. In addition to being computationally less expensive than numerical methods, the compound option approach offers the advantages of being intuitively appealing and easily amenable to comparative statics analysis. Unfortunately, even though the compound option approach is about twenty times faster than numerical methods, it is still not inexpensive because it requires the evaluation of cumulative bivariate and cumulative trivariate normal density functions.

The analytic approximation of American futures option values used in this study is that derived by Barone-Adesi and Whaley [3]. The method is based on MacMillan's [16] quadratic approximation of the American put option on a stock valuation problem and is considerably faster than either the finite difference or the compound option approximation methods.

The quadratic approximation of the American call option on a futures contract, as provided in Barone-Adesi and Whaley [3], is

$$C(F, T; X) = c(F, T; X) + A_2(F/F^*)^{q_2} \quad \text{where } F < F^*$$
$$C(F, T; X) = F - X \qquad \qquad \text{where } F \geq F^* \tag{15.4}$$

and where $A_2 = (F^*/q_2)\{1 - e^{-rT}N[d_1(F^*)]\}$, $d_1(F^*) = [\ln(F^*/X) + 0.5\sigma^2 T]/\sigma\sqrt{T}$, $q_2 = (1 + \sqrt{1 + 4k})/2$, and $k = 2r/[\sigma^2(1 - e^{-rT})]$. F^* is the critical futures price above which the American futures option should be exercised immediately (see Figure 15.1) and is determined iteratively by solving

$$F^* - X = c(F^*, T; X) + \{1 - e^{-rT}N[d_1(F^*)]\}F^*/q_2 \tag{15.4a}$$

Although the valuation equation may appear ominous, its intuition is simple. For a current futures price below the critical stock price F^*, the American call value is equal to the European value plus the early exercise premium, as approximated by the term $A_2(F/F^*)^{q_2}$. Above F^*, the worth of the American call is its exercisable proceeds.

The only parameter to the American option formula (15.4) that requires computational sophistication beyond that required for the European formula (15.2) is the determination of the critical futures price F^*. To this end, Barone-Adesi and Whaley [3] provide an algorithm for solving (15.4a) in five iterations or less.

The quadratic approximation of the American put option on a futures contract is

---

Schwartz [7], who priced American put options on non-dividend-paying stocks. These techniques are reviewed in Brennan and Schwartz [8] and Geske and Shastri [15].

$$P(F, T; X) = p(F, T; X) + A_1(F/F^{**})^{q_1} \quad \text{where } F > F^{**}$$
$$P(F, T; X) = X - F \qquad\qquad\qquad\qquad \text{where } F \leq F^{**}$$

(15.5)

and where $A_1 = -(F^{**}/q_1)\{1 - e^{-rT}N[-d_1(F^{**})]\}$, $q_1 = (1 - \sqrt{1 + 4k})/2$, and where all other notation is as it was defined for the American call. F^{**} is the critical futures price below which the American futures option should be exercised immediately and is determined iteratively by solving

$$X - F^{**} = p(F^{**}, T; X) - \{1 - e^{-rT}N[-d_1(F^{**})]\}F^{**}/q_1 \quad (15.5a)$$

E. Simulation of Early Exercise Premium Values

To demonstrate plausible magnitudes of the early exercise premium on American futures options, the European and American models prices were computed for a range of option-pricing parameters. The results are reported in Table 15.1. It is interesting to note that out-of-the-money futures options have negligible early exercise premiums. For example, when the futures price F is 90, the riskless rate of interest r is 8%, and the standard deviation of the futures price relatives σ is 0.15, an out-of-the-money call option with an exercise price X of 100 and a time to expiration T of 0.5 years has an early exercise premium of 0.0106, only slightly more than 1% of the American option price. Even at-the-money options have small early exercise premiums that account for only a small percentage of the option price. Only when the option is considerably in-the-money does the early exercise premium account for a significant proportion of the price of the option.

In summary, the theory of futures option valuation suggests that the early exercise privilege of American futures options contributes meaningfully to the futures option value. The simulation results, based on option-pricing parameters that are typical for S&P 500 futures option contracts, suggest that this is true, but only for in-the-money options.

II. Empirical Tests

In this section, the performance of the American futures option-pricing models is analyzed using transaction information for S&P 500 equity futures options. After the description of the data in the first subsection, the implied standard deviation methodology is discussed. Volatility estimates are made using nonlinear regression of observed futures option prices on model prices. The third subsection presents an examination of the systematic patterns in the models' prediction errors. This analysis is motivated by the evidence reported in the stock option pricing tests. In the fourth subsection, the hypothesis that the standard deviation of futures price change relatives is the same across call and put options is tested. The final subsection presents the

TABLE 15.1 Theoretical European and American Futures Option Values: Exercise Price (X) = 100

Futures Option Parameters[a]	Futures Price (F)	Call Options			Put Options		
		European $c(F,T;X)$[b]	American $C(F,T;X)$[c]	Early Exercise Premium $\epsilon_C(F,T;X)$	European $p(F,T;X)$[b]	American $P(F,T;X)$[c]	Early Exercise Premium $\epsilon_P(F,T;X)$
$r=0.08$	80	0.0027	0.0029	0.0002	19.6067	20.0000	0.3933
$\sigma=0.15$	90	0.2529	0.2547	0.0018	10.0549	10.1506	0.0957
$T=0.25$	100	2.9321	2.9458	0.0137	2.9321	2.9458	0.0137
	110	10.1752	10.2627	0.0875	0.3732	0.3756	0.0024
	120	19.6239	20.0000	0.3761	0.0199	0.0204	0.0005
$r=0.12$	80	0.0027	0.0030	0.0003	19.4116	20.0000	0.5884
$\sigma=0.15$	90	0.2504	0.2533	0.0029	9.9549	10.1153	0.1605
$T=0.25$	100	2.9029	2.9257	0.0228	2.9029	2.9257	0.0228
	110	10.0740	10.2205	0.1465	0.3695	0.3734	0.0039
	120	19.4286	20.0000	0.5714	0.0197	0.0205	0.0008
$r=0.08$	80	0.3956	0.3986	0.0030	19.9996	20.2032	0.2036
$\sigma=0.30$	90	1.9817	1.9913	0.0096	11.7837	11.8543	0.0707
$T=0.25$	100	5.8604	5.8878	0.0274	5.8604	5.8878	0.0274
	110	12.2527	12.3237	0.0710	2.4507	2.4624	0.0116
	120	20.4776	20.6470	0.1694	0.8737	0.8790	0.0053
$r=0.08$	80	0.0583	0.0603	0.0020	19.2740	20.0000	0.7260
$\sigma=0.15$	90	0.8150	0.8256	0.0106	10.4229	10.6044	0.1815
$T=0.50$	100	4.0637	4.1099	0.0463	4.0637	4.1099	0.0463
	110	10.6831	10.8584	0.1753	1.0752	1.0887	0.0134
	120	19.4105	20.0018	0.5913	0.1947	0.1991	0.0043

a. The notation used in this column is as follows: r = riskless rate of interest; σ = standard deviation of the futures price change relative; and T = time to expiration.

b. The European futures option values are computed using the Black [5] pricing equations.

c. The American futures option values are computed using the Barone-Adesi and Whaley [3] analytic approximations.

results of a joint test of the hypothesis that the American futures option pricing models are correctly specified and that the S&P 500 futures option market is efficient.

A. Data

The data used in this study consist of transaction information for the S&P 500 equity futures and futures option contracts traded on the Chicago Mercantile Exchange (CME) from the first day of trading of the S&P futures options, January 28, 1983, through the last business day of the year, December 30, 1983. The data were provided by the CME and are referred to as "Quote Capture" information. Essentially, the data set contains the time and the price of every transaction in which the price changed from the previously recorded transaction. Bid and ask prices are also recorded if the bid price exceeds or the ask price is below the price at the last transaction. The volume of each transaction and the number of transactions at a particular price are not recorded.

Two exclusionary criteria were applied to the Quote Capture information. First, bid and ask price quotes were eliminated because they do not represent prices at which there were both a buyer and seller available to transact. Both sides of the market transaction were necessary within the market efficiency test design. Second, futures options with times to expiration in excess of 26 weeks were excluded. The trading activity in these options and their underlying futures contracts was too sparse to warrant consideration with the market efficiency test. What remained was a sample of 28,736 transactions, 21,613 in the nearest contract month, and 7,123 in the second nearest contract month.

The futures option-pricing models require the futures price at the instant at which the option is traded. To represent the contemporaneous futures price, the futures price at the trade most closely preceding the futures option trade is used. Because the S&P 500 futures market was so active during the investigation period, the average time between the futures and the subsequent futures option transactions was only 21 seconds.

Table 15.2 offers a summary of the characteristics of the transactions contained in the 232-day sample period. Of the 28,736 transactions, 15,063 were call option transactions and 13,763 were puts. The at-the-money options appear to have been the most active, with 55% of the call option trades and 50% of the put option trades being at futures prices ±2% of the exercise price. Out-of-the-money options were more active than in-the-money options: 25% of total trades to 20% of total trades for calls and 42% to 8% for puts, respectively. Over 64% of the transactions were on options with maturities of less than eight weeks, verifying that most of the trading activity was in the nearest contract month.

TABLE 15.2 *Summary of S&P 500 Futures Option Transactions during the Period January 28, 1983 through December 30, 1983*

Futures Price/ Exercise Price	No. of Transactions			Time to Expiration (in weeks)	No. of Transactions		
(F/X)	Call	Put	Both	(T)	Call	Put	Both
$F/X < 0.90$	11	2	13	$T < 2$	2,307	2,234	4,541
$0.90 \leq F/X < 0.92$	77	9	86	$2 \leq T < 4$	2,375	2,190	4,565
$0.92 \leq F/X < 0.94$	339	42	381	$4 \leq T < 6$	2,567	2,211	4,778
$0.94 \leq F/X < 0.96$	1,014	191	1,205	$6 \leq T < 8$	2,480	2,064	4,544
$0.96 \leq F/X < 0.98$	2,281	773	3,054	$8 \leq T < 10$	1,708	1,623	3,331
$0.98 \leq F/X < 1.00$	4,091	2,615	6,706	$10 \leq T < 12$	1,479	1,371	2,850
$1.00 \leq F/X < 1.02$	4,260	4,252	8,512	$12 \leq T < 14$	1,255	1,164	2,419
$1.02 \leq F/X < 1.04$	1,783	2,559	4,342	$14 \leq T < 16$	337	445	782
$1.04 \leq F/X < 1.06$	830	1,524	2,354	$16 \leq T < 18$	222	173	395
$1.06 \leq F/X < 1.08$	241	875	1,116	$18 \leq T < 20$	175	90	265
$1.08 \leq F/X < 1.10$	78	453	531	$20 \leq T$	158	108	266
$1.10 \leq F/X$	58	378	436				
All	15,063	13,673	28,736	All	15,063	13,673	28,736

The yield on the U.S. Treasury bill maturing on the contract month expiration day[8] was used to proxy for the riskless rate on interest. The yields were computed daily on the basis of the average of the T-bill's bid and ask discounts reported in the *Wall Street Journal*.

B. Implied Standard Deviation Methodology

The American futures option-pricing models have five parameters; F, X, T, r, and σ. Of these, four are known or are easily estimated. The exercise price X and the time of expiration T are terms of the futures option contract, and the futures price F and the riskless rate of interest r are easily accessible market values. The troublesome parameter to estimate is the standard deviation of the futures price change relatives.

The methodology used to estimate the standard deviation of the futures price change relative is described in Whaley [22, pp. 39–40]. Observed futures option prices, V_j, were regressed on their respective model prices, $V_j(\sigma)$, that is,

$$V_j = V_j(\sigma) + \epsilon_j \tag{15.6}$$

---

8. S&P 500 futures option contracts expired the third Thursday of the contract month until the June 1984 contract. Beginning with the June 1984 contract, the third Friday of the month is the expiration day.

where ϵ_j is a random disturbance term,[9] each day during the sample period. All transaction prices for the day were used in each regression. The number of transactions used to estimate σ in a given day ranged from 30 to 300, with the average number being 124. The estimates of σ ranged from 0.1009 to 0.2176, with the average being approximately 0.1555.

The time series of standard deviation estimates indicates that the volatility of the S&P 500 futures price relatives declined during 1983. During the first 116 trading days of the sample period, the average estimate of σ using the American model was 0.1711, while during the last 116 days of the period, it was 0.1399. It is interesting to note that during the same two subperiods, the S&P 500 Index rose by 15.07% and −0.65%, respectively.[10]

C. Tests for Systematic Biases

One way in which the performance of an option-pricing model may be evaluated is by examining its mispricing errors for systematic tendencies. Whaley [22] demonstrates that when the early exercise premium of the American call option on a dividend-paying stock is accounted for in the valuation model, the exercise price and time to expiration biases that had been documented for the European model disappear. Geske and Roll [14] later verify this result and also attempt to explain the variance bias. Here, the variance bias is not of concern since there is only one underlying commodity. The ability of the American futures option models to eliminate the first two biases, however, should be examined.

The tests for systematic biases in the futures option-pricing models involved clustering and then averaging the price deviations by the degree the option is in the money of the option and by the option's time to expiration. Table 15.3 contains a summary of the results for the 15,063 call option and the 13,673 put option transactions in the sample.

Both a "moneyness" bias and a "maturity" bias appear for the call option transaction prices of the sample. The moneyness bias is just the opposite of that reported for stock options.[11] The further the call option is in the money, the lower is the model price relative to the observed price (i.e., out-of-the-money calls are overpriced by the model and the in-the-money calls are underpriced). This is true for the American models when all maturities are

---

9. The relationship between observed and model prices is not exact and is affected by: (1) model misspecification; (2) nonsimultaneity of futures and futures option price quotations; and (3) the bid-ask spread in the futures and futures option markets. If the residuals in the nonlinear regression (15.6) are independent and normally distributed, the resulting value of σ is the maximum likelihood estimate.

10. This evidence is consistent with the notion that the variance rate depends on the price of the underlying asset.

11. See, e.g., Black [4] or Whaley [22].

TABLE 15.3 *Summary of Average Mispricing Errors of American Futures Option-Pricing Models by the Option's Moneyness (F/X) and by the Option's Time to Expiration in Weeks (T) for S&P 500 Futures Option Transactions during the Period January 28, 1983 through December 30, 1983*

	$C - C(F,T;X)$				$P - P(F,T;X)$			
	$T<6$	$6 \leq T<12$	$T \geq 12$	All T	$T<6$	$6 \leq T<12$	$T \geq 12$	All T
$F/X<0.98$	-0.0630[a]	-0.1372	-0.0872	-0.1028	-0.1064	-0.0914	-0.1056	-0.1014
	(1,221)	(1,760)	(741)	(3,722)	(593)	(335)	(89)	(1,017)
$0.98 \leq F/X<1.02$	-0.1228	-0.0775	0.0073	-0.0924	-0.0816	-0.0196	0.1336	-0.0406
	(4,452)	(2,858)	(951)	(8,351)	(3,999)	(2,193)	(675)	(6,867)
$1.02 \leq F/X$	0.0577	0.1175	0.0702	0.0806	0.1286	0.1906	30.3060	0.1929
	(1,486)	(1,049)	(455)	(2,990)	(2,043)	(2,530)	(1,216)	(5,789)
All F/X	-0.0757	-0.0599	-0.0120	-0.0606	-0.0191	0.0808	0.2287	0.0537
	(7,249)	(5,667)	(2,147)	(15,063)	(6,635)	(5,058)	(1,980)	(13,673)

a. The average deviation of the observed option price from the model price for the 1,221 call option transaction prices with in-the-moneyness (F/X) less than 0.98 and time to expiration (T) less than 6 weeks is −0.0630.

clustered together and when the intermediate-term and long-term options are considered separately. For the short-term options, the greatest mispricing occurs for the at-the-money calls, which appear dramatically underpriced relative to the model (e.g., for the American call option-pricing model, the average value of $C - C(F, T; X)$ is -0.1228).

The maturity bias for the calls is also just the opposite of that reported for call options on stocks. Here, model prices are higher than observed prices for short-term options and are lower than observed for long-term options. The relationship is not consistent across the moneyness groupings, however. For out-of-the-money calls, the mispricing is greatest for the intermediate-term options with the model considerably overstating observed values [e.g., the average $C - C(F, T; X)$ is -0.1372], and, for in-the-money options, the mispricing is still greatest for the intermediate-term options, but with the models understating observed values [e.g., the average $C - C(F, T; X)$ is 0.1175]. Overall, however, the maturity bias does not appear to be as serious as the moneyness bias for the sample of call option transaction prices.

The average price deviations for the put options appear to have a more orderly pattern, with the relationships between average price deviation and the moneyness and maturity of the options monotonic. Like the call option results, the maturity bias takes the form of short-term options being underpriced relative to the model and long-term options being overpriced. Unlike the call option results, however, the maturity bias is almost as serious as the moneyness bias, and the moneyness bias takes the form of out-of-the-money options being overpriced relative to the model; and in-the-money options, underpriced. (Recall the put option is in the money where $F/X < 1$.) A possible explanation of this latter result is that floor traders engage in conversion/reversal arbitrage using the European put-call parity relationship,[12]

$$c(F, T; X) - p(F, T; X) = (F - X)e^{-rT} \tag{15.7}$$

If the put-call parity relationship (15.7) is actively arbitraged, overpricing of in-the-money call options should result in overpricing of out-of-the-money put options, and underpricing of out-of-the-money call options should result in underpricing of in-the-money put options, or vice versa.

One final note about the results in Table 15.3 is worthwhile. During the period examined, put options were overpriced on average while call options were underpriced. Obviously, this result is sensitive to the volatility estimate

---

12. The European put-call parity relationship can be found in a variety of papers, including Black [5], Moriarity, Phillips, and Tosini [18], Asay [1], and Wolf [24]. In all of these studies, the futures contract underlying the option contract is treated like a forward, but no problems arise because the European option can be exercised only at expiration.

For American futures options, the assumption of equivalence between forward and futures contract positions can lead to erroneous statements about futures option pricing. Some of these results are outlined in Ramaswamy and Sundaresan [19]. Stoll and Whaley [21] derive the put-call parity relationship for American futures options.

used to price the options, but nonetheless the difference between the average mispricing errors of the put and call option formulas would be approximately the same even if a different estimate of σ were used. This peculiarity indicates that the market's assessment of the volatility of the relative futures price changes may be greater for puts than for calls and provides the motivation for the tests in the next subsection.

D. Stationarity of Volatility Estimates across Options

To test the hypothesis that the standard deviation of futures price change relatives is the same in the pricing of call and put options on the S&P 500 futures contracts, the ratio

$$R = [SSE_C(\sigma_C) + SSE_p(\sigma_p)]/SSE(\sigma) \qquad (15.8)$$

was computed each day during the sample period. In (15.8), $SSE_C(\sigma_C)$ is the sum of squared errors realized by estimating the nonlinear regression (15.6) using only the call option transaction prices during the day, and $SSE_p(\sigma_p)$ is the sum of squared errors using only the put option prices. $SSE(\sigma)$ is the sum of squared errors using both the call and put option prices. If the residuals of the regression are independent and normally distributed, Gallant [12] shows that the test statistic

$$F = (n-2)(1-R) \qquad (15.9)$$

is approximately distributed, $F_{1, n-2}$.[13] The results of these tests are reported in Table 15.4.

The test results indicate that the null hypothesis that the volatility estimates are equal for calls and puts is rejected in 75% of the cases for the American model. The standard deviation of futures price relatives implied by call option prices is lower on average than that implied by put option prices. The cause of this anomaly is difficult to determine. One possible explanation is that the stochastic process governing the futures price movements is ill-defined, so the option-pricing models are misspecified. Another is that perhaps two separate clienteles trade in call options and in put options. But this latter explanation fails to account for the floor traders who could costlessly benefit from such a clientele arrangement.

Regardless of the explanation, the anomaly may be only transitory. The only fact established so far is that the futures option-pricing models do not adequately explain the observed structure of option prices. It may well be the case that the market is mispricing S&P 500 futures options and that abnormal risk-adjusted rates of return may be earned by trading on the basis of the models' prices.

---

13. Barone-Adesi [2] uses a similar maximum likelihood test to compare the structural forms of competing option pricing models.

TABLE 15.4 *Frequency Distribution of Nonrejection/ Rejection of the Null Hypothesis that the Standard Deviations Implied by Option Prices Are Equal for Call-and-Put Options Using S&P 500 Futures Option Transaction Prices during the Period January 28, 1983 through December 30, 1983*

Hypothesis[a, b]	Frequency
H_O: The standard deviation of the futures price relatives for call options is equal to the standard deviation for put options.	59
H_A: The standard deviation of the futures price relatives for call options is *not* equal to the standard deviation for put options.	173
Total	232

a. The probability level used in the evaluation of the test statistics is 5%.
b. The test statistic for the hypothesis test is $F = (n-2)(1-R)$, where n is the number of option transactions and

$$R = [SSE_C(\sigma_C) + SSE_p(\sigma_p)]/SSE(\sigma).$$

Assuming the residuals are independent and normally distributed, the ratio F is approximately distributed as $F_{1, n-2}$.

E. Market Efficiency Test

The systematic biases reported in Table 15.3 and the σ anomaly reported in Table 15.4 may result because the futures option-pricing models are misspecified or because the S&P 500 futures option market is inefficient or both. One way of attempting to isolate the two effects is to test whether abnormal rates of return after transaction costs may be earned by trading futures options on the basis of the models' prices. If abnormal returns after transaction costs can be earned, it is likely to be the case that the market is inefficient. The price deviations, systematic or not, signal profit opportunities. If abnormal profits cannot be earned, there are no grounds for rejecting the null hypothesis that the model is correctly specified and that the S&P 500 futures option market is efficient.

The market efficiency test design involved hedging mispriced futures options against the underlying futures contract. Each day options were priced using the American futures option-pricing models, and the standard deviations were estimated from *all* of the previous day's transaction prices.[14]

---

14. Because both call and put option transaction prices are used in the daily regression to estimate the σ, the estimate is, in essence, an average of the estimates implied by call and puts separately.

Because no estimate of σ was available for the transactions of the first day of the sample period, January 28, 1983, the first day's transactions were eliminated, and only 231 days and 28,493 options remained in the sample.

Each of the 28,493 option transactions was examined to see whether the option was undervalued or overvalued relative to the futures option-pricing models. The hedge formed at that instant in time[15] depended on the nature of the transaction price:

Nature of Transaction Price	Futures Option Position	Futures Position
Undervalued call	Long 1 contract	Short $\delta C/\delta F$ contracts
Overvalued call	Short 1 contract	Long $\delta C/\delta F$ contracts
Undervalued put	Long 1 contract	Long $-\delta P/\delta F$ contracts
Overvalued put	Short 1 contract	Short $-\delta P/\delta F$ contracts

where the partial derivatives of the call and put option prices were computed using valuation Equations 15.4 and 15.5.

Two types of hedge portfolios were considered in the analysis. The first was a "buy-and-hold" hedge portfolio. Each hedge was formed according to the weights described above and was held until the futures option/futures expiration or until the end of the sample period, whichever came first. At such time, the futures option/futures positions were closed, and the hedge profit was computed. The second was the "rebalanced" hedge portfolio. Here, the initial hedge composition was the same as the buy-and-hold strategy, but at the end of each day, the futures position was altered to account for the change in the futures option's hedge ratio. The difference between the profits of these two hedge portfolio strategies was therefore the net gain or loss on the intermediate futures position adjustments within the rebalanced portfolio.[16]

---

15. The hedge portfolio strategy assumed that the hedge is formed at the prices that signaled the profit opportunity. This was done for two reasons. First, floor traders have the opportunity to transact at these prices. If a sell order at a price below the model price enters the pit, the floor trader can buy the options and then hedge his position within seconds using the futures. Second, the transaction price for retail customers may be handled by simply adding the bid-ask spread to the price that triggered a buy and subtracting the bid-ask spread from the price that triggered a sell.

16. To illustrate the mechanics of the buy-and-hold and rebalanced hedge portfolio strategies, consider the following example. A call option with an exercise price of $100 and with two days to expiration is priced at $1, where its theoretical price is $1.50 and its hedge ratio is 0.8. The current futures price is $100. Because the call is underpriced relative to the model, it is purchased, and 0.8 futures contracts are sold. The net investment of both the buy-and-hold and rebalanced hedge portfolios is therefore $1 (i.e., one option contract times $1 per contract).

By the end of the day before expiration, the futures price rises to say, $102. At the new futures price, the model price is $3.00 and the hedge ratio is 0.9. Since the hedge ratio has changed,

Note that the hedge portfolios are assumed to be held until the option's expiration. This is unlike the empirical procedures used in the stock option market efficiency tests, which assume that an option position is opened at one price and then closed at the next available price. If the option-pricing models have systematic mispricing tendencies, an option that is undervalued on one day is likely to be undervalued on the next. By holding the option position open until expiration, at which time the observed and model prices converge to the same value, there is some assurance that the prospective option-mispricing profits are being captured.

In Table 15.5, the average cost, profit, and rate of return of the hedge portfolios formed on the basis of the American futures option prices are presented. When no minimum size restriction was placed on the absolute price deviation, 28,493 hedge portfolios were formed. On an average, the number of futures contracts in each hedge at formation was 0.442 (1.442 less one futures option contract). The average investment cost of each hedge was −$46.75 (−0.0935 × $500),[17] indicating that, on an average, money was collected when the hedge portfolios were formed.

The average profit for the buy-and-hold hedge portfolio was $88 (0.1760 × $500), and the average rebalanced hedge portfolio profit was $77.85. The daily rebalancing of the futures position lowered overall hedge profits. On the other hand, the standard deviation of the buy-and-hold profit was 1.9302 compared with 0.8574 for the rebalanced portfolio profits.[18] The daily rebalancing of the futures position decreased the volatility of the hedge profits portfolio by more than 55%.

Immediately to the right of the rebalanced portfolio profit column is a column with break-even transaction cost rates. These numbers represent the average of the transaction cost rate per contract sufficient to eliminate rebalanced portfolio profit. In other words, if the transaction cost rate was less than $57.60 (0.1152 × $500) per contract, the average portfolio profit was greater than zero. Note that the transaction costs were assumed to be paid only on the contracts bought or sold when the portfolio was formed. The

---

0.1 more futures contracts must be sold in order to maintain the riskless hedge of the rebalanced portfolio. The additional futures contracts are assumed to be bought or sold at the day's closing price—in this case $102.

Now, suppose that on the following day the futures expires at $106 and the futures option at $6.00 (i.e., the futures price $106 less the exercise price $100). The buy-and-hold hedge portfolio profit would be computed as the option position profit, $6 − 1 = $5, plus the futures position profit, −0.8 × ($106 − 100) = −$4.80, or $0.20 in total. The rebalanced hedge portfolio profit is computed as the $0.20 buy-and-hold profit plus the net gain (loss) on the intermediate futures position change, −0.1 × ($106 − 102) = −$0.40, or −$0.20 in total.

17. The value for the S&P 500 futures and futures options are index values. The dollar worth of the contract is obtained by multiplying the index value by $500.

18. The standard deviations are not reported, but they can be inferred from the reported numbers of observations and the t-ratios.

TABLE 15.5 *Average Cost, Profit, and Rate of Return of Hedge Portfolios by Size of Absolute Price Deviation from the American Futures Option-Pricing Models for S&P 500 Futures Option Transaction Prices during the Period January 31, 1983 through December 30, 1983*

Minimum Absolute Price Deviation	No. of Observations	Average Investment[a]	Average No. of Contracts[b]	Buy-and-Hold Portfolio Profit[c]	Rebalanced Portfolio Profit[d]	Break-Even Transaction Cost Rate[e]	Rebalanced Portfolio Excess Rate of Return[f]	Rebalanced Portfolio Excess Return after Transaction Costs[g]	Relative Systematic Risk[h]
All |Δ|	28,493	−0.0935	1.442	0.1760 (15.39)[i]	0.1557 (30.64)	0.1152	0.0905 (35.77)	0.0696 (27.78)	0.1193 (2.11)
|Δ|≥0.05	22,850	−0.1035	1.441	0.2054 (15.83)	0.1854 (31.41)	0.1372	0.1026 (38.48)	0.0850 (32.21)	0.0745 (1.27)
|Δ|≥0.10	17,596	−0.1160	1.437	0.2444 (16.24)	0.2181 (30.70)	0.1615	0.1164 (39.91)	0.1006 (34.81)	0.0375 (0.59)
|Δ|≥0.15	13,116	−0.1370	1.430	0.2507 (14.07)	0.2424 (27.53)	0.1802	0.1247 (37.69)	0.1099 (33.48)	0.0924 (1.30)
|Δ|≥0.20	9,521	−0.1200	1.425	0.2607 (12.18)	0.2696 (23.82)	0.2006	0.1309 (33.64)	0.1168 (30.20)	0.1632 (1.98)

a. The cost of the hedge portfolio is equal to the option price if the option is purchased and minus the option price if the option is sold. The futures position involves no net investment.

b. The average absolute number of option and futures contracts in the hedge.

c. The buy-and-hold portfolio profit assumes the hedge is formed and held until the expiration of the contracts or the end of the sample period.

d. The rebalanced portfolio profit is equal to the buy-and-hold profit plus (less) the net gains (losses) from the futures position adjustments made during the option's life.

e. The break-even transaction cost per contract sufficient to eliminate the rebalanced portfolio profit.

f. The rate of return of the rebalanced hedge portfolio less the riskless rate of interest.

g. The excess rate of return of the rebalanced hedge portfolio after a $10 per contract transaction cost.

h. The relative systematic risk is estimated by regressing the excess rate of return of the hedge on the relative futures price changes over the same period.

i. The values in parentheses are *t*-ratios for the null hypothesis that the parameter is equal to 0.

overall net effect of the incremental transaction costs on the intermediate daily rebalancing of the futures position of the hedge portfolios was assumed to be equal to zero.[19]

The rebalanced portfolio excess rate of return column contains the average rate of return and the net of any interest carrying charge. If the option in the hedge portfolio was purchased, the excess rate of return of the hedge was equal to the rate of return on the hedge less the riskless rate of interest. If the option was sold, interest was assumed to be earned on the proceeds from the sale, so the excess rate of return on the hedge was equal to the rate of return on the hedge plus the riskless rate of interest. The excess rate of return for the rebalanced portfolio using all of the transactions was 9.05% and is significantly greater than zero.

Before proceeding with a description of the remaining two columns, it is worthwhile to point out three facts about the excess rates of return for the rebalanced hedge portfolio. First, the excess return did not fall very much if the proceeds from the futures option sales were assumed to earn no interest. In this case, the average excess rate of return was 8.41%, with a t-ratio of 33.49. Second, the excess rate of return for the American model was only slightly higher than it was for the European model. For the latter model, the average return was 8.91%, with a t-ratio of 35.03. This evidence is consistent with the simulation results in the last section. Finally, the use of student t-ratios to evaluate the significance of the excess rates of return is appropriate since the return distributions were symmetric and only slightly leptokurtic.

The column labeled "Excess Return after Transaction Costs" incorporated a $10 per contract transaction cost assumption. Such a fee is probably appropriate for a floor trader.[20] The average excess rate of return after transaction costs was 6.96%, again significantly greater than zero.

---

19. To account for the transaction costs of the daily readjustment of the futures position within each portfolio separately would dramatically overstate the role of transaction costs within the hedge portfolio because, at the end of the day, some hedges will require that futures contracts be purchased and some that futures be sold. The net overall daily adjustment in the futures position would likely be near zero, so no intermediate transaction costs were imposed.
20. Actually, the assumed $10 per contract overstates the transaction costs a floor trader might face. The only transaction cost paid by floor traders is a clearing fee, which is on the order of $1.50 per contract. The $10 per contract assumption, therefore, presents a conservative view of the floor trader's hedge portfolio profits after transaction costs.

Two other institutional considerations are worthy of note. The transaction cost rates in this market are quoted on a "round-turn" basis. That is, a $50 per contract commission charge covers the cost of entering the market at the time of purchase or sale and the cost of closing the position at a subsequent date. For futures contract positions, the broker charges all of the commission when the position is closed, and, for futures option positions, half the commission is charged when the position is opened and half when it it closed.

Since commission rates are negotiated between each customer and his or her broker, it is difficult to assess what are representative commission charges for the various futures/futures

The final column contains estimated slope coefficients from the regression of rebalanced portfolio excess rates of return on the futures price change relatives over the corresponding period. In essence, this regression is intended to evaluate the effectiveness of the portfolio rebalancing at maintaining a riskless hedge. For the entire sample of hedge portfolios, the relative systematic risk is significantly positive at the 5% level; however its magnitude (0.1193) is very small.

Table 15.5 also contains the hedge portfolio profit characteristics when minimum absolute option price deviations of 0.05, 0.10, 0.15, and 0.20 were imposed. Naturally, the higher the demanded absolute price deviation, the fewer the option transactions to qualify as hedge portfolio candidates. In the case where the minimum absolute deviation was set equal to 0.10, for example, only 17,596 hedges were formed.

With all of the price deviation strategies reported in Table 15.5, the average excess rates of return are significantly greater than zero. For floor traders, demanding a minimum price deviation of 0.05 is reasonable since they face only the cost of clearing their transactions, which is considerably less than $25 per contract. When such a minimum price deviation was imposed, the average hedge portfolio excess rate of return was 10.26% before clearing costs and 8.50% after a $10 per contract clearing cost was applied to both the futures option and futures transactions. Retail customers, however, not only face the commission rates imposed by their broker, but also the bid-ask spread imposed by the market maker. Assuming a commission rate of $50 per contract and a bid-ask spread of $50 per option contract, demanding a minimum price deviation of 0.20 is reasonable. However, in this case the average break-even transaction cost rate was 0.2006, so the retail customer would have earned about $0.30 per hedge after transaction costs.

In the previous section, systematic mispricing errors related to the moneyness of the option were documented. For this reason, the option transactions were categorized by the type of option and by the degree to which the option is in the money. The results are reported in Table 15.6. Most of the abnormal profits associated with the trading strategy appear to be concentrated in out-of-the-money put options. The average excess rate of return after the floor trader's clearing costs was 16.88%. In comparison, none of the other option categories had an average return greater than 3% after clearing costs.

One plausible explanation for this result is that more than 72% of out-of-the-money put options were overpriced (see Table 15.3) and thus sold within

___

option customers. Large institutional customers such as mutual funds typically pay commissions at a rate of $20 to $30 per contract and are allowed to post margin requirement in the form of interest-bearing T-bills. Smaller customers likely pay commissions of $50 or more and are also allowed the T-bill margin-posting privilege. Some brokers quote lower rates for small customers but demand margin money in the form of cash.

TABLE 15.6 *Average Cost, Profit, and Rate of Return of Hedge Portfolios by the Moneyness of the Option for S&P 500 Futures Option Transaction Prices during the Period January 31, 1983 through December 30, 1983*

Futures Option Category	No. of Observations	Average Investment[a]	Average No. of Contracts[b]	Buy-and-Hold Portfolio Profit[c]	Rebalanced Portfolio Profit[d]	Break-Even Transaction Cost Rate[e]	Rebalanced Portfolio Excess Rate of Return[f]	Rebalanced Portfolio Excess Return after Transaction Costs[g]	Relative Systematic Risk[h]
Calls $F/X<1$	7,736	-1.0521	1.339	-0.0077 (-0.34)[i]	0.0204 (2.34)	0.0160	0.0432 (7.00)	0.0159 (2.60)	0.7339 (5.25)
Calls $F/X\geq1$	7,150	0.5963	1.670	0.1052 (4.60)	0.1284 (16.81)	0.0763	0.0295 (12.58)	0.0206 (8.84)	0.4858 (9.02)
Puts $F/X<1$	3,620	-1.9300	1.646	0.0975 (2.98)	0.0497 (1.95)	0.0273	0.0186 (3.99)	0.0074 (1.61)	0.4150 (3.66)
Puts $F/X\geq1$	9,987	0.8208	1.286	0.3979 (21.53)	0.3194 (37.46)	0.2518	0.1968 (42.10)	0.1688 (36.42)	-0.7379 (-7.56)

a. The cost of the hedge portfolio is equal to the option price if the option is purchased and minus the option price if the option is sold. The futures position involves no net investment.

b. The average absolute number of option and futures contracts in the hedge.

c. The buy-and-hold portfolio profit assumes the hedge is formed and held until the expiration of the contracts or the end of the sample period.

d. The rebalanced portfolio profit is equal to the buy-and-hold profit plus (less) the net gains (losses) from the futures position adjustments made during the option's life.

e. The break-even transaction cost per contract sufficient to eliminate the rebalanced portfolio profit.

f. The rate of return of the rebalanced hedge portfolio less the riskless rate of interest.

g. The excess rate of return of the rebalanced hedge portfolio after a $10 per contract transaction cost.

h. The relative systematic risk is estimated by regressing the excess rate of return of the hedge on the relative futures price changes over the same period.

i. The values in parentheses are t-ratios for the null hypothesis that the parameter is equal to 0.

the trading strategy. Over the period January 31, 1983 through December 30, 1983, the S&P 500 Index rose from 145.30 to 164.93, indicating that writing out-of-the-money puts would have been profitable indeed. But, the put options sold within the hedge strategy were balanced against short positions in the futures, so what was gained on the put transactions should have been lost on the futures transactions. Moreover, the estimated systematic risk for the hedge portfolios in this category was significantly negative, indicating that, if anything, not enough put options were sold to immunize the portfolio against movements in the underlying futures price. The overall upward market movement in the equity market during the examination period must therefore be discounted as a potential explanation of the market inefficiency.

Although the results of Table 15.6 indicate that floor traders could profit by writing out-of-the-money puts, it is doubtful whether retail customers could profit by such a strategy. As was noted in Table 15.2, at-the-money options enjoyed the greatest volume of activity and therefore probably experienced the lowest bid-ask spread. Out-of-the-money S&P 500 futures options have less liquidity, and it is not uncommon to find the bid-ask spread as high as 0.15 or 0.20. Assuming a commission rate of $50 per contract and a bid-ask spread of $50 per contract takes the average profit from $159.70 per hedge to an average gain after transaction costs of $45.40.

Overall, the results reported in Tables 15.5 and 15.6 provide evidence that the joint hypothesis that the American futures option valuation models are correctly specified and that the S&P 500 futures option market is efficient is refuted for the period January 31, 1983 through December 30, 1983, at least from the standpoint of floor traders who stood ready to transact based on model prices. From a retail customer's standpoint, however, it is doubtful whether abnormal profits after transaction costs could have been earned.

In Table 15.7, the option transactions in four separate subperiods are considered. In the first subperiod, the average excess rate of return on the hedge portfolio was 0.47%, insignificantly different from zero. In the remaining three subperiods, the excess rate of return was significantly greater than zero, with the return highest in the second subperiod and second highest in the final subperiod. In other words, there does not appear to be any indication that the market became more efficient during 1983. Whether floor traders can continue to earn abnormal rates of return after clearing costs by buying undervalued and selling overvalued S&P 500 futures options must await further empirical investigation.

III. Summary and Conclusions

The purpose of this paper is to review the theory underlying American futures option valuation and to test the theory in one of the recently developed

TABLE 15.7 *Average Cost, Profit, and Rate of Return of Hedge Portfolios by Subperiod for S&P 500 Futures Option Transaction Prices during the Period January 31, 1983 through December 30, 1983*

Subperiod	No. of Observations	Average Investment [a]	Average No. of Contracts [b]	Buy-and-Hold Portfolio Profit [c]	Rebalanced Portfolio Profit [d]	Break-Even Transaction Cost Rate [e]	Rebalanced Portfolio Excess Rate of Return [f]	Rebalanced Portfolio Excess Return after Transaction Costs [g]	Relative Systematic Risk [h]
1/31/83 –4/21/83	9,846	-0.0509	1.454	-0.1758 (-8.73)[i]	0.0308 (7.01)	0.0271	0.0047 (1.56)	-0.1024 (-4.13)	0.8848 (15.40)
4/22/83 –7/14/83	8,237	-0.1623	1.450	0.5118 (22.84)	0.3884 (55.08)	0.2682	0.2067 (50.06)	0.1876 (39.82)	0.8641 (5.66)
7/15/83 –10/6/83	6,001	-0.1902	1.423	0.2323 (8.86)	0.0953 (7.25)	0.0780	0.0737 (10.97)	0.0515 (7.72)	-0.2587 (-0.90)
10/7/83 –12/30/83	4,409	0.0710	1.430	0.2588 (14.55)	0.0968 (4.49)	0.0740	0.0879 (12.48)	0.0567 (8.14)	-1.769 (-4.52)

a. The cost of the hedge portfolio is equal to the option price if the option is purchased and minus the option price if the option is sold. The futures position involves no net investment.

b. The average absolute number of option and futures contracts in the hedge.

c. The buy-and-hold portfolio profit assumes the hedge is formed and held until the expiration of the contracts or the end of the sample period.

d. The rebalanced portfolio profit is equal to the buy-and-hold profit plus (less) the net gains (losses) from the futures position adjustments made during the option's life.

e. The break-even transaction cost per contract sufficient to eliminate the rebalanced portfolio profit.

f. The rate of return of the rebalanced hedge portfolio less the riskless rate of interest.

g. The excess rate of return of the rebalanced hedge portfolio after a $10 per contract transaction cost.

h. The relative systematic risk is estimated by regressing the excess rate of return of the hedge on the relative futures price changes over the same period.

i. The values in parentheses are *t*-ratios for the null hypothesis that the parameter is equal to 0.

futures option markets. The theoretical work begins by focusing on the partial differential equation of Black [5] and by discussing how the boundary conditions to the equation imply different structural forms to the pricing equations. Although no analytic solutions to the American futures option-pricing problems are provided, efficient analytic approximations are presented. Simulations of futures option prices using the European and American models and plausible option-pricing parameters show that the early exercise premium of the American futures option has a significant impact on pricing if the option is in the money.

The empirical work focuses on transaction prices for S&P 500 equity futures options during the first 232 trading days of the market's existence, the period from January 28, 1983 through December 30, 1983. The major empirical results are as follows:

1. A moneyness bias and a maturity bias appear for the American futures option-pricing models. For calls, the moneyness bias is the opposite of that reported for stock options — out-of-the-money options are underpriced relative to the model and in-the-money options are overpriced. For puts, just the reverse is true — out-of-the-money puts are overpriced relative to the model and in-the-money puts are underpriced. The maturity bias is the same for both the calls and the puts — short time-to-expiration options are underpriced relative to the model and long time-to-expiration are overpriced, but the bias appears more serious for put options than for call options.

2. The standard deviation implied by call option transaction prices is lower on average than that implied by put option prices.

3. A riskless hedging strategy using the American futures option-pricing models (as well as the European futures option-pricing models) generates abnormal risk-adjusted rates of return after the transaction costs paid by floor traders or large institutional customers. If a retail customer were to try to capture the profits implied by the futures option mispricing, however, transaction costs will likely eliminate the hedge portfolio profit opportunities.

References

1. M. R. Asay, "A Note on the Design of Commodity Contracts," *Journal of Futures Markets* 2 (Spring 1982), pp. 1–7.
2. G. Barone-Adesi, "Maximum Likelihood Tests of Option Pricing Models," *Advances in Futures and Option Research* 1 (1986).
3. G. Barone-Adesi and R. E. Whaley, "Efficient Analytic Approximation of American Option Values," Working Paper No. 15, Institute for Financial Research, University of Alberta, 1985.

4. F. Black, "Fact and Fantasy in the Use of Options," *Financial Analysts Journal* 31 (July–August 1975), pp. 36–41, 61–72.

5. ———, "The Pricing of Commodity Contracts," *Journal of Financial Economics* 3 (January–March 1976), pp. 167–79.

6. F. Black and M. Scholes, "The Pricing of Options and Corporate Liabilities," *Journal of Political Economy* 81 (May–June 1973), pp. 637–59.

7. M. J. Brennan and E. S. Schwartz, "The Valuation of American Put Options," *Journal of Finance* 32 (May 1977), pp. 449–62.

8. ———, "Finite Difference Methods and Jump Processes Arising in the Pricing of Contingent Claims: A Synthesis," *Journal of Financial and Quantitative Analysis* 13 (September 1978), pp. 461–74.

9. M. Brenner, G. R. Courtadon, and M. Subrahmanyam, "Option on Stock Indices and Stock Index Futures," working paper, New York University, 1984.

10. G. Courtadon, "The Pricing of Options on Default-Free Bonds," *Journal of Financial and Quantitative Analysis* 17 (March 1982), pp. 75–100.

11. J. C. Cox, J. E. Ingersoll, and S. A. Ross, "The Relation between Forward and Futures Prices," *Journal of Financial Economics* 9 (December 1981), pp. 321–46.

12. R. Gallant, "Nonlinear Regression," *American Statistician* 29 (May 1975), pp. 73–81.

13. R. Geske and H. E. Johnson, "The American Put Valued Analytically," *Journal of Finance* 39 (December 1984), pp. 1511–24.

14. R. Geske and R. Roll, "Isolating the Observed Biases in American Call Option Pricing: An Alternative Estimator," working paper, Graduate School of Management, UCLA, 1984.

15. R. Geske and K. Shastri, "Valuation by Approximation: A Comparison of Alternative Valuation Techniques," *Journal of Financial and Quantitative Analysis* 20 (March 1985), pp. 45–71.

16. L. W. MacMillan, "Analytic Approximation for the American Put Option," *Advances in Futures and Options Research* 1 (1986).

17. R. C. Merton, "The Theory of Rational Option Pricing," *Bell Journal of Economics and Management Science* 4 (Spring 1973), pp. 141–83.

18. E. Moriarity, S. Phillips, and P. Tosini, "A Comparison of Options and Futures in the Management of Portfolio Risk," *Financial Analysts Journal* 37 (January–February 1981), pp. 61–67.

19. K. Ramaswamy and S. M. Sundaresan, "The Valuation of Options on Futures Contracts," working paper, Graduate School of Business, Columbia University, 1984.

20. E. S. Schwartz, "The Valuation of Warrants: Implementing a New Approach," *Journal of Financial Economics* 4 (January 1977), pp. 79–93.

21. H. R. Stoll and R. E. Whaley, "The New Options: Arbitrageable Linkages and Valuation," *Advances in Futures and Options Research* 1 (1986).

22. R. E. Whaley, "Valuation of American Call Options on Dividend-Paying Stocks: Empirical Tests," *Journal of Financial Economics* 10 (March 1982), pp. 29–57.

23. ———, "On Valuing American Futures Options," *Financial Analysts Journal* (forthcoming) and Working Paper No. 4, Institute for Financial Research, University of Alberta, 1984.

24. A. Wolf, "Fundamentals of Commodity Options on Futures," *Journal of Futures Markets* 2 (1982), pp. 391–408.

16

Foreign Currency Option Values

*Mark B. Garman & Steven W. Kohlhagen**

Foreign exchange options (hereafter *FX options*) are an important new market innovation. They provide a significant expansion in the available risk-control and speculative instruments for a vital source of risk, namely foreign currency values. The purpose of this paper is to develop the relevant pricing formulas for FX options.

The deliverable instrument of an FX option is a fixed amount of underlying foreign currency. In the standard Black-Scholes (1973) option-pricing model, the underlying deliverable instrument is a non–dividend-paying stock. The difference between the two underlying instruments is readily seen when we compare their equilibrium forward prices. When interest rates are constant (as in the Black-Scholes assumptions), the forward price of the stock must, by arbitrage, command a forward premium equal to the interest rate. But in the foreign currency markets, forward prices can involve either forward premiums or discounts. This is because the forward value of a currency is related to the ratio of the prices of riskless bonds traded in each country. The familiar arbitrage relationship ('interest rate parity') correspondingly asserts that the forward exchange premium must equal the interest rate *differential,* which may be either positive or negative. Thus, both foreign and domestic interest rates play a role in the valuation of these forward contracts,

*The authors gratefully acknowledge comments contributed during the course of this research by Fischer Black, Robert Geske, Richard Roll, and Terry Turner, without implicating them in any errors contained herein.

and it is therefore logical to expect that such a role extends to options as well. That this is indeed the case we shall see below.

I. Development

We use notation as follows:

S = the spot price of the deliverable currency (domestic units per foreign unit)

F = the forward price of the currency delivered at option maturity

K = exercise price of option (domestic units per foreign unit)

T = time remaining until maturity of option

$C(S, T)$ = the price of an FX call option (domestic units per foreign unit)

$P(S, T)$ = the price of an FX put option (domestic units per foreign unit)

r_D = the domestic (riskless) interest rate

r_F = the foreign (riskless) interest rate

σ = volatility of the spot currency price

μ = drift of the spot currency price

$N(\cdot)$ = cumulative normal distribution function

α = the expected rate of return on a security

δ = the standard deviation of the security rate of return.

Our assumptions are the usual ones for an option-pricing model:

1. Geometric Brownian motion governs the currency spot price; that is, the differential representation of spot price movements is $dS = \mu S\,dt + \sigma S\,dz$, where z is the standard Wiener process.
2. Option prices are a function of only one stochastic variable, namely S.
3. Markets are frictionless.
4. Interest rates, both in the domestic and foreign markets, are constant.[1]

As is also usual, our analysis shall pertain to European FX options – options that can be exercised only on their maturity date. The American options, which may be exercised at any time prior to maturity, are discussed later.

The key to understanding FX option pricing is to properly appreciate the role of foreign and domestic interest rates. We do this by comparing the advantages of holding an FX option with those of holding its underlying currency. As is well-known, the risk-adjusted expected excess returns of securities governed by our assumptions must be identical in an arbitrage-free continuous-time economy.[2] That is, we must have

$$\frac{\alpha_i - r_D}{\delta_i} = \lambda \quad \text{for all } i \tag{16.1}$$

where λ does not depend on the security considered.[3] Applying this fact to the ownership of foreign currency, we have[4]

$$\frac{(\mu + r_F) - r_D}{\sigma} = \lambda \tag{16.2}$$

That is, the expected return from holding the foreign currency is μ, the "drift" of the exchange rate (domestic units per foreign unit), plus the riskless capital growth arising from holding the foreign currency in the form of an asset (e.g., foreign treasury notes and CD's) paying interest at the rate of r_F. The denominator of the left-hand side of Equation 16.2 is σ, since this is the standard deviation of the rate of return on holding the currency. (Note that μ, σ, r_F, and r_D are all dimensionless quantities, so there is no issue of conversion between foreign and domestic terms.)

Next, letting $C(S, T)$ be the price of a European call option with time T left to maturity, (16.1) implies

$$\frac{\alpha_C - r_D}{\delta_C} = \lambda \tag{16.3}$$

where α_C and δ_C are the call option's expected rate of return and standard deviation of same, respectively. By Ito's lemma, we have

$$\alpha_C C = \frac{1}{2}\sigma^2 S^2 \frac{\partial^2 C}{\partial S^2} + \mu S \frac{\partial C}{\partial S} - \frac{\partial C}{\partial T} \tag{16.4}$$

and

$$\delta_C S = \sigma S \frac{\partial C}{\partial S} \tag{16.5}$$

Substituting (16.4) and (16.5) into (16.3) yields

$$\frac{\frac{1}{2}\sigma^2 S^2 \frac{\partial^2 C}{\partial S^2} + \mu S \frac{\partial C}{\partial S} - \frac{\partial C}{\partial T} - r_D C}{\sigma S \frac{\partial C}{\partial S}} = \lambda \tag{16.3a}$$

Thus equating (16.2) and (16.3) we have

$$\frac{1}{2}\sigma^2 S^2 \frac{\partial^2 C}{\partial S^2} - r_D C + (r_D S - r_F S)\frac{\partial C}{\partial S} = \frac{\partial C}{\partial T} \tag{16.6}$$

The latter equation is reminiscent of models proposed by Samuelson (1965) and Samuelson and Merton (1969) in which the dividend rate of a stock is presumed to be proportional to the level of the stock price. Indeed, there is a similar interpretation for foreign currency options. Consider r_F as the "dividend rate" of the foreign currency. However, this rate is in foreign terms, so to convert to domestic terms, one would naturally multiply it by the spot exchange rate S. The Samuelson-Merton model has not received a great deal of attention in the literature, probably because of its rather strained assumption of a proportional dividend policy. That is, under their model, a firm must constantly monitor its stock price and adjust a continuously paid dividend as a fixed fraction of that price. This is rather impractical as a realistic dividend policy. But in the foreign exchange context, the "adjustment of dividends" takes place in an automatic fashion, since the conversion from foreign to domestic currency terms at the market exchange rate is natural for dimensional consistency within Equation 16.6.

II. Solutions

The solution to (16.6) for a European FX call option must obey the further boundary condition that $C(S, 0) = \max[0, S - K]$, yielding[5] the valuation formula

$$C(S, T) = e^{-r_F T} SN(x + \sigma\sqrt{T}) - e^{-r_D T} KN(x) \qquad (16.7)$$

where

$$x \equiv \frac{\ln(S/K) + \{r_D - r_F - (\sigma^2/2)\}T}{\sigma\sqrt{T}}$$

Note that both the foreign interest rate r_F and the interest differential $r_D - r_F$ play distinct roles in the solution.

Of course, Equation 16.6 governs all securities satisfying our original assumptions. Thus the European FX put option also satisfies that differential equation, but with the boundary condition $P(S, 0) = \max[0, K - S]$. Hence the solution to the European FX put option is given as

$$P(S, T) = e^{-r_F T} S[N(x + \sigma\sqrt{T}) - 1] - e^{-r_D T} K[N(x) - 1] \qquad (16.8)$$

where x is as defined for the call option.[6]

III. Comparative Statics

The partial derivatives of formula (16.7) are also of interest, and these are computed below. Foremost in significance is the "hedge ratio":

$$\frac{\partial C}{\partial S} = e^{-r_F T} N(x + \sigma\sqrt{T}) > 0 \qquad (16.9)$$

Other partial derivatives are:

$$\frac{\partial C}{\partial K} = -e^{-r_D T} N(x) < 0 \qquad (16.10)$$

$$\frac{\partial C}{\partial \sigma} = e^{-r_D T} K \sqrt{T} N'(x) > 0 \qquad (16.11)$$

$$\frac{\partial C}{\partial r_D} = Te^{-r_D T} K N(x) > 0 \qquad (16.12)$$

$$\frac{\partial C}{\partial r_F} = -Te^{-r_F T} S N(x + \sigma\sqrt{T}) < 0 \qquad (16.13)$$

and

$$\frac{\partial C}{\partial T} \equiv -r_F e^{-r_F T} S N(x + \sigma\sqrt{T}) + r_D e^{-r_D T} K N(x) + \frac{e^{-r_D T}\sigma}{2\sqrt{T}} K N'(x) \qquad (16.14)$$

Interpreting, when other variables (significantly the spot rate) are held constant, FX European call values rise when the domestic interest rate increases and fall when the foreign rate increases. Increases in volatility uniformly give rise to increases in FX option prices, while increases in the strike price cause FX call option prices to decline. However, the sign of the time derivative is ambiguous. In-the-money calls tend to have negative signs for this derivative when the time to maturity is short. The situation is exacerbated when the calls become deep in the money or when foreign interest rates rise well above domestic rates. Of course, a negative time derivative could not pertain to an American FX option, and so we see that the European formulas for calls (and puts) are clearly inadequate descriptions of their American counterparts in these cases. (See also the discussion by Merton [1973] for the proportional dividend case.)

The derivatives of the European FX put options are obtained analogously from (16.8), with the obvious changes in sign for the derivatives involved.

IV. Relationship to Contemporaneous Forward Price

Asserting the familiar relationship known as "interest rate parity" (Keynes [1923]), the forward price of currency deliverable contemporaneously[7] with the maturation of the option is[8]

$$F = e^{(r_D - r_F)T} S \qquad (16.15)$$

Substituting this relation into the solution (16.7) gives the alternate solution[9]

$$C(F, T) = \{FN(x + \sigma\sqrt{T}) - KN(x)\}e^{-r_D T} \qquad (16.16)$$

where

$$x \equiv \frac{\ln(F/K) - (\sigma^2/2)T}{\sigma\sqrt{T}}$$

Note that with this substitution the call value depends only upon F and r_D; it does not depend independently upon S and r_F. That is, given the current domestic rate of interest, all option relevant information concerning the foreign interest rate and the spot currency price is reflected in the forward price.

The European put value formula is analogous:

$$P(F, T) = \{F[N(x + \sigma\sqrt{T}) - 1] - K[N(x) - 1]\}e^{-r_D T} \tag{16.17}$$

We now augment some conclusions regarding comparative statics, this time using the forward-based formula (16.16). The derivative of the call value with respect to forward price is given as

$$\frac{\partial C}{\partial F} = e^{-r_D T}N(x + \sigma\sqrt{T}) > 0 \tag{16.18}$$

However, some caution should be observed in applying this latter derivative as a "hedge ratio." This is because the forward price is not equivalent to the value of a forward contract, the latter being the important determinant of current wealth at risk. Rather, the forward price is a parameter, not unlike a strike price, which is continuously adjusted so as to make the value of the forward contract identically zero. Consequently, the forward price must be discounted by the factor $e^{(r_F - r_D)T}$ to properly reflect current values, and hence the correct "hedge ratio" between wealth at risk in forward and option contract positions is as given previously in (16.9).

With regard to other partial derivatives, we have

$$\frac{\partial C}{\partial K} = -e^{-r_D T}N(x) < 0 \tag{16.19}$$

and

$$\frac{\partial C}{\partial \sigma} = e^{-r_D T}K\sqrt{T}N'(x) > 0 \tag{16.20}$$

exactly as before. However, the sign of the domestic interest rate partial derivative is just the opposite of the previous section:

$$\frac{\partial C}{\partial r_D} = -e^{-r_D T}T\{FN(x + \sigma\sqrt{T}) - KN(x)\} = -TC < 0 \tag{16.21}$$

That is, if the contemporaneous forward rate is held constant, an increase in domestic interest rates results in a decrease in FX call values. Finally, we have

$$\frac{\partial C}{\partial T} = -r_D C + e^{-r_D T}\frac{\sigma}{2\sqrt{T}}KN'(x) \tag{16.22}$$

Again the last derivative is ambiguous in sign, reflecting the European, as opposed to American, nature of the options treated.

V. Comments on American FX Options

As noted previously, the European formulas will not serve to adequately price American FX options. (See also Samuelson [1965], Samuelson and Merton [1969], and Merton [1973].) Early exercise is decidedly a factor in pricing the American options,[10] and affects primarily the deep-in-the-money options (particularly calls on currencies with negative forward premiums and puts on currencies with positive forward premiums). Of course, American FX options must conform to the basic differential equation (16.6). However, the boundary conditions differ from the European case inasmuch as the option prices must never be less than the immediate conversion value, for example:

$$C(S, T) \geq \max[0, S - K]$$

for all T. Following the methodology of Merton (1973), it can also be shown that

$$C(S, T) \geq \max[0, Se^{-r_F T} - Ke^{-r_D T}]$$

for both the European and American cases.

Analytic solutions for the above type of boundary conditions problem seem quite difficult to derive. Therefore numerical methods, such as proposed by Brennan and Schwartz (1977), Parkinson (1977), or Cox, Ross, and Rubinstein (1979) (all recently reviewed by Geske and Shastri [1982]), are indicated for the evaluation of such American options.

VI. Conclusions

The appropriate valuation formulas for European FX options depend importantly on both foreign and domestic interest rates. The present paper has developed such formulas, and these are closely related to the proportional-dividend model when the spot prices are given, and to the commodity-pricing model when contemporaneous forward prices are given. The comparative statics are as might be expected, with two exceptions: The reaction of FX option prices to interest rate changes depends upon the nature of the concomitant changes required in either the spot or forward currency markets. Finally, American FX option values exceed the European FX option values most markedly for deep-in-the-money options, particularly for calls on currencies with negative forward premiums and puts on currencies with positive forward premiums.

Notes

1. The analysis could be extended without much difficulty to stochastic interest rates by assuming that the market is "neutral" toward the sources of uncertainty driving

such rates. In this case, volatility parameters must be redefined to incorporate the variances and covariances of interest rate movements as well as spot price movements. However, we forego this extension in the interest of clarity.

2. This is true, however, only for the case where there is a single source of uncertainty considered; multiple sources give rise to multiple volatility factors and risk premia, which are better expressed in alternative forms. Also, it is important to emphasize that the invariance of the risk-adjusted excess return is a pure arbitrage result and does not depend upon any specific asset-pricing model in a continuous-time (diffusion) setting.

3. In general, λ may depend on time and the state variables involved; however, in this particular case it is a constant.

4. The more usual presentation of our formula (16.2) would be $\mu = (r_D - r_F) + \lambda\sigma$, emphasizing that the expected return can be decomposed into an interest-rate-related drift and a risk premium. The form given emphasizes the invariance of risk premia across securities, in order to compare these.

5. The solution proceeds analogously to Merton's (1973) description of the proportional dividend model, replacing his dividend rate d by the foreign interest rate, as noted previously.

6. Alternatively, we could use put-call parity to determine the put option formula without resolving (16.6).

7. At the current writing, FX options are traded on the Philadelphia Stock Exchange and were designed to mature concurrently with the IMM currency futures contracts in March, June, September, and December.

8. For an introduction to exchange rate relationships, see for example the recent text by Shapiro (1982). This particular relationship is a pure-arbitrage result that employs riskless bonds of maturity identical to the forward contract, which of course can be created when instantaneous interest rates are constant.

9. This solution, although derived in a somewhat different fashion, is equivalent to Black's (1976) commodity option-pricing formula, showing that FX options may be treated on the same basis as commodity options generally, provided that the contemporaneous forward instruments exist.

10. At typical currency parameter values, it is not unusual to see a 10–20% difference between American and European values for certain in-the-money options.

References

Brennan, M., and E. Schwartz. 1977. The valuation of American put options. *J. Finance* 32 (May), 449–462.

Black, F. 1976. The pricing of commodity contracts. *J. Financial Econ.* 3 (January), 167–179.

Black, F., and M. Scholes. 1973. The pricing of options and corporate liabilities. *J. Pol. Econ.* 81 (May/June), 637–654.

Cox, J., S. Ross, and M. Rubinstein. 1979. Option pricing: A simplified approach. *J. Financial Econ.* 7 (September), 229–263.

Geske, R., and K. Shastri. 1982. Valuation by approximation: A comparison of alternative option valuation techniques. Working paper, Graduate School of Management, UCLA.

Keynes, J. 1923. *A Tract on Monetary Reform*. London: Macmillan.

Merton, R. C. 1973. Theory of rational option pricing. *Bell J. Econ. and Management Sci.* 4 (Spring), 141–183.

Parkinson, M. 1977. Option pricing: The American put. *J. Business* 50 (January), 21–36.

Samuelson, P. A. 1965. Rational theory of warrant pricing. *Ind. Management Rev.* 6 (Spring), 13–31.

Samuelson, P., and R. Merton. 1969. A complete model of warrant pricing that maximizes utility. *Ind. Management Rev.* 10 (Winter), 17–46.

Shapiro, A. 1982. *Multinational Financial Management*. Boston: Allyn and Bacon.

PART IV

The Design of Hybrid Instruments and Securities

17

Creating and Pricing Hybrid Foreign Currency Options

*Eric Briys & Michel Crouhy**

For more than ten years, foreign currency markets have been characterized by wide price changes. This high volatility of exchange rates has exposed corporate treasurers and international investors to a significant level of currency risk. Currency options markets have developed to provide new means of dealing with this growing risk. The purchaser of a foreign currency call (put) option has the right, but not the obligation, to buy (sell) a given amount of a foreign currency at a predetermined ("strike") price at any time on or before maturity date for an American option, or only at maturity for a European option.

Currency options have been the subject of considerable professional and academic interest as well.[1] Indeed, these are traded on several security exchanges throughout the world. A sizable over-the-counter market has also developed, offering a variety of specialized currency options. Among such specialized options are the so-called hybrid foreign currency options. These hybrid foreign currency options are based on some use of the put-call parity relation. For example, the exporting corporation buys a put and simultaneously sells a call from the bank so that the overall cost is less than the cost of a straight put, but then the exporter loses any potential gain from an

*We are grateful to the anonymous referees and Hans Stoll, Associate Editor of *Financial Management,* for their insightful comments. The usual caveat applies.
1. For a general background in currency options, see Biger and Hull [1], Garman and Kohlhagen [7], and Giddy [8].

appreciation of the foreign currency above the strike price of the call. Currency risk management has thus become a delicate compromise between flexibility, protection, and cost. The achievement of such a trade-off amounts to tailoring an instrument that perfectly matches the needs of the investor, conditional on his anticipations.

Banks world-wide have been quite successful in marketing those hybrids, although theoretically they can be replicated by combinations of instruments traded on organized markets. A typical hybrid like the Cylinder Option from Citibank or the Range Forward from Salomon Brothers allows its holder to customize the hedge by selecting the appropriate strike price and a maturity that might not be available on an organized exchange. Moreover, hybrid foreign currency options are mostly of the European type, making them less costly than American options. The potential for a wide variety of specifications has attracted many customers. In that respect, the French hybrid foreign currency option market is interesting. While no organized currency option market exists in France, French banks have been actively competing among themselves to market various instruments like the range forward, the participating forward, or the conditional forward—just to cite a few.[2] All these contracts are designed in such a way that the buyer does not have to pay any upfront cost, and they are referred to as zero premium hybrid foreign currency options.[3]

I. Tailoring Hybrid Foreign Currency Options

The buyer of a hybrid foreign currency option (e.g., a corporate treasurer of an exporting firm) aims at the best trade-off between protection, flexibility, and cost. On the one hand, corporate treasurers often claim that put

---

2. See Briys and Crouhy [3, 4].

3. In a range forward contract, the buyer and the bank agree on two prices, S_1 and S_2, at the inception of the contract. At the maturity of the forward contract, the buyer will purchase the foreign currency either at S_1 if the spot price is less than S_1, or at S_2 if the spot price is greater than S_2, or at the spot price if it is between S_1 and S_2. The two prices, S_1 and S_2, are set such that no money exchanges hands at the inception of the contract. A participating forward contract guarantees a minimum exchange rate for a forward sale and a maximum exchange rate for a forward purchase. In addition, the seller (buyer) gets a participation in the foreign currency appreciation (depreciation). Obviously, there is a cost to this participation. Since the contract is structured with no upfront payment, the cost of the seller's upside participation is that the minimum exchange rate guaranteed through a participating forward sale will necessarily be greater than the outright forward price. Analogously, the maximum exchange rate guaranteed through a participating purchase will necessarily be greater than the outright forward price. A conditional forward purchase contract is similar to an outright forward purchase, except that the long side of the contract has the right to pull out of the forward purchase by paying a fee to the short side of the contract on the contract maturity date. The contract can also

FIGURE 17.1   *Put with Proportional Coverage*

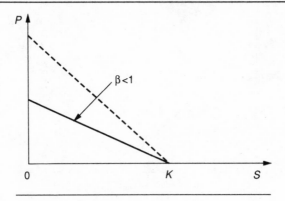

P = payoff,
S = spot rate at expiration,
K = *strike price*,
β = proportional coverage rate.

contracts are too "expensive." On the other hand, standard zero premium hybrid foreign currency options cost nothing to the buyer to initiate, but the residual flexibility of these instruments is slim when they are compared to forward contracts. Three ways of dealing with this issue are considered.

The first way to lower the cost of a put is to slightly reduce the level of protection, as in the "put with proportional coverage" shown in Figure 17.1. If the contract expires in the money, the payoff is limited to a percentage β of what it would be for an ordinary put:

$$P = \beta(K - S) \quad 0 \leq \beta \leq 1 \tag{17.1}$$

When $\beta = 1$, the contract becomes identical to an ordinary put. β can be understood as a coinsurance rate and as a means of reducing the cost of the premium. Obviously, an equivalent payoff can be obtained by holding β puts.

The second way to reduce the cost of the protection of a put is to bound the payoff of the put from above as shown in Figure 17.2. If at maturity the spot rate lies between the strike price K and the limit B, the payoff is that of a regular put (i.e., $K - S$). If the spot rate falls below B, the payoff is bounded

---

be designed in such a way that there is no cancellation fee simply by guarantying a buying price lower than the forward price. Similarly, a conditional forward sale contract is equivalent to an outright forward sale, except that the short side of the forward contract has the right to pull out of the agreement by paying a fee to the long side of the contract.

FIGURE 17.2 *Put with Bounded Payoff*

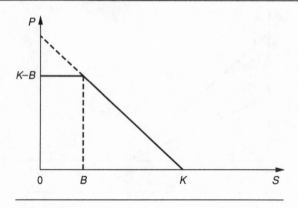

P = payoff,
S = spot rate at expiration,
K = strike price,
B = lower bound of the spot rate at maturity under which
     no additional coverage is provided.

at $K - B$. Such an instrument may be of interest to a corporate treasurer whose view on the currency is one of a moderate decline.[4]

The last case considered here corresponds to the so-called "put with disappearing deductible" as shown in Figure 17.3. In that case, the protection is not effective as long as the spot rate at maturity lies above D. For a spot rate below D, the option is exercised and the payoff corresponds to what would be obtained with a straight put with a strike price K. The payoff profile exhibits a discontinuity at D.

These basic protection schemes are obviously not mutually exclusive and can be easily combined. A tailored hedge can thus be set up to provide the exporter with the desired trade-off between protection, flexibility, and cost.

II. A General Pricing Formula

Instead of pricing each of the above contracts individually, a general pricing formula for put contracts[5] is derived. It can then be adapted to the exact specifications of the hybrid to be priced. Clearly, as long as the payoff func-

---

4. Note that this payoff is similar to that of a spread.
5. Since we are only considering European contracts, the extension to call profiles can easily be shown by applying the well-known put/call parity condition first proposed by Stoll [9].

FIGURE 17.3 *Put with Disappearing Deductible*

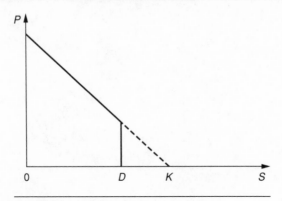

P = payoff,
S = spot rate at expiration.
K = strike price,
D = deductible.

tion of a put contract is given as a stepwise decreasing linear function, it is straightforward to separate it into decreasing continuous segments, as shown in Figure 17.4.[6]

The payoff at maturity is equal to

$$P_j(S_t, 0) = \begin{cases} 0 & \text{if} \quad S_t < K_{j-1} \\ L_j + \alpha_j(S_t - K_j) & \text{if} \quad K_j \ge S_t \ge K_{j-1} \\ 0 & \text{if} \quad K_j < S_t \end{cases} \tag{17.2}$$

where j is the jth segment of the overall payoff profile and S_t is the foreign currency price at maturity date t. An ordinary put is the case with $\alpha_j = -1$, $L_j = 0$, $K_{j-1} = 0$, and $j = 1$ with $K_1 = K$.

Following the risk neutrality approach proposed by Cox and Ross [5] to value options, the current premium for the above generalized payoff segment is equal to its discounted expected value,

$$P_j = e^{-r_d t} \int_{K_{j-1}}^{K_j} (L_j - \alpha_j K_j + \alpha_j S_t) L'(S_t) \, dS_t \tag{17.3}$$

with the following notation:

t = time to maturity,
S_t = the foreign currency spot price at maturity date t,

---

6. See Cox and Rubinstein [6], pp. 371–375.

FIGURE 17.4　*Generalized Payoff Segment*

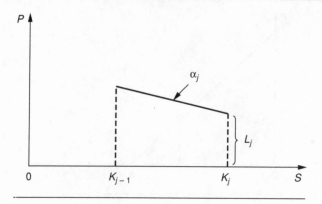

$$P = \text{payoff,}$$
$$S = \text{spot rate at expiration,}$$
$$K_{j-1} - K_j = \text{spot rate range for the payoff function,}$$
$$L_j = \text{payoff at maturity date for } S = K_j,$$
$$\alpha_j = \text{slope of the payoff function.}$$

r_d = the domestic riskless interest rate,

$L'(S_t)$ = the "risk neutral" lognormal density function of the foreign currency price at the maturity of the option (see Appendix).

Integrating this expression yields[7]

$$P_j(S_0, t) = (L_j - \alpha_j K_j)e^{-r_d t}[N(d_2^{j-1}) - N(d_2^j)]$$
$$+ \alpha_j S_0 e^{-r_f t}[N(d_1^{j-1}) - N(d_1^j)] \tag{17.4}$$

with S_0 being the current spot exchange rate, r_f being the foreign riskless interest rate, and where

$$d_2^{j-1} = \frac{\ln(S_0/K_{j-1}) + (r_d - r_f - \sigma^2/2)t}{\sigma\sqrt{t}} \tag{17.5}$$

$$d_2^j = \frac{\ln(S_0/K_j) + (r_d - r_f - \sigma^2/2)t}{\sigma\sqrt{t}} \tag{17.6}$$

$$d_1^{j-1} = d_2^{j-1} + \sigma\sqrt{t} \tag{17.7}$$

$$d_1^j = d_2^j + \sigma\sqrt{t} \tag{17.8}$$

The total premium for a hybrid put contract is therefore

$$P = \sum_j P_j(S_0, t) \tag{17.9}$$

---

7. See the Appendix for a sketch of the proof.

We can verify that (17.4) collapses to the Garman-Kohlhagen pricing formula when $\alpha_j = -1$, $L_j = 0$, $K_{j-1} = 0$, and $j = 1$ with $K_1 = K$, which corresponds to the ordinary put

$$P_j(S_0, t) = Ke^{-r_d t} N(-d_2) - S_0 e^{-r_f t} N(-d_1) \qquad (17.10)$$

where

$$d_2 = \frac{\ln(S_0/K) + (r_d - r_f - \sigma^2/2)t}{\sigma\sqrt{t}} \qquad (17.11)$$

$$d_1 = d_2 + \sigma\sqrt{t} \qquad (17.12)$$

Using the above general pricing formula, the premium on the put with the "disappearing deductible" and with $K_j = D$, $K_{j-1} = 0$, $L_j = K - D$, $j = 1$, and $\alpha_j = -1$ is equal to

$$P_j(S_0, t) = Ke^{-r_d t} N(-d_2) - S_0 e^{-r_f t} N(-d_1) \qquad (17.13)$$

where

$$d_2 = \frac{\ln(S_0/D) + (r_d - r_f - \sigma^2/2)t}{\sigma\sqrt{t}} \qquad (17.14)$$

$$d_1 = d_2 + \sigma\sqrt{t}$$

The pricing of the other schemes is straightforward and follows the same procedure.

Figure 17.5 graphs the premium of the put with "disappearing deductible" as a function of the current spot price for three months, two weeks, and five days to maturity. This can be compared with the graph of a straight European put option at maturity.[8] When the residual life of the option becomes less than two weeks, continuous hedging of the bank's position requires special attention and might become costly. Table 17.1 shows that the delta of the hybrid becomes quite substantial around the critical value D, and is very sensitive to changes in the spot rate. Indeed, one can notice for the option with five days to maturity that when the currency price goes from 5.0 to 5.1 FF per $US, the hedge ratio changes from -3.33 to -1.96 and the gamma "jumps" from 4.31 to 18.3.[9]

III. Conclusion

This paper stresses the wide applicability of the option-pricing theory when it comes to protecting or covering financial assets or a foreign currency posi-

---

8. This example is derived for the $US against the French franc as the domestic currency. The domestic and foreign interest rates are 8.375% and 6.875% respectively, the volatility is 18%, the strike of the straight put is $K = 5.75$ FF, the deductible is $(K - D) = 0.75\%$.
9. Delta $= \partial P/\partial S$ is the hedge ratio, and gamma $= \partial^2 P/\partial S^2$ is the sensitivity of the hedge ratio to the foreign currency price.

FIGURE 17.5   *Graphs of the Premiums for the Put with Disappearing Deductible*

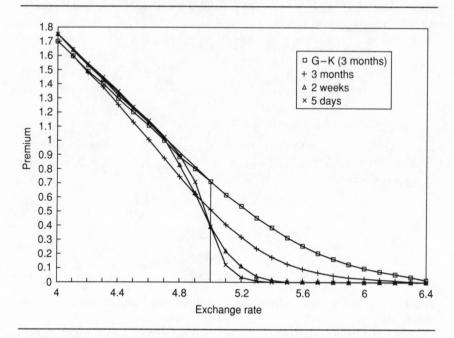

TABLE 17.1   *Deltas and Gammas of the Hybrid with Disappearing Deductible* [a]

				Time to Maturity				
	3 Months		1 Month		2 Weeks		5 Days	
S	Delta	Gamma	Delta	Gamma	Delta	Gamma	Delta	Gamma
4.5	−1.21	−0.44	−1.14	−1.13	−1.02	−0.37	−1.00	0.00
4.6	−1.25	−0.27	−1.28	−1.71	−1.10	−1.44	−1.00	−0.05
4.7	−1.26	−0.01	−1.46	−1.90	−1.34	−3.45	−1.04	−1.13
4.8	−1.25	0.32	−1.63	−1.31	−1.77	−4.73	−1.42	−7.93
4.9	−1.20	0.67	−1.70	0.05	−2.17	−2.59	−2.65	−14.10
5.0	−1.11	0.99	−1.61	1.72	−2.18	2.57	−3.33	4.31
5.1	−1.00	1.23	−1.37	3.01	−1.69	6.55	1.96	18.30
5.2	−0.87	1.37	−1.04	3.47	−1.00	6.62	−0.51	8.92
5.3	−0.73	1.40	−0.70	3.14	−0.45	4.20	−0.06	1.53
5.4	−0.59	1.34	−0.42	2.37	−0.16	1.87	0.00	0.11
5.5	−0.46	1.20	−0.23	1.53	−0.04	0.61	0.00	0.00

a. Where delta $= \partial P / \partial S$ is the hedge ratio, and gamma $= \partial^2 P / \partial S^2$ is the sensitivity of the hedge ratio to the foreign currency price.

tion. The current trend in financial institutions is to propose tailored conditional profiles that are well-suited to match the needs and expectations of customers. The three types of put contracts that have been described above fulfill this goal. Again, constructing payoff profiles from known instruments is a standard exercise.[10] This construction can, however, become an intricate task implying significant transaction costs. This explains why banks have been so successful in marketing these "jigsaw" products to their customers.

---

10. See Breeden and Litzenberger [2].

References

1. N. Biger and J. Hull, "The Valuation of Currency Options," *Financial Management* (Spring 1983), pp. 24–28.
2. D. T. Breeden and R. H. Litzenberger, "Prices of State-Contingent Claims Implicit in Options Prices," *Journal of Business* (March 1978), pp. 621–651.
3. E. Briys and M. Crouhy, "Les Options de Change à Prime Zéro," *Revue Banque* (November 1987), pp. 1046–1050.
4. ———, "Les Hybrides Pour la Gestion du Risque de Change," *Revue Banque* (February 1988), pp. 161–165.
5. J. C. Cox and S. A. Ross, "The Valuation of Options for Alternative Stochastic Processes," *Journal of Financial Economics* (March 1976), pp. 145–166.
6. J. C. Cox and M. Rubinstein, *Options Markets,* Englewood Cliffs, NJ: Prentice-Hall, 1985.
7. M. B. Garman and S. W. Kohlhagen, "Foreign Currency Option Value," *Journal of International Money and Finance* (March 1983), pp. 231–237.
8. I. H. Giddy, "Foreign Exchange Options," *The Journal of Futures Markets* (March 1983), pp. 143–166.
9. H. Stoll, "The Relationship between Put and Call Option Prices," *Journal of Finance* (September 1969), pp. 801–824.

Appendix

Equation 17.3 can be decomposed as the sum of two integrals:

$$P_j = e^{-r_d t} \int_{K_{j-1}}^{K_j} \alpha_j S_t L'(S_t)\, dS_t$$

$$+ e^{-r_d t} \int_{K_{j-1}}^{K_j} (L_j - \alpha_j K_j) L'(S_t)\, dS_t \qquad (17.A1)$$

$$\equiv A - B$$

We first evaluate the first integral A. Define the new variable u such that $e^u = S_t$, which implies that $e^u\, du = dS_t$.

If S_t is the spot price of the foreign currency at maturity date t, being log-normally distributed, then it follows that

$$E(S_t) = e^{(\mu + 0.5\sigma^2)t} \tag{17.A2}$$

where μ and σ^2 are the "risk neutral" distribution mean and variance per unit of time. If we assume that the covered interest arbitrage relationship holds, then

$$\frac{F_t}{S_0} = \frac{e^{r_d t}}{e^{r_f t}} \tag{17.A3}$$

where S_0 is the current spot rate and F_t is the t-period forward rate. By the assumption of risk neutrality, the forward rate is equal to the expected value of the spot rate at expiration, that is, $F_t = E(S_t)$, which when combined with (17.A2) and (17.A3) yields

$$E(S_t) = S_0 e^{(r_d - r_f)t} = e^{(\mu + 0.5\sigma^2)t} \tag{17.A4}$$

It then follows that the parameters of the risk neutral density function are given by

$$(\mu + 0.5\sigma^2)t = \ln(S_0) + (r_d - r_f)t \tag{17.A5}$$

We can then rewrite A as

$$A = \frac{\alpha_j e^{-r_d t}}{\sqrt{2\pi\sigma^2}} \int_{K_{j-1}}^{K_j} e^u e^{-(u - \mu t)^2 / 2\sigma^2} \, du \tag{17.A6}$$

But since $u - (u - \mu t)^2 / 2\sigma^2 t = -[u - (\mu + \sigma^2)t]^2 / 2\sigma^2 t + \mu t + \sigma^2 t / 2$, A thus becomes

$$A = \frac{\alpha_j e^{-r_d t} e^{(\mu + 0.5\sigma^2)t}}{\sqrt{2\pi\sigma^2 t}} \int_{K_{j-1}}^{K_j} e^{-[u - (\mu + \sigma^2)t]^2 / 2\sigma^2 t} \, du \tag{17.A7}$$

Making the new change of variable: $u - (\mu + \sigma^2)t / \sigma\sqrt{t} = y$ and using (17.A4), it follows that

$$A = \frac{\alpha_j S_0 e^{-r_f t}}{\sqrt{2\pi}} \int_{[\ln(K_{j-1}) - (\mu + \sigma^2 t)] / \sigma\sqrt{t}}^{[\ln(K_j) - (\mu + \sigma^2)t] / \sigma\sqrt{t}} e^{-y^2 / 2} \, dy \tag{17.A8}$$

that is

$$A = \alpha_j S_0 e^{-r_f t} \operatorname{Prob}(-d_1^{j-1} \le y \le -d_1^j) \tag{17.A9}$$

where y is the standard normal variable, and where

$$-d_1^{j-1} = \frac{\ln(K_{j-1}) - (\mu + \sigma^2)t}{\sigma\sqrt{t}} \tag{17.A10}$$

$$-d_1^j = \frac{\ln(K_j) - (\mu + \sigma^2)t}{\sigma\sqrt{t}} \tag{16.A11}$$

Denoting by $N(\cdot)$ the univariate cumulative normal distribution, it follows

$$A = \alpha_j S_0 e^{-r_f t} [N(-d_1^j) - N(-d_1^{j-1})] \qquad (17.A12)$$

but

$$(\mu + \sigma^2)t = (\mu + \sigma^2/2)t + \sigma^2 t/2$$
$$= \ln(S_0) + (r_d - r_f)t + \sigma^2 t/2 \qquad (17.A13)$$

thus

$$A = \alpha_j S_0 e^{-r_f t} [N(d_1^{j-1}) - N(d_1^j)] \qquad (17.A14)$$

where we have rewritten

$$d_1^{j-1} = \frac{\ln(S_0/K_{j-1}) + (r_d - r_f + \sigma^2/2)t}{\sigma\sqrt{t}} \qquad (17.A15)$$

$$d_1^j = \frac{\ln(S_0/K_j) + (r_d - r_f + \sigma^2/2)t}{\sigma\sqrt{t}} \qquad (17.A16)$$

The evaluation of integral B would follow the same line of argument.

18

Break Forwards:
A Synthetic Option
Hedging Instrument

Warren Edwardes & Edmond Levy

In managing foreign exchange exposure, the traditional hedges employed are forward exchange contracts or those arising from appropriate transactions in the spot exchange rate and related money markets. The recent experience of high exchange rate volatility and the committed nature of forward contracts created the need for more flexible exposure management instruments. Currency option contracts were a major innovation in this respect. Such contracts are distinguished from conventional forward contracts in that the purchaser of a currency option is merely obliged to deliver an upfront premium to ensure protection against downside currency risk.

Break forwards were developed by Midland Bank as a synthetic currency option hedge that combines the best features of forward contracts and currency options. Break forward contracts provide corporate treasurers with a hedging instrument that can mimic both fully forward hedged and unhedged strategies, *as well as any position along the continuum between these extremes.* Furthermore, the hedge was designed to overcome the corporate treasurer's aversion to upfront premiums and their associated taxation difficulties—that is, there are circumstances in the United Kingdom where option premiums paid may not be tax deductible. Because break forwards do not involve the payment of a premium, this difficulty should not arise. This article clarifies the bridge between traditional hedges and options that break forwards provide. In addition, it carries out a comparative cost analysis of break forwards relative to other hedging instruments.

The Gap in Traditional Hedges

We begin by focusing attention on the case of a U.K. corporate treasurer who seeks to manage the exposure generated by a U.S. dollar principal sum that he anticipates having to pay in three months. Using only traditional hedges, the treasurer has two choices: (1) leave his position exposed to fluctuations in exchange rates or (2) hedge his position completely by buying today in the forward market at, say, 1.50$/£. For completeness assume a current spot exchange rate of 1.513$/£ and an expected annual volatility of 14.6%. (These parameters are not crucial to the discussion other than to provide a possible indicator of the future spot rate in relation to the forward exchange rate.)

The outcome from these two decisions is presented in Figure 18.1. The horizontal axis denotes the spot rate at maturity of the forward contract, while the vertical axis denotes the exchange rate at which the treasurer effectively exchanges currencies under the alternative strategies. Hedging with forwards would ensure that the treasurer receives $1 for every £0.6667 irrespective of the spot rate outcome on maturity; hence the forward position

FIGURE 18.1 *Effective Exchange Rate at Expiration*

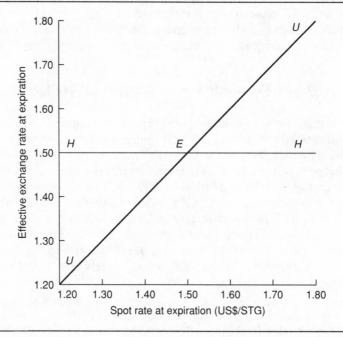

can be represented by the line *HH'*. On the other hand, the unhedged position, represented by *UU'*, enables him to take full advantage of favorable spot movements but leaves him exposed to unlimited downside risk.

Currency exposure relates to the effects of currency movements on the cash flows and financial structure of the firm. A major concern of the treasurer is to adopt hedging strategies that minimize the danger of incurring a serious risk of loss should exchange rates move against him. Few people would disagree that the decisions taken by treasurers in the management of exposure need to be monitored and continually assessed, but there is considerable disagreement about the criterion by which such decisions should be judged.

Generally, exposure management performance is measured relative to some exchange rate yardstick. Sometimes, although seldom explicitly, judgment is made *after the fact* given the more favorable between the forward rate available at the time the exposure is identified and the subsequent spot rate at maturity. In such cases, the treasurer's efforts will inevitably draw criticism as the evaluation will always be made with the benefit of hindsight.

Given this kind of retrospective benchmark, the treasurer would ideally like a hedging instrument that ensures that he has the best of both positions — one that enables him to exchange currencies at the ruling spot rate should it be greater than 1.50 and at 1.50$/£ should spot fall below 1.50. In effect, he would like to ensure the line *HEU'* in Figure 18.1.[1] This requires the ability to make hedging decisions with perfect foreknowledge of the spot exchange rate outcome. Such a product is, of course, unobtainable in the market place. But with the use of break forwards the treasurer can come close to it.

Break Forwards versus Traditional Hedges

Behind a break forward contract is the explicit acceptance by the treasurer of a fixed rate at which he is obliged to purchase dollars — one that is less favorable than the ruling forward rate. The writer of this contract values the spread between this fixed rate and the existing forward rate, and on the basis of its perception of exchange rate volatility, it in turn provides the treasurer with an option to unwind the "fixed" position at a predetermined strike price — the "break rate." The break facility under a break forward contract offers the following right: Having bought dollars at the fixed rate, the treasurer can sell back the dollars at the break rate. He is then free to buy his dollars again in the market but at the ruling spot rate. Clearly this can only be to his

---

1. The case illustrated in this note relates to the exposure management of a U.K. importer. The ideal effective rate for a U.K. exporter would be that represented by the kinked line *UEH'*. This would constitute a hedged position with rates above 1.5000 and an unhedged state below that rate (ignoring bid-ask spreads).

FIGURE 18.2 *Effective Exchange Rate for Various Contracts at Expiration*

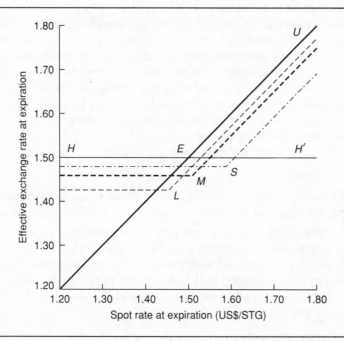

advantage if, at maturity, dollars can be purchased at a rate more favorable than the break rate—that is, when spot is above the break rate. (Of course, he is also free to take advantage of favorable forward rates should they occur at any time throughout the life of the contract, while knowing that the fixed obligation can be unwound at a rate no worse than the break rate.)

Figure 18.2 presents three such break forward contracts. The first break forward contract, *S*, assumes a relatively small loading (1.00%) on the forward rate, yielding a fixed rate of 1.485. Under our market assumptions, this enables the treasurer to break at 1.5825. With the forward rate at 1.50, this three-month European option to break the fixed obligation is out of the money. As one might expect, the higher this loading the more favorable will be the break rate to the treasurer; that is, for a given movement in spot, it is more likely that the break facility will be activated. Thus we might choose to define a medium loading as one that ensures an at-the-money break facility. With our assumed market conditions, an at-the-money break rate will be obtained with a loading of 2.90% (i.e., a fixed rate of 1.4565). The third contract in the diagram above assumes a relatively large loading of 4.80% (fixed rate of 1.4280), yielding a break rate of 1.4505. The effective exchange rates at which currencies are exchanged under each of these contracts is represented by the lines *S*, *M*, and *L*. The kink in these lines represents the point beyond which the treasurer is able to take advantage of favorable spot rates by activating the break facility.

At one extreme, then, we can regard a conventional forward exchange contract as a break forward with a zero loading; it provides no option to unwind. Likewise, the unhedged position can now be given the representation of a break forward contract with an infinite loading; in this case the fixed position is certain to be unwound to take advantage of favorable spot rates (thus the fixed rate would be equal to the break rate). Hence, it only remains for our treasurer to specify a loading that best reflects his views on how much downside risk he is willing to accept.

This choice of loading should depend on three factors:

1. His capacity and willingness to accept risk;

2. His views, if any, on the likely direction or trend in spot movements and the degree of certainty with which such beliefs are held; and

3. His accounting treatment and performance measurement—that is, is he judged against (a) the forward rate at the time the exposure is identified or (b) the spot rate on maturity of the foreign currency exposure. For any chosen loading the break forward provides a backstop should the outcome of spot on maturity be widely at variance with the treasurer's expectations.

We will show that if the choice of hedging instrument is restricted to either a forward exchange contract or dealing spot for the same value date, the opportunity loss—that is, the difference between the actual hedge taken and the ex post optimum—can be unlimited should the wrong instrument be used. With a break forward contract, this loss is always limited.

Exposure Management Evaluation

Consider first the case where the treasurer is judged relative to a forward contract. Here a highly risk-averse treasurer would aim at a minimal loading so as to eliminate all downside risk and effectively lock into the forward rate *irrespective of his views on spot movements.* Such a treasurer forgoes all potential benefits to be earned should the spot move favorably relative to the forward rate. Break forward contracts are aimed at those who are aware of such an opportunity and wish to participate in such beneficial outcomes while maintaining a prudent stance. A loading on the forward rate is precisely the premium due for insurance against this opportunity loss. As in the case of general insurance policies, these premiums can be reduced, but only if the insured is willing to forgo some of the compensation to which he would be entitled. (A good analogy is the acceptance of a £100 excess, or "deductible," on a motor car policy.) The larger is the distance between the break

FIGURE 18.3 *Break Forwards Measured Relative to Forwards*

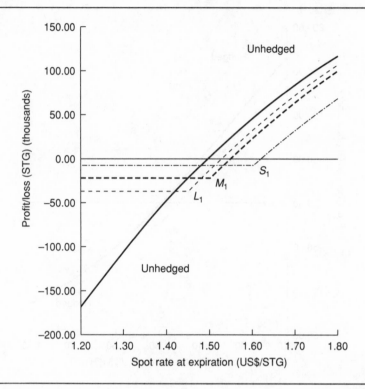

rate and the traditional forward rate (i.e., the larger the excess), the smaller is the loading.

Figure 18.3 is constructed by measuring break forward contracts relative to the fully forward covered position. That is, S_1, M_1, and L_1 are the vertical distances in sterling terms between HH' and S, M, and L, respectively, in Figure 18.2. It is apparent that, for a given loading, break forward contracts offer considerable advantages over the forward contract while still retaining downside protection against exchange rate risk. Note how under these contracts the benefits are obtained earlier, the larger is the loading on the forward exchange rate, thus highlighting the premium-excess trade-off.

When performance is measured relative to the subsequent spot rate (for profits or loss), the highly risk-averse treasurer would adopt a fully unhedged position irrespective of his views on spot rate movements. Here the prime concern becomes the opportunity loss relative to the forward exchange contract should the spot rate move unfavorably. If such movements occurred, the unhedged strategy could lead to a harmful economic exposure. For example, the firm's competitors could have covered themselves in the forward

FIGURE 18.4   *Break Forwards Measured Relative to Spot*

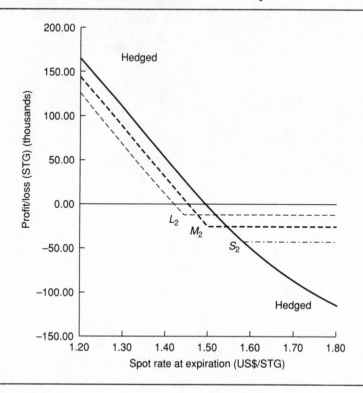

market and guaranteed a price in sterling terms. Our treasurer, however, would be forced either to charge his U.K. customers an exchange surcharge and incur adverse market sentiment or else suffer losses. Again, break forward contracts can be viewed as providing insurance against such losses. In this instance, however, the "premium" is the money value of the difference between the fixed and break rates, with the "excess" being the loading on the forward rate.

Figure 18.4 is constructed in a manner similar to that of Figure 18.3, but now break forward contracts are measured relative to the fully exposed position. The lines S_2, M_2, and L_2 are the vertical distances, in sterling, between UU' and S, M, and L of Figure 18.2.

Choice of Break Forward Loading

The treasurer's choice of break forward loading is dependent not only on his views on spot rate movements and on how firmly such beliefs are held, but also on his willingness or authority to bear risk. These factors should combine to produce an optimal break forward loading, which could in theory be any figure between zero and infinity. The extremes are, as we have already seen, the conventional forward hedge or a fully exposed position. We believe that such positions are rarely the best strategies for the majority of situations.

We have argued that for highly risk-averse treasurers there is no desire to do any better than the criteria by which they are measured. That is, deal forward if performance is measured relative to the forward rate or leave the position exposed and deal at whatever spot rate occurs on the value date if performance is measured relative to that exchange rate. At the other extreme we have the risk lover with a view, however flimsy, that spot (or a subsequent forward rate) will be one side or the other of the ruling forward rate. Such a treasurer will put all his eggs in one basket and either leave his funds exposed or will fully forward cover his funds.

Both such types of treasurers could suffer under one or the other performance criterion should they be applied subsequent to the outcome of the spot rate on the value date (as depicted in Figure 18.1). Consider, however, one who takes out a break forward contract. Recall that for our example the ideal position is represented in Figure 18.2 by the kinked line *HEU'*. The line *M*, representing the medium-loading break forward, remains roughly equidistant from *HEU'*. That is, whatever the spot rate is on the value date (or any subsequent forward rate for the same value date) the treasurer does no worse than exchanging at about 2.90% the wrong side of the optimum rate.

Treasurers typically do not hold identical views on spot movements, nor do they perceive risk in a like manner. Thus a medium-loading break forward will not be suitable to all situations. Those whose performances are measured relative to the forward rate and perceive risk according to that measurement will be tempted toward a smaller-loading break forward contract, such as that depicted by *S*, or (in extreme circumstances) a forward contract. Likewise, those whose performances are measured relative to the spot rate on the value date and perceive risk according to that criterion might well prefer a larger-loading break forward contract, such as that represented by *L*.

An equally important factor is the treasurer's view of how spot will move through the period of the contract. This could either strengthen his demands for a small or large loading or could act as an opposing force. For instance, a moderately risk-averse treasurer (we term him a "risk manager"), who perceives risk as the loss relative to forward cover, may think it quite likely that spot will move favorably relative to the forward rate. In such instances he would prefer a contract that offers flexibility so that, should the outcome of spot coincide with his beliefs, he is able to exchange at the more favorable rate. Thus, although a forward contract or low-loading break forward

FIGURE 18.5 *Choice of Contract for Treasurers Who Measure Their Performance Relative to Forward*

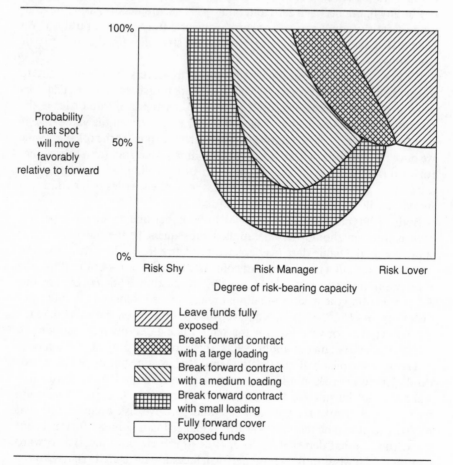

Leave funds fully exposed

Break forward contract with a large loading

Break forward contract with a medium loading

Break forward contract with small loading

Fully forward cover exposed funds

contract might initially be desirable, his views would lead him to accept a medium break forward loading. The extent of this increment will be largely determined by how firmly such beliefs are held and how much risk he is willing to bear.

The number of such examples one could invent are too many to consider here in any detail. We have, however, found it useful to summarize suitable loadings under various scenarios in the form of Figure 18.5 or Figure 18.6 (the choice depends on the choice of performance criterion).[2] These can be used in choosing a break forward loading. The axes measure the probability in the

2. While we understand that such constructions are largely subjective, containing many "grey areas," we hope sensible fine tuning will be applied by the user as necessary.

FIGURE 18.6 *Choice of Contract for Treasurers Who Measure Their Performance Relative to Spot*

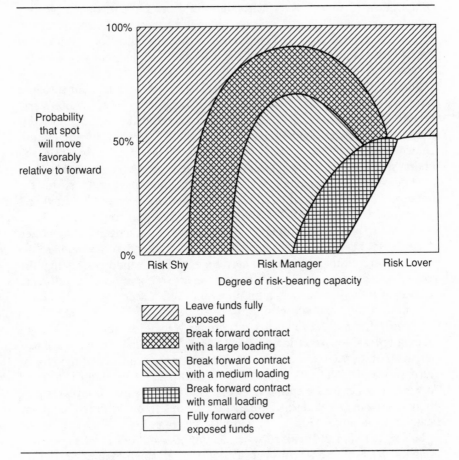

treasurer's view that the spot rate will move favorably relative to the ruling forward rate and his degree of risk-bearing capacity. These together with his chosen performance criterion will indicate the appropriate break forward loading.

Break Forwards versus Currency Options

The evaluation of break forward contracts measured relative to spot, in Figure 18.4 and Figure 18.6, brings out an important interpretation of such contracts as currency options. One of the basic insights of option-pricing theory is that the combination of a put option with a forward purchase is equivalent to a call option. The break facility component of the break forward contract could be viewed as the provision of a European dollar put option. As with all options, their value will depend in part on the intrinsic value of the option—in this case the difference between the strike price and the ruling forward rate. It should not be surprising, therefore, to find that break forward contracts are equivalent to pure option contracts since the former entail a forward commitment coupled with a reversing option.

Suppose that, rather than take out break forward contracts, our treasurer were to purchase dollar call options with strike rates at 1.5825, 1.5000, and 1.4505. The premiums for these options, compounded over three months, represent the maximum loss relative to spot under the respective call option. Under a corresponding break forward (when the break rate is set at the call option strike rate), the maximum loss relative to spot is equal to the difference between the fixed rate and the break rate in money terms. At the extremes we can see that an infinitely large difference between the fixed and break rates (resulting from a zero loading or a forward contract) would be equivalent to an option with an infinite premium (i.e., a deep in-the-money option). On the other hand, a break forward with the fixed rate equal to the break rate (resulting from an infinitely large loading) would be such that the corporate treasurer would suffer no loss versus spot and must therefore be equivalent to an option with a nil premium (i.e., a deep out-of-the-money option, or a fully exposed position).

In general, then, the following rule applies: Small-, medium-, and large-loading break forwards for the purchase (sale) of dollars are equivalent to purchases of, respectively, in-the-money, at-the-money, and out-of-the-money European dollar call (put) options. In every instance the fixed rate in a break forward contract (representing the worst rate the treasurer receives) is precisely the strike rate under the corresponding option but with the premium (suitably compounded) incorporated into that rate.

This recognition of break forwards as synthetic options can be seen diagramatically. Suppose we construct a do-it-yourself small-loading break forward contract by combining an out-of-the-money put option (represented by P_1 in Figure 18.7) with a forward purchase. The overall position is given by the sum of the vertical distances of the lines P_1 and HH' measured from the zero axis at each spot rate. This results in the line S_2.

As can be seen, the premium paid for the put option has been converted via the forward contract into a call option. However, whereas the put option is out of the money, the call option is in the money and hence its associated premium is larger.

It is important to notice that this synthetic call option entails the payment of a premium as required by the put option. Break forward contracts, however, do not require any such payment. The insight by which such contracts can be offered is made immediately obvious once it is seen that S_2 can be constructed in an infinite number of different ways. One in particular is

FIGURE 18.7 *Constructing a Synthetic Call Option*

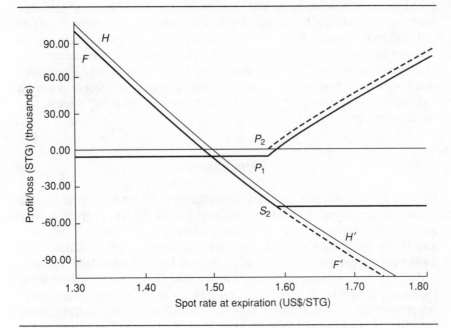

to move P_1 upward until the horizontal segment coincides with the zero axis (thus eliminating the premium) and then to compensate this movement by shifting HH' across to the left accordingly. These two movements give rise to P_2 and FF'. The line P_2 represents a free put option with a strike rate at 1.5825. This option is paid for indirectly through the commitment of a forward purchase of dollars at a fixed rate set worse than the forward rate (i.e., at 1.4850).

It can be seen that the break forward contract can be used whenever options are thought desirable by choosing the break rate to be equal to the desired strike price. Customers liable to capital gains tax treatment on currency forward and option contracts will recognize that the break forward contract has a major tax advantage relative to over-the-counter options. Unlike a currency option, the break forward contract does not entail payment of an initial premium that, in the case of an option, could become a wasting asset affording no tax relief. We believe that break forwards dominate currency options in that, at the time of this writing, they are more tax-efficient instruments when option premiums are not tax deductible.[3]

---

3. The authors do not seek to advise on taxation matters, especially as individual circumstances and the taxation treatment across countries differ and are subject to change. Treasurers must seek their own independent or in-house advice.

Option contracts are flexible instruments for coping with natural option-type exposures. Setting aside any view the treasurer may have on spot rate movements, recall the basic rules for deciding when to use option contracts rather than forward contracts: Whenever a quantity of foreign currency receivable (payable) is uncertain, buy a put (call) option on the currency. If such sums are known then a forward contract is appropriate. *These rules apply equally well to break forwards* — that is, such receivables (payables) can be hedged by selling (buying) the currency forward using a break forward contract.

Conclusion

Break forward contracts are uniquely valuable tools for managing foreign exchange exposure and, with their potential fiscally efficient properties, they mark the beginning of a new generation of treasury instruments. We have seen that the structure of such contracts is flexible enough to imitate both traditional forward and option contracts as well as the unhedged position.

Perhaps the introduction of option and synthetic option foreign exchange products will provide a fairer and more suitable measurement of a treasurer's performance. Currency options limit downside risk while providing scope for taking advantage of favorable rates of exchange over the period of the exposure. It is often remarked that performance should be measured relative to some yardstick that is adjusted in some way to reflect the degree of volatility the market experiences. Break forward contracts can provide a hedge that reflects the market's valuation of a treasurer's views and risk preferences; indeed, the success of a treasurer's exposure management efforts may best be measured relative to this optimal break forward contract. These contracts combine discipline with motivation and a good defence against critics.

19

Pricing and Hedging Capped Options

Phelim P. Boyle* & Stuart M. Turnbull

A number of different financial contracts have been introduced that provide upper and lower bounds to the possible range of outcomes. This gives the user an option written on an asset whose range of values is truncated or capped. By limiting the range of possible outcomes, the risk to the issuer is reduced. Some examples of such contracts are the range forward contract, the Standard Oil indexed notes issued in June 1986,[1] index currency option notes,[2] and collar loans.

There are five purposes to this study. First it is shown that capped options can be viewed as combinations of call and/or put options. Thus, given that it is always possible to value call and put options, it is a straightforward exercise to value capped options. Second, it is shown that for plausible parameter values, the value of a capped option is relatively insensitive to the value of the volatility parameter. This has important practical implications for the pricing of long-term options, when there is usually a larger measure of uncertainty pertaining to the value of the volatility parameter. Third, it is possible to determine the maximum degree of mispricing that occurs if the

---

*Phelim P. Boyle is grateful for ongoing research support from the Natural Sciences and Engineering Research Council of Canada. Comments from the editor and an anonymous referee of the *Journal of Futures Markets* are gratefully acknowledged.
1. A description of this issue is given in a 1986 Prospectus issued by The First Boston Corporation (1986) and Lazard Freres & Co.
2. For a description, see French (1985).

incorrect volatility value is used. It is demonstrated that the degree of mispricing is bounded from above. Fourth, it is shown that the nature of the
contract and the form of truncation has important implications for the hedge
ratio of the contract. Fifth, for indexed options, which can be considered as
a combination of two call options, it is demonstrated that it is generally
optimal to exercise such contracts prematurely, even in the absence of any
form of dividend.

Section I describes different examples and shows that they can be viewed
as combinations of options. The insensitivity of the capped option to changes
in the value of the volatility parameter is demonstrated in Section II. The
maximum degree of mispricing that arises from usage of the incorrect volatility measure is also described in this section. In Section III the effects of the
cap upon the hedging characteristics are examined. The issue of prematurely
exercising indexed options is discussed in Section IV. Conclusions are given
in Section V.

I. Structural Form of Contracts

The Range Forward Contract

Consider a U.S. company that needs to purchase U.K. sterling three months
ahead. The spot rate is \$1.40/£ and the three months forward is \$1.38/£. The
range forward exchange band is \$1.32/£ to \$1.45/£. This range is set such
that the initial value of the contract is zero. If the U.S. company picks the
upper range, the financial institution will set the lower range and vice versa.
At maturity if the spot rate is less than \$1.32/£, the buyer pays \$1.32/£. If
the spot rate is above \$1.45/£, the buyer pays \$1.45/£. If the spot rate is between \$1.32/£ and \$1.45/£, the buyer pays the spot rate.

A forward contract to buy sterling can be viewed as buying a call option
and writing a put option. Thus the value of a forward contract, of maturity
T, is

$$V(S, T, EX) = c(S, T, EX) - p(S, T, EX)$$

where S is the spot rate; EX is the exercise price; c is the value of a European
call option; and p is the value of a European put option. When the contract
is initiated, the exercise price is set such that the value of the contract is zero:

$$V(S, T, EX = f) = c(S, T, f) - p(S, T, f) = 0 \qquad (19.1)$$

where f is the forward rate.[3]

A range forward contract can be viewed as a combination of two contracts. In the first contract the owner buys a call option and writes a put
option. The exercise prices of these options are the forward rate. In the sec-

---

3. Given put-call parity, this implies that $EX = f$. See Equation (6) in Grabbe (1983).

ond contract a cap is placed on the range of possible outcomes by writing a call option with exercise price k_1 ($>f$) and buying a put option with exercise price k_2 ($<f$). Thus the value of the range forward contract is

$$X(S, T, k_1, k_2) \equiv V(S, T, f) - c(S, T, k_1) + p(s, T, k_2) \qquad (19.2)$$

Given that the initial value of $V(S, T, f)$ is zero, then

$$X(S, T, k_1, k_2) = p(S, T, k_2) - c(S, T, k_1) \qquad (19.3)$$

By design the initial premium of a range forward contract is zero. Thus, if a firm buying the contract picks one exercise price, the financial institution picks the other exercise price such that the left-hand side of (19.3) is zero, assuming a competitive market.

Collar Loans

Consider a company that issues a one-year floating rate debt in which the interest rate is adjusted after six months to the six-month LIBOR rate. At the end of six months, if LIBOR is above 9%, the financial institution will pay the difference. If LIBOR is below 6% then the firm pays the difference to the financial institution. Hence the borrowing cost to the firm varies from a minimum of 6% to a maximum of 9%. The spread between the upper and lower limits is set such that when the collar is initiated, the value of the contract is zero.

The collar can be viewed as purchasing a European put option and writing a European call option:

$$X(r, T, k_1, k_2) = p(r, T, k_1) - c(r, T, k_2) \qquad (19.4)$$

where r is the six-month LIBOR rate; k_1 is the price of a six-month default-free pure discount bond priced to yield 9%; and k_2 is the price of a six-month default-free pure discount bond priced to yield 6%.

Indexed Notes

The June 1986 issue of oil-indexed notes by Standard Oil included a capped option. Part of the issue consisted of pure discount bonds that had an attached option feature. In addition to the $1,000 maturity value of the note, the company promised to pay an additional amount based on the price of oil at maturity. Thus, in the case of the 1990 note, this additional amount was equal to the product of 170 and the excess (if any) of the price of a barrel of oil at maturity over $25. The contract also included the stipulation that if the price of oil at maturity was above $40, a price of $40 would be used in computing the payoff to the investor. Thus, for example, if the price of oil is $20 at maturity, the value of the option is zero. If the price of oil is between $25 and $40, say $35, the value of the option is $(35 - 25)170 = \$1,700$. If the price of oil is above \$40, say \$50, the option is worth $\$(40-25)170 =$ \$2,550. Effectively, Standard Oil has written a call option on oil, and by capping the range of outcomes has limited its liability to \$2,550 per contract.

This attached option feature is equivalent to buying a European call option with an exercise price of \$25 and writing a European call option with an exercise price of \$40. Thus in general,

$$X(S, T, k_1, k_2) \equiv c(S, T, k_1) - c(S, T, k_2) \tag{19.5}$$

where k_1 is the exercise price of the long option; and k_2, the exercise price of the short option $(k_2 \ge k_1)$.

Index Currency Option Notes (ICONs)

The first ICON appeared on October 14, 1985, and was issued by the Long-Term Credit Bank of Japan, arranged by Bankers Trust. If the exchange rate (¥/\$) is greater than ¥169/\$ at maturity (ten years) the bondholder receives the face amount of the note, \$1,000. If the exchange rate is less than ¥169/\$, the bondholder receives the face value of the note minus an amount given by the formula $(169/S - 1)1000$, where S is the prevailing exchange rate, ¥/\$. Thus, if the exchange rate is ¥159/\$, the amount deducted is \$62.89 and the bondholder receives \$937.11. Note that ICONs are issued, serviced, and redeemed in dollars. If the exchange rate is less than ¥84.5/\$ $(= 169/2)$, the bondholder receives zero. Thus the payoff to the bondholder has a lower bound of zero and an upper bound of \$1,000.

The value of the ICON at the time of issue is given by

$$B(T) - [c(Y, T, EX) - c(Y, T, 2EX)]1000/EX \tag{19.6}$$

where Y is the spot rate \$/¥; EX is the exercise price \$/¥ $(EX = 1/169)$; $B(T)$ is the market value of the note without the option feature, the note having maturity T; $c(Y, T, k)$ is the dollar value of a European foreign currency call option with maturity T and exercise price k. Comparing Equations 19.6 and 19.5 it is seen that the bondholders have written a capped option. In writing a (naked) call option, the writer's liability is potentially unlimited. The cap limits the writer's liability so that the maximum loss to the writer is \$1,000.

II. The Sensitivity of Capped Option Values to Changes in the Volatility Parameter

Range Forward Contract

The partial differential for a foreign currency option is isomorphic to Merton's (1973) constant dividend yield equation. Thus, the price of a European call option is given by

$$c(S, T, EX) = \exp(-r_f T)SN(d_1) - \exp(-rT)EXN(d_2)$$

where r (r_f) is the domestic (foreign) instantaneous risk-free rate of interest; T is the maturity of the option; S is the spot rate;

$$d_1 \equiv [\ln(S/EX) + (r - r_f + \sigma^2/2)T]/\sigma\sqrt{T}$$

σ^2 being the variance of the proportional change in the exchange rate per unit time; $d_2 = d_1 - \sigma\sqrt{T}$; and $N()$ is the cumulative normal distribution function. The value of a European put option is given by

$$p(S, T, EX) = \exp(-rT)EXN(-d_2) - \exp(-r_f T)SN(-d_1)$$

Note that in deriving these results it is assumed that the exchange rate process can be described by a lognormal process.

The value of the range forward contract is

$$X(S, T, k_1, k_2) = p(S, T, k_2) - c(S, T, k_1)$$

By design, the financial institution picks an exercise price such that the initial value of the contract is zero. This raises the question of the sensitivity of the exercise price to different values of the volatility parameters σ. A 90-day range forward contract to buy sterling is considered. It is assumed that the customer picks the lower bound. The financial institution must determine the upper bound. While a standard deviation of 0.006 per day (11.46% per year) seems reasonable (see Melino and Turnbull [1987]), the financial institution is unsure about the precise value of the volatility and explores a wide range. If the customer picks a lower bound of 136¢/£, the forward rate being 138.03¢/£, then the financial institution sets the upper bound to be 140.16¢/£, assuming a standard deviation of 0.006 per day (see Table 19.1). The value of the call option, which by construction equals the value of the put option so that the value of the range forward contract is zero, is 2.160¢. If the volatility increases by 100% to 0.012 per day from 0.006 per day, this causes the value of the option to more than double. The upper bound increases by 0.10 to 140.26¢/£, a change of 0.071%. Had the lower bound been set at 132¢/£, then the upper bound would have been set at 144.54¢/£, assuming a standard deviation of 0.006 per day. A 100% increase in volatility causes the upper bound to increase by 0.30 to 144.84¢/£, an increase of 0.208%. The sensitivity of the exercise price to changes in the volatility increases as the range between the upper and lower bounds increases.

Degree of Mispricing

It is shown in Appendix A that there exists a value of the volatility σ that maximizes the value of the contract, keeping all of the other parameters constant. This result has important practical implications. It can provide a financial institution with a measure of the dollar cost of mispricing the

TABLE 19.1   *Sensitivity of the Exercise Price to Changes in Volatility*[a]

Exercise Price of Put Option	Range Forward Contract			
	Standard Deviation Per Year	Standard Deviation Per Day	Value of Option	Exercise Price of Call Option
132	0.0382	0.002	0.0079	144.37
	0.1146	0.006	0.9313	144.54
	0.2293	0.012	3.5126	144.84
134	0.0382	0.002	0.0646	142.21
	0.1146	0.006	1.4554	142.33
	0.2293	0.012	4.2858	142.53
136	0.0382	0.002	0.3177	140.10
	0.1146	0.006	2.1606	140.16
	0.2293	0.012	5.1595	140.26

a. Spot rate: 140¢/£.
   Maturity: 90 days.
   Domestic rate of interest: 8%.
   Foreign rate of interest: 14.4%.
   Forward rate: 138.03¢/£.

contract by not setting the appropriate upper and lower bound due to uncertainty about the value of the volatility parameter.

Referring to Table 19.1, if the lower bound is set to be 132¢/£ and the financial institution assumes that volatility, σ, is 0.006 per day, it would set the upper bound at 144.54¢/£. If the upper and lower bounds are fixed at these values, then the value of the range forward contract for different values of its volatility parameters is examined in Table 19.2. It is seen that the value of the contract is maximized when the volatility σ is 0.004 per day. Thus, if the true volatility is 0.004 per day, the real value of the contract is 0.0098¢/£ and not zero. This represents the maximum degree of mispricing, given that the upper bound was set assuming that $\sigma = 0.006$ per day.

Collar Loans

To determine the upper and lower bounds of a collar loan it is necessary to be able to price options written on short-term interest rate investments. It is assumed that the collar loan is written on six-month LIBOR and that a single factor model can be used to describe changes in the term structure. If r represents the one-month LIBOR, then a mean reverting stochastic process is assumed for r:

TABLE 19.2 *Mispricing of Contract Due to Uncertainty about the Volatility,* σ [a]

	Range Forward Contract	
Value of Contract	Standard Deviation Per Day	Standard Deviation Per Year
0.0069	0.0030	0.0573
0.0090	0.0035	0.0669
0.0098	0.0040	0.0764
0.0092	0.0045	0.0860
0.0073	0.0050	0.0955
0.0000	0.0060	0.1146

a. Spot rate: 140¢/£.
   Exercise price of put option: 132¢/£.
   Exercise price of call option: 144.54¢/£.
   Maturity: 90 days.
   Domestic rate of interest: 8%.
   Foreign rate of interest: 14.4%.

$$dr = a(b-r)\, dt + \sigma r^{\beta/2}\, dZ \tag{19.7}$$

where a is a constant representing the rate of reversion; b is a constant that can be interpreted as the mean long-term rate; β is a constant defined between $[0, 2]$; and $\sigma^2 r^\beta$ is the instantaneous variance. If $\beta = 1$ then (19.7) describes the square root process studied by Cox, Ingersoll, and Ross (1985). If $\beta = 2$ then (19.7) describes a lognormal process if $b \equiv 0$. The partial differential equation for interest rate options is[4]

$$\tfrac{1}{2}\sigma^2 r^\beta P_{rr} + [a(b-r) - \lambda \sigma r^{\beta/2}]P_r - rP + P_t = 0 \tag{19.8}$$

where $P(r, t)$ denotes the value of the interest rate option, and λ denotes the price of interest rate risk. It should be noted that this equation depends upon all of the parameters for the stochastic process describing changes in the interest rate and not just the volatility parameter. It also depends upon the price of risk, λ, which must be estimated.

While it is common to assume a square root process to describe changes in the interest rate,[5] there is little empirical evidence to justify such an assumption. Melino and Turnbull (1987), using daily one-month LIBOR data

---

4. For a derivation of this equation and a discussion of how to solve such an equation, see Courtadon (1982). In the Courtadon paper, λ is defined to be negative and thus in Equation 19.6 there is a plus sign.
5. For example, see Brown and Dybvig (1986).

TABLE 19.3 *Empirical Description of the Stochastic Process for Interest Rates* [a]

β	A	B	σ	log-lik
1	0.046603	−0.003318	0.123401	−1592.86
	(0.020210)	(0.002233)	(0.001628)	
2	0.060002	−0.004904	0.039282	−1470.87
	(0.018632)	(0.002345)	(0.000518)	

a. Figures in parentheses are standard errors. These results are taken from Table II, Melino and Turnbull (1987). Note that these parameters are estimated assuming r is expressed in percentage form.

for the period January 2, 1975, to July 9, 1986 (2,875 observations), estimated the parameters for the class of distributions described by

$$dr = (A + Br)\, dt + \sigma r^{\beta/2}\, dZ \qquad (19.9)$$

where $A \equiv ab$ and $B = -a$. The results for two processes are shown in Table 19.3. From Table 19.3, it is seen that the coefficients A and B are not precisely measured, being statistically insignificant from zero. Empirically it was found that the $\beta = 2$ process provided a better description of the data than the square root process.

It is assumed that the one-month LIBOR spot rate is 7.00%. The upper bound for the collar is set and the financial institution must determine the lower bound; that is, the financial institution must determine the exercise price of the call option, so that the initial value of the collar is zero. The results for the two processes are shown in Table 19.4. Part A shows the results for the square root process. The upper bound is set at either 7.35 or 7.45%.[6] The values of A and B are initially set to zero and then to the values given in Table 19.3. The volatility parameter is initially set equal to the appropriate value given in Table 19.3 and then the value is doubled. The price of risk is set equal to zero ($\lambda = 0$). Two points should be noted. First, for the range of parameters considered, the results are not particularly sensitive to the values of A and B that characterize the mean of the process. Second, the lower bound is relatively insensitive to change in the volatility parameter. If the upper bound is set at 7.35%, a 100% increase in the volatility parameter generates a 100% increase in the option price and the lower bound decreases

---

6. If the annual rate of interest is 7.35% per annum for the upper bound, the continuously compounded rate of interest is 7.092% and the exercise price for the option is

$$\$100 \exp(-0.07092 \times 0.5) - \$96.516$$

per $100 face value.

TABLE 19.4 *Collar Loan: Sensitivity of the Exercise Price*[a]

Upper Bound Interest Rate (Per Annum)	Volatility Parameter	Option Price	Lower Bound Interest Rate (Per Annum)
Part A: Square Root Process			
7.35	0.123401	0.1148	7.1487
	0.246802	0.2482	7.1351
7.45	0.123401	0.0969	7.0542
	0.246802	0.2292	7.0442
$A=0$, $B=0$, $\lambda=0.0$, $\beta=1$			
7.35	0.123401	0.1183	7.1856
	0.246802	0.2515	7.1711
7.45	0.123401	0.0999	7.0901
	0.246802	0.2323	7.0800
$A=0.046603$, $B=-0.003318$, $\lambda=0.0$, $\beta=1$			
Part B: Lognormal Process			
7.35	0.039282	0.0189	7.1505
	0.078564	0.0527	7.1519
7.45	0.039282	0.0083	7.0564
	0.078564	0.0375	7.0597
$A=0$, $B=0$, $\lambda=0.0$, $\beta=2$			
7.35	0.039282	0.0217	7.1991
	0.078564	0.0565	7.1943
7.45	0.039282	0.0101	7.0965
	0.078564	0.0404	7.0991
$A=0.060002$, $B=-0.004904$, $\lambda=0.0$, $\beta=2$			

a. Spot rate $=7.00\%$.

by 2 basis points. If the upper bound is set at 7.45%, the lower bound decreases by 1 basis point.

Part B shows the results for the $\beta=2$ process. Two points should be observed. First, the difference in the option prices for the two processes can be substantial, especially for out-of-the-money options. This implies that it is important to empirically identify the correct process when pricing options. Second, for this process the lower bound is less sensitive to change in the volatility parameter when compared to the square root process. A 100% increase in the volatility causes the lower bound to change by less than 1 basis point.

TABLE 19.5   *Hedge Ratio for Range Forward Contract*[a]

Exchange Rate	Maturity 90 Days			
	Value of Contract	Hedge Ratio	Gamma Ratio	Eta Ratio
136	1.7138	−0.4635	0.0259	−52.8306
138	0.8307	−0.4239	0.0132	−68.7743
139.9[b]	0.0412	−0.4114	−0.0002	−74.6477
140	0.0000	−0.4115	−0.0009	−74.6803
142	−0.8339	−0.4269	−0.0142	−69.6795
144	−1.7241	−0.4669	−0.0251	−55.4242

a. Exercise price of put option: 132¢/£.
   Exercise price of call option: 144.54¢/£.
   Spot exchange rate: 140¢/£.
   Domestic rate of interest: 8%.
   Foreign rate of interest: 14.4%.
   Standard deviation: 0.006 per day.
b. Maximum hedge ratio.

III. Hedge Ratio

To hedge a capped option, it is necessary to determine the hedge ratio. For instruments such as the range forward contract, which can be represented as a put minus a call option, the hedge ratio will always be negative, given that the ratio for a put option is negative and for a call option positive. The hedge ratio for different values of the exchange rate is shown in Table 19.5. It is seen that the hedge ratio increases and then starts to decrease as the exchange rate increases, implying the existence of a maximum.[7] For hedging purposes, the hedge ratio (delta) gives the investment in the underlying asset. The sensitivity of the hedge ratio to changes in the exchange rate is referred to as the gamma ratio.[8] It is seen from Table 19.5 that the gamma ratio is relatively small, at least around the spot rate. Similarly, the hedge ratio in this region is also relatively insensitive to change in the volatility. This is measured by the eta ratio.[9]

For capped options such as indexed notes and indexed currency option notes, which depend upon the differences of two call options, the hedge ratio

---

7. The conditions for the existence of a maximum are given in Appendix B.
8. The gamma ratio is defined as $\partial(H)/\partial S$ where H is the hedge ratio.
9. The eta ratio is defined as $\partial(H)/\partial \sigma$ where H is the hedge ratio.

TABLE 19.6 *Hedge Ratio for Indexed Note Standard Oil Option*[a]

Oil Price	Value of Option	Hedge Ratio	Gamma Ratio	Eta Ratio
13.50	1.5281	0.2225	0.0056	−7.2364
15.00	1.8669	0.2286	0.0027	−9.1334
20.00	3.0153	0.2261	−0.0029	−11.8118
25.00	4.0983	0.2055	−0.0049	−11.0499
30.00	5.0621	0.1797	−0.0052	−8.9513
35.00	5.8964	0.1543	−0.0048	−6.6026
40.00	6.6092	0.1313	−0.0043	−4.4657

a. Lower exercise price: $25.
   Upper exercise price: $40.
   Spot price: $13.5.
   Maturity: 4 years.
   Domestic rate of interest: 8%.
   Standard deviation: 0.4 per year.

will generally be positive. Again a maximum usually exists. However, unlike the range forward contract, the hedge ratio will tend to zero as you move away from the maximum. This is illustrated in Table 19.6 for the Standard Oil option.

The difference in the hedge ratios for the range forward contract and indexed notes, or index currency option notes, suggests that for hedging purposes these contracts have very different characteristics. Once the initial hedge is set up, the sensitivity of the hedge ratio to changes in the underlying variables becomes important. Two measures that are commonly used are gamma and eta. It is shown in Appendix B that gamma and eta for the two contracts are very similar. However, gamma and eta will always be less, using the same inputs, for the range forward contract than the indexed note option if the foreign rate of interest is positive.

A collar loan can be represented as a put minus a call option. If interest rates increase, bond prices will decrease, implying that the put option increases and the call option decreases. Thus, the hedge ratio for a collar loan, which measures the change in the value of the option for a unit change in the interest rate, will always be positive. The hedge ratio is shown in Table 19.7 for different values of the spot rate. The hedge ratio decreases and then starts to increase, implying the existence of a minimum. The sensitivity of the hedge ratio to changes in the volatility, as measured by the eta ratio, changes quite dramatically as the value of the contract tends to zero.

TABLE 19.7 *Hedge Ratio for Collar Loan* [a]

Spot Rate	Value of Contract	Hedge Ratio	Gamma Ratio	Eta Ratio
6.20	−0.339	0.470	−0.008	−0.134
6.60	−0.154	0.450	−0.203	−16.384
7.00	0.000	0.329	−0.040	−41.587
7.40	0.153	0.442	0.162	−16.773
7.80	0.335	0.459	−0.005	−0.513
8.20	0.518	0.456	−0.007	−0.022

a. Upper interest rate: 7.35%.
   Lower interest rate: 7.1936.
   Spot interest rate: 7.00%.
   A parameter: 0.060002.
   B parameter: −0.004904.
   Beta: 2.
   Standard deviation: 0.039282.
   Price of risk: 0.0.

IV. American versus European Contracts

Indexed notes such as the Standard Oil option can be viewed as the difference between two call options. In the absence of dividends,[10] it is not optimal to exercise call options prematurely. Thus it is tempting to argue that it is not optimal to exercise indexed notes prematurely. Given a ceiling on the value of the option, there exists a critical price of the underlying asset for which the option owner is indifferent between owning the option and prematurely exercising. If the value of the underlying asset is very large, $S \gg k_2$, where k_2 is the upper exercise price and it is assumed that it is not optimal to exercise the option prematurely, then a contradiction arises. Given that the option will not be prematurely exercised, its maximum value is the present value of receiving $k_2 - k_1$ for certain; that is, $(k_2 - k_1) \exp(-rT)$, where k_1 is the lower price. If the option is exercised, it is worth $k_2 - k_1$. But $k_2 - k_1$ is greater than $(k_2 - k_1) \exp(-rT)$, implying that it is optimal to exercise the option prematurely.

The boundary conditions for an American indexed note are as follows:

1. $X(S, T = 0, k_1, k_2) = \text{Max}\{30, \text{Min}[(S - k_1), (k_2 - k_1)]\}$

---

10. It is assumed that there are no additional carrying costs associated with the underlying asset (oil). See Stoll and Whaley (1986).

TABLE 19.8 *American Indexed Note Standard Oil Option*[a]

Oil Price	Value of Option	Hedge Ratio	Gamma Ratio	Eta Ratio
13.50	2.2699	0.3727	0.0203	3.0377
15.00	2.8502	0.4001	0.0163	0.3248
20.00	5.0100	0.4560	0.0069	−5.5978
25.00	7.3517	0.4765	0.0018	−7.6037
30.00	9.7447	0.4786	−0.0007	−7.3363
35.00	12.1230	0.4718	−0.0019	−6.0181
40.00[b]	15.0000	1.0000	−0.0000	0.0000

a. Lower exercise price: $25.
   Upper exercise price: $40.
   Spot price: $13.5.
   Maturity: 4 years.
   Domestic rate of interest: 8%.
   Standard deviation: 0.4 per year.
b. Left-hand derivatives are used at this value.

2. $X(S, T^-, k_1, k_2) = \begin{cases} \text{Max}\{0, S - k_1, X(S, T^+, k_1, k_2)\} & \text{if } S < k_2 \\ k_2 - k_1 & \text{if } S \geq k_2 \end{cases}$

3. $\lim \dfrac{\partial X}{\partial S} = 0 \quad \text{as } S \to \infty$

The first boundary condition gives the value of the contract at maturity. The second boundary condition arises because it is possible to exercise the contract prematurely. The third boundary condition arises because the maximum value of the contract is fixed, $k_2 - k_1$, independent of the value of the underlying asset.

Values of an American indexed note are shown in Table 19.8. The European values are shown in Table 19.6. The right to exercise the option prematurely results in a higher value of the option. It also alters in a significant way the hedge ratio, which is almost doubled.

V. Conclusions

This study explored the sensitivity of the value of capped options to changes in the value of the volatility parameter. It illustrated that it is possible to determine the maximum degree of mispricing arising from uncertainty about the value of the volatility parameter. For the range forward contract and for a collar loan it was demonstrated that, for plausible parameter values, the determination of the appropriate upper or lower bound by the financial institution is quite insensitive to changes in the volatility parameter. These results also hold for the other types of capped options identified in this study. In limiting the possible range of outcomes, the capped option is written on an asset whose probability distribution is truncated and thus there is less dispersion. Increases in the volatility of the unrestricted process implies that there is a greater chance of the capped process residing at one of the boundaries.

The results of this study have particular relevance for the pricing of long-term foreign currency contracts, such as ICONs. Privately, many financial institutions have expressed concern about the relevant value of the volatility parameter to be used for pricing long-term contracts. It was shown that for capped options the valuation of such options is relatively insensitive to the value of the volatility parameter.

It is important to understand the properties of the hedge ratio for hedging purposes. While the magnitude of the hedge ratio depends upon the type of contract, gamma and eta ratios are very similar in nature. Finally, if contracts are American, this affects the pricing and hedging characteristics and it will, in general, be optimal to exercise such contracts prematurely.

Appendix A

The value of the range forward contract is

$$X(S, T, k_1, k_2) = p(S, T, k_2) - c(S, T, k_1) \tag{19.A1}$$

Given the closed form solutions for European call and put options, then

$$\frac{\partial}{\partial \sigma}[c(S, T, EX)] = \exp(-r_f T)S\sqrt{T}n(d_1) = \frac{\partial}{\partial \sigma}[p(S, T, EX)] \tag{19.A2}$$

where $n(\ )$ is the normal density function and

$$d_1 \equiv \frac{\ln(S/EX) + (r - r_f + \sigma^2/2)T}{\sigma\sqrt{T}}$$

Hence the sensitivity of the value of the contract to comparative static changes in the volatility, σ, is given by

$$\frac{\partial}{\partial \sigma}[X(S, T, k_1, k_2)] = \exp(-r_f T)S\sqrt{T}[n(d_1) - n(h_1)] \tag{19.A3}$$

where

$$d_1 \equiv \frac{\ln(S/k_2) + (r - r_f - \sigma^2/2)T}{\sigma\sqrt{T}} \quad \text{and} \quad h_1 \equiv \frac{\ln(S/k_1) + (r - r_f + \sigma^2/2)T}{\sigma\sqrt{T}}$$

The right-hand side of (19.7) will be zero if

$$d_1 = h_1 \tag{19.A4}$$

or

$$d_1 = -h_1 \tag{19.A5}$$

as $n(\ )$ is a symmetric function. By assumption $k_1 \neq k_2$ so that (19.A5) represents the only solution. Equation 19.A5 will be satisfied if

$$\sigma^2 = \ln\left\{\frac{k_1 k_2}{S^2} \exp[-2(r - r_f)T]\right\} \bigg/ T \tag{19.A6}$$

Provided that $k_1 k_2 \exp[-2(r - r_f)T] > S^2$, the right-hand side of (19.A6) is positive, implying the existence of a meaningful solution.

To examine whether the capped option value is maximized or minimized when (19.A6) holds, it is necessary to compute the second derivative

$$\frac{\partial^2}{\partial\sigma^2}[X(S, T, k_1, k_2)] = -2d_1 \exp(-r_f T) S T n(d_1) < 0 \quad \text{if } d_1 > 0$$

implying that the difference is maximized when (19.A6) holds and $d_1 > 0$.

The value of the range forward contract, given that k_1 and k_2 are set such that (19.A5) and thus (19.A6) hold, is given by

$$X(S, T, k_1, k_2) = \exp(-rT)[k_2 N(-d_1 + \sigma\sqrt{T}) + k_1 N(-d_1 - \sigma\sqrt{T})]$$
$$- 2\exp(-r_f T)SN(-d_1)$$

which is not necessarily equal to zero.

Given (19.A2) this proof also holds for indexed notes and ICONs.

Appendix B

The value of the range forward contract is

$$X(S, T, k_1, k_2) = p(S, T, k_2) - c(S, T, k_1) \tag{19.B1}$$

The hedge ratio for a put option is

$$\frac{\partial p}{\partial S} = -\exp(-r_f T)N(-d_1) \tag{19.B2}$$

and for a call option

$$\frac{\partial c}{\partial S} = \exp(-r_f T)N(d_1) \tag{19.B3}$$

Hence the hedge ratio for the contract is

$$H \equiv \frac{\partial X}{\partial S} = -\exp(-r_f T)[N(-d_1) + N(h_1)] \tag{19.B4}$$

where

$$d_1 \equiv \frac{\ln(S/k_2)+(r-r_f-\sigma^2/2)T}{\sigma\sqrt{T}} \quad \text{and} \quad h_1 \equiv \frac{\ln(S/k_1)+(r-r_f+\sigma^2/2)T}{\sigma\sqrt{T}}$$

To examine the properties of H it is necessary to differentiate again

$$\frac{\partial H}{\partial S} = \exp(-r_f T)[n(d_1)-n(h_1)]/(\sigma S\sqrt{T}) \tag{19.B5}$$

The right-hand side of (19.B5) will be zero if

$$d_1 = h_1 \tag{19.B6}$$

or

$$d_1 = -h_1 \tag{19.B7}$$

as $n(\ )$ is a symmetric function. As $k_1 \neq k_2$, (19.B7) represents the only solution. Note that (19.B7) is identical to (19.A5).

To determine whether the hedge ratio is maximized or minimized at (19.B7), it is necessary to examine the second derivative:

$$\frac{\partial^2 H}{\partial S^2} = -2d_1 \exp(-r_f T)n(d_1)/(\sigma^2 S^2 T) < 0 \quad \text{if } d_1 > 0 \tag{19.B8}$$

implying that the hedge ratio is maximized if $d_1 > 0$.

The derivative of the hedge ratio with respect to the volatility, eta, is

$$\frac{\partial H}{\partial \sigma} = \exp(-r_f T)[n(d_1)(\sqrt{T}-d_1/\sigma)-n(h_1)(\sqrt{T}-h_1/\sigma)]$$

In the case of a contract depending upon the difference of two stock call options,

$$X = c(S, T, k_2) - c(S, T, k_1)$$

then the hedge ratio is

$$H = N(d_1) - N(h_1) \geq 0 \quad \text{as } k_2 > k_1$$

implying $d_1 > h_1$. Thus, the derivative of the hedge ratio with respect to the stock price, gamma, is

$$\frac{\partial H}{\partial S} = [n(d_1)-n(h_1)]/(\sigma S\sqrt{T}) \tag{19.B9}$$

Apart from the $\exp(-r_f T)$ term in Equation 19.B5, Equation 19.B9 is similar in form to (19.B5) and thus a maximum exists.

The derivative of the hedge ratio with respect to the volatility, eta, is

$$\frac{\partial H}{\partial \sigma} = n(d_1)(\sqrt{T}-d_1/\sigma)-n(h_1)(\sqrt{T}-h_1/\sigma)$$

Bibliography

Brown, S. J., and P. H. Dybvig. 1986. The empirical implications of the Cox, Ingersoll, Ross theory of the term structure of interest rates. *Journal of Finance* 41 (July), 617-630.

Cox, J. C., J. E. Ingersoll, Jr., and S. A. Ross. 1985. A theory of the term structure of interest rates. *Econometrica* 53 (March), 385-407.

Courtadon, G. 1982. The pricing of options on default free bonds. *Journal of Financial and Quantitative Analysis* 17 (March), 75-100.

The First Boston Corporation. 1986. *Prospectus Supplement (June 19, 1986), The Standard Oil Company, 37500, Oil Indexed Units.* New York, NY: The First Boston Corporation.

French, M. 1985. Bowing before the icon. *Euromoney* (December), 85-86.

Grabbe, J. O. 1983. The pricing of call and put options on foreign exchange. *Journal of International Money and Finance* 2, 239-253.

Melino, A., and S. M. Turnbull. 1987. *The pricing of foreign currency options.* Working Paper, Department of Economics, University of Toronto.

Melino, A., and S. M. Turnbull. 1987. *Estimation of the parameters describing the LIBOR interest rate process.* Progress Report, Department of Economics, University of Toronto.

Merton, R. C. 1973. Theory of rational option pricing. *Bell Journal of Economics and Management Science* 4 (Spring), 141-183.

Stoll, H., and R. E. Whaley. 1986. The new option markets. In A. E. Peck (ed.), *Futures markets: Their economic role.* Washington, D.C.: American Enterprise Institute for Public Policy Research.

20

The Pricing of Bull and Bear Floating Rate Notes: An Application of Financial Engineering*

Donald J. Smith

Financial engineering can be described as the construction of a security or a portfolio of securities with an otherwise unavailable risk-return configuration. A classic example of financial engineering is the recent issuance of floating rate notes (FRNs) with nontraditional coupon reset formulas. A traditional FRN resets the coupon rate periodically at some fixed margin over (or under) a reference index rate, for example, LIBOR +0.25%. Since 1986, a number of FRNs have been issued with reset formulas at some fixed rate minus the reference rate. These can be called bull or inverse floaters or, as named by some issuers, yield curve notes — see Ogden [8] for further institutional details. The idea is that an investor who is "bullish" on bond prices would be attracted to a security that has a coupon rate that moves inversely to the market rate.

SallieMae (the Student Loan Market Association) has issued several bull floaters, including the initial one that had a reset formula of 17.20% minus

*An earlier version of this paper was presented under the title "The Pricing of Innovative Floaters" at the Southwestern Finance Association Meeting, March 1988, San Antonio, TX, and at the Western Finance Association Meeting, June 1988, Napa, CA. The author thanks the discussants at those sessions, Robert Daigler and Clifford Smith, respectively, and Keith Brown for their comments and suggestions.

LIBOR. Albert Lord, the chief financial officer of SallieMae, said at the time (April 1986) [9]:

> The formula worked out that the bull floater, or yield curve note, plus the swap resulted in us paying 17.20% and receiving fixed rate funds pegged to Treasuries. The end cost of funds, including the cost of the cap, was very competitive—below the five-year Treasury rate.

Evident in this quote is the contention that SallieMae was able to financially engineer a synthetic fixed rate below the comparable Treasury yield by combining the bull floater with interest rate swap and cap agreements.

Bear floaters, which reset at a multiple of the reference rate minus some fixed rate, followed. For instance, Mellon Bank in June 1986 issued three-year, floating rate certificates of deposit (CDs) with a coupon reset formula of twice LIBOR minus 9.12%. In principle, an investor who is "bearish" on bond prices would be attracted to this security, since the coupon rate rises by more than the increase in the market rate. A *Wall Street Journal* article [7] describing the issue observed:

> From the point of view of the issuer, the CD offers conventional floating-rate financing. That's because, like many similar offerings, the CD's structure involves an interest rate swap that eliminates the unusual features of the interest rate on the CDs, leaving Mellon with conventional floating-rate financing.... A swap official at another firm said such a transaction could leave the issuer with a financing cost of about half a percent below LIBOR.

The intent of this article is to analyze these financially engineered structures and to develop equilibrium pricing conditions for bull and bear floating rate notes. Pricing here means the determination of the fixed rate component in the coupon reset formula for a par value FRN (e.g., the fixed rates of 17.20% and 9.12% in the above examples). The methodology is to construct a synthetic fixed-rate portfolio containing the bull or bear floater and interest rate swap, cap, and floor agreements. Equilibrium pricing will be such that the synthetic fixed rate equals an explicit fixed rate alternative. Otherwise, there would be an opportunity for profitable arbitrage.

I. An Example of Equilibrium Pricing on a Bull Floater

Assume that a firm can issue a five-year, semiannual-payment, fixed coupon note that is priced at par value to yield 10%. The firm also can issue a five-year, par value, floating rate note with a semiannual coupon reset formula of six-month LIBOR plus 0.25%. Both types of traditional debt are assumed to have the same documentation and transaction costs and are neither callable nor putable. In sum, the notes are identical on all dimensions except the fixity of the coupon payments on the first alternative.

Assume further that the firm can enter into par value, five-year, semiannual settlement interest rate swaps to either pay or receive a fixed rate of 9.75% versus six-month LIBOR.[1] Such a "fixed-floating" swap is simply a net exchange of coupon cash flows based on a common notional principal amount (see Loeys [6], Felgran [5], Bicksler and Chen [2], or Arnold [1] for institutional details on interest rate swaps). A par value swap entails no initial cash payment; at each subsequent settlement date a payment is made or received for the annual rate difference, adjusted for the fraction of the year elapsed, and multiplied by the notional principal. The fixed rate on the swap is assumed to be 9.75% to rule out the possibility of obtaining a lower cost of funds by issuing one type of traditional debt and directly swapping into the other.

Now suppose that the firm considers issuing a five-year bull floater at par value. The bull floater would have a coupon reset formula of $X - \text{LIBOR}$. The problem is to determine the break-even fixed rate, X_B, such that if $X < X_B$, the firm would be able to lower its cost of funds vis-a-vis the traditional alternatives. An initial approximation for X_B is 19.75%. To see this, let the bull floater be issued at 19.75% − LIBOR, and the firm agree to receive 9.75% and to pay LIBOR on an interest rate swap having a notional principal equal to the par value of the FRN. At each semiannual payment date the cost of funds (COF) is:

$$COF = 19.75\% - \text{LIBOR} - (9.75\% - \text{LIBOR}) = 10\% \qquad (20.1)$$

Since the LIBORs cancel by design, the firm appears to obtain a synthetic fixed rate of 10%, which equals the explicit fixed rate alternative. A break-even rate of 19.75% is only approximate, however, since it neglects the non-negativity constraint on the bull floater. If LIBOR is above 19.75%, the coupon rate is zero but the firm is still obligated to pay LIBOR on the swap. For example, if LIBOR is 21%, the net settlement payment on the swap is 11.25%. Therefore, the synthetic fixed rate is 10% only for LIBOR ≤ 19.75% and rises above 10% if LIBOR > 19.75%.

The firm could resolve this problem by purchasing a five-year, semiannual-settlement, interest rate cap on six-month LIBOR at a strike rate of 19.75% for a notional principal equal to the par value of the bull floater. An interest rate cap agreement is in effect a series of over-the-counter, European, cash

1. The assumption that the firm can either pay or receive at the same fixed rate neglects the swap market maker's bid-ask spread. In fact, a firm will pay a slightly higher fixed rate than it would receive. The bid-ask spread has narrowed considerably in recent years due to competition and is now on the order of ten basis points. The assumption in the paper simplifies the analysis.

settlement put options.[2] The buyer of the cap pays an upfront premium, an amount quoted as a percentage of the contractual notional principal. In return, the cap writer agrees to pay to the buyer at each settlement date the excess of the variable reference rate (typically LIBOR) over the strike rate, adjusted for the fraction of the year elapsed, times the notional principal. If the reference rate is at or below the cap strike rate, no payment is made. With such a cap agreement, the firm would receive cash flows whenever LIBOR exceeds 19.75% in sufficient amount to keep the net interest payments constant at 10%.

The purchase price of a cap agreement, as with any option, will depend on the level of the strike rate, the time to maturity, and the current and expected future levels and volatility of the reference rate. In this example, a cap on LIBOR at 19.75% might well be a deep-out-of-the-money option and therefore not very expensive. Nevertheless, the premium when amortized over the five-year funding period will raise the overall cost of funds above 10%. So the bull floater would have to be priced somewhat below 19.75% at break-even to compensate for the cost of the cap agreement. The investor, in effect, must pay for the nonnegativity constraint.

Since the price of a cap agreement is a function of the strike rate, a closed-form solution to the equilibrium fixed rate component to the coupon reset formula is unobtainable. In any case, to complete the example, suppose that a five-year, semiannual settlement cap on six-month LIBOR at a strike rate of 19.50% costs 96 basis points, that is, 0.96% of the notional principal. The amortized cost of the cap is then about 25 basis points per year, calculated as a ten-period annuity using 5% per period as the interest rate and annualizing the per period cost. Therefore, if the firm issues a par value bull floater at 19.50% − LIBOR, pays LIBOR and receives 9.75% fixed on an interest rate swap, and buys a cap on LIBOR at 19.50% at an upfront premium of 96 basis points, the cost of funds in each period can be summarized as:

$$
\begin{aligned}
COF &= \text{Max}(0, 19.50\% - \text{LIBOR}) - (9.75\% - \text{LIBOR}) \\
&\quad + 0.25\% - \text{Max}(0, \text{LIBOR} - 19.50\%) \\
&= 10\%
\end{aligned}
\tag{20.2}
$$

Figure 20.1 graphically depicts the terms in Equation 20.2. Panel A-1 shows the first term, the coupon rate on the bull floater, to be constrained to nonnegative values. Panel A-2 shows that the payoff on the swap, the second term, is in effect a forward rate agreement. If LIBOR is above 9.75%, the

---

2. A cap agreement is typically documented as a series of put options on an underlying time deposit to conform to Internal Revenue Service regulations for the taxation of exchange-traded options. In practice, many market participants refer to a cap as a "call option on the rate." See Smith [12] for a discussion of the equivalence between a put on a price and call on the rate.

FIGURE 20.1   *Bull Floater*

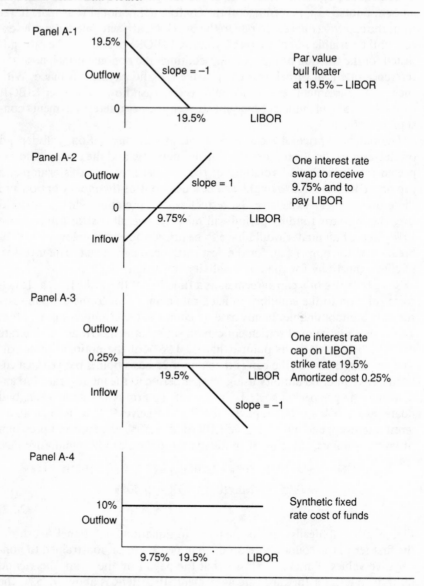

Panel A-1

Par value
bull floater
at 19.5% – LIBOR

Panel A-2

One interest rate
swap to receive
9.75% and to
pay LIBOR

Panel A-3

One interest rate
cap on LIBOR
strike rate 19.5%
Amortized cost 0.25%

Panel A-4

Synthetic fixed
rate cost of funds

firm pays the counterparty; if LIBOR is below 9.75%, the firm receives the
rate difference. Panel A-3 includes the amortized cost of the cap, the third
term, and the receipts on the cap when LIBOR exceeds 19.50%, the fourth

term. These cash flows are vertically summed in Panel A-4 to represent the synthetic fixed rate cost of funds of 10%. Since that equals the explicit cost of traditional fixed rate debt, 19.50% represents the equilibrium pricing on the bull floater.

Now suppose that the firm can in fact issue a par value bull floater at 18.50% – LIBOR. The cost savings, or arbitrage gain, will be somewhat less than 100 basis points, however. First, the premium on a cap at a strike rate of 18.50% will always be higher than at a strike rate of 19.50%. That raises the amortized cost to some degree. Second, the interest rate swap entails bearing the credit risk of the counterparty. If the counterparty were to default when the fixed rate on a replacement swap is less than 9.75%, the cost of funds would rise above 10%. This can be seen by shifting the payoff line on the swap Panel A-2 of Figure 20.1 to the left. Also, there is credit risk on the cap agreement since the firm pays the purchase price at origination and depends on future receipts from the counterparty. Therefore, the expected cost savings should reflect the expected default losses on the swap and cap agreements.

II. An Example of Equilibrium Pricing on a Bear Floater

The firm might also consider issuing a bear floater with a coupon reset formula of the form: $2 \times \text{LIBOR} - Y$. Assume the same rate environment as in the previous section. Now the firm would solve for Y_B, the break-even fixed rate component, such that if $Y > Y_B$ a cost savings is obtained. An initial approximation for Y_B is 9.50%. To obtain a synthetic fixed rate, the firm would issue a par value bear floater at $2 \times \text{LIBOR} - 9.50\%$ and enter *two* interest rate swaps to pay the fixed rate of 9.75% and to receive LIBOR on each. The cost of funds for each period would be:

$$\text{COF} = 2(\text{LIBOR}) - 9.50\% + 2(9.75\% - \text{LIBOR})$$
$$= 10\% \tag{20.3}$$

Note that the firm could use just one swap that has a notional principal of twice the par value of the bear floater.

The nonnegativity constraint on the bear floater becomes binding at low market rates, particularly when LIBOR $< 4.75\%$ if the reset formula is $2 \times \text{LIBOR} - 9.50\%$. Therefore, the structure in Equation 20.3 provides only quasi-fixed funding. If LIBOR is 4%, the coupon rate on the bear floater is zero while the firm pays the counterparty 5.75% on each of two swaps, for a total cost of funds of 11.50%. The firm can complete the structure with the purchase of an interest rate floor agreement. A floor agreement is in effect a series of over-the-counter, European, cash settlement call options.[3] The holder of the floor receives payments from the writer whenever the reference rate is below the strike rate, but none when it is at or above the strike rate. An upfront premium, quoted as a percentage of the notional principal, is paid to the floor writer by the buyer.

The initial approximation for Y_B at 9.50% will be too low, since the amortized cost of a floor on LIBOR at a 4.75% strike rate will raise the all-in synthetic fixed rate above 10%. As in the bull floater example, a closed-form solution for the break-even rate is unobtainable because the purchase price of the floor agreement depends on the specific strike rate, among other factors. Assume, in any case, that a five-year, semiannual settlement floor on six-month LIBOR at a strike rate of 5.75% costs 193 basis points (i.e., 1.93% of the notional principal). That translates to an amortized cost of about 50 basis points per year.

The portfolio that obtains a synthetic fixed rate of 10% in any rate environment consists of a par value bear floater at $2 \times$ LIBOR $- 10.50\%$, two interest rate swaps to pay 9.75% and receive LIBOR, and two interest rate floors at a strike rate of 5.25%. The cost of funds can be summarized as:

$$\text{COF} = \text{Max}[0, 2 \times \text{LIBOR} - 10.50\%]$$
$$+ 2(9.75\% - \text{LIBOR}) + 2(0.50\%)$$
$$- 2[\text{Max}(0, 5.25\% - \text{LIBOR})]$$
$$= 10\% \tag{20.4}$$

The first term is the coupon rate on the bear floater, which is restricted to nonnegative values. The second term is the payoff on the two interest rate swaps. The third and fourth terms are the amortized cost and the cash receipts from the two interest rate floors. These cash flows are displayed in Figure 20.2. Note that the use of two swap and floor agreements, each having a notional principal equal to the par value of the bear floater, doubles the slope of the payoff lines in Panels B-2 and B-3.

III. Generalized Equilibrium Pricing of Bull and Bear Floaters

The numerical examples in the previous sections can now be generalized to cover the equilibrium pricing of any floating rate note. A general expression for the coupon reset formula on an FRN is

---

3. A floor agreement is typically documented as a series of call options on a time deposit but referred to by market participants as a "put option on the rate." See Brown and Smith [3] for further discussion of interest rate caps and floors.

FIGURE 20.2   *Bear Floater*

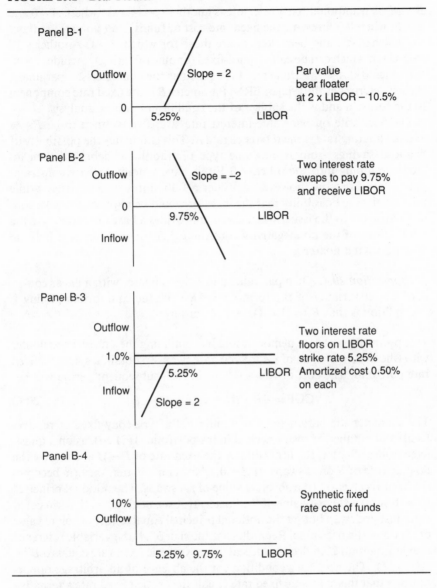

$$C = AR + B \qquad (20.5)$$

where C is the periodic coupon rate, R is the variable reference rate (e.g., LIBOR), and A and B are parameters. A traditional FRN has a coupon reset formula of the form $C = R + M$, where M is the fixed margin over (or under) the reference rate. Hence, a traditional FRN is a special case where $A = 1$ and $B = M$. A traditional fixed rate note is another special case where $A = 0$ and $B = F$, where F represents the fixed rate cost of funds. Bull floaters are those for which $A < 0$ and bear floaters are those for which $A > 1$. Another possible class, which can be called quasi-fixed (or quasi-floating), includes FRNs for which $0 < A < 1$. Parameter A is defined as the characteristic parameter since it determines the type of FRN. Parameter B is the fixed rate component to the formula and is the subject of the equilibrium pricing analysis.

The fixed rate on par value interest rate swaps is assumed to be $F - M$ and the floating rate is the reference rate R. This eliminates the possibility of financial savings from issuing one type of traditional debt and then directly swapping into the other. All FRNs have a nonnegativity constraint that $C \geq 0$. For now, however, consider a fully unrestricted floater. While this permits the possibility that the investor would be required to make coupon payments to the issuer when $C < 0$, it provides a base line to analyze the implications of the nonnegativity constraint. Let the superscript u indicate an unrestricted floater.

Proposition 20.1. On a par value unrestricted floater with a linear coupon reset formula of the form $C^u = AR + B^u$, the equilibrium pricing condition is that $B^u = (1 - A)F + AM$ for any A.

This proposition can be demonstrated by combining the unrestricted floater with (the absolute value of) A interest rate swaps to obtain a synthetic fixed rate portfolio. The cost of funds (COF) in each subsequent period will be

$$COF = AR + B^u + A[(F - M) - R] \tag{20.6}$$

The characteristic parameter A will indicate the type (pay-fixed or receive-fixed) and number of swaps needed in the portfolio. If $A > 0$, as on a quasi-fixed or bear floater, the firm will pay the fixed rate of $F - M$ and receive the floating rate of R on A swaps. If $A < 0$, as on a bull floater, the firm becomes the fixed-receiver on (the absolute value of) A swaps. The notional principal of each swap is the par value of the floater. If A is a noninteger, the firm could enter just one swap but set the notional principal equal to (the absolute value of) A times the par value. Regardless of the sign of A, the variable reference rate in Equation 20.6 drops out, leaving a synthetic fixed rate equal to $B^u + A(F - M)$. The necessary condition for the absence of an arbitrage opportunity is that this synthetic fixed rate equals the explicit fixed rate alternative F. Equating the two and rearranging terms obtains the equilibrium pricing condition in Proposition 20.1.[4]

---

4. An equivalent result obtains if the structure is intended to create a synthetic floating rate. For any A, the cost of funds on the FRN combined with $(1 - A)$ swaps is

Interest rate caps and floors are needed in order to deal with the rate environments when the coupon payment would be negative on a hypothetical unrestricted floater. The nonnegativity constraint becomes binding on bull floaters at high levels of the reference rate, requiring caps, and on bear floaters at low levels, requiring floors. Let $Z_{cap}(X)$ and $Z_{floor}(X)$ stand for the amortized costs of a cap and floor, respectively, having a strike rate of X and a notional principal equal to the par value of the FRN. The payoff on a cap on R at a strike rate of X is $\text{Max}[0, R-X]$ and the payoff on a floor is $\text{Max}[0, X-R]$. Let the superscript r indicate a restricted floater.

Proposition 20.2. On a par value floater with a linear coupon reset formula of the form $C^r = AR + B^r$ restricted to nonnegative values, the equilibrium pricing condition is

$$B^r = \begin{cases} (1-A)F + AM + A[Z_{cap}(-B^r/A)] & \text{if } A < 0 & (20.7) \\ (1-A)F + AM & \text{if } 0 \le A \le 1 & (20.8) \\ (1-A)F + AM - A[Z_{floor}(-B^r/A)] & \text{if } A > 1 & (20.9) \end{cases}$$

These results are obtained by combining the FRN for any A with interest rate swaps and caps (or floors) to create a synthetic fixed rate portfolio. For a bull floater when $A < 0$, the net cost of funds in any period is

$$\text{COF} = \text{Max}[0, AR + B^r] + A[(F-M) - R]$$
$$- A[Z_{cap}(-B^r/A)] + A\{\text{Max}[0, R - (-B^r/A)]\} \quad (20.10)$$

The first term is the coupon rate on the bull floater, restricted to nonnegative values. The second term is the net payoff on (the absolute value of) A receive-fixed swaps. The third term is the amortized cost of (the absolute value of) A interest caps at a strike price of $-B^r/A$, chosen to become in the money exactly when the nonnegativity constraint on the bull floater becomes binding. The fourth term is the receipt on the caps whenever $R > -B^r/A$. Notice that, when $R \le -B^r/A$, the first term is $AR + B^r$ and the fourth term is zero. When $R > -B^r/A$ the first term is zero and the fourth is $AR + B^r$. Therefore, for any R, Equation 20.10 reduces to

$$\text{COF} = AR + B^r + A[(F-M) - R] - A[Z_{cap}(-B^r/A)] \quad (20.11)$$

This expression is set equal to F to rule out any arbitrage opportunities and, after rearranging terms, the condition for $A < 0$ in Proposition 20.2 is obtained.

$$AR + B^u + (1-A)[R - (F-M)]$$

If $A < 1$, the firm receives the fixed rate; if $A > 1$ the firm pays the fixed rate. The cost of funds reduces to $B^u + R + M - (1-A)F - AM$. In the absence of profitable arbitrage opportunities, that variable rate must equal the explicit floating rate of $R + M$. Therefore, $B^u = (1-A)F + AM$ for any A.

For a bear floater when $A > 1$, a synthetic fixed rate results from combining the FRN with A pay-fixed swaps and A interest rate floors. The net cost of funds for each period is:

$$COF = \text{Max}[0, AR + B^r] + A[(F - M) - R]$$
$$+ A[Z_{\text{floor}}(-B^r/A)] - A\{\text{Max}[0, (-B^r/A) - R]\} \qquad (20.12)$$

The nonnegativity constraint on the bear floater becomes binding at $R < -B^r/A$, so the strike rate on the floor agreements is set at that level.

When $R \geq -B^r/A$, the first term, the coupon rate on the FRN, is $AR + B^r$ and the fourth term, the payoff on the floors, is zero. When $R < -B^r/A$, the first term is zero but the fourth becomes $AR + B^r$. Combined with the second and third terms, the settlement on the swaps and the amortized cost of the floors, the net cost is reduced to

$$COF = AR + B^r + A[(F - M) - R]$$
$$+ A[Z_{\text{floor}}(-B^r/A)] \qquad (20.13)$$

The variable reference rate R drops out, providing a synthetic fixed rate that must equal F in order to eliminate any arbitrage opportunities. Rearranging terms obtains the equilibrium condition of $A > 1$ in Proposition 20.2.

The nonnegativity constraint on a quasi-fixed floater when $0 < A < 1$ is never binding so interest rate floors are unnecessary. In Proposition 20.2 then, B^r equals B^u, the pricing condition for an unrestricted floater. Notice that on both bull and bear floaters, B^r is less than B^u. In equilibrium, the issuer is compensated for the amortized costs of the caps or floors via a lower coupon rate. In other words, the investor pays for the advantage of the non negativity constraint by accepting a lower coupon rate than if the FRN had been fully unrestricted.

It should be emphasized that the pricing conditions in Proposition 20.2 are not closed-form solutions for B^r, since the amortized costs of the caps and floors depend on the specific strike rate, which is $-B^r/A$. However, the required strike rates on the caps and floors in practice are likely to represent deep-out-of-the-money options on the reference rate. Then, the amortized costs are likely to be small, and B^u, for which there is a closed-form solution, will be a reasonably good approximation for equilibrium pricing.

IV. The Pricing Sensitivity of Bull and Bear Floaters

The traditional FRN market started in the 1970s in response to the increasing volatility in interest rates. Given no change in the underlying credit worthiness of the issuer or in the marketability of the security, a traditional FRN should trade at par value on each reset date. The minimization of price volatility compared to a fixed rate note for the same maturity is its salient feature. The relative price sensitivity of bull and bear floaters, however, will be quite different than traditional fixed and floating rate instruments because of their innovative coupon reset formulas.

The price sensitivity of bull and bear floaters can be initially examined by returning to the numerical examples of the first sections. The equilibrium pricing of the bull floater is 19.50% − LIBOR, where in the notation of the previous section $F = 10\%$, $R = \text{LIBOR}$, $M = 0.25\%$, and $Z_{\text{cap}}(19.50\%) = 0.25\%$. Substitution into the result in Proposition 20.2 for $A = -1$ obtains $B^r = 19.50\%$. The equilibrium pricing for the bear floater is $2 \times \text{LIBOR} - 10.50\%$. Then, for $A = 2$, $B^r = -10.50\%$ assuming $Z_{\text{floor}}(5.25\%) = 0.50\%$.

Now suppose that on a reset date with four years remaining until maturity, market rates in general rise. In particular, assume that a four-year, par value, fixed rate note would have a coupon rate F equal to 11%. LIBOR too has risen, but a par value traditional FRN can still be issued with a reset formula of LIBOR + 0.25%. The fixed rate on four-year, par value interest rate swaps would now be 10.75% versus LIBOR.

The equilibrium pricing on a new bull floater for $A = -1$ will reflect the higher market rates and will be approximately 21.50% − LIBOR. This assumes that the amortized cost of the requisite cap is still 25 basis points. The cap strike rate is higher, from 19.50% to 21.50%, but so is the current market rate. Those factors offset, and in the absence of a formal cap-pricing model a better assumption is unavailable. The equilibrium pricing on a new bear floater for $A = 2$ will now be approximately $2 \times \text{LIBOR} - 11.50\%$. This also assumes that the amortized cost of the floor agreements remains at 0.50%. A higher strike rate on the floor, from 5.25% to 5.75%, is presumed to offset the higher level for LIBOR.

The key point of this simulation, albeit approximate, is that an investor in the original bull floater experiences an opportunity loss of about 200 basis points per year for the remaining four years. Given the increase in market rates from 10% to 11%, the market price of a bull floater at 19.50% − LIBOR will fall to about 93.67, where par value is 100 and the new fixed rate is used to discount the 100-basis-point-per-period loss over the eight semi-annual periods. On the other hand, an investor in the original bear floater at $2 \times \text{LIBOR} - 10.50\%$ experiences an opportunity gain of about 100 basis points per year. Therefore, the market price will rise to about 103.17. Uncharacteristic to bond-pricing conventions, market rates and the price of a bear floater will be positively related.

Figure 20.3 shows the results for repeating this numerical simulation for a range of market rates, which are represented by the new fixed rate on a par value, four-year note. The amortized costs of the cap and floor agreements are assumed to remain at 0.25% and 0.50%, respectively. The traditional

FIGURE 20.3 *Simulated Price Sensitivities*

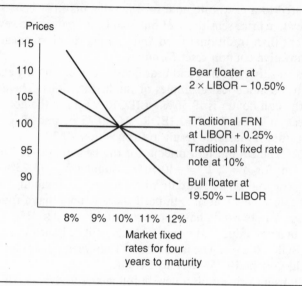

fixed and floating rate instruments represent the usual choice set for an investor. A quasi-fixed floater $(0 < A < 1)$ would have a price-yield curve that falls between those two. Since there is nothing new about its price sensitivity, it is not surprising that quasi-fixed floaters have not appeared in the marketplace. The bull floater, however, is much more price sensitive than a traditional fixed rate note. Intuitively, this is because a higher (lower) market rate both lowers (raises) future coupon cash flows and raises (lowers) the discount rate at which those cash flows are valued. A bear floater has a wholly atypical price-yield configuration. This is because a higher (lower) market rate raises (lowers) future coupon cash flows by more than the change in the discount rate used to value them.

The price sensitivities in Figure 20.3 can also be interpreted as implied durations.[5] A bull floater appears to have a higher duration (i.e., price elasticity with respect to rate changes) than a fixed rate note of comparable maturity, while a bear floater will have a negative duration. These attributes can be generalized by substituting the equilibrium-pricing conditions from Proposition 20.2 into the general expression for the coupon reset formula that $C^r = AR + B^r$, as follows:

---

5. This approach to calculating the implied durations by means of the duration of a replicating portfolio was first seen by the author in Yawitz [13].

$$C^r = \begin{cases} A[R+M+Z_{\text{cap}}]+(1-A)F & \text{if } A<0 \quad (20.14) \\ A[R+M]+(1-A)F & \text{if } 0 \le A \le 1 \quad (20.15) \\ A[R+M-Z_{\text{floor}}]+(1-A)F & \text{if } A>1 \quad (20.16) \end{cases}$$

The strike rate of $-B^r/A$ on the amortized costs of the caps and floors is dropped for simplicity. In this setting the coupon rate on a general floater is replicated by a portfolio of rate-restricted traditional FRNs and fixed rate notes. The terms A and $(1-A)$ represent the portfolio weights. From the investor's perspective, negative weights imply short positions and positive weights imply long positions.

A bull floater for any $A<0$ is replicated by purchasing $(1-A)$ fixed rate notes and selling (the absolute value of) A "capped" floaters. These "capped" floaters have a coupon reset formula of $R+M+Z_{\text{cap}}$, which is higher than on a traditional FRN to offset the maximum rate. This maximum rate is $-F(1-A)/A$ to correspond to the nonnegativity constraint that $C^r \ge 0$. The duration of the bull floater can be inferred from the duration of the replicating portfolio. That will be $(1-A)$ times the duration of a fixed rate note, which is easily calculated, less (the absolute value of) A times the duration of the "capped" floater. The duration of a "capped" floater depends on the proximity of the current coupon rate to the maximum. If the current rate is well below the ceiling, such that the cap is a deep-out-of-the-money option, the duration of the "capped" floater will be close to that of the traditional FRN. A traditional FRN, without a maximum rate, can be assumed to have a short duration equal to the time until the next reset date.[6] As the current rate nears the maximum, the pricing sensitivity of the "capped" floater increases. When the constraint becomes binding, the "capped" floater acts like a fixed rate note and has a comparable duration.

This approach can be clarified with the numerical example. The bull floater at 19.50% − LIBOR can be replicated by an investor via a long position in two fixed rate notes at 10% and a short position in an FRN at LIBOR + 0.50% that has a maximum rate of 20%. Given a remaining maturity of four years, each fixed rate note has a (Macaulay) duration of 3.39 years. If LIBOR is well below 20%, the "capped" floater will have a duration of about 0.50 years. Therefore, the implied duration of the bull floater is approximately 6.28 years. Note that in the earlier exercise the price of the bull floater falls from 100 to about 93.67 when the market rises from 10% to 11%. That percentage price change corroborates an implied duration of over six years, despite a maturity of only four years.

---

6. This necessarily assumes that neither the credit risk of the issuer nor the marketability of the securities has changed. See Yawitz, et al. [14] for analysis of the duration of floating rate notes when the credit risk changes.

A bear floater for $A > 1$ is replicated by long positions in A "floored" floaters and short positions in (the absolute value of) $1 - A$ fixed rate notes. These "floored" floaters have a reset formula of $R + M - Z_{floor}$, which is lower than that of a traditional FRN to reflect the (nonzero) minimum coupon rate. This minimum rate is again specified by $-F(1-A)/A$ to correspond to $C^r \geq 0$. In the numerical example, the bear floater at $2 \times LIBOR - 10.50\%$ can be replicated by buying two FRNs at $LIBOR - 0.25\%$, subject to a 5% minimum rate, and by selling one 10% fixed rate note. The duration of the bear floater will be two times the duration of the "floored" floater minus the duration of the fixed rate note. The price sensitivity of the "floored" floater will be similar to a traditional FRN, namely the time to the next reset date, except when the minimum constraint is binding. In other than low-rate environments, the implied duration of a bear floater is likely to be less than zero because of the negative weight of the long-duration fixed rate note in the replicating portfolio. That gives the uncharacteristic positive relationship beween market rates and the price of a bear floater, as shown in Figure 20.3.

V. Summary and Conclusions

The issuance of bull and bear floaters in recent years is a prototypical example of financial engineering—the construction of a security with a risk-return configuration otherwise unavailable. The anecdotal evidence is that issuers have been able to lower their cost of funds by issuing the bull or bear floater and then transforming that debt to traditional fixed or floating rate funding via interest rate swap, cap, and floor agreements. The optionlike cap or floor agreements are needed to offset the nonnegativity constraint on the underlying security. A bull floater combined with receive-fixed interest rate swaps and cap agreements creates a synthetic fixed rate. A bear floater combined with pay-fixed swaps and interest rate floor agreements also creates a synthetic fixed rate security. A synthetic (traditional) floating rate note could be created instead by altering the number of swaps, caps, and floors.

The initial issuers of a new instrument can exploit arbitrage opportunities. This is a common pattern in financial market innovation. As time passes, those exploitable arbitrage opportunities diminish as learning (reverse engineering) takes place, which leads to the entry of other issuers. Rates and prices are adjusted to reduce or eliminate the arbitrage gain. For instance, institutional investors realize that they can create synthetic bull and bear floaters themselves by combining traditional instruments with swaps, caps, and floors. The equilibrium, or break-even, pricing conditions are those for which the implicit rate on a synthetic structure for both issuers and investors equals the explicit alternative.

An innovative security must be able to transcend the initial arbitrage motivation to attain a lasting presence in the financial marketplace. The unique properties of bull and bear floaters (i.e., their price sensitivities) will have to become the motivating force for issuers and investors. Bull floaters are more sensitive to market rate movements than fixed rate notes of comparable maturity. In fact, the implied duration of a bull floater is typically longer than its maturity. The market price of a bear floater has the atypical characteristic of being positively related to market rates. That implies a negative duration. The addition of bull or bear floaters, then, can dramatically alter overall portfolio price sensitivity. Therefore, bull and bear floating rate notes potentially have a role in interest rate risk management strategies. The question is whether that role can be carried out more efficiently than it could with more traditional products such as futures and options contracts. The early evidence is negative. After an initial flurry in 1986 and 1987, the new-issues market in bull and bear floating rate notes appears to be thinning. Perhaps this is just a further statement of financial market efficiency and the hit-miss process of innovation.

References

1. T. Arnold, "How To Do Interest Rate Swaps," *Harvard Business Review* (September/October 1984), pp. 96–101.
2. J. Bicksler and A. Chen, "An Economic Analysis of Interest Rate Swaps," *Journal of Finance* (July 1986), pp. 645–655.
3. K. Brown and D. Smith, "Recent Innovations in Interest Rate Risk Management and the Reintermediation of Commercial Banking," *Financial Management* (Winter 1988).
4. B. Cornell, "Pricing Interest Rate Swaps: Theory and Empirical Evidence," working paper, UCLA, April 1986.
5. S. Felgran, "Interest Rate Swaps: Use, Risk, and Prices," *New England Economic Review* (November/December 1987), pp. 22–32.
6. J. Loeys, "Interest Rate Swaps: A New Tool for Managing Risk," *Federal Reserve Bank of Philadelphia Business Review* (May/June 1985), pp. 17–25.
7. A. Monroe, "Mellon Issues CDs with Interest Rate Keyed to the Libor," *Wall Street Journal* (June 6, 1986).
8. J. Ogden, "An Analysis of Yield Curve Notes," *Journal of Finance* (March 1987), pp. 99–110.
9. S. Priestley, "Engineering Swaps," *Euromoney Corporate Finance* (April 1986), pp. 25–28.
10. K. Ramaswamy and S. Sundaresan, "The Valuation of Floating Rate Securities," *Journal of Financial Economics* (December 1986), pp. 251–272.
11. C. Smith, C. Smithson, and L. Wakeman, "The Evolving Market for Swaps," *Midland Corporate Finance Journal* (Winter 1986), pp. 20–32.
12. D. Smith, "Putting the Cap on Options," *Euromoney Corporate Finance* (January 1987), pp. 20–21.

13. J. Yawitz, "Pricing and Duration of Inverse Floating Rate Notes," Financial Strategies Group, Goldman Sachs (March 1986).
14. J. Yawitz, H. Kaufold, T. Macirowski, and M. Smirlock, "The Pricing and Duration of Floating Rate Bonds," *The Journal of Portfolio Management* (Summer 1987), pp. 49–56.

21

The Case for Issuing
Synthetic Convertible Bonds

John D. Finnerty

In an article entitled "Equity-Linked Debt," Philip Jones and Scott Mason concluded that a company would be better off, from a tax standpoint at least, by issuing debt with warrants rather than convertible debt with comparable terms.[1] The fact is, however, that issues of units consisting of debt and warrants are much less common than convertible debt issues. Between 1981 and 1985, for example, there were $28.5 billion of new convertible debt issues in the United States, but only $7.4 billion of units of debt and warrants — a ratio of nearly 4 to 1.[2] If Jones and Mason are correct, then how does one account for the preponderance of convertible debt issues? Are corporations routinely neglecting a superior financing alternative, or are there offsetting factors that outweigh the apparent tax advantages?

An Example

To focus the discussion, consider the following example. A corporation plans to issue $50 million principal amount of 20-year 10% subordinated convertible debentures.[3] The debentures are convertible into common stock at a

---

1. See E. Philip Jones and Scott P. Mason, "Equity-Linked Debt," *Midland Corporate Finance Journal* (Winter 1986), pp. 47–58.
2. The source of this information is Securities Data Corp., New York, N.Y.
3. Companies typically issue convertible debt in subordinated form. For a more extended discussion of convertible debt financing, see John D. Finnerty, *Corporate Financial Analysis,* McGraw-Hill, New York, 1986, pp. 358–365.

FIGURE 21.1   *Summary of Terms for Issues of Convertible Debt and Debt with Warrants*

	Convertible Debt	Debt with Warrants Alt #1	Debt with Warrants Alt #2
Price	$1000 per debenture	$1000 per unit ($849.54 per debenture[a] 150.46 per 40 warrants)	$1000 per unit ($849.54 per debenture[a] 150.46 per 40 warrants)
Debt Features			
Security Type	Convertible subordinated debenture	Subordinated debenture Warrant	Subordinated debenture Warrant
Principal Amount	$50 million	$50 million	$50 million
Coupon	10%	10%	10%
Maturity	20 years	20 years	20 years
Sinking Fund	none	none	none

Optional Redemption	Year	Debenture Price	Year	Debenture Price	Year	Debenture Price	Warrant Price	Per Bond Plus 40 Warrants
	1	$1100	1	$1100	1	$1000	$2.50	$1100.00
	2	1090	2	1090	2	1000	2.25	1090.00
	3	1080	3	1080	3	1000	2.00	1080.00
	4	1070	4	1070	4	1000	1.75	1070.00
	5	1060	5	1060	5	1000	1.50	1060.00
	6	1050	6	1050	6	1000	1.25	1050.00
	7	1040	7	1040	7	1000	1.00	1040.00
	8	1030	8	1030	8	1000	0.75	1030.00
	9	1020	9	1020	9	1000	0.50	1020.00
	10	1010	10	1010	10	1000	0.25	1010.00
	11–20	1000	11–20	1000	11–20	1000	0.01	1000.40

Limitations on Redemptions	none	The warrants are non-redeemable.	The warrants are redeemable only if the company simultaneously redeems or else tenders to the trustee $25 principal amount of debentures for each warrant called for redemption. The debentures are redeemable only if the company simultaneously redeems or else tenders to the trustee 40 warrants for each debenture called for redemption.
Limitation on Repurchase	none	The debentures can be repurchased in the market only if an equal percentage of the warrants are simultaneously reacquired.	none

FIGURE 21.1   *Continued*

	Convertible Debt	Debt with Warrants Alt #1	Debt with Warrants Alt #2
Conversion/Warrant Features			
Expiration	20 years	20 years	20 years
Conversion/Exercise Price	$25 per share	$25 per share	$25 per share
Current Share Price	$20 per share	$20 per share	$20 per share
Premium Over Conversion/ Exercise Price	25%	25%	25%
Shares Per Debenture	40	40 (40 warrants per debenture each carrying the right to buy 1 share)	40 (40 warrants per debenture each carrying the right to buy 1 share)
Limitation on Exercise	–	Only with debentures	With cash or debentures

a. Assuming the subordinated debenture yields 12% on a semiannually compounded basis.

25% premium over the company's current stock price of $20 (that is, each debenture of $1,000 face value can be exchanged for 40 common shares, in effect allowing convertible holders to convert at $25 per share). The company's new issue rate for 20-year straight (i.e., nonconvertible) subordinated debt is 12%.

Figure 21.1 provides a brief summary of the terms of the convertible issue. Although convertible debt issues typically contain sinking funds, I have intentionally left out a sinking fund provision in Figure 21.1 in order to simplify the comparison of convertible debt with debt and warrants (although without altering the basic conclusions). The convertible's redemption schedule – the issue is redeemable at the issuer's option at positive but declining premiums over each of the first ten years, and is callable at par thereafter – is typical of convertible debt issues. Aside from the prices set forth in the redemption schedule, there are no other limitations on the issuer's right to redeem or repurchase the issue.[4]

---

4. In practice, convertible debt issues often impose a restriction on the issuer's flexibility to call the issue for redemption within the first few years it is outstanding. One popular form such restriction takes is to prohibit the issuer from calling the issue within three years of its issuance unless the market price of the common stock is at least 150% of the conversion price for at least 20 days within a 30-day trading period. Ignoring this factor does not affect the basic conclusions of my argument.

Figure 21.1 also contains a corresponding list of terms for two comparable issues of debt with warrants — comparable to such a degree that, in the absence of special tax or other factors (which I discuss later), investors should be willing to pay the same price for each of the three securities. Debt with Warrants Alternative #1 (henceforth DW1) has the structure proposed by Jones and Mason as a convertible equivalent. Debt with Warrants Alternative #2 (DW2) differs from DW1 principally in that it permits holders to use *either* cash or debentures to exercise the warrants, whereas DW1 specifies that exercise can be accomplished only with debentures. And, as I shall show later, this additional exercise option offered the holder by DW2 in turn creates a need for differences in redemption and repurchase provisions.

Both of these debt-with-warrants packages, then, in the absence of special tax or other factors, should command the same offering price as the convertible issue in Figure 21.1 for the following reasons: (1) Both the straight debt issue and the warrant mature when the convertible debt does; (2) the conversion terms are identical; (3) the issuer of debt with warrants has the ability to force warrant holders to use the debentures to exercise the warrants; and (4) the redemption terms are effectively identical. Given these conditions, the debt-with-warrants packages can be thought of as "synthetic convertible bonds." The convertible debenture issue is priced at par. Pricing the debt-with-warrants packages at par implies a price of $849.54 per debenture (based on the assumed 12% required yield) and a price of $150.46 for 40 warrants. The warrants entitle the holder to tender one debenture and 40 warrants for 40 shares of common stock.[5]

Once having established that investors would view the above issues of convertible debt and debt with warrants (again, absent special tax or other factors) as securities of equivalent value, we can address the question from the issuer's perspective: Are there important advantages to issues of debt with warrants that would lead corporate issuers to prefer them over conventional convertible bonds?

Analytical Framework

A debt-with-warrants package is clearly superior to a comparable convertible debt issue if all the following conditions hold:

---

5. The warrants portion of the unit can be structured in at least two alternative ways: one warrant per unit to buy 40 shares, or 40 warrants per unit each to buy one share. In practice the latter structure is typical. Also in practice, investors are usually given the option to pay either in cash or by tendering the debenture. They will select the former when the market value of the debenture exceeds the cash exercise price. But as Jones and Mason note, it is necessary to preclude this option in DW1 in order to make the debt with warrants strictly comparable to the convertible debenture.

- The comparable debt-with-warrants package provides the issuer with a larger tax shield per dollar of proceeds, thereby lowering its after-tax cost of funds.

- The debt-with-warrants package affords the issuer greater flexibility to force conversion of the package entirely to equity.

- The debt-with-warrants package affords greater refunding or retirement flexibility, either through the issuer's ability to call the bonds for cash redemption or to repurchase bonds in the open market.

- The debt-with-warrants package has a more favorable impact on reported earnings period by period than the convertible debt issue.

- The debt-with-warrants package results in a smaller amount of debt on the balance sheet.

Even if some of the foregoing conditions do not hold, debt with warrants would still be superior if the conditions that are violated are collectively outweighed by the favorable effect of the conditions that do hold. I now take up each of these factors in more detail. Let me also say here, as an aside, that given that capital markets—and, increasingly, bond rating agencies—are reasonably adept at identifying the economic reality that underlies accounting data, the first three factors listed above are likely to be much more important that the latter cosmetic, accounting effects.

Tax Considerations

As explained by Jones and Mason, the conversion of convertible debentures is not a taxable event for either the issuer or investors. Further, if conversion never takes place, the effective expiration of the embedded conversion option as worthless upon the maturity of the convertible debt has no tax consequences for either issuer or investor.[6]

The tax aspects of the debt-with-warrants packages are more complex. The sale of the debt at a large discount from its face value involves "original issue discount."[7] The issuer—and any taxable purchaser as well—must amortize the discount under the effective yield method over the life of the debt issue. Because the issue's yield to maturity is 12%, the 10% straight issue in Figure 21.1 involves an original issue discount amounting to $150.46

---

6. Jones and Mason, p. 51.
7. Under the Internal Revenue Code, a debt issue has "original issue discount" at the time of issue if the offering price represents a discount from the principal amount of the debenture that equals or exceeds ¼ of 1% multiplied by the maturity of the bond in years. For example, a 20-year bond will have original issue discount if the issuer sells it for 95% or less of its principal amount.

per bond (i.e., the bond with a 10% coupon sells for $849.54). The discount is allocated in such a manner that interest expense for any period is calculated for tax purposes so that the amount of interest paid in cash plus the amount of original issue discount allocated to that period represents an effective interest rate of 12% on the unamortized balance outstanding at the beginning of the period. As a result, the issuer's interest deductions are larger in the case of debt with warrants than with convertibles. But so is the unit holder's interest income.

Table 21.1 illustrates the calculation of the periodic amortization amounts for the straight debentures in Figure 21.1. Note that the value attributed to the warrants on the issuance date ($150.46) equals the amount of original issue discount on the debentures. In effect, the issuance of debt with warrants allows the issuer to deduct the warrant proceeds. As a result, total interest deductions associated with each unit are greater than the interest deductions associated with the convertible debenture. In Table 21.1, the net tax benefit to the issuer (undiscounted) equals the amount of amortization ($150.46) multiplied by the tax rate (46%) — or $69.21 per $1,000 unit. For a $50 million issue, this benefit would amount to almost $3.5 million.

Note, however, that these amortization deductions have a mirror image; they represent income to the holders of these debentures. If debenture holders pay tax at a higher marginal rate than the issuer, there is actually a net tax drain. If fully taxable individual investors represent the marginal purchasers, a debt-with-warrants package would have to provide either a higher interest rate or a smaller conversion premium — or some combination of the two — than an otherwise identical convertible debenture in order to compensate investors for their added tax liability. In fact, these additional taxes borne by holders of debt with warrants could completely offset the tax benefit issuers derive from amortization of the discount.

The exercise of the warrants is a nontaxable event for the issuer, but not necessarily for taxable holders. The exercise of warrants by tendering bonds may or may not be a taxable event; the issue has not been resolved. If it is ruled to be nontaxable, a holder who uses bonds to exercise warrants would receive stock that has the same basis for tax purposes as the investor's purchase price of the unit, and the holding period for the stock would date from when the bonds were purchased. This would parallel the tax treatment accorded the conversion of a convertible bond. The Internal Revenue Service, however, might instead maintain that the exercise terminates the bond investment. Because the value of the shares would presumably exceed the holder's tax basis in the bonds, exercise of the warrants in that case would result in a taxable gain to investors who tender their bonds for warrants.[8] In

---

8. If tendering the debt in exercising the warrants is treated as a taxable exchange, it is unclear under current tax law whether the gain (or loss) recognized on such exchange will be measured by (a) the difference between the principal amount of bonds tendered and the bonds' adjusted

addition, the investor's holding period in this latter case would date from the day the warrants were exercised.

With regard to the tax impact of expiration, under the Tax Reform Act of 1984 (the 1984 Act) the expiration of warrants unexercised no longer triggers a tax liability for the issuer.[9] Prior to passage of the 1984 Act, expiration unexercised would have given rise to ordinary income equal to the original warrant proceeds. It is important to note, however, that an issuer could have avoided this potential tax liability by stipulating in the terms of the warrant that immediately prior to expiration the warrant would automatically convert into a nominal amount of the issuer's common stock.[10] The 1984 Act eliminated the need for such a provision.

The expiration of warrants unexercised does give rise to a capital loss for the holder equal to the holder's purchase price, which generates a tax shield for a taxable holder that is not offset by a tax liability for the issuer. Accordingly, the expiration of warrants unexercised provides a net tax benefit; taxable holders gain to the extent of the tax benefit associated with the capital loss, but at the expense of the government rather than the issuer.[11]

Like the expiration of warrants unexercised, the reacquisition of warrants from holders is also a nontaxable event for the issuer. If the repurchase price is below the selling warrant holder's tax basis, however, there is a net tax benefit equal to the value of the tax deduction to selling warrant holders who are taxable. Conversely, if the repurchase price exceeds the issue price, there is a taxable gain to holders who sell. Readers of the Jones and Mason article will recall that the authors recommended, as a tax-reducing strategy, repurchasing warrants before expiration when the repurchase price exceeds the original issue price. In fact, a repurchase under these circumstances would have an unfavorable tax effect; the corporation would derive no tax savings and taxable holders would realize a taxable gain.

---

tax basis, (b) the difference between the fair market value of the bonds tendered and their adjusted basis, or (c) the difference between the fair market value of the common stock received on exercise and the aggregate adjusted basis of the bonds tendered and warrants exercised.

9. As a result of the 1984 Act, a corporation no longer recognizes gain or loss on the lapse or on the repurchase of a warrant to acquire its own stock. See *Prentice-Hall's Explanation of the Tax Reform Act of 1984*, Prentice-Hall, Englewood Cliffs, NJ, 1984, p. 35. Consequently, the tax advantage that Jones and Mason attribute to the corporate repurchase of outstanding warrants has not existed for the past two years.

10. For example, American Express Company issued 1,832,000 warrants in February and March 1982 that provided that any warrants still outstanding on the expiration date would automatically convert into common shares at the rate of 1 common share for each 100 warrants, which represents 1/100th of the number of shares into which each warrant is freely convertible. See American Express Company prospectus, March 31, 1982. Because they miss this point, Jones and Mason attribute a tax penalty to warrants that a warrant issuer could easily have avoided.

11. Jones and Mason missed the tax asymmetry because they ignored individual income taxes. Jones and Mason, p. 51.

TABLE 21.1 *Interest Expense Associated with Comparable Convertible Debt and Debt with Warrants Issues*

Interest Period	Interest on Convertible Debenture	Interest Expense on Subordinated Debenture			After-Tax Interest on[b]		Book Value of Subordinated Debenture
		Cash	Amortization[a]	Total	Convertible Debenture	Subordinated Debenture	
0	—	—	—	—	—	—	$849.54
1	$50.00	$50.00	$0.97	$50.97	$27.00	$27.52	850.51
2	50.00	50.00	1.03	51.03	27.00	27.56	851.54
3	50.00	50.00	1.09	51.09	27.00	27.59	852.63
4	50.00	50.00	1.16	51.16	27.00	27.63	853.79
5	50.00	50.00	1.23	51.23	27.00	27.66	855.02
6	50.00	50.00	1.30	51.30	27.00	27.70	856.32
7	50.00	50.00	1.38	51.38	27.00	27.75	857.70
8	50.00	50.00	1.46	51.46	27.00	27.79	859.16
9	50.00	50.00	1.55	51.55	27.00	27.84	860.71
10	50.00	50.00	1.64	51.64	27.00	27.89	862.35
11	50.00	50.00	1.74	51.74	27.00	27.94	864.09
12	50.00	50.00	1.85	51.85	27.00	28.00	865.94
13	50.00	50.00	1.96	51.96	27.00	28.06	867.89
14	50.00	50.00	2.07	52.07	27.00	28.12	869.97
15	50.00	50.00	2.20	52.20	27.00	28.19	872.17
16	50.00	50.00	2.33	52.33	27.00	28.26	874.50
17	50.00	50.00	2.47	52.47	27.00	28.33	876.97
18	50.00	50.00	2.62	52.62	27.00	28.41	879.58
19	50.00	50.00	2.78	52.78	27.00	28.50	882.36
20	50.00	50.00	2.94	52.94	27.00	28.59	885.30

21	50.00	50.00	3.12	53.12	27.00	28.68	888.42
22	50.00	50.00	3.31	53.31	27.00	28.79	891.72
23	50.00	50.00	3.50	53.50	27.00	28.89	895.23
24	50.00	50.00	3.71	53.71	27.00	29.00	898.94
25	50.00	50.00	3.94	53.94	27.00	29.13	902.88
26	50.00	50.00	4.17	54.17	27.00	29.25	907.05
27	50.00	50.00	4.42	54.42	27.00	29.39	911.47
28	50.00	50.00	4.69	54.69	27.00	29.53	916.16
29	50.00	50.00	4.97	54.97	27.00	29.68	921.13
30	50.00	50.00	5.27	55.27	27.00	29.85	926.40
31	50.00	50.00	5.58	55.58	27.00	30.01	931.98
32	50.00	50.00	5.92	55.92	27.00	30.20	937.90
33	50.00	50.00	6.27	56.27	27.00	30.39	944.18
34	50.00	50.00	6.65	56.65	27.00	30.59	950.83
35	50.00	50.00	7.05	57.05	27.00	30.81	957.88
36	50.00	50.00	7.47	57.47	27.00	31.03	965.35
37	50.00	50.00	7.92	57.92	27.00	31.28	973.27
38	50.00	50.00	8.40	58.40	27.00	31.54	981.67
39	50.00	50.00	8.90	58.90	27.00	31.81	990.57
40	50.00	50.00	9.43	59.43	27.00	32.09	1000.00
Total	$2000.00	$2000.00	$150.46	$2150.46	$1080.00	$1161.27	

a. The 10% subordinated debenture yields 12% on a semi-annually compounded basis. The $150.46 ($1000 − 849.54) original issue discount is allocated over the 20-year life of the debenture so that total interest expense each year (i.e., cash plus amortization) represents a 12% semi-annually compounded yield on the book value of the debenture at the beginning of the year.

b. At a 46% marginal income tax rate.

As discussed in more detail in a later section, a survey of seven of the largest institutional investors in convertible bonds revealed that approximately 80-90% of the funds invested in convertible bonds are so invested by, or on behalf of, tax-exempt investors such as pension funds. Consequently, we can say with some confidence that the tax savings to issuers of debt with warrants relative to convertible debt should outweigh the actual tax disadvantage to (taxable) holders of debt with warrants.

Forced Conversion and Refunding Flexibility

The principal purpose of the optional redemption provision of a convertible bond is to enable the issuer to force conversion of the bond into common stock. In this regard, it is important to appreciate that even when the value of the underlying common stock exceeds the redemption price of the bond, holders may not convert voluntarily. As long as the annual interest payments on a convertible bond exceed the amount of dividends being paid annually on the underlying common stock into which the bond is convertible, holders (other than corporate holders who receive an 85% dividends received exclusion) will not convert. By continuing to hold the convertible bond, they receive greater income while still benefiting from the full price appreciation in the underlying common stock.

Correspondingly, forcing conversion can benefit the *issuer* whenever the after-tax interest expense per bond exceeds the amount of dividends on the underlying stock. The optional redemption provision is thus of potentially significant value to the issuer; and if the debt-with-warrants package does not afford at least the same degree of flexibility to force conversion of debt to equity as the convertible debentures, the issuer is put at a disadvantage. The issuer can achieve this degree of flexibility either (1) by permitting investors to exercise warrants only with the debentures so that calling the debentures will trigger the exercise of the warrants whenever the market value of the common stock to be received exceeds the debenture's redemption price or (2) by allowing the issuer to call debentures and warrants separately but at redemption prices that make the aggregate redemption price per unit identical to the redemption price per convertible debenture. DW1 (see Figure 21.1) includes the former provision and DW2 includes the latter. Without such provisions, the debt-with-warrants package would afford the issuer much less flexibility in converting each unit of debt with warrants entirely into equity than would a similar convertible debenture.[12]

---

12. If the debentures are callable at par and warrants are exercised voluntarily, the issuer can use the exercise proceeds to retire debt so as to achieve the same effect as conversion. But note that in such a case the effective redemption premium in any year for the straight subordinated

Such provisions also give rise to the need for certain restrictions to protect bondholders. Note that in the case of DW1, if the issuer were permitted to repurchase the associated debt in the marketplace for cash *without* repurchasing an equivalent percentage of warrants, such bond repurchases would cause a portion of the warrants to become worthless. But, at the same time, because of the value of the repurchase option to issuers, restrictions on cash repurchases are highly unusual for public debt issues. For example, the loss of repurchase flexibility could cause the issuer to miss the opportunity to buy back bonds at a discount for sinking fund purposes.[13] Also, without a restriction of this sort, the issuer's right to reacquire bonds for cash would tend to cause investors to insist on holding the warrants and bonds as units rather than to trade them separately. To understand why this is so, picture what could happen just prior to forced exercise if the warrants were exercisable only by tendering bonds. In such a case, the warrants would be worthless without the bonds necessary to exercise them, and the bond would have a value equal only to its redemption value unless the holder has the warrants needed to convert it into stock. Under these circumstances, the value of the debt-with-warrants package would exceed the sum of the value of the bonds and the value of the warrants trading separately (unless arbitrage activity were able to eliminate the differential).[14]

In the case of DW2, the issuer would have the freedom to reacquire the bonds in the open market for cash without purchasing the warrants. Also, by requiring the issuer to tender 40 warrants to the bond trustee along with $1,000 cash for each bond called, the issuer is assured that voluntary exercise of the warrants with cash can be coupled with retirement of the debentures at par, as is the case with a convertible debenture, and investors are assured that the issuer cannot redeem the bonds at par unless the issuer previously acquired or simultaneously calls the associated warrants. This makes

---

debenture in Figure 21.1 is greater than the redemption premium during the same year for the convertible subordinated debenture. For example, during the first year this effective redemption price would be $(\$1000/849.54) \times 100 = 117.71\%$, implying a premium of 17.71%.

13. For example, unless it could reacquire the necessary number of warrants, the issuer would have to forgo the profit that would result from buying bonds at a discount from their par value in the marketplace on the sinking fund date and tendering them to the trustee in lieu of redeeming bonds at par on that date. For a more detailed discussion of this strategy, see John D. Finnerty, *An Illustrated Guide to Bond Refunding Analysis* (Financial Analysts Research Foundation, Charlottesville, VA, 1984); see also Harold Bierman, "The Debt-Equity Swap," *Midland Corporate Finance Journal*, Vol. 1 No. 3 (1983).

14. As Jones and Mason note, there remains the issue of how the difference between the conversion value and the optional redemption value will be allocated between debenture holders and warrant holders. A debenture holder might be able to realize a disproportionate share of the value of this package by collecting the issue, and in the extreme, by acquiring all the debentures and thereby forcing all the warrant holders to sell to the collector or have their warrants expire worthless.

the optional redemption feature identical to that of a convertible bond. In particular, forced exercise will occur only if the company's common stock price appreciates by at least the conversion premium plus the (effective) bond redemption premium, as is the case with a convertible debenture.

In short, DW2 affords the issuer greater redemption and repurchase flexibility than DW1 (which contains the structure proposed by Jones and Mason) because the former allows the issuer greater freedom to reacquire bonds for cash and also permits the issuer to redeem the warrants separately under certain circumstances. It also affords investors greater conversion flexibility by giving them the option to use cash or debentures to exercise the warrants. DW2 affords the issuer roughly the same degree of redemption flexibility as the convertible debt issue pictured in Figure 21.1, but provides greater repurchase flexibility because it allows the issuer to repurchase debt and warrants separately. Both afford investors roughly the same degree of conversion/exercise flexibility.[15]

Financial Reporting Impact

APB Opinion No. 15 requires a supplemental calculation of fully diluted *earnings per share,* which involves treating the convertible debt issue on a pro forma basis as though it had been converted on the first day of the reporting period.[16] When fully diluted earnings per share are less than primary earnings per share, the issuer must report both figures. A convertible debt issue is said to be "dilutive" whenever fully diluted earnings per share are less than primary earnings per share. In addition, under APB Opinion No. 15, if the yield to maturity on the convertible debt issue is less than 2/3 of the AA corporate bond rate, the issuer must treat the convertible debt issue as a common stock equivalent for purposes of calculating primary earnings per share — that is, as though the issue had been converted as of its issuance date (or as of the first day of the reporting period for later periods).[17]

In contrast, a warrant issue is never dilutive as long as the exercise price exceeds the prevailing share price, as is typically the case on the issuance date and for some period thereafter.[18] APB Opinion No. 15 specifies that an issuer

15. There is at least one situation in which DW2 could afford greater conversion exercise flexibility to investors. If there were a period of call deferment, DW2 would give investors the flexibility to use cash or debentures to exercise. If an investor chose to pay cash, he could keep his debentures at least until the period of call protection expires. Once the debentures become callable at $1,000, there is no advantage to holding the debentures and paying cash to exercise the warrants.

16. Accounting Principles Board, "Earnings Per Share," APB Opinion No. 15, AICPA, New York, 1969.

17. Financial Accounting Standard Board, FASB Statement No. 85, Stamford, CT, March 1985.

18. Jones and Mason seem to miss this point (Jones and Mason, p. 53). They state that "fully

of warrants should use the "treasury stock method" to reflect the potentially dilutive effect of warrants when calculating earnings per share.[19] This method assumes that common shares are issued at the exercise price and that the proceeds of exercise are then used to reacquire these shares of stock at the prevailing share price.

In addition, debt with warrants involves a greater interest deduction than a comparable convertible debt issue, as Table 21.1 illustrates. Consequently, the debt-with-warrants package will generally involve lower reported primary earnings per share, at least whenever the yield to maturity of the convertible debt exceeds 2/3 of the AA corporate bond rate. But it will involve greater reported fully diluted earnings per share except when the share price exceeds the exercise price of the warrant by a substantial percentage.[20]

With regard to the balance sheet impact of the two alternatives, convertible debt is recorded as debt from its issuance date. Debt with warrants, on the other hand, is recorded as debt to the extent of the debt portion of the package and as common equity to the extent of the balance.[21] As the original issue discount associated with the debt portion of the unit package is amortized over the life of the debt issue, the periodic amortization is added to the balance of debt outstanding. As the debt issue approaches maturity (assuming it is not tendered in exercise of the warrants), the book value of the debt approaches and eventually equals the prical amount of the debt. The amortization of the OID reduces earnings to the extent that if neither the warrant is exercised nor the convertible debt issue is converted, then just prior to maturity, each alternative would result in book value of debt equal to the $1,000 issue price per convertible debenture or unit; but common equity would be greater under the debt-with-warrants alternative by the amount of the tax shields resulting from amortization of the original issue discount.

Table 21.2 illustrates the financial reporting impact of the two alternatives. Note that the amortization of the OID for tax purposes produces greater cash flow for the units alternative.[22]

On balance, then, debt with warrants will have a more beneficial impact on the issuer's balance sheet because the addition to debt is less than under

---

diluted earnings per share are actually lower as a result of a warrants issue [rather than a common stock issue]." As long as the exercise price exceeds the market price of the stock, the warrants are not dilutive.

19. See Footnote 16 for the reference.

20. For example, in Table 20.2, the higher of the average price during the year and the year-end price would have to exceed $48.29 (a premium of more than 140% over the share price at the time the warrants were issued) in order for the debt-with-warrants alternative to have lower fully diluted earnings per share. During the year of expiration, the higher of the average price during the year and the year-end price would have to exceed $35.97 (a premium of more than 79% over the share price at the time the warrants were issued).

21. The amount of the warrant proceeds is added to additional paid-in capital.

22. The discount is amortized on the same basis for both tax purposes and financial reporting purposes.

TABLE 21.2 *Comparison of the Financial Reporting Impact of the Two Alternatives* [a] *(Dollar Amounts in Millions)*

| | | Pro Forma the Issuance of | |
	Actual	Convertible Debt	Debt with Warrants
Year of Issue			
Operating Income	$50.00	$57.50	$57.50
Interest Expense	–	5.00	5.10
Pre-Tax Income	50.00	52.50	52.40
Taxes	23.00	24.15	24.10
Net Income	$27.00	$28.35	$28.30
Average Shares (Millions)	9.00	9.00[b]	9.00[b]
Earnings Per Share			
Primary	$3.00	$3.15	$3.14
Fully Diluted	$3.00	$2.82	$3.14
Year of Expiration			
Operating Income	$100.00	$107.50	$107.50
Interest Expense	–	5.00	5.92
Pre-Tax Income	100.00	102.50	101.58
Taxes	46.00	47.15	46.73
Net Income	$54.00	$55.35	$54.85
Average Shares (Millions)	9.00	9.00[b]	9.00[b]
Earnings Per Share			
Primary	$6.00	$6.15	$6.09
Fully Diluted	$6.00	$5.28	$6.09
End of Year of Issue			
Long-Term Debt	–	–	$42.6
Convertible Debt	–	$50.0	–
Common Equity	500.0	501.4	508.8
Capitalization	$500.0	$551.4	$551.4
% Debt	–	9.1%	7.7%

TABLE 21.2 *Continued*

| | | Pro Forma the Issuance of | |
	Actual	Convertible Debt	Debt with Warrants
End of Year of Expiration			
Long-Term Debt	–	–	$50.0
Convertible Debt	–	$50.0	–
Common Equity	1000.0	1027.0	1030.5
Capitalization	$1000.0	$1077.0	$1080.5
% Debt	–	4.6%	4.6%

a. Based on the terms contained in Figure 21.1. For the sake of simplicity, it is assumed that the covertible debt or units were issued on the first day of the year, that the issuer's share price averages $20 in both the year of issue and the year of expiration, and that the company earns 15% before taxes each year on the investment of the $50 million of proceeds.
b. Under each alternative, a total of 2,000,000 new shares are issuable.

the convertible debt alternative. In addition, the impact on fully diluted earnings per share will be less severe under that alternative. As suggested earlier, however, it is doubtful whether such financial reporting benefits per se can have a significant and lasting impact on the stock market value of a company.

Marketing Considerations

The preceding analysis implies that a debt-with-warrants package is superior to an otherwise identical convertible bond. Yet, as I mentioned at the outset of this article, convertible bonds clearly dominate debt with warrants in terms of new issue volume. In an attempt to explain this prevalence of convertibles over debt with warrants, I conducted an informal survey of seven of the largest institutional investors in convertible bonds. (For the results of this survey, see Table 21.3.) Collectively they manage more than $4 billion of funds that are invested in convertible bonds and debt with warrants; approximately 80–90% of this amount is invested on behalf of tax-exempt investors such as pension funds. None are prohibited, either by legal restrictions or as a matter of policy, from investing in debt with warrants, and all indicated that a debt-with-warrants package would be subjected to the same scrutiny and evaluated against the same investment criteria as convertible

TABLE 21.3   *Results of Survey of Large Convertible Bond Investors*

Institution	Funds Invested in Convertible Bonds[a] (Millions of Dollars)	Percentage of Funds Tax-Exempt	Limitations on Ability to Invest in Debt with Warrants	
			Legal	Policy
Citibank	$300	100%	Permitted Investment	Permitted Investment
Equitable Life	300	100	Permitted Investment	Permitted Investment
IDS	400	—	Permitted Investment	Permitted Investment
Morgan Guaranty	1,000	80	Permitted Investment	Permitted Investment
Solomon Asset Mgt.	450	90–95	Permitted Investment	Permitted Investment
Swiss Re Holdings	130	N/A	Permitted Investment	Permitted Investment
Trust Company of the West	1,500+	100	Permitted Investment	Permitted Investment
Total	$4,080	80–90%		

a. Including comparable investments such as debt with warrants.

bonds. All noted, however, that debt-with-warrants packages are normally associated with smaller, riskier companies that issue warrants primarily to "sweeten" a straight debt offering rather than to create a convertible bond substitute. As a result, the terms of the debt-with-warrants packages that are trading in the marketplace differ from the customary terms of convertible debt issues in the manner Jones and Mason describe.[23]

Debt with warrants, then, may as yet suffer from an image problem. Prospective investors, and perhaps prospective issuers also, may view warrants accompanying a debt package as a sign of financial weakness. Another potential obstacle to more widespread use of debt with warrants may be the reluctance of issuers to deviate from the more typical convertible bond structure, even if there are advantages to doing so.

Neither of these objections, however, seems insurmountable. In either case, surely the resistance could be overcome by designing a debt-with-warrants

23. Jones and Mason, p. 50.

package that serves as a synthetic convertible bond and then educating investors and prospective convertible bond issuers as to the basic equivalence of the two (except, of course, for the tax advantages provided by debt with warrants). This process of education will involve costs, but it seems unlikely that such costs would be so great as to outweigh the collective value of the tax advantages that issuers could realize by switching from convertible bonds to synthetic convertible bonds.

Conclusion

A convertible bond can be viewed as a package consisting of a straight bond and nondetachable warrants. A company can create an equivalent synthetic convertible bond by combining debt and warrants with principal features that mirror those of the convertible bond (except that the debt and warrants can be traded separately, which could be valuable to corporate treasurers in the process of capital structure planning). Issuing the synthetic convertible bond would be more valuable to a taxable corporate issuer than issuing an otherwise identical convertible bond, at least when the synthetic convertible is purchased by tax-exempt investors (who presently make up roughly 80–90% of the convertible bond market). This tax advantage results from the issuer's ability to amortize the original issue discount on the debenture (which equals the warrant proceeds when the unit price equals the principal amount of the debenture) over the life of the issue.

At the beginning of the article, I posed the following question: Given the apparent tax advantage of debt with warrants over convertible bonds, why do corporate issuers collectively continue to prefer convertible bonds? Based on the results of a survey of several of the largest institutional investors in convertible bonds, it appears that these investors would be receptive to synthetic convertible bonds once they were satisfied that the synthetic convertible bond was fully equivalent to a conventional convertible. This would require, among other things, that the maturity of the debt and the expiration of the warrants be extended to 20 to 25 years, which is customary for a convertible bond but longer than the maturities of debt-with-warrants packages sold to date.[24] Once the marketability of the synthetic convertible bond has been established, its tax advantage to taxable corporations should lead to widespread adoption.

---

24. The list of other complications includes a sinking fund, which convertible debt issues normally contain. The synthetic convertible bond in that case should include a series of warrants the same proportion of which expire on each sinking fund date as the respective sinking fund amounts bear to the aggregate principal amount of the debt issue.

22

Equity-Linked Debt*

E. Philip Jones & Scott P. Mason

Today corporations routinely consider issuing securities far more complex than the classic alternatives of straight debt or equity. One generic form of complex security that has been of continuing interest to issuers is equity-linked debt – that is, corporate debt involving some form of equity participation. The most established market for equity-linked debt is the convertible debt market, where $7.5 billion was raised between January 1983 and April 1984; the largest single issue was Texaco's $1 billion offering in the Euromarket.[1] (Table 22.1 presents a representative list of recent U.S. and Euromarket issues of convertible debt.) Recently, however, corporations have been making greater use of more esoteric forms of equity-linked debt, such as units of debt with warrants, exchangeable debt, and exchangeable units of debt with warrants. Questions naturally arise as to the design and pricing of these alternative forms of equity-linked debt, as well as to their advantages to issuing companies.

Units of debt with warrants are similar to convertible debt except that the debt and warrant portions of the unit are separable into distinct securities. Over $4.5 billion of units of debt with warrants have been issued in the U.S. market, the most notable being MCI Telecommunications Corporation's

*A version of this article was presented at the Harvard Business School's 75th Anniversary Colloquium on New Perspectives on Corporate Financial Decisions.

1. Reported volume figures for all markets pertain to the 15-month period January 1, 1983, to April 1, 1984.

$1 billion offering in July 1983. (See Table 22.2 for a representative list of recent issues of units of debt with warrants.) Exchangeable debt is a form of convertible debt that can be exercised into the common stock of a company other than the issuer's. Over $500 million of exchangeable debt has been recently issued in the U.S. market, the largest issue being InterNorth's $240 million offering in May of 1983 (exchangeable for the common stock of Mobil Corporation). (See Table 22.3 for a list of recent issues of exchangeable debt.) Exchangeable units of debt with warrants are similar to exchangeable debt; the warrant is exchangeable for the common stock of a company other than the issuer's, but the debt and warrant portions of the unit are separable into distinct securities. Two issues, totaling $235 million, of exchangeable units of debt with warrants have been done in the Euromarket: Prudential's $150 million units offering (exchangeable for the common stock of A.T.&T.) and Dart & Kraft's $85 million offering (exchangeable for the common stock of Minnesota Mining and Manufacturing). (Table 22.4 gives the terms of these two issues.) The interrelation among the four types of equity-linked debt is summarized by Figure 22.1.

While complex securities can often be justified by tax considerations or excess investor demand, the corporation is left with the problem of designing and pricing these issues. With convertible debt this problem is lessened by the existence of a well established secondary market, which allows pricing by analogy. Other forms of equity-liked debt, however, can seldom rely upon pricing by analogy because the depth and breadth of their secondary markets are often questionable. It is nonetheless possible to gain valuable insight into the design and pricing of these alternative forms of equity-linked debt by understanding how these securities should be priced relative to convertible debt.

The paper divides into two sections, corresponding to our two basic goals. The first is to offer some practical guidance in the design and pricing of (1) units of debt with warrants, (2) exchangeable debt, and (3) exchangeable units of debt with warrants by clarifying the precise relationship between convertible debt and these forms of equity-linked debt. Our second aim is to make explicit the effect of corporate taxes on the design and pricing of these securities. The second section accordingly reviews the corporate taxation of the various forms of equity-linked debt and comments on the possible role of favorable tax treatment in the market's relative pricing of these issues.

Convertible Debt and Units of Debt with Warrants

It is often stated that units of debt with warrants are equivalent to convertible debt. But the precise nature of the analogy is seldom made clear. Given that

TABLE 22.1 *Convertible Debt*

	Issue Size ($MM)	Date of Issue	Rating Moody's/S&P	Issue Price	Coupon
Texaco Capital N.V.	1000	03/23/84	A1/AA−	100	11.875
Eaton Corporation	75	12/14/83	A3/BBB+	100	8.50
Avnet, Inc.	100	10/04/83	−/A+	100	8.00
COMSAT International N.V.	110	09/28/83	−/−	100	7.75
Burlington Industries	75	09/21/83	Baa2/BBB+	100	8.75
Cessna Aircraft Co.	100	06/23/83	Ba2/BBB	100	8.00
Wang Laboratories Inc.	150	06/08/83	A3/BBB	100	7.75
Olin Corporation	100	05/26/83	Baa1/BBB+	100	8.75
Joseph E. Seagram & Sons	125	05/26/83	A3/A	100	8.25
Singer Company	100	05/18/83	B1/B	100	9.00
Comdisco, Inc.	250	04/27/83	Ba2/BB+	100	8.00
J.P. Stevens	75	04/20/83	Ba2/BB−	100	9.00
Nat'l Medical Enterprises	200	04/06/83	Ba1/BBB	100	8.00
Deere & Co.	200	03/18/83	A3/A	100	9.00
MCI Communications Corp.	400	03/11/83	Baa3/BB+	100	7.75
Hospital Corp. of America	200	03/03/83	Baa1/A−	100	8.50
Northwest Airlines, Inc.	100	02/10/83	−/−	100	7.50
Pan American World Airways, Inc.	150	02/10/83	B3/B	100	15.00

a. Percentage of equity represented by issue if converted.

the market for convertible debt is well established, it would be helpful to understand this analogy as a guide to designing and pricing different units of debt with warrants. Thus, we begin by describing the specific unit of debt with warrants that is precisely equivalent (corporate taxes aside for the moment) to convertible debt. Having identified similarities and differences between the two securities, we then discuss the extent to which the convertible debt market can be used as a benchmark for pricing some of the different units of debt with warrants seen recently in the marketplace.

The pricing of convertible debt is determined by issuer characteristics, interest rates, and the terms of the issue. The primary characteristics of an issuer that affect the pricing of convertible debt are business risk, financial risk, and dividend policy. Some of these factors have a mixed effect on the value of convertible debt. For example, the higher the business and financial risk of an issuer and the higher the level of interest rates, the less valuable is the debt aspect of a convertible bond, and the more valuable is its warrant or equity part. Other factors have an unambiguous effect on pricing. For

Maturity	Optional Redemp- tion	Common Price	Divi- dend per Share ($)	Divi- dend Yield (%)	Con- version Price	Con- version Premium	Shares Per Bond	Dilu- tion[a] Factor (%)
05/01/94	1983	38.875	3.00	7.72	50.00	28.62	20.00	7.9
12/15/08	1986	52.50	0.80	1.52	63.25	20.48	15.81	3.6
10/01/13	1983	42.50	0.50	1.18	52.00	22.35	19.23	5.2
10/15/98	–	42.50	1.15	2.70	48.875	15.00	13.04	7.4
09/15/08	1986	40.625	1.52	3.74	48.50	19.38	20.62	5.1
07/01/08	1985	28.25	0.40	1.42	32.50	15.04	30.77	13.5
06/01/08	1983	40.125	0.10	0.25	52.1625	30.00	19.17	2.0
06/01/08	1983	31.625	1.20	3.79	36.50	15.42	27.40	10.3
06/01/08	1983	32.00	0.68	2.13	37.75	17.97	26.49	3.5
05/15/08	1983	29.75	0.10	0.34	36.00	21.01	13.51	7.4
05/01/03	1983	30.25	0.16	0.53	36.50	20.66	27.40	19.1
05/15/08	1983	25.25	1.20	4.75	30.25	19.80	33.06	12.0
05/15/08	1983	34.00	0.40	1.18	42.25	24.26	23.67	6.5
03/15/08	1983	32.00	–	–	40.00	25.00	25.00	6.8
03/15/03	1983	43.375	–	–	52.125	20.17	19.18	3.1
03/01/08	1983	41.50	0.40	0.96	51.875	25.00	19.28	4.3
02/15/07	1985	42.875	0.80	1.87	50.75	18.37	19.70	8.3
03/01/98	1983	4.75	–	–	5.50	15.79	181.82	20.8

example, the higher the dividend, the less valuable is the convertible debt viewed either as risky debt or warrant.

In addition to these issuer characteristics, it is mainly the terms of a convertible bond that determine its price. Most important among these are (1) issue size or potential dilution,[2] (2) maturity, (3) redemption provisions, (4) coupon rate, and (5) conversion premium.[3] In practice, the issuer typically first decides upon the issue size, maturity, and redemption provisions. Then it identifies a coupon rate and conversion premium that will allow the convertible to be priced at par value. Since there will be more than one possible

---

2. Dilution is used here in the strict sense, that is, the number of shares represented by the cut, n, versus the number of outstanding shares, m, leads to the implicit warrant, W, in the cut being $W = n/n + m \times (C(S + mW/m, E, T))$ where $C(...)$ is the Black-Scholes value of a call, as discussed in Black-Scholes (1973).

3. Only optional redemption provisions are considered here, while mandatory redemption provisions, that is, sinking funds, are ignored.

TABLE 22.2 *Units of Debt with Warrants*

	MCI Communications Corporation	Western Air Lines, Inc.	Pan American World Airways, Inc.	MGM/UA	General Tire & Rubber Company
Issue Size ($mm)	1000	90	100	400	60
Date of Issue	07/25/83	06/16/83	05/05/83	03/14/83	03/22/83
Rating, Moody's/S&P	Baa3/BB+	B3/B−	B3/B−	−/B+	Ba2/−
Issue Price	100	79.30	100	87.85	100
Debt					
Coupon	9.5	10.75	13.50	10.00	11.875
Maturity	07/01/93	06/15/98	05/01/03	03/15/93	09/15/93
Optional Redemption	1983	1983	1983	1983	1983
Warrant					
Common Price	42.00	5.75	5.625	12.875	31.25
Dividend Per Share ($)	0	0	0	0	1.50
Dividend Yield (%)					4.90
Conversion Price	55.00	9.50	8.00	20.00	40.00
Conversion Premium	30.95	65.21	42.22	55.33	28.00
Shares Per Unit	18	100	100	14	12
Maturity	07/01/88	06/15/83	05/01/93	03/14/88	03/15/88
Optional Redemption	1986	1986	1986	1986	1983
Acceptable Scrip	Debt/Cash	Debt/Cash	Debt/Cash	Debt/Cash	Cash
Dilution Factor (%)[a]	7.1	27.2	8.8	15.9	3.0

a. Percentage of equity represented by issue if converted.

TABLE 22.3 *Exchangeable Debt*

	General Cinema Corp.	Signal Companies, Inc.	Fair Lanes, Inc.	Inter-North, Inc.	General Cinema
Issue Size ($mm)	78.2	103.4	24.6	240	100
Date of Issue	01/12/84	01/12/84	05/26/83	05/26/83	03/29/83
Rating, Moody's/S&P	Baa2/BBB	A2/A	–/B	A3/BBB+	–/BBB
Issue Price	100	100	100	100	100
Coupon	10.00	8.00	8.50	10.50	10.00
Maturity	01/15/09	01/15/09	06/01/98	06/01/98	03/15/08
Optional Redemption	1984	1987	–	1983	1986
Underlying Stock	RJR	UTR	BC	MOB	RJR
Common Price	62.50	35.625	36.00	30.00	52.25
Dividend Per Share	3.20	0.20	1.00	2.00	3.00
(Dividend Yield)	(5.12)	(0.56)	(2.78)	(6.67)	(5.74)
Conversion Price	75.00	40.00	41.40	40.00	62.75
Conversion Premium	20.00	12.28	15.00	33.33	20.10
Shares Per Bond	13.33	25.00	24.15	25.00	15.94

TABLE 22.4 *Exchangeable Units of Debt with Warrants*

	Prudential	Dart & Kraft
Issue Size ($mm)	150.0	85.0
Date of Issue	11/25/83	11/07/83
Issue Price	100	100
Debt		
Coupon	10.125	7.75
Maturity	12/15/83	11/30/98
Optional Redemption	1989–91	No
Warrant		
Underlying Stock	AT&T	MMM
Common Price	65.25	83.875
Dividend Per Share	5.46	3.40
(Dividend Yield)	(8.37)	(4.05)
Conversion Price	75.25	99.45
Conversion Premium	15.32	18.56
Shares Per Unit	10	10
Maturity	12/15/88	11/30/98
Optional Redemption	No	No
Acceptable Scrip	Cash	Debt/Cash

FIGURE 22.1 *Equity-Linked Debt*

	Equity Participation	
	Issuer's	Other's
Nonseparable	Convertible Debt	Exchangeable Debt
Separable	Units of Debt with Warrants	Exchangeable Units of Debt with Warrants

combination of coupon rate and conversion premium, the final choice is typically governed by the issuer's or investors' preferences.

The pricing of a unit of debt with warrants depends also on issuer characteristics and interest rates as well as the specification of (1) issue size or potential dilution, (2) the debt's maturity, (3) the debt's redemption provision, (4) the debt's coupon rate, (5) the warrant's maturity, (6) the warrant's redemption provision, (7) the warrant's conversion premium, and (8) acceptable warrant scrip. What we want to determine is which set of terms will result in the unit's being precisely equivalent to convertible debt.

Clearly the maturities of both the debt and the warrant should be the same as the maturity of the convertible debt. Similarly, the coupon rate on the debt, the conversion premium on the warrant, and the issue size should match the coupon rate, the conversion premium, and the issue size of the convertible debt. The specification of acceptable warrant scrip refers to whether the warrants can be exercised by tendering cash, the associated debt, or some combination of the two. If the unit is to be precisely equivalent to convertible debt, then it must be required that the warrants be exercised using *only* the associated debt.

This leaves only the specification of the redemption provisions for the debt and the warrant. Strictly speaking, the precise specification would be to make the debt redeemable under the identical provision as the convertible debt and to make the warrant nonredeemable. This ensures that if the debt is called, the warrant will exercise if profitable to do so, because the only source of acceptable scrip to exercise the warrant is being extinguished through the redemption of the debt.[4]

---

4. There remains the difficult question of how the debt and warrant, when trading separately, would share the profit of exercise.

Also, there are two other possible specifications that deserve mention. The first alternative would be to make the debt nonredeemable and the warrant redeemable for some trivial amount

TABLE 22.5 *Convertible Debt and Analogous Unit of Debt with Warrants*

Convertible Debt		Unit of Debt with Warrants	
Issue Price	$1,000	Issue Price	$1,000
		Debt	
Maturity	20 years	Maturity	20 years
Coupon	10%	Coupon	10%
Mandatory Redemption	None	Mandatory Redemption	None
Optional Redemption	At par	Optional Redemption	At par
Principal Amount	$1,000	Principal Amount	$1,000
		Warrants	
Number of Shares Convertible into	15.38	Number of Warrants	15.38
		Exercise per Warrant	$65
		Payment Upon Exercise	$65 Principal of Debt
		Maturity	20 years
		Optional Redemption	None

To illustrate how we would construct an issue of units of debt with warrants that is completely equivalent to a comparable convertible debt issue, let's use a simple example. Assume that an issue of convertible debt has a maturity of 20 years and can be redeemed at par at any time. Further assume that a coupon rate of 10% and a conversion premium of 30% results in par pricing. Finally, let the underlying stock be selling for $50 per share; therefore, each bond is convertible into 15.38 ($1000/1.3 \times 50$) shares. The correct specification of the analogous unit of debt with warrants is presented in Table 22.5. For this *specific* unit of debt with warrants, the convertible debt market could be used as a benchmark for setting the coupon rate on the debt

once the stock price rises to the conversion price. (This is strictly correct if the analogous convertible debt is redeemable at par. If the convertible debt is call protected and/or has a sliding scale of call prices then the warrant's redemption provision will be different.) But this specification is incorrect since it is possible that interest rates may fall, and the stock price stay sufficiently low such that it makes sense to redeem the debt on interest rate considerations alone. To the extent that redemption for interest rate considerations alone is viewed as an improbable event, then this alternative specification would suffice. The second possible alternative is to make the bond and warrant separately redeemable (i.e., the warrant is redeemable for some trivial amount once the stock price equals the conversion price and the debt is redeemable under the identical provision as the convertible debt). This specification is redundant, since the issuer can accomplish either possible goal, that is, redemption to force conversion or to take advantage of lower interest rates, by making just the debt redeemable.

and the conversion premium on the warrant (again, ignoring taxes for the moment).

The difficulty with pricing by analogy, however, is that those units of debt with warrants that are now trading in the marketplace (see Table 22.2) are not structured along the lines suggested by our example. And, to the extent that the actual units deviate from the terms of the truly analogous unit, its pricing—that is, its coupon rate and conversion premium—should differ systematically from the pricing of convertible debt issues.

As revealed in Table 22.2, actual units of debt with warrants seen in the market fail to be perfect analogues to convertible debt in the following ways:

1. Actual units often contain fewer warrants (i.e., more bonds are issued, via the unit, than are necessary to exercise all of the warrants).

2. The warrant's maturity is significantly shorter than the maturity of the debt.

3. The warrant and the debt are separately redeemable.

4. The maturity of the debt is shorter than the average maturity of convertible debt.

5. Either cash or the associated debt can be used to exercise the warrants.

The first three observations, taken in turn and holding all else constant, would suggest that units of debt with warrants are worth less to the investor than the analogous convertible debt with the same coupon and conversion premium. The last two observations work in the opposite direction; they tend to make units of debt with warrants more valuable. Therefore, with regard to the design of units of debt with warrants, the debt part represents a larger proportion of the unit's value than is true of a comparable convertible bond. This conclusion is supported by the additional observation that, holding issuer quality and issue date reasonably constant, both the coupon rate and the conversion premia tend to be higher for units of debt with warrants than with convertible debt.

Exchangeable Debt and Exchangeable Units of Debt with Warrants

Exchangeable debt and exchangeable units of debt with warrants are securities exercisable into the common stock of a company other than the issuer's. As with convertibles and debt with warrants, it is often stated that exchangeable units of debt with warrants are equivalent to exchangeable debt. But once again, this analogy although useful is imprecise—and for the same reasons. In order for the exchangeable unit to be exactly equivalent to exchangeable debt, there must not only be a match of maturities, coupon, and conversion premia but also, as before, the same specific redemption and scrip provisions.

Unfortunately, the secondary markets for exchangeable issues are not well developed, and thus the equivalence between exchangeable debt and exchangeable units of debt with warrants offers little help with pricing problems. Therefore, the question remains whether any market can offer practical guidance in designing and pricing exchangeable debt or exchangeable units of debt with warrants. The answer would appear to lie in the relation between exchangeable issues and convertible debt. If exchangeable debt and exchangeable debt with warrants can be thought of as forms of convertible debt, then the substantial secondary market for convertible debt can give valuable guidance in the design and pricing of exchangeable issues.

While this approach has merit, there is an important distinction between exchangeable issues and convertible debt that must be taken into account. As has been established, convertible debt can be thought of as a specific combination of debt and *warrants*. By contrast, exchangeable debt and exchangeable units of debt with warrants are actually combinations of debt and *call options*.

A call option is a contract that gives its owner the right to purchase a specified stock on or before a specified date at a specified price. Similar securities are traded on the listed options exchanges — for example, the CBOE — and are not obligations of the companies whose stock is specified in the call option contracts. The shares of stock specified in a call option contract are already outstanding shares of the associated company and the existence of the call options has no effect on the value of these shares.

A warrant also gives its owner the right to purchase a specified stock on or before a specified date at a specified price. Warrants, however, are obligations of the company whose stock is specified in the warrant contract. Furthermore, the actual shares that would be delivered if the warrants were exercised would be new shares in addition to those already outstanding. Since warrants have a potentially dilutive effect on the underlying stock, their existence affects the value of the company's equity.[5] Because of this potential dilution, warrants are worth less than call options. If the dilution potential is small, then the value differential between the warrant and call option will be small. This distinction between warrants and call options leads to the conclusion that exchangeable issues are more valuable, *ceteris paribus,* than convertible bonds and units of debt with warrants.

---

5. Again, we are using dilution here simply to represent the fact that, for example, a one-year call option written on a $50 stock with an exercise price of $50 is worth strictly more than a one-year warrant written on the same stock with the same terms; that is, $C(S, T, E)$ is greater than $W(S, T, E)$.

It is difficult to generalize about the distinctions between actual exchangeable debt and exchangeable units of debt with warrants based on only two examples of exchangeable units. The Prudential deal appears analogous to the regular unit deals, except that the warrants are not redeemable and cash is the only form of acceptable scrip. The first fact would make the Prudential deal more valuable to investors and the second fact would make it less valuable vis-a-vis a regular unit. Given the distinction between warrants and call options, and the fact that the Prudential conversion premium is slightly low, it would appear that this issue is priced favorably to the investor. The Dart & Kraft (D&K) issue is quite distinct from regular units in that neither the debt nor the warrant is redeemable, the warrant's maturity is the same as the debt's maturity, and the exercise price of the warrant is equal to the issue size.[6] The first two facts coupled with the warrant/call option distinction make the D&K unit more valuable than a regular unit. This unit design, plus the low coupon, suggests that in contrast to the Prudential unit and most regular units, a larger portion of the D&K unit value is due to the warrant component. Again this issue appears favorably priced to the investor.

Corporate Taxes and
Equity-Linked Debt

Up to now we have ignored tax considerations in the design and pricing of equity-linked debt. However, it appears that there are significant tax considerations that make (1) a mix of straight debt and equity preferable to units of debt with warrants, (2) units of debt with warrants preferable to convertible debt, and (3) exchangeable debt or exchangeable units of debt with warrants preferable to convertible debt or units of debt with warrants. These considerations have to do with *corporate* taxes. It is assumed that there are no significant considerations related to investor taxes. Given that equity-linked debt is typically issued in the Eurobond market and that domestically held debt is typically owned by nontaxed institutions, this is a reasonable assumption.[7]

In the next two sections we review the corporate tax treatment of the four kinds of equity-linked debt, and then weigh the relative tax advantages of each of the four instruments.

---

6. There are exactly enough bonds to exercise the warrant.

7. Thus the analysis in the spirit of Modigliani and Miller rather than Miller's more recent "Debt and Taxes" model. It is not clear how Miller's model applies with equity-linked debt, given the tax treatment of different types of this debt.

Corporate Tax Treatment of
Equity-Linked Debt

The corporate tax treatment of convertible debt is extremely simple. There is no corporate tax at issue or at conversion. If the debt is issued at par, there is no original issue discount. Coupons are tax deductible.

The tax code treats an issue of units of debt with warrants as two separate transactions: an issue of debt and an issue of warrants. The issuer must allocate the purchase price of the entire issue between a value for the debt and a value for the warrants. The tax treatment of the two parts is then the same as if they were two separate transactions.

Debt with warrants deals are typically designed to sell for par value; the presence of warrants allows the corporation to reduce the coupon rate below that for straight par debt. Hence the allocation of part of the purchase price of the entire deal to the warrants results in an original issue discount (OID) for the debt part. In keeping with the taxation of straight original issue discount bonds, the corporation must amortize the OID according to the effective yield method over the maturity of the debt; this amortization is treated as interest expense.

The warrant part of the deal, as mentioned, is treated as a separate warrant issue. Warrant issues have a corporate tax *disadvantage* because they are not treated as an issue of securities, such as equity or debt. Instead they are treated as a transaction with the investor that is held open until the warrants are either exercised, allowed to expire, or repurchased. If the warrants are exercised, then the original price of the warrants is treated as part of the purchase price of the stock (along with the exercise price); as with direct equity issues, there is no tax.

The tax treatment of warrants that expire unexercised is disputed under current law. The IRS maintains that the original price of the warrants should be treated as ordinary income upon expiration of the warrants. Taxpayers maintain that the original price should be treated as a capital gain upon expiration of the warrants. Under proposed tax law, the basis of the assets that were purchased with the proceeds of the warrant issue must be reduced by the original price of the warrants upon their expiration. Under this proposal, corporations would lose the present value of depreciation tax shields associated with the reduction in basis upon expiration of the warrants. This loss is somewhat less than under the current IRS treatment of the original price as ordinary income. The difference is due to the time value of money applied to foregone future depreciation tax shields under the proposed law as opposed to the immediate ordinary income tax under current IRS treatment.

If the warrants are repurchased before expiration for a price in excess of the original purchase price, then the difference is treated as an ordinary income loss and thus reduces taxes. (If they are repurchased for a price below the original purchase price, then the difference is treated as ordinary income — clearly not a sensible transaction from a tax standpoint.) For example, suppose that a corporation sells warrants where the warrant price is $10 and the exercise price of the warrants is $50. Suppose further that the warrants are not exercised prematurely. If the stock price just before the maturity of the warrants is $80, then the warrants might trade for $30 at that time.

But the warrants are worth more to the corporation itself because a repurchase reduces its taxes. In this example, the corporation could afford to pay $50 for the warrants. This would generate a $40 ordinary income loss (the $50 repurchase cost less the $10 original price), which would save $20 in taxes. The net cost would then be $30, which is what the warrants are worth to outsiders. If the corporation could repurchase the warrants for, say, only $40, this would save $15 in taxes, so that its net cost would be $25. Compared to selling $80 stock at a $50 exercise price, this represents a $5 gain. In this way, the ability of the corporation to repurchase its warrants and generate tax losses tends to offset the aforementioned tax disadvantage of warrants.

The corporate tax treatment of an exchangeable units-of-debt-with-warrants issue is similar to the case of debt with warrants. The proceeds of the issue must be allocated between a value for the bond and a value for the warrant. As before, this allocation leads to an original issue discount for the bond. Also as before, the tax treatment of the warrants is held open until they either expire, are exercised, or are repurchased. If they expire, the tax treatment is disputed, just as it is with its own warrants. If they are exercised, the allocated warrant premium is treated (along with the exercise price) as part of the price paid by investors to the corporation for the third party stock.

For example, suppose the allocated warrant premium is $10 and the exercise price per warrant is $50. Also suppose the warrants are exercised at maturity into a third party stock with a current market price of $70. If the corporation that issued the exchangeable warrants purchases the third party stock, which it has to deliver at that point, then it recognizes a $10 [$70 − ($10 + $50)] capital *loss*. (If the issuing corporation had purchased the third party stock previously at a lower price, then the capital loss just described would be offset to some degree by a holding period capital *gain*. However, this can be considered as a separate transaction.)

Of course, if the warrants are exercised for third party stock that trades at $55, the issuing company will recognize a $5 [($10 + $50) − $55] capital gain. However, given that the warrants are in fact exercised, it is more likely that they will generate a tax loss for the issuing corporation (ignoring any holding period gains if the issuing company buys the third party stock before the warrants are exercised.)

In summary, exchangeable units of debt with warrants have a tax disadvantage associated with the fact that the warrant premium is treated as ordinary income if the warrants expire unexercised, whereas any loss due to exercise is treated as a capital loss.

The corporate tax treatment of exchangeable debt is the same as the treatment of straight nonconvertible debt, with the exception of the treatment of an exchange. If bondholders elect to exchange their debt for third party stock, then the difference between the market value of the third party stock and the exchange price constitutes an *ordinary* income loss for the issuing corporation. For example, suppose that Corporation X issues debt that can be exchanged for stock of Corporation Y at a price of $50 (calculated against the par value of the bonds). If the market value of Corporation Y stock at exchange is $75 then Corporation X recognizes a $25 ordinary income loss.

Corporate Tax Considerations in Choosing Among Types of Equity-Linked Debt

The corporate tax treatment of equity-linked debt can be significant in choosing whether to issue equity-linked debt and which type to issue. One set of tax considerations has to do with the differences in corporate tax treatment as detailed in the previous section. Another set of tax considerations has to do with the corporate tax treatment of dividends; this is especially important in the case of units of debt with warrants and exchangeable debt. The first set of issues is highlighted by considering the choice among convertible debt, units of debt with warrants, and straight debt. Later, the set of issues related to dividends is addressed and the analysis is broadened to include exchangeable securities.

Warrants versus Straight Equity

First consider the choice between issuing convertible debt, units of debt with warrants, or a mix of equity and straight debt over time. Choosing between the last two options—namely, a debt-with-warrants issue versus a strategy of issuing a mix of equity and straight debt over time—boils down to whether a corporation should prefer to issue warrants or to issue equity directly. If the possibility of repurchasing warrants is ignored, then corporations should prefer to finance themselves with equity issues through time rather than with warrants. The reasoning is as follows: Warrants result in potential positive cash flows to the corporation at two points in time. At issuance, the corporation receives the initial warrant price. If the warrants are subsequently exercised, the corporation receives the exercise price. Warrants result in negative cash flows due to taxes if they expire unexercised. A strategy of issuing equity could easily be devised that would result in the same positive cash flows without any negative tax consequences.

The Case of Undervalued Stock

Some corporations prefer to issue warrants (or convertible debt) rather than equity if they think their stock price is undervalued. This makes sense only if it is impractical to issue straight debt. The reason is as follows: If the equity is undervalued, then the warrants will also be undervalued. In fact, since warrants are like a levered security, they will be undervalued by a greater percentage than the equity itself. So, in raising the same sum of money, a warrants issue gives up more value than an equity issue. (Similarly, the "warrants part" of a convertible deal gives up more value than an equity issue. The general principle in such a case is, when your stock is undervalued, issue straight debt if possible; all equity-linked securities will be undervalued.)

Another reason some corporations prefer to issue warrants (and convertible debt) rather than equity is to avoid dilution of earnings per share. However, although current primary earnings per share are not affected by a warrants issue, fully diluted earnings per share are actually lower as a result of a warrants issue. This is because warrants are worth less than shares, so it takes more warrants than shares to raise the same proceeds. Again, corporations concerned about earnings per share should issue straight debt. Warrants or conversion privileges should be introduced only if it is impractical to do a straight debt deal.

In general, then, corporations should prefer to finance by issuing equity rather than by issuing warrants. That is, tax considerations alone suggest that companies should do a traditional mix of equity and straight debt issues rather than combine the two in a units deal of debt plus warrants.

The Tax Advantage of Debt with Warrants over Convertibles

Now consider the comparison between a units-of-debt-with-warrants package and convertible debt. In the absence of corporate taxes, firms might be indifferent between issuing a unit-of-debt-with-warrants package and convertible debt with equivalent terms. However, corporate tax considerations make the units-of-debt-with-warrants package strictly preferable.

To see why, consider the original issue discount in the units-of-debt-plus-warrants package. As was noted, this discount is equal to the imputed value of the warrants part of the package if the debt is issued at par value. The firm is allowed to amortize the original issue discount over time, thus reducing taxes. Now suppose that the warrants remain unexercised at maturity. Even under the most adverse tax ruling, the firm has ordinary income equal to the initial imputed warrant premium, which in turn equals the original issue discount. Even in this case, the corporation comes out ahead because the OID is expensed through time, whereas the warrant premium is recognized as income only at maturity. Furthermore, if the warrants are instead exercised at maturity, the firm gets to amortize the OID without incurring *any* offsetting ordinary income at maturity. Finally, there is the possibility of generating additional tax losses by repurchasing the warrants. In summary, the debt-plus-warrants package is significantly more attractive than the convertible debt alternatives from a corporate tax standpoint.

To recapitulate the conclusions thus far, tax considerations favor straight debt and equity over units of debt with warrants, and favor units of debt with warrants over convertible debt. Thus, of the three strategies, issuing a mix of straight debt and equity is the most attractive from a tax standpoint, and issuing convertible debt is the least attractive.

The Tax Advantages of Exchangeable Debt

By analogy to the tax advantage of debt with warrants relative to convertibles, one might expect that exchangeable units of debt with warrants would dominate an exchangeable debt issue from a corporate tax standpoint. Before addressing this question, however, it is useful to compare (1) convertible debt to exchangeable debt and (2) units of debt with warrants to exchangeable units of debt with warrants. First consider the comparison between convertible debt and exchangeable debt. Recall that there is a difference between the corporate tax treatment of exchangeable debt and convertible debt — namely that the difference between the market value of the third party stock and the exchange price constitutes an ordinary income loss for the issuing corporation in the exchangeable debt case. In contrast, the firm cannot recognize a loss when its own stock is involved, as in the convertible debt case. This feature of the corporate tax treatment of exchangeable debt makes exchangeable debt very attractive. In effect, the government picks up half of any loss due to exchange of exchangeable bonds. Hence exchangeable debt has a considerable tax advantage over convertible debt.

The comparison between units of debt with warrants and exchangeable units of debt with warrants centers on the difference in treatment if the warrants are exercised. The corporate tax treatment is the same in every other respect; most important, the treatment of the OID and of the allocated warrant premium if the warrants expire unexercised is the same in both cases. However, the difference in treatment if the warrants are exercised favors exchangeable units of debt with warrants somewhat over units of debt with warrants.

Remember that if the warrants are exercised, the warrant transaction typically represents a gain for investors and a loss for the issuing corporation. That is, the market value of the stock surrendered typically exceeds the exercise price plus the warrant premium. (Note that any holding period gain on third party stock is being considered as a separate transaction, as before.) If the issue is exchangeable units of debt with warrants, then the issuing corporation gets to recognize a (capital) loss. However, if the issue is units of debt with warrants, then the issuing corporation can only recognize a loss if it repurchases the warrants. In this case, since there is a joint profit to be shared by the issuing corporation and investors, it is not clear that the issuing corporation will be able to repurchase the warrants at a price that allows it to reap all of the joint profit. So exchangeable units of debt with warrants enjoy some corporate tax advantage over units of debt with warrants.

Thus, we are left with the following conclusions: (1) Exchangeable debt dominates convertible debt, and (2) exchangeable debt with warrants dominates debt with warrants. Both conclusions follow from the ability of the issuing corporation to recognize a tax loss upon exercise to a third party stock.

It remains to compare exchangeable units of debt with warrants to exchangeable debt. The tax advantage of the exchangeable units package has to do with the OID features. The tax advantage of exchangeable debt has to do with the fact that any exchange generates an *ordinary* loss (whereas the loss recognized in the case of an exchangeable unit of debt with warrants issue is only a *capital* loss). Which one of these advantages is more important depends on the circumstances and terms of a given deal. Hence it cannot be concluded that one unambiguously dominates the other.

Exchangeables and Tax Arbitrage of Corporate Dividends

It is well known that dividends, as compared to coupons, are a tax-inefficient way to transfer cash from corporations to noncorporate investors. The tax treatment of coupons and dividends is identical for the noncorporate investor; both are treated as ordinary income. But the tax treatment of the two is different at the corporate level; coupons are deductible while dividends are not. Hence, from a tax standpoint corporate payments of dividends to noncorporate investors is inefficient. Indeed it is often argued that a company can increase its value by paying out more coupons and less dividends to noncorporate investors—that is, by financing itself with more debt and less equity.

However, this so-called double taxation of dividends is only applicable when the stockholder is a noncorporate entity. Corporate stockholders are entitled to the intercorporate dividend exclusion, which almost eliminates taxation of dividends payed from one corporation to another.[8] This creates an opportunity for corporations to engage in various forms of tax arbitrage related to dividends.

Both corporations that want to issue equity and corporations that want to issue debt have been able to benefit from tax arbitrage associated with the intercorporate dividend exclusion. Corporations that want to issue equity have used adjustable rate preferred notes (ARPNs), which are typically sold to other companies. To the extent that the companies that own ARPNs are financed in turn by debt, the net effect is to eliminate the double taxation due to direct dividend payments from corporations to noncorporate investors. Note that a key feature of the adjustable rate preferred note is that it is designed to eliminate most of the risk of capital loss or gain to the investing corporation.

Exchangeable debt and exchangeable units of debt with warrants are mechanisms for corporations that want to issue debt to benefit from tax arbitrage associated with the intercorporate dividend exclusion. The key feature of the mechanism is that the company that issues the exchangeable security then uses part of the proceeds to buy the stock into which the security is convertible.[9] Hence, it can always deliver the third party stock whenever the exchangeable bondholders or warrant holders choose to exercise their option. In other words, the company that issues the security immediately hedges its position against capital losses and gains. The resulting position is a pure tax arbitrage associated with the dividends that it receives versus the coupons that it pays. The fact that the dividend receipts are not taxed while the coupon payments are deductible typically generates a positive after-tax "carry" for the issue. Hence the exchangeable mechanism (including the purchase of the third party stock) typically generates both a positive initial cash flow (equal to the proceeds minus the stock purchase) plus a positive annual carry (equal to the dividend minus the coupon after tax).[10] If the security holders ever exchange their debt (or warrants), the issuing firm surrenders its third party stock, and the position is closed out.

The only circumstance that presents a danger to this mechanism is if the third party stock declines in value. In this case the exchangeable bondholders (or warrantholders) will not choose to exercise their options, and the issuing firm will be liable for a principal payment that is greater than the value of

---

8. A corporate stockholder can exclude 85% of dividends from taxation. Thus, for a corporate stockholder in the 46% tax bracket, the effective tax rate on dividends is $(46\%) \times (15\%) =$ 6.31%.

9. The new (Fall 1984) tax law specifically disallows the intercorporate dividend exclusion in this case, where debt proceeds are used to buy stock. However, the arbitrage continues to be available to companies that already own the third party stock.

10. For example, see the terms of the Prudential-AT&T deal.

the third party stock. But the issuing firm can protect itself against this risk by following a "portfolio insurance" strategy — that is, by selling off the third party stock as it declines and shifting into bonds (and doing the reverse if the stock goes back up again).

Thus, it appears that both the exchangeable debt and the exchangeable units-of-debt-with-warrants mechanisms, including purchase of the third party stock as a hedge, allow firms that want to issue debt to engage in tax arbitrage related to the tax treatment of dividends and coupons. The pay-off from this strategy comes in the form of substantial initial net proceeds (equal to the proceeds of the bond issue less the purchase cost of the third party stock) and in the form of a positive annual after-tax carry. As a result, exchangeable debt and exchangeable units of debt with warrants appear to be preferable to convertible debt and units of debt with warrants, and to straight debt as well, as mechanisms for raising cash.

In summary, it appears that exchangeable debt and exchangeable units of debt with warrants are significantly more favorable than convertible debt and units of debt with warrants from a corporate tax standpoint. Recall that this is true even in the case of no coupons and dividends. In addition, the tax arbitrage associated with the intercorporate dividend exclusion and the tax deductibility of interest strengthens this conclusion dramatically.

Conclusion

We have examined the design, pricing, and tax implications of the four types of equity-linked debt: convertible debt, debt with warrants, exchangeable debt, and exchangeable debt with warrants. The analysis indicates that actual units-of-debt-with-warrants issues typically have a larger debt component and a smaller equity component than comparable convertible bonds. Interestingly, tax considerations alone would argue for a larger equity component and smaller debt component for debt with warrants issues. The analysis also indicates that exchangeable issues appear to be favorably priced to investors, as compared to convertible debt and debt with warrants. This is consistent with the observation that exchangeable issues provide a mechanism for corporations to engage in tax arbitrage related to the intercorporate dividend exclusion and the deductibility of interest expense. The tax arbitrage benefits might explain why corporations are willing to issue securities that are priced favorably to investors.

23

LYON Taming*

John J. McConnell & Eduardo S. Schwartz

A liquid yield option note (LYON) is a complex security. It is a zero coupon, convertible, callable, redeemable bond. The complexity of this security is further increased because the prices at which the issuer may call the bond and the prices at which the investor may redeem (or put) the bond escalate through time. Additionally, the bond contains call protection for the investor because the bond may not be called for a prespecified period of time after issuance unless the issuer's stock prices rise above a predesignated level.

This fascinating security was created by Merrill Lynch White Weld Capital Markets Groups in 1985. In the spring of 1985 Waste Management, Inc. and Staley Continental, Inc. were the first two issuers of this security, with Merrill Lynch acting as the underwriter.[1] Because of its novelty and complexity, potential issuers find this security difficult to analyze. Two issues are of paramount concern to LYON issuers. First, is the security "correctly" priced at the initial offering? The issuer is concerned that the security not be underpriced at the initial offering, and the underwriter is concerned that the security not be overpriced. Second, the issuer is concerned that the security not be converted "too soon" after issuance. Issuers are concerned that premature

*Thomas Patrick, Lynne Dinzole, Lee Coles, and Robert Moulton-Ely of Merrill Lynch White Weld Capital Markets Group were especially helpful to us in developing the ideas presented in this paper.
1. Subsequently, LYONs were issued by the G. Heileman Brewing Co., Merrill Lynch & Co., and Joseph E. Seagram & Son, Inc. and others.

conversion will dilute the issuer's earning per share and that the valuable tax savings associated with the LYON will be dissipated.

To address these concerns (and others) we were engaged to analyze the Liquid Yield Option Note. To do so, we developed a LYON-pricing model using modern contingent-claims-pricing techniques. In developing the model we were especially concerned that it be commercially usable. Thus, our goal was to develop a model that is both rich enough to capture the salient ingredients of this complex security and simple enough to be implemented with an enhanced personal computer. Because of the complexity of the security, the final pricing equation can be solved only with numerical techniques. Thus, the focus of this paper is on the practical application of contingent-claim-pricing models that can be solved only with numerical techniques. The contribution of this paper is that it reports on an actual case situation in which numerical solution techniques were used to analyze a security-pricing problem.

We first describe in some detail a specific LYON issue. We then present a pricing model that we shall refer to as the commercially usable LYON-pricing model. As will be quite evident, this simplified pricing model takes a number of liberties with the state of the art in contingent-claim-pricing analysis.[2] Following our presentation of the commercially usable LYON-pricing model, we discuss its limitations and simplifications and suggest ways in which the various limiting assumptions could be relaxed so as to yield a theoretically more sophisticated model. The benefit of a more sophisticated model is that it would likely increase the accuracy of the resulting analysis. The cost is that it would increase the difficulty of implementing and using the model. As it turns out, the commercially usable LYON-pricing model, although quite simple in comparison with a theoretically more sophisticated model, appears to work well in practice in that the theoretical LYON prices generated with the simplified model closely tracked the reported market closing prices for both the Waste Management and the Staley Continental LYONs over the first several weeks following their issuance. Whether the accuracy of the simple model is sufficient for all commercial uses depends, of course, on the needs of the user.

Following our presentation of the simplified LYON-pricing model we present our application of the model to the valuation of the Waste Management LYON. We then investigate the sensitivity of theoretical LYON values to changes in the characteristics of the issuer, the economic environment, and the security. Finally, using the same data, we illustrate the way in which the model can be used to calculate the LYON's optimal conversion price. We end the paper with a brief summary and some concluding remarks.

---

2. An excellent survey of recent applications of contingent-claims-pricing analysis in corporate finance is provided by Mason and Merton [6].

I. The LYON

An appreciation of the LYON-pricing model can perhaps best be gained by considering a specific issue. The one that we consider here was issued by Waste Management, Inc. on April 12, 1985.

According to the indenture agreement, each Waste Management LYON has a face value of $1,000 and matures on January 21, 2001. If the security has not been called, converted, or redeemed (i.e., put to the issuer) prior to that date and if the issuer does not default, the investor receives $1,000 per bond. At any time prior to maturity (or on the maturity date), the investor may elect to convert the bond into 4.36 shares of Waste Management common stock. Additionally, however, the investor can elect to put the bond to Waste Management beginning on June 30, 1988, and on each subsequent anniversary date, at fixed exercise prices that escalate through time.[3] The put exercise prices are:

Date	Put Price	Date	Put Price
June 30, 1988	$301.87	June 30, 1995	613.04
June 30, 1989	333.51	June 30, 1996	669.45
June 30, 1990	375.58	June 30, 1997	731.06
June 30, 1991	431.08	June 30, 1998	798.34
June 30, 1992	470.75	June 30, 1999	871.80
June 30, 1993	514.07	June 30, 2000	952.03
June 30, 1994	561.38		

Finally, Waste Management can elect to call the LYON at fixed exercise prices that escalate through time. Although the issuer may call the LYON immediately after issuance, the investor does receive some call protection because Waste Management may not call the bond prior to June 30, 1987, unless the price of the Waste Management common stock rises above $86.01.[4] On the LYON issue date, the Waste Management stock price was $52.125. The LYON call prices are:

Date	Call Price	Date	Call Price
At Issuance	$272.50	June 30, 1994	563.63
June 30, 1986	297.83	June 30, 1995	613.04
June 30, 1987	321.13	June 30, 1996	669.45
June 30, 1988	346.77	June 30, 1997	731.06
June 30, 1989	374.99	June 30, 1998	798.34
June 30, 1990	406.00	June 30, 1999	871.80
June 30, 1991	440.08	June 30, 2000	952.03
June 30, 1992	477.50	At maturity	1,000.00
June 30, 1993	518.57		

---

3. The investor must give Waste Management at least 30 days notice and not more than 90 days notice prior to exercising the put option.

4. Waste Management must give the investor at least 15 days notice prior to exercising the call option.

Additionally, if the LYON is called between the dates shown above, the call price is adjusted to reflect the "interest" accrued since the immediately preceding call date shown in the schedule.[5]

As our brief description indicates, analysis of a LYON is not a simple matter. To value a LYON it is necessary to take into account the unique characteristics of the security, the issuer, and the economic environment in which the security is issued. Furthermore, the security can be valued only if it is possible to identify the conversion and redemption strategies to be followed by investors and the call strategy to be followed by the issuer. In the spirit of Brennan and Schwartz [2, 4] and Ingersoll [5], we assume that the issuer follows a call policy that minimizes the value of the LYON at each point in time and that the investor follows conversion and redemption strategies that maximize the value of the LYON at each point in time. We refer to these as the optimal call, the optimal conversion, and the optimal redemption strategies, respectively. The optimal call, conversion, and redemption strategies depend upon, among other things, the bond's conversion ratio and upon the call and redemption schedules specified in the bond's indenture agreement.

A. Optimal Conversion Strategy

Because the investor seeks to maximize the value of the LYON, the investor will never convert if the market value of the LYON is greater than the value of the stock into which the LYON can be converted. That is, the LYON will never be converted as long as its market value exceeds its conversion value. Contrarily, because the investor would receive an immediate gain from conversion, the investor would always convert if the value of the LYON were less than its conversion value. Thus, investors will optimally convert the LYON when the value of the security just equals its conversion value. As a consequence, the value of an outstanding LYON must be greater than its conversion value.

B. Optimal Redemption Strategy

On each redemption date the investor must choose between holding the LYON and putting it to the issuer for the prespecified redemption value. However, because the investor seeks to maximize the market value of the security, on any anniversary date the investor will not put the LYON to the issuer if the security's value is greater than its redemption price at that time. Contrarily, because the investor would receive an immediate gain from redemption, the

---

5. The imputed interest is computed by increasing the call prices at a rate of 9.0% per year compounded semiannually.

investor would always redeem the LYON if the LYON value were less than its redemption price on any redemption date. Thus, investors optimally will redeem the LYON when the LYON's market value just equals its redemption value. At no time will the value of the LYON be less than its redemption value.

The redemption value, of course, is the exercise price of a put option. The twist here is that, unlike a conventional put option, the exercise price of the put option embedded in a LYON changes through time.

C. Optimal Call Strategy

On the one hand, because the issuer seeks to minimize the value of the LYON, the issuer will never allow the market value of the security to exceed its call price. On the other hand, the issuer will never call the LYON when its value is less than the call price because this would convey an immediate windfall gain to the investor. Thus, the issuer will optimally call the LYON when the LYON's market value just equals its call price. When the issuer calls the LYON, the investor can elect to receive either the cash call price or the conversion value of the security, whichever is greater. As a consequence, at any point in time, the value of a callable LYON will not exceed the greater of its call price or conversion value.

To determine the equilibrium value of the LYON, we assume that investors and issuers follow the optimal conversion, redemption, and call policies and that each party expects the other to follow the optimal strategy. Under the optimal strategies, the value of the LYON is bounded from above by the maximum of its call price and conversion value, and it is bounded from below by the maximum of its redemption price and conversion value.

II. The LYON-Pricing Model

To derive the LYON-pricing model we assume that the value of the LYON depends upon the issuer's stock price (S) and that instantaneous changes in the issuer's stock price follow a diffusion process with constant variance (σ_S). That is,

$$dS = [S\mu - D(S, t)]dt + S\sigma_S dz_S \tag{23.1}$$

where $S(t)$ is the issuer's stock price at time t; μ is the (possibly stochastic) instantaneous total expected return on the issuer's common stock; σ_S is the standard deviation of the rate of return on the issuer's common stock; and $D(S, t)$ is the total rate of dividends paid to stockholders at time t. In applications of the model, we allow dividend payments to take the general form

$$D(S, t) = d_y S + d e^{g(t - t_0)} \tag{23.2}$$

where d_y is the issuer's dividend yield; d is the issuer's dividend rate; g is the constant growth rate of dividends; and t_0 is the issue date of the LYON. This general form for dividend payments permits either a constant dividend yield (when $d = 0$) or a constant dividend growth rate (when $d_y = 0$).

We further assume that capital markets are perfect, that investors and issuers have costless access to all relevant information, and that the term structure of interest rates is flat and known with certainty. Then, given the usual arbitrage arguments, the value of the LYON must satisfy the partial differential equation

$$\tfrac{1}{2}\sigma_S^2 S^2 L_{SS} + [rS - D(S, t)]L_S + L_t - rL = 0 \qquad (23.3)$$

where r is the known, constant interest rate and subscripts represent partial derivatives.

Solution of (23.3) subject to four boundary conditions gives the theoretical value of the LYON. The boundary conditions follow from the optimal conversion, redemption, and call strategies and from the maturity condition specified in the LYON contract.

A. The Maturity Condition

At the maturity date of the contract, the value of the LYON will be the greater of the conversion value or the face value of the contract:

$$L(S, T) = \text{Max}(C_r S, F) \qquad (23.4)$$

where C_r is the number of shares of the issuer's common stock into which the LYON can be converted (i.e., C_r is the conversion ratio and $C_r S$ is the conversion value of the LYON); F is the face value of the LYON at maturity (typically specified to be $1,000); and T is the maturity date of the contract.

B. The Conversion Condition

At any point in time, the value of the LYON must be greater than or equal to its conversion value:

$$L(S, t) \geq C_r S \qquad (23.5)$$

C. The Redemption (or Put) Condition

At any redemption date the value of the LYON must be greater than or equal to the then prevailing redemption price:

$$L(S, t_p) \geq P(t_p) \qquad (23.6)$$

where $P(t_p)$ is the redemption (or put) price at time t_p.

D. The Call Condition

At every point in time, the value of the LYON must be less than or equal to the greater of the call price and the conversion value:

$$L(S, t) \leq \text{Max}\{C(t), C_r S\} \tag{23.7}$$

where $C(t)$ is the call price of the LYON at time t.

Partial Differential Equation 23.3 subject to the boundary conditions (23.4), (23.5), (23.6), and (23.7) gives the value of the LYON under our set of assumptions. Although there is no known closed form solution to this equation, the virtue of this simplified model is that it can be solved easily by means of numerical methods with an enhanced personal computer. In our applications of the model, the method of finite differences was used to solve (23.3) on an IBM personal computer. Solution of a typical problem required less than ten minutes.

III. Discussion of the Simplified LYON-Pricing Model

It is readily apparent that the commercially usable LYON-pricing model embodies a number of simplifying assumptions. These assumptions were dictated largely by the circumstances under which the model was developed. For the most part, however, the assumptions seem justifiable, given the requirements of the model. In this section we discuss some of these assumptions in more detail, suggest ways in which the assumptions can be relaxed, and consider the costs and benefits of relaxing these assumptions.

Perhaps the most egregious assumptions are that the value of the LYON depends upon the value of the issuer's common stock rather than the total market value of the firm and that the term structure of interest rates is flat and known with certainty.

As an alternative to the assumption that the LYON value depends upon the value of the issuer's common stock, which follows a diffusion process with constant variance, a theoretically more palatable assumption is that the total value of the firm follows a diffusion process with constant variance and that the LYON and the issuer's stock are both contingent claims that depend upon the total value of the firm. This assumption is theoretically more desirable because it would more appropriately capture the default risk of the LYON. The assumption that the value of the LYON depends upon the value of the issuer's common stock precludes the possibility of bankruptcy. Under this assumption, at the maturity date, the investor receives either the face value of the LYON or the conversion value, whichever is greater. Under the alternative assumption, the maturity condition would be altered such that the investor would receive either the greater of the conversion value of the security or the lesser of the face value of the bond or the total value of the firm.[6] Our simplifying assumption, by precluding bankruptcy, means that the simplified model overstates the value of the LYON. Quite clearly, the lower the probability of bankruptcy, the smaller the overstatement of value.

In actual applications of the model, we do, however, compensate for this overstatement of value. Rather than using the risk-free rate of interest as the discount rate, we use an intermediate-term interest rate that is grossed up to capture the default risk of the issuer. This higher discount rate tends to reduce the value of the LYON.[7]

The more vexing assumption is that the term structure of interest rates is flat and known with certainty. This assumption is vexing for two opposing reasons. On the one hand, one of the features of the LYON is the ability of the investor to put the LYON to the issuer at prespecified redemption prices. The redemption feature will be especially valuable if interest rates rise dramatically (and unexpectedly) during the life of the LYON. In that case, the investor would elect to cash in the LYON for the redemption price and invest the proceeds elsewhere. The assumption that future interest rates are known with certainty reduces the value of the put option, and consequently tends to understate the value of the LYON.

On the other hand, the call option is especially valuable to the issuer if interest rates fall dramatically (and unexpectedly) in the future. In that case, the issuer would call the LYON and issue an alternative security with a lower "cost." For this reason, ignoring interest rate uncertainty tends to overstate the value of the LYON. Which of the two opposing interest rate effects is of greater importance in pricing the LYON depends, among other things, upon the call and redemption schedules specified in a specific indenture agreement. Of course, there are ways in which the model could be expanded to account for interest rate uncertainty. One possible approach that has been successful in other contexts is the two-factor model of interest rate uncertainty developed by Brennan and Schwartz [3]. We should note that the simplified model does take into account the level of interest rates through the term, r, in Equation 23.3, and changes in r do permit sensitivity analysis with respect to changes in this variable.

---

6. This assumes that the issuer has only two securities outstanding—common stock and the LYON. A model could be developed (as in Brennan and Schwartz [4]) that would allow for multiple senior securities.

7. A second desirable feature of the alternative assumption is that it is more reasonable to assume that the value of the firm follows a process with constant variance than to assume that the value of the stock follows a process with constant variance. This is because the equity of the firm and all of the firm's senior securities can be considered contingent claims on the total value of the firm. If the total return on the firm follows a process with constant variance, the variance of return on equity must be stochastic because the existence of the firms' senior securities (including the LYON) will affect the stochastic process followed by the stock price.

The disadvantage of the simplified LYON-pricing model is that it may contain errors in valuing the LYON and, because of the various opposing effects, the direction of the errors is unknown. The benefit of the simplified model is that it reduces substantially the difficulty of implementing the model. A theoretically more elegant model would encompass three stochastic variables—the value of the issuing firm and the two interest rate factors. Solution of a partial differential equation with three stochastic variables is substantially more difficult than solving a single-variable model. Perhaps more importantly, though, are the reduced estimation demands of the simplified model. Implementation of a theoretically more complete model would require estimation of the total value of the firm and of the volatility of the total value of the firm, and it would require estimation of the market price of interest rate risk and the parameters of the two-factor interest rate process.

The degree to which a theoretically more sophisticated model would enhance the analysis is, of course, an empirical issue for which we do not have a ready answer. For most reasonably secure issuers a more appropriate accounting for default risk would probably have little effect on the theoretical LYON values. Additionally, as regards the question of introducing a stochastic interest rate, we can take comfort from the conclusions of Brennan and Schwartz. They compare traditional convertible bond prices generated by means of a nonstochastic interest rate model with prices generated by means of a single factor stochastic interest rate process and conclude that "for a reasonable range of interest rates the errors from the certain interest rate model are likely to be slight, and, therefore, for practical purposes it may be preferable to use this simpler model for valuing convertible bonds" [4, pp. 925–926]. Thus, although the commercially usable LYON-pricing model is relatively simple, for most practical purposes it may well be more than adequate given the costs of implementing a more sophisticated model.

IV. Application of the LYON-Pricing Model to Waste Management, Inc.

On April 12, 1985, the Waste Management LYON was issued at a price of $250.00 per bond. On April 11, 1985, the closing price of the Waste Management common stock was $52.125. On the issue day, the closing price of the Waste Management LYON was $258.75.

To apply the LYON-pricing model to Waste Management, Inc. it was necessary to estimate the volatility of the company's common stock and to specify an appropriate interest rate. The common stock volatility used was the standard deviation of daily returns over the 100 trading days prior to issuance of the LYON. The estimated volatility is 30% per year. Whether this is the appropriate estimation period or technique is an open question that we cannot resolve here, but sensitivity analysis does allow us to determine the likely impact of errors in the estimate of the stock price volatility.

The interest rate used is 11.21% per year. The rate was chosen because on the issue date this was the approximate yield of intermediate-term bonds of the same risk rating as the Waste Management bond.

Finally, the dividend yield of the Waste Management common stock was specified as a constant 1.6% per year. This yield was chosen because the company's previous quarterly dividend payment was $.20 per share. With recent stock prices of approximately $50.00 per share, this dividend payment provides an annual yield of 1.6% (i.e., 4×$.20/$50.00).

With these parameters and the data given in the Waste Management prospectus, the theoretical LYON price on the issue date was $262.70. As the data in Table 23.1 indicate, over the first four weeks following issuance the

TABLE 23.1 *Waste Management Common Stock Prices, Theoretical LYON Prices, and Reported LYON Market Prices from April 12, 1985 through May 10, 1985*

Date	Closing Stock Price	Closing LYON Market Price	High LYON Market Price	Low LYON Market Price	LYON Theoretical Price
April 12, 1985	$52¼	$258.75			$262.7
15	53	258.75	$260.0	$258.75	264.6
16	52⅝	257.5	257.5	257.5	263.7
17	52	–	–	–	262.1
18	52⅜	257.5	275.5	255.0	263.0
19	52¾	257.5	257.5	257.5	264.0
22	52½	257.5	257.5	257.5	263.3
23	53¼	260.0	260.0	257.5	265.3
24	54¼	265.0	265.0	262.5	267.9
25	54¼	265.0	265.0	262.5	267.9
26	54	265.0	265.0	265.0	267.2
29	53¾	260.0	265.0	260.0	266.6
30	52⅛	260.0	260.0	257.5	262.4
May 1, 1985	49¾	252.5	257.5	252.5	256.7
2	50½	250.0	252.5	250.0	258.4
3	50¾	252.5	252.5	252.5	259.0
6	50½	252.5	255.5	251.25	258.4
7	50⅞	255.0	256.25	252.5	259.3
8	50¾	253.75	257.5	253.75	259.0
9	51¼	255.0	255.0	253.75	260.3
10	53⅛	260.0	260.0	255.0	265.0

theoretical LYON prices closely track the reported market closing prices, although there is a tendency for the model prices to overstate slightly the reported closing prices. Whether this slight overstatement in prices is due to the simplicity of the model or due to an error in the estimation of the stock volatility is not known. Apparently, though, the model is sufficiently accurate to provide a rough guideline for the pricing of new LYON issues. Other LYON issuers would, of course, have different characteristics than Waste Management and would be issuing the security in other interest rate environments. For that reason it is interesting to investigate the sensitivity of the theoretical LYON value to changes in the values of the parameters used in the base case example.

Panel A of Table 23.2 illustrates the sensitivity of the LYON price to changes in the level of the issuer's stock price and to changes in the issuer's stock price volatility. It should come as no surprise that the LYON value increases monotonically with increases in the issuer's stock price and with increases in the volatility of the issuer's stock price. Additionally, as is the case with other stock price contingent claims, the LYON value is highly sensitive to changes in the volatility of the underlying stock. The result emphasizes the importance of accurate stock volatility measurement procedures — an area in which the volume of research now approaches that of a small cottage industry.

Panel B of Table 23.2 illustrates the sensitivity of LYON values to changes in the issuer's dividend yield. The table indicates that the LYON value declines monotonically with increases in the issuer's dividend yield. This occurs because a higher dividend yield implies a lower expected rate of stock price appreciation. Additionally, the value of dividends is not impounded in the LYON price because the LYON investor does not receive dividend payments. Perhaps somewhat surprisingly, the LYON values are not terribly sensitive to changes in the dividend yield. For example, for the base case stock price of \$52.125, an increase in the dividend yield from 1.6% to 3.0% reduces the LYON value by only about \$3.00 per bond.

In a separate analysis not shown here, LYON values were computed with the dividend specified to grow at a constant rate (rather than being specified as a constant yield). That analysis indicated that the theoretical LYON values are even less sensitive to major changes in the assumed dividend growth rate.

Panel C of Table 23.2 illustrates the sensitivity of the theoretical LYON values to changes in the discount rate. As we would anticipate, the LYON value declines monotonically as the interest rate increases.

In evaluating our example LYON we have proceeded as if the terms of the contract were given and have analyzed the sensitivity of the LYON value to the issuer's stock price volatility and dividend payment policy and the level of interest rates. However, the more likely situation is one in which these parameters are given and the issuer wishes to analyze the effect of changes in the terms of the contract on the LYON price. The LYON-pricing model permits an analysis of the various trade-offs between the terms of the contract and the LYON price. For example, the issuer may wish to examine the effect on the LYON price of changes in the conversion ratio or of changes in the schedules of put prices and call prices specified in the LYON indenture.

Illustrating the sensitivity of the theoretical LYON value to changes in the conversion ratio and the redemption and call schedules is a somewhat more complicated procedure because there exists an infinite number of possible ratios and schedules. However, to give some indication of the sensitivity of the LYON price to changes in the redemption and call schedules, Table 23.3 presents values of the LYON with and without the call and redemption features. Column 1 gives the issuer's stock price; Column 2 presents the value of the LYON with the redemption and call schedules as specified in the Waste Management prospectus; Column 3 gives the value of the LYON without the call option (but with the redemption option); Column 4 gives the value of the LYON without the redemption option (but with the call option); and Column 5 gives the value of the LYON without the call option and without the redemption option. Thus, Column 5 gives the value of a zero coupon convertible bond.

TABLE 23.2 *Sensitivity of the Theoretical LYON Values to Changes in the Issuer's Stock Price, Stock Price Volatility, and Dividend Yield and to Changes in the Interest Rate*

A. Sensitivity of LYON Values to Changes in the Issuer's Stock Price Volatility

Stock Price[a] (per share)	Stock Price Volatility[b] (per year)				
	0.10	0.20	0.30	0.40	0.50
$46.00	$223.23	$236.01	$247.34	$257.22	$265.10
47.00	224.67	237.92	249.48	259.44	267.33
48.00	226.26	239.92	251.69	261.71	269.59
49.00	228.02	242.03	253.96	264.03	271.90
50.00	229.94	244.24	256.30	266.39	274.23
51.00	232.03	246.54	258.71	268.80	276.60
52.00	234.28	248.94	261.18	271.26	279.00
53.00	236.71	251.44	263.71	273.76	281.44
54.00	239.29	254.04	266.31	276.30	283.91
55.00	242.04	256.73	268.97	278.88	286.40
56.00	244.94	259.51	271.68	281.51	288.93
57.00	247.99	262.38	274.46	284.17	291.49
58.00	251.19	265.34	277.29	286.87	294.08
59.00	254.52	268.39	280.18	289.62	296.69

TABLE 23.2 *Continued*

B. Sensitivity of LYON Values to Changes in the Issuer's Dividend Yield

Stock Price[a] (per share)	Dividend Yield[c] (per year)			
	0.0%	1.6%	3.0%	5.0%
$46.00	$250.50	$247.34	$244.84	$241.34
47.00	252.72	249.48	246.90	243.28
48.00	255.00	251.69	249.03	245.31
49.00	257.34	253.96	251.24	247.40
50.00	259.74	256.30	253.52	249.58
51.00	262.20	258.71	255.87	251.83
52.00	264.72	261.18	258.29	254.16
53.00	267.30	263.71	260.78	256.57
54.00	269.93	266.31	263.34	259.05
55.00	272.62	268.97	265.96	261.61
56.00	275.36	271.68	268.65	264.25
57.00	278.14	274.46	271.40	266.96
58.00	280.98	277.29	274.22	269.74
59.00	283.86	280.18	277.10	272.60

C. Sensitivity of LYON Values to Changes in the Interest Rate

Stock Price[a] (per share)	Interest Rate[d] (per year)				
	7.21%	9.21%	11.21%	13.21%	15.21%
$46.00	$301.36	$264.73	$247.34	$235.80	$228.43
47.00	302.19	266.38	249.48	238.27	231.13
48.00	303.07	268.10	251.69	240.82	233.91
49.00	304.01	269.89	253.96	243.43	236.75
50.00	305.00	271.74	256.30	246.10	239.66
51.00	306.04	273.66	258.71	248.85	242.63
52.00	307.14	275.64	261.18	251.66	245.66
53.00	308.29	277.69	263.71	254.53	248.75
54.00	309.49	279.81	266.31	257.46	251.90
55.00	310.76	281.98	268.97	260.45	255.11
56.00	312.07	284.22	271.68	263.50	258.38
57.00	313.44	286.51	274.46	266.60	261.70
58.00	314.87	288.87	277.29	269.77	265.07
59.00	316.35	291.29	280.18	272.98	268.49

a. Base case stock price is $52.125 per share.
b. Base case stock price volatility is 0.20 per year.
c. Base case dividend yield is 1.6% per year.
d. Base case interest rate is 11.21% per year.

TABLE 23.3 *Analysis of the Value of a LYON with and without the Call and Redemption Options*

Stock Price[a] (per share)	Callable[b] Redeemable LYON (per bond)	Noncallable Redeemable LYON (per bond)	Callable Nonredeemable LYON (per bond)	Noncallable Nonredeemable LYON (per bond)
$45.00	$245.28	$264.85	$181.94	$244.08
46.00	247.34	267.26	186.48	246.92
47.00	249.48	269.72	191.02	249.79
48.00	251.69	272.22	195.58	252.69
49.00	253.96	274.76	200.14	255.63
50.00	256.30	277.34	204.72	258.60
51.00	258.71	279.96	209.30	261.60
52.00	261.18	282.62	213.89	264.63
53.00	263.71	285.31	218.49	267.69
54.00	266.31	288.04	223.10	270.78
55.00	268.97	290.81	227.72	273.90
56.00	271.68	293.61	232.34	277.05
57.00	274.46	296.44	236.98	280.22
58.00	277.29	299.31	241.62	283.43
59.00	280.18	302.22	246.27	286.66
60.00	283.13	305.15	250.93	289.92

a. Base case stock price is $52.125 per share.
b. This column represents the base case. The call and redemption schedules in the base case are taken from the Waste Management LYON prospectus (see Section I).

As the table indicates, the call option is valuable to the issuer. When the call option is removed, the LYON value increases. Similarly, the redemption option is valuable to the investor. When the redemption option is removed, the LYON value declines. The two effects are not symmetric. Removal of the call feature in the base case increases the value of the LYON by about $20.00, whereas removal of the redemption option reduces the value of the LYON by almost $50.00. Nevertheless, when both features are removed (in Column 5) the LYON value is almost the same as when the LYON contains both features. Obviously, the value of the LYON is not merely the sum of the values of its individual components. Each of the features of this complex security interacts with the others to determine the security's value.

V. The Optimal Stock Price to Convert a LYON

An important feature of the LYON is that issuers may deduct the imputed interest costs of the security without any offsetting cash outflow to investors.

This tax shelter may be valuable to LYON issuers. Once the LYON is converted, however, this tax shield disappears. For this reason, LYON issuers may be concerned that investors will convert their LYON prematurely.

At any point in time, the investor can choose to convert the LYON. In deciding whether to convert, the investor weighs the value of the dividends he gives up by continuing to hold the LYON against the value of the downside risk protection that he gives up by converting the LYON to the issuer's common stock. The downside risk protection is provided by the redemption option held by the investor.

In general, when the dividend yield of the issuer's stock is relatively low, the benefits of conversion (to obtain the dividend) also will be relatively low. In the extreme, when the underlying common stock pays no dividend, there is no incentive for the investor ever to convert the LYON into common stock. Similarly, for low-dividend-paying stocks there is relatively little incentive for the investor to convert the LYON into common stock. However, even for low-dividend-paying stocks, if the stock price rises high enough, it will be so far above the put price that the downside protection provided by the investor's put option becomes negligible. In that case, the investor will decide optimally to convert to common stock.

The LYON-pricing model can be used to calculate the stock price at which it is optimal to convert a LYON. The optimal conversion stock price is the price at which the investor is just indifferent between holding the LYON and converting to common stock. At any stock price above this critical point, the investor is better off to convert to common stock. At any stock price below this critical point, the investor is better off holding the LYON.

The critical conversion stock price is that price at which the present value of the future dividends forgone by continuing to hold the LYON just equals the present value of the downside protection forgone if the investor converts to common stock. The present value of the downside protection forgone is the expected loss to the investor if he converts now and the conversion value of the LYON at maturity (if the investor had held the LYON) turns out to be less than the security's face value at that date.

In most cases, the critical conversion stock price would imply a LYON value that exceeds the specified call price. Thus, in most cases, if issuers follow the call policy that minimizes the value of the LYON, the issuer would call the bond prior to the point at which the investor would optimally convert. To calculate the stock price at which it is optimal for the investor to convert, it is necessary to assume that the issuer follows a policy of never calling the bond or, alternatively, to assume that the bond is noncallable. With this assumption, the critical stock price can be determined by solving Equation 23.3 subject to boundary conditions (23.4), (23.5) and (23.6). At the critical stock price, the value of the LYON is equal to its conversion value. As an illustration, Column 2 of Table 23.4 displays the stock price at which it would be optimal for an issuer to convert the Waste Management

TABLE 23.4 *The Stock Price at which It Is Optimal to Convert a Waste Management LYON*

Anniversary Date	Optimal Conversion[a] Stock Price (per share)
At Issue	$129.50
June 30, 1985	132.00
June 30, 1986	145.00
June 30, 1987	158.50
June 30, 1988	173.50
June 30, 1989	194.50
June 30, 1990	217.00
June 30, 1991	238.50
June 30, 1992	257.00
June 30, 1993	273.00
June 30, 1994	287.00
June 30, 1995	301.50
June 30, 1996	316.00
June 30, 1997	329.50
June 30, 1998	339.00
June 30, 1999	340.00
June 30, 2000	317.50
January 21, 2001	229.36

a. Data used to calculate the optimal conversion stock price are taken from the base case example and the Waste Management LYON prospectus.

LYON on each anniversary date. At the issue date (or immediately thereafter) the stock price would have to increase to $129.50 per share. As time progresses, the critical stock price increases. The critical stock price increases for two reasons. First, as time passes, the present value of the dividends forgone by holding the LYON declines. Second, because the redemption prices of the LYON increase through time, the value of the downside risk protection for holding the LYON increases. Both of these effects reduce the incentive to convert. However, with two years remaining to maturity, the optimal conversion price declines. This occurs because the critical conversion stock price at the maturity date of the LYON equals the bond's face value divided by the conversion ratio. In this case, that critical value is $1,000/4.36 = $229.36. Because the optimal conversion value previously calculated is above that level, the critical price declines as the term to maturity of the bond becomes shorter.

Table 23.4 presents the optimal conversion price for one set of parameters. However, the model is flexible. Issuers concerned about premature conversion could use the LYON-pricing model to test the sensitivity of the optimal conversion price to changes in the terms of the contract and to changes in dividend policy.

VI. Conclusion

Following the pathbreaking work by Black and Scholes [1] and Merton [7], contingent-claims-pricing methodology has been applied to the pricing and analysis of a wide variety of securities—put options, convertible bonds, warrants, forward contracts, futures contracts, mortgage-backed securities, and many others. Models for analyzing some of these securities give rise to closed-form solutions. Models for many others can be solved only with numerical techniques. Those models with closed-form solutions—especially stock-option-pricing models—have been readily adopted by practical market participants. Those models requiring numerical solution techniques have not yet met wide acceptance, probably because of limitations imposed by the lack of availability of the computer hardware and software needed to implement the models. In this paper we report on one case in which numerical solution techniques were used in a practical situation to solve a simplified model for pricing and analyzing a complex security. Presumably, as more powerful personal computers evolve and as the availability of the software used with numerical solution techniques increases, market practitioners will find other situations in which contingent-claims-pricing models that can be solved only with numerical techniques can be of use in analyzing complex securities.

References

1. F. Black and M. S. Scholes, "The Pricing of Options and Corporate Liabilities," *Journal of Political Economy* 81 (May–June 1973), pp. 637–59.
2. M. J. Brennan and E. S. Schwartz, "Convertible Bonds: Valuation and Optimal Strategies for Call and Conversion," *Journal of Finance* 32 (December 1977), pp. 1699–1715.
3. ———, "A Continuous Time Approach to the Pricing of Bonds," *Journal of Banking and Finance* 3 (July 1979), pp. 133–55.
4. ———, "Analyzing Convertible Securities," *Journal of Financial and Quantitative Analysis* 15 (November 1980), pp. 907–29.
5. J. E. Ingersoll, Jr., "A Contingent-Claims Valuation of Convertible Securities," *Journal of Financial Economics* 4 (May 1977), pp. 289–382.
6. S. P. Mason and R. C. Merton, "The Role of Contingent Claims Analysis in Corporate Finance," in E. I. Altman and M. G. Subrahmanyam (eds.), *Recent Advances in Corporate Finance,* Homewood, IL: Richard D. Irwin, 1985.
7. R. C. Merton, "The Theory of Rational Option Pricing," *Bell Journal of Economics and Management Science* 4 (Spring 1973), pp. 141–83.

24

Putable Stock:
A New Innovation
in Equity Financing*

Andrew H. Chen & John W. Kensinger

One of the problem-solving financial innovations that investment bankers have come up with recently is a putable common stock. It has the potential to reduce the underpricing problem in some initial public offerings, as well as to resolve other problems arising from informational asymmetry. In a putable stock arrangement the investors buy packages (called "units") composed of a share of common stock and a "right" provided by the issuing corporation. The right entitles the unit holder to claim more stock if its market price falls below a stated level. At a predetermined time, say at the end of two years, the issuer guarantees to support a floor value for each unit holder's position. In the event that the market value of the stock has risen above the stated floor value, nothing happens. If the market value has fallen below the floor, however, the issuer is obligated to make up the difference by giving unit holders additional common shares.[1] Like convertible

*Partial support for this work by grants from the Gulf Foundation and the University of Texas College of Business is gratefully acknowledged. We also would like to thank James Ang, Robert Taggart, Jr., John Martin, Ron Masulis, Robert Strong, and the anonymous referees for their valuable comments. An earlier version was presented at the 16th annual meeting of the Financial Management Association, New York, NY, October 1986.
1. For example, if the market value were $10.00 per share of common stock upon maturity and the guaranteed floor were $15.00, the rights would entitle their holders to claim 50 new shares of common stock for every 100 rights they held. Since the terms of the guarantee are public knowledge, dilution effects would be anticipated by the market.

bonds, putable stock allows investors to participate fully in the upside potential of a company but with reduced downside risk.

Although putable stock is classified as equity on the issuing corporation's financial statements, from the investor's point of view it is comparable to a convertible bond. Thus putable stock has attractive features for a corporation that would like to sell convertible bonds but needs a financing arrangement that can be treated as equity for accounting and other purposes. Janjigian [6] recently provided evidence that in some cases (i.e., smaller corporations with high growth potential and volatile stock prices) convertible debt has a large equity component. The observation that putable stock is comparable to a convertible bond is consistent with this evidence.

Chen and Kensinger [3] have recently analyzed several financial innovations that have been used by companies to transform equity into debt for the purpose of gaining tax advantages. With putable stock, however, we encounter the opposite transformation. Tax considerations do not adequately explain the invention of this hybrid security. For corporations that have an existing equity base and an established taxable income stream, convertible bonds (especially the zero coupon variety) are preferable. The corporation issuing zero coupon convertibles incurs no cash outlay before the maturity date but gets a tax deduction for "interest" as it accrues. The holder foregoes cash payment of accrued interest in the event the conversion option is exercised.

We conclude, however, that informational asymmetry and other market imperfections provide good reasons for the putable stock innovation and its potential future use. Based on these conclusions we predict that putable stock has the potential to be a useful tool for initial public offerings, for external financing for companies with relatively high degrees of leverage, or for contingencies that require the sale of equity when management believes that the stock is undervalued by the market.

To meet SEC requirements for treatment as an equity financing, the issuer of putable stock must be able to meet its obligations under the guarantee by issuing more shares of common stock. Other options may also be available to the issuer so that the puts may be paid off in cash, notes (with predefined face value, maturity, and floating interest rates), or preferred stock. We conclude that one of these optional settlement methods would be optimal if the rights were presented for payment at a time when management believed that the common stock is undervalued by the market. These optional settlement methods also provide an efficient means of out-of-court settlement in event of the putable stock equivalent of bankruptcy, when the total market value of equity in the firm is less than the amount of the guarantee. Thus, when the issuer has the option to make the payoff on the puts in cash, notes, or other senior securities, issuing putable stock offers additional advantages over convertible debt.

I. Examples of Putable Stock Use

Putable stock was invented by Drexel Burnham Lambert, an investment banking firm, in a development process involving two separate clients. The first step occurred in November 1984, when Drexel designed a financing package for the $6 million initial public offering (IPO) of stock for Arley Merchandise Corporation. Each unit consisted of a share of common stock with a "right" providing the option to sell the stock back to the company for cash or notes.[2] The Arley units were offered at $8.00 each, with accompanying rights for investors to "put" their stock back to the company for $8.00 per share two years later.[3] These were European-type puts, which could not be exercised early.

However, the SEC subsequently ruled that a package like Arley's must be treated as redeemable equity and placed on the company's books as debt until the puts expired. Soon afterwards, Drexel used this experience to find an innovative solution for the problem of another client. Drexel not only succeeded in satisfying the regulators, but also demonstrated that putable stock can be used in other situations besides initial public offerings.

Gearhart Industries (an oil and gas drilling services company) needed to raise a large amount of money under a short deadline. After a long and sometimes bitter struggle in which Smith International, Inc., tried to take over Gearhart, an agreement was reached in March 1985 for Gearhart to buy back 5.3 million shares of its stock from Smith at $15.00 per share (a total of about $80 million). Unfortunately, the market price of Gearhart's stock was fluctuating around $10.75 per share.[4] Unable to raise the necessary cash by means of an issue of new preferred stock or debt in time to meet the deadline, but concerned about selling common stock at a time when the price was at a record low, Gearhart turned to Drexel for help. Drexel arranged a public offering of common stock as part of a putable stock package, with each share protected by a Gearhart-issued put.[5]

In order to avoid the difficulties created by the SEC ruling on the Arley case, Gearhart's putable stock was made redeemable in cash, debt, preferred

---

2. Details on the case of Arley Merchandise Corporation are reported in [8].

3. Cash settlements were promised to small shareholders, but holders of large blocks could be paid off in senior subordinated notes paying 128% of the 10-year Treasury bond rate.

4. Lest this be seen as a simple case of "greenmail," it should be noted that Smith took a loss of $85 million even at this premium price. Smith paid $165 million for its stake in Gearhart (an average price of $31.00 per share) more than a year earlier, and mounted a serious effort to merge with Gearhart. Gearhart's founder and chief executive, Marvin Gearhart, fought hard and successfully to remain independent. Meanwhile the price of oil plummeted, casting a pall over the oil field services industry.

5. The Gearhart offering was announced by *The Wall Street Journal* on March 28, 1985.

stock, or common stock—at the option of the issuer.[6] This modification overcame the regulatory hurdle. Because the arrangement allowed Gearhart the option of issuing common stock to meet its obligation under the guarantee, the SEC ruled that this was a bonafide equity financing. The putable stock issue was sold in "units," each of which consisted of five shares of common stock and five rights to sell those shares back to Gearhart for a guaranteed price.[7]

The favorable SEC ruling creates a potential cost for the existing shareholders who in effect write the puts. If the puts were redeemed by issuing more shares of common stock, owners of the putable stock units would receive enough extra shares to bring the value of their units back up to the guaranteed amount. By opting to meet the guarantee with additional common stock, the issuer fulfills its obligations by transferring a larger share of ownership to the protected shareholder group at the expense of the original shareholders. If the issuer should experience particularly hard times and the total market value of all outstanding equity falls below the guaranteed floor value of the putable stock issue, the steps taken to satisfy the guarantee would result in a substantial transfer of ownership of the corporation to the holders of the putable stock. The founders and earlier stockholders of the company could be left with very little.

In effect, then, the steps taken to satisfy the guarantee are analogous to bankruptcy. There are legal limits to the issuer's ability to meet the guarantee by issuing more shares, however, necessitating a supplementary mechanism for going "bankrupt" (otherwise, the proceeds from the sale of putable stock would suffer because the guarantee would lack integrity). Such a mechanism is provided when multiple payoff options are available to the issuer, allowing the puts to be paid off with cash, notes, or a special class of preferred stock. An analysis is provided in Section III.

Despite the potential problems created by the issuance of the puts, the market price of Gearhart stock showed no significant reaction to the announcement, suggesting that the terms were perceived as fair. On the announcement date (March 28, 1985) Gearhart stock gained $0.125 (up 2.4%) while the S&P

---

6. Under the terms of the agreement, redeeming a right for cash, notes, or preferred stock required that a share of common stock be surrendered at the time of exercise. No such surrender would be required, however, when exercising a right for additional shares of common stock.

7. The offering price was $75.00 per unit ($15.00 per share). The exercise price per share was set at $21.68 five years after issue (June 1990). Limited opportunities for early exercise were provided at annual intervals, during the last 15 business days in June. During each of these exercise windows, Gearhart was required to honor only 20% of the outstanding puts on a first-come, first-served basis. Exercise prices for early exercise were set by the prospectus at $14.68, $16.18, $17.84, and $19.67 in 1986, 1987, 1988, and 1989, respectively. This graduated scale reflects an increase of 10% compounded semiannually.

500 index held steady. This one-tick gain was well within the normal range of fluctuation for Gearhart. Over the five trading days surrounding the announcement (March 26 to April 1) the average daily residual was a mere 0.12%.[8] Over the period March 4 to May 3, 1985 (18 trading days prior to the announcement and 25 after), the average daily market-adjusted residual was near zero (−.001) with standard deviation of 2.05%. The biggest single-day gain over the interval was 4.98% on April 25, and the biggest loss was 5.92% on March 12. The cumulative residual averaged −1.85% over this period (with standard deviation of 3.16%), and ended the period at 0.6%.

II. Evaluation of Putable Stock

Drexel argues that since listed puts are not available to provide protection for IPO investors, the putable stock innovation provides an attractive investment opportunity that is not otherwise available.[9] Holding the putable stock is not, however, the same as holding the stock and a put together in a portfolio. One difference is that the right conveyed in a putable stock unit is a European-type option that cannot be exercised prior to expiration, while listed puts are American options that can be exercised any time prior to expiration. Furthermore, with putable stock, the puts are written by one group of the company's stockholders (referred to here as the founders) and issued to another group of stockholders, thus creating two distinct stockholder groups. If the puts are exercised, the result will be a transfer of ownership claims from one group to the other.

The key to the valuation of a putable stock lies in the payoffs to be received by the holders in different states of the world (defined in terms of the total market value of the issuing firm). To lay a foundation for understanding the nature of a putable stock, the payoffs to three investment alternatives are analyzed: a putable stock, a convertible bond, and a portfolio containing a common stock and an ordinary protective put.[10] The analysis focuses on the situation of a corporation making its initial public offering and shows that in a frictionless environment the payoffs are identical for holders of a

---

8. The daily returns for the S&P 500 were deducted from the daily returns for Gearhart to calculate the market-adjusted residual. These daily residuals were then cumulated over the period from March 4 to May 3, 1985.

9. Although a homemade "synthetic protective put" can be created by using a dynamic asset allocation scheme, the high transaction costs will prevent individual investors from using such a strategy.

10. An ordinary put is an option that is issued by a party other than the issuer of the underlying common stock, such as those traded on the CBOE.

TABLE 24.1 *List of Symbols*

---

n = number of shares retained by the founders
N = number of shares sold to the public
$\alpha = N/(N+n)$ = proportion of firm offered to public
S = guaranteed value per share
$G = NS$ = total amount of guaranteed payment
S' = market value per share on exercise date, ex-rights
$V' = (N+n)S'$ = value of the firm on exercise date
V = current market value of the firm
m = number of shares transferred under the guarantee
t = time remaining until exercise date

---

putable stock and for holders of zero coupon convertible bonds, showing that Ingersoll's [5] model is applicable to putable stock as well as convertible bonds.[11]

Table 24.1 lists the definitions of the symbols used. The simplifying assumptions are listed below in the order in which they will later be relaxed.

1. The issuing firm starts with a clean slate, having no outstanding debt. All past financing has come from equity investments by the founders. The corporation pays no dividends and intends to continue this policy until maturity of the puts.

2. Information is fully and costlessly available to all participants in the marketplace.

3. The put provision is conveyed by rights that can be exercised only on the expiration date. The guarantee will be honored by transferring additional common stock to the holders of puts, and the capital market fully anticipates the dilution effects of such an issue of additional common stock. The number of additional shares will be determined on the basis of the market value. For example, if the guaranteed floor is $15.00 per unit and the market price of the stock has dropped to $10.00 per

---

11. There is no "standard" putable stock contract. A variety of terms and conditions can be laid out in any given putable stock prospectus, but the essential elements are simple. A putable stock unit contains one put for each share of common stock, and the issuer must be able to satisfy all obligations by issuing more shares of common stock if the puts are exercised. To our knowledge, no putable stock issues have provided the issuer with a recall privilege. The analysis in this section focuses on the most basic situation. Later in the paper we consider the rationale for providing the issuer with alternative means of meeting the obligations arising from the puts (i.e., cash, notes, or preferred stock).

TABLE 24.2 *Payoffs at Expiration*

Strategy	Firm Value at Expiration		
	$V' < G$	$G \leq V' < (N+n)S$	$(N+n)S \leq V'$
Stock plus Put	G	G	$NS' = \alpha V'$
Putable Stock	V'	$(N+m)S' = G$	$NS' = \alpha V'$
Convertible Debt	V'	$NS = G$	$NS' = \alpha V'$

share, an investor holding 100 putable stock units would receive an extra 50 shares.[12]

4. The guarantee will be fully honored, with adjustments to protect the holders of putable stock from dilution. One means of doing so would be for the founders to give up some of their own shares in order to meet the guarantee, so that no new shares would be issued (other adjustment procedures are available which would accomplish the same effect, and are discussed in Section III).

5. In the analysis, convertible bonds are compared to the putable common stock. Each of the bonds is convertible at the end of the period into one share of common stock. N units are sold. The face value of each unit of debt is S, and the total face value of the issue is NS. The holders may take the face value or opt for stock. In event of default on the bonds, bankruptcy is costless.

6. The choice of putable stock or convertible bonds has no impact on the corporation's ability to carry out its business activities; that is, the financing choice does not affect important qualities such as relationships with customers or suppliers.

Table 24.2 summarizes the payoffs from each alternative on the expiration date. If the terminal share value were less than the guaranteed price ($S' < S$), we need to differentiate two separate sets of outcomes that could occur: The value of the firm is less than the total guaranteed payment, so the firm will not be able to fully meet the guarantee even if the founders give up their entire stake (this condition is expressed by $V' < G$); or the value of the firm is equal to or greater than the total amount of the guarantee, so the guarantee

---

12. The exact method for determining the number of shares may vary from case to case and must be described clearly in the prospectus — just like in convertible bond arrangements. In the Gearhart case, for example, the number of additional shares would be calculated by a formula that establishes the "market value" as 90% of the average market price for the 60 days prior to the exercise period. Since the terms of the puts are publicly available information, it is reasonable to expect that the market price of the stock reflects the expected dilution effects.

could be met while leaving the founders with something to spare (this condition is expressed as $G \leq V' < (N+n)S$).

In both of these two cases, holders of stock plus an ordinary put would exercise their puts and in aggregate would receive G, the guaranteed payment. However, if $V' < G$, holders of putable stock would receive no more than the value of the firm. The same is true of holders of convertible bonds because the issuer would default its bond obligations and leave the bondholders with the entire firm.

If the terminal value of a share of stock exceeded the guaranteed price ($S' > S$), holders of stock plus puts would throw away their puts because they expire out of the money. If such investors held a total of N shares, they would hold securities with an aggregate value of NS', and would own an α share of the firm. Another way of expressing the condition in this case is to say that the market value of the firm, V', equals or exceeds the product of the guaranteed price multiplied by the total number of shares outstanding, $(N+n)S$ (this is the way the condition is shown in Table 24.2). Holders of putable stock would enjoy the same aggregate value in this case, as they would not exercise their puts. Holders of convertible debt would convert in this case and their aggregate holding would also be NS'.

Thus it can be seen that the payoffs from holding putable stock are not in all cases the same as the payoffs from holding a portfolio of stock plus the ordinary puts. The payoff from holding putable stock is, however, the same in all cases as the payoff from holding convertible bonds. Figure 24.1 shows graphically the terminal value of the public holding of either putable stock or convertible bonds in relation to the total value of the issuing firm.

The owners of putable stock collectively own a portfolio consisting of an α share of the firm and two put options. One is a long put option to sell an α fraction of the firm for the guaranteed amount. The other is a short put that represents an obligation to accept the *whole* firm in place of the

FIGURE 24.1 *Value of Putable Stock or Convertible Bonds at Maturity*

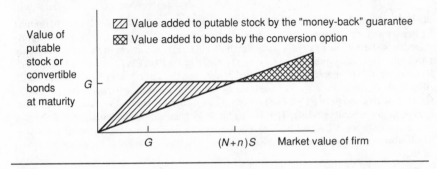

FIGURE 24.2 *Value of Putable Stock or Convertible Bonds Prior to Maturity*

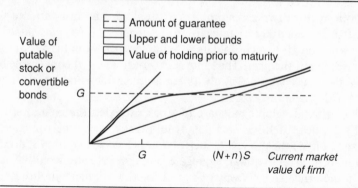

guaranteed amount (the issuers of the guarantee retain the right to make good on it by turning over the whole firm even if it is worth less than the amount of the guarantee). By applying the put-call parity relationship, it can be shown that putable stock fits Ingersoll's [5] valuation model for zero coupon convertible bonds.[13] Prior to expiration, the current market value of the firm (V) is of course the upper bound for the value of putable stock or convertible bonds. The lower bound is αV, and the value of putable stock or convertible bonds prior to expiration must fall between these bounds. The function is expressed graphically in Figure 24.2.

The mechanics of exercising the options in a putable stock package are different from a convertible bond package, so there may be differences in transactions costs that do not show up in Figure 24.2. More complex differences arise when a comparison is made between putable stock and coupon-paying convertible bonds. Holders of putable stock receive any dividends declared, but there are no specific promises as there are in the case of coupon payments for bonds. Failure to pay a coupon, of course, could precipitate bankruptcy. Issuing putable stock does not carry the same risk, therefore, as issuing coupon-paying convertible bonds.

---

13. Stoll [14] and Merton [9] established the put-call parity relationship for European options written on underlying assets with a variety of return-generating functions. A call plus the present value of the exercise price (discounted at the T-bill rate) is equivalent to the underlying asset plus a put. Expressed symbolically: $C(V, G, t) + Ge^{-rt} = V + P(V, G, t)$. Under the assumptions listed above, this relationship can be applied in our analysis. The owners of putable stock hold $\alpha V + P(\alpha V, G, t) - P(V, G, t)$. By transforming the two puts into their equivalents, it can be shown that this equals $V - C(V, G, t) + C(\alpha V, G, t)$, which is Ingersoll's valuation model for zero coupon convertible bonds. That is, the holders of the convertible bonds own the whole firm and are short a call to sell it for G, but have another call to buy an α share of it for $G -$ which works out to be the same package of claims held by the owners of putable stock.

It should be noted that the estimate of the variance rate of the company's market value is one of the key factors in the application of the Black-Scholes OPM (option-pricing model) to evaluate putable stock. For an issuing firm that has a stock price history, the estimation of the variance rate of the company's value can be accomplished by using the historical data of its stock prices. On the other hand, if the putable stock is an IPO situation, one must rely on other measures (such as cash flows of the firm or the price history of a comparable company) to estimate the variance rate for the purpose of pricing the putable stock.

In the foregoing analysis we disregard dividends and bankruptcy resulting from prior borrowings (refer to Assumption 1). Thus the European/American dichotomy that distinguishes putable stock from convertible bonds does not matter. This dichotomy, however, deserves further attention. Even though a convertible bond may be exercised prior to maturity, this privilege does not necessarily make it more valuable than an otherwise identical putable stock. The holders of putable stock also have seniority over unprotected stockholders in the event bankruptcy is declared prior to the maturity of the puts. Therefore, early exercise in event of bankruptcy is in effect provided for. Because an option is generally worth more alive than dead while the underlying asset is still viable, the rational reason for early exercise of a convertible bond is to receive the dividends if the company begins making cash distributions to stockholders. Although the option in a putable stock unit cannot be exercised early, the holder already possesses the stock and therefore automatically receives any dividends that might be declared.

Even so, there is a possibility for a wealth transfer from the putable stockholders to the founding shareholders under extreme circumstances. Consider a situation in which the company experiences severe difficulties and the probability becomes substantial that the value of the company will be less than enough to meet the guarantee. The reasonable expectation in such a circumstance is that the equivalent of bankruptcy will occur, and ownership of the company will shift substantially to the holders of putable stock (with the founding shareholders being left only a remnant). Because the puts cannot be exercised early, the founding shareholders have an opportunity (while they are still in control) to declare dividends in order to receive a portion of the wealth that would otherwise revert to the protected stockholders upon maturity of the puts. A restriction on distributions to shareholders under such circumstances is therefore needed to protect the integrity of the guarantee and reduce the cost of capital for the putable stock issue. In the Gearhart case such restrictions existed in prior covenants. With the proper protection against welching, the European nature of the option in putable stock unit creates no disadvantage for the holder.

III. Advantages of Putable Stock

In the previous section putable stock was shown to be equivalent to convertible bonds under a certain set of assumptions. Relaxing some of the assumptions reveals several advantages putable stock has over convertible bonds.

A. Reduction of Informational Asymmetry Costs

In an IPO, the founders of the firm are fundamentally interested in minimizing the share of ownership they must relinquish in order to obtain the financial resources necessary to realize their firm's potential. When the founders are better informed about the prospects of the firm than are outside investors, they chafe at the prospect of selling what they consider to be undervalued equity claims, but assign a low probability to the prospect that the guarantee in a putable stock issue would be exercised. In that case, there would be informational asymmetry costs associated with the sale of new "plain vanilla" common stock.

Leland and Pyle [7] first described informational asymmetry costs. The problem can arise with any form of external financing and its essence can be explained fairly simply. Managers often possess valuable information about new projects that cannot be unambiguously communicated to the capital market. One potential barrier to communication is the need to keep competitors in the dark in order to maintain the competitive advantage that makes the project potentially profitable. Whenever such an informational asymmetry exists, managers face a problem. If new claims againt the firm are sold in the capital market, they will be undervalued due to the lack of complete information. That is, their market value will be less than their fair value, and the difference constitutes a type of agency cost. Different forms of financing produce different informational asymmetry costs, and the costs are higher for equity than debt. It is management's job to find ways to finance new projects that minimize the informational asymmetry costs borne by existing shareholders.

By using the equivalent of convertible debt to gain the funds it needs, a company can reduce the informational asymmetry cost. The willingness to put existing shareholders on the line in order to protect new shareholders from loss not only reduces the risk faced by the new shareholders, but may also serve as a means of signaling to them the implications of the information held by the insiders. Such signaling could enhance the value of the new issue even beyond what would be justified by the risk reduction alone. Moreover, by packaging the financing as putable stock, the issuing firm is able at the same time to preserve the advantages of equity.

In his recent empirical study of the cost of going public, Ritter [11] concluded that explicit and implicit costs can absorb 30% or more of the proceeds in the case of a small initial public offering (compared to an average of 21% for firm commitment IPOs of all sizes). Ritter identifies informational asymmetry as a significant contributing factor in such high costs, drawing upon earlier work by Rock [12] and Beatty and Ritter [1]. In initial public offerings, informed investors will submit more purchase orders for underpriced offers than for overpriced offers, with the result that uninformed investors (who wind up with the residual) will receive a relatively larger portion of shares in overpriced offers and a relatively smaller portion of shares in underpriced offers. Over several offers, therefore, the uninformed investors can expect to receive more than their fair share of dogs and less than their fair share of good deals (thus they are afflicted by the "winners' curse" familiar to those who often bid too high at auctions and so tend to overpay). Ritter describes the condition of the uninformed investors by saying that their expected return, conditional on receiving shares, is lower than their expected return conditional on submitting a purchase order. To fully subscribe an issue when a large proportion of investors consider themselves uninformed therefore requires a greater degree of underpricing than would be the case if ignorance were less widespread.

A best efforts offering is one way to resolve the problem. The adverse selection problem that confronts the uninformed investors in a firm commitment is reduced in a best efforts offering, since the offer will be withdrawn if it is not fully subscribed. The risk that is borne by uninformed investors in a firm commitment is shifted to the issuer. Thus, the majority of small initial public offerings (less than $4 million proceeds) are best effort offerings. However, a major concern for the issuers is that the offer may be withdrawn, leaving them without the necessary capital.

Putable stock is another alternative that could significantly reduce the costs to uninformed investors (lifting the pall cast over them by the winners' curse) and thus be particularly helpful in facilitating access to public equity capital by small startup companies. Offering the protection of the puts would provide a way of reducing the underpricing required by uninformed investors in a firm commitment. Through the puts, the risk to the uninformed investors would be shifted to the founding shareholders of the issuing corporation, and the corporation could be assured of raising the necessary capital.

The motivation for trying putable stock in the first place was that the owners of Arley Merchandise Corporation were unwilling to accept less than $8.00 per share, but Drexel believed the stock would fetch only about $6.00 in the market. Making the stock putable enabled the package to be offered at $8.00 per unit, with the accompanying rights (the official term for the puts) permitting investors to sell their stock back to the company at $8.00

FIGURE 24.3 *Arley Cumulative Residuals*

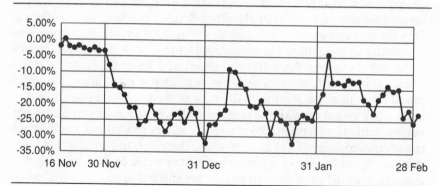

per share two years later (these were European puts that could not be exercised early). The stock and rights could be separated and traded independently, however, at the discretion of the holder.

The rights were listed on the Boston Stock Exchange. The Arley common stock (sans rights) began trading on the American Stock Exchange on November 15, 1984, closing at $7.625 per share, and the "seasoning" of Arley stock took a decidedly different course than the average IPO. Rather than rising substantially in the early rounds of public trading—the fate of the typical underpriced fledgling stock—Arley settled quickly to the $6.00 level predicted by Drexel. Figure 24.3 shows the market-adjusted cumulative residuals for Arley over the first three months of trading.[14] Over the first four full weeks of trading, the cumulative residual dropped off precipitously, falling to −25.65% at the close of December 12. During this time, the average daily residual was −0.35% (with a standard deviation of 1.37%). After this adjustment period, Arley fluctuated randomly (albeit noisily) around $6.00 per share until it began a steady climb in April 1986. The cumulative market-adjusted residual averaged −18.16% (with standard deviation of 5.87%) over the 137 trading days from December 13, 1984, to June 28, 1985. The individual daily residuals averaged nearly zero (.000026) over this postadjustment period, however, with standard deviation of 3.27%.

The willingness of Arley's original owners to shoulder the downside risk for new stockholders allowed Arley to collect a $2.00 premium over the $6.00 market value of its stock. This single experiment does not provide a prudent basis to say that putable stock can do the same on average over a large number of IPOs, but it does provide an incentive for further experimentation.

---

14. The daily returns for the S&P 500 were deducted from the daily returns for Arley to calculate the market-adjusted residual. These daily residuals were then cumulated over the period from November 15, 1984, to June 28, 1985.

A postscript is in order to complete the Arley story. On August 18, 1986, the directors accepted an offer from a group of middle managers to buy Arley for $48.7 million, with public stockholders scheduled to receive $10.00 cash per share. Pending the close of this sale, the stock was trading in the range of $9.00 to $10.00 during the exercise period of the puts, so they expired unused.

The discussion up to this point has been concerned with informational asymmetry that exists at the time of the issue. Informational asymmetry costs could arise at the time the puts mature and can be reduced by the alternative settlement methods (the option to pay off the put-holders in cash, notes, or preferred stock). Suppose that when the puts mature, management has reason to believe that the market value of the corporation is depressed because important information is not available in the marketplace. Paying off the put-holders with undervalued common stock would not be in the best interests of the original (unprotected) shareholders. A payoff in cash, notes, or redeemable preferred stock would then be more advantageous.

B. More Efficient Mechanisms for Handling Default

For purposes of gaining a favorable SEC ruling on the treatment of a putable stock as equity, it is sufficient for common stock to be the only option available to the issuer for meeting the obligations to holders of puts. Additional options (including cash, notes, or preferred stock) are necessary in order to provide a means of effecting the putable stock equivalent of bankruptcy (which occurs when the resources of the corporation are insufficient to meet the obligations created by the guarantee). Due to the legal restrictions on the maximum number of shares a corporation can issue under its charter, such alternatives are required in order to make the puts fully credible to potential investors. If the market value of the issuing corporation falls below the guaranteed amount, a mechanism is needed to effect the transfer of ownership to the holders of putable stock.

A good example is provided by the preferred stock alternative in the Gearhart case, which was described in detail in the prospectus for the putable stock issue. Any new preferred stock issued to satisfy the guarantee would have the same par value and pay the same dividend as common stock, would convey full voting rights, and would convey a prior claim in event of bankruptcy. If the preferred stock alternative were offered, holders of putable stock would have the opportunity to exchange their shares of common stock for an appropriate number of shares of preferred stock.[15] The original stockholders can default on the guarantee, and the lion's share of the company

---

15. The exact wording of the prospectus is as follows: "Any Preferred Stock [exchanged for rights] will pay noncumulative cash dividends at a rate equal to the highest quarterly cash

can be transferred to the putable stockholders without imposing the delays and expense of filing for bankruptcy. Moreover, the process of transferring control is an automatic consequence that follows from fulfilling the contractual obligations imposed by the putable stock agreement.

One of the advantages of putable stock over convertible bonds, therefore, is the relative efficiency with which the transfer of ownership takes place in the event of default. This greater efficiency should be reflected in a higher price paid for putable stock (relative to convertible bonds) at the time of issue, and hence a lower cost of capital. As an illustration, consider the example of a corporation with 500,000 shares outstanding (held, say, by the founders), which issues an additional 500,000 shares of putable stock with a guaranteed floor value of $50 million. The market value of the corporation was $100 million ($100.00 per share) at the time of the issue. The corporate charter, furthermore, limits the total number of shares the firm can issue to 4 million.

Suppose that catastrophe strikes and the value of the corporation drops. The market would anticipate dilution as the expiration of the puts approaches, and the decline in per share values would accelerate. If, for example, the corporation lost 40% of its value and were worth $60 million at the time the puts expired, the holders of putable stock as a group would receive enough new shares so that they would own 5 out of every 6 shares outstanding. Since the founding shareholders own 500,000 shares, the total number of outstanding shares would have to increase to 3 million, and the price per share would drop to $20.00 (an 80% decline). The total value of the founding shareholders' position would be $10 million, while the 2.5 million shares in the hands of the protected stockholders would have a total value of $50 million. Thus, all of the decline would be borne by the founding shareholder group, which is consistent with the spirit of the guarantee.[16] If the market value of the corporation dropped to $55 million, however, the total number of shares would have to be increased to 5.5 million ($10.00 per share) in order to meet the guarantee, but this number exceeds the legal limitation imposed by the corporate charter. Therefore an alternative means of payment is necessary in order to maintain the integrity of the guarantee.

Meeting the obligation with cash would require a substantial liquidation of the company. Paying with notes would create the prospect of bankruptcy at a future date. Thus, either option would result in the realignment of own-

---

dividend rate for the Common Stock from the issuance date of the Rights to the issuance of such Preferred Stock, will have a specified liquidation preference, will be optionally redeemable at any time at liquidation value, will be convertible on a one-for-one basis into Common Stock and will vote together with the Common Stock except as otherwise required by applicable law."
16. It is worth noting that the founding shareholders will not be disenfranchised completely, although their stake in the firm may be reduced to a very small one. In the situation of a small startup company this can provide valuable incentives to the founders, whose continued efforts are critical to the success of the venture.

ership required to make good on the guarantee. The firm might be worth more as a going concern than in liquidation, however – making a cash settlement unattractive. Furthermore, the prospect of costly bankruptcy proceedings could cause the notes to be considered inefficient. In such cases, the option of satisfying the guarantee by offering preferred shares provides the necessary integrity.

C. Improved Relationships with Customers and Suppliers

Putable stock should be considered a worthwhile innovation only if it provides benefits that are not available with convertible debt.[17] The final assumption to be relaxed is that there is no interrelation between the financing decisions of the firm and its value. In the case of a mature corporation, there are many tax considerations, agency problems, and control issues that may make capital structure relevant, and these issues are already familiar to the reader. For the young firm just starting out, tax considerations do not become relevant until a taxable earnings stream has been established. In such a case there are other considerations that may dictate the choice of a financing arrangement that is widely acknowledged to be equity (even if it is a hybrid). Convertible debt would not suffice in such a situation, but putable common stock would be satisfactory.

Alan Shapiro [13] recently provided evidence that the net present value a firm is able to generate derives in substantial part from its ability to maintain a competitive advantage. Potential customers may evaluate a prospective purchase on the basis of the producer's financial strength as well as the average quality of its products. People are often leery of buying from a company that may not survive to give future product support to those customers who get the occasional lemon. Likewise, a firm that projects the appearance of financial strength may enjoy more advantageous relationships with suppliers of everything from loans to labor to nuts and bolts.

Horowitz and Kolodny [4] found evidence of this in a study of the impact of new accounting rules[18] on the level of R&D expenditure by firms. Many of the firms that were forced to switch to immediate expensing of R&D, particularly smaller companies, subsequently reduced their commitment to it. Horowitz and Kolodny concluded that this action, although it hurt the companies' long-term competitive position, was taken in order to avert even more serious near-term harm that might arise purely from accounting effects. Some of the highlights of their list of concerns were: (1) Listing requirements of the various stock exchanges include a minimum reported earnings requirement; (2) Federal Government regulations concerning the determination of a firm's

---

17. This criterion for a worthwhile financial innovation was set forth by Van Horne [15].
18. In 1975 the Financial Accounting Standards Board and the Securities and Exchange Commission banned the use of the deferral, or capitalization, method of accounting for R&D expenditures and required expensing by all firms.

acceptability as a government contractor include a number of accounting ratios that must be within acceptable ranges; and (3) banks and other institutional lenders may also place undue emphasis on accounting numbers as opposed to the economic reality of the firm's financial condition. For similar reasons a firm, particularly a smaller one, may find that equity financing is the only viable way to raise needed capital while preserving the accounting data necessary to allow it to have its stock listed, gain federal contracts, and enjoy good relations with banks and other financial institutions.

D. Putable Stock Can Resolve Special Agency Problems

Even for a corporation that is well beyond the IPO stage, putable stock may provide a solution for agency problems in special circumstances. General Motors, for example, recently issued an "E Class" common stock whose dividends are pegged to the performance of the Electronic Data Systems (EDS) division (they later issued an "H Class" common stock with dividends pegged to the performance of the Hughes Aircraft division). These new classes of common stock create a company within a company. The separate parts have different owners who receive differential rewards, although the whole is controlled by a single management. When these different groups have conflicting interests, complex agency problems arise.

The creation of the "E Class" stock, for instance, has given rise to controversies over transfer pricing for goods and services supplied to other divisions by EDS. High transfer prices are in the best interests of the owners of E Class stock (many of whom are key employees of the EDS division) but hurt the performance of the remainder of the corporation. Likewise, artificially low transfer prices for services supplied by the EDS division would hurt the owners of E Class stock. Given uncertainty over how upper management will resolve transfer-pricing difficulties in the future, the market values of all classes of stock suffer. Owners of E Class stock have cause to be concerned that upper management may enhance the value of the regular stock at the expense of E Class stock.

If a special class of stock were putable to the parent corporation, however, the owners would be assured of redress in the event of a series of adverse decisions by upper management. Investors would therefore be willing to pay a higher price for the special class of stock, and upper management would have an incentive to make better-balanced decisions.

IV. Concluding Comments

Putable stock has been devised to resolve problems arising from the need to raise equity capital when management believes that the market price of ordinary common stock is too low (i.e., when there are significant informational asymmetry costs). Although putable stock is a relatively new financial innovation, it offers promise as a potential means to reduce the underpricing problem for initial public offerings. For a young company seeking funds to finance growth, putable stock also offers a publicly traded alternative to a mezzanine debt financing in which the lender receives warrants to buy common stock.[19] Whether or not putable stock financing is the long-sought solution to the underpricing of IPOs remains to be seen. There is theoretical justification for believing that it can be a solution, and the Arley case provides tantalizing (though tentative) empirical verification. Putable stock may also offer a solution for problems faced by companies that have already gone public but need to raise new common equity in the face of high informational asymmetry costs. Therefore, because of its potential ability to solve significant problems, putable stock deserves to be considered a worthwhile experiment and tried more extensively.

A putable stock is similar to a convertible bond from the investor's perspective, but with several additional benefits to the issuer. The options allowing the issuer to choose cash, notes, preferred stock, or common stock as the means for meeting the guarantee provide an efficient alternative to bankruptcy proceedings. Such provisions may thereby reduce the expected "bankruptcy" costs, and therefore enhance the market value of the corporation. In addition, such provisions allow management to mitigate the cost of informational asymmetries that might exist at the time the puts mature.

If putable stock is to be effective, holders must be adequately protected from possible attempts to "welch" on the guarantee. Therefore it is necessary that well-thought-out default mechanisms be provided in the arrangement. Furthermore, when the issuer retains protection from early exercise, restrictions on the payment of dividends will be necessary to protect the holders of putable stock from potential wealth transfers. In the absence of such antiwelching protection, potential investors will have to protect themselves by anticipating the worst and offering a correspondingly lower price for the putable stock issue. Thus, just as in the case of restrictive covenants in bond contracts, the appropriate restrictions benefit both the holders of putable stock (in the form of reduced risk) and the founding shareholders (in the form of a lower cost of capital for financing the firm's expansion).

---

19. Mezzanine loans are similar to convertible bonds when, as is commonly the case, the lender receives warrants to purchase common stock. In the case of a young company that has attractive growth potential but has not yet established a steady cash flow, the lender may extend an additional line of credit upon which the borrower can draw to make interest payments. In such a case, the mezzanine loan is much like a zero coupon convertible bond.

References

1. R. Beatty and J. Ritter, "Investment Banking, Reputation, and the Underpricing of Initial Public Offerings," *Journal of Financial Economics* 15 (1986), pp. 213–232.

2. F. Black and M. Scholes, "The Pricing of Options and Corporate Liabilities," *Journal of Political Economy* 81 (1973), pp. 637-659.
3. A. Chen and J. Kensinger, "Financing Innovations: Tax-Deductible Equity," *Financial Management* (Winter 1985), pp. 44-51.
4. B. Horowitz and R. Kolodny, "The FASB, the SEC, and R&D," *Bell Journal of Economics* (Spring 1981), pp. 249-262.
5. J. Ingersoll, Jr., "A Contingent-Claims Valuation of Convertible Securities," *Journal of Financial Economics* 5 (1977), pp. 289-322.
6. V. Janjigian, "The Leverage Changing Consequences of Convertible Debt Financing," *Financial Management* (Fall 1987), pp. 15-21.
7. H. Leland and D. Pyle, "Informational Asymmetries, Financial Structure, and Financial Intermediation," *Journal of Finance* (May 1977), pp. 371-387.
8. C. Makin, "The Boom in Uncommon Stock," *Institutional Investor* (June 1985), pp. 101-102.
9. R. Merton, "Theory of Rational Option Pricing," *Bell Journal of Economics and Management Science* 4 (1973), pp. 141-183.
10. S. Myers, "Determinants of Corporate Borrowing," *Journal of Financial Economics* (November 1977), pp. 147-175.
11. J. Ritter, "The Costs of Going Public," *Journal of Financial Economics* (December 1987), pp. 269-281.
12. K. Rock, "Why New Issues Are Underpriced," *Journal of Financial Economics* 15 (1986), pp. 187-212.
13. A. Shapiro, "Corporate Strategy and the Capital Budgeting Decision," *Midland Corporate Finance Journal* (Spring 1985), pp. 22-36.
14. H. Stoll, "The Relationship Between Put and Call Option Prices," *Journal of Finance* (December 1969), pp. 801-824.
15. J. Van Horne, "Of Financial Innovations and Excesses," *Journal of Finance* (July 1985), pp. 621-631.

25

Adjustable Rate
Preferred Stock

*Bernard J. Winger, Carl R. Chen,
John D. Martin, J. William Petty,
& Steven C. Hayden*

I. Introduction

New varieties of securities that mix debt and equity features are being created in increased numbers to meet the real or perceived needs of both issuers and investors. One such security is the adjutable rate preferred stock (ARPS or "floaters"), which first appeared in May 1982.

The ARPS concept is relatively simple, with the dividend rate being adjusted quarterly to recognize the changes in market rates, thereby allowing the value of the security to remain relatively constant. Specifically, the dividend rate on the ARPS issue is set in accordance with a specified "spread" (referred to as the "reset" or "refloat") from the maximum current rate of interest being paid on short-, intermediate-, or long-term government debt. The reset can be either positive or negative. For example, the dividend rate for an ARPS issue might be set each quarter to be 50 basis points above (i.e., a positive reset) the highest of the following three rates: (1) the 91-day Treasury bill rate, (2) the 10-year Treasury note rate, or (3) the 20-year Treasury bond rate. (All ARPS issued through June 1984 used these same three rates.) Thus, the cash manager who purchases an ARPS issue can expect to receive a dividend based on the maximum of the rates offered in the term structure each quarter.[1] Furthermore, the dividend rate on an ARPS issue can only vary within its "upper" and "lower" bounds, commonly referred to as its "collar." For example, the upper limit might be 14% and the lower limit might be 7%.

Investor interest in ARPS has come largely from corporate money managers. As managers of "temporarily" idle cash, this group has historically been hesitant to invest in fixed dividend preferred stock issues.[2] ARPS issues, on the other hand, have proven appealing to corporate money managers for two basic reasons: First, dividends on ARPS issues held by a corporation enjoy an 85% exclusion from federal income taxes.[3] Second, with an ARPS issue the dividend is adjusted quarterly to reflect current interest rates. As a result of this latter feature, the price volatility of ARPS issues is reduced relative to that of a fixed rate preferred stock.

The issuers of ARPS have found the security attractive for four primary reasons: First, pre-tax yields on ARPS are below those on comparable debt securities. Although ARPS dividends are not tax deductible, the pre-tax cost

---

1. The actual dividend received in quarter t is set in the previous quarter, $t-1$; specifically, it is set two weeks after the ex-dividend date in quarter $t-1$. Since the dividend in quarter t reflects interest rates at the end of quarter $t-1$, there is a built-in lag between the ARPS dividend and current Treasury yields. Of course, ARPS prices after the ex-dividend date reflect only the anticipated dividend to be paid at the end of quarter t. In this way, ARPS are described as trading on an "anticipated dividend" basis.

2. In their survey of corporate cash management practices, Gitman et al. [6] found that "market price stability" was the most important investment selection criterion among the cash managers surveyed. In addition, "yield" was ranked third following "marketability." Similar results were found by Kamath et al. [9].

Joehnk et al. [8] and Brown and Lummer [2] explored two alternative cash management investment strategies designed to take advantage of the 85% dividend exclusion on stock held by corporations. Joehnk et al. suggest "preferred dividend rollovers," whereby the corporate cash manager engages in an active trading strategy designed to acquire preferred stock just prior to the ex-dividend date and sell the shares shortly after the dividend is received. The primary risk faced by the cash manager using this strategy is the possibility of a rise in the general level of interest rates leading to a loss of principal.

Brown and Lummer [2] examined the use of a "hedged dividend capture" strategy, whereby the cash manager simultaneously purchases the common stock of one firm and sells a call option on a similar firm with an expiration date near the ex-dividend date on the stock. In this way the risk of an adverse price fluctuation in the common stock price is minimized. Their empirical analysis showed that the cash manager could achieve higher average returns using such a strategy; however, the risk of the strategy was found to be greater than holding more traditional cash management investments.

3. The favorable tax treatment of dividend income to corporate investors allows them to accept lower yields than those offered on debt instruments. Supply and demand in the marketplace, then, should lead to ARPS prices that reflect a type of joint tax optimization on the part of issuers and investors wherein each gains at the expense of the U.S. Treasury. A discussion of this point can be found in McDaniel [10] and Finnerty [5].

advantage is still attractive to an issuer with a low (or zero) marginal tax rate. Second, ARPS provides the issuer with a permanent source of equity capital without the dilution effect that may accompany a common stock issue. This feature was particularly important when ARPS were first utilized in mid-1982. At that time, the primary issuers were large bank-holding companies who felt that their stock prices were depressed as a result of problems stemming from their international loan commitments. Third, the call provisions for ARPS issues have been much less costly to the issuer than is the case with a fixed dividend preferred issue. For example, the call premium on virtually all ARPS issues (offered prior to June 1984) was 3%. Similar fixed rate preferred issues typically carry a call premium of 12% or more. This difference is explained by the fact that there is less incentive to refund a floating rate preferred issue. Fourth, the issuer of a floating rate preferred issue need not be concerned about issuing securities at a time when rates are perceived to be abnormally high since there is obviously no rate "lock-in" effect.

Since ARPS is a new form of security, information to date on the experience of issuers and holders of these securities is relatively limited. Thus, the objectives of the present research are to provide a descriptive study of the nature and offering terms of ARPS issues, and to examine the investment returns that have been realized by investing in ARPS. To accomplish the preceding objectives, we have collected information on all 91 issues of ARPS that were offered between May 1982 and June 1984. In addition, price and volume data have been collected for a sample of 27 actively traded ARPS issues, as well as six mutual funds that invest primarily in ARPS. We then compare the investment performance of these ARPS issues and the ARPS mutual funds with the rates of interest on a variety of money market securities.

The paper is organized as follows: We first provide an overview of the chronological development of the offerings of ARPS. Next, we examine market experience with ARPS, looking first at the factors that have influenced reset values and then at the return performance of ARPS issues. Finally, we offer concluding remarks and a discussion of future research issues.

II. Historical Experience with ARPS

As shown in Table 25.1, there were 91 ARPS issues sold during the period May 1982 through June 1984. These issues accounted for about 69% of all funds raised through preferred-stock offerings during this period. Issuers include industrials, insurance companies, public utilities, and especially commercial banks. This last group accounted for about half of all issues, although their relative importance declined over the period of study. During the period of study, most of the ARPS issuers were large and well known

TABLE 25.1 *Statistical Summaries of the ARPS Market*

Period	Funds Raised ($Billions)			Number of ARPS Issues			
	ARPS[a]	Total Preferreds[b]	Percent ARPS	Banks	Public Utilities	Others	Total
1982							
May–Dec.	$3.022	$4.274	70.7%	18	3	4	25
1983							
Jan.–June	$2.911	$5.046	57.7%	15	7	8	30
July–Dec.	$1.832	$2.167	84.5%	5	5	9	19
1984							
Jan.–June	$1.630	$2.119	76.9%	7	4	6	17
Total	$9.395	$13.606	69.1%	45	19	27	91

a. Source: Dillon, Read and Co., Inc., *Summary of Adjustable Rate Preferred Stocks,* June 1984.

b. Source: Total Preferreds, *Federal Reserve Bulletin,* various issues.

firms, such as Aetna Life and Casualty, BankAmerica, Ensearch, Manufacturers Hanover, McDonald's Corporation, Sears, and Student Loan Marketing ("Sallie Mae"), to mention just a few.

Table 25.2 shows the Standard and Poor's ratings of the ARPS issues at the time of issue. This information, which reflects the risk class of the security, is of interest to corporate money managers who seek a safe investment for temporarily idle cash balances.[4] Ninety percent of the issues were rated BBB– or higher, with the majority (65%) being rated A and BBB.

ARPS issues have generally *not* provided the investor with a conversion feature or a sinking fund provision. Of the 91 issues through June 1984, only five included a conversion feature and only nine had a sinking fund requirement. More recently, however, convertible adjustable preferred have started to receive increased attention as a means for ensuring that the investor can liquidate the investment for an amount equal to the original purchase price.[5]

Table 25.3 uses a sample of four issues to illustrate important ARPS characteristics. Notice in particular their reset formulas, collars, and considerable after-tax yield advantage. (It should be noted, however, that this yield calculation does not include gains or losses stemming from price fluctuations in the ARPS issues.) As long as market interest rates remain within the preferred issue's collar, there should be minimum variation in its price because of changes in market interest rates. However, if market rates continue to rise, once the maximum rate has been reached, then the ARPS price must

---

4. See Kamath et al. [9].

5. See Jaffee [7] and Cook and Hendershott [3].

TABLE 25.2   *Adjustable Rate Preferred Stock by S&P's Rating*[a]

Issue Rating	Number of Issues		Percent
AAA	3		3%
AA+	1		
AA	3	14	15%
AA−	10		
A+	10		
A	17	37	41%
A−	10		
BBB+	9		
BBB	13	28	31%
BBB−	6		
BB+	1		
BB	2	4	4%
BB−	1		
B+	2		2%
NR[b]	3		3%
	91		100%

a. Source: Standard and Poor's Corporation, *Standard and Poor's Stock Guide,* various issues, June 1982–October 1984.
b. Non-rated.

fall as it would with a conventional fixed dividend preferred. Conversely, if the minimum rate is reached, the ARPS price must rise if rates continue falling.

Since long-term rates have exceeded short-term rates in every month of our sample period (May 1982 through July 1984), the dividend rates have effectively been tied to long-term rates. The prescribed ceilings did not represent a constraint until May 1984, at which time there were five issues (out of the 91 issues that were outstanding) where the dividend rate prescribed by formula was *above* the ceiling. Thus, these five issues began trading as *fixed* rate preferred issues in May 1984.

III. Market Performance

ARPS, similar to any floating rate financial instrument, provides a means of transferring interest rate risk from investors to issuers. This fact should lead

TABLE 25.3   *Selected ARPS Issues* [a]

	Chase Man-hattan	U.S. Steel	Citicorp	Houston Lighting and Power
General Information				
1. Date issued	5/13/82	8/25/82	2/18/83	5/16/84
2. Size of issue (millions)	$200	$200	$400	$50
3. Standard and Poor's rating	AA	BBB+	AA	A+
4. Par value	$50	$50	$50	$100
5. Call features				
a. First call	6/1/87	9/30/87	2/1/88	4/1/89
b. Call price	$51.50	$51.50	$51.50	$103.00
Dividend Information				
1. Reset formula: basis points above (+) or below (−) appropriate U.S. Treasury rate	+50.0	+35.0	−412.5	−160.0
2. Collar				
a. Maximum rate	16.25%	15.75%	12.0%	13.0%
b. Minimum rate	7.50	7.50	6.0	6.5
3. Average monthly U.S. Treasury rates in month of issuance				
a. 90-day bills	12.09	8.68	8.11	9.52
b. 10-year rates − constant maturity	13.62	13.06	10.72	12.32
c. 20-year bonds − constant maturity	13.46	12.91	11.03	12.45
4. Pre-tax return based upon reset formula in Line 1 and appropriate rate in Line 3	14.12	13.41	6.91	10.85
5. After-tax return to corporate investor with a 46% marginal tax rate [b]	13.15	12.49	6.43	10.10
6. After-tax returns on other cash instruments in month of issuance [c]				
a. 90-day T-bills	6.53	4.69	4.38	5.14
b. 90-day commercial paper	7.25	5.48	4.50	5.31
c. 90-day CDs	7.45	5.73	4.51	5.44

a. Sources of information: (1) *Federal Reserve Bulletin,* selected issues. (2) Dillon, Read and Co., Inc., *Summary of Adjustable Rate Preferred Stocks,* June 1984.
b. Calculated as follows: $[1-(1-0.85)0.46] \times$ pre-tax return.
c. Calculated as follows: $[1-0.46] \times$ pre-tax return.

to lower yield (cost) than would be available with straight preferreds. Indeed, if ARPS price volatility were no greater than that found with traditional short-term money market securities, we would expect ARPS prices to be bid up so as to reduce their after-tax yields to comparable levels. In this section we examine market experiences with adjustable rate preferred stock, looking first at the history of resets and then at the investor's actual return and risk.

A. Resets over Time

Table 25.3 raises the question of what factors determine the reset values for new ARPS issues. Issuer quality would seem to have some impact, yet the Chase Manhattan issue was far more generous than the similarly rated Citicorp issue. Since Citicorp's ARPS came to market when interest rates were much lower, we might conclude that prevailing rates at the time of issue are also important. However, comparing the U.S. Steel issue to Houston Lighting and Power seems to contradict this hypothesis. Rates were roughly the same when both were issued, but U.S. Steel's reset was much higher.

The foregoing examples lead to the suspicion that the ARPS market in its early stage was an unsettled one. That is, the timing of the issue was a critical variable affecting the reset value. Table 25.4 offers additional evidence of this point. Here we see that between the second and third quarters of 1982, the average reset adjustment rate fell from 56.25 basis points *above* the prevailing Treasury index to 43.75 basis points *below* the Treasury rate index. Simultaneously, the average initial dividend rate fell 83 basis points from 14.21% to 13.38%. This pattern of decreasing reset rates and dividend rates continued through the fourth quarter of 1982 and extended into the first quarter of 1983. However, in the second quarter of 1983 both reset and dividend rates increased sharply. Each then showed an up-down pattern through the second quarter of 1984. Table 25.4 also shows that the 10-year T-note rate declined from its high of 13.82% in the second quarter of 1982 to its lowest value of 10.81% in the second quarter of 1983. From there, it steadily increased to 13.2% in the second quarter of 1984.

To investigate further the variations in resets, the following linear relationship is postulated:

$$R_j = a + \sum_{n=1}^{4} (b_n D_{nj}) + b_5 r_{jt} + b_6 t_j + b_7 t_j^2 + u_{jt} \tag{25.1}$$

where

R_j = the reset rate for security j measured in percentage points;

D_{nj} = dummy variables representing S&P's or Moody's rating for security j such that

$$D_{1j} = \begin{cases} 1 \text{ for AA rating} \\ 0 \text{ otherwise} \end{cases}$$

$$D_{2j} = \begin{cases} 1 \text{ for A rating} \\ 0 \text{ otherwise} \end{cases}$$

$$D_{3j} = \begin{cases} 1 \text{ for BBB rating} \\ 0 \text{ otherwise} \end{cases}$$

$$D_{4j} = \begin{cases} 1 \text{ for BB and B ratings} \\ 0 \text{ otherwise} \end{cases}$$

TABLE 25.4 *Quarterly ARPS Issue Data*

Quarter	No. of Issues	10-year T-Note Average Rate	Issue Rate			Reset (Basis Points Above [+] or Below [−] Treasury)		
			Average	Lowest	Highest	Average	Lowest	Highest
1982								
2nd	4	13.82%	14.213%	14.050%	14.500%	56.25	50	70
3rd	8	12.94%	13.379%	13.200%	13.500%	−43.75	−90	35
4th	13	10.72%	11.135%	10.000%	13.000%	−100.77	−225	25
1983								
1st	24	10.87%	10.085%	9.000%	13.250%	−233.96	−488	175
2nd	6	10.81%	11.667%	11.000%	13.000%	−26.67	−50	75
3rd	11	11.79%	10.681%	8.000%	13.450%	−121.73	−400	100
4th	8	11.90%	11.151%	9.250%	14.000%	−92.50	−280	75
1984								
1st	9	12.09%	10.392%	8.000%	12.500%	−135.00	−250	70
2nd	8	13.20%	10.975%	8.875%	11.375%	−208.00	−450	−25
Total/Average	91	12.02%	11.520%	10.153%	13.175%	−100.68	−243	67

r_t = U.S. Treasury bill rate in month t when security j was initially issued;

t_j = month in which security j was issued, where May 1982 = 0, ..., July 1984 = 27;

t_j^2 = time trend squared; and

u_{jt} = random error term.

The coefficients of the dummy variables measure the impact of quality differentials between AAA and other ratings (the unrated issues were excluded from the sample). *Ceteris paribus,* the lower the quality rating, the higher should be the reset. The maximum of the three treasury rates on the date of issue was included to reflect the possibility that yield spreads between fixed income securities of different quality vary with the general level of interest rates. There is empirical evidence indicating that during periods of rising interest rates and increasing economic uncertainty, yield spreads tend to increase.[6] If so, resets may also increase during such periods.

The third variable, the time trend, is included to see if a learning process took place in the ARPS market. The question here is whether the capital market took a protracted period of time to "season" the ARPS securities. If there was an immediate or very short seasoning process, we would not expect to see a significant trend in resets over time. On the other hand, if it takes time for market participants to settle on appropriate terms for a new instrument, the trend term may be significant. The squared trend term is added to provide a test for convergence in the reset over time. Note that the sign of b_7 should be opposite the sign of b_6 for the system to converge.

Ordinary least squares (OLS) was used to estimate Equation 25.1 using 86 ARPS issues for which complete data were available (of the 91 total issues, five could not be used, primarily because of the absence of quality ratings). The results were as follows:

$$R_j = \ \ 9.65 \ - \ 0.78D_1 + 0.28D_2 + 0.80D_3 + 2.35D_4$$
$$(4.49)^* \ \ (-1.24) \ \ \ (0.45) \ \ \ \ (1.28) \ \ \ \ (3.15)^*$$

$$- \ \ 0.70r_t \ - \ \ 0.51t_j \ + \ 0.02t_j^2 \tag{25.2}$$
$$(-4.91)^* \ \ (-6.81)^* \ \ \ (6.35)^*$$

$$R^2 = 0.52$$

The *t*-statistics are in parentheses and those with an asterisk (*) were significant at the 0.0001 level.

Only one of the four quality dummies had a statistically significant coefficient, and it was positive. This finding is consistent with the expectation that

---

6. The *t*-statistics are in parentheses.

the lower the quality rating, the higher the reset value. However, the difference between resets across quality ratings was only significant for the maximum span across ratings. The maximum Treasury rate at the time of issue had a significant and negative impact on reset values as the coefficient on r_t attests. Thus, other things remaining the same, the higher the interest rate upon which dividends were based, the lower or smaller the reset. Also, the trend terms were highly significant, indicating that the resets followed a negative but converging trend following the introduction of ARPS in May 1982. This latter finding is of interest because traditional economic wisdom suggests that innovators reap any rents inherent in their innovations, while later imitators only sweep up the crumbs. However, the results in Equation 25.2 suggest that later issuers of ARPS obtained more favorable terms than the initial issuers (i.e., they issued securities in the lower resets—hence, other things being the same, a lower required dividend rate). If it always takes time for market participants to become accustomed to an innovative financial instrument and to price it correctly, then this may act as a barrier to financial innovation.[7] Finally, an examination of the correlation matrix obtained from the preceding regression indicates no statistically significant correlations between quality ratings and time-trend variables. This finding was further confirmed in other regressions that expressed quality in rank form (AAA = 7, AA = 6, and so forth). The results do not support the contention that lower quality issuers are attracted first to "gimmick" securities. However, it should be remembered that the nature of ARPS as a substitute for traditional short-term investments demanded a high-quality issuer at the outset.

B. Analysis of Holding Period Returns

The objective in analyzing the returns on ARPS is to compare their performance with that of more conventional investments made by corporate money managers. To accomplish this, we collected data for a sample of ARPS issues that were not closely held and were issued prior to August 1, 1983. We then calculated after-tax holding period returns, and these returns were compared to those of short-term money market securities. In addition, we analyzed the performance of six mutual funds that hold only ARPS issues. These funds are of relatively recent origin, so not as much return data is available for funds as for most of the ARPS issues.

The Test Sample. The key determinant for inclusion of an ARPS issue in the sample was trading activity. Although 91 ARPS issues were outstanding as of July 1984, many of these securities were closely held and therefore not actively traded. For this reason, only 27 ARPS issues were selected for study. The names of the issuing firms and date of issue are included in the Appendix.

---

7. The authors would like to thank Robert A. Taggart for this suggestion.

Daily price and trading volume data were collected for each of the 27 sample firms from August 1, 1983, through July 31, 1984. Interest rate data were also collected for Treasury bills, commercial paper, and certificates of deposit for the sample period. Finally, monthly net asset values and dividend yields were collected for six ARPS mutual funds.

Measuring After-Tax Holding Period Returns. After-tax holding period returns for each ARPS issue were calculated using both 30- and 45-day holding periods. Technically, over the period of study, a corporation could qualify for the 85% dividend exclusion from federal taxes by holding an ARPS for only 16 days. However, we chose not to study this short time period for two reasons: First, the 1984 tax law revision lengthened the mandatory holding period to 45 days. Second, the experience of at least one brokerage house that makes a market in adjustable rate preferreds suggested that corporate money managers generally do not engage in ARPS investments for less than 30 days. Therefore, the 30-day period gave us a minimum holding period for investments in ARPS over the period when the 16-day requirement was in effect, and the 45-day period results provide some insight into the type of investment performance that might be expected under the new tax law.[8] The annualized after-tax holding period returns were calculated in the following manner:

$$\text{ATHPR}_t = \{[(P_t + D_t) - 0.46(P_t - P_{t-n}) - (0.15)(0.46)D_t]/P_{t-n}\}^{365/n} - 1 \qquad (25.3)$$

where

ATHPR_t = the after-tax annualized n-day holding period return for date t,

P_t = the stock price for the end of date t,

D_t = the dividend paid during the holding period ended with date t,

n = the number of days in the holding period (i.e., either 30 days or 45 days).

Annualized holding period returns were calculated using the preceding formula, beginning with August 1, 1983, and continuing through July 31, 1984. Based on these returns, means and standard deviations were then calculated for each security issue.

C. Performance Results: Individual ARPS Issues

Table 25.5 contains the annualized 30-day and 45-day holding period returns (after-tax) as well as the corresponding standard deviation and coefficient of

---

8. We have chosen not to examine specific trading strategies such as buying the stock three days before it went ex-dividend and selling it when the holder is entitled to the 85% dividend exclusion. The research to date (e.g., Joehnk et al. [8]) has demonstrated that any significant return advantage from such strategies requires the cash manager to assume sizable risks.

TABLE 25.5   *ARPS Holding Period Returns*

	30-Day Holding Period			45-Day Holding Period		
Security	Average Annualized HPR's	Return Standard Deviation	Coefficient of Variation	Average Annualized HPR's	Return Standard Deviation	Coefficient of Variation
ARPS						
1	7.34	13.90	1.89	5.71	9.47	1.66
2	3.57	10.15	2.84	12.50	5.42	0.43
3	10.67	9.70	0.91	10.98	9.90	0.90
4	5.00	23.38	4.68	1.77	24.13	13.63
5	3.98	16.47	4.14	2.79	12.81	4.59
6	4.73	20.17	4.26	3.69	11.81	3.20
7	−0.86	21.10	24.54	6.72	10.17	1.51
8	−0.40	26.75	66.88	4.50	32.81	7.29
9	9.75	18.62	1.91	10.43	9.08	0.87
10	6.67	18.99	2.85	1.90	15.51	8.16
11	3.08	22.98	7.46	7.85	18.00	2.29
12	7.67	23.80	3.10	1.08	23.08	21.37
13	14.38	19.83	1.38	13.77	18.19	1.32
14	6.17	21.75	3.53	9.23	27.29	2.96
15	7.98	16.23	2.03	7.40	14.53	1.96
16	−1.14	25.17	22.08	−3.48	25.10	7.21
17	−0.79	28.25	35.76	2.03	18.27	9.00
18	2.09	27.37	13.10	4.80	21.17	4.41
19	11.98	19.28	1.61	12.2	12.61	1.03
20	1.53	17.22	11.26	5.78	23.94	4.14
21	8.3	37.14	4.48	8.54	14.34	1.68
22	6.23	15.08	2.42	6.91	11.94	1.73
23	7.13	16.35	2.29	8.35	16.11	1.93
24	7.09	8.40	1.19	6.75	9.13	1.35
25	8.42	12.38	1.47	7.11	14.98	2.11
26	15.11	12.26	0.81	13.86	9.04	0.65
27	3.47	24.17	6.97	2.03	19.67	9.69
Averages	5.89	19.51		6.49	16.24	2.50

variation for each of the 27 ARPS issues studied. In comparing the 30-day and 45-day returns, the distributions are relatively similar. For the 30-day holding period, the annualizd returns ranged from −1.14% to 15.11%, with an average 5.89% return across the 27 securities. For the 45-day holding periods, the range varied from −3.48% to 13.86%, with the average being 6.49%. The cross-sectional averages of the individual ARPS standard deviations were 19.51% for the 30-day holding period and 16.26% for the 45-day holding period. Thus, the average returns were higher and the standard deviations lower for the 45-day holding period than for the 30-day periods, which accounts for the lower coefficients of variation for the longer holding periods.

TABLE 25.6 *A Comparison of ARPS and Money Market Returns*

Investment Type	After-Tax Average Annualized HPR's	Return Standard Deviation	Coefficient of Variation
ARPS			
30-day holding periods	5.89	19.51	3.31
45-day holding periods	6.49	16.24	2.50
Money-market instruments[a]			
Commercial paper	5.28	0.37	0.07
Certificate of deposit	5.48	0.45	0.08
Treasury bills	5.03	0.25	0.05

a. Average annualized returns assuming a 30-day holding period.

A more meaningful and interesting comparison comes when we look at the ARPS returns vis-à-vis the returns of conventional money market instruments during the same period. Such a comparison is made in Table 25.6 where the ARPS returns are compared to average returns for commercial paper, certificates of deposits, and Treasury bills. A 46% marginal tax rate was assumed in calculating the after-tax yields for the money market instruments, as was done in computing the after-tax returns on the ARPS issues.

A comparison of the average returns earned on the ARPS and the money market instruments reveals that the average returns for ARPS only slightly exceeded the average money market returns. The relatively unattractive average return of the ARPS issues in the 12-month period ending July 1984 was probably due to two factors: (1) the revaluation of ARPS issues following the revelation of the financial distress of Continental Illinois Bank in May 1984, and (2) the rise in interest rates on long-term Treasury notes to levels that pushed many ARPS issues to, or at least very near, their ceiling.

The variation in returns was much greater for the ARPS issues. Without exception, the standard deviations in after-tax holding period returns for the ARPS issues were larger than those of the money market securities. The relative variation is also reflected in the average coefficient of variation (i.e., standard deviation/mean) for the ARPS issues of 3.31 and 2.5 (30 days and 45 days, respectively), as compared with comparable statistics for the money market securities ranging from 0.05 to 0.08.[9] Note, however, that we are

9. Limiting the sample to nonbanking firms (these issues comprised 12 of the 27 issues) produced an average after-tax return for the ARPS of 0.0794 with an average standard deviation of 0.1561. This difference in the overall average and standard deviation in the nonbanking issues reflects the financial turmoil that affected the money market center banks during the Spring of 1984.

evaluating individual ARPS issues and not portfolios, such as the ARPS mutual funds, which should have much more attractive coefficients of variation because of the effect of diversification.

D. Performance Results: ARPS Mutual Funds

At this point we could reasonably conclude that investing in an individual issue of ARPS might provide slightly higher *average* after-tax returns than more traditional cash management investment alternatives over the time period studied. However, the ARPS investments experienced much larger standard deviations in their after-tax holding period returns. The corporate cash manager could have reduced this security-specific risk by diversifying holdings among several issues of ARPS or by simply investing in one of the ARPS mutual funds that appeared beginning in March 1983. These funds offer the same tax exemption as direct investment in ARPS but with two advantages. First, ARPS mutual funds adjust their dividend rate monthly so that the net asset value of the fund should be less volatile than an individual ARPS issue which "refloats" quarterly. Second, the cash manager gains the benefit of diversification and the corresponding reduction in variation of the portfolio's value over time. It also should be noted that prior to the 1984 tax law, these funds could invest up to 25% of their assets in nonARPS investments and the fund's dividends would still qualify for the 85% dividend exemption. This is no longer true, however, and it should be noted that the refund returns reported here were not fully derived from Adjustable Rate Preferred Stock investments but included short-term treasury securities and other investments.

Six ARPS mutual funds were selected for study based on the availability of performance data from those funds.[10] These funds included Colonial, Franklin, Mead, Pilgrim, Putnam, and Vanguard. Table 25.7 contains the mean, standard deviation, and coefficient of variation of the monthly after-tax hold-

---

10. As of the end of our test period (July 1984), the ARPS mutual funds were as follows:

Fund Name	Total Asset Value July 31, 1984 (in $ millions)
Pilgrim PAR Fund	$517
Colonial Corporate Cash Trust II	309
Putnam Corporate Cash Trust/Adj. Rate Portfolio	307
Prudential/Bache ARPS Fund	213
Mead Money Management Fund	192
Vanguard Qualified Dividend Portfolio III	136
First Investors Adjustable Preferred Fund	35
Franklin Corporate Cash Management Fund	17

Prudential and First Investors were excluded from the sample used in evaluating fund performance because of the recent origin of their ARPS funds.

TABLE 25.7 *ARPS Mutual Fund Returns*[a]

Fund Name	Mean Return	Standard Deviation	Coefficient of Variation	Number of Returns[a]
Colonial	4.4	13.1	2.94	5
Franklin	1.9	11.8	6.32	4
Mead	6.0	11.5	1.90	10
Pilgrim	9.5	16.0	1.68	12
Putnam	5.6	12.6	2.25	6
Vanguard	4.6	16.2	3.54	10

a. All returns were annualized and calculated on an after-tax basis using an assumed 46% tax rate; all fund data ended with July 1984 and began with August 1983 or the first month for which data were available.

ing period returns for each of the six funds. Note that the number of months for which data were available varies from four to 12 months depending on how long the fund had been in existence. The results are consistent with those of the individual ARPS issues. For example, the mean return for the sample of 27 ARPS issues, assuming 30-day holding periods, was 5.89%. The same statistic for the six funds ranged from 1.9% to 9.5% with an average of 5.33%. In addition, the standard deviations for the mutual fund returns ranged from 11.5% to 16.2%, which is indeed less than the cross-sectional average standard deviation for the individual ARPS issues (19.51%). This relatively modest reduction in the standard deviation in portfolio returns suggests that the returns earned on the individual ARPS issues are highly positively correlated—as one might expect given that their dividends are derived from the maximum of the *same* three Treasury interest rate series.

IV. Concluding Remarks

Adjustable Rate Preferred Stock was first issued beginning in May 1982 and provided corporate cash managers with what promised to be an attractive investment alternative. ARPS issues offered corporate investors an 85% exclusion from federal income taxes and a dividend rate that adjusted to the higher of the rate being earned on short-, intermediate-, or long-term government debt. On the other side of the market, issuers of Adjustable Rate Preferred Stock found them to be an attractive alternative to the issuance of common stock.

Reset values, an important feature of the offering terms, are inversely related to the quality rating of the ARPS. Moreover, the reset values have followed a negative but converging pattern over time.

The performance of ARPS issues has been disappointing to corporate money managers in that the ARPS issues have experienced substantially more price (and thus return) volatility than expected. When the investment performance of ARPS issues was compared with that of alternative money market investments, we found that ARPS holding period returns have been much more volatile than those of money market instruments normally held by corporate cash managers. In addition, we observed that the rates of return earned by ARPS mutual funds, although less volatile than the individual Adjustable Rate Preferred Stock issues, were also more volatile than those of money market instruments.

An area for further research is the study of the market returns earned by the recently issued convertible ARPS securities and money market ARPS. These securities are designed to reduce the price volatility experienced by the original ARPS issues, and they have begun to rapidly supplant the original Adjustable Rate Preferred Stock concept.[11]

---

11. For example, see Monroe [11].

References

1. Board of Governors of the Federal Reserve System, *Federal Reserve Bulletin,* (June 1982–October 1984).
2. K. C. Brown and S. L. Lummer, "The Cash Management Implications of a Hedged Dividend Capture Strategy," *Financial Management* (Winter 1984), pp. 7–17.
3. T. Q. Cook and P. H. Hendershott, "The Impact of Taxes, Risk and Relative Security Supplies on Interest Rate Differentials," *Journal of Finance* (Sept. 1978), pp. 1173–86.
4. Dillon, Read and Co., Inc., *Summary of Adjustable Rate Preferred Stocks,* January 1984.
5. J. D. Finnerty, "Preferred Stock Refunding Analysis: Synthesis and Extension," *Financial Management* (Autumn 1984), pp. 22–28.
6. L. Gitman, E. A. Moses, and I. T. White, "An Assessment of Corporate Cash Management Practices," *Financial Management* (Winter 1981), pp. 58–69.
7. D. M. Jaffee, "Cyclical Variations in the Risk Structure of Interest Rates," *Journal of Monetary Economics* (July 1985), pp. 309–325.
8. M. D. Joehnk, O. D. Bowlin, and J. W. Petty, "Preferred Dividend Rolls: A Viable Strategy for Corporate Money Managers?" *Financial Management* (Summer 1980), pp. 78–87.
9. R. R. Kamath, S. Khaksari, H. Hylton Meier, and John Winklepleck, "Management of Excess Cash: Practices and Developments," *Financial Management* (Autumn 1985), pp. 70–77.
10. W. R. McDaniel, "Sinking Fund Preferred Stock," *Financial Management* (Spring 1984), pp. 45–52.
11. A. Monroe, "Money Market Preferred Funds Favor with Debt Issuers Source '84 Introduction," *The Wall Street Journal* (August 13, 1985), p. 39.

Appendix: ARPS Sample

Security Company Names	Issue Date
1. Aetna Ins. Co.	07-28-82
2. Allied Corp.	01-31-83
3. American General Corp.	11-04-82
4. Bankamerica	10-22-82
5. Chase Manhattan	01-27-82
6. Chemical Bank	05-25-82
7. Chemical Bank	05-11-82
8. Citicorp 2nd Ser.	08-12-82
9. Ensearch	09-02-82
10. 1st Chicago Corp.	10-15-82
11. 1st Chicago Corp.	02-17-83
12. 1st City B. C. Texas	08-24-82
13. Fleet Financial	02-15-83
14. Illinois Power	02-24-83
15. Irving Bank Corp.	11-18-82
16. Manufacturers Hanover	05-28-82
17. Manufacturers Hanover	07-22-82
18. Marine Midland	03-03-83
19. Morgan, J.P.	02-23-82
20. Niagara Mohawk Power	01-19-83
21. Norstar Bancorp	02-03-83
22. Norwest Corp.	07-20-82
23. Norwest Corp.	07-30-82
24. Republic N.Y. Corp.	05-14-82
25. Texas East Trans.	10-05-82
26. U.S. Steel	08-25-82
27. Wells Fargo	03-08-83

PART V

Regulatory and Accounting

26

The Regulation of
Commodity-Linked Debt
and Depository Instruments*

*James V. Jordan,** Robert S. Mackay,**
& Eugene J. Moriarty***

I. Introduction

Increasingly during the 1980s, firms have been designing commodity-linked debt and depository instruments, even in the face of considerable regulatory uncertainty.[1] Commodities regulation, which is primarily known for its role in regulating futures exchanges, affects the design of commodity-linked instruments. A potentially large array of instruments are affected because the term "commodity" as defined in the Commodity Exchange Act (CEA) includes not only agricultural products, raw materials, and precious metals, but also interest rates, inflation rates, stock indices, currencies, and the like. The emergence of commodity-linked instruments created difficult jurisdictional and regulatory questions for the Commodity Futures Trading Commission

*A shorter version of this paper is forthcoming in the *Journal of Applied Corporate Finance*.
**During preparation of the initial draft of this paper the authors served, respectively, as Consultant, Office of the Chairman; Chief of Staff, Office of the Chairman; and Director of Research, Division of Economic Analysis at the Commodity Futures Trading Commission. The views expressed here are the authors' and do not necessarily reflect the views of the Commission.
1. Complex securities are not unique to the 1980s. Rawls and Smithson (1989) describe securities issued by the Confederacy as dual-currency (French francs and British pounds), cotton-indexed bonds.

(CFTC) because, under one interpretation of the CEA, instruments with futureslike components would have to be prohibited as off-exchange futures contracts and those with optionlike components would have to be regulated by the agency. Such a restrictive interpretation could impede legitimate financial innovation as well as bring the agency into jurisdictional conflict with the Securities and Exchange Commission (SEC) and banking authorities.

The CFTC has addressed these issues in a series of recent releases (CFTC [1989a, b, c]).[2] Potential issuers (and investors) must understand both the economics of commodity-linked instruments and the regulatory framework applied to them. Section II presents an economic framework for analyzing "hybrid" instruments.[3] Section III reviews the development of commodities regulation, and Section IV details the CFTC's recently promulgated regulatory approach. Section V explains the implications of the approach for the design (i.e., financial engineering) of instruments. Section VI analyzes possible motives for the issuance and purchase of these complex instruments, and Section VII is a conclusion.

II. An Economic Framework for Analyzing Hybrid Debt and Depository Instruments

The interpretation and regulations issued by the CFTC were made necessary by the creation of new financial instruments that embed commodity components similar to commodity futures and option positions in debt securities and bank deposits. Three examples that illustrate hybrid design as well as the regulatory questions are Standard Oil of Ohio (SOHIO) oil-indexed notes, Wells Fargo gold-indexed certificates of deposit (CDs), and principal exchange rate linked securities (PERLS) issued by several firms.

A commodity optionlike payoff embedded in a bond issue was offered by SOHIO in the summer of 1986. In addition to a coupon instrument, the package included two zero coupon notes, each of which would trade separately. At maturity the notes paid stated principal plus an additional payment equal to the value of 170 barrels of oil times the excess of the price of oil over $25 per barrel capped at $40 per barrel. The notes appear to be both securities, which are regulated by the SEC, and commodity (oil) options, which are regulated by the CFTC. Although zero coupon nonhybrid debt had been issued prior to this time, the coupling of such debt issued at or near

---

2. The CFTC (1989d) has also recently addressed swap transactions, another difficult off-exchange issue. Swaps are not discussed in this paper.

3. The CFTC refers to commodity-linked instruments as hybrid instruments since they can be viewed as combining elements of straight debt and depository instruments with commodity components that have commodity futureslike and optionlike characteristics.

par with an optionlike payoff raised the question of whether this instrument was simply a means of offering an off-exchange commodity option outside the existing regulatory framework.[4]

Although the CFTC took no action against SOHIO, this instrument first brought into focus the difficult regulatory issues.

The "Gold Market Certificate" offered by Wells Fargo Bank provided for the deposit of from $2500 to $1,000,000 plus a fee or premium. At the end of the deposit period, the depositor received the deposit plus a return, depending on the fee paid, of either 100% or 50% of the increase in the price of gold. This instrument appears to be both a certificate of deposit and a commodity (gold) option, thus crossing banking and commodity regulatory boundaries. In 1987, the CFTC took its first hybrid-related enforcement action against this instrument. The case was settled under a consent decree enjoining Wells Fargo from issuing the certificates.

The third type of instrument was issued in 1988 and had principal and/or coupon payments indexed to foreign currencies. For example, in the PERLS, the payment at maturity was defined as principal plus the difference between the spot value of a stated amount of foreign currency at maturity and the spot value at the time of issue. This design introduced an embedded futures-like component referenced not to a futures price but to the current spot price. The reference to the spot price built a current value into the component and allowed the issuer to set a higher or lower coupon than the coupon on comparable nonhybrid debt. The embedding of a futureslike component raised the question of whether the instrument was simply a means of offering an off-exchange futures contract outside the existing regulatory framework.[5] In two separate instances, the CFTC took a no-action stance on PERLS-type instruments indexed to the dollar/yen exchange rate.

An economic framework for analyzing hybrids can be illustrated using these instruments. Each consists of a straight debt component plus a commodity-related component that has a payoff similar to a futures or option contract. The value of a hybrid instrument can be decomposed as

$$\text{Hybrid Value} = \text{Straight Debt Value} + \text{Commodity Component Value} \qquad (26.1)$$

For a given maturity, default risk, and liquidity, the value of the straight debt component depends on the bond coupon. For a coupon rate equal to

---

4. The CEA generally permits the trading of only commodity options subject to CFTC regulation. The CFTC generally requires that commodity options be traded on or subject to the rules of contract markets (i.e., exchanges) designated by the Commission.

5. With only a few exceptions, the CEA requires that transactions in commodity futures contracts occur on or subject to the rules of contract markets (i.e., exchanges) designated by the CFTC.

the required yield to maturity on comparable debt, the straight bond will sell at par.

The commodity component value depends on the structure of the commodity-related payoff. The SOHIO and Wells Fargo designs have commodity optionlike payoffs. The SOHIO payoff function, which is representative, is

$$N[\max(0, S_m - X)]$$

where N is the number of units of the commodity, S_m the spot price of the commodity at hybrid instrument maturity, and X is the exercise price.[6]

A regulator viewing the hybrid from the perspective of the CEA and trying to discern its nature would be interested in the degree to which the hybrid is more of a "commodity play" than a conventional debt instrument. Is the instrument predominately a commodity option or predominately a debt instrument? The value of an embedded option component relative to the value of the hybrid would provide one measure of predominance that could be used for evaluating how the instrument should be regulated.

In the case of a PERLSlike payoff, the question of the extent to which the instrument is a "commodity play" is more complex. It is helpful to first consider the value of a futures contract. The payoff on a (long) futures contract may be written

$$N(S_m - F)$$

where F is the current futures price. The value of a futures contract, when the contract is initiated, is zero.[7] In the actual PERLS design, however, the payoff was

$$N(S_m - S)$$

where S is the current spot price. For a commodity for which $S < F$, this payoff has a positive current value, since the expected value of $S_m - S$ must be greater than the expected value of $S_m - F$ and both payoffs have the same risk, namely the variation in the spot price at maturity. By choice of reference price, the PERLSlike design can build a valuable commodity component into the instrument. This design allows great flexibility to an issuer. For example, issuers can issue a bond at par that has a lower coupon than the market yield to maturity, because the commodity component value makes up for the lower straight debt value. Similarly, if the commodity price is such that $S > F$, the commodity component will have a negative value and

---

6. For SOHIO, $N = 170$ barrels and $X = \$25$. The cap at $40 is in its effect similar to a short option position. We have omitted the cap for simplicity in this illustration.

7. This is a well-known property of futures contracts. The contract can be initiated with no expenditure of funds except a good-faith margin deposit. F is the delivery price for the commodity in the future, not the current expenditure. Here we are using the term "futures price" somewhat loosely. This is clarified in Section V.

issuers can set a higher than market coupon. Also, a reverse PERLS-type design is possible in which the commodity component is in effect similar to a short commodity position.

Although the relative value of the commodity position may serve a useful evaluative role when a reference price other than the futures price is used, this criterion is more problematic when the futures price is used as the reference price. For example, a hybrid could be designed with the futures price as the reference price so that no value would be imputed to the commodity component. However, with a very large value of N, the actual commodity payoff could easily dwarf the straight bond payments. Because of this consideration the CFTC employed other means to constrain the commodity payoff in such cases; the details are covered in Section V.

In order to fully understand the regulatory approach, it is useful to understand the historical development of commodities regulation. A brief overview is provided in the next section.

III. The Regulatory Environment

Regulation of futures trading began with the Grain Futures Act in 1922, which was revised and renamed the Commodity Exchange Act in 1936.[8] The CEA prohibits the trading of futures contracts other than on a designated "contract market," or futures exchange. The requirement for exchange trading of futures contracts reflects both a recognition of the economic benefits of trading in contracts for future delivery, including risk reduction (through hedging) and price discovery, and long-standing concerns about speculation, price manipulation, and customer abuse in unregulated futures markets.[9] Specific salutary characteristics of exchange trading include reduction of default risk, open price determination, rapid and wide price dissemination, enhancement of liquidity, customer protection, and market protection.

In 1974 the CFTC was created and given exclusive jurisdiction to enforce the CEA. In the same legislation that created the CFTC, the definition of "commodity" was broadened to include virtually everything on which a futures contract can be traded. Due to the emergence of new products, this broader definition can be seen in retrospect as an important development

---

8. An earlier attempt at regulation, the Futures Trading Act of 1921, had been declared unconstitutional by the Supreme Court. See Markham (1987) for a review of futures regulation and Gilberg (1986) for a comparison of the regulation of financial instruments under securities and commodities law.

9. The articles by Peck (1985), Silber (1985), and Stein (1985) review the economic benefits. Markham (1987), particularly in Chapter 1, reviews the early history of alleged and documented problems.

leading up to the CFTC's recent interpretation of the CEA.[10] Prior to the 1974 amendments, hybrids indexed to such commodities as currencies and interest rates clearly would not have been subject to commodities law.

Commodity options, which include both options on futures contracts and options on the underlying commodities, are regulated under the CEA but in a different framework than futures. Options on commodities enumerated in the 1936 CEA, all of which are agricultural commodities, were absolutely banned by that act. Options on "nonenumerated" commodities were not addressed by the CEA.[11] In the early 1970s, options on nonenumerated commodities such as silver, platinum, and coffee were the source of millions of dollars in customer losses due to option sellers' failures to satisfy exercises. With the broadening of the commodity definition in 1974, Congress gave the CFTC the authority to regulate option trading in all nonenumerated commodities. At that time the CFTC allowed off-exchange trading of these options to continue. But in 1978, following further instances of customer abuse,[12] Congress imposed a moratorium on all options trading pending the development of a pilot program for exchange trading by the CFTC. The Commission had the authority, after evaluating the pilot program, to permit exchange and off-exchange trading of commodity options. Also, the ban on "enumerated" commodity options no longer applied. By 1986, following successful pilot programs, CFTC regulations permitted the *exchange trading* of all commodity options.

The important distinction between futures and options regulation, which affects the CFTC's approach to hybrid instruments, is that off-exchange futures contracts are prohibited by act of Congress whereas the CFTC has broad latitude to regulate the trading of commodity options both on and off exchange. Prior to the hybrid releases, only dealer and trade options were exempted from the exchange-trading requirement.[13]

---

10. See Marshall Hanbury's remarks in CFTC (1988).

11. The 1921 act that was declared unconstitutional had sought to stop option trading with a prohibitive tax. Some exchanges and some states prohibited options trading throughout the period prior to the CEA. The 1934 National Industrial Recovery Act included a Code of Fair Competition for grain exchanges, which required an options ban. See Markham (1987), p. 20 and p. 24.

12. See Markham (1987), pp. 79–80 and 194–195.

13. The dealer option exemption applies to options granted by a person who was in the business of granting options on a physical commodity and in the business of buying, selling, producing, or otherwise using that commodity as of May 1, 1978. The trade option exemption applies to off-exchange commodity option transactions that are offered by a person who "has a reasonable basis to believe that the option is offered to a producer, processor or commercial user of, or a merchant handling the commodity underlying the option, or the products or by-products thereof, and that such producer, processor, commercial user or merchant is offered or enters into the commodity option transaction solely for purposes related to its business as such." (CFTC [1988], Rule 37.4(a) 17 CFR 32.4(a).)

The recent actions by the CFTC attempt to avoid unnecessary restriction of securities innovation while retaining the applicability of commodities regulation to hybrids with significant commodities elements.[14]

IV. The New Regulatory Framework for Commodity-Linked Instruments

In January 1989 the CFTC (1989b) issued a statutory interpretation of the CEA that excludes certain categories of hybrid instruments from the Commission's jurisdiction. This "jurisdictional exclusion" from regulation under the CEA applies to all hybrids meeting certain criteria, including hybrids with both futureslike and optionlike components. On the same date, the CFTC (1989a) proposed an exemption from options regulations that applies only to optionlike hybrids that would not already have met the criteria for jurisdictional exclusion. If such optionlike hybrids meet other, more option-specific criteria, they are exempted from the requirement for exchange trading. This "regulatory exemption" was adopted with the issuance of final rules in July (CFTC [1989c]). The details of the exclusion and the exemption are given below.

Jurisdictional Exclusion

The statutory interpretation recognizes a jurisdictional exclusion for two broad categories of hybrid instruments: (1) debt securities within the meaning of Section 2(1) of the Securities Act of 1933 and (2) time deposits within the meaning of 12 CFR 204.2(c)(1) offered by a bank whose deposits are insured by the Federal Deposit Insurance Corporation (FDIC) and marketed and sold directly to a customer. Hybrid instruments in these two categories are excluded from regulation under the CEA if the instruments:

1. Are indexed to a commodity on no greater than a one-to-one basis;

---

14. In contrast to the exchange-trading orientation of commodities regulation, securities regulation has little to say about where stocks and bonds are traded. The greatest dollar volume of bond trading takes place not on the organized exchanges but "over the counter," through a network of brokers and dealers electronically linked. These markets are regulated by the SEC, and the legal and regulatory philosophy is oriented primarily toward disclosure of information about the issuer of a security, which is accomplished through "registration" of the issue in accordance with the Securities Act of 1933. Even registration is not required for certain "exempt securities" and "private placements." Exempt securities include U.S. Government and municipal securities, securities issued by or guaranteed by a bank, and short-term commercial paper. Private placements are sales of securities to "accredited investors," which include certain large institutional investors and wealthy individuals. Exemption from registration does not also mean exemption from other provisions of securities laws, particularly anti-fraud provisions.

2. Limit the maximum loss on the instrument to the commodity-independent face value or coupon or both;

3. Have a commodity-independent yield at the time of issue of at least 50% but no more than 150% of the yield on a comparable nonhybrid instrument;

4. Do not have a commodity component that is severable from the instrument;

5. Do not call for delivery of a commodity by means of an instrument specified in the rules of a futures exchange; and

6. Are not marketed as being or having the characteristics of a futures contract or commodity option.

Items 4, 5, and 6 in this list need little explanation. Essentially, these are intended to maintain a clear separation between the excluded hybrids and exchange-traded commodity contracts and to limit some possible effects of hybrids on those exchange markets. The nonseverability requirement prevents the separate off-exchange trading of a pure commodity contract. The restriction on deliverable instruments provides some protection against interference with deliverable supplies for settlement of exchange-traded contracts. It should be noted, however, that this restriction is not intended to interfere with the ability of issuers to develop physical delivery alternatives to cash settlement. The restriction on marketing prevents misleading representations of the essential nature of the instruments, their legal status, and the regulatory supervision to which they are subject.

The first three items go to the economic characteristics of the hybrids and are designed to address whether the instruments are predominately debt securities or bank depository instruments rather than commodity futures or commodity option contracts. Restricting any indexing to no greater than a one-to-one basis prevents the design of an instrument that offers the equivalent of a levered position in the underlying commodity such that, for example, a 1% increase in the commodity price would produce a 10% increase in the commodity-dependent payment of the hybrid. This reduces the extent to which a hybrid instrument can be a "commodity play." Restricting the maximum loss due to a commodity price movement maintains the similarity between a hybrid instrument and traditional debt and depository instruments. It would indeed be unprecedented if a bond or bank deposit subjected the holder to a potential call for additional funds from the issuer.

The role of the commodity-independent yield (CIY) restriction, particularly the upper bound, may not be immediately obvious. The CIY is a yield-based indicator of the proportion of the value of the instrument that is not commodity related. A CIY lower than the yield on comparable nonhybrid debt at issuance indicates that the commodity component has a positive value and that non-commodity-related interest payments have been reduced. A CIY greater than the comparable nonhybrid yield at issuance indicates that the commodity interest has a negative value and that the non-commodity-related interest payments have been increased. Thus, the CIY criterion acts to preserve the straight-debt character of a hybrid by restricting the absolute value of the commodity interest that can be built into the instrument at issuance.

The one-to-one and CIY criteria also work in tandem to constrain commodity-related value in an instrument excluded from commodity regulation. As just noted, the CIY criterion constrains the embedded commodity value at the time of issue. The one-to-one criterion restricts the potential impact of commodity price changes on the value of the hybrid after issue.

The application and the effects of the one-to-one, maximum-loss, and commodity-independent yield criteria are illustrated by examples in the next section. Before proceeding to these examples, we turn to the regulatory exemption.

Regulatory Exemption

The exemption applies to debt securities, preferred equity securities, and bank deposits. Both securities registered in accordance with the Securities Act of 1933 and those qualifying for specified exemptions from such registration are included. Also exempt are most demand deposits and transaction accounts (1) offered by financial institutions whose deposits are insured by a U.S. government agency or government-chartered corporation, or (2) offered by a foreign bank in the U.S. (if supervised by Federal banking authorities). The intent of this section is to exempt registered securities, securities that are exempt from registration because of other indicia of soundness, and transactions for which such protections should be unnecessary, such as commercial paper and time deposits offered by banks with deposits insured by the FDIC.

Such securities would be exempt if the value of the implied option premium is no greater than 40% of the issue price of the instrument and if any one of the following performance requirements are satisfied:

1. The instrument has been rated in one of the four highest categories by a nationally recognized rating organization, or if not rated, other comparable instruments of the issuer have been so rated;
2. The issuer maintains at least $100 million in net worth;
3. The issuer maintains cover equal to the amount of its commodity-related commitments; and
4. The instrument is eligible for insurance by a U.S. government agency or government-chartered agency.

The exemptive criteria include the same restrictions on severability, deliverable instruments, and marketing as the exclusion criteria.

The implied option premium criterion is similar to the CIY criterion applied in the jurisdictional exclusion. However, since the exemption test is specific to optionlike instruments, measurement of the relative option component in terms of an option premium is a natural choice. The implied option premium is defined as the difference between the present value of the straight debt portion of the hybrid instrument and the issue price of the hybrid instrument. The choice of a 40% maximum at the time of issue reflects an attempt to limit the proportion of the hybrid's value that is due to a commodity optionlike payoff.

The performance requirement is designed to provide some assurance that the issuer of the hybrid instrument will be able to meet the obligations implied by the embedded option component.

Under this exemption, then, hybrid instruments with a limited option component, subject to an alternative regulatory framework, and satisfying several additional requirements including a performance requirement may be traded off-exchange pursuant to the alternate regulatory scheme.

V. Effects of Criteria on Hybrid Instrument Design

The application of the criteria is best explained by examples. First, we present an example of a relatively simple design of a foreign-currency, principal-indexed hybrid that has a long futureslike commodity component and that meets the exclusion test. We discuss in detail the influence of the one-to-one, maximum-loss, and commodity-independent yield criteria on this design. Simple rules for design parameters that keep the instrument within the exclusion criteria are developed. The use of optionlike components in addition to futureslike components is also discussed in the context of this initial example. Second, we introduce variations in the way a futureslike commodity component might be defined and how these variations would fare under the exclusion. Third, we discuss coupon indexing. Fourth, we discuss short, futureslike commodity components. Finally, we show a typical form of an optionlike component and the application of the exclusionary and exemptive criteria to this type of hybrid. The implied option premium criterion is examined in detail.

The first example is a British-pound, principal-indexed bond with a long futureslike commodity component and a coupon rate equal to a comparable nonhybrid coupon rate. This instrument has a $1,000 principal, a 10% coupon rate, and a 5-year maturity. This coupon is assumed to be the same that the issuer would pay on nonhybrid debt of comparable maturity and indentures.

In order to keep the example uncomplicated, it is assumed that the coupon is stated as a percentage of the fixed principal, not the indexed principal. Indexation of the principal is defined as an adjustment to principal equal to the change in the dollar value of 500 British pounds from the reference price of the pounds at issue to the spot price at maturity.

A key feature of this example is that the reference price is chosen to be equal to the price for future delivery of the commodity that could be obtained on a futures or forward contract of the same maturity as the bond maturity at the time of issue. We adopt a generic terminology, *market forward price,* for this price.[15,16] This choice for the reference price affects the maximum loss and the CIY as described in detail below.

The indexed principal, H^*, may be written as

$$H^* = 1000 + 500(S_m - F) \qquad (26.2)$$

where S_m and F represent the price of pounds at maturity and the market forward price of pounds at issue, respectively. The commodity-independent payments of this hybrid are the coupons of $100 and $1000 principal. The commodity-dependent payment is $500(S_m - F)$.

A general expression for the indexed principal in this form of hybrid is

$$H^* = H + N(S_m - R) \qquad (26.3)$$

where H is the principal, N is the number of units of the commodity, and R is the reference price. The commodity-dependent payment is $N(S_m - R)$.

One-to-One Criterion

Under certain conditions, this bond has one-to-one commodity indexing as defined in the exclusion. One-to-one indexing means that the absolute value of the change in any commodity-dependent payment as a percentage of the associated commodity-independent payment (in this example, the principal) may not exceed the absolute value of the percentage change in the commodity price to which the payment is indexed, which in this example is the

---

15. This terminology is generic in the context of the economics literature that distinguishes futures and forward prices principally on the basis of daily resettlement (e.g., Cox, Ingersoll, and Ross [1985]). It is not intended to evoke the regulatory distinction between futures and forward contracts.

16. Theoretically, futures prices may differ from forward prices due to the effect of daily resettlement, default risk, and liquidity. Whether a futures or a forward price is the appropriate reference price depends on the maturity of the hybrid instrument and the particular commodity market. In some cases, futures or forward prices for contracts with the same maturity as the hybrid would be directly observable. In other cases, the issuer would estimate a futures or forward price for the commodity.

current spot price.[17] For example, suppose the spot price of a pound at the time of issue is \$2 and the market forward price at the time of issue is \$1.90. If the spot price at maturity were to be \$2.02, then there would be a 1% increase in the commodity price. The change in the commodity-dependent payment for that 1% assumed change in the spot price would be calculated by comparing the value of the commodity-dependent payment at the spot price at issue, 500(\$2 − \$1.90) = \$50, with its value at the assumed spot price at maturity, 500(\$2.02 − \$1.90) = \$60. This \$10 increase is 1% of the principal of \$1000, so the one-to-one criterion is not exceeded.

A general form of the one-to-one criterion (for the form of hybrid considered in this example) is

$$\frac{N(S_m - R) - N(S - R)}{H} \leq \frac{(S_m - S)}{S} \tag{26.4}$$

where S is the spot commodity price at issue. The term on the left of the inequality is the change in the commodity-dependent payment from its value at the spot price at issue as a percentage of principal. The term on the right is the percentage change in the commodity price. This expression is satisfied only if

$$NS \leq H \tag{26.5}$$

In words, if the value at the issue spot price of the number of units of the commodity specified in the commodity-dependent payment (NS) does not exceed the principal of the instrument then the one-to-one criterion is satisfied. In the example, this means that the instrument meets the one-to-one criterion at an issue spot price of \$2 if the number of pounds specified in the contract for adjusting the principal does not exceed 500. Note that this rule holds for any reference price.

Maximum Loss Criterion

Under certain conditions, this instrument has a maximum potential loss no greater than the principal. The maximum potential loss occurs when the spot price at maturity is zero ($S_m = 0$). In the example, the commodity-dependent payment at $S_m = 0$ is −500 times the forward price (−500F). If the forward price exceeds \$2, this loss will exceed the principal.

In general (for long futureslike positions) the maximum loss criterion is satisfied if

$$H \geq NR \tag{26.6}$$

that is, if the value at the reference price of the number of units of the commodity is less than principal. Note that this rule does not involve current or

---

17. Indexing to a price other than the current spot price is not precluded by the interpretation. However, most of the instruments seen up to now have been indexed with respect to the current spot price.

future spot prices (unless one of these is used as a reference price). If the hybrid instrument were designed so that this condition were violated, the maximum loss criterion would have to be met by specifying an additional contractual restriction. A common restriction would simply specify that a reduction in principal due to indexation could not exceed the principal amount. This would introduce an optionlike component into the instrument.

Commodity-Independent Yield Criterion

Coupon Rate, Yield to Maturity, and Commodity-Independent Yield. In order to understand this criterion, it is important to keep three definitions distinct. These are coupon rate, yield to maturity, and commodity-independent yield (CIY). The *coupon rate* is defined as the coupon (or interest payment on a bank deposit) as a percentage of principal.[18] In the example, the coupon payment is $100 per year (typically, $50 semiannually) and the coupon rate is 10%. The *yield to maturity* (YTM) is the internal rate of return of the stream of payments on a bond, given the bond price. The internal rate of return (in other contexts, also known as the "dollar-weighted" return) is computed as y in the formula

$$P = cH(A_{y,T}) + \frac{H}{(1+y)^T} \qquad (26.7)$$

where P is the issue price, c is the coupon rate, T is the number of periods to maturity, and $A_{y,T}$ is the value of an annuity of $1 for T periods at rate y.[19]

When the bond price equals the principal ($P = H$), the yield to maturity equals the coupon rate ($y = c$). A straight bond selling at par satisfies this condition. Bonds issued (or selling) at a discount have $y > c$; bonds issued (or selling) at a premium have $y < c$. The "estimated annual yield at the time of issuance for a comparable non-hybrid or depository instrument issued by the same or similar issuer"[20] specified in the interpretation is the yield to maturity on the comparable nonhybrid debt. In this context, P, c, and y in (26.7) may be taken as the price, coupon rate, and yield on comparable nonhybrid debt.

The CIY is the internal rate of return of the stream of *commodity-independent* payments on a hybrid debt instrument computed as if that stream were purchased at the issue price. Thus, the CIY is computed from

---

18. In common terminology, the coupon rate is not the same as the coupon yield, which is the coupon as a percentage of the bond (or hybrid) price. The coupon yield is analogous to the dividend yield on preferred or common stock.

19. The annuity factor $A_{y,T}$ is defined by

$$A_{y,T} = \frac{1}{1+y} + \frac{1}{(1+y)^2} + \cdots + \frac{1}{(1+y)^T} = \frac{1-(1+y)^{-T}}{y}$$

20. CFTC (1989b).

$$P' = c'H(A_{\text{CIY},T}) + \frac{H}{(1+\text{CIY})^T} \qquad (26.8)$$

where P' is the hybrid issue price and c' is the hybrid coupon rate. The CIY will be equal to the comparable nonhybrid yield if the hybrid issue price (P') equals the comparable nonhybrid issue price (P) and the commodity-independent payments ($c'H$ and H) are identical to comparable nonhybrid payments (cH and H).

When the embedded commodity component of a hybrid instrument is a futureslike component with a reference price equal to the market forward price, the value of the embedded commodity component at issue is zero. Thus, the value of the hybrid instrument must equal the value of the non-hybrid component ($P' = P$), and this can only be achieved by setting the hybrid coupon equal to the nonhybrid coupon ($c' = c$). The commodity-independent payments will then be identical to the nonhybrid payments, and the CIY will be equal to the comparable nonhybrid yield. This is true regardless of whether the nonhybrid would be issued at par. For example, it is valid for a zero coupon instrument.

In the example, the coupon rate (c), the comparable nonhybrid yield (y), and the CIY are all 10% so the CIY criterion is clearly satisfied—the CIY is at least 50% but no more than 150% of the comparable nonhybrid yield.

CIY as a Limit on Embedded Commodity Value. A reference price less than the market forward price ($R < F$) creates an embedded commodity component with positive current value of $(F-R)(1+y)^{-T}$. This commodity component may be defined as an "in-the-money" commodity component.[21] In order for the hybrid to sell at the nonhybrid issue price, the coupon rate must be reduced so that the value of the nonhybrid instrument is reduced. The CIY, or the internal rate of return of the reduced coupon and unadjusted principal at an issue price of P (see Equation 26.8), will then be less than the yield to maturity of comparable nonhybrid debt.

A reference price greater than the market forward price ($R > F$) creates an embedded commodity component with negative value of $-(F-R)(1+Y)^{-T}$. This is an "out-of-the-money" component. The coupon rate must be increased

---

21. If this were not true an arbitrage opportunity would be available. Suppose an in-the-money futures or forward contract at price $R < F$ could be obtained for zero purchase price. This forward contract could be purchased and a conventional (at-the-money) forward contract at price F could be sold (for zero). At delivery, the profit on the in-the-money contract would be $S_m - R$ and the profit on the conventional contract would be $(S_m - F)$ for a certain net profit of $F - R$. The market could not be in equilibrium if this certain cash flow could be obtained for zero investment. The value of this investment is the discounted value of $F - R$, and since the value of the conventional futures contract is zero, the value of the in-the-money contract is the discounted value of $F - R$. For an in-the-money component embedded in a hybrid, the payment depends on the creditworthiness of the borrower, so the appropriate discount rate is y.

FIGURE 26.1 *Commodity Independent Yield (CIY) and Reference Price (R)*

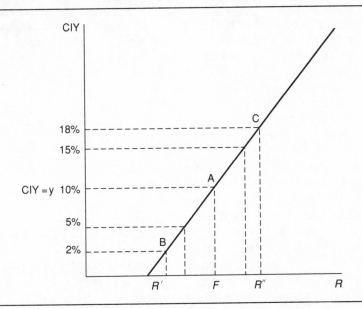

in order to increase the value of the nonhybrid component. The CIY will then be greater than the comparable nonhybrid yield.

The CIY criterion limits the value of the embedded commodity component. Figure 26.1 illustrates this graphically. The CIY is plotted on the vertical axis, and the reference price (R) on the horizontal axis. The point labeled A is the CIY–R combination of the example, in which CIY $= y = 10\%$ and R is the market forward price (F). The point labeled B is the CIY–R combination in which the reference price is R', less than the market forward price. The CIY for this case is assumed to be 2%, an unacceptable CIY under the exclusion. The vertical distance between points A and B, eight percentage points, is a yield-based indicator of the value embedded in the futureslike commodity component. The point labeled C is the CIY–R combination in which the reference price is R'', greater than the market forward price. The CIY for this case is assumed to be 18%, an unacceptable CIY. The difference of eight percentage points from the comparable nonhybrid yield is a measure of the negative value of the commodity component.

Figure 26.1 is useful for illustrating several considerations in the design of hybrids to meet the CIY criterion. One consideration is the inclusion of optionlike components in addition to futureslike components. Consider point A. If a long optionlike component were included in this hybrid, its value would increase the value of the hybrid unless the coupon were decreased.

The coupon could be decreased until the CIY were 5%, and this permissible 5% decrease in the CIY limits the value of the embedded optionlike component. A point to be emphasized here is that the CIY criterion accommodates both futureslike and optionlike designs. Also, a short optionlike component could be embedded that would reduce the value of the hybrid and necessitate increasing the coupon if the nonhybrid issue price were to be maintained. The coupon could be increased until the CIY equals 15%. Thus, the CIY criterion limits the value of such a short optionlike component. These optionlike components could be added to the hybrids represented by points B and C to adjust these points toward the permissible CIY level.

Contango and Backwardation.   A typical choice of reference price when the market forward price is not chosen is the current spot price. In certain markets (known as *contango* markets), the market forward price typically exceeds the spot price. In such markets, this choice for the reference price might correspond to point B in Figure 26.1. Some typically contango commodities are gold and stock indexes. For markets in which the spot price typically exceeds the market forward price (*backwardation* markets), use of the spot price as the reference might correspond to point C in Figure 26.1. Some typical backwardation markets are wheat (during the harvest season) and Treasury bills. In other commodities, the relationship between the spot price and the market forward price varies with market conditions. Currencies and oil are occasionally examples.

The CIY criterion will constrain designers of hybrids with embedded futureslike commodity contracts referenced to the spot price according to the degree of contango or backwardation in the commodity market. This is most easily seen in the context of a one-year hybrid designed with a futureslike component as in the example. If the spot price is chosen as the reference price, the value of the hybrid is

$$P' = \frac{c'H + H + N(F - S)}{1 + y} \tag{26.9}$$

The value of nonhybrid debt in this case is

$$P = \frac{cH + H}{1 + y} \tag{26.10}$$

If the hybrid is to be sold at P, c' must be chosen so that the right-hand sides of (26.9) and (26.10) are equal. This is accomplished when

$$N(F - S) = (c - c')H \tag{26.11}$$

or when the value contributed by the commodity component equals the change in the coupon payment. If the hybrid is designed to just meet the one-to-one test, $N = H/S$. Then (26.11) becomes

$$\frac{F-S}{S} = c - c' \qquad (26.12)$$

which means that the change in the coupon rate must equal the percentage contango or backwardation.[22] If the issue price is par, the coupon rate is also the comparable nonhybrid yield. Then the difference between CIY and the comparable nonhybrid yield must be the percentage contango or backwardation. For example, the 8% difference between points A and B in Figure 26.1 is driven by an 8% contango market.[23] In this example, the CIY criterion cannot be met on a hybrid issued at par if the spot price is chosen as the reference price for a futureslike embedded commodity component.

Of course, the CIY criterion can be met through a different choice of reference price or by adjusting the embedded commodity value by using an option component. In the case of a contango that is too large to meet the CIY criterion, the additional option component would have to subtract value from the commodity component; that is, it would have to have a short optionlike component. The vertical distance between point B and 5% CIY is the value of the short optionlike component as a percentage of par.

For the backwardation case, the excess of CIY over the comparable nonhybrid yield — for example, the 8% positive difference between points C and A in Figure 26.1 — must be the percentage backwardation in the commodity market for par issues. If the percentage backwardation were too large to meet the CIY criterion with the spot price as the reference price, then a value-adding option component could be used, and the vertical distance between the CIY without the option and the 15% CIY needed to meet the criterion is the value of the long option as a percentage of the par issue price.

Table 26.1 shows estimates, based on *Wall Street Journal* data, of coupon rates (c') for hybrids in selected commodities as of February 8, 1989. In each case, the entry in the table is

$$c - \frac{F-S}{S}$$

where c is assumed to be the U.S. Government yield to maturity (YTM). An example of interpreting Table 26.1 is the following. Assume the YTM on one-year comparable nonhybrid debt is 9.94%. If a futureslike component in yen were embedded with the current spot price as the reference price, the hybrid would sell at par at a coupon of 4.88% (because of the degree of contango of yen on this date), and this is also its CIY. This yen-denominated

---

22. For maturities of more than one year, the expression is

$$\frac{F-S}{S} \frac{1}{(1+y)^T} = (c-c')A_{y,T}$$

23. This assumes par issue prices for nonhybrid and hybrid.

TABLE 26.1   *Coupon Rates for Hybrids Denominated in Selected Commodities and Foreign Currencies, February 8, 1989* [a]

	Days		
	30	90	360
U.S. Government YTM	9.25%	9.50%	9.94%
Yen	4.15%	4.54%	4.88%
Ausdollar	15.78%	16.37%	16.93%
Oil	44.82%	36.43%	23.33%
Gold	1.33%	1.46%	1.69%
Copper	41.68%	32.07%	32.72%
Silver	3.57%	0.71%	0.02%
Soybeans	−0.07%	0.37%	10.71%

a. Assumptions: Hybrids contain only long futureslike component with reference price equal to the current spot price. Hybrids sell at par. Comparable nonhybrid debt yield to maturity is U.S. government YTM.

hybrid would then not meet the CIY criterion. The minimum permissible CIY (for being excluded from regulation under the CEA) is 50% of 9.94%, or 4.97%. (The maximum permissible CIY is 14.91%.) However, the would-be issuer of a yen-denominated hybrid has alternatives. For example, a short optionlike component could be added to reduce the total value of the commodity component.

The CIY criterion is perhaps the most controversial of the exclusion criteria. Some commenters argued, in effect, that all commodities are not treated equally by the criterion, as Table 26.1 illustrates. For example, one-year par hybrids could not be issued in yen, the Australian dollar, oil, gold, or copper but could be issued in silver and soybeans. The view underlying the differentiation among commodities is that large deviations of the CIY from the comparable nonhybrid YTM in certain commodities reflects an important distinction between commodity markets and traditional debt markets.[24]

However, one exception was made in the statutory interpretation. For hybrid instruments designed to afford a real rate of return relative to the Consumer Price Index (CPI) or other broadly based inflation measures, the comparable debt yield is defined as a real yield relative to the inflation measure

---

24. The CIY criterion remains a controversial part of the interpretation. See, for example, the Goldman-Sachs comment letter, May 10, 1989. Also, the Federal Reserve Board is moving toward allowing yen-denominated deposits, which behave essentially like PERLS. The CIY criterion could be violated for various currencies unless the forward price is used as the reference price.

TABLE 26.2 *Maximum Commodity Component as Percentage of Par Issue Price, 50% to 150% CIY Criterion*

Comparable Nonhybrid Yield (Coupon)[a]	Years to Maturity						
	1	5	10	15	20	25	30
5%	0.02	0.11	0.19	0.26	0.31	0.35	0.38
10%	0.05	0.19	0.31	0.38	0.43	0.45	0.47
15%	0.07	0.25	0.38	0.44	0.47	0.48	0.49
20%	0.08	0.30	0.42	0.47	0.49	0.49	0.50
25%	0.10	0.34	0.45	0.48	0.49	0.50	0.50
30%	0.12	0.37	0.46	0.49	0.50	0.50	0.50

a. Yield and coupon are equal for nonhybrid debt instruments selling at par.

(see footnote 12 of the Statutory Interpretation). The estimated annual yield of a comparable nonhybrid instrument would be calculated as the bond equivalent yield of the most recently issued one-year Treasury bill less the most recently announced annualized percentage change in the inflation index. More recently, senior staff of the Commission have indicated a willingness to go beyond even this exception for inflation-indexed instruments. They have indicated that the CIY criterion would not have to be met for CPI-indexed instruments that meet the other criteria of the exclusion.

Par Bonds and CIY. The CIY criterion has a special interpretation for instruments issued at par. For such instruments, the CIY criterion is an upper bound on the absolute value of the commodity component as a percentage of par.[25] This is illustrated for hybrids with long futureslike components in Table 26.2. For example, at a CIY of 50% on a 10% YTM, five-year bond,

---

25. Proof:

$$H = c'H \frac{1-(1+y)^{-T}}{y} + \frac{H}{(1+y)^T} + Z$$

where Z denotes the value of the commodity component. Dividing both sides by H and simplifying produces

$$1 = \frac{c'}{y} - \frac{c'-y}{(1+y)^T} + \frac{Z}{H}$$

The upper bound on Z/H can be shown at large y or large T. As y increases, the second term on the right-hand side decreases faster than the first and becomes negligible at very large y. Then

$$\frac{Z}{H} = 1 - \frac{c'}{y}$$

For a par hybrid, the fraction c'/y is the CIY criterion. Thus a criterion of 50% to 150% limits the absolute value of the commodity component to 50%. The effect of long maturity is that the commodity component as a percentage of par is only 19%. The commodity component as a percentage of par approaches (but does not exceed) 50% only at very long maturities and very high YTM.[26]

Variations in Indexing

The foregoing discussion has covered the essential characteristics of a principal-indexed hybrid with an embedded long futureslike position and the effects of the one-to-one, maximum-loss, and commodity-independent yield criteria on this type of instrument. Variations on this type of instrument include different methods of defining the indexing feature, coupon indexing, and embedded short futureslike positions.

Defining the Indexation. Variations include:

1. An adjustment to principal defined as the rate of change in the price of the British pound from the reference price defined as a percentage of the current price, or

$$H^* = H + H\frac{(S_m - R)}{S} \tag{26.13}$$

In this variation the number of ounces involved in the commodity component is defined implicitly as H/S rather than explicitly. This particular definition assures one-to-one indexing. If the denominator of the adjustment is less than the current spot price, then one-to-one indexing cannot be achieved.

2. An adjustment to principal defined as principal times the ratio of the value of British pounds at maturity to the current value, or

$$H^* = H\frac{S_m}{S} \tag{26.14}$$

The right-hand side of this expression can be written as

$$H = c'\frac{H}{y} + Z$$

which is equivalent to the previous equation.

26. Although this characteristic of the criterion provides a useful insight into the impact of the criterion on a potentially large class of hybrids, it is not a general characteristic for nonpar hybrids. For example, consider a comparable nonhybrid zero coupon bond. In order to embed a short in-the-money commodity component, which would reduce the hybrid issue price, a coupon could be attached and adjusted to maintain the hybrid issue price at the nonhybrid issue price. Because the issue price is already relatively low, the absolute value of the commodity component can be shown to exceed 50% of the issue price even though the CIY does not exceed 150% of the nonhybrid yield.

$$H + H\frac{(S_m - S)}{S} \tag{26.15}$$

which is identical to the variation in which the reference price is the issue spot price (see Equation 26.14).

3. An adjustment to principal defined, as in the reverse PERLS, as

$$H^* = 2H - NS_m \tag{26.16}$$

The right-hand side of this expression may be written

$$2H - \left(H + H\frac{(S_m - S)}{S}\right) \tag{26.17}$$

if N is selected to be H/S. This reduces to the right-hand side of (26.13).

4. An adjustment to principal defined in terms of the change in a price other than the spot price. Although this variation has not been seen up to now, it is conceivable and the language in the release was deliberately chosen so as not to exclude such design. For example, the adjustment to principal might be defined as

$$H^* = H + H\frac{(F_m - F)}{F} \tag{26.18}$$

that is, an adjustment based on the rate of change in the market forward price from the time of issue to maturity of the hybrid. (Here the reference price is also the market forward price.) This indexation is similar to (26.14), but the implicit quantity of the commodity is H/F. The one-to-one and maximum loss criteria are satisfied if $H \geq NF$.

Coupon Indexing. Coupon indexation can be achieved either separately or in concert with principal indexation in any of the above forms. In one form, the coupon may vary as a fixed percentage of the indexed principal, where the indexation is computed based on the spot price of the commodity at each coupon payment. The example of the British-pound-indexed principal instrument could be modified so that the 10% coupon is stated as 10% of adjusted principal. The coupon payment at date t is computed as

$$c(H + 500(S_t - F)) \tag{26.19}$$

At $S_t = \$2$ and $F = \$1.90$, the coupon payment is $110. This payment is the same as 10% of the fixed principal plus 10% of the price change on 500 pounds. The commodity-independent payment is $100, or cH, and the commodity-dependent payment is $10, or $c500(S_t - F)$. It is important to remember that when coupons and principal are indexed, the one-to-one and maximum-loss criteria apply separately to the coupons and principal. This example satisfies these criteria. Indeed, the same analysis developed above in terms of how this type of indexation can be designed to satisfy these criteria for principal indexation applies also to coupon indexation.

Identical coupon indexation could be achieved by defining an indexed coupon rate to be multiplied by unadjusted principal. For example, the indexed rate could be defined as

$$c + c \frac{(S_t - F)}{S} \tag{26.20}$$

This is the same form as the principal indexation shown in (26.14).

Variations in which only the coupon, not the principal, is indexed include all of the forms illustrated above. The adjustment in each case is simply applied to the coupon payment rather than the principal payment. An example of this type of instrument is a bank deposit with indexed interest.

Short Futureslike Components.   Short futureslike positions can be embedded in hybrids by simply reversing the definition of the adjustment to principal. For example, the adjusted principal could be defined as:

$$H^* = H + N(R - S_m) \tag{26.21}$$

Based on the analysis of the embedded long futureslike component, it is clear that this design will meet the one-to-one criterion as long as the value at the current spot price of the number of units of the commodity does not exceed the principal. However, the maximum-loss criterion cannot be met without other contractual specifications, since the loss is unlimited as the spot price increases.

The application and effect of the CIY criterion is identical to the case of the long commodity position except that the effect of contango and backwardation is reversed. For example, in a contango market, choice of the spot price for the reference price builds a negative value into the embedded commodity position, necessitating a higher coupon rate and higher CIY.

Optionlike Hybrids

All of the variations considered thus far were presented as primarily futures like hybrids in that optionlike characteristics were added only to meet the maximum-loss or CIY criterion. It is useful to consider an optionlike hybrid in more detail. We present an example that meets the exclusion criterion and then consider the application of the exemptive criteria for a variation that fails the exclusion tests.

The example is a principal-indexed gold bond with a coupon rate below the nonhybrid rate of 10% (for par issues). This example is similar to the indexed certificates of deposit that have been the subject of interpretative letters. The instrument has a maturity of five years, a fixed coupon of 6%, a principal of $1000, and an adjustment to principal equal to 2.5 ounces of gold times the change in the gold price *above* $400 per ounce or

$$H^* = H + (2.5)[\max(0, S_m - 400)] \tag{26.22}$$

If the spot price of gold at issue is $400 per ounce, then this hybrid will satisfy the exclusion criteria. The one-to-one criterion is satisfied, because at an issue spot price of $400 per ounce the principal payment of $1000 is equivalent to 2.5 ounces of gold, the same amount as specified in the adjustment to principal. This will ensure that the percentage change in the commodity-dependent payment as a percentage of the principal does not exceed the percentage change in the price of gold. The maximum-loss criterion will be met by explicit design in this example because of the optionlike payoff function. Finally, if issued at par, the commodity-independent yield will be 6%, or 60% of the comparable nonhybrid yield.

This example may be changed to fail the exclusion by increasing the number of ounces. Suppose, for example, three ounces were specified and that a 5% coupon would allow sale at par. Now the hybrid would fail the one-to-one exclusion criterion because a 1% change in the price of gold would produce a 1.2% adjustment to principal. But since the hybrid has the explicit optionlike character, it could be subjected to the tests for exemption from the exchange-traded option regulations.

We will assume that all of the criteria of the exemption have been successfully applied except the implied option premium test. The application of that test proceeds as follows:

1. Determine the present value at 10% (the comparable nonhybrid yield) of the commodity-independent payments, which are the coupon stream (for five years) and the $1000 principal. This present value turns out to be 810.46. (This calculation is based on annual coupons for simplicity.)

2. The implied option premium is the difference between the issue price and that present value, or $1000 - 810.46 = 189.54$.

3. Determine the proportion of the issue price represented by the implied option premium, which is 189.54/1000, or 18.954%. Since this proportion is not greater than 40%, the implied option premium test is passed.

Thus, this hybrid would be exempted from commodity option regulation.

VI. The Role of Hybrids in Financial Innovation

The financial environment of the 1980s has been marked by the emergence of a host of new financial instruments and financing techniques. These include adjustable rate preferred stock and intermediate-term debt, foreign-denominated bonds, interest rate and currency swaps, and the increased use of futures contracts, forward contracts, and options.[27] In general, the same uncertainties in interest rates, rates of inflation, rates of commodity price change, and changing tax rules that have sparked much of this innovation also underlie the emergence of hybrid financial instruments. Essentially, firms issue hybrid instruments to hedge existing risks, to satisfy investor clienteles, and to capture the gains from product innovation.

For example, a firm producing precious metals or raw materials obtains some hedging benefit by going short the same commodity through a hybrid debt issue. Similarly, if firms have determined that they are effectively in a long position with respect to inflation, currency, or interest rate risk, they may embed an offsetting position in their debt. In many cases, firms may not have a long exposure to such risks. For example, U.S. firms with foreign currency liabilities are effectively short the foreign currency, because if the value of the foreign currency relative to the dollar increases, the firms must use more dollars to obtain the foreign currency to pay its bills. One way to hedge this risk is to embed a long foreign currency position in a hybrid.

The more puzzling question may be why firms should hedge with hybrids rather than through existing futures, option, and forward markets. For most of the hybrids that have been issued (the possible exception is oil-indexed bonds), active forward markets exist in the underlying commodity (for certain maturities). The firms could participate in these markets either on their own or through intermediaries. There must be an advantage to linking the financing instrument with the hedging instrument.

The advantage may involve the appeal of a linked instrument to certain investors. Diversification may be a primary factor. Many investors, both institutional and individual, may be unable to participate directly in commodity markets. The restrictions on widespread investor participation include institutional regulatory restrictions, transaction size limitations for private investors, and unfamiliarity with futures and forward markets. Even where these factors are not restrictive, contracts with desired maturities and other terms may not be available in existing markets. For example, designated futures and option markets have few contracts extending beyond one year. For all these reasons, the diversification achievable by holding, for example, both a straight five-year bond and a five-year gold contract is not obtainable for certain investors. A firm that issues a hybrid has the opportunity to create a unique risk/return combination, and to the extent the combination is unique, the firm obtains the premium investors pay in the form of lower cost financing and hedging.

---

27. Finnerty (1988) discusses the extensive list of new types of securities created in the 1980s, many of which are debt securities.

Taxation also plays a role in the uniqueness of hybrids. The preference of different investors for different combinations of income and capital gains is well recognized. For example, U.S. corporations' preference for high dividends, due to the exclusion of 80% of dividend income from taxation, has led to "dividend-capture" strategies (Seidner [1989]). Similarly, U.S. tax-exempt pension funds have been advised to purchase "yield-tilted" portfolios of securities or portfolios that have relatively high coupons and dividends but are otherwise matched to the funds' usual investment preferences, such as risk level (Sharpe [1985]). Conversely, individuals in a high U.S. tax bracket would prefer lower income-producing securities, all things equal. With the potential for creating high or low coupons as illustrated above, hybrid debt is ideally marketable for tax-differentiated classes of investors. Again, issuing firms will gain the innovation premium.

Finally, hybrids are a new means of changing the risk-sharing arrangement between managers, stockholders, and bondholders. An interesting explanation for the existence of convertible debt is that it provides debtholders with an equity stake in the firm that prevents managers/stockholders from affecting the value of the bond too adversely by increasing the riskiness of the firm. For this reason, it may be the preferred form of debt financing for firms perceived to be facing great uncertainty. Brennan and Schwartz (1986) have shown that bond purchasers and managers can more easily agree on the price of convertible bonds than straight bonds under such conditions. Hybrid debt may be considered an altered form of convertible debt, wherein the "equity" stake is not in equity but in a commodity expected to be correlated with the equity. Certain bondholders may prefer debt that implies corporate hedging (negative correlation with equity). Others may prefer a futureslike or optionlike interest in an underlying factor positively correlated with the value of the firm.

VII. Conclusion

The regulation of off-exchange futureslike and optionlike instruments is one of the most complex and potentially controversial issues facing regulators in the commodities, securities, and banking agencies. The CFTC has addressed a significant component of the off-exchange market by providing exclusion from regulation under the CEA for certain hybrid debt and depository instruments and exemption from the exchange-trading requirement for certain optionlike hybrids that are not so excluded. This approach allows financial innovation to proceed within the constraints of the CEA. The new framework will materially affect the design of future hybrids as well as the evolution of further regulation.

References

Brennan, Michael A., and Edwardo Schwartz. 1986. The case for convertibles. In Joel M. Stern and Donald I. Chew, Jr. (eds.), *The Revolution in Corporate Finance*. Oxford: Basil Blackwell. Reprinted 1987.

Commodity Futures Trading Commission. 1988. Proceedings, Application of the New York Cotton Exchange for designation as a contract market in thirty-day federal funds index futures contracts and the proposed rules on the regulation of hybrid instruments, January 5, p. 45.

————. 1989a. Regulation of hybrid instruments. *Federal Register* 54 (January 11), 1128–1138.

————. 1989b. Statutory interpretation concerning certain hybrid instruments. *Federal Register* 54 (January 11), 1139–1142.

————. 1989c. Regulation of hybrid instruments. *Federal Register* 54 (July 21), 30684–30693.

————. 1989d. Policy statement concerning swap transactions. *Federal Register* 54 (July 21), 30694–30697.

Cox, J. C., J. E. Ingersoll, and S. A. Ross. 1981. The relation between forward prices and futures prices. *Journal of Financial Economics* 9, 321–346.

Davis, Robert. 1986. Are indexed oil instruments also commodity options? *Commodity Law Letter* (July–August).

Finnerty, John D. 1988. Financial engineering in corporate finance: An overview. *Financial Management* 17 (Winter), 14–33.

Gilberg, David J. 1986. Regulation of new financial instruments under the federal securities and commodities laws. *Vanderbilt Law Review* 39, 1599–1689.

Gynn, Robert, and J. J. Tindall. 1987. Intermarket's 1987 hybrid debt innovations directory. *Intermarket* 4 (August), 42–46.

Markham, Jerry W. 1987. *The History of Commodity Futures Trading and its Regulation*. New York: Praeger.

Peck, Anne E. 1985. The economic role of traditional commodity futures markets. In Ann E. Peck (ed.), *Futures Markets: Their Economic Role*. Washington, DC: American Enterprise Institute.

Rawls, S. Waite, III, and Charles W. Smithson. 1989. The evolution of risk management products. *Journal of Applied Corporate Finance* 1 (Winter), 18–26.

Seidner, Alan G. 1989. *Corporate Investments Manual*. Boston: Warren, Gorham and Lamont, pp. 5-25 and 5-26.

Sharpe, William F. 1985. *Investments* (3rd ed.). Englewood Cliffs, NJ: Prentice-Hall, pp. 230–238.

Silber, William L. 1985. The economic role of financial futures. In Anne E. Peck (ed.), *Futures Markets: Their Economic Role*. Washington, DC: American Enterprise Institute.

Stein, Jerome L. 1985. Futures markets and capital formation. In Anne E. Peck (ed.), *Futures Markets: Their Economic Role*. Washington, DC: American Enterprise Institute.

27

The Fundamental Financial Instrument Approach: Identifying the Building Blocks*

Halsey G. Bullen, Robert C. Wilkins, & Clifford C. Woods III

Because of the seemingly endless complexity and diversity of innovative financial instruments, the Financial Accounting Standards Board is taking the approach of breaking down these instruments to resolve the numerous recognition and measurement issues associated with them.

The approach is based on the premise that all financial instruments are made up of a few different "building blocks"—fundamental financial instruments—and that determining how to recognize and measure those fundamental instruments is the key to reaching consistent solutions for the accounting issues raised by other more complex instruments and by various relationships between instruments.

Identifying Fundamental Financial Instruments

To identify which instruments are fundamental, the FASB turned first to its definition of a financial instrument (see the box on page 580). The definition

*Expressions of individual views by the members of the FASB and its staff are encouraged. The views expressed in this article are those of Messrs. Bullen, Wilkins, and Woods. Official positions of the FASB are determined only after extensive due process and deliberation.

What's a Financial Instrument?

The FASB's July 1989 revised exposure draft, *Disclosure of Information about Financial Instruments with Off-Balance-Sheet Risk and Financial Instruments with Concentrations of Credit Risk,* defines a financial instrument as cash, evidence of an ownership interest in an equity, or a contract that is both

- A (recognized or unrecognized) contractual right of one entity to (1) receive cash or another financial instrument from another entity or (2) exchange other financial instruments on potentially favorable terms with another entity.

- A (recognized or unrecognized) contractual obligation of another entity to (1) deliver cash or another financial instrument to another entity or (2) exchange financial instruments on potentially unfavorable terms with another entity.

That definition includes traditional instruments such as receivables, payables, debt securities, and common stock, as well as more innovative financial instruments such as financial futures and forward contracts, interest rate swaps and caps, collateralized mortgage obligations, and financial guarantees. It excludes contracts for the purchase or sale of commodities or other goods, services, inventories, property, plant and equipment, as well as tax obligations.

---

the FASB has established distinguishes between instruments that entail one party's right to receive and another party's obligation to deliver and those that entail rights and obligations to exchange.

If a financial instrument obligates one party to deliver cash or other instruments, that party has a liability—a payable in the broadest sense—and the other party has an asset—a receivable. A right to receive or an obligation to deliver entails a one-way transfer; this transfer would involve no further quid pro quo.

In contrast, a financial instrument that entails a right or obligation to exchange looks to a further transaction that will, if it occurs, consist of a two-way flow of cash and other financial instruments—an exchange. Whether a contract to exchange gives rise to an asset, a liability, or perhaps both is determined by the potential for a favorable or unfavorable result. To be an asset, such a contract must entitle a party to exchange on terms that are at least potentially favorable. (For example, a call option to buy a bond next month for $1,000 has the potential to become favorable to its holder—the market price of the bond could rise above $1,000 by then.) Likewise, to be a liability, such a contract must obligate a party to exchange on terms that are at least potentially unfavorable.

Conditionality of rights and obligations is another characteristic that distinguishes between fundamental financial instruments. A right to receive or an obligation to deliver cash or another instrument—a one-way transfer—may be either unconditional or conditional on some event. The same is true for a right or obligation to exchange cash and other financial instruments—a two-way exchange.

Conditional exchanges can be further subdivided into

- Instruments whose rights and obligations are conditional on events within the control of one party to the contract (for example, in an option contract, the conditional event is generally the option holder's decision to exercise).

- Instruments whose rights and obligations are conditional on events beyond the control of either party to the contract (for example, in a financial guarantee, the conditional event that could take place might be default on some other contract by a third party.

How important that subdivision of conditionality may end up being for accounting recognition and measurement will have to remain to be seen.

Those contractual distinctions between financial instruments helped lead the FASB to its current list of six tentatively identified fundamental financial instruments, which are defined in the box on page 582.

Recognition and Measurement

Recognition and measurement questions to be answered for each fundamental instrument fall into four categories:

Recognition. Whether and when an asset or liability should initially be recorded in the statement of financial position.

Initial measurement. At what amount an asset or liability should initially be recorded.

Subsequent measurement. At what amount an asset or liability should be reported after recognition and initial measurement; in particular, whether gain or loss should be recognized as a result of some or all changes in market value.

Derecognition. Whether and when an asset or liability should be removed from the statement of financial position—and whether gain or loss should be recognized.

While the recognition and initial measurement of financial instruments are not necessarily easy to resolve, the more difficult issues are in subsequent measurement and derecognition.

Six Tentatively Identified Fundamental Financial Instruments

Unconditional receivable (payable). An unqualified right (obligation) to receive (deliver) cash or another financial asset on or before a specified date or on demand. These contracts entail a future one-way transfer of one or more financial assets. Examples are trade accounts, notes, loans, and bonds receivable (payable).

Conditional receivable (payable). A right (obligation) to receive (deliver) cash or another financial asset dependent on the occurrence of an event beyond the control of either party to the contract. These contracts entail a potential one-way transfer of one or more assets. Examples include interest rate caps and floors, insurance contracts without subrogation rights, and compensation promised to a third party if a transaction or other event occurs.

Forward contract. An unconditional right and obligation to exchange financial instruments. Examples include forward purchase and sale contracts, futures contracts, and repurchase agreements that obligate both parties to a future exchange of financial instruments. (Forward and futures contracts for the purchase or sale of metals, grain, or other goods do not qualify as financial instruments because the items to be exchanged are not both financial instruments.)

Option. A right (obligation) to exchange other financial instruments on potentially favorable (unfavorable) terms that is conditional on the occurrence of an event within the control of one party to the contract. Most commonly, the conditional event is an option holder's decision to exercise the right to demand the exchange. Examples include warrants, loan commitments, and exchange-traded and other put or call options. Bonds or stocks with attached warrants, mortgages that allow the borrower to prepay, and convertible bonds are examples of compound financial instruments containing options.

Guarantee or other conditional exchange. A right (obligation) to exchange financial instruments on potentially favorable (unfavorable) terms that is conditional on the occurrence of an event outside the control of either party. Examples include performance bonds, letters of credit, and all other contracts for which the obligor—on occurrence of a specified event—would receive the subrogation or other rights to another financial instrument in exchange for its delivery of a financial instrument.

Equity instrument. An ownership interest in an equity. It typically entitles its holder to a pro rata share of any distributions made to that class of holders but only entails a right (obligation) to receive (deliver) cash or other financial instrument assets on the entity's liquidation. Examples include common stock and partnership interests.

This set of fundamental instruments is being reexamined as the recognition and measurement phase proceeds. Some categories might be combined if analysis shows they should be accounted for similarly, while others might have to be divided.

Mortgages and Mortgage-Backed Securities

A typical fixed rate residential mortgage is a combination of a series of required cash flows — each an unconditional receivable (payable) — and the privilege of prepaying the remaining principal balance at any time — an option written (held). The prepayment option is favorable to the homeowner. If interest rates decline, the borrower can refinance at a lower rate without penalty. And it's that possibility that makes prepayment options unfavorable for banks, thrifts, and other mortgage investors; the prepayment option embedded in everyday residential mortgages is the wild card that makes investing in mortgages (and mortgage-backed securities) so much riskier than it might at first seem to be.

Mortgage-backed securities are created by bundling mortgages into a pool and offering (often through a trust) different interests in that pool to different investors. Mortgage-backed securities take several forms. In some, "senior" investors might be entitled to all cash collected from the pool until they recoup their entire investment plus, say, 9% interest; "subordinated" investors might be entitled to whatever remaining cash is collected.

Alternatively, a pool of mortgages might be split into several classes (or "tranches") of securities, each of which entitles investors to different seniority and rates of return — or split into securities entitling investors to only the interest payments or only the principal payments. Often, financial guarantees are an important part of these securities.

In terms of fundamental instruments, mortgage-backed securities combine unconditional receivables (payables), conditional receivables (payables), guarantees, options, and perhaps equity instruments (representing interests in the residual value of a trust). Examining these components to determine which have been transferred to investors or others and which have been retained by the security's sponsor may help in resolving the troublesome "sale or financing" derecognition question that is raised on many occasions when these securities are first created.

Compound Financial Instruments

Financial instruments that do not meet the definition of one of the fundamental instruments can be analyzed as made up of fundamentals in various combinations. Some of these compound instruments may combine only a few fundamental instruments; for example, a callable zero coupon bond combines (from the issuer's perspective) an unconditional payable and a call option held.

Other compound instruments are more complex. They may contractually link several fundamental instruments. The boxes on this page and on page 584 show how two kinds of compound instruments — mortgages and mortgage-backed securities and interest rate swaps — can be broken down into fundamental instruments.

Interest Rate Swaps

The interest rate swap was invented in the early 1980s to aid companies able to borrow cheaply at floating rates but seeking fixed rates and vice versa. It has become an essential tool of finance since its creation.

A straightforward interest rate swap might require one party — the "fixed rate payer" — to pay a fixed interest rate times a notional principal amount at the end of each of the next five years; the counterparty would be required to pay the floating London interbank offered rate times the same notional principal amount at the same intervals. There are no principal payments and the fixed rate is typically negotiated to eliminate any need for a cash payment at the outset. For convenience, the parties usually agree that a single net payment be made at each due date.

Interest rate swaps are typically entered into in connection with a borrowing, although the swap counterparty usually is not the lender. Some have described the economic position of a floating rate borrower/fixed rate payer in a swap as being the same as that of a fixed rate borrower, but there is a difference. In an interest rate swap, the borrower is exposed to a credit risk since the swap counterparty might default.

The interest rate swap can be analyzed into fundamental financial instruments in at least two ways:

- As a series of forward contracts (to exchange a floating rate cash receipt for a fixed payment).
- As a series of variable rate receivables and a series of fixed rate unconditional payables to be settled by net payments after setoff.

Which of these analyses is more appropriate for swaps, whether the choice affects the accounting result, and whether the relationship between an interest rate swap and a debt incurred at the same time should affect the accounting for either or both instruments are among the questions the financial instruments project is expected to deal with in resolving the diversity in current accounting practice for swaps.

The FASB anticipates that the recognition and measurement of various compound instruments can be approached by analyzing them in terms of their fundamental financial instrument components. Determining the accounting for each fundamental instrument should point the way to the accounting for any compound financial instrument. While that may sound challenging, it mirrors the current business practices of many buyers and sellers of mortgages, corporate bonds, and other compound financial instruments.

Relationships between Financial Instruments

At the same time, the FASB will consider whether some of the contractual and other relationships between financial instruments — whether fundamental or compound—should affect the accounting for one or more of the related instruments. Relationships that raise accounting issues include those between hedging and hedged instruments, assets and liabilities that can be set off against each other, secured debt and securing assets (either with or without recourse to other assets of the borrower), options that are "covered" by particular assets and in-substance defeasances, and other dedications of specific assets to the settlement of specific liabilities.

The Goal: Accounting Standards for Financial Instruments

Breaking down complex financial instruments into their fundamental components is not a new idea. On the contrary, it is often acknowledged by many investment bankers, financial managers, economists, and finance academics (usually in the context of how best to manage financial risks) as the way in which complex financial instruments are created and valued in the marketplace. Similarly, the FASB's approach is intended to break down complex financial instruments to determine their economic substance and thereby develop consistent accounting standards.

As the FASB's financial instruments project proceeds, numerous generally accepted accounting principles will be reconsidered and some surely will have to change. Table 27.1 indicates some of the authoritative accounting literature subject to reconsideration in the project. Another indication of the potential for change in current practice may be the FASB's tentative conclusions on fundamental instruments, which include the tentative decision to measure certain options held or written at their current market values or at estimates of those values based on option-pricing models or other techniques, if this is feasible.

The FASB plans to issue an initial discussion document on the recognition and measurement of financial instruments in 1990. As planned, it would present the fundamental financial instrument approach and the issues the project aims to resolve, expressed in terms of accounting for fundamental instruments, compound instruments, and hedging and other relationships between financial instruments. The document is also expected to provide the FASB's preliminary views on some of those issues. Ultimately—after considering written comments on the discussion document, a public hearing planned for late 1990, and further deliberations and exposure drafts—the project's goal is to issue accounting standards that resolve the accounting issues of financial instruments on a consistent conceptual basis.

The fundamental financial instrument approach is a tool intended to help resolve the recognition and measurement issues of new as well as traditional financial instruments. The approach should help the FASB resolve today's issues and help practicing accountants answer tomorrow's inevitable accounting

TABLE 27.1   *Authoritative Literature that May Be Affected by the Recognition and Measurement Phase of the Financial Instruments Project*

Document	Title	Area that May Be Affected
Accounting Principles Board Opinion no. 21	*Interest on Receivables and Payables*	Accounting and scope restrictions.
FASB Statement no. 12	*Accounting for Certain Marketable Securities*	Entire statement (both debt and equity securities are financial instruments).
FASB Statement no. 15	*Accounting by Debtors and Creditors for Troubled Debt Restructurings*	Entire statement.
FASB Statement no. 52	*Foreign Currency Translation*	Forward exchange contract and hedging provisions.
FASB Statement no. 65	*Accounting for Certain Mortgage Banking Activities*	Mortgage loans, mortgage-backed securities, and the sale of loans with servicing retained.
FASB Statement no. 76	*Extinguishment of Debt*	Entire statement.
FASB Statement no. 77	*Reporting by Transferors for Transfers of Receivables with Recourse*	Entire statement.
FASB Statement no. 80	*Accounting for Futures Contracts*	Entire statement.
FASB Statement no. 91	*Accounting for Nonrefundable Fees and Costs Associated with Originating or Acquiring Loans and Initial Direct Costs of Leases*	Initial and subsequent measurement issues.
Various AICPA accounting and audit guides, especially those for banks, savings and loan associations, finance companies, investment companies and brokers, and dealers in securities.		Some specialized accounting principles will be reexamined. Areas that may be affected include the distinction between trading and investment accounts, allowances for loan losses, and valuing repossessed collateral.

questions about innovative financial instruments and off-balance-sheet financing. The approach is still being developed and the FASB welcomes suggestions and supportive or critical comments from all of its constituents.

28

The Challenges of Hedge Accounting

John E. Stewart*

Increased volatility of interest rates, foreign exchange rates, and other prices has elevated hedging to an important business necessity. A tremendous variety of hedging products has sprung up in recent years to meet this need.

How should these products be reported in financial statements? Because traditional guidance fails to answer this question satisfactorily, the challenge of hedge accounting is here. This article describes hedging and why it's important, some of the financial reporting issues involved, the accounting profession's response, and the significant problems that exist.

What Is Hedging and Why Is It Important?

Hedging is a tool for transferring price, foreign exchange, or interest rate *risk* from those wishing to avoid it to those willing to assume it. Specifically, hedging is the act of taking a position in a hedging instrument—such as in the futures, forward, options, or swap market—opposite to an actual position that's exposed to risk. (See the box on page 588 for definitions.) Hedging

---

*John E. Stewart, CPA, is a partner of Arthur Andersen & Co., Chicago. He serves on the Financial Accounting Standards Board's task force on financial instruments and off-balance-sheet financing and is the chairman of the American Institute of CPAs financial instruments task force. He is a member of the Illinois CPA Society, the National Association of Accountants, and the American Accounting Association.

Definitions of the Basic Hedging Instruments

Forward. An agreement between two parties to exchange specific items — for example, two currencies — at a specified future date and at a specified price.

Futures. An exchange-traded contract for future delivery of a standardized quantity of an item at a specified future date and at a specified price. Changes in the market value of the futures contract are settled in cash daily.

Option. A contract allowing, but *not* requiring, its holder to buy (call) or sell (put) a specific or standard item at a specified price during a specified time period or on a specified date. Options may trade on exchanges or over-the-counter.

Interest rate swap. An agreement between two parties to exchange one interest stream — for example, floating rate — for another — fixed rate — based on a contractual or notional amount. No principal changes hands.

Currency swap. An exchange of two currencies according to an agreement to re-exchange the currencies at the same rate at a specified future date. During the term of the agreement, exchanges of interest payments denominated in the respective currencies also may occur.

reduces the risk of loss from adverse price or rate fluctuations that may occur in owning or owing items over a period of time. Conversely, hedging may limit the gain from favorable changes. Among the items hedged are

- Owned assets including financial instruments or commodities such as grains, metals, and livestock.
- Existing liabilities such as foreign-currency–denominated borrowings.
- Contractual (firm) commitments to buy or sell items such as commodities or financial instruments.
- Anticipated, but not contractually committed, transactions such as purchases or sales or the issuance or refinancing of debt.

Volatility in interest rates, foreign exchange rates, and other prices has created a demand for instruments that could help borrowers, lenders, financial institutions, manufacturers, and other industrial companies reduce their risks — risks that if not properly managed could threaten the very survival of their companies. This volatility — combined with increased internationalization, competition, global deregulation, technology, sophisticated analysis techniques, and tax and regulatory changes — has promoted an almost unbelievable explosion of innovative financial instruments that may be used as hedging vehicles.

Why the Need for Hedge Accounting?

The need for some special accounting for hedges arises in part because of our historical cost, transaction-based accounting system. Under that system, the effects of price or interest rate changes on many existing assets and liabilities aren't recognized in income until realized in a later transaction. If the gains or losses on the underlying assets or liabilities are reported in a time period different from that of the losses and gains reported on the instruments used to hedge these assets and liabilities, the accounting result could be reporting related, offsetting accounts in income during different reporting periods. This reporting would tend to cause fluctuations in income, implying increased exposure to price or interest rate changes when, in fact, the exposure has been reduced.

A somewhat similar result would occur if gains or losses were recognized currently for instruments entered into to hedge firmly committed or probable transactions *not* involving existing assets or liabilities. Under traditional accounting, the unrealized gains or losses associated with these future transactions may not be reflected in the financial statements until realized.

The accounting challenges are to develop special or different accounting (hedge accounting) that addresses these issues and then to specify the conditions under which this hedge accounting is appropriate.

The FASB's Response

How have accounting standard setters, primarily the Financial Accounting Standards Board, responded to the challenge? In general, the standard setters' response has been slow, ad hoc, and inconsistent; but there's some hope in the long run with the FASB's financial instruments project. (See Chapters 27 and 29.)

In 1981, the FASB issued Statement no. 52, *Foreign Currency Translation,* which deals with hedge accounting for foreign exchange forwards, futures, and currency swaps. In 1984, it issued Statement no. 80, *Accounting for Futures Contracts,* which addresses all types of exchange-traded futures, except foreign currency.

However, problems persist. *For many of the new instruments and transactions, the problem is a total absence of accounting guidance.* Not covered are

- Interest rate forwards.
- Almost all types of options.
- Interest rate swaps.

Interest rate swaps were born in the early 1980s and the market has grown to over $1 trillion. The accounting standards say virtually nothing about how either users or market makers should account for these swaps. Similarly, the market for options of all types—exchange-traded and over-the-counter— on commodities, foreign currencies, financial instruments, and futures contracts has soared in recent years, but existing accounting standards address only accounting for options on common stocks (FASB Statement no. 12, *Accounting for Certain Marketable Securities*).

A second problem is that the standards promulgated are *inconsistent*. To the extent instruments covered by existing standards seem analogous to the new financial instruments, the inconsistencies create uncertainty about which rules to follow.

What's Hedge Accounting?

Both Statements no. 52 and 80 provide for hedge accounting. The underlying broad concept of both statements is to achieve some sort of symmetry between accounting for the hedging instrument and the assets, liabilities, or transactions being hedged. If specified criteria are met (reduction of risk, designation, effectiveness, and so forth), gains or losses on the hedging instrument are recorded at the same time and in the same manner as the losses or gains on the hedged item. If the losses or gains on the item being hedged are *deferred*—for example, assets carried at cost or a future transaction—then the gains or losses on the hedging instrument are *deferred* as part of the carrying amount of the heged item rather than recognized currently in income.

Similarly, if unrealized changes in the market price of the hedged item are included in income or in a separate component of stockholders' equity (for example, net investment in a foreign entity), gains or losses on the hedging instrument also are recognized as they occur in income or in the separate component of stockholders' equity—thus providing a match.

If the hedging instrument doesn't meet the specified criteria for hedge accounting, it is accounted for separately at value with gains and losses recorded currently in income.

Despite the similarities in concept between Statements no. 52 and 80, important inconsistencies exist. These inconsistencies relate both to the conditions necessary to qualify for hedge accounting and the application of hedge accounting when the criteria are actually met.

Conflicts between Statements No. 52 and 80

Table 28.1 compares the provisions of Statements no. 52 and 80 in several key areas. Also included are comparisons with the advisory conclusions in the

TABLE 28.1 *Hedge Accounting Comparison*

Hedge Accounting Criteria	FASB 52[a]	FASB 80[b]	AICPA Issues Paper on Options[c]	Interest Rate Swaps in Practice[d]
Designation as a hedge	Yes	Yes	Yes	Frequently but not always
Risk reduction basis	Transaction	Enterprise	Transaction	Sometimes
Degree of correlation	Not explicit	High	High	Matching
Ongoing assessment	Not explicit	Yes	Yes	Usually
Hedge of anticipated transaction (not firm commitment)	No	Yes	Yes	Yes
Cross hedges	Usually not	Yes	Yes	Yes
Hedge of an asset carried at cost	N/A	Yes	No	Yes

TABLE 28.1 *Continued*

	FASB 52[a]	FASB 80[b]	AICPA Issues Paper on Options[c]	Interest Rate Swaps in Practice[d]
Application of Accounting				
Split accounting for inherent elements (premium or discount)	Yes	Usually not	Yes	Frequently not necessary
Amortization of premium on hedge of net investment in a foreign entity	Income or equity	N/A	Income	N/A
Cap on deferred losses to fair value	No	No	Yes	No
Accounting if hedge criteria not met	Formula value	Market	Market	Market or lower of cost or market

a. Statement no. 52 covers foreign exchange forwards, futures and swaps – but not options explicitly.

b. Statement no. 80 covers all (and only) exchange-traded futures except foreign currency futures, which are covered by Statement no. 52.

c. The recommendations included in the AICPA issues paper cover all options (whether or not exchange traded). These recommendations do *not* constitute authoritative generally accepted accounting principles. The chart covers only purchased options.

d. There's no authoritative GAAP for interest rate swaps, although the emerging issues task force has dealt with several swap issues. Existing practice for interest rate swaps is not uniform. Summarized here is the author's perception of practice. The federal banking regulators are working on a release that would provide guidance for regulatory accounting.

American Institute of CPAs issues paper, *Accounting for Options,* and interest rate swap accounting as applied in practice. Many conflicts exist, some of which are discussed below.

Risk Reduction

One criterion for hedge accounting is the hedging instruments must reduce exposure to risk. The statements, however, take different approaches to the determination of risk reduction. Statement no. 80 requires an *enterprise approach:* A futures contract should reduce the enterprise's overall exposure to risk. If the enterprise's other positions already offset the exposure the futures contract is supposed to hedge, the contract won't qualify for hedge accounting. Statement no. 52 provides for a *transaction approach:* Foreign exchange forward contracts or futures need only hedge particular transactions, even if other positions already offset the exposure.

Hedges of Anticipated Transactions

Statement no. 80 allows the designation of futures contracts as an accounting hedge of an anticipated probable transaction (a transaction that an enterprise expects but isn't obligated to carry out in the normal course of business). Statement no. 52 forbids designating foreign currency forward and futures contracts as an accounting hedge of an anticipated foreign currency transaction.

Cross Hedging

Cross hedging involves hedging an exposure, such as commercial paper, with an instrument whose underlying basis differs from the item being hedged, such as U.S. Treasury bill futures. Statement no. 80 permits cross hedging if a clear economic relationship exists and high correlation is probable. Statement no. 52, however, usually does not permit using one currency to hedge another.

Split Accounting for Inherent Elements
(Premium or Discount)

Futures and forward contracts incorporate a premium or discount representing the difference between the current spot price of the underlying commodity or instrument and the future or forward price. This difference reflects, among other things, the time value of money. For futures and forward contracts accounted for as hedges, Statement no. 52 requires the premium or discount be accounted for separately from the changes in value of the futures or forward contract (split accounting). Statement no. 80 forbids separate accounting for the premium or discount except in rare circumstances.

Valuation of Speculative (Nonhedge) Positions

Statement no. 80 requires futures positions that don't qualify for hedge accounting to be valued at market value. However, Statement no. 52 provides for a formula value that ignores the time value of money. (Note that the FASB's emerging issues task force [EITF] reached a consensus in Issue no. 87-2, *Net Present Value Method of Valuing Speculative Foreign Exchange Contracts,* which says that discounting is allowed but not required in applying Statement no. 52.)

Filling the Void

As discussed above, many hedging instruments aren't covered by authoritative generally accepted accounting principles (GAAP)—that is, standards issued by the FASB or its predecessors. To fill the void until the FASB addresses hedge accounting as part of its financial instruments project, accountants have to improvise. They can do this by looking to nonauthoritative guidance and by drawing analogies to existing GAAP. Some of the sources of help and problems in analogizing are described below.

Other Sources of Information

In 1986, the AICPA accounting standards executive committee (AcSEC) finalized an issues paper, *Accounting for Options,* whose conclusions incorporate many of the concepts of FASB Statements no. 52 and 80. However, because the FASB statements' conclusions are inconsistent, AcSEC had to make choices and developed some new ideas along the way, in some cases *adding* to the inconsistencies. (See *Journal of Accountancy,* Jan. 87, p. 87, for how options work and for AcSEC's conclusions.)

The options issues paper has been submitted to the FASB. Although not authoritative, it represents a source of information for practitioners. However, because some of the issues paper's conclusions are inconsistent with existing authoritative literature (for example, Statement no. 12), care must be taken in using it.

Other sources of hedge accounting information CPAs may find useful include

- Another AICPA issues paper published in 1980, *Accounting for Forward Placement and Standby Commitments and Interest Rate Futures Contracts.*

TABLE 28.2 *Hedging Issues Dealt with by the Emerging Issues Task Force*

Issue no.	Topic
84–7	*Termination of Interest Rate Swaps*
84–14	*Deferred Interest Rate Setting*
84–36	*Interest Rate Swap Transactions*
85–6	*Futures Implementation Questions*
86–25	*Offsetting Foreign Currency Swaps*
86–26	*Using Forward Commitments as a Surrogate for Deferred Rate Setting*
86–28	*Accounting Implications of Indexed Debt Instruments*
86–34	*Futures Contracts Used as Hedges of Anticipated Reverse Repurchase Transactions*
87–1	*Deferral Acounting for Cash Securities That Are Used to Hedge Rate or Price Risk*
87–2	*Net Present Value Method of Valuing Speculative Foreign Exchange Contracts*
87–26	*Hedging of Foreign Currency Exposure with a Tandem Currency*
88–8	*Mortgage Swaps*
88–18	*Sales of Future Revenues*

- Articles describing how hedging products work, the accounting issues, and current practice. An example is the article on interest rate swaps in the September 1985 *Journal of Accountancy* (page 63).

Further, the EITF has dealt with several hedging issues (see Table 28.2), but the solutions sometimes have been ad hoc, and in some cases no consensus was reached.

The Problems of Inconsistencies

Despite the fact that some information exists, the inconsistencies among existing FASB standards, AICPA recommendations, and EITF consensuses make it difficult to address accounting for new products by analogy. The result is uncertainty about which accounting should be followed. It's particularly difficult and confusing to resolve practice problems because the instruments—futures, forwards, options, swaps, and so forth—have similarities. Here are some accounting dilemmas:

What Does a CPA Do with Foreign Currency Options?

Does the CPA

- Follow Statement no. 52 and *not* permit hedge accounting for anticipated probable (but not firmly committed) transactions?
- Follow the more recent Statement no. 80 and the AICPA option issues paper and permit it?

Statement no. 52 does not mention options partially because it was written before options became a factor in the market. And even if anticipatory hedge accounting is acceptable for foreign currency options, what does the CPA do with instruments such as foreign-exchange–participating forwards and range forward contracts that have elements of both options and forwards? Statement no. 52 clearly prohibits anticipatory hedge accounting for foreign currency forwards, futures, and swaps.

What Does the CPA Do with Interest Rate Forwards or Interest Rate Swaps?

Does he or she follow

- The designation and enterprise risk reduction criteria of Statement no. 80?
- The designation and transaction risk reduction criteria of Statement no. 52 and the AICPA recommendations?
- None of these?

As indicated in Table 28.1, practice is not uniform. What about an option on an interest rate swap? What about hedging anticipated, but not firmly committed, transactions with interest rate swaps?

What Does a CPA Do with Synthetic Instruments?

Does the CPA

- Analogize to existing hedge accounting criteria and rules?
- If so, which ones?
- Simply account for the instrument?

Synthetic instruments are created in several ways. For example, an entity issues fixed rate debt to creditors and at the same time enters into an interest rate swap with a third party. It receives fixed rate interest and pays floating rate interest on a notional principal amount that equals the principal on the debt. The combination of the debt and the swap converts fixed rate debt to "synthetic" floating rate debt.

Synthetic instrument accounting is accounting for that which the synthetic instrument is meant to replicate—in this case, floating rate debt. Other examples of synthetic instruments include

- Callable debt synthetically changed to noncallable debt through writing (selling) an option on an interest rate swap.
- Synthetic putable debt created from callable debt.
- Synthetically shortening the mandatory maturity of callable debt.
- Synthetic yen debt created from dollar-denominated debt and a currency swap.

All of these synthetic instruments behave like basic identifiable financial instruments in the marketplace, but they're created synthetically because the total cost is perceived to be lower. Synthetic instrument accounting is frequently used in practice. Sometimes the same results could be achieved by applying hedge accounting, but in other cases the criteria for hedge accounting aren't satisfied. For example, the synthetic instrument may well *increase* transaction and enterprise risk.

What Does the CPA Do with Hedging Using Cash Instruments?

Statement no. 52 permits hedge accounting when the *hedging instrument* is a cash instrument, such as foreign-currency–denominated debt or time deposits. However, opinions differ about the acceptability of hedge accounting using cash instruments in other areas, such as U.S. government bonds. In Issue no. 87-1, *Deferral Accounting for Cash Securities That Are Used to Hedge Rate or Price Risk,* the EITF did not reach a consensus, although a majority of the EITF members would prohibit hedge accounting in these other areas.

Compounding Problems

Further compounding the problem are some aspects of Statements no. 52 and 80 that many believe just don't make sense—that is, they don't follow economic substance:

- The prohibition of anticipatory hedge accounting in Statement no. 52.
- The general absence of split accounting for futures in Statement no. 80.
- The effective prohibition of cross hedging (tandem currency) in Statement no. 52.
- The procedures in Statement no. 52 for valuing speculative foreign exchange positions at formula rather than market value.

Hope for Resolution

There's hope for a resolution of these practice problems, but probably not in the near term. That hope is the FASB's project on financial instruments, which includes one segment addressing instruments that transfer risk.

I believe the goals of that project should be to

- Create a level playing field by developing a conceptually based approach that will account for similar instruments similarly and different instruments differently.

- Achieve accounting consistent with economic substance.

- Modernize and generalize accounting standards to deal with new products.

- Address the needs of both product users and market makers.

Any solution should be able to handle existing instruments as well as instruments that will be developed in the future. Many of the new hedging products will be permutations of existing products.

It's worth noting again that the need for hedge accounting is in part—but not completely—driven by our historical cost system. The more *market value accounting* is used for existing assets and liabilities (and that issue is also part of the FASB's project), the less need for special hedge accounting rules. But until the FASB issues new, comprehensive standards, CPAs will have to solve problems by analogizing from existing literature and current practices and by relying on the EITF.

29

The FASB's New ED
on Disclosure

Joan Lordi Amble*

Are companies adequately disclosing information about the new financial instruments with off-balance-sheet risk — interest rate swaps, options written, forward interest rate contracts, and financial guarantees? Some critics claim current information disclosed in the notes to financial statements is incomplete and not comparable.

In July 1989, the Financial Accounting Standards Board issued for comment a revised exposure draft (ED), *Disclosure of Information about Financial Instruments with Off-Balance-Sheet Risk and Financial Instruments with Concentrations of Credit Risk*. This ED is more narrowly focused than the 1987 ED it replaces (see Table 29.1).

First Exposure Draft

Two years ago the FASB issued *Disclosures about Financial Instruments*. The purposes of disclosure set forth in the 1987 ED and retained in the 1989 ED are to

---

*Joan Lordi Amble, CPA, is the project manager at the Financial Accounting Standards Board, Norwalk, Connecticut, on the disclosure phase of the financial instruments project. She will be joining the General Electric Company, Fairfield, Connecticut, as manager — accounting projects. She is a member of the American Institute of CPAs.

Expressions of individual views by the members of the FASB and its staff are encouraged. The views expressed in this article are those of Ms. Amble. Official positions of the FASB are determined only after extensive due process and deliberation.

TABLE 29.1 Summaries of the Major Provisions of the 1987 and 1989 Exposure Drafts

	1987 Exposure Draft	1989 Revised Exposure Draft
Definition of a financial instrument	Contract driven—emphasis on future receipt, delivery, or exchange of cash or other financial instrument that ultimately results in cash.	Same as 1987 ED.
Financial instrument with off-balance-sheet risk	Not defined.	Financial instrument with risk of accounting loss in excess of amount recognized in balance sheet.
Scope	All financial instruments.	Principally financial instruments with off-balance-sheet risk but also all financial instruments with concentrations of credit risk.
Financial instruments excluded	No exclusions.	• Insurance contracts other than financial guarantees and investment contracts. • Lease contracts. • Take-or-pay and throughput contracts. • Pensions and other forms of deferred compensation. • Extinguished debt and related assets held in trust.
Disclosure proposals Nature and terms	—	Information about nature and terms of financial instruments with off-balance-sheet risk and a discussion of the related credit, market and liquidity risk and accounting policy.
Extent of involvement	—	Contract or notional principal amount of financial instruments with off-balance-sheet risk and related amount recognized in the balance sheet.

Credit risk	Maximum credit risk.	Amount of loss due to counterparty failure (maximum credit risk) and information about collateral for financial instruments with off-balance-sheet credit risk.
	Probable credit loss.	—
	Reasonably possible credit loss.	
	Credit risk concentration—information about shared activity or region, and information about credit risk, as noted above, by area of significant concentration.	Credit risk concentration—information about shared activity, region, or economic characteristic, and information about credit risk, as noted above, by area of significant concentration.
	Numerical threshold for individual concentrations.	No numerical threshold specified for individual concentration.
Market risk	Effective interest rates, contractual repricing or maturity dates.	—
	Separate disclosure of above for market risk concentrations involving foreign currencies.	—
Liquidity risk	Contractual future cash receipts and payments.	Narrative discussion only (see requirements under "nature and terms").
	Separate disclosure of above for liquidity risk concentrations involving foreign currencies.	—
Market value	Current market value.	Disclosed only if market value is the measure of (a) maximum credit risk for a financial instrument with off-balance-sheet credit risk or (b) the amount recognized in the balance sheet for a financial instrument with off-balance-sheet risk.

- Describe both recognized and unrecognized items.
- Provide a useful measure of unrecognized items and other relevant measures of recognized items.
- Provide information to help users assess risks and potentials of both recognized and unrecognized items.

Although many respondents agreed with the purposes of disclosure set forth, many also argued that the proposed disclosure requirements in the first ED were too extensive and that the cost of implementing them would be excessive. The FASB viewed the proposals as evolutionary; constituents viewed them as revolutionary.

The due process steps that followed the issuance of the first ED revealed an abundance of hotly debated issues. Many constituents contended off-balance-sheet issues are a driving force behind many of the financial reporting problems facing companies and were an important reason the project was added to the FASB's agenda in 1986. However, they argued that off-balance-sheet issues weren't sufficiently emphasized in the first ED. They urged the FASB to concentrate first on off-balance-sheet issues.

In the fall of 1988 the FASB decided to address the disclosure issues in two phases. Phase 1 resulted in the issuance of the revised ED. As its title implies, the current ED focuses principally on off-balance-sheet issues but also includes concentrations of credit risk for *all* financial instruments. Phase 2, which is expected to begin when a final statement is issued on phase 1, will include all financial instruments and will consider the need for information beyond that proposed in the ED, including information about interest rates, future cash receipts and payments, and market value.

Off-Balance-Sheet Issues

The current ED focuses on the reporting issues in most immediate need of improvement. The set of proposed disclosure requirements draws on information used in managing off-balance-sheet risk. In developing the proposals, the FASB

- Reviewed annual reports of companies that provide additional disclosure of information about financial instruments with off-balance-sheet risk either voluntarily or because of regulatory requirements.
- Reviewed the various Securities and Exchange Commission and regulatory reporting requirements concerning off-balance-sheet items.
- Reviewed how other standard-setting bodies around the world are responding to these issues.
- Requested and reviewed specific comments on those issues from task force members and other interested parties and organizations.

The FASB discussed the proposed disclosure requirements at eight public meetings. In addition, a mini-exposure of an earlier draft of the document's proposals was made to certain task force members and other constituents actively involved in the financial instruments project. The FASB also met with the financial instruments task force in April to discuss the document's proposals.

Implications for 1989 Reporting

The deadline for comments on the revised ED was September 19, 1989, and the final statement is expected in late November 1989. *Most of the disclosure requirements in the ED would be effective for 1989 calendar year reporting.* These include the extent, nature, and terms of financial instruments with off-balance-sheet risk and maximum credit risk for instruments with off-balance-sheet risk. However, the ED's proposed requirements for disclosing information about collateral and concentrations of *credit* risk would be effective for financial statements issued for fiscal years ending after June 15, 1990.

The FASB chose the 1989 effective date for two reasons:

1. Many constituents—including users, preparers, auditors, and regulators—advocated 1989 implementation of the disclosure requirements. Some suggested the disclosure project's first phase be completed and implemented as soon as practicable so the FASB can more effectively consider the remaining disclosure issues as well as the recognition and measurement issues.

2. The FASB concluded that companies should be able to describe the nature and terms of their financial instruments with off-balance-sheet risk and to quantify the related contract amounts *with minimal difficulty.* An entity would need that information to manage its off-balance-sheet risk. The FASB was concerned, however, that some companies may not have systems in place to accumulate information about collateral and concentrations of credit risk. It therefore proposed a delayed effective date for those requirements.

How Does the ED Affect Companies?

At this time, companies that haven't already done so should assess the implications of the revised ED for their particular situations. The ED applies to *all* entities, not just financial institutions. Readers should closely review the illustration in the current ED that identifies some of the more common financial instruments and indicates whether these have off-balance-sheet risk (see the box on page 604). That review will help entities in determining to

Which Financial Instruments Have Off-Balance-Sheet Risk and Which Don't

A financial instrument has off-balance-sheet risk if the risk of accounting loss to the entity exceeds the amount recognized, if any, in the statement of financial position.

The risk of accounting loss on a financial instrument includes

1. *Credit risk.* The possibility of loss, even if remote, from the failure of another party to perform according to the terms of a contract.
2. *Market risk.* The possibility that future changes in market prices may make a financial instrument less valuable or more undesirable.
3. *Liquidity risk.* The possibility that an entity may be obligated to pay cash that it may not have available.
4. *The risk of theft or physical loss.*

The FASB's revised ED addresses credit, market, and liquidity risk only.

The following are examples of some financial instruments that have ("yes") and some that do *not* have ("no") off-balance-sheet risk; not all financial instruments included in the scope of the revised ED are illustrated.

Financial Instrument	Off-Balance-Sheet Risk	
	Holder[a]	Issuer[b]
Traditional items		
Accounts and notes receivable or payable	No	No
Bonds	No	No
Cash	No	No
Common stock	No	No
Loans	No	No
Innovative items		
Collateralized mortgage obligations	No	No
Financial guarantees	No	Yes
Interest rate caps and floors	No	Yes
Loan commitments	No	Yes
Letters of credit	No	Yes
Options	No	Yes
	Both Counterparties[c]	
Swaps (interest rate and currency)	Yes	
Forward contracts	Yes	
Futures contracts	Yes	

a. Holder includes buyer and investor.

b. Issuer includes seller, borrower and writer.

c. For swaps, forward contracts and futures contracts, risks are assessed in terms of the position held by the company; therefore, the holder and issuer categories do not apply.

what extent they're involved in financial instruments with off-balance-sheet risk and to what extent they'll be affected by the final statement. (See the Appendix for how to make the required disclosures.)

Readers also should keep in mind that, although the current ED focuses principally on financial instruments with off-balance-sheet risk, the concentration disclosure requirements cover *all* financial instruments.

A Final Note

The FASB knows that some would prefer a faster pace of evolution and others a more moderate pace. The FASB also knows that not all constituents will endorse all the proposals in its current ED. However, all who stated their views were heard and considered, and comments from constituents on the current ED also will be considered in deliberations leading to issuance of a final statement. After considering the comments on the 1987 ED, the FASB concluded the revised ED would represent a worthwhile improvement in financial reporting. The FASB believes financial reporting for financial instruments is in a transitional stage. Once again, Paragraph 2 of FASB Concepts Statement no. 5, *Recognition and Measurement in Financial Statements of Business Enterprises,* applies: "[T]he Board intends future change [in practice] to occur in the gradual, evolutionary way that has characterized past change."

Appendix: A Sample Disclosure about Financial Instruments with Off-Balance-Sheet Risk

Here's an example of how S&C Bank might disclose information about its off-balance-sheet risk. S&C is a party in these financial instruments with off-balance-sheet risk:

- Commitments to extend credit.
- Standby letters of credit and financial guarantees.
- Interest rate swap agreements.

S&C Bank has no significant concentrations of credit risk with any individual or groups of counterparties. The information present is not comparative. This is permitted in the year of implementation; for all subsequent years, the information would be presented on a comparative basis.

S&C might disclose the following:

Note A: Summary of accounting policies
Interest rate swap agreements

S&C Bank is an intermediary in the interest rate swap market. As an intermediary, the bank maintains a portfolio of generally matched offsetting swap agreements. Those swaps are accounted for at market value, with changes in value reflected in noninterest income. At inception of a swap, the portion of the compensation related to credit risk and ongoing servicing is deferred and recognized as income over the term of the swap agreement.

Note B: Financial instruments with off-balance-sheet risk

The bank is a party to financial instruments with off-balance-sheet risk in the normal course of business to meet the financing needs of its customers. These financial instruments include commitments to extend credit, standby letters of credit and financial guarantees, and interest rate swap agreements. Those instruments involve to varying degrees elements of credit, interest rate, or liquidity risk in excess of the amount recognized in the statement of financial position. The contract or notional amounts of those instruments express the extent of involvement the bank has in particular classes of financial instruments.

S&C's exposure to credit loss from nonperformance by the other party to the financial instruments for commitments to extend credit and standby letters of credit and financial guarantees written is represented by the contractual amount of those instruments. The bank uses the same credit policies in making commitments and conditional obligations as it does for on-balance-sheet instruments. For interest rate swap transactions, the exposure to credit loss is much less than the contract or notional amounts. S&C controls the credit risk of its interest rate swap agreements through credit approvals, limits, and monitoring procedures.

Unless noted otherwise, the bank does not require collateral or other security to support financial instruments with off-balance-sheet credit risk.

	Contract or notional amount
Financial instruments whose contract amounts represent credit risk:	
Commitments to extend credit	$XX
Standby letters of credit and financial guarantees written	XX
Financial instruments whose notional amounts do not represent credit risk:	
Interest rate swap agreements	XX

Commitments to extend credit are legally binding agreements to lend to customers. Commitments generally have fixed expiration dates or other termination clauses and may require payment of fees. Since many of the commitments are expected to expire without being drawn upon, the total commitment amounts do not necessarily represent future liquidity requirements. The amount recognized as a liability in the statement of financial position at December 31, 19XX, for deferred fees on those commitments was $XX. The bank evaluates each customer's credit worthiness on a case-by-case basis. The amount of collateral obtained if deemed necessary by S&C

on extension of credit is based on management's credit assessment of the counter party. Collateral held varies but may include accounts receivable; inventory; property, plant and equipment; and existing income-producing commercial properties.

Standby letters of credit and financial guarantees written are conditional commitments issued by the bank guaranteeing performance by a customer to a third party. Those guarantees are issued primarily to support public and private borrowing arrangements, including commercial paper, bond financing, and similar transactions. The credit risk involved in issuing letters of credit is essentially the same as that involved in extending loan facilities to customers. S&C holds marketable securities as collateral supporting those commitments. The extent of collateral held for those commitments varies from X% to XX%; the average amount collateralized is XX%. The amount recognized in the statement of financial position at December 31, 19XX, as a liability for credit loss and a liability for fees received for standby letters of credit and financial guarantees written approximated $XX.

Interest rate swap transactions generally involve exchanges of fixed and floating rate interest payment obligations without exchanges of the undrlying principal amounts. S&C Bank enters into the interest rate swap market as an intermediary in arranging interest rate swap transactions for customers. The bank, as a principal in the exchange of interest payments between the parties, is exposed to loss if one of the parties defaults. The bank performs normal credit reviews on its swap customers and minimizes its exposure to the interest rate risk inherent in intermediated swaps by entering into offsetting swap positions so that the risks essentially counterbalance each other.

Entering into interest rate swap agreements involves not only the risk of dealing with counterparties and their ability to meet the terms of the contracts but also the interest rate risk associated with unmatched positions. Notional principal amounts often are used to express the volume of these transactions but do not represent the much smaller amounts potentially subject to credit risk. Amounts recognized in the statement of financial position as assets and liabilities for swap agreements entered into as an intermediary approximated $XX and $XX, respectively, which represent the market value of those instruments.

30

Credit Risk and the Scope of Regulation of Swaps*

Clifford W. Smith, Jr., Charles W. Smithson, & Lee Macdonald Wakeman

I. Introduction

Swap contracts represent a new addition to our catalog of financial instruments. Of the various types of swap contracts thus far developed, the U.S. dollar-denominated interest rate swap has generated the greatest volume. Figure 30.1 presents estimates of the volume of interest rate swaps from 1982 through 1986.

The rapid rate of growth in this market has produced heated debates, especially over the credit risk of these instruments. In their joint proposal on capital requirements, the Federal Reserve and the Bank of England (1987, p. 3) assert that, "The credit risks inherent in such contracts now constitute a significant element of the risk profiles of some banking organizations, notably the large multinational banking organizations that act as intermediaries between end-users of these contracts." We believe that such statements reflect a serious misconception about the default risk of interest swaps.

To assess the Federal Reserve/Bank of England proposal we first provide a brief history of the evolution of the swaps market. In Section III we examine the pricing of interest rate swaps, particularly the implications of default

*This research is partially supported by the Managerial Economics Research Center, William E. Simon Graduate School of Business Administration, University of Rochester.

FIGURE 30.1 *Estimated Swap Volume, 1981–1986*

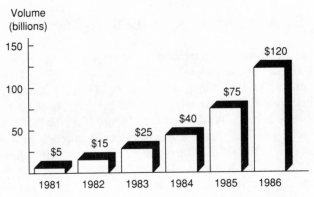

Panel A: Currency swaps.

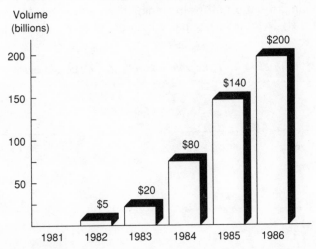

Panel B: Interest rate swaps.

This aggregate notional principal estimate corresponds roughly to estimates of volume from options markets in terms of "equivalent value of underlying shares." Note also that the current estimates of swap volume are unreliable. A swap might go through several intermediaries before reaching the final counterparty and each intermediary could report the swap in its volume. Thus the aggregation of private estimates is likely to result in extreme overstatement. The Federal Reserve and the International Swap Dealers Association have projects to derive more consistent swap volume estimates.

risk. We examine the proposed capital requirements in Section IV. Section V contains our conclusions.

II. A Brief History of the Swap Market

The first swaps developed from parallel loans arranged between companies in different countries, a contractual form popular in the 1970s. To illustrate a parallel loan, suppose an American company (Firm A) makes a loan in dollars to a British firm (Firm B), which in turn makes a loan of equal current value in pounds to Firm A. As illustrated in Figure 30.2, the loans have parallel interest and principal repayment schedules. By entering into this parallel loan agreement, the British firm transforms a debt incurred in pounds into a fully hedged U.S. dollar liability.

Parallel loan agreements developed primarily to avoid exchange rate risk imposed by government controls on capital movement. Thus, they were frequently employed between parent firms and their subsidiaries. There are, however, two important problems in employing parallel loans by two independent firms: (1) Default by one party does not release the other from its

FIGURE 30.2   *Cash Flows to Firm from a Parallel Loan Agreement*

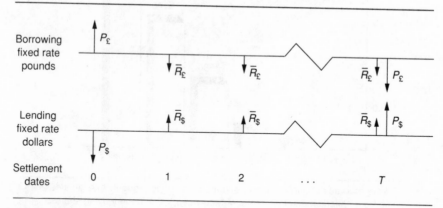

At time 0, Firm A simultaneously borrows pounds at the prevailing *T*-period pound rate and loans an equivalent current amount denominated in dollars at the *T*-period dollar rate. During the term of the loan, Firm A makes interest payments in pounds to Firm B, while Firm B makes interest payments in dollars to Firm A. At maturity (time *T*) the two firms make their final interest payments and return the principals; Firm A returns pounds and Firm B returns dollars. Note that inflows are denoted by up arrows and outflows by down arrows; the magnitude of the cash flow is indicated by the arrow's length.

contractually obligated payments; (2) although the loans effectively cancel one another, they remain on-balance-sheet items for accounting and regulatory purposes. In 1981 a new transaction, the currency swap, overcame these problems and by its success effectively replaced parallel loans.

Currency Swaps. A currency swap involves the same patten of cash flows as a parallel loan. Indeed, Figure 30.2 can be used to illustrate a fixed currency swap where Firm A receives fixed rate dollars and pays fixed rate pounds (while the counterparty, Firm B, receives fixed rate pounds and pays fixed rate dollars). Although a swap is defined in terms of an exchange of cash flows, there is no actual exchange of payments. Instead, at specified intervals, only the net cash flows are exchanged; the party that would have received the lower cash flow pays the other the difference.

By simplifying the older parallel loan transaction to a netting of the cash flows, the probability and magnitude of default are reduced. Furthermore, current regulatory and accounting practice treats swaps as off-balance-sheet items. In this way the currency swap accomplishes the goals of the parallel loan agreement while eliminating its problems. The currency swap's success has led to a variety of adaptations.

In a currency coupon swap, the counterparties again agree on the timing of the exchanges and the principal amounts; however, the interest rate in one currency is fixed and the other floating.

Interest Rate Swaps. Introduced in 1982, the interest rate swap is a special case of a currency coupon swap, one in which all the cash flows are denominated in a single currency. Figure 30.3 illustrates the cash flows of an interest rate swap for the party who is paying a series of cash flows determined by a fixed interest rate $(\bar{R})$ in return for a series of cash flows determined by a floating interest rate $(\tilde{R})$. The reverse would be true for the counterparty.

FIGURE 30.3 *Cash Flows from an Interest Rate Swap*

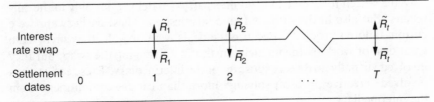

The party pays a series of cash flows determined by the T-period fixed interest rate $(\bar{R}_t)$ at the origination in return for a series of cash flows $(\tilde{R}_t)$ determined by the relevant floating interest rate.

In a basis rate swap both interest rates are floating, thus allowing floating rate cash flows calculated on one basis to be exchanged for floating rate cash flows calculated on another. For example, it permits firms to make conversion from one-month LIBOR (London Inter Bank Offer Rate) to six-month LIBOR, or from LIBOR to U.S. commercial paper rates. A basis rate swap is equivalent to pairing two simple interest rate swaps such that the flows are converted from floating to fixed, and then converted from fixed to floating (but on a different basis).

Commodity Swaps.   Swaps defined in prices other than interest rates and foreign exchange rates are also possible. Once a notional principal is agreed on and converted to a flow, any set of forward prices can be used to calculate the difference checks. The counterparties could agree to a notional principal and to the conversion of this principal to flows using a fixed dollar interest rate and the U.S. price of wheat. Such a swap is analytically no different than a currency swap; forward wheat prices replace forward currency prices. Neither firm need be in the wheat business; the difference checks are paid in dollars, not grain. Moreover, in a swap where the firm pays wheat, it can receive either fixed or floating rates in any currency or commodity.

Swaps with Optionlike Payoffs.   Swaps can be constructed with optionlike provisions limiting the range of outcomes. If a firm wanted protection against a substantial interest rate rise and was willing to limit its gains from a dramatic decline, it could modify a simple interest rate swap contract to read, "As long as the interest rate neither rises by 200 basis points nor falls more than 100, the firm pays a floating rate and receives fixed; but if the interest is more than 200 basis points above or 100 below the current rate, the firm receives and pays a fixed rate."

The Evolution of the Market.   As we noted, currency swaps were the first to appear. The earliest swaps were negotiated on a one-off basis, which involved a search for a matching counterparty—matching not only in the currencies, but also in the principal amounts desired. These early swaps were custom-tailored products. Because the deals were one-off, they involved a great deal of work by the financial institution arranging the swap, but they involved virtually no direct exposure for the intermediary. These early swaps involved "creative problem solving" more than capital commitment from the intermediary.

As interest rate swaps began to appear, the movement toward a more standardized product began. With the U.S. dollar interest rate swaps, there were fewer dimensions necessary for counterparties to match; the product had become more homogeneous. More frequently, instead of requiring exactly matching counterparties, the intermediary could bundle counterparties. With the move toward homogeneity and the reduced reliance on an identifiable counterparty, swap markets (especially the interest rate swap market) began to look more like commodities markets. Competition forced spreads down. And intermediaries began to accept swaps without counterparties, taking the risk on their own books and either matching it or hedging it with government securities or financial futures. Hence the evolution of the swap market was like that of many markets — from a customized, client-specific product to a standardized product.

With the customized product, the role of the intermediary had been one of problem solving. The dominant intermediaries in this early stage of development were investment banks. As the product became more standardized, the role of the intermediary changed considerably — there is now less emphasis on arranging the deal and more on transactional efficiency and capital commitment. As the market has evolved, the intermediaries have changed to more highly capitalized commercial banks.

III. Pricing Interest Rate Swaps

The cash flows from a swap contract can be decomposed into equivalent cash flows from portfolios of other, more familiar contracts — loans and forward contracts. These decompositions prove useful as we examine components of the pricing of a simple interest rate swap contract.

A. An Interest Rate Swap as a Portfolio of Loans

Figure 30.4 decomposes the interest rate swap in Figure 30.3 into a pair of loan contracts, borrowing at a fixed rate and lending at a floating rate. Using market interest rates, the value of the swap at origination must be zero. However, after origination the value of the swap is determined by the relation between the fixed and realized floating rates. Obviously, rate structure changes can produce large transfers between the counterparties. Note that this arbitrage result does not depend on the assumption that the contracts are default risk-free. With default risk, as long as the borrowing is collateralized with the lending agreement, the cash flows in Figures 30.3 and 30.4 are always equivalent.

Unfortunately, the apparent similarity between loans and swaps has led some to argue that the default risk in swaps is underpriced. For example, the chairman of the International Swap Dealers Association summarized the views of many market participants when he asserted, "The credit aspect of swaps is not being adequately remunerated in the market. There's a credit

FIGURE 30.4   *Decomposition of an Interest Rate Swap into a Portfolio of Loans*

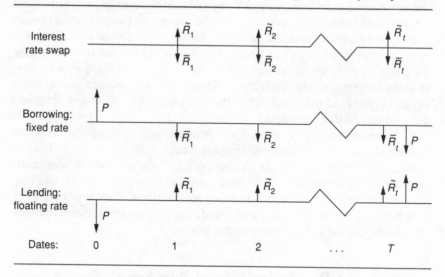

The cash flows from an interest rate swap where the party pays fixed is equivalent to the cash flows of a portfolio of two loan contracts: Borrowing at a T-period fixed rate ($\bar{R}_t$) and lending at a floating rate ($\tilde{R}_t$) and P is the loan principal.

spread of 150 basis points in the loan market but of only 5 to 10 basis points in swaps. The weakest credits are getting a terrific deal." [Shirreff (1985)]

We believe that there are several important differences between the default implications of loans versus swaps: First, the principal in a swap is not at risk—it is only notional; however, a significant component of the default risk of a loan has to do with the failure to repay the principal. Second, the swap cash flows are proportional to the difference in rates, not the level of rates. This potential exposure to default can be quantified by considering again the decomposition into borrowing at a fixed rate and lending at a floating rate. If rates have fallen since contract origination, the value of the above-market fixed rate coupons will be higher. This is illustrated in the off-market-rate swap in Figure 30.5. With lower market rates, the required initial principal exchange, $P'-P$, reflects the current market value of the loss to the counterparty were the fixed rate payer to default. However, there is a third, crucial difference between default on swaps and loans: Rational default requires both that the party to the swap be in financial distress and that the value of the remaining contract to that party be negative. Thus, for a customer using the swap to hedge, outflows are required when the customer's core business is expected to be strong. (We will return to this point.)

FIGURE 30.5   *An Off-Market-Rate Swap*

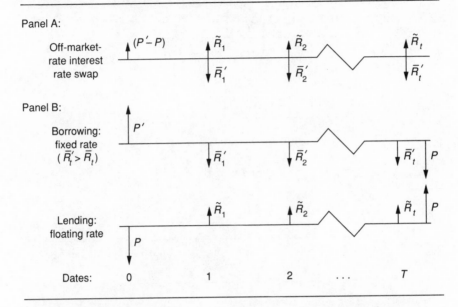

The party pays cash flows $(\bar{R}'_t)$ determined by a fixed interest rate above the current market rate and receives cash flows $(\tilde{R}_t)$ determined by the relevant floating interest rate. In Panel A, a principal exchange $(P'-P)$ occurs at origination, with P' equal to the market value of a bond with coupons $\bar{R}'_t$ and a principal repayment of P. In Panel B this swap is decomposed into two loan contracts: borrowing at a fixed rate higher than the prevailing market rate and lending at the market floating rate.

B. An Interest Rate Swap as a Portfolio of Forwards

Figure 30.6 indicates the fact that this swap contract can also be decomposed into a portfolio of simpler, single-payment contracts. These simple contracts are forward contracts. At each settlement date, the party to this swap contract has an implicit forward contract on interest rates—the obligation to sell a fixed rate cash flow for an amount agreed on at contract origination. Hence, the swap contract is like a portfolio of forward contracts, one corresponding to each settlement date.

But there are two important differences between an interest rate swap and an explicit portfolio of forward contracts: (1) The exercise price for the embedded forward contracts is the par rate, not the forward rate. So unlike a simple portfolio of forwards the value of each of the embedded forwards is not zero at origination (except in the special case where the term structure is

FIGURE 30.6   *An Interest Rate Swap as a Portfolio of Forwards*

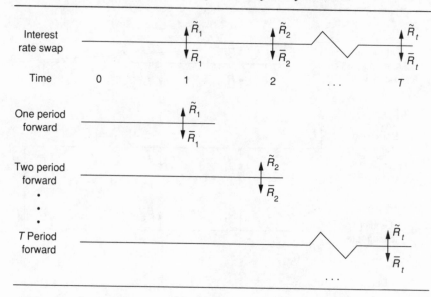

The cash flows of interest rate swap are equivalent to a portfolio of T forward contracts in which the party illustrated has agreed at origination to pay at period t in the future a known amount $(\bar{R}_t)$ to receive an amount determined by the prevailing single-period interest rate $(\tilde{R}_t)$.

flat). (2) In a swap, the forwards are not independent in the sense that default on any settlement check accelerates the maturity of the remaining embedded forwards.

We have noted that the analogy between swaps and loans invites a misleading analysis of default risk. However, we believe that the analogy between swaps and forwards is more productive. The payoff profile in Figure 30.7 can be used to illustrate either a forward, futures, or swap contract. Note that in each case the default risk is two-sided: If interest rates rise, the owner of the contract is required to make a payment; conversely, if interest rates fall, the owner of the contract receives a payment.

Closely allied to the two-sided risk issue is the issue of the use of the instrument. The payoff profile illustrated in Figure 30.7 could be used either to speculate on or hedge against changes in the interest rate. Clearly, the credit risk (the risk of default on the contract) is influenced by the use of the instrument. A firm with fixed obligations faces some probability of financial distress and bankruptcy. If the firm's cash flows are sensitive to interest rate changes and if it enters into a forward, futures, or swap contract as a hedge,

FIGURE 30.7   *Payoff Profile for a Swap at a Representative Settlement Date*

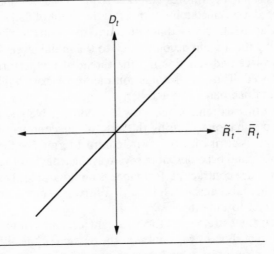

The value of a typical swap difference check, D_t, received by the party paying fixed and receiving floating. The value of the check increases as the realized floating rate, $\tilde{R}_t$, is greater than the fixed rate at origination, $\bar{R}_t$. This figure also can be used to illustrate the relation between swap, forward, and futures contracts. The value to the seller of a forward contract behaves similarly, but the fixed rate is replaced by the forward rate. The value of the day T settlement to the seller for a futures contract also behaves similarly, but the rate difference is between the futures rate calculated on day t and that from day $t-1$.

the probability of bankruptcy is actually reduced. In establishing a hedge, an outflow is required only when the contract owner's core business produces net inflows.

The manner in which default risk is treated differs substantially among forward, swap and futures contracts. A major difference is in the mechanism guaranteeing contract performance.

At one extreme is the futures contract. With futures contracts, there are three mechanisms designed specifically to deal with the threat of nonperformance. First, the futures contract is cash settled daily, reducing the performance period to one day. Second, a maximum daily price fluctuation is specified for most contracts. Third, futures contracts require an explicit performance bond to be posted. The owner of the futures contract has been required to post an initial margin, typically equal in value to the maximum daily fluctuation permitted in the value of the contract. Each day the contract is settled by drawing down or adding to the contract owner's margin account. Further, the futures contract requires that the margin account balance exceed a specified minimum. If as the result of daily settlements the account balance falls below that minimum, the contract owner must replenish it, bringing the margin account back to the initial level. With these mechanisms in place and functioning, the threat of nonperformance is substantially reduced. Thus, the futures contract involves virtually no extension of credit from one party to the other.

At the other extreme is the forward contract. No payments are made at contract origination or during the term of the contract. The total value of the contract is at risk for the entire contract term. The threat of nonperformance exists and becomes more severe as the length of the forward contract increases, since contract performance is not guaranteed either by a bond or by any other mechanism. Thus, with a forward contract each party has extended credit to the other.

Between the extremes of forward contracts and futures contracts is the swap contract. For a swap contract, the passing of the difference check provides only a periodic, partial settlement of the contract. Since only the maturing embedded forward contract is settled, the swap contract generally maintains some value after the difference check is passed.

The three contracts also differ with respect to the manner in which the contracts are traded. In the early stages of the evolution of the swap market, swap contracts were arranged on an individual basis, particularly in the case of currency swaps. The financial intermediary would arrange a swap between two parties who were known to each other. In such a system, the problems of two-sided risk are potentially severe. Each party has to expend resources to evaluate the counterparty's credit risk. Moreover, in such an environment, development of a secondary market that allows firms to divest themselves of the swap is necessarily limited. Hence, in a system with matched counterparties, there was understandable reluctance to permit transfer of the swap contract. As the interest rate swap market evolved, it became increasingly like the forward market for foreign exchange. Today the vast majority of interest rate swaps involve a bank as a counterparty. While the bank and the counterparty must still evaluate each other's credit risk, the problem of transferring the swap contract has been substantially reduced. If a firm enters into an interest rate swap contract with a bank and subsequently wishes to cancel it, there is no need to search for a third party to assume the contract obligation. The swap can be canceled with a cash settlement.

Futures contracts are exchange-traded instruments. The exchange takes no positions itself; instead, through its clearinghouse, the exchange guarantees the performance of all participants. Hence, the problem of two-sided risk is addressed by the exchange interposing itself between the parties to every transaction. In addition, the futures contract transaction must be executed through a firm that is a member of the exchange. The member firm endorses the transaction, effectively imposing a potential liability on the member firm if its customer fails to perform. Moreover, this broker endorsement increases the broker's incentive to monitor its customers' performance by monitoring the margin accounts.

While some forward contracts are also exchange traded, the recent experience with the default in tin contracts on the London Metal Exchange indicates clearly that, in a market characterized by two-sided risk, the creation of an exchange does not in and of itself eliminate nonperformance risk. By setting up an exchange, individual traders view the exchange as the counterparty, but the threat of nonperformance by individual traders remains. If a contract owner defaults, it becomes the responsibility of the exchange to cover the default. Most forward foreign exchange contracts – and, more recently, the forward interest rates contracts – are traded by brokers and banks.

IV. Capital Adequacy for Swap Contracts

With the dramatic growth in volume has come concern about the credit risk of swaps, including proposals for the imposition of capital adequacy requirements on the banks that intermediate swaps. Obviously, intermediation in the swap market imposes claims on a firm's capital. (This would seem the most reasonable explanation of the differential participation of commercial and investment banks as intermediaries in this market.) Equally obvious, capital reserves perform a valuable function by bonding the performance of the financial intermediary, thereby reducing the risk of nonperformance by the intermediary. Hence, nonperformance risk declines as the size of the capital reserve increases. However, as pointed out by Smith, Smithson, and Wakeman (1988), these facts alone are insufficient justification for capital adequacy requirements like those in the Federal Reserve/Bank of England (1987) proposal. Since banks can fully capture the benefits of adequately bonding themselves, the argument that additional bonding increases social welfare must be based on the existence of some unspecified externality or market impediment. In a functioning marketplace, financial intermediaries will be forced to provide the optimal bond (the optimal level of capital reserves). It follows that in a well-functioning market any additional reserve requirement imposed by a regulatory authority must have the effect of lowering social welfare. Thus, we contrast the Federal Reserve/Bank of England capital requirement with that of a market-determined capital reserve.

The proposed capital requirement is expressed as a product of three terms: the credit equivalent exposure, the credit conversion factor, and the capital ratio. In examining the proposed capital requirement for swap contracts, we focus first on the credit equivalent exposure, and then the credit conversion factor.

Credit Equivalent Exposure. As we have argued, Figure 30.5 illustrates the current replacement cost of a swap and thus the cost of default to the originating institution. Since rational default occurs only when the value of the contract is negative, the potential credit exposure looks like an option. By employing put-call parity we can reexpress the embedded forward in Figure 30.7 as equivalent to writing a call and buying a put on bonds. Since options have only one-sided credit risk, the change in the price of the forward associated with the customer's credit risk will be equal to the change in the value of the call. As Stulz and Johnson (1987) show, the value of a call subject to default can be derived using option-pricing techniques. Specifically, its value depends on the correlation between the value of the underlying asset and the value of the writer's other assets. The problem is more complex for swaps than forwards or options because of the specified sequence of settlement checks. Deriving an optimal default strategy thus requires consideration of the compound option issues discussed by Geske (1977).

Rather than explicitly solving for the credit equivalent exposure, the Federal Reserve/Bank of England (1987) employ a simulation. As described in the technical analysis, ex post values for exposures from a matched pair of swaps were simulated using as data the interest rate prevailing at contract origination, the volatility of interest rates, and the time remaining to contract maturity. The simulation results were then subjected to a statistical analysis. From this analysis, estimates of potential credit exposure as a percent of the notional principal and by time remaining to maturity are obtained.

We believe that there are a number of specific technical problems with their simulation: First, the density function for interest rates used in their simulation results in an upward drift (trend) in rates. Also, since potential credit exposures are determined by changes in the interest rate from that which prevailed at contract origination, the upward drift is also imparted to the potential credit exposures. Hence, to the extent that the distribution does not accurately portray the probability density function for interest rates, the calculated credit exposures are biased upward. Second, the volatility estimates inputted into the simulations are likely to be unrealistically high. These estimates were obtained using data from the period 1981–1986. As Figure 30.8 illustrates, this six-year period includes one and one-half years when the volatility of interest rates was at its peak (i.e., 1981 through mid-1982). If indeed the volatility estimates used overestimate future volatilities, the potential credit exposures are biased upward. Third, the technical analysis suggests that replacement costs are calculated every six months and that their absolute values are summed. Since the swap is being evaluated at origination,

FIGURE 30.8 *Interest Rate Volatility, 1960–1986*

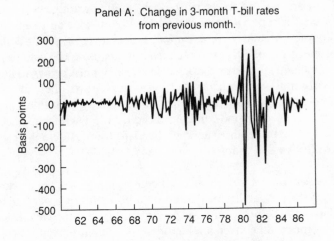

Panel A: Change in 3-month T-bill rates from previous month.

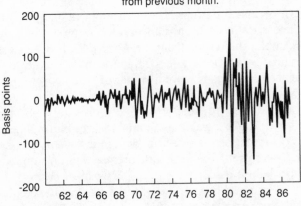

Panel B: Change in 10-year Treasury bond yield from previous month.

all of the future replacement costs must be discounted to time 0. They do not indicate that this has been done. If not, the calculated potential credit exposures are biased upwards. Fourth, as with loans, diversification effects exist such that the exposure of the sum is less than the sum of the individual exposures. However, there are features of swaps that reduce the exposure of a portfolio of swaps more than a corresponding portfolio of loans. A difference between a portfolio of swaps and a portfolio of loans recognized by all observers of this market is the netting arrangements that exist for swaps. As noted by the Federal Reserve and the Bank of England, these arrangements effectively reduce the notional principal of swap contracts and must therefore reduce both the current replacement cost and the potential credit exposure of a swap. Failure to recognize these netting arrangements overstates the exposure for a portfolio of swaps. Finally, default on swaps should be more idiosyncratic than default on loans. As has been noted, default on a swap requires two conditions to occur simultaneously: The value of the contract to the financial intermediary's counterparty must be negative, and the counterparty must be in financial distress. In contrast, the value of a loan contract to the borrower (the financial intermediary's counterparty) is always negative, so only one condition need occur. Therefore, since default on swaps will be more idiosyncratic, diversification of default risks should be more effective for swaps than for loans.

Credit Conversion Factor.   The credit conversion factor can be viewed as a function of the probability of default on a portfolio of a particular instrument relative to the probability of default for a portfolio of loans. Hence, to consider the credit conversion factor for swap contracts, it is necessary to consider the probability of default for swaps relative to that for loans.

The issue of the default risk of swaps was discussed in Section III. The probability of default for swaps is dramatically less than for a comparable loan. This theoretical prediction is apparently borne out by market experience. For example, the results from the April 1987 Touche-Ross survey of the International Swap Dealers Association members indicate that the default experience for swaps is more like that of AAA corporate bonds than that of a portfolio of loans. This should not be surprising since bank loan portfolios include loans to small firms and individual consumers, but the counterparties in swap contracts are limited to large banks, financial institutions, and those investment-grade firms with independent access to the capital markets. Therefore, from both a theoretical and an empirical view, the probability of default associated with a portfolio of swaps is significantly less than for a comparable portfolio of loans. Hence, the credit conversion factor should be strictly less than 100%.

Our analysis suggests that the probability of default for a swap contract is determined primarily by four significant factors. First, the creditworthiness of the customer. Second, the counterparty's inherent exposure to interest rate movements. Whether or not the firm is using the swap as a hedge will have a significant effect on the probability of default. A swap used as a hedge has a lower probability of default. While for more creditworthy counterparties, the financial institution is less concerned with the use to which the swap is put, for the lower-rated counterparties, it is clearly in the financial institution's interest to know the use of the swap. Third, the shape of the term structure. If the term structure is upward sloping (as it has been), the probability of default is reduced if the counterparty pays fixed and receives floating. If the term structure is upward sloping, the expectations hypothesis implies that the party paying fixed and receiving floating should expect to pay difference checks early in the term of the swap and receive net payments in later periods. Thus, the default risk of the fixed-rate payer is less than would be the case if the term structure were flat. An overview of the market for interest rate swaps indicates that the less creditworthy counterparties have been, by and large, paying cash flows based on a fixed interest rate. Hence, the probability of default for the portfolio of swaps is lower than if the counterparties were reversed. Fourth, whether the contract is bonded, for example, through collateralization.

None of these factors are reflected in the calculation of the credit conversion factor. Indeed, using the proposed rule, two-swap portfolios could be constructed that have dramatically different default characteristics but have the same capital requirements. When regulation deviates from marginal cost pricing in this way, regulatorily induced capital misallocations are likely. We believe that the current form of the regulation can be justified only on the grounds that it is simple for the regulators to calculate. We believe this is the wrong objective.

V. Conclusions

If the capital requirement is effective (if the capital requirement is set higher than optimal), the resulting regulatory tax will lead to reallocations in the swap market. We believe that reallocations will occur in three primary dimensions: volume, location, and credit quality. First, the regulatory tax would raise costs and thereby lower volume. And as swaps become more expensive, firms will be restricted in their ability to manage their exposure to financial price risks. Second, if the Federal Reserve/Bank of England proposal were adopted, some of the booking of swap business would move from the regulated institutions (U.S. and U.K. commercial banks and U.K. investment banks) to unregulated institutions (investment banks in the United States and financial intermediaries outside the United States and the United Kingdom). This suggests a potentially perverse outcome of the proposed regulation: The very reason for the proposed capital adequacy requirements (the fact that intermediation of swaps imposes a claim on the intermediary's capital) is the reason that commercial banks are replacing investment banks as the principal arrangers of swaps. If imposed, the capital adequacy requirement could block this movement and would, ceteris paribus, locate more of the swap business in those financial intermediaries that have less, not more, capital. Third, the imposition of a regulatory tax will affect the pricing of credit risk and therefore the composition of the users of swaps. As the default-risk price for swaps increases, more creditworthy users will opt to switch to other markets. For example, AAA credits are more likely to disintermediate and return to brokered, one-off transactions to avoid the tax. Thus, the effect of the regulation may well be opposite that desired: The regulation could increase rather than decrease the average default rate faced by the regulated institutions in the swaps market.

References

Bank for International Settlements. 1986. *Recent Innovations in International Banking.*

Bicksler, James, and Andrew H. Chen. 1986. An economic analysis of interest rate swaps. *The Journal of Finance* 41 (No. 3), 645–655.

Federal Reserve Board and Bank of England. 1987. "Agreed Proposal of the United States Federal Banking Supervisory Authorities and the Bank of England on Primary Capital and Capital Adequacy Assessment" and Staff Memo: "Treatment of Interest Rate and Exchange Rate Contracts in the Risk Asset Ratio." March 3, 1987.

Geske, Robert. 1977. The valuation of corporate liabilities as compound options. *Journal of Financial and Quantitative Analysis* 12, 541–552.

Jensen, Michael C., and Clifford W. Smith, Jr. 1985. Stockholder, manager, and creditor interests: Applications of agency theory. In E. Altman and M. Subrahmanyam (eds.), *Recent Advances in Corporate Finance.* Homewood, IL: Irwin, pp. 93–131.

Keslar, Linda. 1986. Season of the elusive floating rate payer. *Euromoney Corporate Finance* (April), 29–31.

Layard-Liesching, Ronald. 1986. Swap fever. *Euromoney* (January 1986 Supplement), 108–113.

Levich, Richard M. 1986. On the microeconomics of swaps and hedges. Unpublished manuscript, New York University.

Priestly, Sarah. 1986. When swaps make foreign debt easier to live with. *Euromoney Corporate Finance* (April), 33–35.

Shirreff, David. 1985. The fearsome growth of swaps. *Euromoney* (October), 247–261.

Smith, Clifford, Charles W. Smithson, and Lee M. Wakeman. 1986. The evolving market for swaps. *Midland Corporate Finance Journal* 3, 20–32.

Smith, Clifford, Charles W. Smithson, and Lee Macdonald Wakeman. 1988. The market for interest rate swaps. *Financial Management* 17, 34–44.

Stulz, René M., and Herb Johnson. 1985. An analysis of secured debt. *Journal of Financial Economics* 14 (No. 4), 501–522.

31

Patent and Copyright Protection for Innovations in Finance*

Christopher Petruzzi, Marguerite Del Valle, & Stephen Judlowe

---

The originator of a new financial product bears substantial risk and expense in both creating the product and in introducing it to the market. If successful innovations can be quickly copied by competitors who bear none of the risk and expense but can divert profits from the innovator, then the potential diversion of profits reduces the incentives to create a new product. Recent court decisions, however, have recognized that protection can be accorded to some innovations in finance. These protections are due to a broad interpretation of copyright and patent laws, along with the fact that many of the recent innovations in finance require the use of a computer for practical implementation. The different laws that may be used to protect innovations in finance will be described, along with examples showing that innovators who avail themselves of legal protection may receive substantial financial rewards. Those rewards are lost forever to innovators who fail to seek the appropriate legal protection in a timely manner. Even if qualification for legal protection is uncertain, the enormous potential from a monopoly in finance makes the investigation of patents and other legal protection worth the innovator's while.

---

*The authors are grateful for comments from James Ang and two anonymous referees.

I. Trade Secrets

In addition to patents, some legal protection is available to financial innovators through copyrights and trade secret laws. While these provide less protection than a patent, they may be obtained more cheaply and easily.

A trade secret may consist of any formula, pattern, device, or compilation of information that is used in business and that gives the trade secret proprietor an opportunity to obtain advantage over competitors who do not know or use it. One protects a trade secret by keeping it secret. This involves employee confidentiality, nondisclosure agreements, and other devices designed to ensure that no one but authorized personnel have access to the trade secret. Trade secret law is based largely on common law, and the trade secret is good as long as it is protected by the owner. A trade secret owner may recover only actual damages from someone who misappropriates a trade secret.

Trade secret law protects against the secret being used by those who obtain it through improper means, such as theft or breach of obligation to preserve confidentiality. However, the trade secret owner's only redress is against the misappropriator, not against any subsequent user who gained the trade secret by lawful means. Trade secret law does not protect against the person who independently develops the secret or obtains the secret through the negligence of the trade secret owner.

A competitor can also legally obtain a trade secret through reverse engineering. This amounts to taking apart the invention in order to determine how the invention works. Reverse engineering is done most easily with a physical product, but it can also be done with software—even when only output from the software is sold. The party desiring to appropriate the trade secret of the software may experiment with various inputs, and by observing the outputs then determine the sequence of operations for the software system. When the software itself is sold, it can be a relatively simple task for a skilled programmer to determine the trade secret.

While marketing a financial innovation will normally require disclosures that reveal the trade secret, developing expertise in the use of the trade secret, document preparation, SEC filing requirements, and determination of marketing possibilities may produce substantial time lags between the conception of a financial innovation and the final sale of a product. Trade secret law has historically been the principal protection for financial innovations, and the period of protection has often been limited to the lag time required for competitors to market a similar product.

II. Copyrights

A copyright protects "writings" that possess some minimal degree of originality and are fixed in tangible form. A copyright protects any works created on or after January 1, 1978, from the date of creation until 50 years after the death of the author. Joint-authored works are protected until 50 years after the death of the last surviving author. A copyright may be registered merely by filing certain formalities with the copyright office within three months of the creation of the protected work. As with trade secret law, a copyright provides no protection against the independent creation of the exact work by another.

Damages awarded against a copyright infringer may be any one of three types. The first type is actual damages incurred by the copyright's holder plus profits realized by the infringer due to the infringement. In lieu of actual damages, the holder of a registered copyright may elect to receive statutory damages. Statutory damages for a nonwillful copyright infringement range from $250 to $10,000 per infringement, at the discretion of the court. Statutory damages for a willful infringement may be up to $50,000 per infringement. If the infringer did not play an active role in the violation (such as a bookstore owner who unwittingly sold a work that infringes a copyright) the court may reduce the statutory damages to as little as $100 per infringement.

Computer software is copyrightable. The copyright provides remedies against another party who copies the software program. This protection may be of limited value, however, since a creative programmer can often write a new program able to duplicate all of the functions of the original program without infringing the copyright. Recently, however, courts have extended the protection of copyrights on software so that the original program is protected from new programs that have the same "concept and feel," even if the programming code for the new program is substantially different from that of the original program [13]. This protection will prevent competition from programs that have more or less the same prompts and user inputs, but it will not prevent competition from a program that has the same functionality in an original format.

III. Patents

The strongest legal protection that has been granted to financial innovators is a patent. Throughout history patents have been awarded to protect an inventor's work and to provide incentives for future innovations. Upon receiving a patent from the Doge of Venice in 1594, Galileo stated, "It is not fit that this invention which is my own, discovered by me with great labor and expense, be made the common property of everyone" [3]. However, the social dangers of monopoly require that patents be given only when, in the words of Thomas Jefferson (a member of the first U.S. Board of Patents), the invention was "worth to the public the embarrassment of an exclusive patent" [9]. In order to avoid this "embarrassment," the U.S. Patent and Trademark Office (PTO) exercises considerable discretion before issuing a patent, and courts overturn any patent that does not strictly meet the statutory criteria.

In the United States a patent is a 17-year granting of the exclusive right to make, use, or sell an invention. It gives the owner the right to preclude competition in the invention or to extract royalties from others who wish to use the patented invention. The scope of the patent is defined by claims that set forth the metes and bounds of the patent owner's rights. Those claims are broadly interpreted relative to the narrow protection of a copyright, so that the holder of a patent is protected against anyone using the claimed technology or its equivalent, even if the infringer has made minor changes in the practice of the invention.

A patent protects the owner against all willful copiers and reverse engineers, as well as against innocent infringers. Someone who independently develops an invention that has already been patented or who practices an invention without knowledge of the patent still infringes the patent. Obtaining a patent involves extensive review of the application by an examiner trained in the art on which protection is sought. If the patent is issued, it is a comprehensive legal protection.

The patent law requires that certain conditions be met before a patent is issued for an invention. For instance, the claimed invention must have utility. It must also be novel. The invention must be nonobvious to someone having ordinary skill in the art to which the invention pertains. The invention must be fully disclosed and described in such clear terms that one of ordinary skill in the art would be able to practice the invention. Finally, the subject matter of the sought patent must be within the area recognized as protectable. That is, it must be a new and useful process, manufacture, machine, or composition of matter made by a person. It must represent an advancement over the prior art that is of benefit to the public so as to justify the issuance of the patent [14].

The novelty requirement is that the inventor be first. A prior discovery of the claimed subject matter will bar the issuance of a patent, even if the patent applicant did not know the prior discovery. A patent claim must be filed with the patent office by the applicant within one year of the date the patented subject matter was first manufactured, used, or sold, or else the patent will be barred because it will be deemed that the prior manufacture, use, or sale destroyed the novelty of the claimed invention.

The criterion of nonobviousness is more complicated. "Obviousness" is a term of art in patent law. The patent may not be obtained if the subject matter as a whole "would have been obvious at the time the invention was made to a person having ordinary skill in the art" [15]. While the factual questions of who is a practitioner and what is obvious to that person may be disputed in courts of law, it is generally accepted that the person having ordinary skills is just that. The subject matter may be obvious to the leading finance professors doing research related to the patentable subject matter but still meet the criterion of nonobviousness.

A series of cases, beginning approximately in 1980, suggested that the Supreme Court advocated strong patent protection for innovative companies. These cases (and subsequent ones in the lower courts) laid the groundwork on which an inventor can hope to base patent claims on a financial innovation.

In the case of *Diamond v. Chakrabarty* (1980), the Supreme Court majority opinion pointed out that the Committee Reports accompanying the 1952 Patent Act indicated that Congress intended to "include anything under the sun that is made by man" [1]. Though not directly addressed by the court, this may be assumed to include computer programs.

In the case of *Diamond v. Diehr and Lutton* (1981), the defendants had devised a process for molding synthetic rubber. The "invention" improved on previous technology by automatically feeding temperatures into a digital computer that then instructed an operator on subsequent actions in the process. The application was initially rejected by the patent office on the grounds that the only novelty was the control of the operation by the computer. The appeal went to the Supreme Court, where it was determined that the subject matter of the application was patentable and the patent was awarded [2].

IV. Merrill Lynch's Cash Management Account Patent

A seminal case in the patenting of computer programs was *Paine Webber v. Merrill Lynch,* concerning Merrill Lynch's Cash Management Account (CMA).[1] Merrill Lynch had been awarded a patent on its method of keeping customer accounts. The CMA integrated idle funds into money market accounts, brokerage margin accounts, and charge accounts (such as Visa) with such features as a periodic sweep of idle funds into interest bearing accounts

---

1. CMA is a trademark registered to Merrill Lynch.

and a hierarchical debiting of accounts so as to maximize the interest accrued by the customer. It enabled the customer to make charges on his Visa card and automatically pay the charge bill when due out of credit available from stock margin. Merrill Lynch's method for implementing the CMA contained safeguards against check kiting and other potential abuses. The use of a digital computer was of key importance in implementing the invention, since the costs of administering by hand would be prohibitive.

The law recognizes that patentability is not precluded by the use of previously known elements. Most inventions are combinations of other inventions or known technologies in nonobvious ways. The Merrill Lynch CMA was a combination of this type. Each of the parts of the CMA (hierarchical debiting of accounts, money market funds, Visa accounts, idle fund sweep, brokerage accounts, and digital computers) existed before the patent, but these elements had never been combined in this manner. In order for the combination to be determined patentable, it was necessary that the statutory criteria for patentability be satisfied. After rigorous prosecution of the application, the patent office determined that all the conditions had been met.

The CMA proved to be an effective device for Merrill Lynch to gain customers, and this success presumably prompted several other brokerage firms to institute similar systems. Merrill Lynch notified those firms that practice of these similar systems infringed the CMA patent. Paine Webber was one of those firms notified by Merrill Lynch, and it sued Merrill Lynch in Federal District Court, seeking a judgment of "noninfringement, invalidity, and unenforceability" of the CMA patent. Merrill Lynch countersued seeking monetary damages from Paine Webber and third party Dean Witter for patent infringement.

No one disputed the utility of the CMA or that Merrill Lynch had been the originator. The Paine Webber argument was that the CMA system was not patentable — citing long-standing law that methods of doing business cannot be the subject matter of a valid patent. The court rejected Paine Webber's argument and upheld the patent, finding that the computer implementation of the data processing methodology at issue was patentable subject matter [7]. In the face of this judicial construction, Dean Witter paid Merrill Lynch $1 million for a license to continue operating its version of the CMA [11]. Paine Webber later settled with Merrill Lynch and paid an amount that by mutual agreement was not to be disclosed.

V. Implications for New Financial Products

While in many cases it is not clear which inventions would be eligible for a patent, the doubt as to whether or not to award a patent must be weighed against the value of the strong legal protection that the patent may provide. Some recent financial innovations that were not patented make clear the importance of investigating patent possibilities. Visicalc, developed in 1979 by a Harvard Business School student and a programmer, was the first electronic spreadsheet [12]. As an invention, Visicalc clearly had utility and novelty. Furthermore, it appears that Visicalc was not obvious to a person having ordinary skill in the "art," whatever the relevant art may have been. Visicalc was a likely candidate for a patent.

How valuable could a patent on Visicalc have been? Lotus 1-2-3 is a user of the technology invented for Visicalc, and Lotus' 1987 profits were $72 million on sales of $395.6 million [6]. This is after numerous Lotus "look-alikes" that also use the Visicalc technology have made significant inroads into the spreadsheet market. By comparison, Visicorp had cumulative profits of approximately $4.6 million through 1982, and losses every year after that [8]. Visicorp could have had the right to exclude other software developers from using the patented technology. Alternatively, it could have continued to sell its own product and license the technology to other software developers who made improvements. Either way, profits from the innovation could have accrued to the original inventors, thereby encouraging further development of original computer software.

The current ambiguity in patent law makes it unclear which other recent financial innovations might have been eligible for a patent. Many of the most recent innovations have, however, been "instructions for a digital computer" (software) to perform novel and nonobvious useful tasks, since performing those tasks by hand is not economically feasible. Some systems for program trading in which the computer selects stocks to purchase and sell as substitutes for the exact stocks in an index may have been eligible for a patent.

The current ambiguity even suggests that algorithms such as the Black-Scholes options valuation formula may have been eligible. Although the courts have held that "laws of nature, physical phenomena, and abstract ideas" are excluded from patent protection (Einstein's $E = mc^2$ is given as an example of excluded matter [2]), financial formulas are different from laws of mathematics and physics in important ways. Financial valuation formulas rarely if ever involve a universal truth. Validity of the Black-Scholes formula, for example, is dependent on the probability distributions of possible stock returns, estimates of variance in stock price changes, and the absence of arbitrage profits. Since the assumed conditions may or may not exist, the formula is neither a mathematical identity nor a universal truth, either of which would be unpatentable. Furthermore, selection of the proper period of previous returns for estimation of a stock's variance may have been the subject of experimentation by patent applicants, and the option-pricing method would in part be the result of that experimentation. A computer program that estimated a stock's variance and applied that variance estimate to the Black-Scholes formula may have been eligible for a patent had Fischer Black and Myron Scholes applied in a timely manner.

On a more general level, current law expressly states that "a claim is not unpatentable merely because it includes a step or element directed to a law of nature, mathematical algorithm, formula, or computer program so long as the claim as a whole is drawn to subject matter which is otherwise statutory" [2]. While $E = mc^2$ was not patentable, a computer program that applies the formula in a useful and previously nonobvious way may be deserving of a patent. By analogy, the accounting identity of assets equal to liabilities plus equities is not patentable, but various methods of applying the formula may qualify.

VI. Costs of Obtaining and Enforcing a Patent

The out-of-pocket costs for a patent application, including attorney's fees and fees to the PTO, are generally not prohibitive. The costs of litigation against patent violators may be considerably more expensive, and those costs must be borne by the patentee. Court decisions in favor of the patent holder, however, may require the infringer to reimburse attorney's costs, and a willful patent violation may result in an award of punitive damages up to three times the actual damages. In addition to these costs, there may be opportunity costs that make alternative forms of protection (such as trade secrets) more desirable.

The academic literature on patents discusses several reasons for not seeking patent protection. Horstmann, MacDonald, and Slivinski [5] argue that competitors may derive valuable information from a patent. Since information on the patent application is not disclosed to the public prior to the patent award, there is no loss of proprietary information during the patent pending period. Competitors may, however, use information from the patent after it is awarded to develop similar innovations that do not, however, infringe the patent. Innovators who consider this possibility may choose not to patent some innovations, keeping them instead as a trade secret. While this argument describes behavior in some industries, it has only a limited application to financial innovations, since the successful marketing of a financial product frequently requires full disclosure to customers and/or to the SEC. This disclosure may provide competitors with as much useful information as the patent itself.

Innovators may also choose not to seek patent protection because they believe that their innovation has a short useful life. Prosecution of an application to patent is a lengthy process. At best, there is a wait of two years from the filing of a patent application to the actual award of a patent. Changes in markets and technologies may mean that a monopoly on the innovation would have no value after even the best case, two-year period.

Scherer [10] notes that in an industry that is oligopolistic or monopolistic prior to an invention, there may be no need to protect a patent on an invention that may only be used in that one industry. His argument is dependent on barriers to entry that are sufficiently high (i.e., factors of production owned exclusively by the innovator). A similar argument may be used for the capture of a variety of positive externalities.

The applicability of Scherer's argument to innovations in finance depends on the nature of the innovation. A technology with a narrow application (such as to stock exchanges only) may not warrant a patent. Furthermore, the theory of industrial organization demonstrates that a monopoly at any one stage of production will under certain conditions result in the same prices and profits as a monopoly at the final stage. This suggests that research and development of new financial products that require the use of a monopolistic institution (such as the New York Stock Exchange) might be financed by that institution as a means of internalizing benefits without the legal costs of obtaining and enforcing a patent. This strategy may be more efficient than the joint research ventures made by companies in industries that lack a monopoly in one stage of production.

Hirshleifer [4] uses similar logic to show that an innovator may effectively reap the benefits of his innovation through speculation on relative price changes that occur as a result of changed technology. He provides the example of Eli Whitney, who was not able to effectively enforce his patent on the cotton gin but who might have gained from changes in the prices of cotton and various production factors. While Whitney's problems might dissuade an innovator from patenting an invention, we must keep in mind that those problems arose in part from the fact that the technology of the cotton gin had low economies of scale, so that many small gins operated in violation of Whitney's patent. Since there is some fixed cost to preventing each patent infringement, patent enforcement may be uneconomical when there are likely to be many small violators.

Hirshleifer's suggestion of using speculation on price changes as an alternative to patent protection would have only limited appeal, even in the hypothetical world of frictionless markets for all possible claims in all possible states of the world. Even in such a market, the informed purchases of the inventor may influence prices and thereby reduce profits. Furthermore, even if the exact technology of the new invention were not anticipated by markets, the effects of the invention may be anticipated so that no relative price changes occur as a result of the invention. Perhaps it is due to these considerations that there are not any known cases in which Hirshleifer's interesting suggestion has been employed.

VII. Conclusion

In recent years, the financial industry has produced a wide variety of valuable and sophisticated innovations. The popular press has even referred to the inventors of those innovations as "rocket scientists." Real rocket scientists carefully consider the available means of legal protection for their innovations, and a broad interpretation of the patent laws means that the same choices of legal protection are now available to some innovations in finance. This legal protection provides incentives for increased innovation in financial areas, and may therefore reward both the innovator and society at large.

References

1. *Diamond v. Chakrabarty,* 447 U.S. 303 (1980).
2. *Diamond v. Diehr,* 450 U.S. 175 (1981).
3. B. J. Fererico, "History of the Patent Office," *Journal of the Patent Office Society* (July 1936), p. 23.
4. J. Hirshleifer, "The Private and Social Value of Information and the Reward to Inventive Activity," *American Economic Review* (September 1971), p. 561.
5. I. Horstmann, G. MacDonald, and A. Slivinski, "Patents as Information Transfer Mechanisms," *Journal of Political Economy* (December 1985), p. 837.
6. M. Ozanian, *Financial World* (April 5, 1988), p. 17S.
7. *Paine, Webber, Jackson, and Curtis, Inc. v. Merrill, Lynch, Pierce, Fenner, and Smith, Inc.* 564 F. Supp. 1358 (D.Del. 1983).
8. P. Petre, *Fortune* (May 28, 1984), p. 70.
9. G. Rich, "Principles of Patentability," in J. F. Witherspoon (ed.), *Nonobviousness: The Ultimate Condition of Patentability,* The Bureau of National Affairs, 1980.
10. F. Scherer, *The Economic Effects of Compulsory Patent Licensing,* Monograph 1977-2, Center for the Study of Financial Institutions, New York, NY: New York University, p. 23.
11. P. Sudo, "Litigation," *American Banker* (December 28, 1983), p. 7.
12. A. Taylor, "Small-Computer Shootout," *Time* (March 2, 1981), p. 93.
13. *Whelan Associates, Inc. v. Jaslow Dental Laboratory,* 797 F.2d 1222 3rd Cir. (1986).
14. *35 U.S.C.,* sec. 101.
15. *35 U.S.C.,* sec. 103.

32

Monopoly, Manipulation, and the Regulation of Futures Markets*

Frank H. Easterbrook

In the textbook model of competition, all buyers and sellers are tiny compared with the market as a whole. These people trade fungible commodities in an ongoing auction. Every seller's product is the same as every other's. All participants in the market are sophisticated. Every buyer continues to purchase as long as the price is less than the value he places on the commodity; every seller continues to sell as long as the price is greater than the marginal cost of production. New buyers and sellers can jump in at an instant's notice, and if they find the going rough they can jump out again. No one can take advantage of a trading partner because someone else will offer the prospective victim a better deal. Information about bids and offers spreads instantly to all participants and would-be entrants. Every beneficial trade takes place. The trading leads to an outcome that is best for each buyer, each seller, and society as a whole.

Of course textbook economies occur only in textbooks. It is commonplace to lament the fact that traders are not microscopic compared with the market; that traders are gullible; and that entry and exit are not quick and free, information not cheap and ubiquitous, and products not identical. These departures from the utopian vision of perfect competition give rise to calls

*I thank Dennis W. Carlton, Tom Coleman, Daniel R. Fischel, John H. Stassen, Lester Telser, and the participants in the Workshop in Applied Price Theory at the University of Chicago for helpful comments on an earlier draft. This paper was substantially completed before I joined the court of appeals and was revised in minor ways thereafter.

for intervention by the government to "perfect" the operation of our regrettably imperfect markets. If the intervention of the government is afflicted with the same costs and failures as the markets, we shall have to sigh in resignation.

Yet some markets come close to the model. Agricultural and financial markets have standard products handled by many sophisticated traders. Products are comparable. Information spreads quickly. True, all of us can't be farmers or bankers, and even farmers cannot produce more wheat instantly or move it costlessly to where it is demanded, so the free entry and exit condition does not hold. Farmers and bankers do not always honor their contracts, so their promises are not really interchangeable. And of course all of us can't be glued to video monitors displaying price information. So perfection cannot be achieved. But a market can come close.

Futures markets come closer than cash markets. A futures contract is a claim to the underlying commodity, but because of its standard terms it is more easily traded than the commodity itself. Every contract (for a given commodity and time) is identical to every other, so contracts are fungible. The contracts are made with or guaranteed by a clearing house, so the performance of a contract does not depend on the identity, wealth, or inclinations of the person holding it. Anyone can buy a contract; entry and exit are quick and cheap; contracts can be sold nationwide without transportation cost; the supply of contracts can grow or shrink quickly. Traders in futures markets are largely professionals — both those who use futures contracts to hedge and those who trade for a living. They have up-to-the-minute information on price. Futures markets are accordingly all but indistinguishable from the textbook models of perfect competition.

In most product markets, from razor blades to iron ore to computers, firms may introduce products as they wish. If they fail, both the firms and the customers suffer. (Customers may be left without service or performance of warranties.) Few people think that the departure of the computer market from the model of perfect competition is a reason to restrict entry, which would force the market even farther away from the model.

Yet both entry into and the daily conduct of futures markets are heavily regulated. The usual reason given is that futures markets suffer from monopoly and manipulation: Traders can "corner the market" to their profit, or they can manipulate prices. So they can. The question I investigate is whether the threat of monopoly and manipulation is so serious (compared with the threat in other markets) that entry should be restricted. Section I shows how monopolization could occur and assesses the costs of monopoly in futures markets. Section II takes up the way futures markets respond to these costs. It looks at the kinds of precautions exchanges take and whether they are apt to take the appropriate level of precaution. Section III looks at some cases of actual or asserted monopolization to see whether there were substantial losses and whether the private mechanisms worked. Finally, Section IV evaluates the case for regulation of entry and compares the costs of monopoly against the costs of preventing the operation of markets altogether.

I. The Nature and Effects of Monopoly in Futures Markets

In markets for commodities such as wheat and automobiles, monopoly means controlling the supply. A merger or effective cartel of all automobile manufacturers would enable the sellers to reduce output. Consumers bid more for the remaining supply. Producers get monopoly profits. Consumers who would buy at the competitive price but are unwilling to pay the higher price lose the difference between the value they place on a car and the real cost of producing one. The foregone consumers' surplus is the allocative welfare loss of monopoly. The prospect of obtaining the monopoly profit also induces would-be monopolists to spend resources getting and keeping their position, which increases the total cost of monopoly (see Posner [1976], pp. 8–22, 237–255). The higher price attracts new entry, however, and the monopolist cannot hold onto its position without barricading this entry. The cartel must not only prevent entry but also prevent "cheating" by members — that is, the practice of increasing one's own output hoping to sell more at the enhanced price. The allocative loss is limited by cheating and new entry; the sooner and the more the cheating, and the quicker the entry, the less the loss.[1]

A futures market is a slice of the market in the underlying commodity. A contract may entitle the buyer to delivery of wheat in Chicago in March. Accordingly it seems simpler to monopolize the supply. The would-be monopolist need not capture the entire supply of wheat; it is enough to get hold of wheat deliverable in Chicago in March. But it turns out not to be so easy. The monopolist of cars, wheat, or ore can extract an overcharge because people need the commodity. Someone who needs wheat does not need a futures contract for wheat; he can purchase the wheat directly. Thus, a person with a monopoly of futures contracts to deliver wheat in Chicago in March cannot easily extract an overcharge. People who want wheat will not transact with him.

The general point is that for many purposes transactions in the commodity are substitutes for transactions in futures contracts.[2] Because buyers can

---

1. If entry is immediate, even the producer of 100% of the supply must charge the competitive price (Baumol, Panzar, and Willig [1982]).

2. The cash commodity is not a perfect substitute, for otherwise we would not see futures markets. Futures are useful in hedging risks, and they also create additional liquidity akin to money. See Telser and Higinbotham (1977) and Telser (1981). I return to these features below.

use whichever is cheapest, they cannot easily be exploited in futures markets. The "monopolist" of a futures contract must find someone to stand on the other side of the transaction, and no one voluntarily subjects himself to monopoly when a competitive price is available. If it becomes known that one person has a monopolistic position on one side of the market, the contract dies. The putative monopolist cannot find anyone to exploit.

"Monopoly" in a futures market therefore turns out to be a species of fraud. The putative monopolist must conceal his position and intentions from his would-be trading partners, for otherwise he won't have partners. People do not knowingly submit to exploitation. In fact, a reasonable definition of monopolization of a futures market is any explicit or implicit misrepresentation of the size of one's position in relation to the rest of the open interest. The misrepresentation may take two forms. (Each can occur on either the buying or the selling side, and for ease of exposition I do not distinguish them.)

The first, which I call a *position fraud,* is the unexpected assembly or maintenance of a large position on one side of the market. (I forswear the usual terminology of "squeezes," "corners," and the like, not only because people do not agree on the meaning of these terms, but also because this jargon makes the argument hard to follow.) The party may acquire a large portion of the existing contracts, thus undercutting the usual assumption that every trader is "small" in relation to the market. Or the party may simply decline to liquidate his position, so that at the very close of trading a formerly small holding becomes large in relation to the open contracts. The holder of these contracts then demands or tenders delivery (depending on whether he is long or short). Holders of opposite positions, surprised by the sudden demand or tender, unable either to make or take delivery without incurring large costs, and unable to find other parties with whom to close out their positions, must pay a premium to negotiate around the demand. If the adverse parties had been aware of the large position, they could have stayed out of the market, liquidated their positions earlier, or prepared to take or make delivery (such preparations could greatly reduce the costs of compliance and therefore the premium available to the holder of the large position).

The second maneuver, the *ownership fraud,* entails owning both futures contracts and the underlying commodity. For example, the perpetrator buys up the supplies of wheat available for delivery in Chicago in March. Then he enters "long" contracts giving him a right to delivery, and he insists on delivery. The "shorts" (the people who have promised to deliver wheat) are embarrassed by their inability to obtain supplies to fulfill their obligations. They are shocked to discover that the person entitled to delivery already owns the deliverable supply. They must either spend large sums to put more supplies into a deliverable position or pay a premium to the holder of the long interests. Again secrecy is important. People would not knowingly sell wheat short to someone who already owned the wheat; and if they did so by accident and found out in time, they could bring new supplies to market to reduce the premium they must pay to cancel their obligations. Of course the defrauder must pay a premium to get control of the deliverable supply; when the fraud is over he must unload the commodity at a loss.[3] He seeks to make more by jacking up the price of the futures contract than he loses on the cash commodity.

Both types of fraud leave a characteristic trail. There will be substantial concentration of ownership on one side of the market and sudden changes of price around the end of the contract's term. As soon as the contracts have been settled, prices return to the level established by the terms of supply and demand in the underlying commodity. The sudden price fluctuation produces a transfer of wealth among participants in the market and also enables us to identify suspicious events. The manipulation may be secret at the start but cannot be secret at the end. An undisclosed manipulation is an unsuccessful manipulation. (A flurry of wash sales might lengthen the period during which the price change occurs but cannot eliminate the change, at least not without eliminating the profit from the transaction.)

What are the losses from these frauds? There are transfers of wealth from victim to perpetrator, but these shifts of wealth are not real economic loss. No resources are used up. The transfers are not even unambiguous losses to the victims. The risk of manipulation in futures markets is known. People transact in these markets voluntarily, and they will not do so if the anticipated costs (including the loss on becoming a victim) are less than the anticipated returns. The opportunities outside futures markets (including investing in the cash commodity) will determine the returns required to justify participation in futures. When manipulation is possible, the terms of trade adjust; there is no reason to think that participants in futures markets make smaller net profits on account of manipulation.

The real costs of manipulation *come from the adjustments* of terms that prevent the occurrence of anticipated net losses. The adjustment for the risk of manipulation drives a wedge between the futures price and the anticipated price of the cash commodity. This gap—needed to compensate the participants for risk—also makes the futures contract less valuable as a tool for hedging. Someone who owns the underlying commodity and wants to reduce

---

3. Some traders have control of the deliverable supply because they monopolize it. Governments monopolize the production of their currencies, and some nations participate in cartels monopolizing physical commodities (such as tin and cocoa) traded in futures markets. These markets are therefore more open to manipulation by the monopolist, and we should expect to see less trading in them relative to the trade in the underlying commodity. I put these unusual markets to one side in this paper. For treatment of their special properties, see Anderson and Sundaresan (1983).

the risk of a change in its price cannot obtain an exactly offsetting position in the futures contract but must continue to bear some of the risk. The futures contract becomes a little less liquid and therefore a little less useful as a money substitute. The price signals sent by the futures market also become a little less accurate. A farmer looking at futures prices in order to decide how much corn to plant will miscalculate by a little on account of the change.[4] And if a futures exchange alters the contract to reduce the possibility of manipulation — say, by permitting delivery in three places instead of one, thus enlarging the deliverable supply and making it harder to commit the ownership fraud — the change creates the same sorts of loss. A contract with a defined supply spanning three cities is less useful to someone who wants to hedge against wheat in Chicago, and so forth. The larger area means that there is no single index of value; a greater supply produces greater uncertainty in price.

Manipulations also create some direct welfare loss. People who are surprised by the state of the market may expend extra resources moving new supplies to a deliverable condition. The costs of shipping commodities at the last minute are wasted. People may take precautions, such as moving additional supplies earlier; again, these are wasteful. Finally, people may spend resources trying to execute these manipulations or to shift the costs of manipulations to others. These resources are lost to society.

It is not possible to quantify these costs, but they are not likely to be large. Manipulations are rare: Since they must be disclosed eventually, it is hard to commit more than one. Each manipulation affects only a single contract among the many that cover each commodity. The number of recorded manipulations is a minuscule fraction of the total number of futures contracts that have been traded. Thus, the change in price needed to compensate people for the risk of manipulation will be small, and the losses entailed in creating and taking precautions against manipulations also must be small. Hedgers can obtain almost perfect hedges; farmers can obtain almost perfect price signals to guide future conduct.

Although we cannot know the social costs of monopoly and manipulation in futures markets, we can know the *maximum* costs. They will be less than the social benefits of the futures contract itself. No one enters into a futures transaction unless he expects to obtain benefits exceeding expected costs — including the costs of being the victim of manipulation. When private costs

---

4. A farmer who looked at the prices during a manipulation would of course be sent wildly astray. But no one makes planting decisions on the basis of the price in the last few days of the current contract, the only price seriously affected by a manipulation. People make decisions on the basis of prices predicted for some time hence by open contracts. See Marcus and Modest (1984), explaining how futures markets influence production decisions. See also Forsyth, Palfrey, and Plott (1984), confirming predictions that futures markets lead to more accurate prices in spot markets.

become too high, people shift to using forward contracts and other transactions in the underlying commodity rather than futures markets. For reasons I have sketched, the private costs of being a victim, which include the transfer of wealth to the perpetrator, exceed the social costs. Similarly the social gains from futures markets exceed the expected private gains. The social gains include benefits derived from more accurate planting by farmers, more accurate investing by owners of Treasury bills, and so on; yet the futures exchanges cannot charge the farmers or investors for all these benefits. The benefits flow from the price signals sent by the futures markets, not from the actual purchase and sale of contracts. Thus, those who never trade get some benefits from futures markets. (A process of linkage discussed in Section II ensures, however, that the futures exchanges take into account some of the value these people place on information.)

Because participation in futures markets is voluntary, people will cease dealing in a given contract when expected private gains fall to zero. Expected private gains fall to zero while social gains are still positive (because social gains exceed private ones, while social costs of monopoly are less than private costs). The futures market in a given commodity will close down — with or without regulation — before monopoly and manipulation create net social costs. Thus, whenever we observe a futures market in operation, we may be confident that there are net social benefits; however large the costs of monopoly and manipulation may be, they are not large enough to extinguish the gains from having the market.

II. Market Responses to the Costs of Monopoly

Traders can protect themselves against monopoly and manipulation by withdrawing. As soon as they learn of the existence of a manipulative strategy, they close their positions. They can go on to transact in another contract free from the attempted manipulation. Entry and exit are so easy that monopoly cannot thrive.

This is not an interesting response, though, when the would-be monopolist can keep his position secret. Then the response must be organized rather than individual. The exchange on which the futures contract trades will handle the collective response.

Some futures contracts hardly require an organized response to the possibility of monopoly. Both the frauds discussed above depend on the ability of the manipulator to obtain a "large" position in relation to the open interest and the deliverable supply. For some futures contracts this is all but impossible. Consider, for example, a futures contract covering Treasury securities of a particular maturity. The securities are readily available. They can be carried from one end of the country to the other quickly and for trivial cost, and so all of them are potentially available for delivery. No one could corner the supply of them. Futures in precious metals or other easily shipped, fungible commodities are also almost impossible to manipulate because of the large deliverable supply.[5]

Or consider a contract based on the price of some other security, such as a contract on the Standard and Poors 500 stock index. The value of this index depends on the price of a large basket of stocks. The futures contract on the index is not settled by delivery or even by transactions to set a price; the cash settlement price of the futures contract is derived mechanically by inspecting the value of the index. No one can manipulate this contract even by having 100% of the futures interest. To manipulate the futures price you must manipulate the price in the other market that determines the futures price.

Because the reference market is much larger than the futures market, manipulation becomes almost impossible. Suppose someone wanted to manipulate the price of an index in stocks of the electronic industry. He would have to jack up the closing price of IBM, Xerox, and other electronics stocks on the day specified in the futures contract. This is no mean feat; if he makes a higher bid price, he must be prepared to buy. Securities markets are very liquid, and even a small increase in the bid price may bring a flood of offers. The manipulator must accept these offers through the closing, else the price will return to where it was. Few people or institutions have the assets to manipulate the price of IBM stock even for an instant.[6] And things get worse. Having jacked up the price of the securities in the index, and thus having realized more on the futures contract, the manipulator is stuck with a lot of IBM and Xerox stock that cannot be sold for what the manipulator paid.

---

5. Every once in a while someone tries. Between 1978 and 1980 the price of silver futures rose rapidly and then fell. The result: a welter of charges and countercharges of manipulation. The principal targets of lawsuits are members of the Hunt family who, it is alleged, took substantial long positions and demanded delivery, driving up the price. (For example, *Friedman v. Bache Halsey Stuart Shields, Inc.,* 738 F.2d [D.C. Cir. 1984], one of the many suits.) I do not try to sort out these charges. But if it is true that the Hunts were trying to monopolize silver and silver futures, they were apparently the largest victims of their scam. Their desire to take delivery month after month became known, and people scoured the world to find deliverable supplies. The price rose, but the Hunts discovered that they could not sell the silver for what they paid; the price was driven by their demand, not by the demands of others. Apparently they lost more than a billion dollars. Not the stuff that encourages future manipulations! When a tactic generates only losses for the perpetrators, it suffocates itself. Neither the exchange nor the government need be concerned.

6. It would be easier to affect the price of IBM or any other stock by spreading lies about the firm's prospects. Fraud could affect the value of any commodity, from stock to oil, underlying a futures contract. The defrauder would need to make the false news believable, however, and then escape detection. No set of precautions can prevent futures frauds that involve lies about the commodity—but then this sort of fraud does not appear to be common. I have not seen any claim that a futures fraud has been committed in this way.

The manipulator supported the price; with the manipulator selling rather than buying, the price will fall. The manipulator's gain in the futures market must exceed his loss in the securities market, and because the securities market is so much larger, this is unlikely.[7] Manipulation of this sort is not logically impossible, but it should be sufficiently rare that this risk may be discounted in the absence of evidence that such manipulations occur. None has ever been established. (See Federal Reserve System [1985], pp. VII-5–VII-13.)

I return, then, to commodities such as grains in which manipulation is more likely. Here a few simple precautions will go a long way to reducing the amount of manipulation. Because monopolization of futures markets is a form of fraud, the best antidote is information. A futures exchange can monitor the positions the traders hold; if a trader appears to have too large a share of the open interest, the exchange can instruct him to reduce his holdings. (Position limits perform some of this task automatically, and an exchange can monitor holdings to ensure that even amounts less than the limit do not become excessive in relation to the rest of the market.) If the trader will not sell, the exchange can publicize the situation. Most traders believe that publicity would prevent the realization of profit and will act to avoid it.[8] Publicity enables other traders to make appropriate responses; it also means that in the future other people will be less likely to trade with the potential offender. The exchange might formally bar a person from trading (sanctions can include bans for life). "Shunning" of professional traders by other traders could also be effective. The value of a trader's seat is open to forfeiture if the trader misbehaves. Traders who commit an ownership fraud

---

7. In late April 1984 the press expressed concern that the Chicago Board Options Exchange's (CBOE) options contract on the Standard and Poors 100 stock index had been manipulated through coordinated last-minute bloc transactions that jacked up the price of the securities. A quick check revealed that the implied losses on reselling the securities would be approximately five times the apparent gains on the futures contract. (See 16 Securities Regulation and Law Report 723, 750 [April 27, May 4, 1984].) The CBOE established that no manipulation had occurred. (Report of the Special Index Study Committee, CBOE [August 22, 1984].) As far as I can tell, this is the only time a manipulation in a financial options contract has been alleged, and no one has ever seriously alleged, let alone documented, a manipulation of a financial futures contract (Federal Reserve System [1985], pp. VII-5–VII-13). In principle a defrauder could sell the underlying securities short to "recover the corpse." This, too, seems to be significant only in principle. Short sales require the posting of 100% margin and thus are very expensive; they are also so closely monitored that a strategy involving large-scale buying and simultaneous short selling would be detected.

8. Secrecy is the order of the day in futures markets, and for good reasons. Hedgers do not want others to learn their positions because that would convey information valuable to their competitors in the underlying commodity. Traders seek secrecy even knowing that the secrecy possessed by others facilitates frauds. That traders subject themselves to occasional frauds as the price of general secrecy speaks volumes about both the value of secrecy and the infrequency of fraud.

may find people unwilling to sell them the cash commodity in the future for the market price, and this, too, is an effective sanction. (Recall that the ownership fraud involves buying the cash commodity for less than the perpetrator will demand to settle the contract, which implies a loss for its trading partners.)

A futures exchange has a large arsenal of other weapons against monopolization. By establishing daily price change limits, the exchange reduces the ability of a manipulator to capitalize on a position. The exchange may elect to require liquidation of a contract at a fixed price if the probability of monopolization becomes too high. It could change the terms of delivery, enlarging the deliverable supply to frustrate a manipulative maneuver. Indeed, the exchange could build any of these precautions into the terms of the contract.

Every futures exchange uses some or all of these methods — and every exchange used at least some of them before federal regulation began with the Grain Futures Act of 1922 (42 Stat. 998). The exchanges today frequently impose position limits more restrictive than those required by regulations, and they frequently intervene quietly to require traders to reduce their positions. (See Federal Reserve System [1985], pp. VII-17–VII-35.) Although interventions that alter the terms of the contract or require immediate liquidation are much less frequent, these too occur.[9]

It is plainly in the interest of exchanges to define the terms of contracts and establish rules that reduce the amount of monopoly and manipulation. Each exchange must attract business, which will not be forthcoming in the desired volume if the contracts are needlessly risky. Traders control the terms by their ability not to trade. They can buy forward contracts on the underlying commodity or simply stay out of the market. Each exchange also faces competition from contracts designed by other exchanges. Traders can take their business elsewhere in a twinkling of an eye. This competition, together with the availability of substitutes for futures markets, ensures that the exchanges will do a great deal to police transactions (see D. R. Fischel [1986]). An exchange that neglects to take precautions — and to find ways to certify that it will make these precautions effective — cannot long survive.

The question remains whether an exchange will take the right precautions. To say it will take some is not to say it will take enough. There is an optimal amount of precaution in any market, an amount that stops short of eliminating fraud. After all, the only way to have no manipulation is to have no market. Traders are willing to suffer the risk of manipulation in exchange for the benefits of the futures market, and they want to conserve on enforcement costs. The exchange should continue taking additional precautions only

9. For example, *Sam Wong & Son, Inc. v. New York Mercantile Exchange,* 735 F.2d 653 (2d Cir. 1984), recounting in some detail the New York Mercantile Exchange's handling of Maine potato futures in the spring of 1979.

until the social gains at the margin just equal the social costs. Of course, an exchange looks only at the private costs and benefits — those it can appropriate for itself and its members. The question, then, is whether the private costs and benefits facing a futures exchange closely approximate the social costs and benefits.

The answer is almost certainly yes. The traders incur both the private and the social gains and suffer the losses from futures trading and manipulation. These traders constantly transact with the exchanges and among themselves. As long as no significant effects are felt by third parties, strangers to these contracts, the exchanges have the proper incentives to design optimal contracts and take optimal precautions.[10] And here almost every affected party is in on the contract.

Only "almost" because those who plan transactions in reliance on the price information produced by a futures exchange may stand outside the circle of contracting parties. For example, people deciding whether to plant wheat may rely on the information about future prices of wheat contained in the quotations from a futures exchange. These producers (and therefore the rest of us) gain when the prices permit more astute decisions about production, yet the futures exchange has no obvious way to charge for this service. Accordingly, the exchanges will take too few precautions designed to preserve the accuracy of price.

This is not likely to be a serious shortcoming, however. Many who deal in wheat are likely to hedge by transacting in the futures markets, and if they do so, the exchanges will be induced to take the appropriate precautions. Even if the occasional farmer disdains the futures markets, the farmer expects to sell to someone else who does. If the person to whom the farmer sells hedges by trading in the futures market, this again transmits the appropriate incentives to the exchange. The social benefits of accurate prices that are not reflected in futures transactions of one sort or another are likely to be small. Certainly there is no reason to think that futures markets take less care than other markets to make prices accurate for the benefit of such parties.[11] (This is not to say that they take the optimal degree of care; it is only

---

10. Coase (1960) points out that the private solution will diverge from the optimal one when transactions costs are high and that they are likely to be so in multiparty cases. But the exchanges themselves are in a position to coordinate the actions of the many traders. The exchanges set the terms of the contracts and then see whether people want to trade. The action of the exchanges replaces the need for an express series of negotiations among the many potential traders.

11. The difficulty of appropriating the value of accurate prices extends beyond futures markets and is only casually related to the problem of monopoly and manipulation. For example, the interest rates at auctions of Treasury bills may be used by many people to plan transactions, and it is not possible to charge those who refer to this information. Because of the webs of contracting among producers, hedgers, and other traders, futures markets probably come closer than other markets to taking optimal precautions.

to say that they are likely to be driven in the appropriate direction to a greater degree than many markets that are unregulated.)

It has been argued, however, that futures markets do not respond to these (and other) costs and benefits completely because of the way they operate. The futures exchanges sell trading services. They charge by the trade, and they cannot engage in price discrimination to collect extra from those who gain the most from less manipulation and more accurate prices. A reduction in the number of episodes of monopolization does not necessarily lead to more trading. Consequently, the argument concludes, the exchange will not take optimal precautions (Edwards and Edwards [1984], pp. 354–55). This argument is fallacious. Although a futures exchange sells transactional services, and although a reduction in manipulation does not necessarily lead to an increase in the number of transactions precisely reflecting the gains from less manipulation, it does not follow that the futures exchange cannot charge for the value of its precautions. The exchange can increase the price it collects per trade. Traders will pay higher prices per trade as long as the change is less than the value of the reduction in the costs of manipulation. The futures exchange can charge for its precautions even if, by increasing the accuracy of the price signals, the precautions lead to fewer trades.

In sum, there is no reason to think that futures exchanges will systematically take suboptimal precautions against monopoly and manipulation. Edwards and Edwards (1984) eventually come to this conclusion. The traders (and the traders' trading partners) reap the gains and suffer the losses of manipulation, so they will compensate the exchanges for taking the appropriate steps. Each exchange must do so, or it will lose business to another exchange that selects the appropriate mix of precautions. No exchange will stamp out manipulation, because that is not worth the cost. The cost of catching each episode rises as they become more rare, and the value of staming out that last offense is small; hence, the optimal rate of crime is always greater than zero. For similar reasons, no manufacturer tries to eliminate all defects from its products.

If it is necessary to choose between the level of precaution set by the exchanges and the level set by a regulatory agency, several considerations suggest that the exchange will do better than the agency. One consideration favors the regulator: the regulator can consider 100% of the social gains and losses from monopoly and manipulations; a futures exchange, while approaching that, will always fall short. In principle, then, the regulator could promulgate the perfect rule. But practice falls far short of principle. Consider these three difficulties.

First, a regulatory agency must act on the basis of estimates of costs and benefits. The exchange, too, acts on the basis of estimates. A regulator who estimates wrongly suffers no loss; loss falls rather on private parties for whom beneficial transactions have been foreclosed. The regulator may suffer a political loss, but the political "market" does not transmit price signals very well. A futures exchange that estimates wrongly suffers real losses. The exchange can reward employees who analyze correctly and penalize those who do not. The regulatory agency pays its employees at a fixed civil service scale quite impervious to profit and loss. You should trust those who wager with their own money to do the calculations correctly. They may be wrong, but they are less likely to err than are regulators, who are wagering with other people's money.

Second, the futures exchanges compete with one another. We may suppose (despite the first consideration above) that both exchanges and regulators make haphazard estimates of the appropriate level of precautions to take. When an exchange estimates wrongly, people do less trading there and move their business to other exchanges that are more nearly right. When a regulatory agency guesses wrong, it is hard for "customers" to take their business elsewhere. Armen Alchian and Gary Becker have shown that, even if participants in markets are stupid and respond poorly to incentives, the reactions of their customers lead the market in the direction of efficiency (see Alchian [1950], Becker [1976], and Sowell [1980]). A form of natural selection is at work. Businesses that miscalculate are sifted out. Certainly a process of selection is at work in the futures business. Carlton (1984) illustrates the rapid birth and death of both contracts and exchanges. No similar process eliminates regulatory agencies.

Third, regulatory agencies can cause futures exchanges to diverge from efficient practices in ways the exchanges cannot achieve by themselves. Regulators can impose costly rules that make it hard for new futures exchanges to compete with existing ones. They can prevent the entry of new exchanges altogether or delay existing exchanges from offering new contracts. They can award new contracts to the least successful exchanges in order to buoy them up, protecting them from competition by others. Traders lose as the penalty for failure goes down and as contracts migrate toward less efficient forums. The exchanges cannot do these things; only the government can. Yet as I emphasized at the outset, persistent monopoly is possible only if new competition may be nipped in the bud. The ability of government to reduce competition and produce monopoly profits for the exchanges makes it an attractive nuisance (see Stigler [1975]; and Salop, Scheffman, and Schwartz [1986]). Consider the airline business. For a long time, the Civil Aeronautics Board justified its existence as necessary to ensure safe, low-cost air transport. To that end it excluded new entry and tightly regulated existing firms. It awarded "plum" routes to failing airlines. Since deregulation in 1978, fares have fallen, air travel is safer, and there is more frequent service (provided by new commuter airlines) to small cities. The experience showed that the principal function of regulation had been to prop up a cartel of the major carriers. We should incur the risk that regulation will be put to anticompetitive ends only if there is strong evidence that government has a comparative advantage over private conduct in solving important failures in markets. There is neither a logical argument nor evidence showing such a comparative advantage in futures markets.[12]

III. Regulation and the History of Manipulation

No one seeking to demonstrate the existence of monopoly and fraud in futures markets would have much difficulty doing so. The Hutchinson wheat fraud of 1867, the Harper Deal of 1887, the Cargill wheat corner of 1963, and many others are part of the lore of the markets.[13] Of course, no one wanting to demonstrate the existence of monopoly in the underlying commodities or fraud in the issuance of securities of firms that deal in commodities would lack examples, either. The question is not whether there is monopoly and manipulation, but how much there is — and whether the amount has declined with the recent increase in the amount of regulation by enough to cover the costs of that regulation.

These questions are not easily answered. One problem is the lack of a benchmark. The number of futures contracts offered has increased through the years. This naturally leads to an increase in the opportunities for manipulation. But we cannot count the total number of attempted manipulations. Perhaps exchanges handle attempted manipulations with greater secrecy now than they used to. I have been unable to persuade the exchanges to furnish me with any data about the number or circumstances of private interventions.

Then there is a problem of determining whether any change in the amount of manipulation was produced by the exchanges or the government. Both the exchanges and the government have altered their rules over time. Even if we could determine whether the exchanges' rules or governmental regulations were responsible for a change in the frequency of manipulation (which is unlikely) we could not determine who was responsible for the rules and regulations. Do futures exchanges adopt their rules freely, or are some of the rules responses to or anticipations of regulatory pressure? Do regulators adopt their regulations on the basis of independent judgments about the benefits of regulation, or are some of these regulations merely copies of the

---

12. The Federal Reserve System's 1985 study does not perform any comparative analysis. It also finds few problems and recommends little additional regulation. It never considers whether the current level of regulation is excessive.

13. These and others discussed below are discussed in Hieronymus (1977), Johnson (1981), and McDermott (1979). See also *Cargill, Inc. v. Hardin*, 452 F.2d 1154 (8th Cir. 1971), cert. denied, 406 U.S. 932 (1972) (finding liability for the conduct in 1963).

exchanges' private rules (or, worse, efforts to reduce rather than enhance competition)? These difficulties make it all but impossible to determine whether the amount of monopoly and manipulation has decreased and, if so, why.

It may be helpful to recall that monopoly and manipulation (which I have used almost as synonyms) are not the same as exploiting an advantageous position in the market. Markets offer people the opportunity to assess anticipated supply and demand. Someone who takes a long position (buying the right to delivery or to settlement) does so because he believes or fears the price will rise. The stronger his belief, the more long contracts he will buy. Hedgers and speculators on both sides of the market serve valuable functions in bringing to light new information, about supply and about demand, that makes the price more accurate and the futures market more useful. The reward for this effort (and the associated risk) is the ability to obtain a profit from coming to the right conclusion. If a shortage of supply develops and the price rises, we cannot logically turn around and accuse the holder of a large long position of "manipulation"; that would remove the lure of profit that makes the market work.

Any effort to find and denounce "manipulation" must therefore differentiate that conduct from astute anticipation of changes in the conditions of supply and demand. The usual legal definitions of manipulation invoke notions such as "intentional wrongdoing" or creation of "artificial" conditions. The definition cited most often is that behavior is manipulative when "conduct has been intentionally engaged in which has resulted in a price which does not reflect basic forces of supply and demand."[14] This gets us nowhere.

An effort to isolate which "forces of supply and demand" are "basic" and which are not is doomed to failure. What is a "basic" demand? Economists think of supply and demand as givens. People demand what they demand, and never mind the reasons why. If people want to purchase wheat to admire its beauty rather than to mill it into flour, they may be weird, but their demand is real. Is a demand for gold to be put into a safe "basic"? How about a demand for wheat to be held in silos in anticipation of famine? People may want warehouse receipts for wheat in order to bake bread, but they may also want them (as they want Treasury bills) for their close equivalence to money. There is no way to say what demand is real and what is artificial. The addition of "intent" does not help. No one accumulates futures contracts—for reasons good or ill—unaware of what he is doing. Everyone in the futures market intends to make as much money as he can. Scrutiny of intent is therefore not likely to assist in the search for manipulation.

Nonetheless, the legal tests point in the right direction. For reasons I have explained, manipulation is a form of fraud. A person who accumulates a

---

14. *Cargill, Inc. v. Hardin* (n. 13 above), 452 F.2d at 1163. See also, e.g., in re Cox, CCH Commodity Futures Law Reports, ¶21.767 at 27.076 (CFTC 1983).

substantial long position could be counting on one of two things to produce profit: either a shortage of the commodity, or the ignorance of other traders about what the first trader is doing. Someone who buys long positions because he understands the supply of the commodity better than other traders is engaged in normal economic behavior; his actions drive the price in the direction it should move. Someone who is betting on his ability to conceal his own position from others and to profit solely from that concealment is engaged in fraud; his actions likely drive the price in the wrong direction. The person who seeks profit solely from concealment makes today's price less, not more, accurate as a predictor of future prices. The decrease in accuracy is a source of economic loss. Moreover, the inaccurate price is likely to cause people to ship the commodity toward the place where the price suddenly rises, only to ship it back again later. This, too, is source of economic loss.

Concealment by itself may be beneficial. Concealing one's position may be useful in obtaining the profit from one's ability to predict actual conditions of supply and demand, and hedgers need secrecy to avoid revealing their positions in the cash commodity. Secrecy is a valuable commercial strategy that increases the value of searching for new information. The essential distinction is between secret strategies necessary to capture the value of new information about underlying conditions and secrecy designed to cause prices to diverge from those that reflect the underlying conditions.

A reasonable economic definition of manipulation is conduct whereby (1) the profit flows solely from the trader's ability to conceal his position from other traders and (2) the trades do not move price more quickly in the direction that reflects long-run conditions of supply and demand. Someone searching for manipulation might look for asymmetric information. He also might look for the telltale sign of sudden price fluctuations. When the closing price on a futures contract significantly diverges from the price of the cash commodity immediately before and after, this is strong evidence that someone has reduced the accuracy of the market price and inflicted real economic loss on participants in the market. Courts usually look for both concealment and sudden swings in price.

A search for examples of manipulation in light of this test turns up remarkably few. You can find one in 1931, another in 1957, and a few more before and since.[15] While thousands of suits are filed each year alleging violations of the antitrust statutes and goodly numbers of plaintiffs win antitrust judgments every year, most years go by without a single judgment of

---

15. *Peto v. Howard,* 101 F.2d 353 (7th Cir. 1939) (July 1931 corn in Chicago); *Volkart Bros., Inc.,* 20 A.D. 306 (1961) (October 1957 cotton in New Orleans), reverse sub nom. *Volkart Bros., Inc. v. Freeman,* 311 F.2d 52 (5th Cir. 1962). See also the cases collected in the sources cited in n. 13 above.

liability for a futures manipulation. Even some of the adjudicated incidents of manipulation demonstrate its rarity.

Take, for example, the ownership fraud involving the May 1963 wheat contract on the Chicago Board of Trade. Cargill secured 2,471,000 of the 2,804,000 bushels of wheat available for delivery in Chicago. Then it took a long position of almost 2,000,000 bushels and demand delivery. On the last day of trading Cargill owned about 62% of the long interest. The shorts discovered to their chagrin that Cargill owned the wheat available to be delivered and would not sell to them for less than $2.28¼ per bushel — the same price it wanted to settle delivery obligations under the contract. Cargill got its $2.28¼. Just before the last day of trading on the May contract, however, Cargill had sold 600,000 bushels of wheat for $2.09, and cash wheat in Chicago sold for between $2.03 and $2.15 right after the settlement. The court found Cargill liable for manipulation, pointing out that this situation could be called "artificial" because such a price fluctuation had never been observed before; that is, the court made the rarity of the price changes the tip-off of the offense.[16] It also concluded that Cargill had used its special knowledge to advantage — it profited not because it knew more about the demand and supply of wheat in the cash market but because it alone knew who owned the deliverable wheat in Chicago.[17] (The court might also have observed that Cargill alone knew that it would demand delivery, which most longs do not.)

When there is no fraud, there is no manipulation. The May 1979 Maine potato futures contract, like the May 1963 Chicago wheat contract, was marked by a sudden price rise. This time, evidence showed that the rise was caused by an unexpectedly poor crop. One trader accumulated almost all the long interest in the contract, but others knew what this trader was doing, and, according to the opinion of the court, they also anticipated that he would stand for delivery.[18] The exchange ultimately stopped trading in the contract and required an orderly liquidation — a demonstration of the ability and willingness of a futures exchange to prevent even suspicious conduct.[19]

---

16. Rarity of the fluctuation is a common element of the claim of manipulation. For example, in re Cox (n. 14 above) (comparative tables showing rapid price fluctuations, a dramatic change in the relation among Chicago, Kansas City, and Minneapolis prices that could not be accounted for by transportation costs, and the lack of similar fluctuations and price relations in other years).

17. *Cargill, Inc. v. Hardin* (n. 13 above), 452 F.2d at 1159: "It is important to note here that Cargill was in possession of a valuable piece of information that other traders and grain dealers in Chicago did not have access to, namely that it owned the bulk of deliverable wheat in Chicago." (See also 452 F.2d at 1170.)

18. *Sam Wong & Son, Inc. v. New York Mercantile Exchange* (n. 9 above).

19. The court held that the exchange was not liable for failure to stop trading sooner or to redefine delivery obligations to increase deliverable supply. It concluded, however, that Anthony Spinale, the disappointed holder of the long contracts, might be entitled to recover if he could prove that the exchange stopped trading out of malice or in order to give other traders an

The point: there is often a large price change and a large profit without manipulation. The number of cases of real manipulation seems to be small indeed.

IV. The Methods and Limits of Regulation

Regulation of futures markets may take three principal forms. The first is to punish monopolistic or manipulative behavior. The second is to establish rules for the administration of futures contracts. The third is to prohibit the writing of contracts unless a regulator concludes that the contract is not subject to manipulation.

The first approach allows the exchanges to offer such products and take such precautions as they choose. Then an agency or the courts may punish those who engage in monopolistic or manipulative conduct. This form of regulation by deterring wrongful conduct prevails in most markets. People make their own arrangements, and the antitrust laws (administered by the courts, the Department of Justice, and the Federal Trade Commission) punish wrongdoers. It has also been the method of regulating futures markets for most of our history.

The second approach allows exchanges to offer futures contracts freely but requires them to establish precautions, such as reporting requirements and position limits, that reduce the probability of manipulation. An agency reviews the requirements the exchanges establish and requires changes if it concludes that these are inadequate. This approach has been used (though to varying degrees) since the Grain Futures Act of 1922.[20] It relies heavily on the self-interest of the futures exchanges to identify and implement effective precautions. If the markets function well without rigorous constraints, then the agency does not intervene. This approach is also the one in use today for the securities markets. Anyone may offer a new security without obtaining the SEC's approval. The regulatory agency requires some disclosure by the issuer of the characteristics of the security, and it also requires the stock exchanges to adopt and enforce some simple rules of honest conduct. This system of regulation assumes that informed traders should be left to their own judgment to decide well or poorly, as they choose, both in buying stocks and in designing rules. The SEC largely defers to the exchanges' rules — especially

---

advantage. As the court observed, there is nothing wrong with guessing the deliverable supply and insisting on maximum profit. "The Exchange is not a social club. We see no reason to believe that if a surplus of potatoes had developed, the shorts would have exhibited a higher quality of mercy to Spinale than he did to them" (*Sam Wong & Son, Inc. v. New York Mercantile Exchange* [n. 9 above], 735 F.2d at 678).

20. See Grain Futures Act, 42 Stat. 998 (1922); Commodity Exchange Act, 49 Stat. 1491 (1936), both amended and substantially superceded by the Commodity Futures Trading Commission Act of 1974, 7 U.S.C. §§2–22.

those that have been successful through the years. (Loss [1983] describes the rules.)

The third approach, entry regulation, requires that an exchange demonstrate both that futures contracts are not subject to manipulation and that they are otherwise in the public interest. Entry regulation was applied to futures markets for the first time by the Commodity Futures Trading Commission Act of 1974 (7 U.S.C. §§2-22). Under this approach, the exchange must justify each contract. The burden is on the exchange to support the contract rather than on a court or an agency to expose flaws in the contract. It is obviously the most effective in preventing monopolization—you can't monopolize a market that does not exist—but also has the highest costs.

The costs of deterrence, the first method, are least. The costs of regulation of the exchanges, the second method, are higher because the regulator may require the exchanges to take excessive precautions. The regulator may set the position limit too low, for example, thus reducing the value of the contract in hedging and also reducing the liquidity of the market. This form of regulation is unlikely to be beneficial unless regulators systematically do better than the exchanges at finding the optimal precautions. For the reasons discussed in Section II, it is unlikely that the government has a comparative advantage here.

Entry controls almost certainly are not cost justified. For the reasons discussed in Section I, the costs of monopoly and manipulation in a futures market cannot exceed the other benefits of the futures contract in question. The participants in futures markets bear the costs of monopoly and manipulation; if these costs exceed the benefits from the futures contract, they will stop trading.

Even if the costs of monopoly are high and futures exchanges do not take appropriate precautions, the costs of having no contract at all exceed the costs of having a manipulable contract. Recall from Section I that the cost of monopoly is the forgone value that the buyers of a product could receive. Monopoly means a lesser output at a higher price; people do less trading in monopoly-prone contracts because the implicit price (including the cost of being victimized) is higher. The value to the buyers is lost altogether, however, when the contract is abandoned or not introduced. Consider which is worse: a world in which videocassette recorders (VCRs) are subject to monopolization, or one in which VCRs do not exist at all because of fear that, if they existed, someone might monopolize them? In the former world the buyers priced out of the market lose the value they place on having a VCR; in the latter world, everyone who would buy a VCR loses. We do not prohibit the manufacture of products that might become monopolized; we do not even prohibit the manufacture of products, such as power lawn mowers, that might prove dangerous. Instead, we punish misconduct when it occurs. What is true of the market in VCRs and lawn mowers is true of the market in futures contracts.

To make matters worse, the absence of a futures contract makes it easier to monopolize the market in the underlying commodity. Recall again how monopoly works. The sellers reduce their output, so customers pay more for what remains. As long as they can keep output down and keep new entrants out, they stand to profit. New entry and cheating by members of the cartel ultimately undercuts the monopoly, and prices fall again. The existence of a futures market makes cartels harder to form and maintain. Producers participate in futures markets to hedge their risks. They will sell futures contracts, locking in a price for some time ahead. The existence of these price commitments on the part of producers is a form of prearranged "cheating" on the cartel. It is very hard to organize to drive down output when sellers have commitments to deliver. The futures market commits sellers to deliver and enables buyers to obtain the competitive price for some time to come. By the time all these prearranged commitments have expired, new entry from other producers is likely, so the cartel never really gets off the ground.

There is another perspective from which to assess the costs and benefits of both entry control and regulation of the exchanges. That is to ask how often the costs are incurred. The costs of prohibiting the introduction of a contract apply to every transaction that would have been consummated. The costs of regulation of the operation of the futures exchanges apply to every transaction, too. If a stringent position limit makes a contract less useful for hedging or makes the market less liquid, that cost is reflected in every transaction because the price of the futures contract becomes less accurate. The gains of regulation, on the other hand, are realized only to the extent that regulation prevents particular episodes of monopoly or manipulation. As Section I showed, the beneficiaries from a reduction in monopoly are the marginal traders—those who are priced out of the market if monopoly raises the effective cost of participating. Regulation, therefore, balances a certain loss on all trades under existing contracts against a possible gain on some trades on some contracts. This is worthwhile only if monopoly and manipulation, when it occurs, is quite costly indeed. We have no reason to conclude that monopoly in futures markets is particularly costly. There are so many substitutes for futures markets (the purchase of the underlying commodity on forward contracts and the purchase of options on securities are just two among them) that the allocative welfare loss from monopoly and manipulation of futures markets is bound to be small. The swap of certain losses on many trades for possible gains on a few trades is unlikely to be worthwhile.[21]

---

21. This discussion is closely related to the trade-off between allocative losses and productive efficiency gains in mergers. A merger may enable the surviving firm to reduce its real costs of production even while it gets the monopoly power to increase price. The lower costs of production increase efficiency, while the monopolistic reduction in output decreases efficiency. The lower costs of production apply to all units of output, however, while the efficiency loss from

Whether this trade-off is worth making depends in part on how often manipulation occurs and whether deterrence of violations is likely to be effective. If monopoly and manipulation are rare, it is cheaper to penalize the wrongdoer in that rare case than to penalize all participants in every case by establishing costly precautions.[22] Why spend resources scrutinizing each contract and each trade in advance when very few are undesirable? Regulation by deterrence comes at lower cost than regulation by prior scrutiny.

Of course whether manipulation is "rare" depends in turn on the effectiveness of the sanctions meted out on offenders. The discussion in Section III suggests that offenses are indeed rare. It is easy to see why. Sanctions deter undesirable conduct by increasing the loss associated with that conduct. The effective sanction depends on the probability that the offense will be detected and on the size of the penalty imposed when detection occurs. The penalty is the sum of any fine actually collected by the government and the effective private sanction.

It is very hard to commit an undetected monopoly or manipulation in futures markets. All futures exchanges require traders to report substantial holdings. These reports are confidential, but they provide evidence with which holdings can be traced. (In litigation arising out of asserted monopolization and manipulation, courts customarily can compute to the hundredth of a percent every trader's share of the open interest throughout the life of the contract.) When one trader owns a large portion of the open interest at the end of a contract, others find out—and fast. The trader with the big stake can't capitalize on his position except by demanding a higher price to settle the contract. The traders quickly learn with whom they must deal to close their positions. The holder of a large position may say that the position was not acquired with the purpose or effect of manipulation; large positions and manipulation certainly are not synonymous. Rather, the point is that no one is likely to obtain gains from monopoly or manipulation without being identified, so penalties can be imposed. This is not like robbery, where the principal task is finding the culprit.

---

monopoly applies only to the forgone units (the reduction in output). Unless the loss from each unit is forgone, the savings from lowering the actual costs of production on each unit will exceed the losses from the cutback in output (for discussions, see Williamson [1968]; and Fisher, Lande, and Vandaele [1983]). This is one reason why antitrust law does not bar all mergers but concentrates instead on the very large mergers that could cause substantial reductions in output. The parallel to futures contracts is plain. A futures contract with fewer precautions is "more efficient" because it can be "produced" at lower cost, and these savings apply to all transactions. Unless the contract creates a substantial prospect of monopoly and consequent cutbacks in output, the savings from the lower-cost production of transactions exceed the potential losses from the monopoly, which apply only to the marginal units.

22. Several scholars discuss the trade-offs between regulation and the use of penalties and show why, as the number of violations falls, the use of penalties becomes relatively more attractive (Shavell [1984a, 1984b]; Wittman [1977, 1984]).

Offenses may be harder to detect when they involve more than one market. For example, an effort to influence the price of a futures contract that reflects the value of a stock index will take the form of an effort to change the price of the stocks in the index. The offender will attempt to disguise these efforts as normal trading, perhaps the trading of a few large blocs at the last minute. A regulatory agency may have a comparative advantage at monitoring substantial trades in order to determine whether they have cross-market effects. Even here, however, it is possible to use computers to detect abnormal price movements, and the markets can investigate appropriately. If the bloc traders also hold substantial positions in the futures markets, there are grounds for investigation. It should be rare indeed for someone to engage in manipulation without attracting notice. (A manipulation too small to notice also does not impose substantial costs. Because we do not want to deter all offenses, however trivial, the existence of such small manipulations is not a compelling reason for regulation.)

Once a person has been certified as a monopolist or manipulator, it is relatively easy to impose a substantial penalty. Traders are not judgment-proof. Many have substantial wealth. People holding seats on the exchange may forfeit the value of the seats; traders who do not hold seats may forfeit the value of their reputations (shunning by other traders can impose enormous losses). So deterrence is likely to be an effective, low-cost method of dealing with wrongdoing in futures markets.

Notwithstanding the utility of deterrence, many people believe that futures markets impose substantial costs on unsuspecting third parties and that futures exchanges systematically underestimate the size of these costs. For example, they may contend that futures markets are especially risky and that because the professional traders can protect themselves the bulk of the cost of manipulation will fall on "outsiders"—less sophisticated, less wealthy investors. Certainly most traders in futures markets are sophisticated, and many are wealthy. It is hard to evaluate arguments that these traders arrange for losses to fall elsewhere. But let us suppose for the moment that they do. What is the appropriate response? One possibility is that the government should prevent sophisticated, wealthy people from trading a futures contract with their eyes open just on the off chance that widows and orphans might gain from the ban. The other possibility is that the government should prevent widows and orphans from doing themselves injury. This is the less costly alternative. In securities markets, certain privately sold, risky securities may be sold only to "accredited investors"—people of substantial income, wealth, or knowledge.[23] Similar restrictions could protect less sophisticated

---

23. See Section 4(6) of the Securities Exchange Act of 1934 and SEC Rules 215.501-5 defining "accredited investor" and specifying certain securities for which status as an accredited investor is a necessary condition of purchase.

investors in futures markets without injuring people who use futures markets for hedging. I do not recommend such restrictions; there is no solid evidence that exchanges fail to take adequate precautions against the exploitation of the unsophisticated. (Some exchanges and dealers establish minimum account sizes designed to keep unsophisticated traders from the markets.) But if there were such evidence, the response should be limited.

What remains is the persistent belief that the existence of futures contracts increases the likelihood of manipulation in other markets. This is the stated ground of the legislative and regulatory antipathy to contracts on "narrow-based" indices (see Federal Reserve System [1985], making an argument of a sort characterized in Fischel [1986] and Fischel and Grossman [1984]). I have indicated in earlier discussion that such cross-market manipulation is unlikely to be profitable, but assume that this is wrong and that futures contracts create opportunities for profitable manipulation. It still does not follow that prohibition of the futures contract is the optimal solution. Regulation by deterrence remains the least-cost option, just as in markets for other products. It is possible to detect manipulatory conduct and impose appropriate sanctions.

No one believes that the right response to corporate officers' trading on material inside information is to prohibit corporate officers from owning or trading stock. The officers' ownership of stock is highly valuable to other participants in the corporate venture because it aligns the officers' interests with those of other investors. It is foolish to sacrifice these gains in order to reduce the amount of inappropriate trading. We therefore permit trading but penalize wrongful trades. The same principles apply to futures markets. Futures contracts are highly valuable in hedging or distributing risk, in creating liquidity, and so on. It is foolish to sacrifice these benefits when a system of penalties imposed on wrongful conduct can preserve them.

V. Conclusion

The exchanges that establish futures contracts are led by the demands of traders to establish the optimal precautions against monopoly and manipulation. These offenses are not nearly as costly in futures markets as they are in the underlying product markets, so "optimal" precautions do not seek to eradicate the misconduct. Instead, a futures exchange seeks some mix of care and deterrence that reduces the frequency of these offenses as long as it is beneficial to do so. The existing evidence suggests that there are some episodes of monopoly and manipulation, but not very many. This is what we should expect to see.

Because the exchanges seek to select the right mix of precaution and penalty, there is no strong justification for either imposing regulations on trading or restricting the creation of new contracts. Because the loss from manipulation cannot exceed the value of the contract itself, it is never right to limit new entry.

References

Alchian, A. A. 1950. Uncertainty, evolution, and economic theory. *Journal of Political Economy* 58 (June), 211–21.

Anderson, R., and M. Sundaresan. 1983. Futures markets and monopoly. Working Paper no. CSFM-63 (July). New York: Columbia University, Business School.

Baumol, W. J., J. C. Panzar, and R. D. Willig. 1982. *Contestable Markets and Industry Structure*. New York: Harcourt Brace Jovanovich.

Becker, G. S. 1976. Irrational behavior and economic theory. In G. S. Becker, *The Economic Approach to Human Behavior*. Chicago: University of Chicago Press.

Carlton, D. W. 1984. Futures markets: Their purpose, their history, their growth, their successes and failures. *Journal of Futures Markets* 4 (Fall), 237–71.

Coase, R. H. 1960. The problem of social cost. *Journal of Law and Economics* 3 (October), 1–44.

Edwards, L. N., and F. R. Edwards. 1984. A legal and economic analysis of manipulation in futures markets. *Journal of Futures Markets* 4 (Fall), 333–66.

Federal Reserve System. 1985. *A Study of the Effects on the Economy of Trading in Futures Markets*. Washington, DC: U.S. Government Priting Office.

Fischel, D. R. 1986. Regulatory conflict and entry regulation of new futures contracts. *Journal of Business* 59, S85–S102.

Fischel, D. R., and S. J. Grossman. 1984. Customer protection in futures and security markets. *Journal of Futures Markets* 4 (Fall), 273–95.

Fisher, A. A., R. H. Lande, and W. Vandaele. 1983. Could a merger lead to both a monopoly and a lower price? *California Law Review* 71 (December), 1697–1706.

Forsyth, R., T. R. Palfrey, and C. R. Plott. 1984. Futures markets and informational efficiency: A laboratory examination. *Journal of Finance* 39 (September), 955–81.

Hieronymus, T. A. 1977. *The Economics of Futures Trading for Commercial and Personal Profit* (2d ed.). New York: Commodity Research Bureau.

Johnson, P. McB. 1981. Commodity market manipulation. *Washington and Lee Law Review* 38 (Summer), 725–79.

Loss, L. 1983. *Fundamentals of Securities Regulation*. Boston: Little Brown.

McDermott, E. T. 1979. Defining manipulation in commodity future trading: The futures "squeeze." *Northwestern University Law Review* 74 (Spring), 202–25.

Marcus, A. J., and D. M. Modest. 1984. Futures markets and production decisions. *Journal of Political Economy* 92 (June), 409–26.

Posner, R. A. 1986. *Antitrust Law: An Economic Perspective*. Chicago: University of Chicago Press.

Salop, S., D. Scheffman, and W. A. Schwartz. 1986. A bidding analysis of special interest regulation: Raising rivals' costs in a rent-seeking society. In R. Rogowski and B. Yandle (eds.), *Regulation and Competitive Strategy*. Washington, DC: Federal Trade Commission.

Schavell, S. 1984a. Liability for harm versus regulation of safety. *Journal of Legal Studies* 13 (June), 357–74.

Schavell, S. 1984b. A model of the optimal use of liability and safety regulation. *Rand Journal of Economics* 15 (Summer), 271–80.

Sowell, T. 1980. *Knowledge and Decisions*. New York: Basic.

Stigler, G. J. 1975. *The Citizen and the State*. Chicago: University of Chicago Press.

Telser, L. G. 1981. Margins and futures contracts. *Journal of Futures Markets* 1 (Summer), 225–53.

Telser, L. G., and H. N. Higinbotham. 1977. Organized futures markets: Costs and benefits. *Journal of Political Economy* 85 (October), 969–1000.

Williamson, O. E. 1968. Economics as an antitrust defense: The welfare tradeoffs. *American Economic Review* 58 (March), 18–36.

Wittman, D. 1977. Prior regulation versus post liability: The choice between input and output monitoring. *Journal of Legal Studies* 6 (January), 193–211.

Wittmann, D. 1984. Liability for harm or restitution for benefit? *Journal of Legal Studies* 13 (January), 57–80.

CREDITS

Chapter 2 reprinted from Clifford W. Smith, Jr., Charles W. Smithson, and D. Sykes Wilford, "Managing Financial Risk," *Journal of Applied Corporate Finance,* Vol. 1 No. 4 (1989), pp. 27–48.

Chapter 3 reprinted from John D. Finnerty, "Financial Engineering in Corporate Finance: An Overview," *Financial Management,* Vol. 1 No. 4 (1988), pp. 14–33.

Chapter 4 reprinted from Donald J. Smith, "The Arithmetic of Financial Engineering," *Journal of Applied Corporate Finance,* Vol. 1 No. 4 (1989), pp. 49–58.

Chapter 5 reprinted from Clifford W. Smith, Jr., Charles W. Smithson, and D. Sykes Wilford, "Financial Engineering: Why Hedge?" *Intermarket,* Vol. 6 No. 7 (1989), pp. 12–16.

Chapter 6 reprinted from Kenneth R. French, "A Comparison of Futures and Forward Prices," *Journal of Financial Economics,* Vol. 12 No. 3 (1983), pp. 311–342.

Chapter 7 reprinted from Phelim Boyle, "The Quality Option and Timing Option in Futures Contracts," *Journal of Finance,* Vol. 44 No. 1 (1989), pp. 101–113.

Chapter 8 reprinted from Clifford W. Smith, Jr., Charles W. Smithson, and Lee Macdonald Wakeman, "The Evolving Market for Swaps," *Midland Corporate Finance Journal,* Vol. 3 No. 4 (1986), pp. 20–32.

Chapter 9 reprinted from Clifford W. Smith, Jr., Charles W. Smithson, and Lee Macdonald Wakeman, "The Market for Interest Rate Swaps," *Financial Management,* Vol. 17 No. 4 (1988), pp. 34–44.

Chapter 10 reprinted from Larry D. Wall and John J. Pringle, "Interest Rate Swaps: A Review of the Issues," *Economic Review of the Federal Reserve Bank of Atlanta,* (1988), pp. 22–40.

Chapter 11 reprinted from Clifford W. Smith, Jr., "Option Pricing: A Review," *Journal of Financial Economics,* Vol. 3 No. 1: 2 (1976), pp. 3–52.

Chapter 12 reprinted from Fischer Black, "How to Use the Holes in Black-Scholes," *Journal of Applied Corporate Finance,* Vol. 1 No. 4 (1988), pp. 67–73.

Chapter 13 reprinted from John C. Cox, Stephen A. Ross, and Mark Rubinstein, "Option Pricing: A Simplified Approach," *Journal of Financial Economics,* Vol. 7 No. 3 (1979), pp. 229–263.

Chapter 14 reprinted from Mark Pitts, "The Pricing of Options on Debt Securities," *Journal of Portfolio Management,* Vol. 9 (1985), pp. 41–50.

Chapter 15 reprinted from Robert E. Whaley, "Valuation of American Futures Options: Theory and Empirical Tests," *Journal of Finance,* Vol. 41 No. 1 (1986), pp. 127–150.

Chapter 16 reprinted from Mark B. Garman and S. W. Kohlhagen, "Foreign Currency Option Values," *Journal of International Money and Finance,* Vol. 2 (1983), pp. 231–237.

Chapter 17 reprinted from Eric Briys and Michel Crouhy, "Creating and Pricing Hybrid Foreign Currency Options," *Financial Management,* Vol. 17 No. 4 (1988), pp. 59–65.

Chapter 18 reprinted from Warren Edwardes and Edmond Levy, "Break-Forwards: A Synthetic Option Hedging Instrument," *Midland Corporate Finance Journal,* Vol. 5 No. 2 (1987), pp. 59–67.

Chapter 19 reprinted from Phelim P. Boyle and Stuart M. Turnbull, "Pricing and Hedging Capped Options," *Journal of Futures Markets,* Vol. 9 No. 1 (1989), pp. 41–54.

Chapter 20 reprinted from Donald J. Smith, "The Pricing of Bull and Bear Floating Rate Notes: An Application of Financial Engineering," *Financial Management,* Vol. 17 No. 4 (1988), pp. 72–81.

Chapter 21 reprinted from John D. Finnerty, "The Case for Issuing Synthetic Convertible Bonds," *Midland Corporate Finance Journal,* Vol. 4 No. 3 (1986), pp. 73–82.

Chapter 22 reprinted from E. Philip Jones and Scott P. Mason, "Equity-Linked Debt," *Midland Corporate Finance Journal,* Vol. 3 No. 4 (1986), pp. 46–58.

Chapter 23 reprinted from John J. McConnell and Eduardo S. Schwartz, "LYON Taming," *Journal of Finance,* Vol. 41 No. 3 (1986), pp. 561–577.

Chapter 24 reprinted from Andrew H. Chen and John W. Kensinger, "Puttable Stock: A New Innovation in Equity Financing," *Financial Management,* Vol. 17 No. 1 (1988), pp. 27–37.

Chapter 25 reprinted from B. J. Winger, C. R. Chen, J. D. Martin, J. W. Petty, and S. C. Hayden, "Adjustable Rate Preferred Stock," *Financial Management,* Vol. 15 No. 1 (1986), pp. 48–57.

Chapter 26 reprinted from James V. Jordan, Robert S. Mackay, and Eugene J. Moriarty, "The Regulation of Hybrid Debt Instruments."

Chapter 27 reprinted from Halsey F. Bullen, Robert C. Wilkens, and Clifford C. Woods III, "The Fundamental Financial Instrument Approach," *Journal of Accountancy,* Vol. 168 No. 5 (1989), pp. 71–78.

Chapter 28 reprinted from John E. Stewart, "The Challenges of Hedge Accounting," *Journal of Accountancy,* Vol. 168 No. 5 (1989), pp. 48–62.

Chapter 29 reprinted from Joan Lordi Amble, "FASB's New ED on Disclosure," *Journal of Accountancy,* Vol. 168 No. 5 (1989), pp. 63–70.

Chapter 30 reprinted from Clifford W. Smith, Charles W. Smithson, and Lee Macdonald Wakeman, "Credit Risk and the Scope of Regulation of Swaps," *Bank Structure and Competition,* (1987), pp. 166–185.

Chapter 31 reprinted from Christopher Petruzzi, Marguerite Del Valle, and Stephen Judlowe, "Patent and Copyright Protection for Innovations in Finance," *Financial Management,* Vol. 17 No. 4 (1989), pp. 66–71.

Chapter 32 reprinted from Frank Easterbrook, "Monopoly, Manipulation, and the Regulation of Futures Markets," *Journal of Business,* Vol. 59 No. 2 (1986), pp. 103–127.

INDEX

663

ABOUT THE EDITORS

Clifford W. Smith, Jr., Clarey Professor of Finance at the William E. Simon Graduate School of Business Administration at the University of Rochester, has published over 40 papers and 5 books in the fields of option pricing, corporate financial policy, and financial intermediation. Students gave Mr. Smith their Superior Teaching Award on twelve occasions and he was chosen from among the University of Rochester faculty as one of ten University Mentors in recognition of his scholarship and teaching. He is an editor of the *Journal of Financial Economics,* associate editor of the *Journal of Financial and Quantitative Analysis,* the *Journal of Accounting and Economics,* the *Journal of Real Estate Finance and Economics,* and *Financial Management;* a member of the editorial review board of the *Journal of the American Real Estate and Urban Economics Association;* and a member of the advisory board of the Continental Bank *Journal of Applied Corporate Finance.*

Charles W. Smithson is a Managing Director at Chase Manhattan Bank. His research has focused on a wide range of microeconomic issues including derivative instruments, regulation, production, labor markets, and natural resources. His current research is focused on financial instruments and risk management. Charles is the author of numerous articles which have appeared in scholarly journals, the trade press, and the popular press. He is also the author of several books, including *Managerial Economics* and *The Doomsday Myth.* He holds a B.A. and M.A. from the University of Texas at Arlington, and received his Ph.D. at Tulane University.